Perspectives on Property Law

Perspectives on Property Law

Second Edition

Robert C. Ellickson

Walter E. Meyer Professor of Property and Urban Law,
Yale University

Carol M. Rose

Gordon Bradford Tweedy Professor of Law
and Organization,
Yale University

Bruce A. Ackerman

Sterling Professor of Law and Political Science,
Yale University

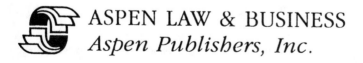 ASPEN LAW & BUSINESS
Aspen Publishers, Inc.

Library of Congress Catalog Card No. 95-75250

ISBN 0-316-23157-6

Second Edition

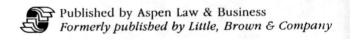 Published by Aspen Law & Business
Formerly published by Little, Brown & Company

Printed in the United States of America

To Jenny and Owen
R.C.E.

To Hugh and Marie
C.M.R.

Contents

Preface   *xi*
Acknowledgments   *xv*

Chapter 1
The Debate Over Private Property

A. Culture and Human Nature
Erving Goffman, Asylums: Essays on the Social
    Situation of Mental Patients and Other Inmates   1
Margaret Jane Radin, Property and Personhood   8
Carol M. Rose, Property as Storytelling: Perspectives
    from Game Theory, Narrative Theory, Feminist
    Theory   20

B. Property and Prosperity
William Blackstone, Commentaries on the Laws of
    England   37
Richard A. Posner, Economic Analysis of Law   45
Duncan Kennedy & Frank Michelman, Are Property
    and Contract Efficient?   55

C. Diffusion of Political Power
Milton Friedman, Capitalism and Freedom   71
Cass R. Sunstein, On Property and Constitutionalism   88

D. Distributive Justice
John Rawls, A Theory of Justice   101
James Q. Wilson, The Moral Sense   114
Robert C. Ellickson, The Untenable Case for an
    Unconditional Right to Shelter   118
Yoram Barzel, Economic Analysis of Property Rights   125

Chapter 2
The Problem of the Commons

A. Tragedy or Comedy?
Garrett Hardin, The Tragedy of the Commons   132
James M. Acheson, The Lobster Gangs of Maine   141

B. The Economics of the Commons
Harold Demsetz, Toward a Theory of Property
   Rights   148
Robert C. Ellickson, Property in Land   158

Chapter 3
The Significance of Possession
Robert Sugden, The Economics of Rights,
   Cooperation and Welfare   172
Carol M. Rose, Possession as the Origin of Property   181
Thomas W. Merrill, Property Rules, Liability Rules,
   and Adverse Possession   191

Chapter 4
The Coase Theorem and its Limitations
Ronald H. Coase, The Problem of Social Cost   200
Robert Cooter, The Cost of Coase   209
Robert C. Ellickson, Order Without Law: How
   Neighbors Settle Disputes   215
Jack L. Knetsch, The Endowment Effect and Evidence
   of Nonreversible Indifference Curves   226

Chapter 5
Property Rules, Liability Rules
Guido Calabresi & A. Douglas Melamed, Property
   Rules, Liability Rules, and Inalienability: One View
   of the Cathedral   236
Arthur Hoppe, A License to Steal   259
Thomas W. Merrill, Trespass, Nuisance, and the
   Costs of Determining Property Rights   261

Chapter 6

**Property Rights that Arise Outside
the Legal System**

Robert Axelrod, The Evolution of Cooperation   275
Elizabeth Hoffman & Matthew L. Spitzer,
  Entitlements, Rights, and Fairness: An
  Experimental Examination of Subjects' Concepts
  of Distributive Justice   287
Hanna Papanek, To Each Less than She Needs, From
  Each More Than She Can Do: Allocations,
  Entitlements and Value   302

Chapter 7

Transacting and Trading

A. Ground Rules for Exchange
Ian Ayres & Robert Gertner, Filling Gaps in
  Incomplete Contracts: An Economic Theory of
  Default Rules   313
Carol M. Rose, Crystals and Mud in Property Law   320

B. Markets and Morals
Margaret Jane Radin, Market-Inalienability   336
Albert O. Hirschman, Rival Interpretations of Market
  Society: Civilizing, Destructive, or Feeble?   345

Chapter 8

**Subdividing Property in Time: Of Estates,
Landlords and Tenants**

A. Neighbors in Time: Of Future Interests
Richard A. Posner, Economic Analysis of Law   360
Douglas W. Allen & Dean Lueck, The "Back Forty" on
  a Handshake: Specific Assets, Reputation, and the
  Structure of Farmland Contracts   368

B. Rental Housing Markets
Irving Welfeld, Poor Tenants, Poor Landlords, Poor
  Policy   374
John C. Weicher, Private Production: Has the Rising
  Tide Lifted All Boats?   382

C. Minimum Housing Standards
Richard A. Posner, Economic Analysis of Law   393
Bruce A. Ackerman, Regulating Slum Housing
Markets on Behalf of the Poor   398

D. Rent Control
Richard Arnott, Rent Control: The International
Experience   404
Margaret Jane Radin, Residential Rent Control   410

Chapter 9
Land Use and the Environment

A. Servitudes and Private Communities
Richard A. Epstein, Covenants and Constitutions   424

B. Public Land Use Controls
Andrew J. Cappel, A Walk Along Willow: Patterns of
Land Use Coordination in Pre-Zoning New Haven
(1870–1926)   439
William A. Fischel, Do Growth Controls Matter? A
Review of Empirical Evidence on the Effectiveness
and Efficiency of Local Government Land Use
Regulation   457

C. Housing Segregation
Richard F. Muth, Cities and Housing   470
Thomas C. Schelling, Micromotives and
Macrobehavior   478

D. The Takings Issue
Frank I. Michelman, Property, Utility, and Fairness:
Comments on the Ethical Foundations of "Just
Compensation" Law   487
William A. Fischel & Perry Shapiro, Takings,
Insurance, and Michelman: Comments on
Economic Interpretations of "Just Compensation"
Law   514

E. Environmental Protection
Thomas C. Schelling, Prices as Regulatory
Instruments   532

Preface

Property is a term that triggers strong emotions. For some, including the Founders, it carries the promise of prosperity and freedom from tyranny. For others, it signifies blind defense of a status quo characterized by unequal wealth. Issues of property have inspired philosophical comment at least since Plato; unlike many philosophic issues, however, they have also provoked intense popular concern. Wars and revolutions are commonly fought over property rules and property distributions. Property teachers can deservedly note that issues in torts and contracts (the other foundational private-law subjects) are rarely so explosive.

Despite its highly charged subject matter, property law often strikes law students as a confusing jumble of doctrines that apply to relatively unconnected sets of disputes. To counter that impression, we have designed this reader primarily for use in an introductory course on property law, most predictably as a supplement to a casebook or other compendium of primary legal materials. Because the structure of property institutions has increasingly attracted interdisciplinary study, we expect that students and researchers in other fields may also benefit from both the selections and our notes and questions.

Although we have consciously included a highly diverse set of readings in this volume, we aim not to add to the confusion but to help the student to identify fundamental questions linking conventionally separated pockets of property law. An understanding of these interconnections should provide a foundation for advanced study in highly diverse property-related fields: to name just the most obvious, environmental policy, poverty law, intellectual property, real estate, family wealth transactions, taxation, urban government, natural resources, and legal history.

This reader builds on and indeed is a successor to Bruce Ackerman's Economic Foundations of Property Law, published in 1975. In his preface to that edition, Ackerman observed that "[t]he institution of private property . . . serves as the linchpin of our economic organization, and it would be remarkable if its proper study could not enlighten the fundamental premises of a wide range of legal phenomena." Whether supported by law or customary practice, *private property* denotes a regime that entitles an individual owner to exercise dominion over a scarce resource. At maximum, this control includes the rights to use the resource, to exclude others from it, and to transfer it to others. In many contexts, however, societies—including our own—dilute this pure form of private property; for example, the legal system may support a political protester's right to leaflet in a shopping center whose legal title belongs to someone else. Moreover, societies routinely make room for other forms of property. University students who jointly use a dormitory's common room have a casual form of *communal property*. Streets, beaches, and even languages and jokes may be *open-access property*, available for all to use. The selections in this volume should help the reader to untangle these different property regimes and to reflect upon the reasons why every society ends up with such an eclectic variety of them.

In the first edition of this collection, Ackerman included *Economic* in the title. His decision to do so was faithful to the spirit of the time—as is our collective decision to delete the word from the title of this second edition. The 1970s were an ascendant period for law and economics. Ackerman's preface to the first edition unassailably asserted that scholars applying tools of economics had produced "the most dynamic body of research in the field" of property. In the 1990s, however, most observers no longer regard law and economics as a dynamic upstart, but rather as "normal science" (to borrow a phrase from Thomas Kuhn), at least in a predominantly private-law field such as property.

This edition does contain many seminal works in law and economics—indeed, eleven of the twenty-four that appeared in the first edition. But we have widened our net to take in authors adopting newly "upstart" perspectives that aim either to complement or to displace the normal science of law and economics. Even in the first edition, Ackerman noted that "the insights of the economist must be placed in a larger structure in which sociological, psychological and historical theory have their rightful place. Consequently, it would be quite appropriate for the instructor to supplement the readings in this volume with others. . . ." Because recent interdisciplinary work on property has been so rich, the editors now can assist instructors who share this aspiration. We include here selections taken not only from sociology, psychology, and history (the disciplines Ackerman mentioned), but also philosophy, gender studies, game theory, critical legal studies, and law and literature. Which, if any, of these perspectives will make lasting contributions to legal thought presently remains murky; the readers of this volume are members of one of the juries that will decide.

To the extent that this second edition varies from the first, it is entirely the work product of Robert Ellickson and Carol Rose, who acknowledge here a particular debt to Bruce Ackerman—not only for permitting us to become meddlesome co-owners of this small part of his voluminous intellectual property, but even more for pioneering the first edition. Bruce's 1975 preface asserted that property courses at the time often consisted of a thin base of historical accounts of struggles between English landowners and the Crown, a Langdellian superstructure of American common-law precedent, all incongruously finished off with oddments of constitutional law and recent statutory reforms. The success of his first edition demonstrated even then the strong latent demand for a volume that added spice and structure to property instruction. Moreover, simply by its appearance, the first edition helped establish a canon that has significantly influenced the course of scholarship on property law. In the 1960s, property was generally regarded as a sleepy field. By the 1990s it had become one of the most vibrant, varied, and contested fields of legal scholarship. Bruce's first edition was a decisive stroke in this transformation. While the editors of the present edition can scarcely hope to have so dramatic an impact, we do aspire not only to endorse Bruce's stress on interdisciplinary work, but also to stretch that work in new directions.

The selections appearing here have been rigorously edited. Most footnotes have been deleted; those that remain retain their original numbers, and readers will notice large gaps in the sequences. Any reader who finds an excerpt stimulating is urged to consult the fuller original. After all, these excerpts were chosen not only to clarify, but to provoke.

Robert C. Ellickson
Carol M. Rose

February 1995
New Haven

Acknowledgments

Acheson, James M., The Lobster Gangs of Maine, 48–49, 73–76, 142–144. Copyright © 1988 by University Press of New England. Reprinted by permission.

Ackerman, Bruce A., Regulating Slum Housing Markets on Behalf of the Poor: Of Housing Codes, Housing Subsidies and Income Redistribution Policy, 80 Yale Law Journal, 1102–1106. Copyright © 1971. Reprinted by permission of The Yale Law Journal Company and Fred B. Rothman & Company.

Allen, Douglas W. & Lueck, Dean, The "Back Forty" on a Handshake: Specific Assets, Reputation, and the Structure of Farmland Contracts, The Journal of Law, Economics, and Organization 8(2), 366–371, 375. Copyright © 1992. Reprinted by permission of Oxford University Press.

Arnott, Richard, Rent Control: The International Experience, 1 Journal of Real Estate, Finance, and Economics, 203–206, 209–210. Copyright © 1988. Reprinted by permission of Kluwer Academic Publishers.

Axelrod, Robert, The Evolution of Cooperation, 3–5, 7–12, 19–21, 30–35. Copyright © 1984 by Robert Axelrod. Reprinted by permission of BasicBooks, a division of HarperCollins Publishers, Inc.

Ayres, Ian & Gertner, Robert, Filling Gaps in Incomplete Contracts: An Economic Theory of Default Rules, 99 Yale Law Journal, 87–89, 91–94, 97–100, 125–127. Copyright © 1989. Reprinted by permission of The Yale Law Journal Company and Fred B. Rothman & Company.

Barzel, Yoram, Economic Analysis of Property Rights, 76–81. Copyright © 1989. Reprinted by permission of Cambridge University Press.

Blackstone, William, 2 Commentaries on the Laws of England, *2–*11. This excerpt appeared in the first edition, published in 1766 (facsimile of the first edition published in 1979).

Calabresi, Guido & Melamed, A. Douglas, Property Rules,

pensation" Law, 17 The Journal of Legal Studies, 269–289, 292–293. Copyright © 1988. Reprinted by permission of The University of Chicago Law School.

Friedman, Milton, Capitalism and Freedom, 7–10, 13–20, 22, 25–32. Copyright © 1962 by the University of Chicago Press. Reprinted by permission of the publisher.

Goffman, Erving, Asylums: Essays on the Social Situation of Mental Patients and Other Inmates, 18–21, 244–254. Copyright © 1961 by Erving Goffman. Used by permission of Doubleday, a division of Bantam Doubleday Dell Publishing Group, Inc.

Hardin, Garrett, The Tragedy of the Commons, 162 Science, 1243–1248. Copyright © 1968 by AAAS. Reprinted by permission.

Hirschman, Albert O., Rival Interpretations of Market Society: Civilizing, Destructive, or Feeble?, 1463–1474, 20 Journal of Economic Literature. Copyright © 1982. Reprinted by permission of the American Economic Association. (See also, Rival Views of Market Society and Other Recent Essays. Copyright © 1986 by Viking / Penguin. Paperback edition with new introduction, 105–141. Copyright © 1992 by Harvard University Press.)

Hoffman, Elizabeth & Spitzer, Matthew L., Entitlements, Rights, and Fairness: An Experimental Examination of Subjects' Concepts of Distributive Justice, 14 The Journal of Legal Studies, 259–273, 275–277, 280–284. Copyright © 1985. Reprinted by permission of The University of Chicago Law School.

Hoppe, Arthur, A License to Steal, San Francisco Chronicle, February 8, 1971. Copyright © 1971 by The Chronicle Publishing Company. Reprinted by permission of the author.

Kennedy, Duncan & Michelman, Frank, Are Property and Contract Efficient?, 8 Hofstra Law Review, 711–732, 734–737. Copyright © 1980. Reprinted by permission of the Hofstra Law Review.

Knetsch, Jack L., The Endowment Effect and Evidence of Nonreversible Indifference Curves, 79 American Economic Review, 1277–1283. Copyright © 1989. Reprinted by permission of the American Economic Association.

Merrill, Thomas W., Property Rules, Liability Rules, and Adverse Possession, 79, Northwestern University Law Review, 1122–1128, 1133–1135, 1152–1153, (1984–1985). Copyright © 1985. Reprinted by special permission of Northwestern University School of Law.

Merrill, Thomas W., Trespass, Nuisance, and the Cost of Determining Property Rights, 14 The Journal of Legal Studies, 13–21, 23–26, 35–39, 41–42, 45–48 Copyright © 1985. Reprinted by permission.

Michelman, Frank I., Property, Utility, and Fairness: Comments

Law & the Humanities, 37–57. Copyright © 1990 by the Yale Journal of Law & the Humanities. Reprinted by permission.

Schelling, Thomas C., Micromotives and Macrobehavior, 140–141, 146–155. Reprinted from Micromotives and Macrobehavior by Thomas C. Schelling, with the permission of W.W. Norton & Company, Inc. Copyright © 1978 by W.W. Norton & Company, Inc.

Schelling, Thomas C., Prices as Regulatory Instruments, in Incentives for Environmental Protection (Thomas C. Schelling ed.), 1–11, 13–21, 24–26, 28–30, 32. Copyright © 1983. Reprinted by permission of The MIT Press.

Sugden, Robert, The Economics of Rights, Cooperation, and Welfare, 87–97 (from Chapter 5, "Possession"). Copyright © 1986. Reprinted by permission of Blackwell Publishers.

Sunstein, Cass R., On Property and Constitutionalism, 14, note 95, Cardozo Law Review, 907–922. Copyright © 1993. Reprinted by permission.

Weicher, John C., Private Production: Has the Rising Tide Lifted All Boats?, in Housing America's Poor, 45–46, 48–59, 61, edited by Peter Salins. Copyright © 1987 by The University of North Carolina Press. Used by permission of the publisher.

Welfeld, Irving, Poor Tenants, Poor Landlords, Poor Policy, The Public Interest, 110–117. Copyright © 1988 by National Affairs, Inc. Reprinted with permission of the author and The Public Interest, No. 92 (Summer 1988).

Wilson, James Q., The Moral Sense, 73–76. Reprinted with the permission of The Free Press, a division of Simon & Schuster, from The Moral Sense by James Q. Wilson. Copyright © 1993 by James Q. Wilson.

Perspectives on Property Law

Chapter 1

The Debate over Private Property

A. Culture and Human Nature

Asylums: Essays on the Social Situation of Mental Patients and Other Inmates*

Erving Goffman

The admission procedure can be characterized as a leaving off and a taking on, with the midpoint marked by physical nakedness. Leaving off of course entails a dispossession of property, important because persons invest self feelings in their possessions. Perhaps the most significant of these possessions is not physical at all, one's full name; whatever one is thereafter called, loss of one's name can be a great curtailment of the self. . . .

Once the inmate is stripped of his possessions, at least some replacements must be made by the establishment, but these take the form of standard issue uniform in character and uniformly distributed. These substitute possessions are clearly marked as really belonging to the institution and in some cases are recalled at regular intervals to be, as it were, disinfected of identifications. With objects that can be used up — for example, pencils — the inmate may be required to return the remnants before obtaining a reissue. Failure to provide inmates with individual lockers and periodic searches and confiscations of accumulated personal property reinforce prop-

*Source: pp. 18-21, 244-254 (1961).

1

erty dispossession. Religious orders have appreciated the implications for self of such separation from belongings. Inmates may be required to change their cells once a year so as not to become attached to them. The Benedictine Rule is explicit:

> For their bedding let a mattress, a blanket, a coverlet, and a pillow suffice. These beds must be frequently inspected by the Abbot, because of private property which may be found therein. If anyone be discovered to have what he has not received from the Abbot, let him be most severely punished. And in order that this vice of private ownership may be completely rooted out, let all things that are necessary be supplied by the Abbot: that is, cowl, tunic, stockings, shoes, girdle, knife, pen, needle, handkerchief, and tablets; so that all plea of necessity may be taken away. And let the Abbot always consider that passage in the Acts of the Apostles: "Distribution was made to each according as anyone had need."[21]

One set of the individual's possessions has a special relation to self. The individual ordinarily expects to exert some control over the guise in which he appears before others. For this he needs cosmetic and clothing supplies, tools for applying, arranging, and repairing them, and an accessible, secure place to store these supplies and tools — in short, the individual will need an "identity kit" for the management of his personal front. He will also need access to decoration specialists such as barbers and clothiers.

On admission to a total institution, however, the individual is likely to be stripped of his usual appearance and of the equipment and services by which he maintains it, thus suffering a personal defacement. Clothing, combs, needle and thread, cosmetics, towels, soap, shaving sets, bathing facilities — all these may be taken away or denied him, although some may be kept in inaccessible storage, to be returned if and when he leaves. In the words of St. Benedict's Holy Rule:

> Then forthwith he shall, there in the oratory, be divested of his own garments with which he is clothed and be clad in those of the monastery. Those garments of which he is divested shall be placed in the wardrobe, there to be kept, so that if, perchance, he should ever be persuaded by the devil to leave the monastery (which God forbid), he may be stripped of the monastic habit and cast forth.[22]

As suggested, the institutional issue provided as a substitute for what has been taken away is typically of a "coarse" variety, ill-suited, often old, and the same for large categories of inmates. The

---

21. The Holy Rule of St. Benedict, Ch. 55.
22. The Holy Rule of St. Benedict, Ch. 58.

impact of this substitution is described in a report on imprisoned prostitutes:

> First, there is the shower officer who forces them to undress, takes their own clothes away, sees to it that they take showers and get their prison clothes — one pair of black oxfords with cuban heels, two pairs of much-mended ankle socks, three cotton dresses, two cotton slips, two pairs of panties, and a couple of bras. Practically all the bras are flat and useless. No corsets or girdles are issued.
>
> There is not a sadder sight than some of the obese prisoners who, if nothing else, have been managing to keep themselves looking decent on the outside, confronted by the first sight of themselves in prison issue.[23] . . .

In mental hospitals and similar institutions the basic kind of personal territory is, perhaps, the private sleeping room, officially available to around five or ten per cent of the ward population. In Central Hospital such a room was sometimes given in exchange for doing ward work. Once obtained, a private room could be stocked with objects that could lend comfort, pleasure, and control to the patient's life. Pin-up pictures, a radio, a box of paper-back detective stories, a bag of fruit, coffee-making equipment, matches, shaving equipment — these were some of the objects, many of them illicit, that were introduced by patients.

Patients who had been on a given ward for several months tended to develop personal territories in the day room, at least to the degree that some inmates developed favorite sitting or standing places and would make some effort to dislodge anybody who usurped them. Thus, on one continued treatment ward, one elderly patient in contact was by mutual consent accorded a free-standing radiator; by spreading paper on top, he managed to be able to sit on it, and sit on it he usually did. Behind the radiator he kept some of his personal effects, which further marked off the area as his place. A few feet from him, in a corner of the room, a working patient had what amounted to his "office," this being the place where staff knew they could find him when he was wanted. He had sat so long in this corner that there was a soiled dent in the plaster wall where his head usually came to rest. On the same ward, another patient laid claim to a chair that was directly in front of the TV set; although a few patients would contest this place, he generally could sustain his claim upon it.

Territory formation on wards has a special relation to mental disorder. In many civilian situations an equalitarian rule such as

23. John M. Murtagh & Sara Harris, Cast the First Stone (New York: Pocket Books, 1958), pp. 239-240. . . .

"first come, first served" prevails, and some disguise conceals another organizing principle, "strongest takes what he wants." This last rule operated to some extent on bad wards, just as the first rule did on good wards. Another dimension must be introduced, however. The alignment to ward life that many back-ward patients took, for whatever voluntary reason or from whatever involuntary cause, led them to remain silent and unprotesting and to move away from any commotion involving themselves. Such a person could be dislodged from a seat or place regardless of his size or strength. Hence, on the bad wards, a special pecking order of a sort occurred, with vocal patients in good contact taking favorite chairs and benches from those not in contact. This was carried to a point where one patient might force a mute one off a footrest, leaving the vocal patient with a chair *and* a footrest, and the mute patient with nothing at all — a difference that is not negligible considering the fact that except for breaks at mealtime some patients spent the whole of the day on these wards doing nothing but sitting or standing in one place.

Perhaps the minimum space that was built into a personal territory was that provided by a patient's blanket. In some wards, a few patients would carry their blankets around with them during the day and, in an act thought to be highly regressive, each would curl up on the floor with his blanket completely covering him; within this covered space each had some margin of control.

As may be expected, a personal territory can develop within a free place or group territory. For example, in the recreation room of a chronic male service one of the two large wooden armchairs favorably situated close to the light and the radiator was regularly taken by an elderly respected patient, both patients and staff recognizing his right to it.

One of the most elaborate illustrations of territory formation in a free place in Central Hospital occurred in the disused basement of one of the continued-treatment buildings. Here a few of the more intact rooms had been taken over by lower-echelon staff to use as supply rooms; thus there was a paint room and a room where grounds-care equipment was stored. In each of these rooms a patient helper held semi-official dominion. Pin-ups, a radio, a relatively soft chair, and supplies of hospital tobacco were to be found. A few of the remaining less usable rooms had been appropriated by aging long-term parole patients, each of whom had managed to stock his nest with something, if only a broken chair and stacks of old Life magazines. In the rare event of any of these patients being needed during the day by a member of staff, a message would be sent directly to his basement office, not his ward.

In some cases, an assignment provided a personal territory. For example, the working patients who looked after their ward's clothing and supply room were allowed to stay in this room when no chores were to be done; and there they could sit or lie on the floor away from the alterations of commotion and pall in the day room. . . . In everyday life, legitimate possessions employed in primary adjustments are typically stored, when not in use, in special places of safekeeping which can be gotten to at will, such as footlockers, cabinets, bureau drawers, and safe deposit boxes. These storage places protect the object from damage, misuse, and misappropriation, and allow the user to conceal what he possesses from others. More important, these places can represent an extension of the self and its autonomy, becoming more important as the individual foregoes other repositories of selfhood. If nothing can be kept only for oneself, and everything one uses is used by others, too, then little protection from social contamination by others is possible. Further, some of the things one must give up are those with which one has become especially identified and which one employs for self-identification to others. It is thus that a man in a monastery may be concerned about his one privacy, his letterbox, and a man on a frigate about his canvas clothes bag.

Where such private storage places are not allowed, it is understandable that they will be illicitly developed. Further, if one is to possess an object illicitly, then the place in which it is stored may itself have to be concealed. A personal storage space that is concealed and/or locked not merely to thwart illegitimate interlopers but also legitimate authority is sometimes called a *stash* in the criminal and near-criminal world, and will be called this here. It may be noted that these illicit storage places represent a more complex matter, organizationally, than do simple make-do's, since a stash can ordinarily safeguard more than one kind of illicit possession. I would like to add that one important object that may be stashed is the human body (dead or alive), giving rise to special terms such as hideout, stowaway, laying low, and to one of the inevitable scenes of detective fiction.

When patients entered Central Hospital, especially if they were excited or depressed on admission, they were denied a private, accessible place to store things. Their personal clothing, for example, might be stored in a room that was beyond their discretionary use. Their money was kept in the administration building, unobtainable without medical and/or their legal agents' permission. Valuables or breakables, such as false teeth, eyeglasses, wrist watches, often an integral part of body image, might be locked up safely out of their owners' reach. Official papers of self-identification might also be retained by the institution. Cosmetics, needed to present oneself properly to others, were collectivized, being made accessible to patients only at certain times. On convalescent wards, bed boxes were available, but since they were unlocked they were subject to theft from other patients and from staff, and in any case were often located in rooms locked to patients during the day.

If people were selfless, or were required to be selfless, there would of course be a logic to having no private storage place. . . . But all have some self. Given the curtailment implied by loss of places of safekeeping, it is understandable that patients in Central Hospital developed places of their own.

It seemed characteristic of hospital life that the most common form of stash was one that could be carried around on one's person wherever one went. One such device for female patients was a large handbag; a parallel technique for a man was a jacket with commodious pockets, worn even in the hottest weather. While these containers are quite usual ones in the wider community, there was a special burden placed upon them in the hospital: books, writing materials, washcloths, fruit, small valuables, scarves, playing cards, soap, shaving equipment (on the part of men), containers of salt, pepper, and sugar, bottles of milk — these were some of the objects sometimes carried in this manner. So common was this practice that one of the most reliable symbols of patient status in the hospital was bulging pockets. Another portable storage device was a shopping bag lined with another shopping bag. (When partly full, this frequently employed stash also served as a cushion and back rest.) Among men, a small stash was sometimes created out of a long sock: by knotting the open end and twisting this end around his belt, the patient could let a kind of moneybag inconspicuously hang down inside his trouser leg. Individual variations of these portable containers were also found. One young engineering graduate fashioned a purse out of discarded oilcloth, the purse being stitched into separate, well-measured compartments for comb, toothbrush, cards, writing paper, pencil, soap, small face cloth, toilet paper — the whole attached by a concealed clip to the underside of his belt. The same patient had also sewn an extra pocket on the inside of his jacket to carry a book. Another male patient, an avid newspaper reader, invariably wore a suit jacket, apparently to conceal his newspapers, which he carried folded over his belt. Still another made effective use of a cleaned-out tobacco pouch for transporting food; whole fruit, unpeeled, could easily be put in one's pocket to be taken back to the ward from the cafeteria, but cooked meat was better carried in a grease-proof stash.

I would like to repeat that there were some good reasons for these bulky carryings-on. Many of the amenities of life, such as soap, toilet paper, or cards, which are ordinarily available in many depots of comfort in civil society, are not thus available to patients, so that the day's needs had to be partly provided for at the beginning of the day.

Fixed stashes, as well as portable ones, were employed, too; they were most often found in free places and territories. Some patients attempted to keep their valuables under their mattresses but, as previously suggested, the general hospital rule making dormitories off-limits during the day reduced the usefulness of this device. The half-concealed lips of window sills were sometimes used. Patients with private rooms and friendly relations with the attendant used their rooms as stashes. Female patients sometimes hid matches and cigarettes in the compacts they left in their rooms. And a favorite exemplary tale in the hospital was of an old man who was claimed to have hid his money, $1200, in a cigar box in a tree on the hospital grounds.

NOTES AND QUESTIONS ON PROPERTY AND THE SENSE OF SELF

1. The author writes of the inmates' being stripped of "possessions," but also mentions that they lose personal "property." Is there any difference between *possessions* and *property*? Which of the inmates' possessions count as property? Is the first-mentioned "possession," the inmate's name, a kind of property? Why or why not?

2. Why does the author make so much of an inmate's use of property (or possessions) to present a personal appearance? Are such uses of property a good thing, or do they imply that property merely serves vanity and deception? Why did the Benedictines restrict the monks' property, anyway? What other institutions do so, and why? For related critiques of property, see, for example, E.M. Forster, My Wood, in Abinger Harvest 22 (1964), suggesting that property makes the holder pompous and self-important; Thorstein Veblen, The Theory of the Leisure Class (1899), arguing that the wealthy use property for "conspicuous consumption."

3. Why is "first come, first served" a principle identified with the asylum's "good wards," whereas "strongest takes what he wants" is a principle identified with the "bad wards"? What is the matter with the rule of the stronger? See Thomas Hobbes, Leviathan (1651). First possession is an extremely widespread rule for property formation; see Chapter 3, infra, on The Significance of Possession infra. But does this make first possession more morally justifiable than the rule of the stronger? Which would latecomers prefer? Is first possession justifi-

able on efficiency grounds? Compare Duncan Kennedy and Frank Michelman, Are Property and Contract Efficient? infra, p.55.

4. How do you account for the pervasive "territory formation" among inmates? Do you see similar patterns in other persons, such as the homeless, who ostensibly own very little property? Do these patterns suggest that some sort of territoriality is "hardwired" in the human psyche, as is argued by the sociobiologists? For variations on this theme, see Elizabeth Cashdan, Spatial Organization and Habitat Use, in Eric Alden Smith & Bruce Winterhalder, Evolutionary Ecology and Human Behavior (1992). Or is the inmates' territory formation grounded on functional needs, culture, or both?

Property and Personhood *

Margaret Jane Radin

This article explores the relationship between property and personhood, a relationship that has commonly been both ignored and taken for granted in legal thought. The premise underlying the personhood perspective is that to achieve proper self-development — to be a *person* — an individual needs some control over resources in the external environment. The necessary assurances of control take the form of property rights. Although explicit elaboration of this perspective is wanting in modern writing on property, the personhood perspective is often implicit in the connections that courts and commentators find between property and privacy or between property and liberty. In addition to its power to explain certain aspects of existing schemes of property entitlement, the personhood perspective can also serve as an explicit source of values for making moral distinctions in property disputes, and hence for either justifying or criticizing current law. . . . It is not surprising that personhood has played a part in property theories all along the political spectrum. Conservatives rely on an absolute conception of property as sacred to personal autonomy. Communitarians believe that changing conceptions of property reflect and shape the changing nature of persons and communities. Welfare rights liberals find entitlement to a minimal level of resources necessary to the dignity of persons even when the entitlement must curtail the property rights of others. This article does not emphasize how the notion of person-

*Source: 34 Stanford Law Review 957-973, 977-979, 984-991, 1002-1006 (1982).

hood might figure in the most prevalent traditional lines of liberal property theory: the Lockean labor-desert theory, which focuses on individual autonomy, or the utilitarian theory, which focuses on welfare maximization. It rather attempts to clarify a third strand of liberal property theory that focuses on personal embodiment or self-constitution in terms of "things." . . .

In what follows I shall discuss the personhood perspective as Hegel developed it in Philosophy of Right, trace some of its later permutations and entanglements with other perspectives on property, and try to develop a contemporary view useful in the context of the American legal system. . . .

I.   Property for Personhood: An Intuitive View

Most people possess certain objects they feel are almost part of themselves. These objects are closely bound up with personhood because they are part of the way we constitute ourselves as continuing personal entities in the world. They may be as different as people are different, but some common examples might be a wedding ring, a portrait, an heirloom, or a house.

One may gauge the strength or significance of someone's relationship with an object by the kind of pain that would be occasioned by its loss. On this view, an object is closely related to one's personhood if its loss causes pain that cannot be relieved by the object's replacement. If so, that particular object is bound up with the holder. For instance, if a wedding ring is stolen from a jeweler, insurance proceeds can reimburse the jeweler, but if a wedding ring is stolen from a loving wearer, the price of a replacement will not restore the status quo — perhaps no amount of money can do so.

The opposite of holding an object that has become a part of oneself is holding an object that is perfectly replaceable with other goods of equal market value. One holds such an object for purely instrumental reasons. The archetype of such a good is, of course, money, which is almost always held only to buy other things. A dollar is worth no more than what one chooses to buy with it, and one dollar bill is as good as another. Other examples are the wedding ring in the hands of the jeweler, the automobile in the hands of the dealer, the land in the hands of the developer, or the apartment in the hands of the commercial landlord. I shall call these theoretical opposites — property that is bound up with a person and property that is held purely instrumentally — personal property and fungible property respectively. . . .

Once we admit that a person can be bound up with an external "thing" in some constitutive sense, we can argue that by virtue of this connection the person should be accorded broad liberty with respect to control over that "thing." But here liberty follows from property for personhood; personhood is the basic concept, not liberty. Of course, if liberty is viewed not as freedom from interference, or "negative freedom," but rather as some positive will that by acting on the external world is constitutive of the person, then liberty comes closer to capturing the idea of the self being intimately bound up with things in the external world.

It intuitively appears that there is such a thing as property for personhood because people become bound up with "things." But this intuitive view does not compel the conclusion that property for personhood deserves moral recognition or legal protection, because arguably there is bad as well as good in being bound up with external objects. If there is a traditional understanding that a well-developed person must invest herself to some extent in external objects, there is no less a traditional understanding that one should not invest oneself *in the wrong way* or *to too great an extent* in external objects. Property is damnation as well as salvation, object-fetishism as well as moral groundwork. In this view, the relationship between the shoe fetishist and his shoe will not be respected like that between the spouse and her wedding ring. At the extreme, anyone who lives only for material objects is considered not to be a well-developed person, but rather to be lacking some important attribute of humanity.

II.   The Role of the Concept of Person . . .

A.   Theories of the Person

The polymorphous nature of the word "person" inevitably creates problems for a moral thesis about property built upon notions of personhood. "Person" stems from the Latin *persona*, meaning, among other things, a theatrical role. In Roman law, *persona* came to mean simply an entity possessing legal rights and duties. Today it commonly signifies any human being. . . .

B.   Property Theories and Theories of the Person

[L]et us begin with the person conceived as bodily continuity. Locke says that "every Man has a *Property* in his own *Person*," from which it immediately follows that "[t]he *Labour* of his Body, and the

Work of his hands . . . are properly his."[28] Though . . . Locke elsewhere considers the person as reflective consciousness and memory, he may well mean here that one literally owns one's limbs and hence must own their product. If not, perhaps property in one's person should be understood to mean simply that an individual has an entitlement to be a person or to be treated as a person. This would probably include the right to self-preservation on which Locke bases the right to appropriate.

If it makes sense to say that one owns one's body, then, on the embodiment theory of personhood, the body is quintessentially personal property because it is literally constitutive of one's personhood. If the body is property, then objectively it is property for personhood. This line of thinking leads to a property theory for the tort of assault and battery: Interference with my body is interference with my personal property. Certain external things, for example, the shirt off my back, may also be considered personal property if they are closely enough connected with the body.

The idea of property in one's body presents some interesting paradoxes. In some cases, bodily parts can become fungible commodities, just as other personal property can become fungible with a change in its relationship with the owner: Blood can be withdrawn and used in a transfusion; hair can be cut off and used by a wigmaker; organs can be transplanted. On the other hand, bodily parts may be too "personal" to be property at all. . . .

Finally, let us consider the view that what is important in personhood is a continuing character structure encompassing future projects or plans, as well as past events and feelings. The general idea of expressing one's character through property is quite familiar. It is frequently remarked that dogs resemble their masters; the attributes of many material goods, such as cars and clothes, can proclaim character traits of their owners. Of course, many would say that becoming too enthralled with property takes away time and energy needed to develop other faculties constitutive of personhood. But, for example, if you express your generosity by giving away fruits that grow in your orchard, then if the orchard ceases to be your property, you are no longer able to express your character. This at least suggests that property may have an important relationship to certain character traits that partly constitute a person.

This view of personhood also gives us insight into why protecting people's "expectations" of continuing control over objects seems so important. If an object you now control is bound up in your fu-

28. J. Locke [Second Treatise of Government], ch. V, §27.

ture plans or in your anticipation of your future self, and it is partly these plans for your own continuity that make you a person, then your personhood depends on the realization of these expectations. . . .

C. The Problem of Fetishism

We must construct sufficiently objective criteria to identify close object relations that should be excluded from recognition as personal property because the particular nature of the relationship works to hinder rather than to support healthy self-constitution. A key to distinguishing these cases is "healthy." We can tell the difference between personal property and fetishism the same way we can tell the difference between a healthy person and a sick person, or between a sane person and an insane person. In fact, the concepts of sanity and personhood are intertwined: At some point we question whether the insane person is a person at all. Using the word "we" here, however, implies that a consensus exists and can be discerned. Because I seek a source of objective judgments about property for personhood, but do not wish to rely on natural law or simple moral realism, consensus must be a sufficient source of objective moral criteria — and I believe it can be, sometimes, without destroying the meaning of objectivity. In the context of property for personhood, then, a "thing" that someone claims to be bound up with nevertheless should not be treated as personal vis-à-vis other people's claimed rights and interests when there is an objective moral consensus that to be bound up with that category of "thing" is inconsistent with personhood or healthy self-constitution.

Judgments of insanity or fetishism are both made on the basis of the minimum indicia it takes to recognize an individual as one of us. There does not seem to be the same reason to restrain a private fetishist as there would be to restrain an insane person prone to violence against others. But the restraint of denying the fetishist's property special recognition as personal is less severe than that imposed on someone deemed violently insane. To refuse on moral grounds to call fetishist property personal is not to refuse to call it property at all. The immediate consequence of denying personal status to something is merely to treat that thing as fungible property, and hence to deny only those claims that might rely on a preferred status of personal property.

A broader aspect of the problem of fetishism is suggested by Marx's "fetishism of commodities."[47] Marx attributed power in a

47. K. Marx, Capital, ch. 1.

market society to the commodities that form the market. He believed that people become subordinate in their relations to these commodities. In other words, under capitalism property itself is antipersonhood.

Even if one does not accept that all capitalist market relations with objects destroy personhood, it is probably true that most people view the caricature capitalist with distaste. Most people might consider her lacking in some essential attribute of personhood, such as the capacity to respect other people or the environment. If there is some moral cut-off point, beyond which one is attached too much or in the wrong way to property, the extent to which someone may emulate the caricature capitalist and still claim property for personhood is not clear, but is not unlimited. Although the caricature capitalist cannot express her nature without control over a vast quantity of things and other people, her need for this control to constitute herself the complete capitalist could not objectively be recognized as personal property because at some point there is an objective moral consensus that such control is destroying personhood rather than fostering it.

III.   Hegel, Property, and Personhood

A.   Hegel's Philosophy of Right

The property theory of Hegel's Philosophy of Right,[49] although based on a conception of persons, does not immediately invoke the intuitive personhood perspective. . . .

Because the person in Hegel's conception is merely an abstract unit of free will or autonomy, it has no concrete existence until that will acts on the external world. "[T]he person must give its freedom an external sphere in order to exist as Idea."[52] At this level of particularization, the external sphere "capable of embodying [the person's] freedom" consists of the rest of the world, everything that is distinct from the person.

From the need to embody the person's will to take free will from the abstract realm to the actual, Hegel concludes that the person becomes a real self only by engaging in a property relationship with something external. Such a relationship is the *goal* of the person. . . . Hegel at least clearly makes the claim that a human being can only become properly developed — actualize her freedom — in the context of a community of others. Thus, though he speaks of the person

49. . . . (T. Knox trans. 1942) [hereinafter cited as PR]. . . .
52. PR §41.

in the sphere of abstract right only in the Kantian sense of abstract rationality, he implicitly claims that personhood in the richer sense of self-development and differentiation presupposes the context of human community. If accepted, this claim has important ramifications for a theory of personal property which does rely on that richer sense of personhood. . . .

IV.   Two Kinds of Property: The Dichotomy as Critique

One element of the intuitive personhood perspective is that property for personhood gives rise to a stronger moral claim than other property. This division of property resembles a recurrent kind of critique of real-world property arrangements. The underlying insight of the many dualist property theories seems to be that some property is accorded more stringent legal protection than other property, or is otherwise deemed more important than other property by social consensus. . . .

B.   A Utilitarian Dichotomy

In apparent contrast to these assertions that certain property claims are stronger than others, some utilitarians might claim that since there is only one social goal, maximization of welfare, so there is only one kind of property — that which results in maximization of welfare. In this utilitarian scheme, there will also be no reason for distinctions between property entitlements and other kinds of individual entitlements except for deference to linguistic tradition. Posner's position represents this view: Efficiency will be maximized only when anything that is scarce in the relevant human society during the relevant time period (thus, a "good" and not merely an undifferentiated attribute of the environment) is the subject of an entitlement.[92]

Yet those who espouse utilitarianism in the form of instrumental economics have elaborated a hierarchy of *remedies*. The Calabresi-Melamed distinction between protecting entitlements with "property rules" or "liability rules" is now a widely recognized tool of economic analysis.[93] An entitlement is protected by a property rule if *B* can obtain it from *A* only by paying whatever

92. R. Posner [Economic Analysis of Law (2d ed. 1977)].
93. . . . Property Rules, Liability Rules, and Inalienability: One View of the Cathedral, 85 Harv. L. Rev. 1089 (1972). . . .

price A sets as a willing seller, or if A can obtain an injunction to prevent B's interference. An entitlement is protected by a liability rule if B can obtain it from A by paying some extrinsically determined price (such as the "market" price), even if A is not a willing seller, or if A can obtain only damages on account of B's interference. To some extent, this system does not correspond to the ordinary meaning of property. Most rights traditionally called property are protected against the government only by a liability rule. On the other hand, some rights not traditionally called property, like freedom from bodily intrusion, are protected by property rules. . . .

C. The Personhood Dichotomy

The personhood dichotomy comes about in the following way: A general justification of property entitlements in terms of their relationship to personhood could hold that the rights that come within the general justification form a continuum from fungible to personal. It then might hold that those rights near one end of the continuum — fungible property rights — can be overridden in some cases in which those near the other — personal property rights — cannot be. This is to argue not that fungible property rights are unrelated to personhood, but simply that distinctions are sometimes warranted depending upon the character or strength of the connection. Thus, the personhood perspective generates a hierarchy of entitlements: The more closely connected with personhood, the stronger the entitlement.

Does it make sense to speak of two levels of property, personal and fungible? I think the answer is yes in many situations, no in many others. Since the personhood perspective depends partly on the subjective nature of the relationships between person and thing, it makes more sense to think of a continuum that ranges from a thing indispensable to someone's being to a thing wholly interchangeable with money. Many relationships between persons and things will fall somewhere in the middle of this continuum. Perhaps the entrepreneur factory owner has ownership of a particular factory and its machines bound up with her being to some degree. If a dichotomy telescoping this continuum to two end points is to be useful, it must be because within a given social context certain types of person-thing relationships are understood to fall close to one end or the other of the continuum, so that decisionmakers within that social context can use the dichotomy as a guide to determine which property is worthier of protection. For example, in our social context a house that is owned by someone who resides there is generally understood to be toward the personal end of the continuum. There is both a positive sense that people are bound up with their homes and a normative sense that this is not fetishistic. . . .

D.   Welfare Rights and A Dichotomy in Property . . .

A welfare rights or minimal entitlement theory of just distribution might hold that a government that respects personhood must guarantee citizens all entitlements necessary for personhood. If the personhood dichotomy in property is taken as the source of a distributive mandate as part of such a general theory, it would suggest that government should make it possible for all citizens to have whatever property is necessary for personhood. But a welfare rights theory incorporating property for personhood would suggest not only that government distribute largess in order to make it possible for people to buy property in which to constitute themselves but would further suggest that government should rearrange property rights so that fungible property of some people does not overwhelm the opportunities of the rest to constitute themselves in property. That is, a welfare rights theory incorporating the right to personal property would tell the government to cease allowing one person to impinge on the personhood of another by means of her control over tangible resources, rather than simply tell the government to dole out resources.

Curtailing fungible property rights that impinge on others' opportunities for self-constitution may seem a more radical sort of reform than wealth redistribution through taxation. But purely fungible property is just like any other form of wealth. If a welfare rights theory of distribution makes personhood interests take precedence over some claims to wealth, permitting taxation to provide largess for the poor, it may equally permit curtailing fungible property rights that impinge on the poor, unless doing so only for the holders of certain assets would under the circumstances violate accepted norms of equality.

V.   Two Kinds of Property: A Selective Survey

This Part surveys a number of disparate legal issues from the viewpoint of property for personhood. These issues represent types of cases in which the rough dichotomy between personal and fungible property approximates the world well enough to be useful. . . .

[Professor Radin first discusses several legal rules providing special consideration to the "sanctity of the home," notably privacy protections, allowing persons to own and read the literature of their choice in the privacy of their homes. She also discusses laws protecting tenants and constitutional safeguards against unreasonable searches.]

B. Aspects of the Taking Problem

The whole question of government regulation and "taking" of private property is the most difficult, yet most promising area for applying the personhood dichotomy. The personhood perspective cannot generate a comprehensive theory of property rights vis-à-vis the government; it can only add another moral inquiry that helps clarify some cases. But this is a field in which a unified theory has not been forthcoming. . . .

[T]he theory of personal property suggests that not all object-loss is equally important. Some objects may approach the fungible end of the continuum so that the justification for protecting them as specially related to persons disappears. . . .

On the other hand, a few objects may be so close to the personal end of the continuum that no compensation could be "just." That is, hypothetically, if some object were so bound up with me that I would cease to be "myself" if it were taken, then a government that must respect persons ought not to take it. If my kidney may be called my property, it is not property subject to condemnation for the general public welfare. Hence, in the context of a legal system, one might expect to find the characteristic use of standards of review and burdens of proof designed to shift risk of error away from protected interests in personal property. For instance, if there were reason to suspect that some object were close to the personal end of the continuum, there might be a prima facie case against taking it. That prima facie case might be rebutted if the government could show that the object is not personal, or perhaps that the object is not "too" personal compared with the importance to the government of acquiring that particular object for social purposes.

This suggests that if the personhood perspective is expressed in law, one might expect to find an implied limitation on the eminent domain power. That is, one might expect to find that a special class of property like a family home is protected against the government by a "property rule" and not just a "liability rule." Or one might expect to find that a special class of property is protected against taking unless the government shows a "compelling state interest" and that taking it is the "least intrusive alternative."

This general limitation has not developed. Perhaps the personhood perspective is not strong enough to outweigh other concerns, especially the government's need to appear even-handed and the lower administrative costs associated with simpler rules. For example, perhaps we are unwilling to presume that all single-family homes are personal because many houses are held only for investment, and a subjective inquiry into each case slows down government too much. On the other hand, perhaps the personhood perspective is so deeply embedded that, without focusing on the problem, we expect that the condemning authority will take fungible property where possible. We may simply take for granted that the government will not take homesteads when parking lots will do. Still, the fact that the personhood perspective has not surfaced to give some explicit protection to family homes from government taking, such as stricter scrutiny, seems to be anomalous. . . .

NOTES AND QUESTIONS ON THE "PERSONHOOD" THEORY OF PROPERTY

1. Reconsider the selection from Goffman: Does Radin's account of "personhood" property explain the inmates' distress at losing what seem to be relatively trivial items, or their anxiety to establish ways to keep such items? By her account, which entitlements should be most important to them? Why?

2. How plausible are Radin's intuitions about the sort of property that people become "bound up with"? For evidence on the matter, see Mihaly Csikszentmihalyi & Eugene Rochberg-Halton, The Meaning of Things: Domestic Symbols and the Self (1981).

3. Does the distinction between personhood property and fungible property stand up, in the sense that some identifiable properties are more important than others in people's ability to carry out their personal projects? Might a business be personhood property? What about the bank account that an elderly couple has saved for retirement?

Consider the remark that a quadriplegic law student made to one of the editors of this volume: He regards money (rather than heirlooms, clothes, or any other specific item) as his most important asset, because money enables him to hire the assistants he needs for dressing, eating, transportation, writing, and the like; thus money enables him to carry out a meaningful and useful life. Is his money personhood property? Or is it fungible property? How do you know the difference?

4. Note that Radin characterizes a wedding ring "in the hands of the jeweler" as instrumental or fungible property. If the per-

sonhood/fungible attributes of a given item depend on the characteristics of the individual in possession of that item, can the personhood/fungible distinction function as a rule of law? Why does the distinction carry some implicit legal weight in protecting the privacy of the home, but do little to protect the home from eminent domain? For more on eminent domain and takings of property, see Chapter 9 D., infra. For another author's contemporaneous and somewhat similar thesis about the graded importance of different kinds of property, and some suggestions about the legal consequences for eminent domain, see William Rogers, Bringing People Back: Toward a Comprehensive Theory of Taking in Natural Resources Law, 10 Ecol. L.Q. 205 (1982).

5. What is wrong with fetishism? How does anyone know a healthy attachment from a sick or fetishistic one?

One of the editors of this book has repeatedly urged Professor Radin to consider the challenge to fetishism presented by Scrooge McDuck, Donald Duck's hugely wealthy and thoroughly capable elderly relative. McDuck, as some readers of Disney comics may recall, enjoys rolling about and diving in his great vats of money. That is, McDuck seems to take great personal pleasure in the most thoroughly fungible of resources, namely: cold cash. Is McDuck, so clearly an example of the "caricature capitalist," an unhealthy fetishist? If so, what accounts for his great personal competence, and why is he, according to informal reports of numerous Disney readers, the most popular character in Donald Duck's entourage? On the other hand, if McDuck's tastes are merely personal quirks rather than unhealthy fetishes, can any attachment to property be considered fetishistic? The editors are sorry to report that Professor Radin has never responded publicly to the issues so dramatically raised by McDuck.

6. Radin discusses a "personhood" interest in a minimal level of economic support. Who should provide this support, and how? Are the personhood claims of recipients compatible with the personhood claims of what may be involuntary donors?

A seminal article on the property-like characteristics of welfare payments and other governmentally-created benefits is Charles Reich, The New Property, 73 Yale Law J. 957 (1964). Reich argued that recipients of such benefits should have a cognizable property interest in what had previously been thought to be mere governmental "largesse." Among other things, Reich suggested that welfare recipients need secure property in order to play genuine roles as citizens. How does that argument compare to Radin's personhood thesis? Is political participation an aspect of personhood, and how does it depend on property ownership? Reich's article spawned an enormous literature on the "new property," as well as some well-known caselaw, notably Goldberg v. Kelly, 397 U.S. 254 (1970).

For other arguments on minimal levels of support, see John Rawls, A Theory of Justice, infra, p.101, and the notes following that selection.

7. For further consideration of the idea of body parts as property, see the selection from Radin's Market-Inalienability, infra p.336.

Property as Storytelling: Perspectives from Game Theory, Narrative Theory, Feminist Theory *

Carol M. Rose

Introduction

Many of our modern views about property, and indeed about political and economic matters generally, come from the works of seventeenth and eighteenth century theorists who hoped to find a firmly scientific basis for the study of "political economy."[1] Their systematic approach suggests that these theorists' accounts of property might be purely analytic — "synchronic" as the linguists call it. An account of this sort would treat the subject as if all its parts occur at once, in an interlocking whole whose various aspects can be inferred logically and verified empirically, without reference to origins or to transformative changes over time. On such an account, one might indeed perceive that things change as time passes, but if one has a proper grip on the overall analytic framework, any changes would occur according to set patterns, so that future states are predictable from past states. This would be, more or less, a scientific approach: all changes in a given system are predictable from a proper synchronic analysis of the system itself.

But however much these early modern theorists hoped to ground political economy as a science, one notices that their discussions of property at some point take a striking turn towards a narrative or "diachronic" explanatory mode, treating property regimes as if they had origins and as if they developed over time. Locke is undoubtedly the most influential of the classic property theorists,

*Source: 2 Yale J.L. & Humanities 37-57 (1990).
1. T. Hobbes, Leviathan, ch. 20, at 261 (C.B. McPherson ed. 1968) (1651): "The skill of making, and maintaining Common-wealths, consisteth in certain rules, as doth Arithmetique and Geometry; not (as Tennis-play) on Practice onely"; see also J. Locke, Two Treatises of Government, editor's introduction at 104 (P. Laslett rev. ed. 1963) (3d ed. 1698) [hereinafter Locke]. . . .

and Locke used this narrative approach in his famous discussion of property in the Second Treatise of Government. Although the parts are somewhat scattered, the Treatise clearly unfolds a story line, beginning in a plenteous state of nature, carrying through the growing individual appropriation of goods, then proceeding to the development of a trading money economy, and culminating in the creation of government to safeguard property. Indeed Locke's choice of a narrative mode is all the more striking because he appears to have been indifferent to the factual accuracy of the story as a genuine history.

Almost a century later, William Blackstone launched into a quite similar pseudo-history in explaining property as an institution with an origin and evolution: he too described human beings as beginning in a state of plenty, gradually accumulating personal and landed property, and finally creating government and laws to protect property.[9] And in more recent days, the modern economist Harold Demsetz has chosen to illustrate his theory of property rights by reference to a narrative history of an evolving property regime among fur-hunting Indians on the American continent.[10]

Why have these theorists turned to storytelling to discuss property? Why have they chosen a narrative explanatory mode, which often diverges from scientific/predictive modes, and instead envisions events as unfolding in ways that, at least arguably, are only understandable after the fact? That is the subject of this paper, or at least one of its subjects. The larger subject is the relation of property to storytelling generally: the reasons why in our general discussions of who has what, and how property gets distributed, we turn to narratives instead of looking exclusively to scientific or predictive analytic approaches. In treating that subject, the paper will borrow especially from game theory, narrative theory and feminist theory. . . .

I. The Preference Orderings in the Classical Analysis of Property

We often think of property as some version of entitlement to things: I have a right to this thing or that. In a more sophisticated version of property, of course, we see property as a way of defining our relationships with other people. On such versions, my right to this thing or that isn't about controlling the "thing," so much as it is about my

9. 2 W. Blackstone, Commentaries on the Laws of England 3-9 (1766 & reprint 1979) [hereinafter Blackstone].
10. Demsetz, Towards a Theory of Property Rights, 1967 Am. Econ. Rev. 347 (Papers & Proceedings).

relationship with *you*, and with everybody else in the world: if I have a property right to this thing or that, I can keep you from exercising any control over it or having any access to it at all. That was Blackstone's benchmark for property: property was not just a "sole and despotic dominion," but it was a dominion that empowered the holder to the "total exclusion of the right of any other individual in the universe."[14]

In fact, that is the standard economic version of property: property as an institution revolves around the desire for resources themselves, but it also revolves around the desire to control others' access to those resources, at least when the resources are scarce. On this classical view, the institution of property mediates peoples' conflicting desires about resources, and it does so by allocating exclusive rights. If there were no property rights in the berry patch, all of us would just have to fight all the time for the berries. But instead, a property regime allocates this part of the patch to X, and that part to Y; and this (or any other) allocation gives each owner a sense of security, so that she invests in cultivation and tending the plants — which she won't do if she thinks she is going to wind up having to share the berries later with a lot of interloping loafers. Besides that, exclusive property rights identify who has what, and allow all of us owners to trade instead of fighting. As a result, everything gets more valuable. It all gets more valuable because the property regime encourages us to work, and then to trade the results of our work, instead of wasting time and effort in bickering and fighting.

So when we break down this very standard version of property, we find several critical points. The first point is that desire — that is, a desire for resources — is at the center of the whole institution of property. The second point is that we need the capacity to shut out others from the resources that are the objects of our desire, at least when those objects become scarce. And the third point is that by allocating exclusive control of resources to individuals, a property regime winds up by satisfying even more desires, because it mediates conflicts between individuals and encourages everyone to work and trade instead of fighting, thus making possible an even greater satisfaction of desires.

There is another element hidden in this analysis, though: it is the idea that we already know, at least roughly, how people are going to order their desires, or more technically, their *preferences* about themselves and others, and about their respective access to desired resources.

What is that understood ordering? Like many of our interesting ideas in this area, it comes to us from the seventeenth century, and

14. 2 Blackstone 2.

most particularly from Hobbes first and later Locke. Hobbes' major point about human preferences is that individuals want to *live*. Our desire to stay alive is just *there*, omnipresent and undeniable; it needs no further explanation. When push comes to shove, Hobbes thought, we will prefer our own lives over other peoples',[20] and by and large, we will also prefer our lives over highfalutin' causes, however noble. That is why in battle, for example, as Hobbes put it, "there is on one side, or both, a running away."[21]

Locke's major addendum to this picture was to show the relevance of property to the desire to live. He pointed out that life depends on property, in a very primitive sense; if one cannot literally *appropriate* those berries and fruits, one will simply die.[22]

And so acquisitiveness, the desire to have property, is "just there" too, also universal and omnipresent; thus one can always predict a human desire to have things for one's self, or as they say more lately, the human propensity to be a self-interested rational utility maximizer. The propensity is just a kind of fact of life, and the eighteenth century political economists took it for granted, rejecting as unrealistic the earlier condemnations of acquisitiveness. They attempted instead to carry forward the new science of political economy on the firm ground of irreducible self-interest, and indeed they toned down the language of "avarice" into that of the more benign "interest."

Indeed, if we do take these preferences for life and acquisition as givens, then economics can make a bid to be a kind of logical science in politics and law. With these preferences understood, we can sensibly talk about how the law gives people incentives to do this thing and that, and we can manipulate future welfare by institutionalizing the proper ex-ante approaches. Shifts of entitlements become predictable because we know how people order their preferences; with that knowledge, we can predict their responses and moves under different states of affairs.

That is what modern neoclassical economists do, more or less taking these utility-maximizing preference orderings for granted, and using them to perform some very powerful and sophisticated predictions of property-related behavior under varying circumstances. They make predictions about the production or consumption shifts that follow from shifts of costs, and may predict, for example, a lowered provision of rental housing in the wake of added landlord repair costs. Underlying such predictions is an idea that people prefer more for themselves rather than less, and that this

20. Hobbes, ch. 13, at 184.
21. Hobbes, ch. 21.
22. Locke, 2d Treatise §28.

preference ordering is an irreducible fact that needs no further explanation — it is just there.

Note, however, that if we do *not* have that starting point of a
predictable set of preferences for "more" rather than "less," then the
ways that people trade and otherwise shift their entitlements will be
a little weird and unpredictable; and in talking about property, and
about the ways people deal with it, at least sometimes we may have
to turn to post-hoc explanatory approaches to supplement our logical predictions. That is, we may only be able to understand property
arrangements through narrative discourses like literature and history, discourses that construct a story of how things got to be that
way — a story in which there were genuine choices along the way,
and in which things were not really predictable in advance, and did
not have to wind up the way they did.

II.   The Humdrum and the Weird; or, Predictable and
Unpredictable Preferences

This part of the paper questions the idea that any given preference
orderings are "just there," as they seem to be in the standard classical and neoclassical economic view. It suggests instead that even if
one is quite sympathetic to the classical view of self-interest, there
are a lot of leftover preference orderings that would not have been
predicted, and that have to be explained in some way through an
after-the-fact story. This part makes that point through a series of
thought experiments on the ways that people order their preferences about their own and other people's access to resources.

These thought experiments present scenarios about preference
orderings, in a situation where there are two people (you and I) and
some Resource X that both of us desire. The scenarios presume five
possible outcomes, to wit:

> I get a lot of X, and so do you;
> I get pretty much X (where "pretty much" is something over
>   one-half of "a lot"), and so do you;
> I get a little X, and so do you;
> I get a lot of X, and you get nothing; and
> I get nothing, and you get a lot of X.

Obviously these outcomes would not be exhaustive in the real
world, but they are enough to work with for now. In each of the
following scenarios, "I" order my preferences among these possible
outcomes, beginning with the outcome that I desire most, and mov-

ing downward to the outcome that I desire least. Again, there is some mathematically large number of ways that people might line up these outcomes, but I have chosen six that are probably familiar to most readers, and have given them names so that they can be identified more easily:

Number 1: John Doe (JD). This perfectly ordinary person has the following order of preferences:

Choice #1: I get a lot, you get a lot.
       2: I get a lot, you get zip.
       3: I get pretty much, you get pretty much.
       4: I get a little, you get a little.
       5: I get zip, you get a lot.

JD seems to be quite compatible with classical property thinking. His order of preferences is based on a kind of self-interest that is "just there." He is not mean, and is happy to have you get a lot of X where there is plenty to be had, but not if your share cuts into his. In general, he just prefers getting more over getting less, no matter what you get.

Number 2: King of the Mountain (KOM). A somewhat more competitive type orders his preferences as follows:

Choice #1: I get a lot, you get zip.
       2: I get a lot, you get a lot.
       3: I get pretty much, you get pretty much.
       4: I get a little, you get a little.
       5: I get zip, you get a lot.

KOM is getting a bit slippery, from the point of view of the standard predicted preferences. He reverses John Doe's first and second preferences: he doesn't prefer the situation of maximum combined utility (both get a lot), but rather prefers the situation where he is the only winner. Still, economic prediction might be able to accommodate KOM; after all, KOM is just like JD insofar as he maximizes his own take, and his choices always put getting *more* over getting *less*. He just competes a bit more with the other guy. A little later, I will argue that with respect to property, JD and KOM are pretty much identical.

Number 3: Malice Aforethought (MA). This is a nastier character:

Choice #1: I get a lot, you get zip.
       2: I get a little, you get a little.
       3: I get pretty much, you get pretty much.
       4: I get a lot, you get a lot.
       5: I get zip, you get a lot.

MA is *very* slippery. MA would rather lose a great deal than have the other guy win; his preference ordering is based on keeping the other guy down. He is not looking very self-interested any more, at least in the usual sense. The reason is that he is "distracted" by interpersonal matters.

Number 4: Mom (or Good Citizen). Mom is a more comfortable figure, and orders her preferences this way:

Choice #1:   I get a lot, you get a lot.
2:   I get pretty much, you get pretty much.
3:   I get zip, you get a lot.
4:   I get a lot, you get zip (?).
5:   I get a little, you get a little (?).

Interestingly enough, Mom too is out of line for a prediction based on self-interest: her first choice is like JD's (both get a lot), but after that she prefers that both get a reasonably good deal, and thereafter she puts the other person first. Why would a self-interested utility maximizer do that? S/he wouldn't. Again, Mom seems to be distracted by interpersonal matters. But note, Mom's orderings choose highest *joint* utility first, the next highest next and so forth. As for the question marks by 4 and 5: if Mom gets a lot, maybe she can give you some; if she can't do that, she might prefer 5 to 4.

Number 5: Portnoy's Mom (PM). She will be the first to tell you that her order of preference is:

Choice #1:   I get zip, you get a lot.
2:   I get a lot, you get a lot.
3:   I get pretty much, you get pretty much.
4:   I get a little, you get a little.
5:   I get a lot, you get zip.

PM is even more out of line with a predicted preference ordering of self-interested maximization. She would rather have the other person come in first — but she's not completely crazy, either, since her second choice is to do well herself, as long as the other guy does too.

Number 6: Hit Me. This is a kind of natural victim:

Choice #1:   I get zip, you get a lot.
2:   I get a little, you get a little.
3:   I get pretty much, you get pretty much.
4:   I get a lot, you get a lot.
5:   I get a lot, you get zip.

This character is out of the economic predictor's ballpark. She is a mirror image of Malice Aforethought: She wants to lose, she wants to be beaten, preferably by somebody else. . . .

Now I want to return to the main argument. Which of our preference orderings can be predicted on the classical assumptions of self-interested maximization? John Doe certainly can be, and King of the Mountain too, if we assume that self interest simply means indifference about others. Both are maximizing their own "take," both consistently choosing more over less; and preference orderings like that are assumed to be "just there," without any need for further explanation.

But how about the others? However odd they are, and however small their numbers, characters with the offbeat and unpredicted preference orderings of Numbers 3 to 6 do indeed seem to be around too, at least in most people's repertoire of experience. How do we know that? Well, for one thing, we see these characters in actual narratives, both historical and fictional. Shakespeare and Gibbon, to take two illustrious examples, are all full of tales about Malice Aforethought and his vengeance and spite. Mom and the Good Citizen might be less dramatic, but they too are all over the place in heroic novels and tales; and according to feminist literature, the cooperative, helpful character is really quite common. Roth of course told the story of Portnoy's Mom,[34] in a way that is apparently readily recognizable by a substantial segment of the population; and feminist literature has a good deal to say about Hit Me and about victimization generally.

Those other characters certainly make themselves felt in the law as well. Here as in literature and history, some of the most interesting examples revolve about the Malice Aforethought character. In property law, there is a whole category of cases about people who build the so-called "spite fence"; their story revolves about a character who goes to considerable expense to wall in a neighbor's windows, or put up some repulsive object to ruin the neighbor's view of the sunset. An example from a few years ago involved a disappointed Vermont landowner, whose neighbors blocked his efforts to rezone his lot for motel use; he decided to use the property for a piggery instead. One needs to know the story, the narrative, to figure out how such people got that way.

Much sadder are the cases of Hit Me, the victims. The criminal law is now seeing persons who give away all they have, even their lives, and appear to defer consistently to some others in what seems to be a kind of pathology of other-regarding behavior. Perhaps such persons are not very common, and perhaps their motives are exceedingly complex, but their plight does seem to attract

34. P. Roth, Portnoy's Complaint (1969).

an extraordinary level of popular fascination, and perhaps self-comparison.

The Good Citizen or Mom is another category that shows up constantly in law, and generally speaking, the law tries to encourage her cooperative behavior. The law allows people to set up all kinds of cooperative arrangements; people can form contracts and partnerships, hold joint bank accounts, and own property in various forms of common tenure. The law also polices cooperative arrangements and disfavors those in which one person seems to take advantage of another, even though the advantage-taking may fall within the formal terms of a given agreement. Moreover, while the law does not generally require that anyone assist another who is in trouble, it does recognize that some people will volunteer anyway, and protects those "Good Samaritans." Thus if John Doe's carelessness causes an accident, and Mom stops to assist the victim, tort law may make John Doe responsible for Mom as well as for the original victim, on the theory that he should have realized that she would try to help.

The point of all this is that legal doctrines reflect the knowledge that these other preference orderings exist; certainly there is no monolithic legal expectation that everyone will behave as an individual self-interested utility maximizer. The further point is that all these offbeat preference orderings suggest an element of indeterminacy in the ways that people use property, trade it, transfer it. There is no single ordering of preferences in the real world, and everyone knows it. . . .

What does that mean? It means that even if we think the classical property view is generally true, we are going to have to make some allowances for oddities in the way people actually do order their preferences, at least some of the time. And that in turn means that the way we fix and trade entitlements is not going to be perfectly predictable, from a set of maximizing preferences that are just there. At least some of the time, in order to figure out how entitlements have shifted and settled as they have, we are going to have to explain things after the fact, post hoc — that is, we are going to have to tell a story.

III.   Narrativity and the Property Regime

I want to go now to the point where the weakness of a single ordering of preferences is most telling. That point has to do with the very regime of property itself. But to get to that point, I have to begin with an explanation of a particular kind of property, that is, common property.

Common property is a kind of property system that often emerges when it is impractical or expensive to have individualized property in a given resource. For example, it might be awfully expensive to establish and police individual rights to fish in a large lake. At the same time, though, the fish are a finite resource, and it might be important to restrain the total "take," so that the fishery doesn't get overused or ruined, and so that the fish can regenerate. What our fishermen have to do, then, is to agree on some way that they can limit the times they fish, or the numbers they take, or the way they re-stock the lake — or do something else to protect the fish against decimation.

Note that our fishermen now cannot follow the preference choice "I get a lot, you get a lot," and just let all the fishermen take all the fish they want. That is the choice of plenty, and these fish are not infinitely plenteous, but are rather a limited resource. But the fishery resource is not easily divided up among the fishermen, either; it would be conserved and used most productively if all the parties were simply to exercise some forbearance. And so, they could be faced with what is conventionally called the "Prisoner's Dilemma": all parties have to give up something for the sake of a higher long-term collective total, but it is not at all clear that they will do so, especially since each has some individual motive to cheat on any cooperative arrangement.

Now, this common-property problem creates a modification of the way we can picture the preference choices that were available to our earlier cast of characters. If we rule out the choice of Plenty (i.e., "I get a lot, you get a lot,"), the remaining options fall into the familiar Prisoner's Dilemma square:

	You cooperate	*You cheat*
I cooperate	(A) I get pretty much, you get pretty much.	(B) I get zip, you get lots.
I cheat	(C) I get lots, you get zip.	(D) I get little, you get little.

Of course, the best choice from the point of view of joint utility maximization is Box (A), where each fisherman cooperates and curtails some of his fishing for the sake of preserving the resource indefinitely for the whole group; that choice would mean that everyone would get pretty much over the long run, and the total fish taken would be maximized because the underlying resource would be able to renew itself. But for each fisherman, the *individual's* maximizing choice would be Box (C), in which he cheats while the others cooperate; thus he would prefer that all the others follow the rules and cooperate to curtail overfishing, while he "defects," or cheats, and takes all he can. But if each fisherman chooses this strategy of cheating, the whole system is driven toward Box (D), where all parties cheat, and the joint product winds up at a relatively puny level, because the fish are too depleted to regenerate. Thus the "cheating" choice can turn a renewable resource — a "positive-sum game" resource where there are gains from cooperation — into a wasting asset, a "zero-sum" resource in which all individual gains are at the expense of others, and in which the resource eventually depletes, to the ultimate detriment of all the players.

Now let us review the choices of our cast of characters: How would each character choose, if we rule out the option of Plenty (I get a lot, you get a lot)? And most important, would any of these characters be able to sustain a cooperative arrangement, and choose the optimal Box (A), where everyone acts to get "pretty much," but not the individual maximum?

First and most important, John Doe and King of the Mountain would not choose this cooperative Box (A). Where the option of Plenty is gone, they would have identical preference orderings. In a situation of finite or scarce resources, when we have to strike out the preference for everyone getting a lot, we see for both JD and KOM the following ordering:

1: C) I get lots, you get zip.
2: A) I get pretty much, you get pretty much.
3: D) I get little, you get little.
4: B) I get zip, you get lots.

When resources are limited, the cooperative management of common property is a second choice for both John Doe and King of the Mountain. Instead, in this situation of scarcity, they both have the same first choice: to take the mostest fustest. Hence the standard political economists' prediction, which is based on these characters, is what is called the Tragedy of the Commons: unless restrained by some outside compulsion, each tries to get the most for himself, and in the ensuing race, a resource that could be renewable is driven toward ruination instead.[45]

45. Hardin, The Tragedy of the Commons, 162 Science 1243 (1968).

Malice Aforethought wouldn't put Box (A) first either. Striking the option of Plenty makes no difference to his first choice, which is (C) (I get lots, you get zip). In this he is like John Doe and King of the Mountain, even though his next choices would diverge from theirs. Mrs. Portnoy wouldn't choose box (A) either: her first choice remains (B) (I get zip, you get lots), which of course just encourages Malice Aforethought. And Hit-Me is like Portnoy's Mom in putting choice (B) first.

The heroine of the piece, then, is Mom (or the Good Citizen) who does not put her own well-being above yours, but is not a fool about needless self-sacrifice either: After the ruled-out choice of Plenty (I get a lot, you get a lot), her next — and now first — choice is the cooperative choice (A), (I get pretty much, you get pretty much). This is the most productive choice in a world where scarce resources have to be managed cooperatively; it is the choice that forbears from taking the largest individual portion and instead maximizes the joint product.

Now, here is the kicker. The larger implication of all this is that a property *regime* generally, taken as an entire system, has the same structure as a common property. This is most notable at the formative stage. At the outset of private property, people have to cooperate to set up the system — they have to get themselves organized, go to the meetings, discuss the options, figure out who gets what and how the entitlements will be protected. Even if the property regime is just a matter of customary practices that develop over time, the participants have to cooperate to the extent of recognizing and abiding by the indicia of ownership that their customs set out. And indeed, even after a property regime is in place, people have to respect each others' individual entitlements out of cooperative impulses, because it is impossible to have a continuous system of policing and/or retaliation for cheating. Thus a property system depends on people not stealing, cheating and so forth, even when they have the chance — that is, all the participants, or at least a substantial number of them, have to cooperate to make a property regime work.

A property regime, in short, presupposes a kind of character who is *not* predicted in the standard story about property. And that, I suggest, is why the classic theories of property turned to narrative at crucial moments, particularly in explaining the origin of property regimes, where the need for cooperation is most obvious: Their narrative stories allowed them to slide smoothly over the cooperative gap in their systematic analyses of self-interest.

One can see the point in the various parts of Locke's story about property. He starts off with a tale of people in a state of nature, acquiring natural products like acorns and apples through the very labor of gathering them; and then realizing that wealth could be stored through the collection of durables (like nuts and little pieces of gold); and finally, growing nervous at the "very unsafe, very un-secure" enjoyment of property in the state of nature, and joining with others to establish the civil society that will protect everyone's hard-earned property.[52]

Hold it right there: joining with others? Just how did they form that civil society and its government, anyway? Who put in the time and effort of schmoozing, and getting the special committees to-gether, and hammering out the terms? Why didn't they all just loaf around, as John Doe would, choosing Box (C) in the hopes that other people would do all the organizing work? And if they did let George do it, who is this George character anyway? If there is a George, he looks an awful lot like Mom, or the Good Citizen — somebody who would be willing to do some work for the sake of the common good.

Blackstone's story is a more connected narrative, but it slides over the point even more easily. After a long tale of the way in which people started to hold onto increasing numbers of objects for them-selves, as they became more talented and numerous, he points out that the "earth would not produce her fruits in sufficient quantities, without the assistance of tillage: but who would be at the pains of tilling it, if another might watch an opportunity to seize upon and enjoy the product of his industry, art and labour?" Here is the happy conclusion: "Necessity begat property, and in order to insure that property, recourse was had to civil society."[56] And that's it.

Now wait a minute: If nobody would be at pains of tilling un-less they could capture the rewards, why should they be at pains of setting up a civil society? Why don't Blackstone's characters sit around waiting for George too?

In short, there is a gap between the kind of self-interested indi-vidual who needs exclusive property to induce him to labor, and the kind of individual who has to be there to create, maintain, and pro-tect a property regime. The existence of a property regime is not predictable from a starting point of rational self-interest; and con-sequently, from that perspective, property needs a tale, a story, a post-hoc explanation.

That, I think, is one reason Locke and Blackstone, and their modern-day successors, are so fond of telling stories when they talk about the origin of property. It is the story that fills the gap in the classical theory, and, as Hayden White might put it, that makes property "plausible." Narrative gives us a smooth tale of property

52. [Locke] §123.
56. [2 Blackstone, at 2-8.]

as an institution that could come about through time, effort, and above all through cooperative choices.

Cooperation, then, is a preference ordering that the classical property theorists weren't counting on in theory, but that they can't do without. And so they have to tell a story to explain it, and rely on our imaginative reconstruction from narrative to paint a plausible picture about how we got these property regimes in the first place.

IV.   Reprise: The "Natural-ness" of Self-Interest and the "Moral-ness" of the Property Story

Quite aside from the thought experiments we have run through, and quite aside from the striking case of the cooperative preferences that we need for the institution of property itself, it should be pretty obvious that John Doe's self-interested preference ordering is only one among a number of options. In the real world, his orderings have to be explained too; they have a history too, and need a story just like anybody else's. The Critical Legal Studies movement has been around long enough to get across the idea that John Doe is just another story; it is instead the endless repetition of JD's "naturalness" that has made us think that his preferences are "just there," needing no further explanation or narration.

Feminist theorists have made the point in another way: at least since Carol Gilligan,[60] and really for some time before, we have realized that Mom or the Good Citizen — the caring, cooperative person generally — is just as much "there" as the indifferent non-cooperator, John Doe. Indeed, the feminist theorists have pointed out the importance of narrative in arriving at preference choices: Mom talks things over, and arrives at her preference orderings through discussion and negotiation — perhaps at least sometimes because she has little to begin with, and hence little capacity to retaliate against non-cooperators. Presumably, from Mom's (or Good Citizen George's) perspective, cooperation would be the predictable set of preferences, while John Doe's self-interest would be the oddity, and John Doe would have to be explained by some kind of story about how he got that way.

So why is cooperation the preference ordering that seems to need the story? There is, of course, the point that is made so tellingly by critical theory, and even more so by feminist theory: the dominant story-teller can make his position seem to be the natural one. It is not too hard to envision the bland John Doe (or perhaps the more competitive King of the Mountain) as the surrogate for the Liberal,

60. C. Gilligan [In a Different Voice (1982)].

the dominating storyteller and *bête noire* of the Crits; while Malice Aforethought could stand in for the Patriarch, another dominating storyteller and enemy of feminist theory. And one should note that John Doe, King of the Mountain, and Malice Aforethought all have a disturbing similarity in their patterns of preferences: where there is not enough to go around, where Plenty is ruled out as an option, each of these characters prefers as a first choice: "I get a lot, you get nothing." Perhaps this is why it is sometimes difficult to tell these characters apart.

But there is more to be said about these characters than their identity as a dominating group of storytellers. Consider Mom's big problem: suppose that she encounters John Doe, the blandest of these three noncooperating characters. However much she may prefer cooperative solutions, when she meets this non-cooperator, she has to choose between two roles she does not want. One of her choices is to be a Hit-Me victim, since her choice to cooperate would only meet John Doe's choice to cheat, which would put her in the worst of all possible positions. Her other choice is to mimic John Doe himself, by choosing mutual non-cooperation — but that is a role that she realizes would lead to a collective loss, which she also does not want. Thus unless she is dealing with another Mom, another cooperator, she is stuck with a choice between Boxes (B) or (D): the choice between cooperating and the great risk of domination, or of cheating and the certainty of the relative mutual impoverishment of "I get a little, you get a little."

And that, I would suggest, is a big reason why John Doe seems like nature, like something that is "just there," while Mom seems to need a narrative. John Doe chooses the safe route, the route that might lead to the jackpot if the opposite number is a cooperator/sucker, and that at least lets him get a little bit if the other guy is another noncooperative John Doe.

But Mom the cooperator takes risks for a common good. When it works, everyone is better off, but when it doesn't, she may lose horribly. And she makes you wonder, how did she get that way? Why didn't she take the safe route and cheat, like John Doe? Why does she hang in there, hoping the frog will become a prince? What gives her the nerve to take a risk that the other guy might be a cooperator too? More importantly, is it really a matter of her nerve at all, or only of having no alternatives — of using imagination in the face of hopelessness, of creativity when she has no leverage for retaliation? *What's her story, anyway?*

Thus we are back to storytelling — and not just the story about Mom, but also to the story that she can tell: her storytelling can both create a sense of commonality, and reorder her audience's ways of dealing with the world. According to the narrative theorists, the teller of the tales has a vision of some kind of community, even if it is only a community of two.[64] The storyteller places herself with the audience experiencing the tale; she takes a clutch of occurrences and through narrative reveals them for her audience as *actions*, with beginnings, middles, and ends — actions in which the audience can imagine themselves as common participants or common observers. When she tells us, "Here is what we (or they) did, and how we (or they) did it," she transforms events into our experienced or imagined actions, and in the process tells us who we are, as real or imaginable actors. Thus the storyteller, by structuring the audience's experience and imagination, helps to turn her audience into a moral community. Moreover, by structuring our experience of events, the storyteller in effect constructs our memories and consciousness, so that we can draw on this new stock to act in the future. In this sense, narratives change our minds, and give us an opportunity to reconsider and reorder our approach to events; we can recollect them as actions taken and not taken, and act differently in the future, instead of endlessly repeating some formulaic, repetitive, and predictable response, as rocks respond to gravity. Perhaps this is what Mom is aiming at: Narrative theory coincides with feminist theory in suggesting that preference orderings don't just come out of nowhere; they may be constructs of narrative and negotiation, and may change over time, as we digest the stories of the places that our preferences have led us, or may lead us in the future, unless we act to lead them instead.

Thus as the feminist theorist Robin West has pointed out — though in somewhat different terms — narrative gives Mom a way to get John Doe to exercise a little imagination, and get him to take a chance on cooperating too, for the sake of a larger good. She can tell him a story, she can let him know that things don't have to be the way they are; she can put together a narrative to show how it feels to be in the other guy's shoes, and how it is that mutual trust and cooperative efforts are not only possible but preferable from everyone's point of view.[68] In fact, there is even a story about this storytelling endeavor, in a way: it is the tale of Scheherazade. But even that is a particularly haunting story-of-storytelling, since the captive Scheherazade had no weapons but her wits, and her tale suggests that storytelling may begin in weakness, telling tales to power.

Perhaps now we can take another guess at why Locke and Blackstone and their successors have been telling those siren tales

---

64. D. Carr, Time, Narrative and History, 61-62, 153-156 (1986).
68. West [Economic Man and Literary Woman: One Contrast, 39 Mercer L. Rev.], at 868-870.

about property, too. Their theoretical self-interest had a fatal weakness too when it came to establishing a property regime. But if their tales could just get us John Does over the hump of our conservative, unimaginative, play-it-safe self-interest, they might get us to establish property regimes; they might get us to recognize that if we all respect each others' claims, we can encourage everyone to expend labor on the resources of the world, and we all will be better off in the end.

And maybe that is the real story about why they told those stories, and why their successors continue to tell them. They may have been right or wrong in their argument that property improves the lot of humankind; and their smooth tales of property's cooperative origins may well have slighted the emotional context in which cooperation takes place. But those tales are moral ones all the same, just as much as Aesop's Fables, speaking to and constituting a kind of moral community, and urging that community to change its ways.

NOTES AND QUESTIONS ON NARRATIVE APPROACHES

1. Several of the authors discussed here are represented in selections in this volume, including William Blackstone, Harold Demsetz, and Garrett Hardin.

2. What is the picture of human nature and human desires that Rose attributes to the classical property thinkers? How does this differ from the picture presented by Goffman? By Radin? What consequences might follow for the structuring of property regimes? For other depictions of human preferences about property, see the selections from Sugden, infra p.172, Knetsch, infra p.226, and Hoffman & Spitzer, infra p.287.

3. Rose's analysis of the supposed flaws of the classical property theory revolves around the problem conventionally identified as the "Prisoner's Dilemma" (PD). Rose says that a character like "Mom" — someone with some level of altruistic or other-directed preferences — is needed to overcome PD problems. Is this true? Robert Axelrod, The Evolution of Cooperation (1984), reproduced in part at p.275, infra, argues that cooperation can emerge from purely self-interested motivations. But compare Robert Frank, Passions Within Reason: The Strategic Role of the Emotions (1988), who argues that cooperation rests fundamentally on emotions that cannot be derived from rational self-interest.

4. Rose's "post-modern" presentation suggests that there is no

single dominating set of human preferences. Is that true? Why, then, is the classical property story so persuasive? Does its persuasive power suggest some kind of underlying dominating preferences? Or does it only suggest that stories help people to believe inconsistent things?

5. In discussing the theory of narrative as a persuasive strategy, Rose relies chiefly on David Carr, Time, Narrative and History (1986), which relates narrative to the theory of action. The classical study of rhetoric, which revolved around the question of persuasion, is no longer studied in a systematic fashion at most universities. Interest in rhetoric is increasing, however, stimulated by the view that even persons in the predictive sciences are influenced by arguments that are merely *persuasive* without being *demonstrative* — sometimes on the premise that there is no conclusively demonstrable truth at all. For a version of this position with respect to the physical sciences, see Thomas Kuhn, The Structure of Scientific Revolutions (1962); for the argument that economics is also basically rhetorical, see Donald McCloskey, The Rhetoric of Economics (1985).

Do people really use "stories" to change their own and other peoples' minds and behaviors? How important, for example, are stories for lawyers? The burgeoning literature on legal storytelling receives a stinging critique in Daniel Farber & Suzanna Sherry, Telling Stories Out of School: An Essay on Legal Narratives, 45 Stan. L. Rev. 807 (1993).

6. Isn't this selection a piece of rhetoric too? Why, for example, do the characters have the names they do? Why do the possible preference orderings ("I get a lot, you get a little," for instance) wind up falling so neatly into a Prisoner's Dilemma box?

B.   Property and Prosperity

Commentaries on the Laws of England*

William Blackstone

There is nothing which so generally strikes the imagination, and engages the affections of mankind, as the right of property; or that sole and despotic dominion which one man claims and exercises over the external things of the world, in total exclusion of the

*Source: Vol. 2, *2-*11 (1766).

right of any other individual in the universe. And yet there are very few that will give themselves the trouble to consider the original and foundation of this right. Pleased as we are with the possession, we seem afraid to look back to the means by which it was acquired, as if fearful of some defect in our title; or at best we rest satisfied with the decision of the laws in our favor, without examining the reason or authority upon which those laws have been built. We think it enough that our title is derived by the grant of the former proprietor, by descent from our ancestors, or by the last will and testament of the dying owner; not caring to reflect that (accurately and strictly speaking) there is no foundation in nature or in natural law, why a set of words upon parchment should convey the dominion of land: why the son should have a right to exclude his fellow-creatures from a determinate spot of ground, because his father had done so before him: or why the occupier of a particular field or of a jewel, when lying on his death-bed, and no longer able to maintain possession, should be entitled to tell the rest of the world which of them should enjoy it after him. These inquiries, it must be owned, would be useless and even troublesome in common life. It is well if the mass of mankind will obey the laws when made, without scrutinizing too nicely into the reason for making them. But, when law is to be considered not only as a matter of practice, but also as a rational science, it cannot be improper or useless to examine more deeply the rudiments and grounds of these positive constitutions of society.

In the beginning of the world, we are informed by holy writ, the all-bountiful Creator gave to man "dominion over all the earth, and over the fish of the sea, and over the fowl of the air, and over every living thing that moveth upon the earth." [a] This is the only true and solid foundation of man's dominion over external things, whatever airy metaphysical notions may have been started by fanciful writers upon this subject. The earth, therefore, and all things therein, are the general property of all mankind, exclusive of other beings, from the immediate gift of the Creator. And, while the earth continued bare of inhabitants, it is reasonable to suppose that all was in common among them, and that every one took from the public stock to his own use such things as his immediate necessities required.

These general notions of property were then sufficient to answer all the purposes of human life; and might perhaps still have answered them had it been possible for mankind to have remained in a state of primeval simplicity: as may be collected from the manners of many American nations when first discovered by the Euro-

(a) Gen. i. 28.

peans; and from the ancient method of living among the first Europeans themselves, if we may credit either the memorials of them preserved in the golden age of the poets, or the uniform accounts given by historians of those times. . . . Not that this communion of goods seems ever to have been applicable, even in the earliest stages, to aught but the *substance* of the thing; nor could it be extended to the *use* of it. For, by the law of nature and reason, he, who first began to use it, acquired therein a kind of transient property, that lasted so long as he was using it, and no longer: or, to speak with greater precision, the *right* of possession continued for the same time only that the *act* of possession lasted. Thus the ground was in common, and no part of it was the permanent property of any man in particular; yet whoever was in the occupation of any determined spot of it, for rest, for shade, or the like, acquired for the time a sort of ownership, from which it would have been unjust, and contrary to the law of nature, to have driven him by force: but the instant that he quitted the use or occupation of it, another might seize it, without injustice. Thus also a vine or other tree might be said to be in common, as all men were equally entitled to its produce; and yet any private individual might gain the sole property of the fruit, which he had gathered for his own repast. A doctrine well illustrated by Cicero, who compares the world to a great theatre, which is common to the public, and yet the place which any man has taken is for the time his own.

But when mankind increased in number, craft, and ambition, it became necessary to entertain conceptions of more permanent dominions; and to appropriate to individuals not the immediate *use* only, but the very *substance* of the thing to be used. Otherwise innumerable tumults must have arisen, and the good order of the world be continually broken and disturbed, while a variety of persons were striving who should get the first occupation of the same thing, or disputing which of them had actually gained it. As human life also grew more and more refined, abundance of conveniences were devised to render it more easy, commodious, and agreeable; as, habitations for shelter and safety, and raiment for warmth and decency. But no man would be at the trouble to provide either, so long as he had only an usufructuary property in them, which was to cease the instant that he quitted possession; if, as soon as he walked out of his tent, or pulled off his garments, the next stranger who came by would have a right to inhabit the one, and to wear the other. In the case of habitations in particular, it was natural to observe, that even the brute creation, to whom every thing else was in common, maintained a kind of permanent property in their dwellings, especially for the protection of their young; that the birds of the air had nests, and the beasts of the field had caverns, the invasion of which they esteemed a very flagrant injustice, and would sacrifice their lives to preserve them. Hence a property was soon established in every man's house and home-stall: which seem to have been originally mere temporary huts or movable cabins, suited to the design of Providence for more speedily peopling the earth, and suited to the wandering life of their owners, before any extensive property in the soil or ground was established. And there can be no doubt, but that movables of every kind became sooner appropriated than the permanent substantial soil: partly because they were more susceptible of a long occupancy, which might be continued for months together without any sensible interruption, and at length by usage ripen into an established right; but principally because few of them could be fit for use, till improved and ameliorated by the bodily labor of the occupant, which bodily labor, bestowed upon any subject which before lay in common to all men, is universally allowed to give the fairest and most reasonable title to an exclusive property therein.

The article of food was a more immediate call, and therefore a more early consideration. Such as were not contented with the spontaneous product of the earth, sought for a more solid refreshment in the flesh of beasts, which they obtained by hunting. But the frequent disappointments incident to that method of provision, induced them to gather together such animals as were of a more tame and sequacious nature, and to establish a permanent property in their flocks and herds, in order to sustain themselves in a less precarious manner, partly by the milk of the dams, and partly by the flesh of the young. The support of these their cattle made the article of *water* also a very important point. And therefore the book of Genesis (the most venerable monument of antiquity, considered merely with a view to history) will furnish us with frequent instances of violent contentions concerning wells; the exclusive property of which appears to have been established in the first digger or occupant, even in such places where the ground and herbage remained yet in common. Thus we find Abraham, who was but a sojourner, asserting his right to a well in the country of Abimelech, and exacting an oath for his security, "because he had digged that well." [e] And Isaac, about ninety years afterwards, reclaimed that as his father's property, and after much contention with the Philistines was suffered to enjoy it in peace. [f]

All this while the soil and pasture of the earth remained still in common as before, and open to every occupant: except perhaps in

(e) Gen. xxi. 30.
(f) Gen. xxvi. 15, 18, etc.

the neighborhood of towns, where the necessity of a sole and exclusive property in lands (for the sake of agriculture) was earlier felt, and therefore more readily complied with. Otherwise, when the multitude of men and cattle had consumed every convenience on one spot of ground, it was deemed a natural right to seize upon and occupy such other lands as would more easily supply their necessities. This practice is still retained among the wild and uncultivated nations that have never been formed into civil states, like the Tartars and others in the east; where the climate itself, and the boundless extent of their territory, conspire to retain them still in the same savage state of vagrant liberty, which was universal in the earliest ages, and which, Tacitus informs us, continued among the Germans till the decline of the Roman empire. We have also a striking example of the same kind in the history of Abraham and his nephew Lot. [h] When their joint substance became so great that pasture and other conveniences grew scarce, the natural consequence was, that a strife arose between their servants; so that it was no longer practicable to dwell together. This contention Abraham thus endeavored to compose: — "Let there be no strife, I pray thee, between thee and me. Is not the whole land before thee? Separate thyself, I pray thee, from me. If thou wilt take the left hand, then I will go to the right; or if thou depart to the right hand, then I will go to the left." This plainly implies an acknowledged right, in either, to occupy whatever ground he pleased, that was not preoccupied by other tribes. "And Lot lifted up his eyes, and beheld all the plain of Jordan, that it was well watered everywhere, even as the garden of the Lord. Then Lot choose him all the plain of Jordan, and journeyed east; and Abraham dwelt in the land of Canaan."

Upon the same principle was founded the right of migration, or sending colonies to find out new habitations when the mother-country was overcharged with inhabitants; which was practiced as well by the Phœnicians and Greeks, as the Germans, Scythians, and other northern people. And, so long as it was confined to the stocking and cultivation of desert uninhabited countries, it kept strictly within the limits of the law of nature. But how far the seizing on countries already peopled, and driving out or massacring the innocent and defenceless natives, merely because they differed from their invaders in language, in religion, in customs, in government, or in color; how far such a conduct was consonant to nature, to reason, or to Christianity, deserved well to be considered by those who have rendered their names immortal by thus civilizing mankind.

As the world by degrees grew more populous, it daily became more difficult to find out new spots to inhabit, without encroaching

(h) Gen. c. xiii.

upon former occupants: and, by constantly occupying the same individual spot, the fruits of the earth were consumed, and its spontaneous produce destroyed, without any provision for future supply or succession. It therefore became necessary to pursue some regular method of providing a constant subsistence; and this necessity produced, or at least promoted and encouraged, the art of agriculture. And the art of agriculture, by a regular connection and consequence, introduced and established the idea of a more permanent property in the soil than had hitherto been received and adopted. It was clear that the earth would not produce her fruits in sufficient quantities without the assistance of tillage; but who would be at the pains of tilling it, if another might watch an opportunity to seize upon and enjoy the product of his industry, art, and labor? Had not therefore a separate property in lands as well as movables been vested in some individuals, the world must have continued a forest, and men have been mere animals of prey, which, according to some philosophers, is the genuine state of nature. Whereas now (so graciously has Providence interwoven our duty and our happiness together) the result of this very necessity has been the ennobling of the human species, by giving it opportunities of improving its *rational* faculties, as well as of exerting its *natural*. Necessity begat property; and, in order to insure that property, recourse was had to civil society, which brought along with it a long train of inseparable concomitants, — states, government, laws, punishments, and the public exercise of religious duties. Thus connected together, it was found that a part only of society was sufficient to provide, by their manual labor, for the necessary subsistence of all; and leisure was given to others to cultivate the human mind, to invent useful arts, and to lay the foundations of science.

The only question remaining is, how this property became actually invested, or what it is that gave a man an exclusive right to retain in a permanent manner that specific *land*, which before belonged generally to everybody, but particularly to nobody. And, as we before observed that occupancy gave the right to the temporary *use* of the soil, so it is agreed upon all hands, that occupancy gave also the original right to the permanent property in the *substance* of the earth itself; which excludes every one else but the owner from the use of it. There is indeed some difference among the writers on natural law concerning the reason why occupancy should convey this right, and invest one with this absolute property: Grotius and Puffendorf insisting that this right of occupancy is founded on a tacit and implied assent of all mankind that the first occupant should become the owner; and Barbeyrac, Titius, Mr. Locke, and others, holding that there is no such implied assent, neither is it necessary that there should be; for that the very act of occupancy alone, being a degree of bodily labor, is, from a principle of natural justice, without any consent or compact, sufficient of itself to gain a title; — a dispute that savors too much of nice and scholastic refinement. However, both sides agree in this, that occupancy is the thing by which the title was in fact originally gained; every man seizing to his own continued use such spots of ground as he found most agreeable to his own convenience, provided he found them unoccupied by any one else.

Property, both in lands and movables, being thus originally acquired by the first taker, which taking amounts to a declaration that he intends to appropriate the thing to his own use, it remains in him, by the principles of universal law, till such time as he does some other act which shows an intention to abandon it; for then it becomes, naturally speaking, *publici juris* once more, and is liable to be again appropriated by the next occupant. So if one is possessed of a jewel, and casts it into the sea or a public highway, this is such an express dereliction, that a property will be vested in the first fortunate finder that will seize it to his own use. But if he hides it privately in the earth, or other secret place, and it is discovered, the finder acquires no property therein; for the owner hath not by this act declared any intention to abandon it, but rather the contrary: and if he loses or drops it by accident, it cannot be collected from thence that he designed to quit the possession; and therefore in such a case the property still remains in the loser, who may claim it again of the finder. And this, we may remember, is the doctrine of the law of England with relation to treasure trove.

But this method of one man's abandoning his property, and another seizing the vacant possession, however well founded in theory, could not long subsist in fact. It was calculated merely for the rudiments of civil society, and necessarily ceased among the complicated interests and artificial refinements of polite and established governments. In these it was found, that what became inconvenient or useless to one man, was highly convenient and useful to another, who was ready to give in exchange for it some equivalent that was equally desirable to the former proprietor. Thus mutual convenience introduced commercial traffic, and the reciprocal transfer of property by sale, grant, or conveyance; which may be considered either as a continuance of the original possession which the first occupant had, or as an abandoning of the thing by the present owner, and an immediate successive occupancy of the same by the new proprietor. The voluntary dereliction of the owner, and delivering the possession to another individual, amount to a transfer of the property: the proprietor declaring his intention no longer to occupy the thing himself, but that his own right of occupancy shall be vested in the new acquirer. . . .

The most universal and effectual way of abandoning property, is by the death of the occupant: when, both the actual possession and intention of keeping possession ceasing, the property which is founded upon such possession and intention ought also to cease of course. For, naturally speaking, the instant a man ceases to be, he ceases to have any dominion: else, if he had a right to dispose of his acquisitions one moment beyond his life, he would also have a right to direct their disposal for a million of ages after him: which would be highly absurd and inconvenient. All property must therefore cease upon death, considering men as absolute individuals, and unconnected with civil society: for, then, by the principles before established, the next immediate occupant would acquire a right in all that the deceased possessed. But as, under civilized governments, which are calculated for the peace of mankind, such a constitution would be productive of endless disturbances, the universal law of almost every nation (which is a kind of secondary law of nature) has either given the dying person a power of continuing his property, by disposing of his possessions by will; or, in case he neglects to dispose of it, or is not permitted to make any disposition at all, the municipal law of the country then steps in, and declares who shall be the successor, representative, or heir of the deceased; that is, who alone shall have a right to enter upon this vacant possession, in order to avoid that confusion which its becoming again common would occasion. . . .

NOTES AND QUESTIONS ON THE BLACKSTONIAN VISION

1. Blackstone begins by remarking on people's uneasiness about the basis of property. Does this suggest, as some have said, that property is ultimately based on theft, and that, moreover, people realize this and hence are nervous about their own titles? The view that property is theft was most famously stated by P.J. Proudhon, What is Property? (1840). Marx's view was somewhat similar; see The So-Called Primitive Accumulation, in Capital, pt. 8 (3rd ed. 1883).

2. Blackstone gives several "principles" upon which property may be based, including (a) God's bequest to all mankind, (b) an analogy to animal nesting behavior, (c) reward to labor, (d) "necessity" for agriculture, and (e) occupancy. How do these principles fit together, if they do? Which, if any, overcome the charge that property is theft? Do you think that Blackstone really cared? (Note, for example, his comment on the "scholastic" dispute between Grotius and Locke.)

3. Blackstone suggests that certain types of objects were turned into property before others, and that property rights themselves evolved from temporary usage to more permanent entitlement. What accounts for these evolutionary patterns? Are there modern sequels, in the American West, for instance? See Terry L. Anderson & P.J. Hill, The Evolution of Property Rights: A Study of the American West, 18 J. Law & Econ. 163 (1975), describing evolving property regimes in such resources as water and livestock range. Are there contemporary examples of emerging property rights in previously unowned resources, in such places as the South American rainforest or the ocean seabed?

4. On Blackstone's account, what does private property *do* for people? Why have property regimes if property makes people uneasy?

5. Rose, Storytelling, suggested that Blackstone's account was just a "story," and indeed basically the same optimistic story that is told by Demsetz, p.148 infra. How persuasive is the story? Is it any more persuasive than the story that "property is theft"? Does your answer depend on your views about whether human beings are naturally cooperative? See Robert Axelrod, The Evolution of Cooperation, infra p.275.

6. In the final two paragraphs of this selection, Blackstone offers reasons why owners of private property should be entitled to transfer their belongings by sale and by disposition at death (either by will or rules of intestate succession). How persuasive are these passages? These issues — alienability and the appropriate time span of private ownership — are revisited infra at pp. 336–359 and 367–368.

Economic Analysis of Law*

Richard A. Posner

§3.1   The Economic Theory of Property Rights: Static and Dynamic Aspects

To understand the economics of property rights, it is first necessary to grasp the economist's distinction between *static* and *dynamic* analysis. Static analysis suppresses the time dimension of economic activity: All adjustments to change are assumed to occur instanta-

*Source: pp. 32–40 (4th ed. 1992).

neously. The assumption is unrealistic but often fruitful; the attentive reader of Chapter 1 will not be too disturbed by a lack of realism in assumptions.

Dynamic analysis, in which the assumption of instantaneous adjustment to change is relaxed, is usually more complex than static analysis. So it is surprising that the economic basis of property rights was first perceived in dynamic terms. Imagine a society in which all property rights have been abolished. A farmer plants corn, fertilizes it, and erects scarecrows, but when the corn is ripe his neighbor reaps it and takes it away for his own use. The farmer has no legal remedy against his neighbor's conduct since he owns neither the land that he sowed nor the crop. Unless defensive measures are feasible (and let us assume for the moment that they are not), after a few such incidents the cultivation of land will be abandoned and society will shift to methods of subsistence (such as hunting) that involve less preparatory investment.

As this example suggests, legal protection of property rights creates incentives to use resources efficiently. Although the value of the crop in our example, as measured by consumers' willingness to pay, may have greatly exceeded its cost in labor, materials, and forgone alternative uses of the land, without property rights there is no incentive to incur these costs because there is no reasonably assured reward for incurring them. The proper incentives are created by parceling out mutually exclusive rights to the use of particular resources among the members of society. If every piece of land is owned by someone — if there is always someone who can exclude all others from access to any given area — then individuals will endeavor by cultivation or other improvements to maximize the value of land. Of course, land is just an example. The principle applies to all valuable resources.

All this has been well known for hundreds of years.[1] In contrast,

---

1. See, e.g., 2 William Blackstone, Commentaries on the Laws of England 4, 7 (1766). And property-rights systems are prehistoric in their origins. Vernon L. Smith, The Primitive Hunter Culture, Pleistocene Extinction, and the Rise of Agriculture, 83 J. Pol. Econ. 727 (1975).

The proposition that enforcing property rights will lead to a greater output is questioned by Frank I. Michelman in Ethics, Economics, and the Law of Property, 24 Nomos 3, 25 (1982). He suggests that the farmer who knows that half his crop will be stolen may just plant twice as much. This suggestion overlooks

    (1) the added incentive to theft that will be created by planting a larger crop and the resulting likelihood that more than one-half of the larger crop will be stolen;

    (2) the unlikelihood that farming would be so much more profitable than substitute activities not entailing preparatory investment as to keep people in farming; and

    (3) the likelihood that the farmer, if he remained in farming, would divert some of his resources from growing crops to protecting them with walls, guards, etc.

the static analysis of property rights is little more than 50 years old. Imagine that a number of farmers own a pasture in common; that is, none has the right to exclude any of the others and hence none can charge the others for the use of the pasture. We can abstract from the dynamic aspects of the problem by assuming that the pasture is a natural (uncultivated) one. Even so, pasturing additional cows will impose a cost on all the farmers. The cows will have to graze more in order to eat the same amount of grass, and this will reduce their weight. But because none of the farmers pays for the use of the pasture, none will take this cost into account in deciding how many additional cows to pasture, with the result that more cows will be pastured than would be efficient. (Can you see an analogy to highway congestion?)

The problem would disappear if someone owned the pasture and charged each farmer for its use (for purposes of this analysis, disregard the cost of levying such a charge). The charge to each farmer would include the cost he imposes on the other farmers by pasturing additional cows, because that cost reduces the value of the pasture to the other farmers and hence the price they are willing to pay the owner for the right to graze.

The creation of exclusive rights is a necessary rather than a sufficient condition for the efficient use of resources: The rights must be transferable. Suppose the farmer in our first example owns the land that he sows but is a bad farmer; his land would be more productive in someone else's hands. Efficiency requires a mechanism by which the farmer can be induced to transfer the property to someone who can work it more productively. A transferable property right is such a mechanism. Suppose Farmer A owns a piece of land that he anticipates will yield him $100 a year above his labor and other costs, indefinitely. Just as the price of a share of common stock is equal to the present value of the anticipated earnings to which the shareholder will be entitled, so the present value of a parcel of land that is expected to yield an annual net income of $100 can be calculated and is the minimum price that A will accept in exchange for his property right. Suppose Farmer B believes that he can use A's land more productively than A. The present value of B's expected earnings stream will therefore exceed the present value calculated by A. Suppose the present value calculated by A is $1,000 and by B $1,500. Then at any price between $1,000 and $1,500 both A and B will be made better off by a sale. Thus there are strong incentives for a voluntary exchange of A's land for B's money.

This discussion implies that if every valuable (meaning scarce as well as desired) resource were owned by someone (the criterion of universality), ownership connoted the unqualified power to exclude everybody else from using the resource (exclusivity) as well as to use it oneself, and ownership rights were freely transferable, or as lawyers say alienable (transferability), value would be maximized. This leaves out of account, however, the costs of a property-rights system, both the obvious and the subtle ones. Those costs are a particular focus of this chapter.

An example will illustrate a subtle cost of exclusivity. Suppose our farmer estimates that he can raise a hog with a market value of $100 at a cost of only $50 in labor and materials and that no alternative use of the land would yield a greater net value — in the next best use, his income from the land would be only $20. He will want to raise the hog. But now suppose his property right is qualified in two respects: He has no right to prevent an adjacent railroad from accidentally emitting engine sparks that may set fire to the hog's pen, killing the hog prematurely; and a court may decide that his raising a hog on this land is a nuisance, in which event he will have to sell the hog at disadvantageous (why disadvantageous?) terms before it is grown. In light of these contingencies he must reevaluate the yield of his land: He must discount the $100 to reflect the probability that the yield may be much less, perhaps zero. Suppose that, after this discounting, the expected revenue from raising the hog (market value times the probability that it will reach the market) is only $60. He will not raise the hog. He will put the land to another use, which we said was less valuable;[4] the value of the land will fall.

But the analysis is incomplete. Removing the hog may increase the value of surrounding residential land by more than the fall in the value of the farmer's parcel; or the cost of preventing the emission of engine sparks may exceed the reduction in the value of the farmer's land when he switches from raising hogs to growing, say, fireproof radishes. But, the alert reader may interject, if the increase in value to others from a different use of the farmer's land exceeds the decrease to him, let them buy his right: The railroad can purchase an easement to emit sparks; the surrounding homeowners can purchase a covenant from the farmer not to raise hogs; there is no need to limit the farmer's property right. But . . . the costs of effecting a transfer of rights — transaction costs — are often prohibitive, and when this is so, giving someone the exclusive right to a resource may reduce rather than increase efficiency.

We could, of course, preserve exclusivity in a purely notional sense by regarding the property rights in a given thing as a bundle of distinct rights, each exclusive; that is in fact the legal position. The economic point however is that the nominal property owner will rarely have exclusive power over his property.

4. The anticipated profit from raising the hog is now only $10 (the farmer's costs are $50). The next best use, we said, would yield a profit of $20.

§3.2   Problems in the Creation and Enforcement of Property Rights

Property rights are not only less exclusive but less universal than they would be if they were not costly to enforce. Imagine a primitive society in which the principal use of land is for grazing. The population of the society is small relative to the amount of land, and its flocks are small too. No technology exists for increasing the value of the land by fertilizer, irrigation, or other techniques. The cost of wood or other materials for fencing is very high and, the society being illiterate, a system for publicly recording land ownership is out of the question. In these circumstances the costs of enforcing property rights might well exceed the benefits. The costs would be the costs of fencing to keep out other people's grazing animals, and would be substantial. The benefits might be zero. Since there is no crowding problem, property rights would confer no static benefits, and since there is no way of improving the land, there would be no dynamic benefits either. It is therefore not surprising that property rights are less extensive in primitive than in advanced societies and that the pattern by which property rights emerge and grow in a society is related to increases in the ratio of the benefits of property rights to their costs.

The common law distinction between domestic and wild animals illustrates the general point. Domestic animals are owned like any other personal property; wild animals are not owned until killed or put under actual restraint (as in a zoo). Thus, if your cow wanders off your land, it is still your cow; but if a gopher whose burrow is on your land wanders off, he is not your property, and anyone who wants can capture or kill him, unless he is tame — unless he has an *animus revertendi* (the habit of returning to your land). (Can you think of an economic argument for the doctrine of *animus revertendi*?)

The reason for the difference in legal treatment between domestic and wild animals is that it would be both difficult to enforce a property right in a wild animal and pretty useless; most wild animals, as in our gopher illustration, are not valuable, so there is nothing to be gained from creating incentives to invest in them. But suppose the animals are valuable. If there are no property rights in valuable fur-bearing animals such as sable and beaver, hunters will hunt them down to extinction, even though the present value of the resource will be diminished by doing so. The hunter who spares a mother beaver so that it can reproduce knows that the beavers born to her will almost certainly be caught by someone other than him (so long as there are many hunters), and he will not forgo a present benefit to confer a future benefit on someone else. Property rights would be desirable in these circumstances but it is hard to imagine a feasible scheme for giving the hunter who decided to spare the mother beaver a property right in her unborn litter. The costs of enforcing such a property right would still exceed the benefits, though the benefits would now be substantial.

There are two possible solutions. The more common is to use the regulatory powers of the state to reduce hunting to the approximate level it would be at if the animals were hunted at an optimal rate; this is an example of how regulation can be a substitute for property rights in correcting a divergence between private and social costs or benefits. The other solution is for one person to buy up the entire habitat of the animals; he will then regulate hunting on his property optimally because he will obtain all the gains from doing so.

Another example of the correlation between property rights and scarcity is the difference in the water law systems of the eastern and western states of the United States. In the eastern states, where water is plentiful, water rights are communalized to a significant extent, the basic rule being that riparian owners (i.e., the owners of the shore of a body of water) are each entitled to make reasonable use of the water — a use that does not interfere unduly with the uses of the other riparians. In the western states, where water is scarce, exclusive rights can be obtained, by appropriation (use).

Now consider the example of things, often very valuable things such as the treasure in a shipwreck, which were once owned but have been abandoned. Here the general rule is finders keepers. In a sense this is the same rule as for wild animals and for water in western states. Ownership of the thing is obtained by reducing it to actual possession. Until then the thing is unowned (the unborn beavers, the abandoned ship), and it is this gap in ownership — this interval when no one has a property right — that is the source of the economic problem.

But the problem is slightly different in the animal and treasure cases. In the case of wild animals the problem is too rapid exploitation; in the case of abandoned property it is too costly exploitation. Suppose the treasure in the shipwreck is worth $1 million and it will cost $250,000 to hire a team of divers to salvage it. Because the expected profit of the venture is so high, someone else may decide to hire his own team and try to beat the first team to it. A third and even a fourth may try, too, for if each one has the same chance (25 percent) of reaching the treasure first, then the expected value of the venture to each one ($1 million × .25) will still cover each one's expected cost. If four try, however, the cost of obtaining the treasure, $1 million, will be four times what it would have been if only one had tried.[3] Actually the net social loss from this competition will be less than $750,000, because the competition probably will result in the treasure's being found sooner (thus increasing its present value) than if only one were trying. But the gain in time may be modest and not worth the additional expenditures that accelerated the search.

There would be no problem of excessive cost if the treasure had not been abandoned; for then the owner would simply have hired one of the four salvagers for $250,000. But when we call property abandoned in the legal sense, we mean that the cost of revesting the property in the original owner is prohibitive, either because he cannot be found at reasonable cost or he considers the property (perhaps incorrectly) to be worth less than the cost of finding or using it. The problem of too costly exploitation of a valuable resource, like the problem of too rapid exploitation, is rooted ultimately in the sometimes prohibitive costs of enforcing property rights.

The law can do something about the abandonment problem and to some extent has done so. The common law sometimes gives the first committed searcher for abandoned property a right to prevent others from searching so long as his search is conscientiously pursued. Another common law rule makes abandoned treasure trove (currency and bullion), if found, escheat to the government rather than becoming the property of the finder. This rule reduces the investment in finding to whatever level the government thinks proper; the government determines that level by determining how much reward to give the finder. In the case of currency (as distinct from treasure that has historical, aesthetic, or collectors' value), the optimal level is very low, perhaps zero. Finding money does not increase the wealth of society; it just enables the finder to have more of society's goods than someone else. The optimal reward may therefore be very low — maybe zero. The trend in the common law is to expand the escheat principle of treasure trove into other areas of found property and thus give the finder a reward rather than the property itself; this makes economic sense.

It might appear that nothing could be more remote from sunken treasure than patented inventions, and yet the economic problem created by patents is remarkably like that of abandoned property. Ideas are in a sense created but in another sense found. Suppose that whoever invents the widget will, if allowed to exclude

3. The tendency of an expected gain to be translated into costs through competitive efforts is called rent-seeking, recurs many times in this book, and is the subject of a growing literature. See essays collected in Toward a Theory of the Rent-Seeking Society (James Buchanan, Robert Tollison & Gordon Tullock eds. 1980). . . .

others from its use by being granted a patent, be able to sell the patent to a manufacturer for $1 million. And suppose that the cost of invention is $250,000. Others will try to be first to invent the widget. This competition will cause it to be invented sooner. But suppose it is invented only one day sooner; the value of having the widget a day earlier will be less than the cost of duplicating the entire investment in invention.

§3.3   Intellectual Property

As the preceding paragraph illustrates, the economist experiences no sense of discontinuity in moving from physical to intellectual property. In particular, the dynamic rationale for property rights is readily applied to the useful ideas that we call inventions. Suppose that it costs $10 million to invent a new type of food blender, the marginal cost of producing and selling the blender once it is invented is $50 (why is the $10 million not a marginal cost?), and the estimated demand is for 1 million of the blenders (we can for present purposes ignore the fact that demand will vary with the blender's price). Unless the manufacturer can charge $60 per blender, he will not recoup his costs of invention. But if other manufacturers face the same marginal cost as he, competition will (in the absence of patents) bid the price down to $50, the effort at recoupment will fail, and anticipating this the manufacturer will not make the invention in the first place; he will not sow if he won't be able to reap. Moreover, in a world without patents, such inventive activity as did occur would be heavily biased toward inventions that could be kept secret, in just the same way that a complete absence of property rights would bias production toward things that involve minimum preparatory investment.... So we have patents; but the law uses several devices to try to minimize the costs of duplicating inventive activity that, as we saw in the preceding section, a patent system invites. Here are four of them:

1. A patent expires after 17 years, rather than being perpetual. This reduces the value of the patent to the owner and hence the amount of resources that will be devoted to obtaining patents.

2. Inventions are not patentable if they are "obvious." The functional meaning of obviousness is discoverable at low cost. The lower the cost of discovery, the less necessary patent protection is to induce the discovery to be made, and the greater is the danger of overinvestment if patent protection is allowed. If an idea worth $1 million costs $1 rather than $250,000 to discover, the amount of wasteful duplication to get a patent will be greater, perhaps $249,999 greater.

3. Patents are granted early — before an invention has been carried to the point of commercial feasibility — in order to head off costly duplication of expensive development work.

4. Fundamental ideas (the laws of physics, for example) are not patentable, despite their great value. Until the advent of costly atomic-particle accelerators, basic research did not entail substantial expenditure, and patent protection might therefore have led to too much basic research. By confining patentability to "useful" inventions in rather a narrow sense, the patent law identifies (though only crudely) inventions likely to require costly development before they can be brought to market. The nonpatentability of basic discoveries, like the limited term of patents, reflects more than just a concern with costs of acquiring patents, however; there are also serious identification problems, as in the case of wild animals. An idea does not have a stable physical locus, like a piece of land. With the passage of time it becomes increasingly difficult to identify the products in which a particular idea is embodied; and it is also difficult to identify the products in which a basic idea, having many and varied applications, is embodied. Here then is another example of how the costs of property rights limit their extent.

The costs of the patent system include (besides inducing potentially excessive investment in inventing) driving a wedge between price and marginal cost. . . . Once an invention is made, its costs are sunk; in economic terms, they are zero. Hence a price that includes a royalty to the inventor will exceed the opportunity cost of the product in which the invention is embodied. This wedge, however, is analytically the same as the cost of a fence to demarcate a property right in land; it is an indispensable cost of using the property rights system to allocate resources.

NOTES AND QUESTIONS ON THE ECONOMICS OF PROPERTY RIGHTS

1. Posner self-consciously views property issues from an economic perspective. In The Expanding Domain of Economics, 7 Am. Econ. Rev. 53 (Dec. 1985), Jack Hirshleifer identifies and evaluates the core principles of economics. This core consists of simple — some would say simplistic — conceptions of human motivation and method. As Hirshleifer puts it (at p.54), "Economic man is characterized by *self-interested goals* and *rational choice of means*." Hirshleifer recognizes that this rational-actor model is overdrawn but asserts that, even in unalloyed form, it has proven to have great explanatory power in many contexts. In Posner's hands, does the eco-

nomic paradigm generate important insights? This reader includes many selections by both proponents and critics of the rational-actor model, and should provide ample opportunities for appraisal of the approach.

2. Economists make use of two quite different definitions of *efficiency*. The first is *Pareto superiority*. An outcome is Pareto superior to the status quo if the outcome would make at least one individual better off and no one worse off. The second is the *Kaldor-Hicks* test, according to which an outcome is efficient if, after the outcome occurs, the gainers value its occurrence more than the losers disvalue it. Because the Kaldor-Hicks criterion does not require that gainers actually compensate losers, many outcomes that satisfy the Kaldor-Hicks test do not satisfy the Pareto-superiority test. Assume, for instance, that closing an utterly obsolete military base would be Kaldor-Hicks efficient. The shutdown nevertheless would not be Pareto superior unless compensation were actually paid to local merchants, base employees, and others sustaining losses, in amounts sufficient to make each loser at least indifferent to the closure.

In a prior passage in the excerpted work Posner states that "because the conditions of Pareto superiority are almost never satisfied in the real world," he himself normally employs the Kaldor-Hicks standard for efficiency. Was this his practice in the passages just reproduced? For Posner's full defense of his use of the Kaldor-Hicks approach, see Economic Analysis of Law pp.12-16 (4th ed. 1992). Does the Kaldor-Hicks test assume that policy analysts are capable of making interpersonal comparisons of utility? Bruce A. Ackerman, Economic Foundations of Property Law xi-xiv (1975), provides a memorably skeptical inquiry into the normative soundness of departures from Paretian criteria.

The preexisting distribution of wealth may determine whether a particular measure satisfies the Kaldor-Hicks criterion. How much a person demands as compensation for a loss is apt to be positively correlated with how much he has. (See Kennedy and Michelman's discussion of "Crusoes," infra pp.65-69.) In practice, would legislators considering amendments to, say, landlord-tenant statutes take into account the relative wealths of prospective gainers and losers? Symposium on Efficiency as a Legal Concern, 8 Hofstra L. Rev. 485-770 (1980), is a leading collection of essays on the ethics of the Kaldor-Hicks test. See also the sources on cost-benefit analysis, infra p.234, Note 4.

3. Posner restates Blackstone's economic rationale for the alienability of resources: A trade between willing parties can be expected to generate gains for both sides. Does this rationale undergird the common-law doctrine that limits the powers of bargainers and donors to create restraints on alienation? Or, contrarily, is that doctrine

in tension with freedom of contract? Most legal systems sharply limit the alienation of, for example, babies, body parts, and sexual services. Could Posner account for these policies? A selection by Margaret Radin, infra p.336, revisits issues of inalienability.

4. Posner draws on wild animals, treasure troves, and scientific inventions to illustrate how a legal system might efficiently bestow an exclusive right to *pursue* a resource. At what stage, if ever, should the editorial board of a law review give a student member an exclusive right to develop a particular Note topic?

Are Property and Contract Efficient?*

Duncan Kennedy & Frank Michelman

Introduction

This is an article about economic justifications for the legal institutions of private property and enforceable contract. There is, of course, an enormous literature addressed to such questions. . . .

This Article . . . neither argues for (nor against) any legal rules or institutions nor proposes a proper role or technique for economic analysis. It is concerned, in the first place, with what may appear to be a task of mere intellectual housekeeping: that of cataloguing and refuting in detail a number of *false* arguments and suppositions about the economic virtues of private property and free contract. The arguments that concern us are those purporting to justify the legal institutions in question by reference only (a) to a very weak, highly plausible value judgment that we should do things that make or could make everyone affected more satisfied than they would otherwise be, and (b) to a very weak, highly plausible factual judgment that people tend most of the time to act as though they had goals and were trying to achieve them — i.e., that people are rational maximizers of satisfactions. . . .

I. Five False Arguments for Private Property

In this Part, we take up a series of arguments for private property, and show that each depends on empirical assumptions additional to that of rational maximizing behavior. Throughout, we will be

*Source: 8 Hofstra Law Review 711-737 (1980).

contrasting the property regime, or PP, with two other regimes, since economic arguments for PP always make some implicit comparison with alternative possibilities. The two other regimes are the state of nature (SON) and the regime of forced sharing for needs (FSN).

A property regime (PP) is one in which things of value are assigned to owners, who have the following rights with respect to them: (a) they can consume them, or use them to produce other things of value, which they will also own; (b) they can get the state's help in preventing any nonowner from consuming them or using them for production without the owner's consent; and (c) owners have exclusive power to transfer ownership to others, with the state recognizing and then enforcing the transfer. This is admittedly a very rough, and in a number of respects a weasel-worded definition, but it is adequate for our present purposes. In Part III, where we take up the problems of the boundaries and internal structure of the property concept, we will offer a much more technically precise definition.

In the state of nature (SON) there is no ownership of anything, and no institution of legally enforced contract either. People may simply do as they wish, using whatever means are available to them — subject to everyone else doing likewise. Conceptually, the distinction between PP and SON is that in PP ownership rights are assumed to be automatically and universally respected — or, equivalently, perfectly and costlessly protected by an absolutely reliable and irresistible force ("the state"); whereas in SON, while there is always the contingent possibility of some people, perhaps by prearrangement, coming forcefully to the aid of others seeking protection or vindication for ownership-like positions, actual protection or vindication will always depend on the hazards of specific, concrete tests of strength (will, wit, etc.).

Forced sharing for needs (FSN) resembles private property, except that ownership is qualified in the following way: Anyone who "needs" a thing and doesn't own it (or its equivalent in cash or credit) may take or requisition it from anyone else who owns it and doesn't "need" it, and the state will intervene, if necessary, on the side of the needy taker. We can imagine rules defining need objectively, either in very general terms (e.g., having in one's ownership at this moment less than two-thirds of the per capita average share of privately held national wealth) or in terms of a series of particular situations, equally objectively described (e.g., being diabetic and lacking insulin for an overdue shot). Alternatively, we can imagine an official body administering a much vaguer and more subjective standard (e.g., being needy is having so little that a person of good conscience would feel guilty about your state of deprivation, supposing the deprivation was not your fault).

We have cast our five arguments in terms of comparisons between PP and SON or FSN. In each case we compare the valued experiences generated, or sometimes the hours worked, under the various regimes.[7] But we have set aside all arguments that refer to the good (or ill) that may be wrought by, or ascribed to, the *mere existence* of property rights. It might be that because people believe that property is right or fair, they will stop working under SON or FSN, whether out of depression or a desire to bring a property regime into existence. Moreover, it is of course true that if people want property for its own sake, irrespective of its impact on how many valued experiences of other kinds they have, then people will be worse off under an alternative regime. Finally, it may be that property is a good or right arrangement on grounds having nothing to do with the volume or distribution of valued experiences. Because we are specifically interested here in exploring the economic, instrumental virtues of property, we suppose throughout that none of these is the case: people, we assume, want or don't want a property regime because of its impact, *as a means,* on their supply of goods,

7. We have construed the several arguments for property as all designed to show that property is relatively efficient by the test variously known as "Kaldor-Hicks," or "hypothetical compensation," or "potential Pareto superiority" — i.e., that property will generate a higher-valued periodic total output of goods, services, and leisure for the members of society taken altogether than will any alternative regime. Some economists may object that such is not the sense in which they ordinarily speak of "efficiency;" that in calling a regime "efficient" a careful economist would mean only that it was a "Pareto *optimum*," an arrangement that could not be altered without worsening the lot of at least one person; that, indeed, comparison of regimes in terms of *total* values *across* society is meaningless without an objective, or at least intelligible, metric for comparing one person's gain with another's loss; that the only such metric known is that of (actual or constructed) offer or asking prices, which is unsatisfactory because it suppresses the important but unfathomable effects of changes in distribution on the total of individual welfare levels.

Our response is, first, that the strict criterion of actual Pareto superiority — better for each person, or at least as good — cannot be the one intended by claims that property is relatively efficient, because it is plain without argument that the strict criterion cannot select among PP, SON, and FSN; second, that a great deal of policy analysis, as distinguished from work in economic theory, in fact aims, if only mediately, at maximization of social welfare by way of "educated guesses" about cross-personal welfare comparisons; third, that if we succeed with our project of showing that PP is not demonstrably more efficient than SON or FSN in the less demanding "potential" sense, we shall also have shown, a fortiori (supposing any such showing were needed), that PP is not efficient vis-a-vis the alternatives in the strict Paretian sense; and, finally, that the nature of our attacks on the economic arguments for property is such that specification of output metrics is not crucial for us: in some instances, the arguments we are attacking will imply their own metrics (e.g., total labor time in the case of the First Argument); in others, our position holds no matter what metric you choose to consider — offer/asking prices ("wealth"), labor time, product output by weight, utiles, whatever.

services, and leisure; and property is good or right (bad or wrong) just insofar as it is (is not) truly such a means.

A. First Argument for PP: Security Increases Production

In both SON and FSN no one can expect with certainty to be able to retain the fruits of her labor. It follows, according to the First Argument, that people will not work as much as under conditions of legally guaranteed security. . . .

There are two mistakes in the First Argument. The first, particularly relevant to SON, is that it confuses the legal "permission" of violence and chaos with the actual social practice of violence and chaos. Even if no one has any legal right to protection, and everyone is legally entitled to do anything they want and can get away with, it does not follow that among rational maximizers there must arise either random depredations or actual freedom to refrain from production. There might, in SON, evolve a balance of physical and social force such that both the "weak" and the "strong" have very distinct ideas about what will probably happen to them if they do or don't produce. And the particular, highly discernible pattern of force might be one that induces the population as a whole to produce more rather than less than they would under PP.

In a two person SON, for example, the stronger won't necessarily kill the weaker. The stronger may be more interested in the consumption of products of labor than in perfect safety or in aggression for its own sake. Even according to the usual, very pessimistic models of human nature used in this kind of analysis, the stronger in that case will rather force the weaker to work, and extract from him as much surplus as is compatible with stability. It might very well be that he would impose something analogous to a tax on everything except what the weaker needed to survive at a level that permitted the kind of production the stronger desired. There is no reason to expect this arrangement to generate great "uncertainty." The weaker would know pretty well what to expect and so would the stronger.

To be sure, the weaker may receive less return for his labor than under a two-person property regime, while the stronger receives a large income without working at all. But the weaker's incentive to work will not necessarily be lessened by the low return to labor. The stronger may force him, by threatening him with even less palatable alternatives, to work more hours for less return than he would in a property regime. As for the stronger, he is provided by the weaker with a steady flow of products, but there are two reasons why he may also work more than under property. First, he must supervise and direct the weaker, and the return to supervision may be very high. Second, he may choose to spend his time producing, of his own free will, "luxuries" that he prefers to leisure, given that his "necessities" have been otherwise supplied.

Of course, this picture of an industrious state of nature is no more logically necessary than that which is usually implicit in economic discussions of property. . . .

The second objection to the First Argument, relevant to both SON and FSN, is that even if holdings and harvests are more secure under PP than SON and FSN, people may respond to the hazards of the latter regimes by working more rather than less. Under the chancy, non-property regimes people are doubtful whether they will enjoy the fruits of their productive undertakings, so the reward for each unit of work or investment is less, ex ante, than it would be under property. Because the reward is less, according to the First Argument, they will work less. The objection is that reducing the probable share of product retained by the producer may induce people to work more rather than less, in order to maintain the same level of welfare-from-consumption. For example, a farmer may respond to the threat of theft by planting more crops, in the hope that he can thereby offset depredations and keep his income up — with the result of increasing the consumption of society as a whole, the thieves included. In technical terms, it all depends on the relation between the income and the substitution effects of the reduced rewards from work.

The argument that property has desirable effects on productive effort thus amounts to no more than an empirical assertion. It remains such when we take into account that people who live off the work of others in the state of nature or in a regime of forced sharing might have to work for their livings under a property regime (though they might, too, live on voluntary charity). The question whether adding their product, if any, would overcome whatever *reduction* in product might be caused by giving people greater security can be resolved only by looking at the circumstances of particular cases.

B. Second Argument for PP: Theft is Inefficient

Suppose a thief takes something, in the SON, that the thief would willingly have paid only five dollars for in PP, while the possessor would have offered ten dollars to the thief at the moment of theft, if it had been possible thereby to bind the thief not to steal the object. It is a common intuition that it is somehow not economically sound to let the theft happen under these circumstances. It is, one might think, inefficient because the law is sanctioning a change that makes one person worse off (the possessor, by ten dollars) while making another better off by considerably less (the thief, by five dollars).

The argument that theft is inefficient plainly depends on an assumption of substantial transaction costs, which in turn imports motivational assumptions regarding individual wants and proclivities, not at all implicit in the bare postulate of rational maximizing behavior. If there are no transaction costs, there will be no theft, even without the coercive legal institution of property, unless the property is worth more to the thief than to the victim. Otherwise, the possessor will offer the thief some sum to go away, they will negotiate, and strike a bargain in which the thief receives something between five and ten dollars in exchange for desisting. The end result is that the prior possession is respected but the possessor ends up, say, out $9.95, rather than the $10 value of the object, while the thief ends up pocketing $9.95 rather than what would have been (for him) $5.00 worth of stolen goods. The only difference between this outcome and the one that would have occurred under a property regime is "distributional." The object is finally allocated to the same use (unless the possessor's impoverishment causes him to change that use). Some are better off and some worse off than they would have been under PP, but we cannot rank either outcome as Pareto superior to the other.

Let us, however, grant arguendo that substantial transaction costs are an inevitable accompaniment of essential human nature. The theft, then, may well occur in SON but not in PP, apparently leaving society $5 poorer in SON. On the other hand, transaction costs also disrupt the functioning of a PP regime. For example, transaction costs in PP may prevent the transfer of an object from a possessor who values it at $5 to another who values it at $10; whereas in SON, the other might simply take the object. For ought the rationality postulate can tell us, the disruption in PP may on the whole be more damaging to wealth or welfare than that in SON. We cannot say a priori which way the balance of systemic advantage lies.

The problem is further complicated by obscurity in the relationship between dollar evaluations and real satisfaction levels. Suppose, again, that in SON but not in PP a theft will occur that costs the victim $10 while the thief gains only $5. Obviously, one cannot say that either the SON or the PP result is Pareto superior in the strictest sense of better for both parties. Nor can one say with assurance that the PP result is "socially" preferred. The dollar figures are supposed to represent sums of money the parties respectively would be willing to exchange for the object in question, not the absolute (interpersonally comparable) amounts of satisfaction possession would bring them. So if the initial possessor is very rich and the thief is very poor, an observor might feel that the theft probably results in a net gain in total satisfaction — since, given the standard assumption of diminishing marginal utility of wealth, a dollar means relatively less to the possessor than to the thief.

The concept of efficiency does tell us that as between the theft and a deal in which the possessor pays the thief to desist, we should prefer the latter. If the possessor and the thief can agree on a bribe, both will be better off (according to their own evaluations of the matter) than if the theft actually occurs. From this we can infer that if there were no property, it would be inefficient to criminalize the exaction of a payment to prevent the theft. But as between the theft and respect for the property *without* a bribe, we cannot say that either alternative makes both parties' prospects, or the total of their prospects, better than the other does. In other words, efficiency provides no basis for choosing between them.

C.   Third Argument for PP: PP Reduces Uncertainty

The third argument for PP is that SON and FSN involve an unpleasant psychological state of anxiety about whether or not one will be able to keep what one has and to enjoy the fruits of one's labor. Since this anxiety is a psychic "bad," we can make everyone better off by eliminating it through a property regime. . . .

The basic response to the argument that property maximizes the psychic good of certainty is that, under all three regimes, to enhance certainty for one person is to impair certainty for another. Under a property regime people are all certain that they and no one else will receive the fruits of their labor, but all uncertain of access to the fruits of others' labor. In moving from one regime to another, some will have gained security at the expense of others, and everyone will have traded certainty and uncertainty of one kind for certainty and uncertainty of another.

1.   THE CERTAINTY OF A PROPERTY REGIME VIS-A-VIS THE STATE OF NATURE

In the state of nature, the strong are certain that no automatic, irresistible force will stop them from exploiting the weak. Thus secure in the knowledge of their strength, they are certain of receiving benefits they cannot be as certain of receiving under property. . . .

The more one speculates about the multiple changes in expectations generated by the shift from the state of nature to a regime of property, the less clear it is what might be meant by the argument about the psychic good of certainty. The only thing that is certain to be certain under property is effective protection of the weak against violent dispossession by the strong, and vice versa. Yet in the state of nature there is an exactly equivalent certainty that no absolutely dominant force will intervene to frustrate the dispossessing strong. Depending on their initial positions, their preferences, and their ideas about likely courses of events, some people may prefer one kind of certainty, others the other kind. . . .

2.   THE CERTAINTY OF PROPERTY VIS-A-VIS FORCED SHARING

If what we have been saying about the certainty argument in the context of the state of nature is true, then it should be plain that certainty arguments won't work any better against forced sharing. If what we are interested in is the certainty provided by *law*, then forced sharing is a legal regime, by any definition, just like property. It should provide no more and no less certainty than any other set of rules and standards about the application of public force.

If, on the other hand, we are concerned with people's sense of confidence that their expectations about substantive outcomes will be fulfilled, then life under forced sharing will be *differently* certain and uncertain than life under property. Forced sharing ties the fortunes of the individual to the group. It therefore eliminates some fundamental uncertainties of a property regime. Under FSN, one need not fear that one's own unproductiveness will expose one to isolated deprivation as long as others are producing. But forced sharing introduces its own forms of insecurity, since the fortunes of the group depend on a complex process of interaction, with no guarantees against a disastrous slide into uncooperative behavior.

As we did in the comparison with the state of nature, we might illustrate possible impacts of forced sharing on different sorts of people. But at this point perhaps an analogy is enough: those who are "good at production" under private property, or who have large holdings of property, would obviously have more to fear from forced sharing than those who are weak producers and have no property. They are analogous to "the strong" in the state of nature, who have a lot to lose from a property regime. But the gainers from property are like the strong in that they are also vulnerable, in a property regime, to mischance that leaves them in need, whereas under forced sharing they would not be. . . .

D.   Fourth Argument for PP: Coordinational Failure

The Fourth Argument for PP is that life under SON or FSN will be an organizational nightmare, whereas coordination under property will be easily managed. . . .

1. THE COORDINATION PROBLEM IN FSN

In the state of forced sharing, each person's level of welfare is directly dependent on each other person's. The question is whether the people involved will respond to this situation by working a lot or by working only very little, in each case by comparison to the property regime. (As with the First Argument, we here grant arguendo that less work means less total satisfaction.) They might work only a little, if each person expected others to work a lot, and hoped to be able to enjoy a share without working himself. The law does not prevent this outcome, and it intervenes positively to prevent the others from punishing the freeloader by denying him his "needed" share of the labor of others.

There is a way, however, for the group to sanction the freeloader: if everyone cuts back work, then the freeloader will find himself at a low level of welfare. If everyone decides to live off the labor of others, everyone will starve. When everyone is starving, either there will be a group reaction to reverse the slide, or there will not be. In other words, the state of forced sharing can easily be conceptualized as a strategic game, in which the structure of incentives is ambiguous.

As is generally the case with games of this kind, our best guess about the outcome depends on the precise assumptions we make about the situation. In a small group, with easy communication and much mutual knowledge and trust, it is more likely that a cooperative solution will occur and will persist; if everyone has the same capacity for work, the agreement process will be easier; and so on. The only general point of importance for us is that the bare postulate of rational maximizing behavior tells us little about the outcome. It is possible to flesh out the situation so that people work a great deal, more than under many imaginable property regimes; and it is possible to construct it so that they end by working less.

2. THE COORDINATION PROBLEM IN SON

Just as in FSN, in SON each person's welfare is dependent on each other person's, but here the interdependence is brought about by the absence of self-enforcing rules, rather than by irresistible enforcement of sharing. Again the question is how things will go when people realize that they can steal what they are strong, shrewd, and swift enough to get away with. It is easy to imagine a situation in which some give up work, and subsist on meager gains by stealing from those who continue working, while the workers have to invest so much time and energy in precautions that they are not much better off than the freeloaders. It is even possible to imagine that people will become so preoccupied with defense of the products of their labor that they will take to launching preemptive strikes against one another, and that the world will be ceaselessly embroiled in lethal conflict. Or we might foresee the gradual depletion through overuse of the world's scarce, but unowned resources until the race simply dies out.

But, as we saw in considering the First Argument for private property, there is nothing inevitable about such a slide into mutual self-destruction. It is quite imaginable that a single Amazon might emerge who was strong enough to force everyone to work all the time, so that, far from discoordination, we had a situation of continuous, centrally directed labor. Or the people involved might achieve through nonbinding agreements and informal arrangements many of the benefits of property, while avoiding many of the drawbacks of rights relentlessly enforced.

As with FSN, a lot depends on particular aspects of the SON we are imagining — things like the number of people, the ease of communication, the existence of powerful family, tribal, or local groups with internally effective norms of cooperation and some set of practices for dealing with "others." If all we know is that people are rational maximizers, we cannot say that they will or that they will not manage to prevent the slide into chaos.

3.   THE COORDINATION PROBLEM IN PP

In a complex economic system, with extensive division of labor and little production for autoconsumption, the economic process as a whole requires an extraordinary amount of social cooperation. If everyone has property in his labor, and if property in the means of production is widely dispersed, this cooperation requires great numbers of complex chains of bargains among individual right holders, and these bargains will be costly to organize and vulnerable to strategic failure. The situation under property may be a "prisoners' dilemma" such that each owner rationally pursuing his view of his own interest will behave antisocially. For example, every owner may withdraw his property from production because of fear of economic collapse, and thereby fulfill as fact what began as only prophecy. If there were no transaction costs, each property owner would see that the sum of all the individual exercises of rights was a social disaster, and the group could strike a bargain to keep production going. But the atomization of control might make such a solution impossible. By contrast, a single "strong man" who controlled the whole economy might avert the disaster by forcing everyone to behave in the socially appropriate fashion. Likewise, communal ownership might result in "planning" that prevented crisis.

The point, then, is not that some or any property regime can never be superior on efficiency grounds to the state of nature. Rather, if there are no transaction costs preventing bargaining, each regime is necessarily efficient, in the sense of Pareto optimal (on the production-possibility frontier), whereas in the presence of transaction costs the question of efficiency is an empirical one. Given transaction costs, it may be that people in SON would be blocked from moving to a property regime that would unleash such a flood of commodities that the gainers could compensate the strong for their losses. But it might also work the other way around: the dispersal of control among property holders might prevent the strong from reorganizing production along lines that would produce enormous surpluses, which would in turn permit the strong to buy off the weak.

E.   Fifth Argument for PP: Distribution of the Tradeoff Between Work and Leisure

We have now arrived at the argument for private property that seems most plausible to people who have some technical knowledge of economics. It is that a property regime maximizes welfare because it provides individuals with both the information and motivation they require to make the choices among different kinds of work and investment, and between work and leisure, that will allow the group to get the maximum of satisfaction from the resources available to them. One form of the argument is to assert that departures from private property always cause a "distortion" of incentives. The distortion argument is complex, and in order to address it we will have to elaborate our model of a property regime considerably beyond what has been necessary up to this point.

1.   THE CRUSOE ECONOMY

The idea that underlies the "distortion" argument is that of the single producer on a desert island who "owns" both his own labor and a defined set of natural resources, simply because there is no one else around to make conflicting claims. This solitary producer will spend some time at work and some time not working. The postulate of rational maximizing behavior is helpful in figuring out what particular division he will make between the two uses of time. He will work until the psychic rewards of another unit of work fall below those of a unit of leisure. In equilibrium he will arrange things so that the marginal yield of utility from work and leisure is equal.

He will follow the same procedure in deciding what to work on. In equilibrium, the marginal yield of a further minute spent on shelter will exactly equal that of a minute spent on food gathering.

These marginal equalities guarantee that Crusoe is getting the most possible satisfaction out of both his time and his resources. There is a quite real sense in which the actual quantities of work of different kinds, and of leisure, that Crusoe chooses are "natural." They reflect the natural surround of physical resources, and Crusoe's "nature," in the sense in which nature means simply a set of preferences.

2. THE MULTIPLE-CRUSOE ECONOMY

The next step in the development of the distortion argument is to imagine a multiplicity of islands, each different from the others, each with a different Crusoe on it. At first, the Crusoes are ignorant of each others' existence. Each behaves as though he were the only person in the world, producing in such a way as to generate marginal equality of satisfactions from different kinds of work, and from the mix of work and leisure. Then they become aware of one anothers' existence.

Let's suppose they respond to this knowledge by agreeing that each Crusoe will "own" his island, and by creating a state to enforce their property regime. Each will continue to produce as before, except now there is the possibility of trade and the division of labor. Imagine a first phase of trade in resources only. Two Crusoes discover that each would prefer the other's island to his own. That is, given the first Crusoe's preferences and his capacities for labor and leisure, he would prefer to own the second's island rather than his own; and vice versa for the second Crusoe. A round of trading of islands ensues, until there is no trade left that anyone wants to make. On each island, the Crusoe owner produces until the marginal equalities are achieved. . . .

It would be misleading to describe as "natural" the various quantities of different kinds of work and of leisure that the Crusoes are now doing. These amounts depend on what island each Crusoe has, and this in turn depends on the initial distribution. This is an important point, which we can illustrate as follows. Suppose three Crusoes and three islands, with the Crusoes' rankings as follows:

A prefers 1 to 2 and 2 to 3
B prefers 1 to 2 and 2 to 3
C prefers 1 to 3 and 3 to 2

Initial distribution I:
A gets 1
B gets 2
C gets 3
Result: no trades

Initial distribution II:
A gets 1
B gets 3
C gets 2
Result: A keeps 1; B gets 2; C gets 3 (same as I)

Initial distribution III:
A gets 2
B gets 1
C gets 3
Result: no trades (different from I)

Initial distribution IV:
A gets 3
B gets 1
C gets 2
Result: B keeps 1, A gets 2, C gets 3 (same as III, different from
I and II)

It seems unnecessary to continue through all the permutations, since the result is clear: who ends with which island depends on who has which island to start with, and on the preferences as among islands of different Crusoes. After the islands have been finally distributed, each Crusoe will equalize the marginal returns of work and leisure. But the result of this equalization process, the *actual* division of time, depends on who has which island rather than on anything in "nature." There is no particular work/leisure tradeoff that is natural, any more than there is a natural distribution of islands. Another way to put the same point is to say that there are multiple possible efficient outcomes given a set of Crusoes and a set of islands. Once the trading process is completed, and each Crusoe has equalized the marginal returns of different kinds of work and leisure, the situation will be Pareto optimal. But there are as many actual contents for the optimal solution as there are post-trading distributions of islands. . . .

c.   *Crusoes in the State of Nature*—Now suppose that the Crusoes fail to institute a property regime on becoming aware of one anothers' existence. The ordering that emerges from their interactions is strictly alegal, and the only constraints on individual behavior are those arising from the balance of force and the structure of preferences. Each Crusoe will have to decide how much and what kind of work to do. Some will base the decision on an expectation of being able to take the fruits of the labor of others; others will expect to be victims. The original distribution of islands and parts of islands will undergo all kinds of vicissitudes as coalitions or kingdoms form and reform.

It is obvious that the incentives associated with work of different kinds and with leisure will be radically different in the state of nature than under either of our two property regimes. Under property, each Crusoe knew he could keep what he produced on his island, but had no claim on what anyone else produced, except that under the second property regime there was a limited right to assistance in an emergency. In the state of nature, one knows what one can keep only to the extent one can accurately predict the balance of force. But there are nonetheless a number of crucial ways in which the two situations are similar.

First, each Crusoe will still try to equate his expected marginal returns from different kinds of work and from leisure. Each will, according to the postulate of rational maximizing, make himself as well off as possible given his expected access to resources and products. Some will do much better under SON, some much worse. But all will make the same marginal equations they made under the property regime. The results will be different, but the form of private rationality will not.

Second, it is no more true of the results in the state of nature than of the results under one or another property regime that they are "natural." Once the Crusoes find themselves as a matter of fact in a state of society, *all* of the possible structures of incentives available to them are social, rather than natural, so there is no sense in which the particular choices among kinds of work and between work and leisure are "distorted" in one situation or another. Distortion implies an undistorted norm. If there are no "natural" incentive structures, then the word "distortion" seems appropriate only if we *define* one or another regime as correct, and compare all other regimes to it. But we have found no basis in economic reasoning for choosing a norm.

d. Labor "Wasted" on Protection Against Theft—Our last proposition may seem easy to refute simply by pointing out that in the state of nature people will have an incentive to produce goods that the stronger cannot so easily take from them, rather than the goods they want most, and also have an incentive to spend time on devices designed to make theft more difficult. Since they would prefer to have the products of an equal amount of time spent under a property regime, it would appear that property *must* generate a net increase in welfare.

An easy answer is that PP involves its own kinds of "unproductive" activities, like lawyering, prosecuting, judging, and housing the legal system. Whether, under any particular set of circumstances, these will cost more or less than fences (etc.) is an empirical question.

Furthermore, we cannot treat the argument about precautions as conclusive, even assuming costless enforcement of legal property rights. The argument assumes that the diversion of production into theft-proof goods and into precautions is a pure loss, from the point of view of social welfare, so that eliminating the diversion is a pure gain. But it is obvious that the production is diverted because some people are trying to live off the products of others. Eliminating the diversion by introducing private property means preventing the freeloaders from freeloading, as well as reducing the wages available to those whose strongest talents are for serving as guards. It seems, on the face of it, that this should decrease the welfare of the latter groups. When the diversion argument ignores the impact of property rules on their welfare, it is patently inconclusive. The gain to the industrious from being able to produce what they most want, and from dismantling their defensive measures, may or may not be greater than the loss to former thieves and Pinkertons. In order to decide, we need a social welfare function that allows us to compare these gains and losses. . . .

NOTES AND QUESTIONS ON CRITICAL APPRAISALS OF PRIVATE PROPERTY

1. Kennedy and Michelman (K & M) seek to prove that the efficiency of private property (PP) cannot be deduced from the bare-bones premises of economics. If K & M think that economists need to enrich their initial assumptions, why do they assert that the traditional economic rationales for PP are "false," as opposed to "incomplete"? More broadly, is deductive logic a helpful tool for appraising the relative merits of PP and alternative institutions? How empirically inclined are K & M in comparison to, say, Blackstone and Posner?

2. K & M identify two mistakes in the argument that the security of PP serves to enhance production. First, in SON the strong may coerce the weak to produce even more than they would under PP. K & M give an example in which there is one strong person and one weak person. Does this example load the dice in their favor? Why might the weak be substantially less productive in SON if many strong persons were competing to extract the surplus of their labor? See the selection by Hardin on the "tragedy of the commons,"

infra p.132. See also Thomas Hobbes, Leviathan, ch. 13 (1651), arguing that the state of nature is a more or less egalitarian war of all against all. In settled societies, why did even slave-owners sometimes give informal property rights to slaves? See the Barzel selection, infra p.125.

Second, K & M argue that individuals might work *harder* if their holdings were insecure, perhaps to attain a margin of safety in consumption. Reread Posner's response to this criticism, supra p.46, Note 1. Who has the better of this exchange? For a more formal economic inquiry that supports parts of Posner's rejoinder, see Stergios Skaperdas, Cooperation, Conflict, and Power in the Absence of Property Rights, 82 Am. Econ. Rev. 720 (1992). K & M's position receives reinforcement in Mark Kelman, A Guide to Critical Legal Studies 155-157 (1987).

Neither Posner nor K & M cite evidence about the effects of insecurity on work effort. Anthropological studies indicate that, in virtually all preliterate societies, an individual or kinship group that cultivates a crop is granted private property rights in that crop. See Martin J. Bailey, Approximate Optimality of Aboriginal Property Rights, 35 J.L. & Econ. 183, 191-192 (1992); Melville J. Herskovits, Economic Anthropology, 350-370 (1952). Does this empirical regularity strengthen Posner's side of the debate? Prove as a logical matter that PP inevitably increases crop production?

3. Theft is regarded as a crime in all societies. See James Q. Wilson & Richard J. Herrnstein, Crime and Human Nature 22-23, 448-450 (1985). Does the universality of this norm undermine K & M's attack on the proposition that "theft is inefficient"?

The common-law doctrine of private necessity entitles a starving hiker to break into an uninhabited mountain cabin to obtain food. Does this rule support K & M's arguments about theft? Would Posner think the private-necessity doctrine inefficient? The law of adverse possession may end up rewarding thievery. Is it inefficient? Consult the selection by Merrill, infra p.191.

4. K & M argue that PP may not reduce uncertainty. Is risk allocation a zero-sum game? If so, what explains the existence of insurance companies, which sell the service of risk-bearing? Do the selections by Goffman and Radin, supra pp.1 and 8, show that in practice certain forms of PP enhance aggregate security? Do those selections suggest premises about human nature that economists might add to their models in order to satisfy K & M's demands for deductive rigor?

5. In their "Crusoes" discussion, K & M demonstrate the possibly profound influence of initial entitlements. For other sources on this issue, see infra pp.207-208, Note 3.

6. Michelman provides an even richer and more expansive version of his views in Frank I. Michelman, Ethics, Economics, and the Law of Property, in Ethics, Economics, and the Law 3 (NOMOS XXIV) (J. Roland Pennock & John W. Chapman eds. 1982).

C. Diffusion of Political Power

Capitalism and Freedom*

Milton Friedman

I. The Relation Between Economic Freedom and Political Freedom

It is widely believed that politics and economics are separate and largely unconnected; that individual freedom is a political problem and material welfare an economic problem; and that any kind of political arrangements can be combined with any kind of economic arrangements. The chief contemporary manifestation of this idea is the advocacy of "democratic socialism" by many who condemn out of hand the restrictions on individual freedom imposed by "totalitarian socialism" in Russia, and who are persuaded that it is possible for a country to adopt the essential features of Russian economic arrangements and yet to ensure individual freedom through political arrangements. The thesis of this chapter is that such a view is a delusion, that there is an intimate connection between economics and politics, that only certain combinations of political and economic arrangements are possible, and that in particular, a society which is socialist cannot also be democratic, in the sense of guaranteeing individual freedom.

Economic arrangements play a dual role in the promotion of a free society. On the one hand, freedom in economic arrangements is itself a component of freedom broadly understood, so economic freedom is an end in itself. In the second place, economic freedom is also an indispensable means toward the achievement of political freedom.

The first of these roles of economic freedom needs special emphasis because intellectuals in particular have a strong bias against

*Source: pp. 7-32 (1962).

regarding this aspect of freedom as important. They tend to express contempt for what they regard as material aspects of life, and to regard their own pursuit of allegedly higher values as on a different plane of significance and as deserving of special attention. For most citizens of the country, however, if not for the intellectual, the direct importance of economic freedom is at least comparable in significance to the indirect importance of economic freedom as a means to political freedom.

The citizen of Great Britain, who after World War II was not permitted to spend his vacation in the United States because of exchange control, was being deprived of an essential freedom no less than the citizen of the United States, who was denied the opportunity to spend his vacation in Russia because of his political views. The one was ostensibly an economic limitation on freedom and the other a political limitation, yet there is no essential difference between the two.

The citizen of the United States who is compelled by law to devote something like ten percent of his income to the purchase of a particular kind of retirement contract, administered by the government, is being deprived of a corresponding part of his personal freedom. . . .

A citizen of the United States who under the laws of various states is not free to follow the occupation of his own choosing unless he can get a license for it, is likewise being deprived of an essential part of his freedom. So is the man who would like to exchange some of his goods with, say, a Swiss for a watch but is prevented from doing so by a quota. So also is the Californian who was thrown into jail for selling Alka Seltzer at a price below that set by the manufacturer under so-called "fair trade" laws. So also is the farmer who cannot grow the amount of wheat he wants. And so on. Clearly, economic freedom, in and of itself, is an extremely important part of total freedom.

Viewed as a means to the end of political freedom, economic arrangements are important because of their effect on the concentration or dispersion of power. The kind of economic organization that provides economic freedom directly, namely, competitive capitalism, also promotes political freedom because it separates economic power from political power and in this way enables the one to offset the other.

Historical evidence speaks with a single voice in the relation between political freedom and a free market. I know of no example in time or place of a society that has been marked by a large measure of political freedom, and that has not also used something comparable to a free market to organize the bulk of economic activity.

Because we live in a largely free society, we tend to forget how limited is the span of time and the part of the globe for which there has ever been anything like political freedom: the typical state of mankind is tyranny, servitude, and misery. The nineteenth century and early twentieth century in the Western world stand out as striking exceptions to the general trend of historical development. Political freedom in this instance clearly came along with the free market and the development of capitalist institutions. So also did political freedom in the golden age of Greece and in the early days of the Roman era.

History suggests only that capitalism is a necessary condition for political freedom. Clearly it is not a sufficient condition. Fascist Italy and Fascist Spain, Germany at various times in the last seventy years, Japan before World Wars I and II, tzarist Russia in the decades before World War I — are all societies that cannot conceivably be described as politically free. Yet, in each, private enterprise was the dominant form of economic organization. It is therefore clearly possible to have economic arrangements that are fundamentally capitalist and political arrangements that are not free.

Even in those societies, the citizenry had a good deal more freedom than citizens of a modern totalitarian state like Russia or Nazi Germany, in which economic totalitarianism is combined with political totalitarianism. Even in Russia under the Tzars, it was possible for some citizens, under some circumstances, to change their jobs without getting permission from political authority because capitalism and the existence of private property provided some check to the centralized power of the state.

The relation between political and economic freedom is complex and by no means unilateral. In the early nineteenth century, Bentham and the Philosophical Radicals were inclined to regard political freedom as a means to economic freedom. They believed that the masses were being hampered by the restrictions that were being imposed upon them, and that if political reform gave the bulk of the people the vote, they would do what was good for them, which was to vote for laissez faire. In retrospect, one cannot say that they were wrong. . . .

Fundamentally, there are only two ways of coordinating the economic activities of millions. One is central direction involving the use of coercion — the technique of the army and of the modern totalitarian state. The other is voluntary co-operation of individuals — the technique of the market place.

The possibility of coordination through voluntary cooperation rests on the elementary — yet frequently denied — proposition that both parties to an economic transaction benefit from it, *provided the transaction is bilaterally voluntary and informed.*

Exchange can therefore bring about co-ordination without coercion. A working model of a society organized through voluntary exchange is a *free private enterprise exchange economy* — what we have been calling competitive capitalism.

In its simplest form, such a society consists of a number of independent households — a collection of Robinson Crusoes, as it were. Each household uses the resources it controls to produce goods and services that it exchanges for goods and services produced by other households, on terms mutually acceptable to the two parties to the bargain. It is thereby enabled to satisfy its wants indirectly by producing goods and services for others, rather than directly by producing goods for its own immediate use. The incentive for adopting this indirect route is, of course, the increased product made possible by division of labor and specialization of function. Since the household always has the alternative of producing directly for itself, it need not enter into any exchange unless it benefits from it. Hence, no exchange will take place unless both parties do benefit from it. Cooperation is thereby achieved without coercion.

Specialization of function and division of labor would not go far if the ultimate productive unit were the household. In a modern society, we have gone much farther. We have introduced enterprises which are intermediaries between individuals in their capacities as suppliers of service and as purchasers of goods. And similarly, specialization of function and division of labor could not go very far if we had to continue to rely on the barter of product for product. In consequence, money has been introduced as a means of facilitating exchange, and of enabling the acts of purchase and of sale to be separated into two parts.

Despite the important role of enterprises and of money in our actual economy, and despite the numerous and complex problems they raise, the central characteristic of the market technique of achieving coordination is fully displayed in the simple exchange economy that contains neither enterprise nor money. As in that simple model, so in the complex enterprise and money-exchange economy, cooperation is strictly individual and voluntary *provided:* (a) that enterprises are private, so that the ultimate contracting parties are individuals and (b) that individuals are effectively free to enter or not to enter into any particular exchange, so that every transaction is strictly voluntary.

It is far easier to state these provisos in general terms than to spell them out in detail, or to specify precisely the institutional arrangements most conducive to their maintenance. Indeed, much of technical economic literature is concerned with precisely these questions. The basic requisite is the maintenance of law and order to prevent physical coercion of one individual by another and to enforce contracts voluntarily entered into, thus giving substance to "private." Aside from this, perhaps the most difficult problems arise from monopoly — which inhibits effective freedom by denying individuals alternatives to the particular exchange — and from "neighborhood effects" — effects on third parties for which it is not feasible to charge or recompense them. These problems will be discussed in more detail in the following chapter.

So long as effective freedom of exchange is maintained, the central feature of the market organization of economic activity is that it prevents one person from interfering with another in respect of most of his activities. The consumer is protected from coercion by the seller because of the presence of others sellers with whom he can deal. The seller is protected from coercion by the consumer because of other consumers to whom he can sell. The employee is protected from coercion by the employer because of other employers for whom he can work, and so on. And the market does this impersonally and without centralized authority.

Indeed, a major source of objection to a free economy is precisely that it does this task so well. It gives people what they want instead of what a particular group thinks they ought to want. Underlying most arguments against the free market is a lack of belief in freedom itself.

The existence of a free market does not of course eliminate the need for government. On the contrary, government is essential both as a forum for determining the "rules of the game" and as an umpire to interpret and enforce the rules decided on. What the market does is to reduce greatly the range of issues that must be decided through political means, and thereby to minimize the extent to which government need participate directly in the game. The characteristic feature of action through political channels is that it tends to require or enforce substantial conformity. The great advantage of the market, on the other hand, is that it permits wide diversity. It is, in political terms, a system of proportional representation. Each man can vote, as it were, for the color of tie he wants and get it; he does not have to see what color the majority wants and then, if he is in the minority, submit.

It is this feature of the market that we refer to when we say that the market provides economic freedom. But this characteristic also has implications that go far beyond the narrowly economic. Political freedom means the absence of coercion of a man by his fellow men. The fundamental threat to freedom is power to coerce, be it in the hands of a monarch, a dictator, an oligarchy, or a momentary majority. The preservation of freedom requires the elimination of such concentration of power to the fullest possible extent and the dispersal and distribution of whatever power cannot be eliminated — a system of checks and balances. By removing the organization of economic activity from the control of political authority, the market eliminates this source of coercive power. It enables economic strength to be a check to political power rather than a reinforcement.

Economic power can be widely dispersed. There is no law of conservation which forces the growth of new centers of economic strength to be at the expense of existing centers. Political power, on the other hand, is more difficult to decentralize. There can be numerous small independent governments. But it is far more difficult to maintain numerous equipotent small centers of political power in a single large government than it is to have numerous centers of economic strength in a single large economy. There can be many millionaires in one large economy. But can there be more than one really outstanding leader, one person on whom the energies and enthusiasms of his countrymen are centered? If the central government gains power, it is likely to be at the expense of local governments. There seems to be something like a fixed total of political power to be distributed. Consequently, if economic power is joined to political power, concentration seems almost inevitable. On the other hand, if economic power is kept in separate hands from political power, it can serve as a check and a counter to political power.

The force of this abstract argument can perhaps best be demonstrated by example. Let us consider first, a hypothetical example that may help to bring out the principles involved, and then some actual examples from recent experience that illustrate the way in which the market works to preserve political freedom.

One feature of a free society is surely the freedom of individuals to advocate and propagandize openly for a radical change in the structure of the society — so long as the advocacy is restricted to persuasion and does not include force or other forms of coercion. It is a mark of the political freedom of a capitalist society that men can openly advocate and work for socialism. Equally, political freedom in a socialist society would require that men be free to advocate the introduction of capitalism. How could the freedom to advocate capitalism be preserved and protected in a socialist society?

In order for men to advocate anything, they must in the first place be able to earn a living. This already raises a problem in a socialist society, since all jobs are under the direct control of political authorities. It would take an act of self-denial whose difficulty is underlined by experience in the United States after World War II with the problem of "security" among Federal employees, for a socialist government to permit its employees to advocate policies directly contrary to official doctrine.

But let us suppose this act of self-denial to be achieved. For advocacy of capitalism to mean anything, the proponents must be able to finance their cause — to hold public meetings, publish pamphlets, buy radio time, issue newspapers and magazines, and so on. How could they raise the funds? There might and probably would be men in the socialist society with large incomes, perhaps even large capital sums in the form of government bonds and the like, but these would of necessity be high public officials. It is possible to conceive of a minor socialist official retaining his job although openly advocating capitalism. It strains credulity to imagine the socialist top brass financing such "subversive" activities.

The only recourse for funds would be to raise small amounts from a large number of minor officials. But this is no real answer. To tap these sources, many people would already have to be persuaded, and our whole problem is how to initiate and finance a campaign to do so. Radical movements in capitalist societies have never been financed this way. They have typically been supported by a few wealthy individuals who have become persuaded — by a Frederick Vanderbilt Field, or an Anita McCormick Blaine, or a Corliss Lamont, to mention a few names recently prominent, or by a Friedrich Engels, to go farther back. This is a role of inequality of wealth in preserving political freedom that is seldom noted — the role of the patron.

In a capitalist society, it is only necessary to convince a few wealthy people to get funds to launch any idea, however strange, and there are many such persons, many independent foci of support. And, indeed, it is not even necessary to persuade people or financial institutions with available funds of the soundness of the ideas to be propagated. It is only necessary to persuade them that the propagation can be financially successful; that the newspaper or magazine or book or other venture will be profitable. The competitive publisher, for example, cannot afford to publish only writing with which he personally agrees; his touchstone must be the likelihood that the market will be large enough to yield a satisfactory return on his investment.

In this way, the market breaks the vicious circle and makes it possible ultimately to finance such ventures by small amounts from many people without first persuading them. There are no such possibilities in the socialist society; there is only the all-powerful state.

Let us stretch our imagination and suppose that a socialist government is aware of this problem and is composed of people anxious to preserve freedom. Could it provide the funds? Perhaps, but it is difficult to see how. It could establish a bureau for subsidizing subversive propaganda. But how could it choose whom to support? If it gave to all who asked, it would shortly find itself out of funds, for socialism cannot repeal the elementary economic law that a sufficiently high price will call forth a large supply. Make the advocacy of radical causes sufficiently remunerative, and the supply of advocates will be unlimited.

Moreover, freedom to advocate unpopular causes does not require that such advocacy be without cost. On the contrary, no society could be stable if advocacy of radical change were costless, much less subsidized. It is entirely appropriate that men make sacrifices to advocate causes in which they deeply believe. Indeed, it is important to preserve freedom only for people who are willing to practice self-denial, for otherwise freedom degenerates into license and irresponsibility. What is essential is that the cost of advocating unpopular causes be tolerable and not prohibitive.

But we are not yet through. In a free market society, it is enough to have the funds. The suppliers of paper are as willing to sell it to the Daily Worker as to the Wall Street Journal. In a socialist society, it would not be enough to have the funds. The hypothetical supporter of capitalism would have to persuade a government factory making paper to sell to him, the government printing press to print his pamphlets, a government post office to distribute them among the people, a government agency to rent him a hall in which to talk, and so on.

Perhaps there is some way in which one could overcome these difficulties and preserve freedom in a socialist society. One cannot say it is utterly impossible. What is clear, however, is that there are very real difficulties in establishing institutions that will effectively preserve the possibility of dissent. So far as I know, none of the people who have been in favor of socialism and also in favor of freedom have really faced up to this issue, or made even a respectable start at developing the institutional arrangements that would permit freedom under socialism. By contrast, it is clear how a free market capitalist society fosters freedom.

A striking practical example of these abstract principles is the experience of Winston Churchill. From 1933 to the outbreak of World War II, Churchill was not permitted to talk over the British radio, which was, of course, a government monopoly administered by the British Broadcasting Corporation. Here was a leading citizen of his country, a Member of Parliament, a former cabinet minister, a man who was desperately trying by every device possible to persuade his countrymen to take steps to ward off the menace of Hitler's Germany. He was not permitted to talk over the radio to the British people because the BBC was a government monopoly and his position was too "controversial."

Another striking example, reported in the January 26, 1959 issue of Time, has to do with the "Blacklist Fadeout." Says the Time story:

"The Oscar-awarding ritual is Hollywood's biggest pitch for dignity, but two years ago dignity suffered. When one Robert Rich was announced as top writer for The Brave One, he never stepped forward. Robert Rich was a pseudonym, masking one of about 150 writers . . . blacklisted by the industry since 1947 as suspected Communists or fellow travelers. The case was particularly embarrassing because the Motion Picture Academy had barred any Communist or Fifth Amendment pleader from Oscar competition. Last week both the Communist rule and the mystery of Rich's identity were suddenly rescripted.

"Rich turned out to be Dalton (Johnny Got His Gun) Trumbo, one of the original "Hollywood Ten" writers who refused to testify at the 1947 hearings on Communism in the movie industry. Said producer Frank King, who had stoutly insisted that Robert Rich was "a young guy in Spain with a beard": "We have an obligation to our stockholders to buy the best script we can. Trumbo brought us The Brave One and we bought it." . . .

"In effect it was the formal end of the Hollywood black list. For barred writers, the informal end came long ago. At least 15% of current Hollywood films are reportedly written by blacklist members. Said Producer King, "There are more ghosts in Hollywood than in Forest Lawn. Every company in town has used the work of blacklisted people. We're just the first to confirm what everybody knows."

One may believe, as I do, that communism would destroy all of our freedoms, one may be opposed to it as firmly and as strongly as possible, and yet, at the same time, also believe that in a free society it is intolerable for a man to be prevented from making voluntary arrangements with others that are mutually attractive because he believes in or is trying to promote communism. His freedom includes his freedom to promote communism. Freedom also, of course, includes the freedom of others not to deal with him under those circumstances. The Hollywood blacklist was an unfree act that destroys freedom because it was a collusive arrangement that used coercive means to prevent voluntary exchanges. It didn't work precisely because the market made it costly for people to preserve the blacklist. The commercial emphasis, the fact that people who are running enterprises have an incentive to make as much money as they can, protected the freedom of the individuals who were blacklisted by providing them with an alternative form of employment, and by giving people an incentive to employ them.

If Hollywood and the movie industry had been government enterprises or if in England it had been a question of employment by the British Broadcasting Corporation it is difficult to believe that the "Hollywood Ten" or their equivalent would have found employment. Equally, it is difficult to believe that under those circumstances, strong proponents of individualism and private enterprise — or indeed strong proponents of any view other than the status quo — would be able to get employment.

II.   The Role of Government in a Free Society ...

I turn now to consider more specifically, though still in very broad terms, what the areas are that cannot be handled through the market at all, or can be handled only at so great a cost that the use of political channels may be preferable.

Government as Rule-Maker and Umpire

It is important to distinguish the day-to-day activities of people from the general customary and legal framework within which these take place. The day-to-day activities are like the actions of the participants in a game when they are playing it; the framework, like the rules of the game they play. And just as a good game requires acceptance by the players both of the rules and of the umpire to interpret and enforce them, so a good society requires that its members agree on the general conditions that will govern relations among them, on some means of arbitrating different interpretations of these conditions, and on some device for enforcing compliance with the generally accepted rules. As in games, so also in society, most of the general conditions are the unintended outcome of custom, accepted unthinkingly. At most, we consider explicitly only minor modifications in them, though the cumulative effect of a series of minor modifications may be a drastic alteration in the character of the game or of the society. In both games and society also, no set of rules can prevail unless most participants most of the time conform to them without external sanctions; unless that is, there is a broad underlying social consensus. But we cannot rely on custom or on this consensus alone to interpret and to enforce the rules; we need an umpire. These then are the basic roles of government in a free society: to provide a means whereby we can modify the rules, to mediate differences among us on the meaning of the rules, and to enforce compliance with the rules on the part of those few who would otherwise not play the game.

The need for government in these respects arises because absolute freedom is impossible. However attractive anarchy may be as a philosophy, it is not feasible in a world of imperfect men. Men's freedoms can conflict, and when they do, one man's freedom must be limited to preserve another's — as a Supreme Court Justice once put it, "My freedom to move my fist must be limited by the proximity of your chin."

The major problem in deciding the appropriate activities of government is how to resolve such conflicts among the freedoms of different individuals. In some cases, the answer is easy. There is little difficulty in attaining near unanimity to the proposition that one man's freedom to murder his neighbor must be sacrificed to preserve the freedom of the other man to live. In other cases, the answer is difficult. In the economic area, a major problem arises in respect of the conflict between freedom to combine and freedom to compete. What meaning is to be attributed to "free" as modifying "enterprise"? In the United States, "free" has been understood to mean that anyone is free to set up an enterprise, which means that existing enterprises are not free to keep out competitors except by selling a better product at the same price or the same product at a lower price. In the continental tradition, on the other hand, the meaning has generally been that enterprises are free to do what they want, including the fixing of prices, division of markets, and the adoption of other techniques to keep out potential competitors. Perhaps the most difficult specific problem in this area arises with respect to combinations among laborers, where the problem of freedom to combine and freedom to compete is particularly acute.

A still more basic economic area in which the answer is both difficult and important is the definition of property rights. The notion of property, as it has developed over centuries and as it is embodied in our legal codes, has become so much a part of us that we tend to take it for granted, and fail to recognize the extent to which just what constitutes property and what rights the ownership of property confers are complex social creations rather than self-evident propositions. Does my having title to land, for example, and my freedom to use my property as I wish, permit me to deny to someone else the right to fly over my land in his airplane? Or does his right to use his airplane take precedence? Or does this depend on how high he flies? Or how much noise he makes? Does voluntary exchange require that he pay me for the privilege of flying over my land? Or that I must pay him to refrain from flying over it? The mere mention of royalties, copyrights, patents; shares of stock in corporations; riparian rights, and the like, may perhaps emphasize the role of generally accepted social rules in the very definition of property. It may suggest also that, in many cases, the existence of a well specified and generally accepted definition of property is far more important than just what the definition is.

Another economic area that raises particularly difficult problems is the monetary system. Government responsibility for the monetary system has long been recognized. It is explicitly provided for in the constitutional provision which gives Congress the power "to coin money, regulate the value thereof, and of foreign coin." There is probably no other area of economic activity with respect to which government action has been so uniformly accepted. This habitual and by now almost unthinking acceptance of governmental responsibility makes thorough understanding of the grounds for such responsibility all the more necessary, since it enhances the danger that the scope of government will spread from activities that are, to those that are not, appropriate in a free society, from providing a monetary framework to determining the allocation of resources among individuals. . . .

In summary, the organization of economic activity through voluntary exchange presumes that we have provided, through government, for the maintenance of law and order to prevent coercion of one individual by another, the enforcement of contracts voluntarily entered into, the definition of the meaning of property rights, the interpretation and enforcement of such rights, and the provision of a monetary framework.

Action Through Government on Grounds of Technical Monopoly and Neighborhood Effects

The role of government just considered is to do something that the market cannot do for itself, namely, to determine, arbitrate, and enforce the rules of the game. We may also want to do through government some things that might conceivably be done through the market but that technical or similar conditions render it difficult to do in that way. These all reduce to cases in which strictly voluntary exchange is either exceedingly costly or practically impossible. There are two general classes of such cases: monopoly and similar market imperfections, and neighborhood effects.

Exchange is truly voluntary only when nearly equivalent alternatives exist. Monopoly implies the absence of alternatives and thereby inhibits effective freedom of exchange. In practice, monopoly frequently, if not generally, arises from government support or from collusive agreements among individuals. With respect to these, the problem is either to avoid governmental fostering of monopoly or to stimulate the effective enforcement of rules such as those embodied in our anti-trust laws. However, monopoly may also arise because it is technically efficient to have a single producer or enterprise. I venture to suggest that such cases are more limited than is supposed but they unquestionably do arise. A simple example is perhaps the provision of telephone services within a community. I shall refer to such cases as "technical" monopoly.

When technical conditions make a monopoly the natural outcome of competitive market forces, there are only three alternatives that seem available: private monopoly, public monopoly, or public regulation. All three are bad so we must choose among evils. Henry Simons, observing public regulation of monopoly in the United States, found the results so distasteful that he concluded public monopoly would be a lesser evil. Walter Eucken, a noted German liberal, observing public monopoly in German railroads, found the results so distasteful that he concluded public regulation would be a lesser evil. Having learned from both, I reluctantly conclude that, if tolerable, private monopoly would be the least of the evils.

If society were static so that the conditions which give rise to a technical monopoly were sure to remain, I would have little confidence in this solution. In a rapidly changing society, however, the conditions making for technical monopoly frequently change and I suspect that both public regulation and public monopoly are likely to be less responsive to such changes in conditions, to be less readily capable of elimination, than private monopoly.

Railroads in the United States are an excellent example. A large degree of monopoly in railroads was perhaps inevitable on technical grounds in the nineteenth century. This was the justification for the Interstate Commerce Commission. But conditions have changed. The emergence of road and air transport has reduced the monopoly element in railroads to negligible proportions. Yet we have not eliminated the ICC. On the contrary, the ICC, which started out as an agency to protect the public from exploitation by the railroads, has become an agency to protect railroads from competition by trucks and other means of transport, and more recently even to protect existing truck companies from competition by new entrants. Similarly, in England, when the railroads were nationalized, trucking was at first brought into the state monopoly. If railroads had never been subjected to regulation in the United States, it is nearly certain that by now transportation, including railroads, would be a highly competitive industry with little or no remaining monopoly elements.

The choice between the evils of private monopoly, public monopoly, and public regulation cannot, however, be made once and for all, independently of the factual circumstances. If the technical monopoly is of a service or commodity that is regarded as essential and if its monopoly power is sizable, even the shortrun effects of private unregulated monopoly may not be tolerable, and either public regulation or ownership may be a lesser evil.

Technical monopoly may on occasion justify a de facto public monopoly. It cannot by itself justify a public monopoly achieved by making it illegal for anyone else to compete. For example, there is no way to justify our present public monopoly of the post office. It may be argued that the carrying of mail is a technical monopoly and that a government monopoly is the least of evils. Along these lines, one could perhaps justify a government post office but not the present law, which makes it illegal for anybody else to carry mail. If the delivery of mail is a technical monopoly, no one will be able to succeed in competition with the government. If it is not, there is no reason why the government should be engaged in it. The only way to find out is to leave other people free to enter.

The historical reason why we have a post office monopoly is because the Pony Express did such a good job of carrying the mail across the continent that, when the government introduced transcontinental service, it couldn't compete effectively and lost money. The result was a law making it illegal for anybody else to carry the mail. That is why the Adams Express Company is an investment trust today instead of an operating company. I conjecture that if entry into the mail-carrying business were open to all, there would be a large number of firms entering it and this archaic industry would become revolutionized in short order.

A second general class of cases in which strictly voluntary exchange is impossible arises when actions of individuals have effects on other individuals for which it is not feasible to charge or recompense them. This is the problem of "neighborhood effects." An obvious example is the pollution of a stream. The man who pollutes a stream is in effect forcing others to exchange good water for bad. These others might be willing to make the exchange at a price. But it is not feasible for them, acting individually, to avoid the exchange or to enforce appropriate compensation.

A less obvious example is the provision of highways. In this case, it is technically possible to identify and hence charge individuals for their use of the roads and so to have private operation. However, for general access roads, involving many points of entry and exit, the costs of collection would be extremely high if a charge were to be made for the specific services received by each individual, because of the necessity of establishing toll booths or the equivalent at all entrances. The gasoline tax is a much cheaper method of charging individuals roughly in proportion to their use of the roads. This method, however, is one in which the particular payment cannot be identified closely with the particular use. Hence, it is hardly feasible to have private enterprise provide the service and collect the charge without establishing extensive private monopoly.

These considerations do not apply to long-distance turnpikes with high density of traffic and limited access. For these, the costs of collection are small and in many cases are now being paid, and there are often numerous alternatives, so that there is no serious monopoly problem. Hence, there is every reason why these should be privately owned and operated. If so owned and operated, the enterprise running the highway should receive the gasoline taxes paid on account of travel on it.

Parks are an interesting example because they illustrate the difference between cases that can and cases that cannot be justified by neighborhood effects, and because almost everyone at first sight regards the conduct of National Parks as obviously a valid function of government. In fact, however, neighborhood effects may justify a city park; they do not justify a national park, like Yellowstone National Park or the Grand Canyon. What is the fundamental difference between the two? For the city park, it is extremely difficult to identify the people who benefit from it and to charge them for the benefits which they receive. If there is a park in the middle of the city, the houses on all sides get the benefit of the open space, and people who walk through it or by it also benefit. To maintain toll collectors at the gates or to impose annual charges per window overlooking the park would be very expensive and difficult. The entrances to a national park like Yellowstone, on the other hand, are few; most of the people who come stay for a considerable period of time and it is perfectly feasible to set up toll gates and collect admission charges. This is indeed now done, though the charges do not cover the whole costs. If the public wants this kind of an activity enough to pay for it, private enterprises will have every incentive to provide such parks. And, of course, there are many private enterprises of this nature now in existence. I cannot myself conjure up any neighborhood effects or important monopoly effects that would justify governmental activity in this area.

Considerations like those I have treated under the heading of neighborhood effects have been used to rationalize almost every conceivable intervention. In many instances, however, this rationalization is special pleading rather than a legitimate application of the concept of neighborhood effects. Neighborhood effects cut both ways. They can be a reason for limiting the activities of government as well as for expanding them. Neighborhood effects impede voluntary exchange because it is difficult to identify the effects on third parties and to measure their magnitude; but this difficulty is present in governmental activity as well. It is hard to know when neighborhood effects are sufficiently large to justify particular costs in overcoming them and even harder to distribute the costs in an appropriate fashion. Consequently, when government engages in activities to overcome neighborhood effects, it will in part introduce an additional set of neighborhood effects by failing to charge or to compensate individuals properly. Whether the original or the new neighborhood effects are the more serious can only be judged by the facts of the individual case, and even then, only very approximately. Furthermore, the use of government to overcome neighborhood effects itself has an extremely important neighborhood effect which is unrelated to the particular occasion for government action. Every act of government intervention limits the area of individual freedom directly and threatens the preservation of freedom indirectly for reasons elaborated in the first chapter.

Our principles offer no hard and fast line how far it is appropriate to use government to accomplish jointly what it is difficult or impossible for us to accomplish separately through strictly voluntary exchange. In any particular case of proposed intervention, we must make up a balance sheet, listing separately the advantages and disadvantages. Our principles tell us what items to put on the one side and what items on the other and they give us some basis for attaching importance to the different items. In particular, we shall always want to enter on the liability side of any proposed government intervention, its neighborhood effect in threatening freedom, and give this effect considerable weight. Just how much weight to give to it, as to other items, depends upon the circumstances. If, for example, existing government intervention is minor, we shall attach a smaller weight to the negative effects of additional government intervention. This is an important reason why many earlier liberals, like Henry Simons, writing at a time when government was small by today's standards, were willing to have government undertake activities that today's liberals would not accept now that government has become so overgrown.

NOTES AND QUESTIONS ON PROPERTY'S RELATION TO LIBERTY

1. In Friedman's litany of legal restraints on freedom early in this selection, he leaves out several quite widespread kinds of laws that curtail voluntary transactions. Some examples are laws limiting the contractual capacities of minors (including statutory rape laws), laws restraining the use of narcotics, and laws requiring the use of automobile seat belts or motorcycle helmets. Do any of these differ from Friedman's examples? Would you expect him to accept any of these laws? Why or why not? Are there rationales for such con-

straints that might be compatible with an overall libertarian commitment? Consider Cass R. Sunstein, Legal Interference with Private Preferences, 53 U. Chi. L. Rev. 1129 (1986) arguing that some legislation reflects "preferences about preferences" — that is, we know we are likely to be tempted by X or Y, but wish we weren't; thus we willingly pass legislation in order to restrain ourselves from following preferences that we consider shortsighted in our more sober moments. See also Jon Elster, Ulysses and the Sirens (1984).

2. Is it in fact true that a private property/free market economic system diffuses political power? Why isn't political power more diffused if major economic assets are owned by the public, that is, by the entire citizenry, as in socialist regimes? Compare Charles E. Lindblom, Politics and Markets 170-188 (1977) (concentrations of private wealth lead to plutocracy). One response, deriving from the economics-influenced literature of "public choice," is that publicly owned or managed goods tend to be siphoned off by special interests. Two classics on this subject are Mancur Olson, The Logic of Collective Action (1st ed. 1965); and James Buchanan & Gordon Tullock, The Calculus of Consent (1962).

3. How great a concession does Friedman make when he observes that government properly may prevent violence, operate the monetary system, enforce contracts, define property rights, provide antitrust protection, and manage at least some streets, parks, and pollution problems? Do such responses to "market failure" swallow up the claim that the market can coordinate without coercion — and with it, the claim that the market can diffuse power and protect individualism? Might not a government act quite repressively in, say, antitrust or environmental enforcement?

4. Friedman's arguments interestingly echo some political claims from an earlier time, described in Joyce Appleby's Capitalism and the New Social Order: The Republican Vision of the 1790s (1984). Here Appleby explores the liberating influence of early capitalism in republican political thought. She points out that prior to the mid-eighteenth century, most people thought that hierarchical governance was essential to the ordering of human behavior (including economic behavior), since human beings were thought to be generally too unruly to operate without detailed and intimate supervision.

Undermining this hierarchical world view, according to Appleby, was the eighteenth century growth of commerce and an accompanying popular discussion of a single metaphoric "market," composed of all trading activity rather than simply a particular town marketplace. If goods that were bought and sold could reach a rough equilibrium or "market" price in this larger market, then the "market" itself appeared to be a self-regulating mechanism, operating without the need for political supervision — or as Friedman put it, capable of "coordination without coercion." In the eighteenth century, according to Appleby, the next step was an extension of this economic idea into the political arena: If human beings did not need hierarchic rulers to govern their economic affairs, then why did they need rulers in politics generally? In this way, Appleby claims that the development of free market economic thinking was a crucial step towards the early republican political theory of democracy and popular self-governance.

As of 1984, when Appleby's book appeared, she was considerably less sanguine than Friedman about the *actual* liberating effect of the market. She thought it was an interesting and historically important idea, but she ultimately hinted that the experience of capitalism should teach observers that the market creates its own patterns of domination and subordination.

5. Friedman's references to Russia are of course now out of date. Did the Eastern European overthrow of socialist regimes reflect a Friedman-like view associating economic and political freedom? If so, will Eastern Europe be a test case? Do the post-1989 events in Europe bear out Friedman's views, Appleby's, both, or neither? For more on the role of private property and liberty in the new Eastern European constitutional regimes, see the next selection by Cass Sunstein.

On Property and Constitutionalism *

Cass R. Sunstein

It is generally understood that the recent revolutions in Eastern Europe are producing a large-scale transition. . . . The new reform movements actually involve three distinct transitions. . . .

[F]or the foreseeable future, it seems clear that the transition to markets, and the accompanying efforts to promote economic development, will be foremost in the minds of the reformers. Democratization also appears on the agenda, but it usually takes a secondary role. In the meantime, the movement for constitutional reform generally draws little public attention, and indeed has been dwarfed by other matters. . . .

*Source: 14 Cardozo L. Rev. 907-922 (1993).

In fact, the transitions are closely related. The right kind of constitution could play an important role in fueling economic development and democratic reform; . . . [t]he wrong kind of constitution — or no constitution at all — could be devastating to progress in both of these areas.

To offer only one example: Firm constitutional protection of property rights, combined with an independent judiciary, is an excellent way of encouraging international investment in one's nation. Such devices should spur domestic investment and initiative as well. Without constitutional protection, . . . [a]nyone who engages in economic activities in these nations will do so with knowledge that the state may take their property or abrogate their contracts. To say the very least, this will be an obstacle to economic development.

In Eastern Europe, there is a more pressing need for constitutional protection of economic and democratic rights than there was in the United States or the West. In the United States, for example, the process of constitution-making was simplified by the fact that well before that process began, private property, the common law, and civil society were firmly in place. . . . The market and the institutions of civil society — private intermediate associations operating between the individual and the state, including religious organizations, charitable trusts, local community groups, business enterprises — antedated the Constitution.

The task of constitution-making in Eastern Europe is both more critical and more daunting, precisely because of the absence of well established institutions protecting market ordering and civil society. The emerging constitutions must not only create the basic governmental structures and protect the conventional catalog of liberal rights, but also concern themselves with the creation of safeguards for the transition to [a] market ordering. . . .

I.   Property, Prosperity, Democracy

. . . Westerners often think that the constitutions of Eastern European countries before the downfall of communism are not constitutions at all. In fact, however, they embody a distinct conception of constitutionalism. Crucially, such constitutions do not distinguish between public and private spheres. . . .

Moreover, such constitutions . . . do not merely grant privileges to citizens, but also impose obligations on them. Finally, and most important of all, the central provisions of these constitutions set out very general social aspirations or commitments. Their provisions are designed to state those aspirations, not to create concrete entitlements that citizens can attempt to vindicate, through an independent judiciary, against government officials. . . .

Thus, for example, the Soviet Constitution includes the right to work, the right to rest and leisure, the right to health protection, and the right to maintenance in old age, sickness, and disability. It imposes on citizens the duty to preserve and protect socialist property and to enhance the power and prestige of the Soviet State. The Polish Constitution includes the right to work, the right to rest and leisure, and the right to health protection. The Romanian Constitution includes the right to leisure, the right to work, including equal pay for equal work and measures for the protection and safety of workers. The Bulgarian Constitution offers the right to a holiday, the right to work, the right to labor safety, the right to social security, and the right to free medical care.

Along each of these dimensions, western constitutions are quite different. . . . Most important, they aim to create solid individual rights, ones that can be invoked by individual citizens, as of right, in an independent tribunal authorized to bar governmental action. Western constitutions generally do not include broad aspirations. Positive rights are the exception, and when they exist they are usually not subject to judicial enforcement.

The individual rights protected by western constitutions are not, of course, limited to private property and economic liberties. They include other political and civil liberties and rights as well, and these are indispensable safeguards. My principal goal here, however, is to explain how constitutionalism might work simultaneously to promote the transition to economic markets and the transition to democracy, and for this reason it will be valuable to focus on the right to private property. . . .

A. Private Property and Economic Prosperity

It is generally agreed that a system of private property helps to bring about economic prosperity. . . .

First, the institution of private property creates and takes advantage of the powerful human inclination to bring goods and services to oneself and to people one cares about. This claim does not depend on a proposition about human selfishness. The desire to acquire goods might be deeply altruistic, in the sense that people may want to give their goods to others, including the most vulnerable members of society.

In a system of private property, the gains from the use and cultivation of ownership rights accrue to a designated owner. A system without private property stifles incentives and thus induces both sloth and waste. These points, too, do not depend on especially cyni-cal accounts of human nature. It is necessary only to glance briefly at history, past and present, and to acknowledge that human beings will frequently attempt to accumulate resources. Social institutions that appeal to this inclination will increase social productivity.

Second, a system of private property performs a crucial coor-dinating function. It ensures that the multiple desires of hundreds, thousands, or millions of consumers will be reflected in market out-comes. In this way it protects against the perverse forms of scarcity produced by a command economy. Public officials cannot possibly know what and how much people will want in advance. Official decisions will thus create both too much and too little production. By contrast, a system of ownership rights signals people to devote their productive activity to areas in which that activity is most valued. . . .

Third, the institution of private property solves, all at once, a serious collective action problem faced by people in any system without that institution. When property is unowned, no one has a sufficient incentive to use it to its full advantage or to protect it against exploitation. . . .

The point can be made more vivid by a glance at the problem of environmental deterioration. In recent years, it has been increas-ingly recognized that that problem — especially severe in Eastern Europe but of critical importance in the West as well — is in signifi-cant part a product of the collective action problem produced by the fact that the air and water are public goods, that is, collectively rather than privately owned. The consequence is that the environ-mental costs of polluting activity are widely diffused among the public and not "internalized," or taken into account, by polluters. Because they do not bear the direct cost, polluters lack an incentive to limit their polluting activity. This system creates a built-in ten-dency toward excessive pollution levels.

A system without private property can be understood as a mas-sive version of this unfortunate state of affairs. If property is un-owned, everyone has an incentive to exploit it, and no one has an incentive to use it to its full advantage. Activity levels will have no relationship to their actual social costs and benefits. Ownership rights overcome this difficulty. They operate like a well-functioning system of environmental law; they ensure that people have incen-tives to take account of both the benefits and the harms of what they do. This is an exceedingly important task for a constitutional democracy.

Finally, a system of private property creates the kind of stability and protection of expectations that are preconditions for investment and initiative, from both international and domestic sources. A company deciding whether to invest in a country will have a greater incentive to do so if it knows that its investment will be protected, and that government confiscation is prohibited by the nation's highest law. A citizen who is seeking to begin a business will be far more likely to do so if he can operate against a secure and stable background, protected against the vicissitudes of government policy. . . .

B. Property and Democracy

The connection between property and prosperity may be reasonably well understood, but the right to private property has not always been considered a precondition for democracy. On the contrary, private property has frequently been thought to present an obstacle to democracy. . . .

There is indeed some tension between a system of property rights and a system of democracy. If property rights are secure, there is a firm limit on what the democratic process is entitled to do. . . . Notably, a new market economy will likely impose conspicuous short-term costs — unemployment and inflation — and in the emerging Eastern European democracies, there will probably be a continuous temptation to slow the transition to markets, or perhaps to reject it altogether. For this reason, the simultaneous transition to democracy and to economic markets — without the protection of constitutionalism — will be exceptionally difficult.

In important respects, however, it is quite plausible to think that the right to a stable system of property rights — one with which the state will interfere only occasionally or in a limited way, with a provision for compensation — is actually necessary to democracy and not opposed to it at all.

The most fundamental point about the relationship between property and democracy is that a right to own private property has an important and salutary effect on the citizens' relationship with the state and — equally important — on their understanding of that relationship. Because of this effect, it can be seen as a necessary precondition for the status of citizenship. Personal security and personal independence from the government are guaranteed in a system in which rights of ownership are protected through public institutions.

This theme has played a large role in republican thought. In the republican view, the status of the citizen implies a measure of independence from government power. . . .

In [a] sense, the ownership of private property is closely associated with the role of law. Both of these create a realm of private autonomy in which the citizenry can operate without fear of public intrusion. That realm is indispensable to the public sphere itself. Only people with a degree of security from the state are able to participate without fear, and with independence, in democratic deliberations. In this sense, a sharp, legally-produced distinction between the private and the public can usefully serve the public sphere. Contrary to a conventional understanding, it need not harm it at all. . . .

A central point here is that in a state in which private property does not exist, citizens are dependent on the good will of government officials, almost on a daily basis. Whatever they have is a privilege and not a right. They come to the state as supplicants or beggars rather than as right holders. Any challenge to the state may be stifled or driven underground by virtue of the fact that serious challenges could result in the withdrawal of the goods that give people basic security. A right to private property, free from government interference, is in this sense a necessary basis for a democracy. . . .

The final point is that one of the best ways to destroy a democratic system is to ensure that the distribution of wealth and resources is unstable and constantly vulnerable to reevaluation by the political process. A high degree of stability is necessary to allow people to plan their affairs, to reduce the effects of factional or interest group power in government, to promote investment, and to prevent the political process from breaking down by attempting to resolve enormous, emotionally laden issues about who is entitled to what. Stability and security — a sense of context — are important individual and collective goods. A system in which property rights are open to continuous readjustment will produce serious harm. . . .

Like the right to freedom of religious conscience, moreover, the right to property helps create a flourishing civil society, an intermediate level between the government and the individual. The development of a civil society can in turn be understood as a mechanism both for creating economic prosperity and for promoting democratic self governance. A constitutional system that respects private property should be regarded not as an effort to oppose liberal rights to collective self-government, but instead as a way of fortifying democratic processes.

. . . In the West, enthusiasm for property rights is often thought to entail a reluctance to allow redistribution, or (worse) complete indifference to the poor. The proper response is twofold. First, property rights help create wealth, and greater wealth will often benefit the most vulnerable as well. Time and again it has been shown that economic growth does more than welfare and employment programs to benefit the disadvantaged. Of course, growth does not do everything, and it must be supplemented. The second point, then, is that welfare and employment programs are a necessary part of any system of property rights. . . . Indeed, it is important to ensure not merely that everyone has a right to private property, but also that everyone has private property. Property rights without property ownership involve a degree of dependence that is debilitating to citizenship.

Properly understood, the defense of property rights is a defense of programs of redistribution as well. These programs are not designed to produce economic equality — a truly disastrous goal — but instead to bring about at least rough equality of opportunity and, even more important, freedom from desperate conditions, or from circumstances that impede basic human functioning.

II. Property and Constitution Making

I have said that the task of economic development cannot be rigidly separated from the task of constitution-making. Without constitutional protection of property rights, there will be continuous pressure to adjust distributions of property on an ad hoc basis. When a group of people acquires a good deal of money, it will be tempting to tax them heavily. When another group verges on bankruptcy, there will be a temptation to subsidize them. After the fact, these steps may seem fair or even necessary; but if everyone knows that government might respond in this way, there will be a powerful deterrent to the development of a market economy. No citizen — and no international or domestic investor — can be secure of his immunity from the state.

A pervasive risk is that governmental control over property rights will undo the decision, made in the basic system creating such rights, to solve a collective action problem faced by public ownership. If property rights are insecure if they are subject to continuous governmental examination — the system will approach equivalence to one in which there are no such rights at all. . . . [I]t will create individual vulnerability to government and at the same time produce both too little and too much use of existing resources. It will deter economic development and impair the movement toward democracy as well.

A. In General

I have claimed that a constitution can accomplish a great deal in easing the transition to economic markets and private property.

In order for it to do so, constitutional protections must be judicially enforceable — that is, a court must be available to vindicate any rights that the constitution creates. . . . To be sure, some nations in the West have prospered with little or nothing in the way of judicial enforcement of constitutions. But these nations benefited from the background of civil society, market economies, and well-defined property rights. For them, constitutional protections were far less important.

For Eastern Europe in general, the drafting of a constitution appears to pose two especially distinctive challenges. The first is to begin the process of creating a legal culture with firm judicial protection of individual rights. By individual rights I mean, first and foremost, traditional "negative" rights against government, prominent among them property ownership and freedom of contract. It is, of course, misleading to think of these as genuinely negative rights. They depend for their existence on governmental institutions willing to recognize, create, and protect them. . . .

The second challenge is to facilitate the creation of a market economy and of a civil society — that is, a realm of private action containing institutions (churches, markets, corporations, labor unions, women's organizations, and so forth) that are independent of the state and minimally constrained by it. . . .

To carry out this task, constitution-makers should avoid three strategies that contain serious risks. All of these strategies are characteristic features of communist constitutionalism. Unfortunately, all of them appear to be influencing current debates in the post-communist era. The draft constitutions tend to replicate the errors of the communist constitutions themselves.

1. ASPIRATIONS

The first such strategy is to use a constitution as a place for setting out very general social aspirations, or for imposing positive duties on government (such as the provision of a social welfare state including such guarantees as equitable remuneration, leisure time, social security, and occupational safety and health). There are three reasons why this would be a dangerous strategy, at least under current conditions.

First, to state aspirations and impose positive duties — prominent of course in the Soviet Constitution — runs the risk of turning a constitution into something other than a legal document with real-world consequences. . . . [A] constitution should not list all things to which a country aspires. It should limit itself, for the most part, to rights that it is genuinely able to enforce. A constitution that creates positive rights is not likely to be subject to judicial enforcement because these rights are vaguely defined, simultaneously involve the interests of numerous people, and depend for their existence on active management of government institutions — something for which judges are ill-suited. The existence of unenforceable rights will in turn tend to destroy the negative rights — freedom of speech, freedom of religion, and so forth — that might otherwise be genuine ones. If some rights are shown to be unenforceable, it is likely that others will be unenforceable as well.

The second problem with positive rights is that they will work against the general current efforts to diminish the sense of entitlement to state protection, and to encourage individual initiative and self-reliance. Both markets and democracy tend to develop these highly salutary characteristics. Sometimes liberal constitutionalism is praised because it responds accurately to "human nature," and does not try to tinker with it. There is undoubtedly something to this idea; efforts fundamentally to revise human character are usually doomed to failure. But liberal constitutionalism might be defended precisely on the ground that it has healthy effects on human character. Markets and democracy tend to create certain types, with many valuable characteristics.

To say this is emphatically not to say that in the post-reform era, nations in Eastern Europe should eliminate social welfare protections and leave their citizens to the vicissitudes of the market. Such a route would be a recipe for disaster, since it would allow for mass suffering of the kind that is unacceptable in any nation. But these protections should be created at the level of ordinary legislation, and subject to democratic discussion, rather than placed in the foundational document.

The third problem with positive rights is that they establish government interference with markets as a constitutional duty. The current trend is to limit such interference, and to establish the preconditions for private markets, free trade, and free contract. To impose a constitutional duty of interference is to move in precisely the wrong direction.

. . . At most, any positive rights and aspirations should be understood to be unenforceable.

2. DUTIES

Another strategy, posing similar risks, is to use the constitution as a place for creating "duties" as well as rights. Such duties are not likely to be enforceable through courts. Their statement in a constitution tends to weaken the understanding that the document creates protected rights, with real meaning, against the state. . . .

3. NO DISTINCTION BETWEEN PUBLIC AND PRIVATE SPHERES

Yet another dangerous strategy is to make constitutional provisions binding against private people and private organizations as well as against the state. In almost all western systems, the constitution applies only to the government, not to the people in general. This is extremely important, because it recognizes and helps create a private sphere — a civil society that operates independently of the state. It also frees up private organizations — employers, religious organizations, unions, and so forth — to act as they choose. If the people want to apply particular constitutional provisions to particular private organizations, of course they can do so, through ordinary legislation. . . .

Ironically, these dangers are more serious for the East than for the West. In the United States, for example, the institutions of private property and civil society are firmly in place, and social injustice frequently occurs precisely because of the absence of positive protections and of safeguards against the power of private institutions. The case for a firm right to some forms of social assistance is at least a plausible one in America. Such a right would not seriously jeopardize existing legal and social institutions; it could not possibly threaten the general belief in markets, solid property rights, and civil society.

In systems that are seeking to establish free markets and civil society for the first time, and that already have a strong public commitment to a social welfare state, the relevant considerations point in precisely the opposite direction. A dramatic legal and cultural shift, creating a belief in private property and a respect for markets, is indispensable. . . .

We might draw a more general conclusion from this discussion. It is often said that constitutions, as a form of higher law, must be compatible with the culture and mores of those whom they regulate. In one sense, however, the opposite is true. Constitutional provisions should be designed to work against precisely those aspects of a country's culture and tradition that are likely to produce harm through that country's ordinary political processes. There is a large difference between the risks of harm faced by a nation committed by culture and history to free markets, and the corresponding risks in a nation committed by culture and history to social security and general state protection. Constitutions should work against the particular nation's most threatening tendencies. This point explains why extremely powerful safeguards against sex discrimination and ethnic and religious oppression are necessary in Eastern Europe (a point that would, however, take me well beyond the scope of this Essay). It is for this reason above all that constitutions designed for one nation are ill-adapted for use by others. . . .

NOTES AND QUESTIONS ON PROPERTY IN POST-SOCIALIST CONSTITUTIONS

1. Some of Sunstein's arguments are essentially psychological: The protection of property gives people a sense of security and makes them feel that their lives are protected from governmental disruption. Is this merely an illusion? Why does it really matter for democracy how people *feel*? What hinges on a mere sense of security and independence?

There are quite a number of conflicting views about the effects of market relations on the human psyche. For some of them, see the selection from Albert O. Hirschman, Rival Interpretations of Market Society, infra p.345.

2. Sunstein outlines a number of ways in which property enhances individual and social wealth, and he also notes that more prosperous societies can more easily alleviate poverty. Is prosperity connected to political stability in other ways? If citizens are caught up in the pleasures of making money, are they likely to feud with each other over such matters as religious or ethnic differences? Are they likely to be very interested in politics at all? For the argument that the American founders hoped that commerce and private property would assure democracy, essentially by distracting citizens from political issues, see Martin Diamond, The Federalist, in Joseph Cropsey & Leo Strauss, History of Political Philosophy 648-649 (2d ed. 1972). Does this mean that property promotes democracy by making politics boring? Does political activity suffer from a resulting citizen disinterest and even contempt? Compare Albert O. Hirschman, Shifting Involvements (1982), arguing that people oscillate between private and public concerns.

3. Sunstein argues that welfare programs are an essential part of democratic property regimes. Why? Economic arguments are often made *against* welfare. According to one such argument, welfare programs mean taxing the better-off; hence, welfare may discourage and weaken the most industrious and successful group, thus undermining general prosperity. According to another argument, welfare may reduce the incentives of the recipients to work, again undermining general prosperity. For fuller discussion see Ellickson, Right to Shelter, infra p.118.

In linking democracy to prosperity, does Sunstein become vulnerable to antiwelfare arguments like these? How might he respond? If he thinks welfare is so important, why does he resist constitutionalizing it? Does this suggest some doubts on his part?

4. Sunstein, like Friedman, supra p.71, seems to think that property rights depend on government. If so, what is the difference between "negative" protections of property (and of free speech and other rights) and the "positive" rights of which Sunstein is so skeptical? Do not both categories of rights make the citizen dependent on government?

5. In what sense does the security of property actually depend on government? Consider a "safe" neighborhood or street, where people feel free to leave their doors unlocked: Is property secure because of the police, because of people's habits and customs, or because of some interaction of law and culture? What about commercial dealings: Why do business people trust each other? Is it just because they know they can sue for breach of contract? Consider whether there might be such a thing as a "cultural infrastructure" of property and commerce, and how law upholds and enhances it. Is that what Sunstein's article is really about? If the Eastern Europeans have lost such a cultural infrastructure, as Sunstein may be suggesting, will they have to become police states again in order to enforce private property rights?

6. Sunstein has an interestingly contrarian view of constitutions — that they should provide for the measures that the people of a nation are unlikely to take, left to their own traditions and history. Compare the classic constitutional theory of Montesquieu, in The Spirit of the Laws (1748), arguing that the laws must be *compatible* with the habits, traditions, and mores of a people. Who is right, Sunstein or Montesquieu?

D.   Distributive Justice

Introductory Note on Past and Present Theories of Distributive Justice

The institution of private property tends to preserve existing — and invariably unequal — distributions of wealth. Not surprisingly, ideological opponents of private property have consistently stressed its association with inequality. Theorists critical of private property were especially prominent in the nineteenth century, a period of unprecedented industrial expansion. Karl Marx, the most influential of the critics, called for the State, once it had been reconstituted to represent the "proletariat," to seize ownership of capital, land, and other means of production from the "bourgeoisie." In practice, does State ownership empower individual workers? Enrich them? Decrease their alienation? Or, as critics of Marxist regimes have asserted, entoil workers in huge unresponsive bureaucracies?

Henry George, a member of the generation following Marx's, provided an enduringly influential critique of the justice of private property in land. George's core concern was tax policy. He was chary of taxes on orchards, buildings, and other *land improvements*, on the grounds that taxes of this stripe discourage investment and unfairly reduce returns to enterprises. George's central insight was that *land sites*, as distinguished from improvements on land, are almost completely inelastically supplied (at least outside Holland). "A tax on date trees, imposed by the Mohammed Ali, caused the Egyptian fellahs to cut down their trees: but a tax of twice the amount imposed on land produced no such result." The upshot, for George, was that government should impose steep taxes to appropriate "unearned" increments in land values. As he saw it, these taxes would not crimp production and would justly transfer site values (which arise from growth of the community and not from owner enterprise) to the collectivity that created them. A concise statement of his views is Henry George, Our Land and Land Policy, 9 Writings of Henry George 108 (1898). Are there any economic or ethical differences between taxing site values and taxing the *natural* human capital that especially intelligent or athletic persons are born with?

This section includes several contemporary selections on the crucial question of distributive justice, starting with an excerpt from John Rawls's influential A Theory of Justice. Later in this volume, a selection by Hoffman & Spitzer, infra p.287, considers informal norms of fair distribution.

Consider, prior to embarking on these readings, to what extent the United States Constitution embodies principles of distributive justice. Jennifer Nedelsky associates certain views with James Madison and the other framers, and contrasts them with egalitarianism:

> In the conception crystallized and articulated during the formation of the Constitution, the relationship between inequality, property, liberty, and limited government was as follows: The acquisition and use of property were essential elements of liberty. Given free rein, "men's different and unequal faculties of acquiring property" would result in unequal possessions. Justice required the protection of these acquisitions from the predatory claims of the less successful. The object of government was to provide both this liberty and this justice. . . .

The egalitarian vision is practically a reversal of this founding conception: Whether the inequality of property is the result of liberty or not, it stands in the way of liberty and justice for all. The freedom to use and acquire property and the security of one's acquisitions are no longer defining elements of liberty and justice, but the potential objects of regulation and redistribution — aimed at assuring justice and liberty. In the stronger versions of egalitarianism, this objective entails a governmental responsibility either to assure that the ability to exercise one's rights is not contingent on wealth or to provide the resources necessary to make that exercise possible. . . .

Jennifer Nedelsky, Private Property and the Limits of American Constitutionalism 261-262 (1990).

For echoes of the views that Nedelsky associates with the framers, see Richard A. Epstein, Takings (1985); Milton Friedman, Capitalism and Freedom, ch. 10 (1962); and Robert Nozick, Anarchy, State, and Utopia (1974). In a more egalitarian vein are Bruce A. Ackerman, Social Justice in the Liberal State (1980), and Ronald M. Dworkin, Taking Rights Seriously (1977).

Nedelsky herself welcomes the eclipse of the Madisonian stress on property, in part because she sees it as resting on the flawed conception that individuals achieve autonomy on their own, not through social relationships. See Private Property and the Limits of American Constitutionalism at 264-276. According to one reviewer, "Nedelsky's failure to consider the additional material prosperity introduced by a system of private property means that, if anything, her own account of the Madisonian Constitution is 'distorted': Constitutional protection for private property is far easier to attack in a zero-sum society than in a world where private property creates incentives that encourage a better life for all." Thomas W. Merrill, Zero-Sum Madison, 90 Mich. L. Rev. 1392, 1393 (1992).

A Theory of Justice*

John Rawls

. . . I shall be satisfied if it is possible to formulate a reasonable conception of justice for the basic structure of society conceived for the time being as a closed system isolated from other societies. The significance of this special case is obvious and needs no explanation. It is natural to conjecture that once we have a sound theory for this case, the remaining problems of justice will prove more tractable in

*Source: pp. 8-22, 60-65, 274-275, 279-282 (1971).

the light of it. With suitable modifications such a theory should provide the key for some of these other questions.

The other limitation on our discussion is that for the most part I examine the principles of justice that would regulate a well-ordered society. Everyone is presumed to act justly and to do his part in upholding just institutions. Though justice may be, as Hume remarked, the cautious, jealous virtue, we can still ask what a perfectly just society would be like. Thus I consider primarily what I call strict compliance as opposed to partial compliance theory (§§25, 39). The latter studies the principles that govern how we are to deal with injustice. It comprises such topics as the theory of punishment, the doctrine of just war, and the justification of the various ways of opposing unjust regimes, ranging from civil disobedience and militant resistance to revolution and rebellion. Also included here are questions of compensatory justice and of weighing one form of institutional injustice against another. Obviously the problems of partial compliance theory are the pressing and urgent matters. These are the things that we are faced with in everyday life. The reason for beginning with ideal theory is that it provides, I believe, the only basis for the systematic grasp of these more pressing problems. . . .

3.   The Main Idea of the Theory of Justice

My aim is to present a conception of justice which generalizes and carries to a higher level of abstraction the familiar theory of the social contract as found, say, in Locke, Rousseau, and Kant. In order to do this we are not to think of the original contract as one to enter a particular society or to set up a particular form of government. Rather, the guiding idea is that the principles of justice for the basic structure of society are the object of the original agreement. They are the principles that free and rational persons concerned to further their own interests would accept in an initial position of equality as defining the fundamental terms of their association. These principles are to regulate all further agreements; they specify the kinds of social cooperation that can be entered into and the forms of government that can be established. This way of regarding the principles of justice I shall call justice as fairness.

Thus we are to imagine that those who engage in social cooperation choose together, in one joint act, the principles which are to assign basic rights and duties and to determine the division of social benefits. Men are to decide in advance how they are to regulate their claims against one another and what is to be the foundation charter of their society. Just as each person must decide by rational reflection what constitutes his good, that is, the system of ends which it is rational for him to pursue, so a group of persons must decide once and for all what is to count among them as just and unjust. The choice which rational men would make in this hypothetical situation of equal liberty, assuming for the present that this choice problem has a solution, determines the principles of justice.

In justice as fairness the original position of equality corresponds to the state of nature in the traditional theory of the social contract. This original position is not, of course, thought of as an actual historical state of affairs, much less as a primitive condition of culture. It is understood as a purely hypothetical situation characterized so as to lead to a certain conception of justice. Among the essential features of this situation is that no one knows his place in society, his class position or social status, nor does any one know his fortune in the distribution of natural assets and abilities, his intelligence, strength, and the like. I shall even assume that the parties do not know their conceptions of the good or their special psychological propensities. The principles of justice are chosen behind a veil of ignorance. This ensures that no one is advantaged or disadvantaged in the choice of principles by the outcome of natural chance or the contingency of social circumstances. Since all are similarly situated and no one is able to design principles to favor his particular condition, the principles of justice are the result of a fair agreement or bargain. For given the circumstances of the original position, the symmetry of everyone's relations to each other, this initial situation is fair between individuals as moral persons, that is, as rational beings with their own ends and capable, I shall assume, of a sense of justice. The original position is, one might say, the appropriate initial status quo, and thus the fundamental agreements reached in it are fair. This explains the propriety of the name "justice as fairness": It conveys the idea that the principles of justice are agreed to in an initial situation that is fair. The name does not mean that the concepts of justice and fairness are the same, any more than the phrase "poetry as metaphor" means that the concepts of poetry and metaphor are the same.

Justice as fairness begins, as I have said, with one of the most general of all choices which persons might make together, namely, with the choice of the first principles of a conception of justice which is to regulate all subsequent criticism and reform of institutions. Then, having chosen a conception of justice, we can suppose that they are to choose a constitution and a legislature to enact laws, and so on, all in accordance with the principles of justice initially agreed upon. Our social situation is just if it is such that by this sequence of hypothetical agreements we would have contracted into the general system of rules which defines it. Moreover, assuming that the original position does determine a set of principles (that is, that a particular conception of justice would be chosen), it will then be true that whenever social institutions satisfy these principles those engaged in them can say to one another that they are cooperating on terms to which they would agree if they were free and equal persons whose relations with respect to one another were fair. They could all view their arrangements as meeting the stipulations which they would acknowledge in an initial situation that embodies widely accepted and reasonable constraints on the choice of principles. The general recognition of this fact would provide the basis for a public acceptance of the corresponding principles of justice. No society can, of course, be a scheme of cooperation which men enter voluntarily in a literal sense; each person finds himself placed at birth in some particular position in some particular society, and the nature of this position materially affects his life prospects. Yet a society satisfying the principles of justice as fairness comes as close to a society can to being a voluntary scheme, for it meets the principles which free and equal persons would assent to under circumstances that are fair. In this sense its members are autonomous and the obligations they recognize self-imposed. . . .

In working out the conception of justice as fairness one main task clearly is to determine which principles of justice would be chosen in the original position. To do this we must describe this situation in some detail and formulate with care the problem of choice which it presents. These matters I shall take up in the immediately succeeding chapters. It may be observed, however, that once the principles of justice are thought of as arising from an original agreement in a situation of equality, it is an open question whether the principle of utility would be acknowledged. Offhand it hardly seems likely that persons who view themselves as equals, entitled to press their claims upon one another, would agree to a principle which may require lesser life prospects for some simply for the sake of a greater sum of advantages enjoyed by others. Since each desires to protect his interests, his capacity to advance his conception of the good, no one has a reason to acquiesce in an enduring loss for himself in order to bring about a greater net balance of satisfaction. In the absence of strong and lasting benevolent impulses, a rational man would not accept a basic structure merely because it maximized the algebraic sum of advantages irrespective of its permanent effects on his own basic rights and interests. Thus it seems that the principle of utility is incompatible with the conception of social cooperation among equals for mutual advantage. It appears to be inconsistent with the idea of reciprocity implicit in the notion of a well-ordered society. Or, at any rate, so I shall argue.

I shall maintain instead that the persons in the initial situation would choose two rather different principles: the first requires equality in the assignment of basic rights and duties, while the second holds that social and economic inequalities, for example inequalities of wealth and authority, are just only if they result in compensating benefits for everyone, and in particular for the least advantaged members of society. These principles rule out justifying institutions on the grounds that the hardships of some are offset by a greater good in the aggregate. It may be expedient but it is not just that some should have less in order that others may prosper. But there is no injustice in the greater benefits earned by a few provided that the situation of persons not so fortunate is thereby improved. The intuitive idea is that since everyone's well-being depends upon a scheme of cooperation without which no one could have a satisfactory life, the division of advantages should be such as to draw forth the willing cooperation of everyone taking part in it, including those less well situated. Yet this can be expected only if reasonable terms are proposed. The two principles mentioned seem to be a fair agreement on the basis of which those better endowed, or more fortunate in their social position, neither of which we can be said to deserve, could expect the willing cooperation of others when some workable scheme is a necessary condition of the welfare of all. Once we decide to look for a conception of justice that nullifies the accidents of natural endowment and the contingencies of social circumstance as counters in quest for political and economic advantage, we are led to these principles. They express the result of leaving aside those aspects of the social world that seem arbitrary from a moral point of view. . . .

4.   The Original Position and Justification . . .

It seems reasonable to suppose that the parties in the original position are equal. That is, all have the same rights in the procedure for choosing principles; each can make proposals, submit reasons for their acceptance, and so on. Obviously the purpose of these conditions is to represent equality between human beings as moral persons, as creatures having a conception of their good and capable of a sense of justice. The basis of equality is taken to be similarity in these two respects. Systems of ends are not ranked in value; and each man is presumed to have the requisite ability to understand

and to act upon whatever principles are adopted. Together with the veil of ignorance, these conditions define the principles of justice as those which rational persons concerned to advance their interests would consent to as equals when none are known to be advantaged or disadvantaged by social and natural contingencies. . . .

. . . I have emphasized that this original position is purely hypothetical. It is natural to ask why, if this agreement is never actually entered into, we should take any interest in these principles, moral or otherwise. The answer is that the conditions embodied in the description of the original position are ones that we do in fact accept. Or if we do not, then perhaps we can be persuaded to do so by philosophical reflection. Each aspect of the contractual situation can be given supporting grounds. Thus what we shall do is to collect together into one conception a number of conditions on principles that we are ready upon due consideration to recognize as reasonable. These constraints expresses what we are prepared to regard as limits on fair terms of social cooperation. One way to look at the idea of the original position, therefore, is to see it as an expository device which sums up the meaning of these conditions and helps us to extract their consequences. On the other hand, this conception is also an intuitive notion that suggests its own elaboration, so that led on by it we are drawn to define more clearly the standpoint from which we can best interpret moral relationships. We need a conception that enables us to envision our objective from afar: The intuitive notion of the original position is to do this for us.

5.   Classical Utilitarianism

There are many forms of utilitarianism, and the development of the theory has continued in recent years. I shall not survey these forms here, nor take account of the numerous refinements found in contemporary discussions. My aim is to work out a theory of justice that represents an alternative to utilitarian thought generally and so to all of these different versions of it. I believe that the contrast between the contract view and utilitarianism remains essentially the same in all these cases. Therefore I shall compare justice as fairness with familiar variants of intuitionism, perfectionism, and utilitarianism in order to bring out the underlying differences in the simplest way. With this end in mind, the kind of utilitarianism I shall describe here is the strict classical doctrine which receives perhaps its clearest and most accessible formulation in Sidgwick. The main idea is that society is rightly ordered, and therefore just, when its major institutions are arranged so as to achieve the greatest net balance of satisfaction summed over all the individuals belonging to it. . . .

11.   Two Principles of Justice

I shall now state in a provisional form the two principles of justice that I believe would be chosen in the original position. . . . The first statement of the two principles reads as follows:

> First: each person is to have an equal right to the most extensive basic liberty compatible with a similar liberty for others.
> Second: social and economic inequalities are to be arranged so that they are both (a) reasonably expected to be to everyone's advantage, and (b) attached to positions and offices open to all. . . .

By way of general comment, these principles primarily apply, as I have said, to the basic structure of society. They are to govern the assignment of rights and duties and to regulate the distribution of social and economic advantages. As their formulation suggests, these principles presuppose that the social structure can be divided into two more or less distinct parts, the first principle applying to the one, the second to the other. They distinguish between those aspects of the social system that define and secure the equal liberties of citizenship and those that specify and establish social and economic inequalities. The basic liberties of citizens are, roughly speaking, political liberty (the right to vote and to be eligible for public office) together with freedom of speech and assembly; liberty of conscience and freedom of thought; freedom of the person along with the right to hold (personal) property; and freedom from arbitrary arrest and seizure as defined by the concept of the rule of law. These liberties are all required to be equal by the first principle, since citizens of a just society are to have the same basic rights.

The second principle applies, in the first approximation, to the distribution of income and wealth and to the design of organizations that make use of differences in authority and responsibility, or chains of command. While the distribution of wealth and income need not be equal, it must be to everyone's advantage, and at the same time, positions of authority and offices of command must be accessible to all. One applies the second principle by holding positions open, and then, subject to this constraint, arranges social and economic inequalities so that everyone benefits.

These principles are to be arranged in a serial order with the first principle prior to the second. This ordering means that a departure from the institutions of equal liberty required by the first principle cannot be justified by, or compensated for, by greater social and economic advantages. The distribution of wealth and income, and the hierarchies of authority, must be consistent with both the liberties of equal citizenship and equality of opportunity.

It is clear that these principles are rather specific in their content, and their acceptance rests on certain assumptions that I must eventually try to explain and justify. A theory of justice depends upon a theory of society in ways that will become evident as we proceed. For the present, it should be observed that the two principles (and this holds for all formulations) are a special case of a more general conception of justice that can be expressed as follows.

> All social values — liberty and opportunity, income and wealth, and the bases of self-respect — are to be distributed equally unless an unequal distribution of any, or all, of these values is to everyone's advantage.

Injustice, then, is simply inequalities that are not to the benefit of all. Of course, this conception is extremely vague and requires interpretation.

As a first step, suppose that the basic structure of society distributes certain primary goods, that is, things that every rational man is presumed to want. These goods normally have a use whatever a person's rational plan of life. For simplicity, assume that the chief primary goods at the disposition of society are rights and liberties, powers and opportunities, income and wealth. (Later on in Part Three the primary good of self-respect has a central place.) These are the social primary goods. Other primary goods such as health and vigor, intelligence and imagination, are natural goods; although their possession is influenced by the basic structure, they are not so directly under its control. Imagine, then, a hypothetical initial arrangement in which all the social primary goods are equally distributed: everyone has similar rights and duties, and income and wealth are evenly shared. This state of affairs provides a benchmark for judging improvements. If certain inequalities of wealth and organizational powers would make everyone better off than in this hypothetical starting situation, then they accord with the general conception.

Now it is possible, at least theoretically, that by giving up some of their fundamental liberties men are sufficiently compensated by the resulting social and economic gains. The general conception of justice imposes no restrictions on what sort of inequalities are permissible; it only requires that everyone's position be improved. We need not suppose anything so drastic as consenting to a condition of slavery. Imagine instead that men forego certain political rights when the economic returns are significant and their capacity to influence the course of policy by the exercise of these rights would be marginal in any case. It is this kind of exchange which the two principles as stated rule out; being arranged in serial order they do not permit exchanges between basic liberties and economic and social gains. . . .

Now the second principle insists that each person benefit from permissible inequalities in the basic structure. This means that it must be reasonable for each relevant representative man defined by this structure, when he views it as a going concern, to prefer his prospects with the inequality to his prospects without it. One is not allowed to justify differences in income or organizational powers on the ground that the disadvantages of those in one position are outweighed by the greater advantages of those in another. Much less can infringements of liberty be counterbalanced in this way. Applied to the basic structure, the principle of utility would have us maximize the sum of expectations of representative men (weighted by the number of persons they represent, on the classical view); and this would permit us to compensate for the losses of some by the gains of others. Instead, the two principles require that everyone benefit from economic and social inequalities. . . .

43. Background Institutions for Distributive Justice

The main problem of distributive justice is the choice of a social system. The principles of justice apply to the basic structure and regulate how its major institutions are combined into one scheme. Now, as we have seen, the idea of justice as fairness is to use the notion of pure procedural justice to handle the contingencies of particular situations. The social system is to be designed so that the resulting distribution is just however things turn out. To achieve this end it is necessary to set the social and economic process within the surroundings of suitable political and legal institutions. Without an appropriate scheme of these background institutions the outcome of the distributive process will not be just. Background fairness is lacking. I shall give a brief description of these supporting institutions as they might exist in a properly organized democratic state that allows private ownership of capital and natural resources. These arrangements are familiar, but it may be useful to see how they fit the two principles of justice. Modifications for the case of a socialist regime will be considered briefly later.

First of all, I assume that the basic structure is regulated by a just constitution that secures the liberties of equal citizenship (as described in the preceding chapter). Liberty of conscience and freedom of thought are taken for granted, and the fair value of political liberty is maintained. The political process is conducted, as far as circumstances permit, as a just procedure for choosing between governments and for enacting just legislation. I assume also that there is fair (as opposed to formal) equality of opportunity. This means that in addition to maintaining the usual kinds of social overhead capital, the government tries to insure equal chances of education and culture for persons similarly endowed and motivated either by subsidizing private schools or by establishing a public school system. It also enforces and underwrites equality of opportunity in economic activities and in the free choice of occupation. This is achieved by policing the conduct of firms and private associations and by preventing the establishment of monopolistic restrictions and barriers to the more desirable positions. Finally, the government guarantees a social minimum either by family allowances and special payments for sickness and employment, or more systematically by such devices as a graded income supplement (a so-called negative income tax). . . .

. . . In practice we must usually choose between several unjust, or second best, arrangements; and then we look to nonideal theory to find the least unjust scheme. Sometimes this scheme will include measures and policies that a perfectly just system would reject. Two wrongs can make a right in the sense that the best available arrangement may contain a balance of imperfections, an adjustment of compensating injustices.

The two parts of the distribution branch derive from the two principles of justice. The taxation of inheritance and income at progressive rates (when necessary), and the legal definition of property rights, are to secure the institutions of equal liberty in a property-owning democracy and the fair value of the rights they establish. Proportional expenditure (or income) taxes are to provide revenue for public goods, the transfer branch and the establishment of fair equality of opportunity in education, and the like, so as to carry out the second principle. . . .

So far I have assumed that the aim of the branches of government is to establish a democratic regime in which land and capital are widely though not presumably equally held. Society is not so divided that one fairly small sector controls the preponderance of productive resources. When this is achieved and distributive shares satisfy the principles of justice, many socialist criticisms of the market economy are met. But it is clear that, in theory anyway, a liberal socialist regime can also answer to the two principles of justice. We have only to suppose that the means of production are publicly owned and that firms are managed by workers' councils say, or by agents appointed by them. . . .

Some socialists have objected to all market institutions as inherently degrading, and they have hoped to set up an economy in which men are moved largely by social and altruistic concerns. In regard to the first, the market is not indeed an ideal arrangement, but certainly given the requisite background institutions, the worst aspects of so-called wage slavery are removed. The question then becomes one of the comparison of possible alternatives. It seems improbable that the control of economic activity by the bureaucracy that would be bound to develop in a socially regulated system (whether centrally directed or guided by the agreements reached by industrial associations) would be more just on balance than control exercised by means of prices (assuming as always the necessary framework). To be sure a competitive scheme is impersonal and automatic in the details of its operation; its particular results do not express the conscious decision of individuals. But in many respects this is a virtue of the arrangement; and the use of the market system does not imply a lack of reasonable human autonomy. A democratic society may choose to rely on prices in view of the advantages of doing so, and then to maintain the background institutions which justice requires. This political decision, as well as the regulation of these surrounding arrangements, can be perfectly reasoned and free.

Moreover the theory of justice assumes a definite limit on the strength of social and altruistic motivation. It supposes that individuals and groups put forward competing claims, and while they are willing to act justly, they are not prepared to abandon their interests. There is no need to elaborate further that this presumption does not imply that men are selfish in the ordinary sense. Rather a society in which all can achieve their complete good, or in which there are no conflicting demands and the wants of all fit together without coercion into a harmonious plan of activity, is a society in a certain sense beyond justice. It has eliminated the occasions when the appeal to the principles of right and justice is necessary.[19] I am not concerned with this ideal case, however desirable it may be. We should note though that even here the theory of justice has an important theoretical role: it defines the conditions under which the spontaneous coherence of the aims and wants of individuals is neither coerced nor contrived but expresses a proper harmony consistent with the

19. Some have interpreted Marx's conception of a full communist society as a society beyond justice in this sense. See R.C. Tucker, The Marxian Revolutionary Idea (New York, WW. Norton, 1969), chs. I and II.

ideal good. I cannot pursue these questions further. The main point is that the principles of justice are compatible with quite different types of regime.

NOTES AND QUESTIONS ON THE RAWLSIAN THEORY OF WEALTH AND DISTRIBUTION

1. Rawls sets his scenario by isolating his hypothetical society from all others. What if he instead supposed that all societies permitted easy entry and departure, and then asked, to what society would people gravitate? Rawls asserts that people in fact cannot voluntarily choose the society in which they live. But if they could easily move about, would the quest for "justice as fairness" be an unnecessary exercise? Might we then find a plurality of just societies, perhaps having quite different characteristics?

2. Does Rawls make things too easy for himself by supposing that "everyone is presumed to act justly and to do his part in upholding just institutions"? With this assumption, can he even address some of the central problems in property and contract regimes, such as the "prisoner's dilemma" and "tragedy of the commons," where individual self-interest diverges from the common good? Do property regimes always raise problems of "partial compliance," which Rawls purposefully avoids?

3. Consider the "original position": Would a person so ignorant of herself that she did not know her status, abilities, or conceptions of the good really have any basis for choice about the just society? For a critique on the thinness of personality supposed by Rawls, see Michael J. Sandel, Liberalism and the Limits of Justice 62 (1982).

4. Elsewhere in A Theory of Justice (at §§12-13), Rawls discusses at length his central principle of just wealth distribution, which he calls "the difference principle." As Rawls states it, "[t]he intuitive idea is that the social order is not to establish and secure the more attractive prospects of those better off unless doing so is to the advantage of those less fortunate." Id. at 75. Thus, for example, an inequality in the distribution of income among social classes "is justifiable only if the difference in expectation is to the advantage of the representative man who is worst off, in this case the unrepresentative unskilled worker. The inequality in expectation is permissible only if lowering it would make the working class even more worse off." Id. at 78.

How does the difference principle differ from the principle of Pareto superiority, described supra p.54, Note 2? How does it differ from the utilitarian (or Kaldor-Hicks) principle that Rawls rejects (for example, the principle of choosing those institutions that would "achieve the greatest net balance of satisfaction" to all participants in the society)?

5. Would people behind a veil of ignorance really choose Rawls's difference principle over the utilitarian principle? What if the difference principle entailed some loss in net social wealth due to lessened incentives, administrative costs, and so on? Might a rational person instead choose utilitarian institutions on the theory that *ex ante*, such institutions would improve her chances for a slice of a larger pie? What does Rawls's difference principle implicitly presume about people's attitudes toward risk? See the next selection by James Q. Wilson; see also Carol M. Rose, "Enough, and As Good" of What? 81 Nw. U. L. Rev. 417 (1987).

6. Progressive income taxes are logical sources of revenue for redistributive programs. For many observers, although not Rawls, a central issue of policy is the effect of higher taxes on work effort. As Kennedy and Michelman observed, while a higher tax rate might cause some workers to choose more leisure (a substitution effect), the same taxes could induce *more* work from individuals striving to avoid diminution in after-tax income (an income effect). Which effect is greater is not obvious. Some investigators assert that higher taxes on balance do discourage work, and redistributive efforts therefore significantly diminish the total pie. See Edgar K. Browning & William R. Johnson, The Trade-Off Between Equality and Efficiency, 92 J. Pol. Econ. 175 (1984). Others think the effect is small. See Thomas MaCurdy, Work Disincentive Effects of Taxes, 82 Am. Econ. Rev. 243 (Pap. & Proc. 1992). See generally How Taxes Affect Economic Behavior (Henry J. Aaron & Joseph A. Pechman eds. 1981).

7. Should private law take into account the wealth of litigants involved in a particular civil case, in order to accomplish a more progressive distribution of income? Most law-and-economics scholars argue it should not, on the grounds that private-law rules are relatively inferior distributive mechanisms. A. Mitchell Polinsky, in An Introduction to Law and Economics 119-127 (2d ed. 1989), provides a succinct version of the argument. Polinsky states that it is nearly impossible to use legal rules to redistribute income among parties to contractual disputes because the parties can contract around them, for example, by changing the contract price. In addition, because not all members of given income classes are involved in disputes, Polinsky asserts that, even in noncontractual disputes, redistribution through private law is inherently less "precise" than redistribution through broad tax and welfare programs. In Why the Legal System is Less Efficient than the Income Tax in Redistributing

Income, 23 J. Legal Stud. 667, 677 (1994), Louis Kaplow and Steven Shavell similarly conclude that "it is appropriate for economic analysis of legal rules to focus on efficiency and to ignore the distribution of income in offering normative judgments."

On most civil issues, it is prejudicial — indeed often a reversible error — for a trial judge to allow admission of evidence concerning the wealth of the parties. Does this mean that the law on the books is already consistent with the economists' approach? Is the law in action as insensitive to distributive considerations?

8. Rawls's Theory of Justice elicited voluminous commentary. For a sampling of the early reactions, see Reading Rawls (Norman Daniels ed. 1975). Rawls updates and elaborates his views in Political Liberalism (1993). On the issue of distributive justice, he asserts:

> . . . [M]easures are required to assure that the basic needs of all citizens can be met so that they can take part in political and social life.
> About this last point, the idea is not that of satisfying needs as opposed to mere desires and wants; nor is it that of redistribution in favor of greater equality. The constitutional essential here is rather that below a certain level of material and social well-being, and of training and education, people simply cannot take part in society as citizens, much less equal citizens.

Id. at 166.

The Moral Sense*

James Q. Wilson

. . . As I understand him, everybody in Rawls's universe is averse to risk; each wants to make certain that, if he winds up on the bottom of the heap, the bottom is as attractive as possible.

But many people are in fact not averse to risk, they are risk takers; to them, a just society would be one in which inequalities in wealth were acceptable provided that the people at the top of the heap got there as a result of effort and skill. And even people who are not risk takers may endorse this position because they think it fair that rewards should be proportional to effort, even if some people lose out entirely. (These same people might also expect their church or government to take care of those who lost out.) They have this view of fairness because they recognize that people differ in talent, energy, temperament, and interests; that conflicts among such people are inevitable; and that matching, as best one can, rewards to contributions is the best way of handling that conflict.

*Source: pp. 73-76 (1993).

To test this view, let us imagine a society in which property is distributed more or less equally. . . . Indeed, we can more than imagine such a society, we can study it.

The San are African bushmen who live in small groups, or bands, that until quite recently foraged widely through inhospitable parts of Namibia, Botswana, and Angola, hunting animals and picking edibles. Only a few simple possessions were required by their livelihood or permitted by their mobility. With few fixed places of abode, their sense of land tenure was more directed to the broad territory that they canvassed than to a specific residence that they occupied. Under these circumstances it is not surprising that most differences among people were not thought sufficiently great to warrant large differences in treatment. Food brought back to the camp was distributed equally among all, with the successful hunter having no greater claim than anyone else. Arrowheads that had killed animals did not remain as trophies of the hunter but were exchanged among other members of the band, women as well as men.[37] Contrary to what some Western observers have suggested, San life was not idyllic, nor were they quite the "harmless people" sometimes depicted: not only were the San very poor, their children (although raised in the most tender fashion) were cruel to animals, husbands (although sharing in child care) occasionally beat their wives, and adults (though they were hospitable to strangers and unfamiliar with war) committed homicides at a rate that exceeds that found in many American cities.

But if not idyllic, San society was indisputably egalitarian. The weak division of labor, the need for cooperation, and the difficulty of accumulating or transporting possessions fostered the view that everyone's contribution (or in terms of equity theory, input) was roughly the same as everybody else's, and so everyone's benefits (or output) should be about the same. Culture reinforced necessity: the San engaged in ritual joking designed to deflate any claims to status or prowess. Though the San are the best-known hunter-gatherer societies, there are others and once were many others and, insofar as we can tell, most tended toward an egalitarian structure.

When these peoples became settled, however, things changed. They may have acquired a sedentary life voluntarily (as when it became possible to raise crops and keep cattle), involuntarily (as when an outside power compelled them to live on reservations), or opportunistically (as when the chance arose to work for cash wages for other people). Whatever the process, the people now live in fixed abodes from whence they herd cattle, raise crops, or earn cash incomes. Living in one place requires less cooperation and permits a

37. [Richard L. Lee, The !Kung San (1979).]

greater division of labor than being on the move. Cash, unlike fresh meat, can be stored and hidden. Proximity to industrial societies means that cash and crops can be exchanged for manufactured goods, not the least of which is alcohol. They can even become actors in movies such as *The Gods Must Be Crazy*. One San woman who had a part in that film used her wages to buy things that she would not share with her kin, thereby provoking a fight.

Jean-Jacques Rousseau might have had the settled San [in] mind when he wrote, with heavy sarcasm, this famous line to explain the origin of human inequality: "The first man who, having enclosed a piece of ground, bethought himself of saying, *This is mine*, and found people simple enough to believe him, was the real founder of civil society." The entire Discourse on the Origin of Inequality [1758] can be read as a commentary on what we know about the transition from hunter-gatherer to sedentary societies. Building huts meant acquiring property, "the source of a thousand quarrels and conflicts." Settled into those huts, the men "went abroad in search of their common subsistence" while the women "became more sedentary and accustomed themselves to mind the hut and their children." Tools become valuable and their possession possible, and so men became beholden to them and alert to the differences in status implied by differences in their ownership.

The many contemporary followers of Rousseau read these words as an argument against inequality, but if anything, they are an argument against civilization, by which I mean settled living and the division of labor. Rousseau clearly preferred premodern man to modern man and opposed political society, which, arising out of the need to protect property, "bound new fetters on the poor and gave new powers to the rich; irretrievably destroyed natural liberty, fixed externally the law of property and inequality, converted clever usurpation into unalterable right, and, for the advantage of a few ambitious individuals, subjected all mankind to perpetual labour, slavery, and wretchedness."

But this unhappy state of affairs did not arise because men were naturally equal; rather, it arose because the conditions of settled life forced men to recognize, act upon, and reinforce their natural inequalities, inequalities that hunter-gatherers could afford — indeed, were obliged — to overlook. In settled societies, Rousseau wrote, "equality might have been sustained, had the talents of individuals been equal." But they are not: Once the division of labor took effect, "the strongest did the most work; the most skilful turned his labour to best account; the most ingenious devised methods of diminishing his labour." While all might work equally, the one would gain much while the other "could hardly support himself." Though laws may legitimate and even magnify these differences, "all the inequality which now prevails owes its strength and growth to the development of our faculties and the advance of the human mind."

Equality is a special and, as it turns out, rare and precarious case of equity. Settled living, and in particular the accumulation of private property, makes equality of outcomes impossible because inequality of contributions become manifest. The task of settled societies is to devise ways of assuring that outcomes are proportional to worth, reasonably defined.

NOTES AND QUESTIONS ON THE COMPARATIVE WEALTH OF SOCIETIES

1. For a sweeping historical study that links establishment of private property rights with economic growth, see Douglass C. North & Robert Paul Thomas, The Rise of the Western World (1973).

2. What does it mean for a society to be wealthy? Marshall P. Sahlins argues that "the original affluent society" was that of paleolithic hunter-gatherers, who enhanced their well-being by *wanting less* rather than *producing more*. See Sahlins, The Original Affluent Society, in Stone Age Economics 1-39 (1972). This relaxed attitude permitted them to meet their needs quite adequately without a great deal of labor, and to spend a considerable amount of time chatting, loafing, and sleeping. Similarly, H.D.F. Kitto, in The Greeks 131-35 (1951), noted that the ancient Greeks' philosophizing, politicking, and other creative uses of leisure were only possible because they willingly accepted austere living conditions, a point that Kitto thinks far more important than the Greeks' use of slaves. James Axtell, The Invasion Within: The Contest of Cultures in Colonial North America 302-327 (1985) argues that seventeenth-century Native Americans were far more successful in wooing renegades and war-raid captives to their nomadic lifestyle than the European settlers were at "converting" Native Americans to a sedentary life; this was at least in part because of the attractions of adventure and what a pair of "white Indians" called "'the most perfect freedom, the ease of living, [and] the absence of those cares and corroding solicitudes which so often prevail with us.'" Id. at 327. Eighteenth- and nineteenth-century American history is replete with stories of European-origin settlers who refused to return to "civilization" after being captured by the Indians. See, for example, John Demos, The Unredeemed Captive: A Family Story from Early America (1994).

Which society was wealthier? Is the definition of wealth as material goods, associated with a sedentary and industrious lifestyle, simply an example of what Sahlins calls "neolithic ethnocentrism," whereas persons given a choice may prefer nomadic or hunter-gatherer ways of life? If hunter-gatherer ways are so appealing, what prompted the San to give them up?

The Untenable Case for an Unconditional Right to Shelter*

Robert C. Ellickson

As homelessness has become a prominent domestic issue, numerous advocates have called for constitutional recognition of an individual's unconditional right to enjoy a minimum level of shelter. I argue here that these advocates have failed to deal with the fundamental fact that a society must maintain incentives to work. Both theory and data indicate that an unconditional shelter right, presumably coupled with ironclad rights to enjoy other material benefits, could be counterproductive, even for the poor. . . .

II.   Three Approaches to Welfare Rights . . .

If individuals are in fact partly motivated by material ends, the recognition of unconditional welfare rights might diminish society's aggregate wealth in several ways. First, a person who is guaranteed sustenance has less reason to work. Second, if income taxes or other taxes on labor are used to fund welfare guarantees, welfare programs diminish the marginal material rewards of wage-earners, thereby decreasing their labor incentives. Third, a welfare state invariably gives rise to administrative costs and wasteful rent-seeking efforts. Finally, as more and more individuals and households in an area receive government assistance, neighborhood residents may no longer be able to sustain the traditional informal norm that an employable person has a duty to be in the workforce.[17] Although there is no consensus on the magnitude of the various costs of maintaining a welfare state, even left-liberal social scientists and politicians are concerned about these issues.

*Source: 15 Harv. J.L. & Pub. Pol'y 17, 20-28, 32-34 (1992).
    17. This possibility, which is often couched as the "dependency" or "underclass" issue, is deeply contested. See Isabel V. Sawhill, Poverty in the U.S.: Why Is It So Persistent?, 26 J. Econ. Literature 1073, 1097-1109 (1988).

To simplify the analysis drastically, assume that a society may adopt one or another of three possible strategies to resolve the inherent tension between providing welfare and encouraging work. The three, which I now briefly outline, are (1) the no-welfare approach, (2) the conditional-welfare approach, and (3) the unconditional-welfare approach.

In a market economy such as the United States, each individual essentially owns his own labor. This endowment of rights to labor creates direct material incentives to participate either in self-employment, household production, or labor markets. In a market economy, each worker serves as the primary monitor against his own shirking. However, some workers will inevitably be mentally or physically incapable of performing marketable tasks, or will simply be unqualified to perform the jobs available in the market. A government that adopts a *no-welfare approach* does little or nothing to relieve an individual of the consequences of being unemployable or unemployed.

Many voters apparently regard the laissez-faire system just described as unacceptably cruel to those who either cannot work or are jobless for reasons largely beyond their control. As a result, over the last century the democratic nations with market economies have all instituted welfare-state programs to supplement (and, perhaps unintentionally, to supplant) more traditional systems of social insurance such as the extended family, the voluntary association, and organized religion.

Policymakers in the United States have generally opted for the second strategy, a *conditional-welfare approach*. Few U.S. programs render all applicants eligible for long-term welfare benefits. Eligibility for benefits is instead typically restricted to limited categories of persons, notably those who either cannot work (because of age or disability), or should not be in the workforce (because they are caretakers of small children). Persons who fall outside these categories are expected to make their way without significant governmental assistance. This approach to welfare is conditional in the sense that applicants for benefits must prove that they should be excused from the presumptive duty to be self-supporting. The welfare benefits that are made more broadly available, such as food stamps and general assistance, typically are conditional in another sense: A beneficiary's entitlement depends on continuing compliance with specified "workfare" obligations. The lawmakers who create these conditional-welfare programs intend to soften the harsh consequences of the laissez-faire system, while at the same time minimizing harm to work incentives.

A society that pursues the third strategy, the *unconditional-*

welfare approach, promises all of its members certain minimal material comforts with no questions asked. Most advocates of a right to shelter appear to contemplate an entitlement of this variety. If a society were able to deliver on this set of promises, it would free its members from much of the stress of being personally responsible for providing for themselves. The unconditional-welfare approach inherently places in the hands of central authorities the task of distributing most social largesse. In practice, these same central authorities must also assume great responsibility for policing against shirking — a responsibility that a market economy largely decentralizes to each individual. Because the managers of an unconditional-welfare state have little discretion in distributing material benefits (at least in theory), they are likely to institute elaborate nonmaterial incentives to induce people to work.

Unconditional-welfare systems appear to be most viable within small, closely-knit societies that are capable of administering informal sanctions. For example, a kibbutz that assures housing to each of its members may be able to correlate social status positively with industriousness and to ostracize or even expel able-bodied shirkers. By contrast, experience abroad suggests that a nation-state is too large and too loosely-knit to generate informal social forces that successfully support norms of work. In practice, a state that adopts the unconditional-welfare approach therefore tends to resort to heavy-handed coercion to enforce legal duties to work. Even though the unconditional-welfare approach may eliminate certain stresses that individuals bear when they must be self-sufficient, this approach introduces the new stresses that arise when an individual is monitored by a powerful centralized bureaucracy.

Communist states, of course, provide the crispest examples of the unconditional-welfare approach. Communist bills of rights contain an array of positive rights including, typically, an express right to shelter.[23] These constitutions also set out what might be called "bills of duties," which invariably include an express duty to work. Although the authorities who have managed Communist regimes have tried exhortation and other noncoercive techniques, they have also resorted to criminal prosecutions to enforce duties to work.[26]

---

23. See, e.g., Cuba Const. art. 8c . . . ("The socialist state . . . works so that no family be left without a comfortable place to live."); . . . U.S.S.R. Const. art. 44 . . . ("Citizens of the U.S.S.R. have the right to housing").

26. See Ian M. Kennedy, Cuba's Ley Contra La Vagancia — The Law on Loafing, 20 UCLA L. Rev. 1177 (1973). Because the United States offers welfare only on a conditional basis, it can dispense with criminal prosecutions for failure to work. See Papachristou v. City of Jacksonville, 405 U.S. 156, 156-157 (1972) (voiding vagrancy ordinance for vagueness and for encouraging arbitrary arrests).

III.   Do Shelter Rights Lead to Improved Housing Conditions?

It is theoretically possible that the guarantee of a right to shelter (and related welfare benefits) would, by weakening work incentives, shrink the aggregate social welfare pie so much that everyone, including the poor, would end up materially worse off. This prospect may seem utterly fanciful on its face. In this section, I introduce some evidence that it is not. Poor persons in the United States, who lack a constitutional right to shelter, tend to live in more spacious and better-maintained housing than do poor persons in nations that recognize a right to shelter. Moreover, the housing conditions of poor households in the United States have been steadily improving with time. Although these facts hardly prove that the United States would injure the poor by embracing an unconditional right to shelter, they do demonstrate that our conditional-welfare system has proven to be much more successful than its detractors would have us believe. In general, the United States deserves high commendation for the housing its people enjoy. American housing is much larger, better-equipped, and cheaper than that in Japan, for example.

A.   Housing in Jurisdictions that Recognize a Right to Shelter

Comparative housing data are of poor quality. In addition, an analysis cannot readily control for the many factors, other than the presence or absence of a right to shelter, that might determine a nation's housing success. Despite these difficulties, a brief look at housing conditions in different nations is instructive.

International evidence shows that proclaiming a right to shelter does not magically lead to better housing conditions. It is hardly news that the Communist states that have long espoused a right to housing have done a dreadful job of delivering on that promise. The median household in the Soviet Union lives in two rooms and has about 130 square feet per capita;[30] the median U.S. household occupies five rooms and has nearly 600 square feet per capita.[31] Only 2% of United States households, compared to 76% of Soviet households, live in two rooms or less. To put it bluntly: Americans below the poverty line typically live far more spaciously than do middle-class Soviets.

More pertinent to debates over housing in western democracies

---

30. See International Monetary Fund et al., 3 A Study of The Soviet Economy 322 (1991). . . .
31. See Bureau of the Census, Statistical Abstract of the United States 45, 720 (1990).

are the housing patterns in Sweden and the Netherlands, two nations that Professor [Curtis] Berger praises for having embraced a constitutional right to housing. The scant evidence available suggests that poor households in these nations live in worse housing than do their counterparts in the United States. In the early 1980s, for example, 5% of Swedish housing units and 4.1% of Dutch housing units lacked full plumbing facilities, whereas only 2.7% of U.S. housing units did. At the same time, it is perhaps relevant that 64.4% of United States dwelling units were occupied by homeowners, while only 41.4% of Swedish and 42.7% of Dutch dwelling units were. Despite the legal promises of their nations, observers in Sweden and Holland report shortages of low-rent housing units. Because housing-production costs in Sweden are more than double what they are in the United States, housing affordability is a much more serious problem there.

Because advocates of shelter rights aspire to change current law, they are likely to stress nonlegal theories of American housing triumphs, such as unusually plentiful endowments of land and other resources, or the good fortune of having avoided wartime destruction. These particular hypotheses are weak; Sweden, for example, has a lower population density than does the United States and did not suffer war damage. More credible is the hypothesis that federal income tax incentives have led to greater — some economists would say excessive — investment in U.S. housing.

This tax hypothesis, however, underscores the potential effects of basic legal choices on economic performance. Observers who believe that natural resources and deep-rooted cultural traditions are paramount should heed the divergent trajectories of the economies of East and West Germany, and of North and South Korea. Should not the advocates of unconditional shelter rights be wary of importing the general welfare strategy of nations with inferior housing records?

B. Trends in Housing Conditions in the United States

Contrary to the commentators' perceptions of a housing "crisis," during this century most poor American households — despite their lack of a right to shelter — have benefited from steadily improving housing conditions. For example, the percentage of black households lacking complete plumbing plunged from 79.6% in 1940 to 6.1% in 1980, and the percentage living with more than one person per room dropped from 28.3% in 1960 to 9.1% in 1980. Contrary to what some advocates might have predicted for the Reagan decade, the available data indicate that these auspicious trends have continued since 1980. The residential situation of the institutionalized poor has also improved as prisons, mental hospitals, and similar accomodations have become much more livable.

The nation's progress in housing is often overlooked because panhandlers and other impoverished people have become increasingly visible in conspicuous downtown locations during the past decade. Although advocates for the homeless tend to link this "homelessness" problem with changes in housing markets, I have argued elsewhere that it is more plausibly attributed to the deinstitutionalization of the mentally ill, the drug epidemic, the loosening of police supervision of street behavior, and the deepening of underclass subcultures.[42] Observers should be cautious about inferring a "housing crisis" from a rise in panhandling. The fragmentary evidence on the subject suggests that many panhandlers dwell permanently in conventional housing.[43] . . .

V. Conclusion: The Grand Constitutional Design

Why has our political system balked at expressly recognizing "a right to shelter," "a right to a minimum income," and other similar rights, when for more than a century it has guaranteed self-ownership of labor and a right to schooling? The essential reason is both simple and manifest: The proposed entitlements tend to discourage work, while the existing entitlements tend to encourage it.

The current constitutional provisions reject the unconditional-welfare approach. To secure the value of the rights that our constitutions presently confer, a recipient must complement the conferrals with personal labor. Owning one's own labor is valuable only to the extent that one is willing to work. The value of receiving an education depends significantly on one's willingness to apply oneself in school. By increasing the rewards of work, the present constitutional guarantees help induce individuals to contribute to the nation.

Events in several American cities illustrate the drawbacks of establishing unconditional rights to material aid. During the early 1980s, New York City, Philadelphia, and Washington, D.C. each guaranteed their citizens unqualified rights to receive emergency shelter. These open-door shelter policies attracted unexpected numbers of able-bodied entrants, and the shelters apparently fostered

42. See Robert C. Ellickson, The Homelessness Muddle, Pub. Interest, Spring 1990, at 45. For a somewhat different view, see Peter H. Rossi, Down and Out in America: The Origins of Homelessness 181-194 (1989).

43. See Brandt Goldstein, An Empirical Study of the Panhandlers of York and Broadway Streets in New Haven, Connecticut 19-21 (1991) (unpublished manuscript, on file with author) (noting that at least 8 of 12 panhandlers interviewed had customary and regular access to a conventional dwelling); Interagency Council on the Homeless, 1990 Annual Report 25 (1991).

dependency. In Philadelphia, housing advocates eventually agreed to allow the city to deny shelter to employable persons who had refused to comply with job-hunting requirements. When the D.C. City Council backtracked from that jurisdiction's right to shelter, D.C. voters declined to reverse that retreat. Many New York City shelter administrators came to favor imposing some sort of workfare obligation on able-bodied members of the shelter population, but encountered resistance from lawyers who represented the homeless.

Remarkably, despite these events and the magnitude of the issue involved, most of the advocates of unconditional shelter rights either ignore the tension between welfare and work, or dismiss its importance. Those who have drafted our constitutions and conditional welfare programs have served us better. They have been attuned to the desirability of having a decentralized system for monitoring against shirking. They have been aware of the inherent tension between positive and negative liberties, and aware that a bill of rights that delivers on promises of unconditional welfare rights would be hard-pressed to deliver on promises to shield the individual from an intrusive state. Moreover, international evidence does not support the proposition that recognition of an unconditional right to shelter actually results in better housing for the poor. Shifting jobs from carpenters to lawyers is not the way to improve housing conditions.

NOTES AND QUESTIONS ON GAINERS AND LOSERS FROM PRIVATE PROPERTY

1. For counterpoint to this selection see, among many others, Curtis Berger, Beyond Homelessness: An Entitlement to Housing, 45 U. Miami L. Rev. 315 (1990-1991) (advocating federal legislation to establish entitlements to housing); and Frank I. Michelman, Welfare Rights in a Constitutional Democracy, 1979 Wash. U. L.Q. 659 (restating Michelman's long-held position that the Equal Protection Clause can be construed to confer unconditional welfare rights).

2. Ellickson argues that unconditional welfare rights are unlikely to serve the long-run interests of individuals born into poverty. Is his normative outlook at odds with Rawls's? Is it similar to the classical utilitarian position that Rawls associates with Sidgwick?

3. How might Kennedy and Michelman take exception to the assertion, at p.118 of this selection, that income taxes reduce work incentives?

4. Is it true, as an historical matter, that a state that creates un-

conditional welfare rights must also enforce a duty to work? Are state-enforced work obligations inherently more oppressive than the pressures to work that arise when labor is self-owned?

5. Housing consumption is hardly the only measure of individual welfare. What have been the trends in the nutrition consumed and medical care received by poor people in the United States? For more on trends in U.S. housing conditions, see the selection by Weicher, infra p.382.

6. To measure poverty, should an analyst focus on the housing or other goods and services a household consumes, or on its cash income? See Susan E. Mayer & Christopher Jencks, Poverty and the Distribution of Material Hardship, 24 J. Human Resources 88 (1989) (authors' survey suggests that family income explains only about 14 percent of the variance in material hardship).

The Census Bureau's official poverty rate is based on reported cash income. Critics have leveled two major criticisms against this statistic. First, the official poverty rate excludes the benefits of in-kind transfers, such as food stamps, Medicaid, and Section 8 housing allowances. In 1990, federal outlays on the various in-kind transfers to the poor were more than double the amount of federal cash transfers to the poor. (Should analysts count receipt of a dollar of, say, Medicaid benefits as the equivalent of a dollar in cash?) Second, federal surveys of consumer expenditures suggest that many households underreport their cash income to census takers. See Morton Paglin, The Underground Economy: New Estimates from Household Income and Expenditure Surveys, 103 Yale L.J. 2239, 2249 (1994) (estimating underground economy in 1990 at 8.4 percent of Gross Domestic Product).

For a spectrum of views on poverty trends, see Uneven Tides: Rising Inequality in America (Sheldon Danziger & Peter Gottschalk eds. 1992); Symposium on The Transfer Society, 6 Cato J. 1-352 (1986). For an international assessment, see Timothy M. Smeeding, Michael O'Higgins & Lee Rainwater, Poverty, Inequality and Income Distribution in Comparative Perspective (1990).

Economic Analysis of Property Rights*

Yoram Barzel

By the beginning of this century slavery had largely disappeared. But comparing slaves and free laborers and exploring the

*Source: pp. 76-81 (1989).

forces that permitted slavery to flourish in some circumstances and not in others not only provide insight into an extinct institution; such study also sheds light on contemporary ones, enhancing especially the understanding of policing and ownership practices.

The Slave Contract

Labor services, routinely exchanged in the market, are subject to contract. The typical contract for the services of a free worker transfers a rather narrow, and usually short-term, set of attributes from the labor owner to its buyer. Slavery, too, may be viewed as a labor contract — one, however, that gave slave owners extensive rights over their slaves. In the case of forced slavery, the contract extended over the slave's entire time horizon. The voluntary slave contract typically specified a shorter duration and gave the owner fewer rights over the slave than did the forced slave contract.

Forced slavery was initiated by theft — free people were captured and, as the term suggests, were forced into slavery. Voluntary slavery was the result of an explicit contract — a contract to which both parties agreed, presumably with the belief that signing the contract would be beneficial to each. In some cases, voluntary slavery resulted from a loan default, when, for whatever reason, persons who posted themselves as collateral against debt defaulted and lenders took over the collateral, assuming ownership of the persons. Indentured servitude, a form of voluntary slavery, was a direct method of repaying loans. Such loans often served to finance the passage of the servant from Europe to America. To repay the loan, indentured servants worked in America for a number of years virtually as slaves. The duration of the servitude was determined in an auction in which the winning bidder was the person who bid the smallest number of years of service and bought the loan contract from its previous holder — often the captain of the passage ship; the servant worked out her or his debt for the final lender, usually an American farmer.

The term "contract" normally implies a voluntary relationship; indeed, a relationship from which both parties expect to gain. The term fits voluntary slavery well but forced slavery less well. Free persons, having been forced into slavery, obviously did not expect any gain from their change in status. Thus, if the term can apply at all to forced slavery, it applies only to the period of time after the persons have already become slaves. Even then, such usage stretches the definition of "contract" to its limit. Nevertheless, it will be seen that the notion of a slave contract is still useful in analyzing the institution of slavery.

Slaves' Supply of Labor

. . . The owner of a forced slave will require the effort that, net of maintenance expenses, will yield the highest present-value income stream. Thus, a forced slave may be compared to a free person who has contracted to operate in exactly the same way the slave is required to. Given that the slave (or her or his ancestors) was stolen, she or her operates under a contract the terms of which have just been described. Manumission is the act of buying out that contract.

In the era when the law permitted slavery, the question of manumission was pertinent. As indicated in the opening paragraph of this book, the observation of self-purchase poses a major puzzle: How could a slave, another person's piece of property, purchase her or his own contract? In order to resolve this puzzle, transaction costs, in particular policing costs, must be considered.

The Costs of Supervision

Since slaves were the full-fledged property of their owners, all the income they could generate was legally their owners'. Owners who took anything from their slaves were simply taking something that was legally theirs to start with. Owners had the legal right to take; they also had the might. How could slaves, then, accumulate wealth, sometimes to an extent that enabled them to purchase their own contracts? Had both slaves' capabilities and the net output they produced been costlessly measurable, wealth-maximizing slave owners would indeed have extracted every last ounce of productiveness from their slaves. Under these conditions, conditions that would have permitted owners to be owners in the most complete sense of the word, it is ironic that the slave status itself would have been inconsequential. Had policing been costless, the owner could have let the debtor operate as a free person and still obtain the same income, for instance, by receiving an explicit debt payment of the same value as that generated by the slave's services without requiring a slave contract. The free person, however, would still have had to work exactly like a slave in order to be able to pay her or his debt. Since in reality the evaluation of inputs and outputs is costly, policing is required to induce effort; as we shall see, accumulation by slaves is then possible.

When the net output of a free worker can be determined at low cost, it is advantageous for her or him to operate as an independent worker, since then no problems of incentive arise in motivating her or him to work. Such was not the case with slaves; the labor services slaves could provide belonged to their owners. Even when output was easily measured, slaves would have gained from producing less and thus had to be induced to produce more. The distinction between slaves' and free workers' incentive became even more acute for tasks that free workers performed by the hour. Free workers will do best if they can convince their future employers that they are more productive than they actually are, since, as it is difficult to ascertain their true productiveness, their wages will then be higher. Slaves, on the other hand, would have done best if they could have convinced their owners that they were no good, since little would then have been expected of them.[4] Slave owners, then, had to spend resources to figure out how productive the slaves were and how hard they could be driven and to actually supervise their efforts or output.

Assuming that the supervision of effort is subject to diminishing marginal productivity, owners would, in their supervision effort, have stopped short of extracting the maximum output of which slaves were capable. The difference between slaves' maximum output and their actual output became, in practice, the slaves' property. It did not, as a rule, come in the same form as the product they produced for their owners, but mostly in reduced effort. Still, slaves were able to convert some of this potential into property, property that owners had an interest in protecting.

Owners had the choice between supervising their slaves' output, which is comparable to what employers have to do when the free workers they employ work by the piece, and supervising their effort, which is comparable to what employers have to do when they employ free workers by the hour. The latter required continuous supervision, since whenever slaves were not watched over they had little incentive to perform. The former required overseeing output as to its quantity, its quality, and, indirectly, its effect on other productive services such as equipment. Slaves' output supervision also required output quotas, since, left to their own devices, they would have produced as little as they could. Moreover, quotas could not have been set by simply observing past performance, since slaves' incentive to produce little during the demonstration period would have been strong indeed. Since quotas were subject to error, and since too high a quota would have resulted in the destruction of slaves, the quotas owners would have selected to maximize their own wealth were expected to leave their slaves with the difference between the quota and the maximum they could produce, a differ-

---

4. Slaves had to be careful not to do too good a job at deceiving their owners, since owners who thought their slaves were not worth their cost would have found them expendable.

ence they could take advantage of. Since owners' confiscation of slaves' accumulation would have been equivalent to raising the quota, confiscation would have defeated the purpose for which the quota was set to begin with. In pursuit of their self-interest, owners permitted slaves to own and to accumulate.

Slaves seldom became rich. Nevertheless, the free time they were able to gain enabled them, among other things, to grow vegetables, to fish and hunt, and also to steal. Their owners and neighbors were ready buyers for what slaves had to sell. Slaves who were ultimately able to buy their contracts were, as a rule, household slaves, sometimes well-trained ones. Because their tasks were diverse, they were difficult to supervise, a difficulty that increased with the skill of the performer. Household slaves, therefore, especially skilled ones, had better opportunities to accumulate than did the slaves who worked in the fields.

The need for supervision and the desire to economize on its cost made ownership of slaves less than fully delineated. Slaves were able to capture some of these undelineated rights — in this case, rights to themselves. Success, partly due to skills in feigning inability on the one hand and to activities such as fishing on the other, and partly due to the luck of having errors made in their favor, eventually enabled some slaves to buy their own contracts.

Slaves' Consumption

The sharp conflict between slaves' and owners' interests was not confined to slaves' effort and its supervision; it also affected consumption practices. Owners could not drive their slaves hard unless they made sure that they were properly maintained — that the nutrition, medical care, and other services slaves received were commensurate with the effort required of them. Correspondingly, in the United States, as Fogel and Engerman (1972) show, slaves received that appears, by nineteenth-century standards, to have been good medical care and a nutritious diet.[6] Owners, however, had little incentive to let their slaves consume food other than that included in the least-cost diet or to let them consume other services beyond the lowest-cost ones required for maintenance. Slaves, on the other hand, were not necessarily harmed when their productivity was lowered. Obviously, they preferred more palatable food, which they

---

6. Fogel and Engerman, however, do not interpret their findings on nutrition the way I do. In general, they do not systematically apply transaction cost notions to the analysis of slavery.

would have substituted, in part, for less pleasant if more nutritious food. One major tool owners possessed for minimizing maintenance costs was the ability to control consumption directly; they attained this control by simply providing consumption items in kind rather than allowing slaves a budget, which would have permitted choice. Thus, slaves' diet in the American South contained much corn and sweet potatoes, then considered nutritious but less desirable than the more expensive wheat and white potatoes even poor free farmers chose to consume. Owners' control of slaves' consumption, however, was not absolute. Slaves would, on occasion, avoid taking medicine, since in their eyes remaining ill was sometimes preferable to returning to work.

NOTES AND QUESTIONS ON OWNERSHIP OF AND BY SLAVES

1. John Locke, Second Treatise of Government, §85 (1690) observed that a distinctive attribute of slavery is the slave's inability to own property. Does Barzel's argument support that view? What is the relationship, if any, between *being treated as property* and *being unable to own property*? Reconsider the situation of asylum inmates described by Goffman, supra p.1, or consider the situation of some third-world women described by Papanek, infra p.303. Do those conditions of relative "propertylessness" resemble enslavement? Why or why not?

2. Barzel suggests that monitoring costs put limitations on enslavement even when slavery was legal. Where these costs were high, why might even a slaveowner have thought it more profitable to treat the slave as "owning" his or her labor, and paying for output, instead of using punishment as the exclusive motivator? Do the monitoring costs of different kinds of work suggest why, when slavery was legal, some jobs were performed by slave labor and other jobs by free labor? Did "employers" have different monitoring costs for, say, carpentry as compared to field work? What about factory labor? How might the possibility of sabotage affect the employer's preference for free or slave labor?

3. Now that enslavement is formally illegal, does the monitoring-cost approach reveal anything about labor relations? For example, does the approach predict that some types of work might still be organized in ways approaching enslavement? Are those predictions borne out in the context of, say, agricultural field work? Sweatshop garment production? Prostitution? Are there

ways (legal or illegal) in which modern employers might lower their monitoring costs to make slavery-like conditions feasible?

4. Why does it matter to the author to establish at the outset that involuntary slavery is larceny? Does the rightful ownership of the slave's labor have any real bearing on his argument?

5. The question of slavery's "efficiency" and its larger relationship to capitalism has received extensive historical treatment, particularly among the generation of historians active during and following the modern civil rights movement. For an early work, see Eric Williams, Capitalism and Slavery (1944). A very controversial work arguing that slavery, however unjust, was efficient was Robert W. Fogel & Stanley L. Engerman, Time on the Cross: The Economics of American Negro Slavery (1974) ; a later revision was Robert W. Fogel, et al., Without Consent or Contract: The Rise and Fall of American Slavery (1989). For a very critical discussion, see Thomas L. Haskell, The True & Tragical History of "Time on the Cross," N.Y. Rev. of Books, Oct. 2, 1975, at 33. For the related theme of capitalism and abolitionism, see Thomas Bender, ed., The Anti-slavery Debate: Capitalism and Abolitionism as a Problem in Historical Interpretation (1992).

Chapter 2

The Problem
of the Commons

A. Tragedy or Comedy?

The Tragedy of the Commons*

Garrett Hardin

. . . We can make little progress in working toward optimum population size until we explicitly exorcize the spirit of Adam Smith in the field of practical demography. In economic affairs, The Wealth of Nations (1776) popularized the "invisible hand," the idea that an individual who "intends only his own gain," is, as it were, "led by an invisible hand to promote . . . the public interest." Adam Smith did not assert that this was invariably true, and perhaps neither did any of his followers. But he contributed to a dominant tendency of thought that has ever since interfered with positive action based on rational analysis, namely, the tendency to assume that decisions reached individually will, in fact, be the best decisions for an entire society. If this assumption is correct it justifies the continuance of our present policy of laissez-faire in reproduction. If it is correct we can assume that men will control their individual fecundity so as to produce the optimum population. If the assumption is not correct, we need to reexamine our individual freedoms to see which ones are defensible.

*Source: 162 Science 1243-1248 (1968).

The Tragedy of Freedom in a Commons

The rebuttal to the invisible hand in population control is to be found in a scenario first sketched in a little-known pamphlet in 1833 by a mathematical amateur named William Forster Lloyd (1794-1852). We may well call it "the tragedy of the commons," using the word "tragedy" as the philosopher Whitehead used it: "The essence of dramatic tragedy is not unhappiness. It resides in the solemnity of the remorseless working of things." . . .

The tragedy of the commons develops in this way. Picture a pasture open to all. It is to be expected that each herdsman will try to keep as many cattle as possible on the commons. Such an arrangement may work reasonably satisfactorily for centuries because tribal wars, poaching, and disease keep the numbers of both man and beast well below the carrying capacity of the land. Finally, however, comes the day of reckoning, that is, the day when the long-desired goal of social stability becomes a reality. At this point, the inherent logic of the commons remorselessly generates tragedy.

As a rational being, each herdsman seeks to maximize his gain. Explicitly or implicitly, more or less consciously, he asks, "What is the utility to *me* of adding one more animal to my herd?" This utility has one negative and one positive component.

1. The positive component is a function of the increment of one animal. Since the herdsman receives all the proceeds from the sale of the additional animal, the positive utility is nearly +1.
2. The negative component is a function of the additional overgrazing created by one more animal. Since, however, the effects of overgrazing are shared by all the herdsmen, the negative utility for any particular decision-making herdsman is only a fraction of − 1.

Adding together the component partial utilities, the rational herdsman concludes that the only sensible course for him to pursue is to add another animal to his herd. And another; and another. . . . But this is the conclusion reached by each and every rational herdsman sharing a commons. Therein is the tragedy. Each man is locked into a system that compels him to increase his herd without limit— in a world that is limited. Ruin is the destination toward which all men rush, each pursuing his own best interest in a society that believes in the freedom of the commons. Freedom in a commons brings ruin to all.

Some would say that this is a platitude. Would that it were! In a sense, it was learned thousands of years ago, but natural selection favors the forces of psychological denial. The individual benefits as an individual from his ability to deny the truth even though society as a whole, of which he is a part, suffers. Education can counteract the natural tendency to do the wrong thing, but the inexorable succession of generations requires that the basis for this knowledge be constantly refreshed.

A simple incident that occurred a few years ago in Leominster, Massachusetts, shows how perishable the knowledge is. During the Christmas shopping season the parking meters downtown were covered with plastic bags that bore tags reading: "Do not open until after Christmas. Free parking courtesy of the mayor and city council." In other words, facing the prospect of an increased demand for already scarce space, the city fathers reinstituted the system of the commons. (Cynically, we suspect that they gained more votes than they lost by this retrogressive act.)

In an approximate way, the logic of the commons has been understood for a long time, perhaps since the discovery of agriculture or the invention of private property in real estate. But it is understood mostly only in special cases which are not sufficiently generalized. Even at this late date, cattlemen leasing national land on the western ranges demonstrate no more than an ambivalent understanding, in constantly pressuring federal authorities to increase the head count to the point where overgrazing produces erosion and weed dominance. Likewise, the oceans of the world continue to suffer from the survival of the philosophy of the commons. Maritime nations still respond automatically to the shibboleth of the "freedom of the seas." Professing to believe in the "inexhaustible resources of the oceans," they bring species after species of fish and whales closer to extinction.

The National Parks present another instance of the working out of the tragedy of the commons. At present, they are open to all, without limit. The parks themselves are limited in extent—there is only one Yosemite Valley—whereas population seems to grow without limit. The values that visitors seek in the parks are steadily eroded. Plainly, we must soon cease to treat the parks as commons or they will be of no value to anyone.

What shall we do? We have several options. We might sell them off as private property. We might keep them as public property, but allocate the right to enter them. The allocation might be on the basis of wealth, by the use of an auction system. It might be on the basis of merit, as defined by some agreed-upon standards. It might be by lottery. Or it might be on a first-come, first-served basis, administered to long queues. These, I think, are all the reasonable possibilities. They are all objectionable. But we must choose—or acquiesce in the destruction of the commons that we call our National Parks.

Pollution

In a reverse way, the tragedy of the commons reappears in problems of pollution. Here it is not a question of taking something out of the commons, but of putting something in—sewage, or chemical, radioactive, and heat wastes into water; noxious and dangerous fumes into the air; and distracting and unpleasant advertising signs into the line of sight. The calculations of utility are much the same as before. The rational man finds that his share of the cost of the wastes he discharges into the commons is less than the cost of purifying his wastes before releasing them. Since this is true for everyone, we are locked into a system of "fouling our own nest," so long as we behave only as independent, rational, free-enterprisers.

The tragedy of the commons as a food basket is averted by private property, or something formally like it. But the air and waters surrounding us cannot readily be fenced, and so the tragedy of the commons as a cesspool must be prevented by different means, by coercive laws or taxing devices that make it cheaper for the polluter to treat his pollutants than to discharge them untreated. We have not progressed as far with the solution of this problem as we have with the first. Indeed, our particular concept of private property, which deters us from exhausting the positive resources of the earth, favors pollution. The owner of a factory on the bank of a stream—whose property extends to the middle of the stream—often has difficulty seeing why it is not his natural right to muddy the waters flowing past his door. The law, always behind the times, requires elaborate stitching and fitting to adapt it to this newly perceived aspect of the commons.

The pollution problem is a consequence of population. It did not much matter how a lonely American frontiersman disposed of his waste. "Flowing water purifies itself every ten miles," my grandfather used to say, and the myth was near enough to the truth when he was a boy, for there were not too many people. But as population became denser, the natural chemical and biological recycling processes became overloaded, calling for a redefinition of property rights. . . .

Freedom to Breed Is Intolerable

The tragedy of the commons is involved in population problems in another way. In a world governed solely by the principle of "dog eat dog"—if indeed there ever was such a world—how many children a family had would not be a matter of public concern. Parents who bred too exuberantly would leave fewer descendants, not more, because they would be unable to care adequately for their children. David Lack and others have found that such a negative feedback demonstrably controls the fecundity of birds. But men are not birds, and have not acted like them for millenniums, at least.

If each human family were dependent only on its own resources; *if* the children of improvident parents starved to death; *if,* thus, overbreeding brought its own "punishment" to the germ line—*then* there would be no public interest in controlling the breeding of families. But our society is deeply committed to the welfare state, and hence is confronted with another aspect of the tragedy of the commons. . . .

Pathogenic Effects of Conscience . . .

If we ask a man who is exploiting a commons to desist "in the name of conscience," what are we saying to him? What does he hear?—not only at the moment but also in the wee small hours of the night when, half asleep, he remembers not merely the words we used but also the nonverbal communication cues we gave him unawares? Sooner or later, consciously or subconsciously, he senses that he has received two communications, and that they are contradictory: (1, the intended communication) "If you don't do as we ask, we will openly condemn you for not acting like a responsible citizen"; (2, the unintended communication) "If you *do* behave as we ask, we will secretly condemn you for a simpleton who can be shamed into standing aside while the rest of us exploit the commons."

Everyman then is caught in what Bateson has called a "double bind." Bateson and his co-workers have made a plausible case for viewing the double bind as an important causative factor in the genesis of schizophrenia. The double bind may not always be so damaging, but it always endangers the mental health of anyone to whom it is applied. "A bad conscience," said Nietzsche, "is a kind of illness."

To conjure up a conscience in others is tempting to anyone who wishes to extend his control beyond the legal limits. Leaders at the highest level succumb to this temptation. Has any President during the past generation failed to call on labor unions to moderate voluntarily their demands for higher wages, or to steel companies to honor voluntary guidelines on prices? I can recall none. The rhetoric used on such occasions is designed to produce feelings of guilt in noncooperators.

For centuries it was assumed without proof that guilt was a valuable, perhaps even an indispensable, ingredient of the civilized life. Now, in this post-Freudian world, we doubt it.

Paul Goodman speaks from the modern point of view when he says: "No good has ever come from feeling guilty, neither intelligence, policy, nor compassion. The guilty do not pay attention to the object but only to themselves, and not even to their own interests, which might make sense, but to their anxieties."

One does not have to be a professional psychiatrist to see the consequences of anxiety. We in the Western world are just emerging from a dreadful two-centuries-long Dark Ages of Eros that was sustained partly by prohibition laws, but perhaps more effectively by the anxiety-generating mechanisms of education. . . .

Since proof is difficult, we may even concede that the results of anxiety may sometimes, from certain points of view, be desirable. The larger question we should ask is whether, as a matter of policy, we should ever encourage the use of a technique the tendency (if not the intention) of which is psychologically pathogenic. We hear much talk these days of responsible parenthood; the coupled words are incorporated into the titles of some organizations devoted to birth control. Some people have proposed massive propaganda campaigns to instill responsibility into the nation's (or the world's) breeders. But what is the meaning of the word responsibility in this context? Is it not merely a synonym for the word conscience? When we use the word responsibility in the absence of substantial sanctions are we not trying to browbeat a free man in a commons into acting against his own interest? Responsibility is a verbal counterfeit for a substantial *quid pro quo*. It is an attempt to get something for nothing.

If the word responsibility is to be used at all, I suggest that it be in the sense Charles Frankel uses it. "Responsibility," says this philosopher, "is the product of definite social arrangements." Notice that Frankel calls for social arrangements—not propaganda.

Mutual Coercion Mutually Agreed Upon

The social arrangements that produce responsibility are arrangements that create coercion, of some sort. Consider bank robbing. The man who takes money from a bank acts as if the bank were a commons. How do we prevent such action? Certainly not by trying to control his behavior solely by a verbal appeal to his sense of responsibility. Rather than rely on propaganda we follow Frankel's lead and insist that a bank is not a commons; we seek the definite social arrangements that will keep it from becoming a commons. That we thereby infringe on the freedom of would-be robbers we neither deny nor regret.

The morality of bank robbing is particularly easy to understand because we accept complete prohibition of this activity. We are willing to say "Thou shalt not rob banks," without providing for exceptions. But temperance also can be created by coercion. Taxing is a good coercive device. To keep downtown shoppers temperate in their use of parking space we introduce parking meters for short periods, and traffic fines for longer ones. We need not actually forbid a citizen to park as long as he wants to; we need merely make it increasingly expensive for him to do so. Not prohibition, but carefully biased options are what we offer him. A Madison Avenue man might call this persuasion; I prefer the greater candor of the word coercion.

Coercion is a dirty word to most liberals now, but it need not forever be so. As with the four-letter words, its dirtiness can be cleansed away by exposure to the light, by saying it over and over without apology or embarrassment. To many, the word coercion implies arbitrary decisions of distant and irresponsible bureaucrats; but this is not a necessary part of its meaning. The only kind of coercion I recommend is mutual coercion, mutually agreed upon by the majority of the people affected.

To say that we mutually agree to coercion is not to say that we are required to enjoy it, or even to pretend we enjoy it. Who enjoys taxes? We all grumble about them. But we accept compulsory taxes because we recognize that voluntary taxes would favor the conscienceless. We institute and (grumblingly) support taxes and other coercive devices to escape the horror of the commons.

An alternative to the commons need not be perfectly just to be preferable. With real estate and other material goods, the alternative we have chosen is the institution of private property coupled with legal inheritance. Is this system perfectly just? As a genetically trained biologist I deny that it is. It seems to me that, if there are to be differences in individual inheritance, legal possession should be perfectly correlated with biological inheritance—that those who are biologically more fit to be the custodians of property and power should legally inherit more. But genetic recombination continually makes a mockery of the doctrine of "like father, like son" implicit in our laws of legal inheritance. An idiot can inherit millions, and a trust fund can keep his estate intact. We must admit that our legal system of private property plus inheritance is unjust—but we put up with it because we are not convinced, at the moment, that anyone has invented a better system. The alternative of the commons is too horrifying to contemplate. Injustice is preferable to total ruin.

It is one of the peculiarities of the warfare between reform and the status quo that it is thoughtlessly governed by a double standard. Whenever a reform measure is proposed it is often defeated when its opponents triumphantly discover a flaw in it. As Kingsley Davis has pointed out, worshippers of the status quo sometimes imply that no reform is possible without unanimous agreement, an implication contrary to historical fact. As nearly as I can make out, automatic rejection of proposed reforms is based on one of two unconscious assumptions: (1) that the status quo is perfect; or (2) that the choice we face is between reform and no action; if the proposed reform is imperfect, we presumably should take no action at all, while we wait for a perfect proposal.

But we can never do nothing. That which we have done for thousands of years is also action. It also produces evils. Once we are aware that the status quo is action, we can then compare its discoverable advantages and disadvantages with the predicted advantages and disadvantages of the proposed reform, discounting as best we can for our lack of experience. On the basis of such a comparison, we can make a rational decision which will not involve the unworkable assumption that only perfect systems are tolerable.

Recognition of Necessity

Perhaps the simplest summary of this analysis of man's population problems is this: The commons, if justifiable at all, is justifiable only under conditions of low population density. As the human population has increased, the commons has had to be abandoned in one aspect after another.

First we abandoned the commons in food gathering, enclosing farm land and restricting pastures and hunting and fishing areas. These restrictions are still not complete throughout the world.

Somewhat later we saw that the commons as a place for waste disposal would also have to be abandoned. Restrictions on the disposal of domestic sewage are widely accepted in the Western world; we are still struggling to close the commons to pollution by automobiles, factories, insecticide sprayers, fertilizing operations, and atomic energy installations.

In a still more embryonic state is our recognition of the evils of the commons in matters of pleasure. There is almost no restriction on the propagation of sound waves in the public medium. The shopping public is assaulted with mindless music, without its consent. Our government is paying out billions of dollars to create supersonic transport which will disturb 50,000 people for every one person who is whisked from coast to coast three hours faster. Advertisers muddy the airwaves of radio and television and pollute the view of travelers. We are a long way from outlawing the commons in matters of pleasure. Is this because our Puritan inheritance makes us view pleasure as something of a sin, and pain (that is, the pollution of advertising) as the sign of virtue?

Every new enclosure of the commons involves the infringement of somebody's personal liberty. Infringements made in the distant past are accepted because no contemporary complains of a loss. It is the newly proposed infringements that we vigorously oppose; cries of "rights" and "freedom" fill the air. But what does "freedom" mean? When men mutually agreed to pass laws against robbing, mankind became more free, not less so. Individuals locked into the logic of the commons are free only to bring on universal ruin; once they see the necessity of mutual coercion, they become free to pursue other goals. I believe it was Hegel who said, "Freedom is the recognition of necessity."

The most important aspect of necessity that we must now recognize, is the necessity of abandoning the commons in breeding. No technical solution can rescue us from the misery of overpopulation. Freedom to breed will bring ruin to all. At the moment, to avoid hard decisions many of us are tempted to propagandize for conscience and responsible parenthood. The temptation must be resisted, because an appeal to independently acting conscience selects for the disappearance of all conscience in the long run, and an increase in anxiety in the short.

The only way we can preserve and nurture other and more precious freedoms is by relinquishing the freedom to breed, and that very soon. "Freedom is the recognition of necessity"—and it is the role of education to reveal to all the necessity of abandoning the freedom to breed. Only so, can we put an end to this aspect of the tragedy of the commons.

NOTES AND QUESTIONS ON THE COMMONS

1. What attributes make a resource subject to commons problems? Are examples drawn from overgrazing and water pollution really comparable to the example of "freedom to breed"? What is a population "problem," anyway? If other resources (like grazing land, air, and water) were not subject to unrationed open access, would overpopulation be a problem?

2. Hardin mentions several ways to avoid the commons problem by rationing, including the creation of private property, auctions, merit-based allocation, lotteries, and first-come-first-served

by queue. Can you think of other rationing methods? Which is best for which kinds of resources?

3. Private property is often said to avert the tragedy of the commons. But does it? Who enforces property limitations? Does another kind of "commons" problem lurk in the organization and maintenance of a property regime? See James Krier, The Tragedy of the Commons, Part II, 15 Harv. J.L. & Pub. Pol. 325, 332-339 (1992).

4. Hardin's article has generated an enormous literature, some of it critical of his view that the commons is inherently tragic. One critic is Elinor Ostrom. In Governing the Commons (1990), she joins with other authors in sharply distinguishing "open access" resources from "common property" resources. The latter term designates resources that are owned or controlled by finite numbers of people who manage to organize themselves (and exclude outsiders) in such a way that they use the "commons" productively. Ostrom compiles many examples from all over the world, including fisheries, irrigation works, and grazing areas. Still another example appears in the selection that follows, by James Acheson. As you read it, consider what kinds of common resources might be tragic, and what kinds might lend themselves instead to common management. Consider also the role of culture in solving (or creating) commons problems.

5. The "tragedy of the commons" is sometimes described as an "n-person prisoner's dilemma." Can you see why? For more on the prisoner's dilemma, see Axelrod, The Evolution of Cooperation, infra p. 275.

6. The phrase "tragedy of the commons" was itself a huge hit. Several similar ideas, however, were developed earlier and in a more systematic way by H. Scott Gordon, in The Economic Theory of a Common-Property Resource: The Fishery, 62 J. Pol. Econ. 124 (1954). Does Gordon's title perhaps suggest why he is not as well-known as Hardin?

The Lobster Gangs of Maine*

James M. Acheson

While lobstermen themselves often subscribe to the stereotype of the independent man-at-sea, they are in fact part of a complicated social network. The industry has rules that all men are expected to

*Source: pp. 48-49, 73-76, 142-144 (1988).

obey, its own standards of conduct, and its own mythology. To succeed in lobstering a man not only must have certain technical skills and work hard, but also must be able to operate in a particular social milieu.

Beyond the kinship group, the most important people in a lobster fisherman's life are the men who fish from the same harbor. Such social groupings, while they are recognized by everyone in the lobster-fishing industry, have no universally accepted name. People refer to the "Monhegan boys," or the "Friendship fishermen," or the "Port Clyde gang." Sometimes men refer to those in their own harbor as "the men I fish with." I have called these groups "harbor gangs," although this term is only rarely used by the fishermen themselves (Acheson 1972).

Membership in a harbor gang strongly influences many aspects of a lobster fisherman's career. Most importantly, it controls entry into the industry. To go lobster fishing, a man must first become a member of a harbor gang. Once he has gained admission, he can go fishing only in the territory "owned" communally by members of that gang. Fishermen who place their traps in the territory of another gang can expect swift retribution, normally the purposeful destruction of their gear. Although these territories and the gangs that own them are completely unrecognized by the state, they are a long-standing reality. Fishermen identify with a particular harbor gang and are identified as members of it. Members of harbor gangs obtain a great deal of valuable information from one another on fishing locations and innovations. They also assist one another in times of emergency at sea. If a motor breaks down or someone runs out of gas, other members of the gang are called for a tow. This is one of the reasons that people in a harbor gang keep their radios on the same channel. . . .

Lobster fishermen in the same harbor gang ordinarily have long-term, multistrand ties with one another. Almost all live in the town where the harbor is located. Many are members of long-established families and share kinship ties as well. The men of the same generation have grown up together, and members of their families have known one another and intermarried for generations. . . .

Defense of Boundaries

Violation of territorial boundaries meets with no fixed response. An older person from an established family with a long history of fishing might infringe on the territorial rights of others almost indefinitely. Those being infringed upon are especially reluctant to accuse a gang leader or the member of a large family, either of whom could have a large number of allies. An unpopular person, a young fisherman, or a newcomer encounters trouble more quickly. Sooner or later, however, someone decides to take action against the interloper. Sometimes a small group of fishermen decide to act in concert, but boundary defense is often effected by one person acting alone.

The violator is usually warned, sometimes by verbal threats and abuse, but usually by surreptitious molestation of lobstering gear. Two half-hitches of rope may be tied around the spindle of the buoy, or legal-sized lobsters may be taken out and the doors of the traps left open. Fishermen have been known to leave threatening notes in bottles inside the offending traps, and one colorful islander carves a representation of female genitalia in the styrofoam buoys. Most interlopers move their gear when warned in these ways. If the violations persist, the traps are destroyed. Fishermen have destroyed traps by "carving them up a little" with a chain saw or by smashing them with sledge hammers. When such traps are pulled, the owner has little doubt as to what has happened. Usually, however, the offending traps are cut off: they are pulled, the buoy toggles and warp line are cut, and the trap is pushed into deep water, where there is little chance of finding it. There is no practical way to protect traps in the water. Removing the traps not only removes the symbol of another person's intrusion but also limits the intruder's capacity to reduce the defender's own catch. Destruction of traps does not usually lead to direct confrontation since the owner can only guess who destroyed them or even whether they were destroyed on purpose.

In a few instances, gangs defend their boundaries as a group. It is well known that anyone invading the traditional territories of such islands as Metinic, Monhegan, and Green Island can expect coordinated resistance from men fishing those islands. Once in a while, groups goaded beyond endurance launch a full scale "cut war" in which hundreds of traps are destroyed, boats sunk, and even docks and fish houses burnt. These so-called lobster wars lead to long-standing bitterness, violence, and court action.

It is a rare day in a harbor when someone does not suspect that his traps have been tampered with. Many incidents occur as a result of feuds and competition within a particular area. Much of this small-scale molestation stems from the fact that maintaining territorial lines means constantly utilizing one's own territory and perhaps a little more—a process known as "pushing the lines." Even in slow months, a few traps are left in certain peripheral areas to maintain local territorial claims. However, fishermen touch another's gear only with great reluctance, knowing that their own gear is vulnerable to retaliation. The whole industry is aware that the individuals whose traps have been cut off may well take vengeance, but frequently against the wrong person. The result, they know, can be a comic and costly chain of events in which the innocent and the guilty retaliate blindly against one another. The norms are therefore widely obeyed, and although the entire coast is patrolled by only a few wardens, there is little trouble. Fishermen are very careful to punish intruders in ways that will not provoke a massive, violent response. According to one fisherman, "The trick to driving a man [out of the area] is to cut off just one or two traps at a time." This harassment makes it unprofitable to fish an area but does not challenge a man to open warfare, since he can only guess who cut his traps.

A conspiracy of silence surrounds all trap-cutting incidents and efforts to enforce boundaries. Those who resort to cutting traps rarely advertise their "skill with the knife," to reduce both the possibility of retaliation and the chance of losing their lobster licenses for destroying the traps of other men. Destruction of another's gear is always considered immoral, regardless of the circumstances, because it interferes with the victim's ability to feed his family. Victims may growl and threaten but they rarely report the incident to any law enforcement agency. The culprit's identity may be unknown, and chances of successful prosecution are small. Fishermen feel strongly that the law should be kept at bay and that people should handle their own problems. Any fisherman who goes to the police to complain about trap cuttings not only looks ineffectual and ridiculous but is somewhat of a threat. When a man's traps are missing, taking the law into his own hands is not only more effective but also maintains his standing among fellow fishermen. . . .

Fishermen say that a man is allowed to fish within the entire territory owned by the harbor gang to which he belongs. This statement is not strictly accurate. A man is expected to keep his distance from other fishermen and not "dump" his traps on top of another's, where they can become entangled. Fishermen with traps in a saturated location have usufructuary rights; others cannot enter until someone leaves. The older, more skilled fishermen are likely to have their traps prepositioned in the best locations. When lobsters do appear, those who have "camped out" in good spots have monopolized all or most of the available space. Younger fishermen—particularly those who have joined the gang recently—are well advised to stay out of the way of men with status in the hierarchy of skill and prestige. Men of lower status can lose a great deal by coming into conflict with highliners.

Sometimes groups of men use a particular spot or set of spots for such a long time that they begin to feel proprietary rights over these locations. Within harbor gangs in the study area, however, such men have only usufructuary rights, not permanent ownership. Should the men who regularly fish in a location move their traps elsewhere, others from the harbor gang can move their traps into it. . . .

Common-Property Resources

According to the theory of common-property resources, resources such as fish, air, water, and publicly owned parks and forests are overexploited and abused in ways that privately owned resources are not. Owners of private property protect their resources, while those exploiting publicly owned or open-access resources are locked into a system that makes unlimited exploitation rational. Why should one cattleman, logger, or polluter conserve the resources, since he cannot capture the benefits for himself? Under these circumstances, it is only logical for such a person to expand the amount of capital he uses and strive to use as much of the resources as possible and as fast as possible. The result is what Garrett Hardin has called the "tragedy of the commons." In the case of fisheries, the "tragedy" is said to result in overexploitation of fish stocks, decline of the breeding stock, "overcapitalization," and "economic inefficiency." Two different kinds of solutions have been suggested for such common-property problems. Many of the economists who have developed this body of theory see salvation in establishing private property rights of one kind or another. Hardin, a biologist, is more pessimistic. He believes such problems can be solved only by draconian government controls.

Although the theory of common-property resources has played a key role in shaping current conceptions of resource management, little empirical work has been done to verify this theory. . . . One axiom of the theory is that property rights help to conserve resources, promote economic efficiency, and result in higher incomes. This case study confirms this axiom. In the perimeter-defended areas, where access is more limited and property rights are more vigorously enforced, the stock of lobsters is larger, catches of fishermen are larger, and the breeding stock is larger. However, the theory assumes that there are really only two kinds of ownership: private ownership and having no control over access at all. As . . . a number of other authors have recently pointed out, there are really three different kinds of property: private property, communal or jointly owned property, and "open access." Maine lobstering territories are an instance of joint or communal property. Such institutions, which can be generated by local communities operating on their own, can be effective in conserving the resources. This case study reinforces [the] point . . . that the problem is not "common property" but "open access," or no controls at all on usage. It also helps to modify Hardin's theory by pointing out that governmental action and private property are not the only solutions to resource problems. An alternative solution is a communal property arrangement.

Maine lobster territories are not unique in this respect. A large number of local communities have generated a wide variety of institutions to control exploitation of the resources on which their livelihood depends. Though tragedies of the commons (more accurately, tragedies of "open access") do exist in both the third world and the developed world, they are not inevitable in the absence of private property.

Maine lobstering territories have not been an unqualified success in conserving the resource. They have limited the numbers of fishermen entering the fishery, but except in those few places where informal or formal trap limits are imposed (e.g., Swans Island), they have not helped to limit the number of traps and the escalation of fishing effort.

NOTES AND QUESTIONS ON COMMUNAL PROPERTY REGIMES

1. Acheson describes three kinds of property, locating them on a spectrum of exclusivity: private property, an intermediate communal property, and the completely non-exclusive "open access." Open-access property is thought to be particularly subject to the "tragedy of the commons." How do these categories apply to property normally considered "public"? Which kind of property is, say, a post office building? The White House? A small neighborhood park? Yellowstone National Park? Are any or all of these properties subject to the "tragedy of the commons"? What might account for differences?

2. What accounts for the intermediate communal property that Acheson posits? The Maine fishermen appear to have certain elements of individual entitlement in their practices; why have they not gone the whole way to individual property?

3. Would you describe the Maine lobstermen's territory as a kind of "property," as Acheson does? Why or why not? Does the

lobstermen's example suggest that property is a creature of law, as is often argued, or rather an institution that can arise informally? See generally Robert C. Ellickson, Order Without Law: How Neighbors Settle Disputes (1991).

4. Why do lobstermen generally retaliate against interlopers in a surreptitious manner? Note the danger of secret retaliation: The victim may counter-retaliate against the wrong person. Why would the community of lobster fishers engage in a "conspiracy of silence" when they themselves might bear the brunt of mistaken responses? Compare Jon Elster, Norms of Revenge, 100 Ethics 862 (1990), describing the extremely open (and communally-encouraged) practices of retaliation in certain Balkan countries, particularly in response to slights to family honor. Under what circumstances would you expect norms of secret revenge? Open and public revenge? Are norms of revenge necessary to maintain a property regime?

5. Is it true that open-access property is always "tragic"? Compare Carol Rose, The Comedy of the Commons, 53 U. Chi. L. Rev. 711 (1986), describing a kind of "inherently public property" in the history of Western law, where a number of persistent legal devices have retained certain types of property in a state of open access. These public property doctrines have historically applied not only to lanes of transportation, such as roads and waterways, but also to some traditional recreational areas, like cricket fields and maypole dancing areas. Modern counterparts are the various doctrines opening beaches and waterfronts to public use. Are these doctrines simply irrational encouragements of wasteful resource practices—that is, the tragedy of the commons? Or might some kinds of property be in their *best* use when open to the public at large?

Consider transportation lanes: Why might a community generally want to encourage public travel and transport by keeping travel lanes open, even to the point of subsidizing roads and other transport methods? What would happen to a community isolated by, say, the collapse of bridges during flooding? Given the costs of isolation, is it really "tragic" to guarantee open access to such properties as roads or bridges, or might it rather be a good idea? How about telephone systems? Public squares? Maypole dance fields? Playgrounds? Beaches? Is there a stronger case for "privatization" of some of these properties than others? Why or why not?

6. Might some "hard-wired" aspect of human nature generate solutions to commons problems? See Edna Ullmann-Margalit, The Emergence of Norms (1978), arguing that prisoner's dilemmas and commons problems, or at least some of them, predictably give rise

to norms that help solve the problems. If this is true, does it simply add to the mystery? Where do such norms come from? Bear this question in mind when you read the next selection by Harold Demsetz.

B.   The Economics of the Commons

Toward a Theory of Property Rights*

Harold Demsetz

When a transaction is concluded in the marketplace, two bundles of property rights are exchanged. A bundle of rights often attaches to a physical commodity or service, but it is the value of the rights that determines the value of what is exchanged. Questions addressed to the emergence and mix of the components of the bundle of rights are prior to those commonly asked by economists. Economists usually take the bundle of property rights as a datum and ask for an explanation of the forces determining the price and the number of units of a good to which these rights attach.

In this paper, I seek to fashion some of the elements of an economic theory of property rights. The paper is organized into three parts. The first part discusses briefly the concept and role of property rights in social systems. The second part offers some guidance for investigating the emergence of property rights. The third part sets forth some principles relevant to the coalescing of property rights into particular bundles and to the determination of the ownership structure that will be associated with these bundles.

The Concept and Role of Property Rights

In the world of Robinson Crusoe property rights play no role. Property rights are an instrument of society and derive their significance from the fact that they help a man form those expectations which he can reasonably hold in his dealings with others. These expectations find expression in the laws, customs, and mores of a society. An owner of property rights possesses the consent of fellowmen to al-

*Source: 57 Am. Econ. Rev. Pap. & Proc. 347-358 (1967).

low him to act in particular ways. An owner expects the community to prevent others from interfering with his actions, provided that these actions are not prohibited in the specifications of his rights.

It is important to note that property rights convey the right to benefit or harm oneself or others. Harming a competitor by producing superior products may be permitted, while shooting him may not. A man may be permitted to benefit himself by shooting an intruder but be prohibited from selling below a price floor. It is clear, then, that property rights specify how persons may be benefited and harmed, and, therefore, who must pay whom to modify the actions taken by persons. The recognition of this leads easily to the close relationship between property rights and externalities.

Externality is an ambiguous concept. For the purposes of this paper, the concept includes external costs, external benefits, and pecuniary as well as nonpecuniary externalities. No harmful or beneficial effect is external to the world. Some person or persons always suffer or enjoy these effects. What converts a harmful or beneficial effect into an externality is that the cost of bringing the effect to bear on the decisions of one or more of the interacting persons is too high to make it worthwhile, and this is what the term shall mean here. "Internalizing" such effects refers to a process, usually a change in property rights, that enables these effects to bear (in greater degree) on all interacting persons.

A primary function of property rights is that of guiding incentives to achieve a greater internalization of externalities. Every cost and benefit associated with social interdependencies is a potential externality. One condition is necessary to make costs and benefits externalities. The cost of a transaction in the rights between the parties (internalization) must exceed the gains from internalization. In general, transacting cost can be large relative to gains because of "natural" difficulties in trading or they can be large because of legal reasons. In a lawful society the prohibition of voluntary negotiations makes the cost of transacting infinite. Some costs and benefits are not taken into account by users of resources whenever externalities exist, but allowing transactions increases the degree to which internalization takes place. . . .

The Emergence of Property Rights

If the main allocative function of property rights is the internalization of beneficial and harmful effects, then the emergence of property rights can be understood best by their association with the emergence of new or different beneficial and harmful effects.

Changes in knowledge result in changes in production functions, market values, and aspirations. New techniques, new ways of doing the same things, and doing new things—all invoke harmful and beneficial effects to which society has not been accustomed. It is my thesis in this part of the paper that the emergence of new property rights takes place in response to the desires of the interacting persons for adjustment to new benefit-cost possibilities.

The thesis can be restated in a slightly different fashion: property rights develop to internalize externalities when the gains of internalization become larger than the cost of internalization. Increased internalization, in the main, results from changes in economic values, changes which stem from the development of new technology and the opening of new markets, changes to which old property rights are poorly attuned. A proper interpretation of this assertion requires that account be taken of a community's preferences for private ownership. Some communities will have less well-developed private ownership systems and more highly developed state ownership systems. But, given a community's tastes in this regard, the emergence of new private or state-owned property rights will be in response to changes in technology and relative prices.

I do not mean to assert or to deny that the adjustments in property rights which take place need be the result of a conscious endeavor to cope with new externality problems. These adjustments have arisen in Western societies largely as a result of gradual changes in social mores and in common law precedents. At each step of this adjustment process, it is unlikely that externalities per se were consciously related to the issue being resolved. These legal and moral experiments may be hit-and-miss procedures to some extent but in a society that weights the achievement of efficiency heavily, their viability in the long run will depend on how well they modify behavior to accommodate to the externalities associated with important changes in technology or market values.

A rigorous test of this assertion will require extensive and detailed empirical work. A broad range of examples can be cited that are consistent with it: the development of air rights, renters' rights, rules for liability in automobile accidents, etc. In this part of the discussion, I shall present one group of such examples in some detail. They deal with the development of private property rights in land among American Indians. These examples are broad ranging and come fairly close to what can be called convincing evidence in the field of anthropology.

The question of private ownership of land among aboriginals has held a fascination for anthropologists. It has been one of the intellectual battlegrounds in the attempt to assess the "true nature" of man unconstrained by the "artificialities" of civilization. In the process of carrying on this debate, information has been uncovered that bears directly on the thesis with which we are now concerned. What appears to be accepted as a classic treatment and a high point of this debate is Eleanor Leacock's memoir on The Montagnes: "Hunting Territory" and the Fur Trade.[3] Leacock's research followed that of Frank G. Speck[4] who had discovered that the Indians of the Labrador Peninsula had a long-established tradition of property in land. This finding was at odds with what was known about the Indians of the American Southwest and it prompted Leacock's study of the Montagnes who inhabited large regions around Quebec.

Leacock clearly established the fact that a close relationship existed, both historically and geographically, between the development of private rights in land and the development of the commercial fur trade. The factual basis of this correlation has gone unchallenged. However, to my knowledge, no theory relating privacy of land to the fur trade has yet been articulated. The factual material uncovered by Speck and Leacock fits the thesis of this paper well, and in doing so, it reveals clearly the role played by property right adjustments in taking account of what economists have often cited as an example of an externality—the overhunting of game.

Because of the lack of control over hunting by others, it is in no person's interest to invest in increasing or maintaining the stock of game. Overly intensive hunting takes place. Thus a successful hunt is viewed as imposing external costs on subsequent hunters—costs that are not taken into account fully in the determination of the extent of hunting and of animal husbandry.

Before the fur trade became established, hunting was carried on primarily for purposes of food and the relatively few furs that were required for the hunter's family. The externality was clearly present. Hunting could be practiced freely and was carried on without assessing its impact on other hunters. But these external effects were of such small significance that it did not pay for anyone to take them into account. There did not exist anything resembling private ownership in land. And in the *Jesuit Relations*, particularly Le Jeune's record of the winter he spent with the Montagnes in 1633-34 and in the brief account given by Father Druilletes in 1647-48, Leacock

3. Eleanor Leacock, American Anthropologist (American Anthropological Asso.), Vol. 56, No. 5, Part 2, Memoir No. 78.
4. Cf., Frank G. Speck, The Basis of American Indian Ownership of Land, Old Penn Weekly Rev. (Univ. of Pennsylvania), Jan. 16, 1915, pp. 491-495.

finds no evidence of private land holdings. Both accounts indicate a socioeconomic organization in which private rights to land are not well developed.

We may safely surmise that the advent of the fur trade had two immediate consequences. First, the value of furs to the Indians was increased considerably. Second, and as a result, the scale of hunting activity rose sharply. Both consequences must have increased considerably the importance of the externalities associated with free hunting. The property right system began to change, and it changed specifically in the direction required to take account of the economic effects made important by the fur trade. The geographical or distributional evidence collected by Leacock indicates an unmistakable correlation between early centers of fur trade and the oldest and most complete development of the private hunting territory. . . .

The principle that associates property right changes with the emergence of new and reevaluation of old harmful and beneficial effects suggests in this instance that the fur trade made it economic to encourage the husbanding of fur-bearing animals. Husbanding requires the ability to prevent poaching and this, in turn, suggests that socioeconomic changes in property in hunting land will take place. The chain of reasoning is consistent with the evidence cited above. Is it inconsistent with the absence of similar rights in property among the southwestern Indians?

Two factors suggest that the thesis is consistent with the absence of similar rights among the Indians of the southwestern plains. The first of these is that there were no plains animals of commercial importance comparable to the fur-bearing animals of the forest, at least not until cattle arrived with Europeans. The second factor is that animals of the plains are primarily grazing species whose habit is to wander over wide tracts of land. The value of establishing boundaries to private hunting territories is thus reduced by the relatively high cost of preventing the animals from moving to adjacent parcels. Hence both the value and cost of establishing private hunting lands in the Southwest are such that we would expect little development along these lines. The externality was just not worth taking into account.

The lands of the Labrador Peninsula shelter forest animals whose habits are considerably different from those of the plains. Forest animals confine their territories to relatively small areas, so that the cost of internalizing the effects of husbanding these animals is considerably reduced. This reduced cost, together with the higher commercial value of fur-bearing forest animals, made it productive to establish private hunting lands. Frank G. Speck finds that family proprietorship among the Indians of the Peninsula included retaliation against trespass. Animal resources were husbanded. Sometimes conservation practices were carried on extensively. Family hunting territories were divided into quarters. Each year the family hunted in a different quarter in rotation, leaving a tract in the center as a sort of bank, not to be hunted over unless forced to do so by a shortage in the regular tract. . . .

The Coalescence and Ownership of Property Rights

I have argued that property rights arise when it becomes economic for those affected by externalities to internalize benefits and costs. But I have not yet examined the forces which will govern the particular form of right ownership. Several idealized forms of ownership must be distinguished at the outset. These are communal ownership, private ownership, and state ownership.

By communal ownership, I shall mean a right which can be exercised by all members of the community. Frequently the rights to till and to hunt the land have been communally owned. The right to walk a city sidewalk is communally owned. Communal ownership means that the community denies to the state or to individual citizens the right to interfere with any person's exercise of communally-owned rights. Private ownership implies that the community recognizes the right of the owner to exclude others from exercising the owner's private rights. State ownership implies that the state may exclude anyone from the use of a right as long as the state follows accepted political procedures for determining who may not use state-owned property. I shall not examine in detail the alternative of state ownership. The object of the analysis which follows is to discern some broad principles governing the development of property rights in communities oriented to private property.

It will be best to begin by considering a particularly useful example that focuses our attention on the problem of land ownership. Suppose that land is communally owned. Every person has the right to hunt, till, or mine the land. This form of ownership fails to concentrate the cost associated with any person's exercise of his communal right on that person. If a person seeks to maximize the value of his communal rights, he will tend to overhunt and overwork the land because some of the costs of his doing so are borne by others. The stock of game and the richness of the soil will be diminished too quickly. It is conceivable that those who own these rights, i.e., every member of the community, can agree to curtail the rate at which they work the lands if negotiating and policing costs are zero. Each can agree to abridge his rights. It is obvious that the costs of reaching such an agreement will not be zero. What is not obvious is just how large these costs may be.

Negotiating costs will be large because it is difficult for many persons to reach a mutually satisfactory agreement, especially when each hold-out has the right to work the land as fast as he pleases. But, even if an agreement among all can be reached, we must yet take account of the costs of policing the agreement, and these may be large, also. After such an agreement is reached, no one will privately own the right to work the land; all can work the land but at an agreed upon shorter workweek. Negotiating costs are increased even further because it is not possible under this system to bring the full expected benefits and expected costs of future generations to bear on current users.

If a single person owns land, he will attempt to maximize its present value by taking into account alternative future time streams of benefits and costs and selecting that one which he believes will maximize the present value of his privately-owned land rights. We all know that this means that he will attempt to take into account the supply and demand conditions that he thinks will exist after his death. It is very difficult to see how the existing communal owners can reach an agreement that takes account of these costs.

In effect, an owner of a private right to use land acts as a broker whose wealth depends on how well he takes into account the competing claims of the present and the future. But with communal rights there is no broker, and the claims of the present generation will be given an uneconomically large weight in determining the intensity with which the land is worked. Future generations might desire to pay present generations enough to change the present intensity of land usage. But they have no living agent to place their claims on the market. Under a communal property system, should a living person pay others to reduce the rate at which they work the land, he would not gain anything of value for his efforts. Communal property means that future generations must speak for themselves. No one has yet estimated the costs of carrying on such a conversation.

The land ownership example confronts us immediately with a great disadvantage of communal property. The effects of a person's activities on his neighbors and on subsequent generations will not be taken into account fully. Communal property results in great externalities. The full costs of the activities of an owner of a communal property right are not borne directly by him, nor can they be called to his attention easily by the willingness of others to pay him an appropriate sum. Communal property rules out a "pay-to-use-the-property" system and high negotiation and policing costs make ineffective a "pay-him-not-to-use-the-property" system.

The state, the courts, or the leaders of the community could attempt to internalize the external costs resulting from communal property by allowing private parcels owned by small groups of person with similar interests. The logical groups in terms of similar interests, are, of course, the family and the individual. Continuing with our use of the land ownership example, let us initially distribute private titles to land randomly among existing individuals and, further, let the extent of land included in each title be randomly determined.

The resulting private ownership of land will internalize many of the external costs associated with communal ownership, for now an owner, by virtue of his power to exclude others, can generally count on realizing the rewards associated with husbanding the game and increasing the fertility of his land. This concentration of benefits and costs on owners creates incentives to utilize resources more efficiently.

But we have yet to contend with externalities. Under the communal property system the maximization of the value of communal property rights will take place without regard to many costs, because the owner of a communal right cannot exclude others from enjoying the fruits of his efforts and because negotiation costs are too high for all to agree jointly on optimal behavior. The development of private rights permits the owner to economize on the use of those resources from which he has the right to exclude others. Much internalization is accomplished in this way. But the owner of private rights to one parcel does not himself own the rights to the parcel of another private sector. Since he cannot exclude others from their private rights to land, he has no direct incentive (in the absence of negotiations) to economize in the use of his land in a way that takes into account the effects he produces on the land rights of others. If he constructs a dam on his land, he has no direct incentive to take into account the lower water levels produced on his neighbor's land.

This is exactly the same kind of externality that we encountered with communal property rights, but it is present to a lesser degree. Whereas no one had an incentive to store water on any land under the communal system, private owners now can take into account directly those benefits and costs to their land that accompany water storage. But the effects on the land of others will not be taken into account directly.

The partial concentration of benefits and costs that accompany private ownership is only part of the advantage this system offers. The other part, and perhaps the most important, has escaped our notice. The cost of negotiating over the remaining externalities will be reduced greatly. Communal property rights allow anyone to use the land. Under this system it becomes necessary for all to reach an agreement on land use. But the externalities that accompany private ownership of property do not affect all owners, and, generally speaking, it will be necessary for only a few to reach an agreement that takes these effects into account. The cost of negotiating an internalization of these effects is thereby reduced considerably. The point is important enough to elucidate.

Suppose an owner of a communal land right, in the process of plowing a parcel of land, observes a second communal owner constructing a dam on adjacent land. The farmer prefers to have the stream as it is, and so he asks the engineer to stop his construction. The engineer says, "Pay me to stop." The farmer replies, "I will be happy to pay you, but what can you guarantee in return?" The engineer answers, "I can guarantee you that I will not continue constructing the dam, but I cannot guarantee that another engineer will not take up the task because this is communal property; I have no right to exclude him." What would be a simple negotiation between two persons under a private property arrangement turns out to be a rather complex negotiation between the farmer and everyone else. This is the basic explanation, I believe, for the preponderance of single rather than multiple owners of property. Indeed, an increase in the number of owners is an increase in the communality of property and leads, generally, to an increase in the cost of internalizing.

The reduction in negotiating cost that accompanies the private right to exclude others allows most externalities to be internalized at rather low cost. Those that are not are associated with activities that generate external effects impinging upon many people. The soot from smoke affects many homeowners, none of whom is willing to pay enough to the factory to get its owner to reduce smoke output. All homeowners together might be willing to pay enough, but the cost of their getting together may be enough to discourage effective market bargaining. The negotiating problem is compounded even more if the smoke comes not from a single smoke stack but from an industrial district. In such cases, it may be too costly to internalize effects through the marketplace.

Returning to our land ownership paradigm, we recall that land was distributed in randomly sized parcels to randomly selected owners. These owners now negotiate among themselves to internalize any remaining externalities. Two market options are open to the negotiators. The first is simply to try to reach a contractual agreement among owners that directly deals with the external effects at issue. The second option is for some owners to buy out others, thus changing the parcel size owned. Which option is selected will depend on which is cheaper. We have here a standard economic problem of optimal scale. If there exist constant returns to scale in the ownership of different sized parcels, it will be largely a matter of indifference between outright purchase and contractual agreement if only a single, easy-to-police, contractual agreement will internalize the externality. But, if there are several externalities, so that several such contracts will need to be negotiated, or if the contractual agreements should be difficult to police, then outright purchase will be the preferred course of action.

The greater are diseconomies of scale to land ownership the more will contractual arrangement be used by the interacting neighbors to settle these differences. Negotiating and policing costs will be compared to costs that depend on the scale of ownership, and parcels of land will tend to be owned in sizes which minimize the sum of these costs.[8]

NOTES AND QUESTIONS ON DEMSETZ'S THEORY OF PROPERTY RIGHTS

1. When Demsetz speaks of communal ownership, does he mean open-access property or property controlled by a limited group? If, as Demsetz asserts, "communal property results in great externalities," why do nations with private property systems allocate a significant fraction of their lands to streets, sidewalks, parks, and other open-access areas? See supra p.147, Note 5.

2. In sharp contrast to Hardin's pessimism, Demsetz predicts that efficient property rights tend to "emerge" after technological shocks or other events have created new cost-saving opportunities. Similarly optimistic is Terry L. Anderson & P.J. Hill, The Evolution of Property Rights: A Study of the American West, 18 J.L. & Econ. 163 (1975), cited supra p.45, Note 3.

Gary Libecap is less sanguine. He argues that the likelihood of property rights evolving adaptively is positively associated with:

    a.   the magnitude of the aggregate gains the institutional reform could be expected to engender;

    b.   the smallness of the number of parties involved;

    c.   the homogeneity of the parties;

    d.   the quality of shared information about the incidence of gains and losses; and

    e.   the extent of deconcentration of wealth both before and after the institutional reform.

8. Compare this with the similar rationale given by R. H. Coase to explain the firm in The Nature of the Firm, Economica, New Series, 1937, pp. 386-405.

See Gary D. Libecap, Contracting for Property Rights 19-28 (1989). Apply these criteria to: the Labrador tribe that serves as Demsetz's chief example; Acheson's lobstermen; settlers on the American frontier; the world population (whose growth is Hardin's central concern).

Libecap's caution stems in part from his involvement in a study of whether parties sharing a common pool of oil succeed in contracting to prevent its premature exploitation. To oversimplify the results, the study found that contractual solutions were reached only when there were four or fewer parties. See Gary D. Libecap & Steven N. Wiggins, Contractual Responses to the Common Pool, 74 Am. Econ. Rev. 87 (1984).

3. "We all know that [if a single person owns land] he will attempt to take into account the supply and demand conditions that he thinks will exist after his death." Demsetz, at p.154. Is it indeed a virtue of the institution of private property that it prompts mortal owners to consider the welfare of future generations? This issue receives fuller treatment infra p.367, Note 5.

4. This selection concludes with Demsetz's assertion that parcels of land tend to be efficiently sized. Is his reasoning persuasive? Given your answer, should a city employ zoning ordinances to set minimum sizes for lots? Should a city invoke the power of eminent domain to assemble large land parcels for redevelopment?

Property in Land*

Robert C. Ellickson

I. The Case for Individual Ownership of Land . . .

A. Three Simple Land Regimes

. . . Suppose that a close-knit group of 25 adults, identified by letters *A* through *Y*, were to control the land within the perimeter of the large square pictured in Figures 1 and 2. Suppose further that this group had to choose to govern this territory either as open-access property, group property, or individual property—regimes that it could establish either by formal rule or informal practice. Recall that under the first of these three alternatives, the open-access

*Source: 102 Yale L.J. 1315, 1322-1335, 1341-1344 (1993).

regime, anyone at all, including persons other than $A \ldots Y$, would be completely privileged to enter and use the land within the perimeter. Both theory and practice suggest that this regime would likely be beset by tragedy.

Under the second alternative, group ownership, the 25 members would jointly own both privileges to use the land within the perimeter and rights to exclude all others from it. The 25 would manage the land collectively by means of some relatively democratic governance system. Figure 1, in which there are no internal division lines within the perimeter, illustrates group ownership by $A \ldots Y$.

To create the third regime, individual ownership, $A \ldots Y$ would subdivide all of the land within the square into 25 parcels, one of which would be assigned to each member. Figure 2 shows one of the many possible divisions they might create. In this instance, all land within the perimeter of the square has been subdivided into 25 rectangles of unequal area, and each rectangle has been allotted to the individual owner indicated in its upper left corner. At this point in the inquiry, an individual owner of a parcel can be regarded as having unfettered privileges of use as well as absolute rights to exclude.

A person's action (or inaction) may affect the physical condition of land. To highlight the significance of differences in the spatial consequences of actions, both Figures 1 and 2 include identical sets of concentric circles drawn around a common center at which a human action is hypothesized to occur. These circles deserve highly sophisticated adjectives. The innermost circle illustrates the minor land area that is substantially affected by a *small event,* such as the cultivation of a tomato plant. The intermediate region circumscribes the territory substantially affected by a *medium event,* such as the building of a small dam to create a pond in a stream. Lastly, the outside circle delimits the domain substantially affected by a *large event,* such as a fire that emits choking fumes over a wide-ranging area.

Before these Figures can be employed to elucidate the relative efficiency of alternative land regimes, the potentially ambiguous term *efficiency* must be clarified. The rational-actor model assumes that an individual calculatingly pursues his self-interest. This implies that a member of a social group will be tempted at times to undertake a land activity that is individually rewarding but socially wasteful. Whatever the land regime, an individual's self-interested, opportunistic act will create a *deadweight loss* whenever the costs it inflicts on others exceed the individual's benefits from the act. When

Figure 1.
Group Ownership.

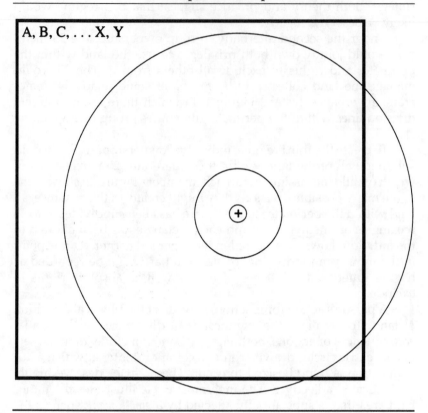

A, B, C, . . . X, Y

land is group-owned, each group member may be tempted to grab too many of the parcel's assets, to pollute the property with wastes, and to shirk from useful work that would enhance the land's value. Conversely, when land is individually owned, a self-interested owner may be tempted to use it without regard to the costs and benefits conferred on neighbors or others. Individuals may be able to reduce deadweight losses by (1) enforcing existing property rights; (2) transferring property rights to better managers; or (3) redefining property rights so as to create better-tailored incentives for appropriate economic activity. Each of these responses, however, would give rise to *transaction costs*. Different land regimes therefore involve different combinations of transaction costs and deadweight

Figure 2.
Individual Ownership.

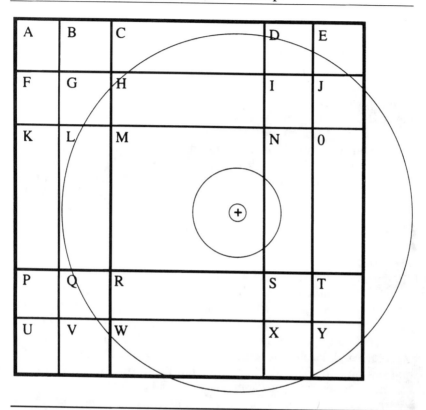

losses. A change in land rules is *efficient* when it reduces the sum of these two sorts of costs.

B. *Small Events: The Relative Ease of Monitoring Boundaries*

1. THE GENIUS OF INDIVIDUAL LAND OWNERSHIP

In his classic work, Demsetz showed that individual ownership of land completely internalizes to owners the effects of what this article calls small events. In essence, the parcelization of land is a relatively low-transaction-cost method of inducing people to "do the right thing" with the earth's surface, the vernacular for avoiding deadweight losses. Compared to group ownership, not to mention an open-access regime, private property tends best to equate the personal product of an individual's small actions with the social product of those actions.

Suppose, for example, that the small event pictured by the innermost circle in Figures 1 and 2 was to be the cultivation of a garden of tomato plants. Under the group ownership regime portrayed in Figure 1, the 25 co-owners would be forced to use their internal governance mechanisms to prevent deadweight losses in the growing and harvesting of the tomatoes. They might succeed in doing this, but only by incurring the transaction costs of monitoring potential shirkers and grabbers within the group's membership.

For three basic reasons, monitoring tends to be cheaper under the individual ownership regime illustrated in Figure 2. First, self-control by one person (in this instance, owner M) by means of his own central nervous system is much simpler than the multiperson coordination entailed in intragroup monitoring. When land uses have no spillover effects, individual ownership directly and precisely punishes land misuse and rewards productive labor.

Second, individual ownership not only greatly reduces the number of instances in which people have to be watched, but it also makes that task simpler when it must be performed. Demsetz incautiously implied that an individual landowner is entirely free of the burden of monitoring others' behavior within the borders of his parcel. Not so. A landowner must still be on the lookout for wasteful grabbing by trespassers who enter land without authorization. *A key advantage of individual land ownership is that detecting the presence of a trespasser is much less demanding than evaluating the conduct of a person who is privileged to be where he is.* Monitoring boundary crossings is easier than monitoring the behavior of persons situated inside boundaries. For this reason, managers are paid more than night watchmen. To illustrate, suppose that the 25 owners in Figure 1 wanted to deter a deviant member from stealing tomatoes from one of their common gardens. Because each member would have the privilege of entering all gardens, the group might have to assign overseers to scrutinize the minute-to-minute behavior of all persons present in cropgrowing areas to guard against pilferage.[41] If the tomato garden were individually owned, by contrast, the sole owner would merely need to watch for an unauthorized entry. Upon seeing a trespasser cross a physically marked boundary, the owner in the

---

41. The hypothetical is realistic. The stealing of sheaves of grain from fields was a common problem in open-field villages. See Warren O. Ault, Open-Field Farming in Medieval England: A Study of Village By-Laws 34-38 (1972).

usual case could expel him without having to marshal evidence of misconduct beyond the unauthorized entry itself.

Third, Demsetz has recently pointed out that an individual landowner is much more highly motivated than a group member to police boundaries or to carry out any other sort of monitoring function. A sole owner bears the entirety of any loss stemming from his slack oversight, whereas a group member bears only a fraction. The institution of private land ownership thus not only simplifies monitoring tasks, but also tends to ensure that those tasks are in the hands of conscientious agents.

2. TECHNOLOGIES FOR MARKING, DEFENDING, AND PROVING BOUNDARIES

Because private property in land necessitates the policing of boundaries, advances in surveying and fencing techniques may enhance the comparative efficiency of the institution. Preliterate societies developed many simple technologies that a landowner could use to detect and deter trespassers. During Hammurabi's reign around 1750 B.C., pegs were used to mark borders. Cairns, dikes, and stone walls are even more graphic and immovable. In social environments in which neighbors are inclined to cooperate, physically marked boundaries, if uncontroversially placed, are largely self-enforcing. A four-year old can understand the convention that one does not cross a marked boundary. By contrast, the internal work rules that govern behavior within group-owned land are not nearly as plain to observers.

For millennia, absentee owners have employed simple technologies such as hedges, moats, and impregnable fencing to keep out persons and animals that do not respect boundaries. In addition, domesticated dogs, especially ones that instinctively bark at or attack strangers, are superb boundary defenders. By contrast, dogs are quite useless in enforcing a group's internal rules of conduct. Can a dog be trained to bark when a familiar person has shirked or pilfered? A modern-day landowner intent on detecting boundary violations can resort, in lieu of a dog, to an inexpensive electronic motion detector. "Shirking detectors"—devices that would sound an alarm when a worker was simply going through the motions—have yet to be invented.

In sum, a shift from group to individual ownership of land substitutes the relatively cheap systems of self-control and boundary monitoring for the relatively costly system of pervasive intragroup monitoring. In contexts where the satisfaction of basic human needs entails the coordination of many small events—such as the planting and harvesting of crops, caring for children and animals, and maintaining dwellings and other structures—the parcelization of land is a major institutional achievement.

Individual ownership does, however, generate some new transaction costs, mainly those arising from the proliferation of boundaries and ownership entities. The boundaries in the parcelized regime in Figure 2 are three times the length of the boundaries in the group-ownership regime in Figure 1. Disputes may arise over both the location of these boundaries and the identities of parcel owners. Because land boundaries are human artifacts, a group must develop rules concerning adequate means of delineating parcels and proving ownership. Partly to reduce outlays for erecting indestructible boundary monuments, ancient groups that had developed written languages strove to establish authoritative off-site records of boundaries and owners. Some of the earliest surviving human texts, the Mesopotamian kudurrus dating from c. 2500 B.C., record private land transfers on stone stelae about two feet high; these stones eventually came to be kept in temples. A Sumerian proverb refers to a "Registrar of Deeds." In Egypt, the vizier was keeping comprehensive land records by 2350 B.C., and by 650 B.C. an Egyptian staff of "land-measurers" was working under an "overseer of farmlands." Four thousand years after the Mesopotamian experience, the Puritans, with land becoming scarce in Massachusetts, began a major effort to improve the quality of land registries.

The efficiency thesis predicts that innovations in technologies for marking, defending, and proving boundaries lead to more parcelization because they reduce the transaction costs of private property regimes. According to this view, for example, Glidden's invention of barbed wire in 1874 should have stimulated more subdivision of rangeland in the American West. And this indeed appears to have occurred. In Shasta County, California, innovations in fencing and irrigation enhanced the cost-effectiveness of fenced pasture and spurred the parcelization of unfenced ranges on which cattlemen had previously run herds at-large. Conversely, the viability of group ownership might be enhanced by the advent of inexpensive video cameras or other technologies for monitoring behavior within a group setting.

C. Medium Events: A Simple Way
to Promote Cooperative Relations

Demsetz' second major argument for private property in land rested on the social dynamics of medium events. Suppose, as Demsetz himself did, that the intermediate circle in Figures 1 and 2 were to demarcate the expected territorial effects of the proposed construction of a small dam. The parcelization of group land, Demsetz pointed out, would greatly reduce the number of persons concerned with this event. In the democratic group-ownership situation portrayed in Figure 1, all 25 co-owners would have to become knowledgeable about the proposed dam in order to help decide whether it was a cost-justified project. In the parcelized regime of Figure 2, by contrast, only the two substantially affected landowners, M and N, would have to be involved in the externality adjustment process. Embracing the consensus position that transaction costs tend to increase with the number of individuals involved, Demsetz saw land parcelization as having the virtue of increasing small-number situations. Picking up on this assertion, Michelman rightly stated that practitioners of transaction-cost economics stress avoidance of "excessive dependence of coordination on large-number transactions."[57]

When medium events are at issue, parcelization has two additional advantages that Demsetz did not mention. First, besides reducing the number of persons who must coordinate, parcelization is a low-transaction-cost device for knitting these individuals closely together, thereby inclining them toward cooperative behavior. In most societies, land ownership changes slowly. Two adjoining landowners therefore usually enjoy a continuing multiplex relationship—the sort that is most likely to engender cooperation. To be sure, a democratic commune of twenty-five members might be so close-knit that the average twosome of its members, chosen at random, would be even more intimate than two adjoining individual landowners. To achieve that degree of close-knittedness, however, the group might have to convene regular evening meetings of the entire membership. By contrast, two abutting landowners in a parcelized regime may be able to maintain amicable relations with only an occasional exchange of pleasantries across their common fence. The *sum* of transaction costs and deadweight losses arising out of medium events is therefore likely to be lower when land is individually owned.

Parcelization also relegates the settlement of disputes arising out of medium events to those persons most likely to be informed about the matter in controversy. A sole owner of a land parcel is apt to have better knowledge of its immediate environment than virtually anyone else does. For example, if a dam were proposed for a site on parcel M in Figure 2, M and N, the owners of the only two

---

57. [Frank I. Michelman, Ethics, Economics, and the Law of Property, in NOMOS xxiv, Ethics, Economics and the Law 3, 20 (J. Roland Pennock & John W. Chapman eds. 1982).]

parcels substantially affected, probably could appraise the total costs and benefits of the dam better than could a random pair of members in the *A . . . Y* group.

In short, for activities that result in mostly small and medium events, individual ownership is better than both open-access and group ownership for minimizing the sum of deadweight losses and transaction costs. According to the efficiency thesis, this insight explains why family farming is ubiquitous, why collectivized agriculture almost always fails, and why virtually no dwelling units are shared by groups as large as 25. Indeed, the historical record supports the following private-property thesis: *a close-knit group virtually always entitles its members to own, as private property, lands used for dwellings, crops, and other intensive activities.*

II. The Advantages of Group Ownership of Land

The discussion up to this point has given short shrift to the merits of group (and other forms of public) ownership of land. Staying entirely within Demsetz's general framework, one can enrich his analysis by explicitly incorporating the possibilities of increasing returns to scale and the desirability of spreading risks. . . .

A. When Returns Increase with Parcel Size

Bigger land parcels are sometimes better. As tracts increase in area, the costs of fencing and other forms of perimeter monitoring drop per acre enclosed. This mathematical relationship has prompted many traditional societies to graze livestock on expansive group-owned pastures. A large territory also permits a landowner to use more specialized equipment and workers and to marshal gangs of workers for projects for which returns to scale exist. . . .

When Demsetz posed an example that involved a large event, he rightly qualified his enthusiasm for land parcelization. For example, if the large event pictured in Figure 2 were to be a smoky fire on parcel M, the transaction costs of large-number coordinations might prevent the many affected parcel owners from cooperating to resolve the dispute through some external institution. By contrast, if the governing body of the group portrayed in Figure 1 already had controls in place to monitor internal small and medium events, it might be able to respond to this large event much more expeditiously than the diffuse group of individual neighbors could. When a group's system of internal social control is itself characterized by increasing returns to scale, the identity of the land regime that best minimizes costs depends in part on what sorts of events—small, medium, or large—carry the highest stakes for group welfare.

The case for private ownership of farms and homesteads rests on the plausible assumption that vital agricultural, construction, homemaking, and child-rearing activities entail mostly small and medium events.[73] For the reasons just suggested, however, industrial activities that cause local air pollution might be better placed on large tracts which, because of the investment required, are likely to be group-owned. Group ownership does not necessarily imply government ownership, of course. The sorry environmental records of federal land agencies and Communist regimes are a sharp reminder that governments are often particularly inept managers of large tracts. Large events are inherently difficult to regulate. Identifying the institutions that govern them best—or, more bluntly, least badly—should be an exercise in experience, not logic. This points up the value of history. Under what circumstances, if any, have pioneers establishing land regimes from scratch chosen to own land collectively?

B. Three Pioneer Settlements

Three of the most famous remote habitations in U.S. history were the Jamestown settlement of 1607, the Plymouth settlement of 1620, and the Mormon settlement at Salt Lake in 1847. [Discussion omitted.]

Although these three pioneer settlements differed, their land histories are remarkably similar. In each case the settlers started with group ownership of land, but after a period began parcelling out plots to individuals and households, a move that improved agricultural productivity. These events support the private-property thesis, but are unlikely to surprise anyone familiar with the history of collectivized agriculture. It is more intriguing to ask why the settlers declined to establish private property in croplands from the start. The prior section suggested one possibility. The pioneers at the three settlements may have started off with group-owned land in order to exploit returns to territorial scale presented by initial public

---

73. Marx and Engels tragically exaggerated the efficiencies of scale that are present in agriculture. See [Frederic L.] Pryor, [The Red and the Green 34-35, 372-373 (1992)]. . . . In 1987 in Cuba, an extreme case, the average state farm employed 1448 workers on 14,084 hectares (roughly 35,000 acres). [Id.] at 144 (table showing sizes of collective and state farms in Marxist regimes). By contrast, family farms still dominate American agriculture. In 1987, non-family-held corporations with eleven or more shareholders accounted for only 1.8% of the value of farm products sold in the United States. See Bureau of the Census, Statistical Abstract of the United States 647 (1991).

works such as defensive palisades and, at Salt Lake, irrigation facilities. There is evidence, however, that high risks, not scale economies, were the main impetus for the initial collectivization of land at these outposts.

C. Group Ownership as a Risk-Spreading Device

A sole landowner bears the entire risk that his land will be damaged, devalued, or unproductive. Group ownership, by contrast, pools risk. Because most individuals are risk-averse, the risk-spreading feature of group property is advantageous—even decisive in certain situations.

As alternatives to group ownership of property, a group may employ numerous other risk-spreading mechanisms, including reciprocal altruism within a family or social group, insurance markets, and government welfare programs. In comparison, group ownership of land is in most contexts a mediocre method of spreading losses. It concentrates group investments in a single, highly undiversified, asset. Moreover, for reasons presented in Part I, intensive uses are usually less efficiently conducted on group land than on private land, a fact that makes group land ownership a comparatively costly insurance vehicle.

The efficiency thesis predicts that group land ownership will be more prevalent in situations in which risks are high and a group cannot employ a superior insurance mechanism. The settlers of the three pioneer communities initially faced conditions of precisely this sort. That the risks were acute cannot be doubted. All three pioneer settlements were remote outposts, located weeks or months away from civilization. The first parties of settlers faced lethal dangers, including raids by Indians, infections from exotic diseases, and difficulties in learning how to farm in their strange environments. Remoteness precluded risk-spreading through multigenerational kinship networks, insurance markets, or government welfare programs. The settlers could spread risks only among themselves, and one option was to have a collective economy that guaranteed each member some share of total group output.

Risk analysis also suggests why the pioneers would begin to parcelize their lands after a period of time. Settlers would lower their probability estimates of disaster and be less attentive to risk-spreading as they gradually learned how to prevent tribal raids, avoid disease, and grow crops. Moreover, as the months passed, the settlers could develop more efficient social-insurance mechanisms, such as informal mutual-aid relationships, tithe-supported churches, and tax-supported governments. In sum, after a few years, the risk-spreading benefits of group land ownership would no longer outweigh its familiar shortcomings, such as the shirking that notably afflicted Jamestown and Plymouth. At that point, the settlers understandably would switch to private land tenure, the system that most cheaply induces individuals to accomplish small and medium events that are socially useful.

Jamestown's history provides particular support for the proposition that high levels of risk promote group ownership. Fatalities from disease, famine, and Indian raids were higher at Jamestown than at the other [two] settlements. Historians have engaged in a spirited debate about why the Jamestown settlers bowled in the streets as they starved. . . . [S]eventeenth-century observers tended to stress the system of property rights in early Jamestown. At first, most land was held collectively, and each resident was fed no matter how much he worked. Later, when the colony began systematically to parcelize its lands, the reports of idleness ceased. Edmund S. Morgan, an eminent colonial historian, nevertheless has been reluctant to attribute much of Jamestown's work problem to its collectivized economy. Instead, Morgan has argued that the Jamestown settlers were handicapped by a culture of idleness that afflicted Englishmen of their background.[123]

By historical fluke, there is convincing evidence that the settlers' ideas and attitudes about work were not the problem at Jamestown. In 1609, the flagship of a Virginia Company fleet heading for Jamestown encountered rough weather and landed in Bermuda instead. Bermuda proved to be a much safer place. The island was uninhabited, and disease was far less prevalent than at Jamestown. Bermuda's first settlers had early success in growing corn. In 1612, the Virginia Company sent another 50 colonists to make the settlement permanent. In 1615, the Bermuda settlers began a process of meting out twenty-five acre plots to each member; by comparison, the Jamestown colony had endured for seven years before it officially doled out three-acre plots. Contrary to what Morgan's thesis would predict, idleness was not a problem on Bermuda, where settlers were building substantial houses at a time when the Virginians were still dwelling in "little better than shanties."[127]

Risk analysis provides a simple explanation of why events unfolded differently at Jamestown and Bermuda. In the high-risk environment at Jamestown, settlers persevered with a collectivist economy that included group land ownership partly because that institution served to spread an individual's risk of becoming incapacitated. In Bermuda, a low-risk environment, the settlers moved

123. [Edmund S. Morgan, The Labor Problem at Jamestown, 1607-18, 76 Am. Hist. Rev. 595, 611 (1971).]

127. [Virginia Bernhard, Bermuda and Virginia in the Seventeenth Century: A Comparative View, 19 J. Soc. Hist. 57, 60 (1985).]

more promptly to the risk-concentrating regime of individual land ownership, which generated pronounced productivity gains (as a similar move eventually did at Jamestown). In short, the unusually deadly environment at Jamestown not only decimated the labor force, but also helped perpetuate institutions that spread risks but put less food on the table.

NOTES AND QUESTIONS ON LAND REGIMES

1. According this selection, an *efficient* rule is one that minimizes the sum of (a) transaction costs, and (b) deadweight losses stemming from externalities. Is this simply a version of the Kaldor-Hicks test, described supra p.54, Note 2? Would Demsetz concur in this usage?

2. Ellickson shares Demsetz's optimism about the evolution of property institutions, but only where social groups are close-knit. In light of Libecap's criteria, supra p.157, Note 2, how might a close-knit group be defined?

3. Do dogs and fences warrant the attention this selection gives them? Is it indeed easier for land occupants to monitor boundary crossings by trespassers than the behavior of members who are privileged to use group lands? If communal farming is inherently inefficient, what explains the long survival of the kibbutzim of Israel and the communal Hutterite farms of the Great Plains? See Ellickson's discussion at pp. 1344-1362 of this article, and the sources cited therein. Are not most family farms communes of a sort? A valuable essay on the rise and fall of communal agriculture is Barry C. Field, The Evolution of Property Rights, 42 Kyklos 319 (1989).

4. While the selection asserts that the institution of private land ownership is apt to give rise to problems such as air pollution, it concludes that events of large territorial scope will bedevil a society whatever its mix of land regimes. Is this too pessimistic? On approaches to controlling air pollution, see Schelling infra p.532.

5. The selection highlights risk-spreading as one of the advantages of group ownership and contends that risk factors explain why land was owned communally in Jamestown longer than it was in Bermuda. What other differences between these two settlements might have been significant?

The Kwakiutl Indians of British Columbia were renowned for potlatching, a reciprocal exchange institution that required ostentatious gift-giving by those who had enjoyed particularly bountiful salmon harvests. According to one analyst, this system evolved because it enabled the tribe's subgroups to maintain exclusive property rights in salmon fisheries. Potlatching provided each subgroup with insurance against a poor salmon harvest and thereby reduced its likelihood of encroaching on another subgroup's fishing territory. See D. Bruce Johnsen, The Formation and Protection of Property Rights Among the Southern Kwakiutl Indians, 15 J. Legal Stud. 41 (1986). Is a system of this sort likely to wither in the face of growing insurance markets and government welfare programs?

6. Efficiencies of scale may be present in the use of resources other than land. Consider money: How might a dozen poor individuals coordinate with one another to periodically provide useful clumps of capital to each of the dozen? See Ivan Light, Ethnic Enterprise in America (1972); Timothy Besley, Stephen Coate & Glenn Loury, The Economics of Rotating Credit Associations, 83 Am. Econ. Rev. 792 (1993).

Chapter 3

The Significance
of Possession

The Economics of Rights, Cooperation
and Welfare*

Robert Sugden

5.1 Nine Points of the Law

When oil and gas reserves were discovered under the North Sea the
problem arose of who had the right to exploit them. The potential
claimants were nation states. Given the power of most nation states
to inflict harm on most others, it was important to find some way of
dividing up the reserves that would be generally acceptable. In effect, nations were involved in a variant of the division game, but
with many players instead of just two.

The solution reached was to allocate each portion of the sea bed
to the country whose coastline happened to be nearest. In terms of
any abstract theory of justice, this seems completely arbitrary. The
main beneficiaries from this arrangement were the United Kingdom
and Norway. West Germany, despite its large population and its
considerable length of North Sea coastline, came out badly. Why did
West Germany acquiesce in such an unfair partition? Why, for that
matter, should the share-out have been restricted to countries with
a North Sea coastline? The poor countries of Africa and Asia might
have used arguments of distributive justice to support claims to
North Sea oil. If it is replied that these countries lack the military

*Source: pp. 87-97 (1986) (from Chapter 5, "Possession").

172

power to support such claims, how much military power does Norway have? And the United States and the Soviet Union are overwhelmingly more powerful than any of the North Sea countries; yet they too got nothing.

One answer might be that this peculiar division of the sea bed was prescribed by international law. In 1958 an international conference in Geneva had drafted a convention which was to come into force when it had been ratified by 22 states; the 22nd state signed in 1964. According to this convention, each state has a right to exploit the continental shelf adjacent to its coastline. International boundaries on the continental shelf are to be fixed by agreement between the states concerned, but in case of dispute, median lines (i.e. lines equidistant from the coasts of two countries) are to be used. In fact, however, the agreement among the North Sea countries departed from this convention quite significantly. There is a deep trench between the Norwegian coast and the North Sea oilfields; according to the Geneva Convention these oilfields were all on the British continental shelf, even though in some cases the closest coastline was Norway's. In the event the North Sea countries opted for the simpler rule of ignoring the depth of the sea bed and allocating every portion of continental shelf to the country with the closest coastline. So the partition of the North Sea was not arrived at simply by applying existing international law. And in any case, we should need to explain why the Geneva Convention was agreed in the first place. The participants in the Geneva Conference were also playing a kind of division game: Why did the median line solution appeal to them?

Suppose, suggests Milton Friedman, that:

> you and three friends are walking along the street and you happen to spy and retrieve a $20 bill on the pavement. It would be generous of you, of course, if you were to divide it equally with them, or at least blow them to a drink. But suppose you do not. Would the other three be justified in joining forces and compelling you to share the $20 equally with them? I suspect most readers will be tempted to say no. (Friedman, 1962, p. 165)

This is another example of the division game, this time with four players. Friedman suggests that if his readers played the game they would recognize the rule of "finders keepers." Although we may tell our children that the right thing to do is to take the money to a police station, I feel sure Friedman is right: most people *would* recognize that the person who finds the $20 bill keeps it. At any rate, the finder's claim is far stronger than that of the friends who happen to be with him when he finds it.

Suppose you are driving your car and approaching a long bridge over a river. The bridge is only wide enough for one car. Another car is approaching the bridge from the other side. It reaches the bridge before you do and begins to cross. Do you stop and allow the other car to cross, or continue on in the expectation that the other driver will see you coming and reverse? My observation is that most drivers recognize a convention that the first car on the bridge has the right of way.

In each case, I suggest, a conflict is resolved by appeal to a convention. In each case the convention works by assigning each disputed object to the claimant with whom the object is already most closely associated — "associated" in some sense that is itself conventional. The first driver on the bridge has a special association with it — the relation of being the first claimant, or of being the person in possession. The person who first picks up the $20 bill has a similar relation to it. In the case of the North Sea, each portion of the sea bed is assigned to the nation whose land is closest to it.

In the rest of this chapter I shall argue that many of the property conventions that are used to resolve human conflicts work in this way: They exploit existing associations between claimants and objects. Such conventions inevitably tend to favour possessors, since to be in possession of something is to have a very obvious association with it. The maxim that possession is nine points of the law is more than a description of a feature of a particular legal system; it describes a pervasive tendency in human affairs. . . .

5.2   Asymmetries in the Structure of a Game . . .

. . .[S]uppose that at the start of every contest one individual is in possession of the disputed resource while the other is not. I shall call the first player the possessor and the second the challenger. This is an asymmetry of labelling. However, we might expect that in reality the asymmetry would go a little deeper than this, for two main reasons. First, we might expect an individual, on average, to value disputed resources more highly when he is the possessor than when he is the challenger, because at any time the things a person has in his possession are likely to be things he particularly values. (That is why he is carrying them around with him, keeping close watch on them, or whatever. And people develop habits of life around, and acquire skills to use, the things they have long possessed.) Second, we might expect that in the case of a fight, possession confers some advantage; thus an individual may be slightly more likely to win fights when he is the possessor than when he is the challenger. . . .

This line of argument supplies one reason why conventions favouring possessors might tend to be relatively successful in a world of natural selection. However, many other conventions have similar advantages. Take, for example, the convention that a disputed resource goes to the best fighter, or the convention that it goes to the person who needs it most. Either of these seems more directly connected with a relevant asymmetry than the convention favouring possessors. Wouldn't these conventions be more likely to establish themselves?

5.3   Prominence and Possession

If a convention is to develop it must first be recognized by people: Each person must come to see that there is some pattern in the behaviour of his fellows, and that it is in his interest to follow this pattern himself. In the early stages of the development of a convention, when only a small proportion of the population are following it, these patterns are likely to be hard to spot. People are more likely to find those patterns that — consciously or unconsciously — they are looking for. Thus a convention is more likely to develop if people have some prior expectation that it will.

This is not as circular as it sounds. Such prior expectations correspond with Schelling's concept of prominence. Despite the elusiveness of this concept, and the way it seems to lie beyond the reach of rational analysis, there can be no doubt that some solutions *are* more prominent than others.

Hume seems to have had in mind something like Schelling's notion of prominence when writing his Treatise on Human Nature — particularly the two penetrating passages entitled "Of the origin of justice and property" and "Of the rules, which determine property" (Hume, 1740, Book 3, Part 2, Sections 2-3). As I have pointed out before, Hume argued that rules of property are conventions that have evolved spontaneously — that have arisen, as he put it, gradually and acquired force by slow progression and by our repeated experience of the inconveniences of transgressing them. He tried to answer the question I am confronting: Why does one particular convention of property evolve rather than another? To answer this question, he wrote, we must look to "the imagination" rather than to "reason and public interest" (1740, Book 3, Part 2, Section 3).

Hume presents the following example of a division game:

> I first consider men in their savage and solitary condition; and suppose, that being sensible of the misery of that state, and foreseeing the advantages that wou'd result from society, they seek each other's company, and make an offer of mutual protection and assistance. I also suppose, that they are endow'd with such sagacity as immedi-

ately to perceive, that the chief impediment to this project of society and partnership lies in the avidity and selfishness of their natural temper; to remedy which, they enter into a convention for the stability of possession, and for mutual restraint and forbearance. I am sensible, that this method of proceeding is not altogether natural; but besides that I here only suppose those reflexions to be form'd at once, which in fact arise insensibly and by degrees; besides this, I say, 'tis very possible, that several persons, being by different accidents separated from the societies, to which they formerly belong'd, may be oblig'd to form a new society among themselves; in which case they are entirely in the situation above-mention'd.

'Tis evident, then, that their first difficulty, in this situation, after the general convention for the establishment of society, and for the constancy of possession, is, how to separate their possessions, and assign to each his particular portion, which he must for the future inalterably enjoy. This difficulty will not detain them long; but it must immediately occur, as the most natural expedient, that every one continues to enjoy what he is at present master of, and that property or constant possession be conjoin'd to the immediate possession. (1740, Book 3, Part 2, Section 3)

. . . Hume is claiming that the rule favouring possessors has a natural prominence; this leads people to converge on it as a solution in a game in which any agreement is better than none.

Why is this solution particularly prominent? Hume appeals to what he claims is a natural tendency of the human mind to seek out relations between objects:

'Tis a quality, which I have already observ'd in human nature, that when two objects appear in a close relation to each other, the mind is apt to ascribe to them any additional relation, in order to compleat the union. . . . Thus for instance, we never fail, in our arrangement of bodies, to place those which are *resembling* in *contiguity* to each other, or at least in *correspondent* points of view; because we feel a satisfaction in joining the relation of contiguity to that of resemblance, or the resemblance of situation to that of qualities . . . As property forms a relation betwixt a person and an object, 'tis natural to found it on some preceding relation; and as property is nothing but a constant possession, secur'd by the laws of society, 'tis natural to add it to the present possession, which is a relation that resembles it. (1740, Book 3, Part 2, Section 3)

I think there is an important truth here. If we are playing a game in which we have to agree on a way of assigning objects to persons, there *is* a natural prominence to solutions that base the assignment on some pre-existing relation between persons and objects. And the closer the resemblance between the pre-existing relation and the one to be determined in the game, the more prominent is the solution based on that relation.

If this sounds like a conservative rationalization of the law of

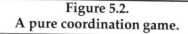

Figure 5.2.
A pure coordination game.

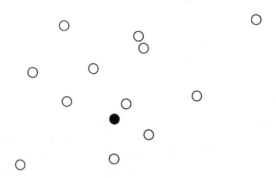

Join the black circle to one of the white circles. If you choose
the same circle as your partner, you win £10; otherwise,
you win nothing.

property, consider the following pure coordination game. . . . You
and a partner are separated and not allowed to communicate. Then
you are each shown the pattern of circles drawn in Figure 5.2. You
are told to draw a line joining the black circle to any one white circle.
If you both hit on the same white circle, you will each be given £10;
otherwise, you get nothing. Which circle would you choose? My
hunch is that most people would choose the white circle closest to
the black one. The reason, I think, is the one given by Hume. You are
asked to establish a relation between the black circle and a white
one (the relation of being linked by a line). It is natural to look for
some other relation, already there in the diagram, by which one and
only one white circle can be linked to the black one; the most prominent such relation, surely, is that of being closest. (I cannot *prove* that
this is the most prominent relation. Why not the relation of lying
directly below the black circle, or of being farthest away from it? I
can only say that closeness seems the most prominent relation to me,
and hope the reader has the same reaction.)

Prominence, as I argued in Section 3.3, is often dependent on
analogy. When people face new problems of the kind that are resolved by convention, they tend to look for prominent solutions by
drawing analogies with other situations in which conventions are
well established. Thus conventions can spread from one context to
another. The conventions that are best able to spread are those that

are most general (i.e. that can be applied in the greatest range of cases) and most fertile (i.e. most susceptible to extension by analogy). The idea that disputes are resolved in favour of possessors seems to be peculiarly fertile and general.

Conventions favouring possessors can be found everywhere. Perhaps the purest case is the principle, embodied in English law, that a right to a parcel of land or to a right of way can be established by a long period of undisputed occupation or use. However arbitrary this principle may be from any moral point of view, it seems to be generally recognized as a working convention, even in cases in which litigation is out of the question. Consider minor disputes between neighbours, between workmates, or between employers and employees. Think how much importance is attached to precedents, to "custom and practice." If your neighbour or workmate or employer starts doing something that annoys you, the time to complain is *straight away* — before a precedent is established. Why do precedents matter so much, if not because there is some convention that established practices are allowed to continue? And notice how very general this convention is — how many different kinds of disputes it can be used to resolve.

Closely analogous with conventions favouring possessors are conventions favouring first claimants — those people who first register, in a way that is itself defined by convention, their claims on disputed resources. Take the convention of the queue, or of "first come, first served." The principle here is that, of all the people who might dispute over something — perhaps the opportunity to use a public telephone, or to be served in a shop, or to get on a bus — the person who was there first has established the strongest claim. Or take the principle of "last in, first out" for determining who must go when someone in a factory or office has to be made redundant. Or take the convention, well established on planes and trains, that once a person has occupied a seat it is his for the rest of his journey, even if he leaves it temporarily.

The author Leo Walmsley has described a convention that was recognized on the Yorkshire coast up to the 1930s. After a storm, valuable driftwood could be washed up. The first person to go on to any stretch of the shore after high tide was allowed the pick of the driftwood; anything he collected into piles and marked with two stones was regarded as his, to carry away when he chose. This is an interesting mixture of two principles — the principle of first claims and the principle that property can be acquired by labour. When driftwood is washed up on the shore it belongs to no one, but by gathering it into piles a person makes it his.

This latter principle is formulated most famously by Locke,

who gives it the status of natural law — a moral law that is evident to the natural reason of man:

> Though the Water running in the Fountain be every ones, yet who can doubt, but that in the Pitcher is his only who drew it out? His *labour* hath taken it out of the hands of Nature, where it was common, and belong'd equally to all her Children, and *hath* thereby *appropriated* it to himself.
>
> Thus this Law of reason makes the Deer, that *Indian's* who hath killed it . . . And amongst those who are counted the Civiliz'd part of Mankind, who have made and multiplied positive Laws to determine Property, this original Law of Nature for the *beginning of Property,* in what was before common, still takes place; and by vertue thereof, what Fish any one catches in the Ocean, that great and still remaining Common of Mankind . . . is *by* the *Labour* that removes it out of that common state Nature left it in, *made* his *Property* who takes that pains about it. (1690, Second Treatise, Ch. 5)

Like Hume, I am not convinced that this principle of property can be discovered out of nothing, by reason alone. But Locke is surely right in saying that, in the absence of "positive laws," this principle *is* widely recognized as a way of resolving disputes. It is, I suggest, a convention that has evolved. . . .

Hume suggests another form of prominence that is related to possession:

> We acquire the property of objects by *accession,* when they are already connected in an intimate manner with objects that are already our property, and at the same time inferior to them. Thus the fruits of our garden, the offspring of our cattle, and the work of our slaves, are all of them esteem'd our property, even before possession. (1740, Book 3, Part 2, Section 3)

In other words, conventions may exploit two-step relations between persons and objects: If I am in possession of object X, and if there is some especially prominent relation between object X and some "inferior" object Y, then this may be enough to establish a prominent relation between me and Y. This idea may help to explain the attraction of the median-line solution to the problem of partitioning the North Sea. Among geographical features, the relation of closeness seems to have an inescapable prominence, and in this sense it is natural to associate each portion of the sea bed with the closest land mass, and thus with the nation that is in possession of that land.

An alternative explanation of the median-line solution is that it derived its prominence from the existence of long-standing conventions about fishing rights. It has long been recognized that each nation has the right to control fishing off its own coasts, although how far this right extends has often been a matter of dispute — as in the "cod wars" between Britain and Iceland. The median-line rule is a natural extension of this principle, and so this may be an example of the spread of conventions by analogy. But then why did the convention of coastal fishing rights become established? Hume's idea of accession may help to explain why this convention seems a natural solution to fishing disputes.

NOTES AND QUESTIONS ON CLAIMS DERIVED FROM PROXIMITY

1. Sugden talks as if an "association" between people and things is a matter of convention, but in discussing "prominence," does he implicitly assume some element of human nature to explain the conventions? If so, what is it? A territorial instinct? If so, how can the term "property" be extended to matters as abstract and intangible as a patent or a stock option? Toward the end of the selection, he notes the example of a person who collects a bundle of driftwood and marks it with stones. In what sense are the stones "prominent"? Does "prominence" have any unifying thread at all?

2. Sugden says that "first in time" is analogous to spatial proximity. What if anything is the analogy? Is physical likeness equally analogous to proximity? Consider, for example, the belief among some peoples that physical representations (photos, pictures, etc.) give power over the represented person (as exemplified in voodoo dolls), or the belief that naming gives power over the thing or person named. Does naming and magical representation represent a kind of property? Is allocation according to promixity (or "first in time") just our version of voodoo? On the subject of magic and property (perhaps the original voodoo economics), see Mark C. Suchman, Invention and Ritual: Notes on the Interrelation of Magic and Intellectual Property in Preliterate Societies, 89 Colum. L. Rev. 1264 (1989), describing intellectual property in magical skills.

3. Might proximity itself be a proxy for power or control over a given resource? For example, could the allocation of North Sea oil rights to nearby countries simply be a tacit recognition that those countries could sabotage anyone else's efforts to take these resources? Are those countries simply larger versions of the Monhegan lobster gangs described by Acheson, supra? If so, the ability to exert control is the chief element in the "association" of things with persons, and proximity is simply one factor in such control. Compare Yoram Barzel, supra, and Stefano Fenoaltea, Slavery and Supervision in Comparative Perspective, 44 J. Econ. History 635 (1984). These authors try to explain why slaves (who in theory owned noth-

ing) were quite frequently given formal or informal property rights in their labor; this was most likely when their work had to be done with care (with skilled carpentry, for instance), giving them a *de facto* ability to sabotage output.

4. Allocation of property rights on the basis of proximity seems rather arbitrary, but it is not necessarily unattractive on distributional grounds. For example, some proposals for protection of tropical rainforest resources would allocate property rights in the forest to local indigenous populations. See Lee Breckenridge, Protection of Biological and Cultural Diversity: Emerging Recognition of Local Community Rights in Ecosystems under International Environmental Law, 59 Tenn. L. Rev. 735 (1992). Similarly, a number of proposals for pharmaceutical uses of rainforest genetic materials would allocate to source-nations property shares in any products actually developed. See Roger A. Sedjo, Property Rights, Genetic Resources and Biotechnological Change, 35 J. Law & Econ. 198 (1992). How might these allocations of property rights, based on proximity, help to preserve rainforest resources?

5. What does "possession" mean? The next selection addresses this issue.

Possession as the Origin of Property *

Carol M. Rose

How do things come to be owned? This is a fundamental puzzle for anyone who thinks about property. One buys things from other owners, to be sure, but how did the other owners get those things? Any chain of ownership or title must have a first link. Someone had to do something to anchor that link. The law tells us what steps we must follow to obtain ownership of things, but we need a theory that tells us why these steps should do the job.

John Locke's view, once described as "the standard bourgeois theory,"[1] is probably the one most familiar to American students. Locke argued that an original owner is one who mixes his or her labor with a thing and, by commingling that labor with the thing, establishes ownership of it. This labor theory is appealing because it appears to rest on "desert," but it has some problems. First, without a prior theory of ownership, it is not self-evident that one owns even

*Source: 52 U. Chi. L. Rev. 73-88 (1985).
1. Richard Schlatter, Private Property: The History of an Idea 151 (1951).

the labor that is mixed with something else. Second, even if one does own the labor that one performs, the labor theory provides no guidance in determining the scope of the right that one establishes by mixing one's labor with something else. Robert Nozick illustrates this problem with a clever hypothetical. Suppose I pour a can of tomato juice into the ocean: Do I now own the seas?[5]

A number of thinkers more or less contemporary to Locke proposed another theory of the basis of ownership. According to this theory, the original owner got title through the consent of the rest of humanity (who were, taken together, the first recipients from God, the genuine original owner). Locke himself identified the problems with this theory; they involve what modern law-and-economics writers would call "administrative costs." How does everyone get together to consent to the division of things among individuals?

The common law has a third approach, which shares some characteristics with the labor and consent theories but is distinct enough to warrant a different label. For the common law, *possession* or "occupancy" is the origin of property. This notion runs through a number of fascinating old cases with which teachers of property law love to challenge their students. Such inquiries into the acquisition of title to wild animals and abandoned treasure may seem purely academic; how often, after all, do we expect to get into disputes about the ownership of wild pigs or long-buried pieces of eight? These cases are not entirely silly, though. People still do find treasure-laden vessels, and statesmen do have to consider whether someone's acts might support a claim to own the moon, for example, or the mineral nodes at the bottom of the sea. Moreover, analogies to the capture of wild animals show up time and again when courts have to deal on a nonstatutory basis with some "fugitive" resource that is being reduced to property for the first time, such as oil, gas, groundwater, or space on the spectrum of radio frequencies.

With these more serious claims in mind, then, I turn to the maxim of the common law: first possession is the root of title. Merely to state the proposition is to raise two critical questions: What counts as possession, and why is it the basis for a claim to title? In exploring the quaint old cases' answers to these questions, we hit on some fundamental views about the nature and purposes of a property regime.

Consider Pierson v. Post,[16] a classic wild-animal case from the early nineteenth century. Post was hunting a fox one day on an abandoned beach and almost had the beast in his gunsight when

5. . . . Anarchy, State and Utopia 175 (1974). . . .
16. 3 Cai. R. 175 (N.Y. Sup. Ct. 1805).

an interloper appeared, killed the fox, and ran off with the carcass. The indignant Post sued the interloper for the value of the fox on the theory that his pursuit of the fox had established his property right to it.

The court disagreed. It cited a long list of learned authorities to the effect that "occupancy" or "possession" went to the one who killed the animal, or who at least wounded it mortally or caught it in a net. These acts brought the animal within the "certain control" that gives rise to possession and hence a claim to ownership.

Possession thus means a clear act, whereby all the world understands that the pursuer has "an unequivocal intention of appropriating the animal to his individual use." A clear rule of this sort should be applied, said the court, because it prevents confusion and quarreling among hunters (and coincidentally makes the judges' task easier when hunters do get into quarrels).

The dissenting judge commented that the best way to handle this matter would be to leave it to a panel of sportsmen, who presumably would have ruled against the interloper. In any event, he noted that the majority's rule would discourage the useful activity of fox hunting: who would bother to go to all the trouble of keeping dogs and chasing foxes if the reward were up for grabs to any "saucy intruder?" If we really want to see that foxes don't overrun the countryside, we will allocate a property right — and thus the ultimate reward — to the hunter at an earlier moment, so that he will undertake the useful investment in keeping hounds and the useful labor in flushing the fox.

The problem with assigning "possession" prior to the kill is, of course, that we need a principle to tell us when to assign it. Shall we assign it when the hunt begins? When the hunter assembles his dogs for the hunt? When the hunter buys his dogs?

Pierson thus presents two great principles, seemingly at odds, for defining possession: (1) notice to the world through a clear act, and (2) reward to useful labor. The latter principle, of course, suggests a labor theory of property. The owner gets the prize when he "mixes in his labor" by hunting. On the other hand, the former principle suggests at least a weak form of the consent theory: The community requires clear acts so that it has the opportunity to dispute claims, but may be thought to acquiesce in individual ownership where the claim is clear and no objection is made.

On closer examination, however, the two positions do not seem so far apart. In *Pierson*, each side acknowledged the importance of the other's principle. Although the majority decided in favor of a clear rule, it tacitly conceded the value of rewarding useful labor. Its rule for possession would in fact reward the original hunter most of the time, unless we suppose that the woods are thick with "saucy intruders." On the other side, the dissenting judge also wanted some definiteness in the rule of possession. He was simply insisting that the acts that sufficed to give notice should be prescribed by the relevant community, namely hunters or "sportsmen." Perhaps, then, there is some way to reconcile the clear-act and reward-to-labor principles.

The clear-act principle suggests that the common law defines acts of possession as some kind of *statement*. As Blackstone said, the acts must be a *declaration* of one's intent to appropriate. . . .[23]

Possession now begins to look even more like something that requires a kind of communication, and the original claim to the property looks like a kind of speech, with the audience composed of all others who might be interested in claiming the object in question. Moreover, some venerable statutory law obligates the acquiring party to *keep on* speaking, lest he lose his title by "adverse possession."

Adverse possession is a common law interpretation of statutes of limitation for actions to recover real property. Suppose I own a lot in the mountains, and some stranger to me, without my permission, builds a house on it, clears the woods, and farms the lot continuously for a given period, say twenty years. During that time, I am entitled to go to court to force him off the lot. But if I have not done so at the end of twenty years, or some other period fixed by statute, not only can I not sue him for recovery of what was my land, but the law recognizes him as the title owner. The doctrine of adverse possession thus operates to transfer property to one who is initially a trespasser if the trespasser's presence is open to everyone, lasts continuously for a given period of time, and if the title owner takes no action to get rid of him during that time.

Here again we seem to have an example of a reward to the useful laborer at the expense of the sluggard. But the doctrine is susceptible to another interpretation as well; it might be designed, not to reward the useful laborer, but to require the owner to assert her right publicly. It requires her to make it clear that she, and not the trespasser, is the person to deal with if anyone should wish to buy the property or use some portion of it. . . .

Possession as the basis of property ownership, then, seems to amount to something like yelling loudly enough to all who may be interested. The first to say, "This is mine," in a way that the public understands, gets the prize, and the law will help him keep it against someone else who says, "No, it is *mine*." But if the original

23. [2 Commentaries on the Laws of England] 9, 258.

communicator dallies too long and allows the public to believe the interloper, he will find that the interloper has stepped into his shoes and has become the owner.

Similar ideas of the importance of communication, or as it is more commonly called, "notice," are implicit in our recording statutes and in a variety of other devices that force a property claimant to make a public record of her claims on pain of losing them altogether. Indeed, notice plays a part in the most mundane property-like claims to things that the law does not even recognize as capable of being reduced to ownership. "Would you please save my place?" one says to one's neighbor in the movie line, in order to ensure that others in line know that one is coming back and not relinquishing one's claim. In my home town of Chicago, one may choose to shovel the snow from a parking place on the street, but in order to establish a claim to it one must put a chair or some other object in the cleared space. The useful act of shoveling snow does not speak as unambiguously as the presence of an object that blocks entry.

Why, then, is it so important that property owners make and keep their communications clear? Economists have an answer: Clear titles facilitate trade and minimize resource-wasting conflict. If I am careless about who comes on to a corner of my property, I invite others to make mistakes and to waste their labor on improvements to what I have allowed them to think is theirs. I thus invite a free-for-all over my ambiguously held claims, and I encourage contention, insecurity, and litigation — all of which waste everyone's time and energy and may result in overuse or underuse of resources. But if I keep my property claims clear, others will know that they should deal with me directly if they want to use my property. We can bargain rather than fight; through trade, all items will come to rest in the hands of those who value them most. If property lines are clear, then, anyone who can make better use of my property than I can will buy or rent it from me and turn the property to his better use. In short, we will all be richer when property claims are unequivocal, because that unequivocal status enables property to be traded and used at its highest value.

Thus, it turns out that the common law of first possession, in rewarding the one who communicates a claim, *does* reward useful labor; the useful labor is the very act of speaking clearly and distinctly about one's claims to property. Naturally, this must be in a language that is understood, and the acts of "possession" that communicate a claim will vary according to the audience. Thus, returning to Pierson v. Post, the dissenting judge may well have thought that fox hunters were the only relevant audience for a claim to the fox; they are the only ones who have regular contact with the subject matter. By the same token, the mid-nineteenth-century California courts gave much deference to the mining-camp customs in adjudicating various Gold Rush claims; the Forty-Niners themselves, as those most closely involved with the subject, could best communicate and interpret the signs of property claims and would be particularly well served by a stable system of symbols that would enable them to avoid disputes.

The point, then, is that "acts of possession" are, in the now fashionable term, a "text," and that the common law rewards the author of that text. But, as students of hermeneutics know, the clearest text may have ambiguous subtexts. In connection with the text of first possession, there are several subtexts that are especially worthy of note. One is the implication that the text will be "read" by the relevant audience at the appropriate time. It is not always easy to establish a symbolic structure in which the text of first possession can be "published" at such a time as to be useful to anyone. Once again, Pierson v. Post illustrates the problem that occurs when a clear sign (killing the fox) comes only relatively late in the game, after the relevant parties may have already expended overlapping efforts and embroiled themselves in a dispute. Very similar problems occurred in the whaling industry in the nineteenth century: The courts expended a considerable amount of mental energy in finding signs of "possession" that were comprehensible to whalers from their own customs and that at the same time came early enough in the chase to allow the parties to avoid wasted efforts and the ensuing mutual recriminations.

Some objects of property claims do seem inherently incapable of clear demarcation — ideas, for example. In order to establish ownership of such disembodied items we find it necessary to translate the property claims into sets of secondary symbols that our culture understands. In patent and copyright law, for example, one establishes an entitlement to the expression of an idea by translating it into a written document and going through a registration process — though the unending litigation over ownership of these expressions, and over which expressions can even be subject to patent or copyright, might lead us to conclude that these particular secondary symbolic systems do not always yield widely understood "markings." We also make up secondary symbols for physical objects that would seem to be much easier to mark out than ideas; even property claims in land, that most tangible of things, are now at their most authoritative in the form of written records.

It is expensive to establish and maintain these elaborate structures of secondary symbols, as indeed it may be expensive to establish a structure of primary symbols of possession. The economists have once again performed a useful service in pointing out that there are costs entailed in establishing *any* property system. These costs might prevent the development of any system at all for some objects, where our need for secure investment and trade is not as great as the cost of creating the necessary symbols of possession.

There is a second and perhaps even more important subtext to the "text" of first possession: the tacit supposition that there is such a thing as a "clear act," unequivocally proclaiming to the universe one's appropriation — that there are in fact unequivocal acts of possession, which any relevant audience will naturally and easily interpret as property claims. Literary theorists have recently written a great deal about the relativity of texts. They have written too much for us to accept uncritically the idea that a "text" about property has a natural meaning independent of some audience constituting an "interpretive community" or independent of a range of other "texts" and cultural artifacts that together form a symbolic system in which a given text must be read. It is not enough, then, for the property claimant to say simply, "It's mine" through some act or gesture; in order for the "statement" to have any force, some relevant world must understand the claim it makes and take that claim seriously.

Thus, in defining the acts of possession that make up a claim to property, the law not only rewards the author of the "text," it also puts an imprimatur on a particular symbolic system and on the audience that uses this system. Audiences that do not understand or accept the symbols are out of luck. . . .

In the history of American territorial expansion, a pointed example of the choice among audiences made by the common law occurred when one group did not play the approved language game and refused to get into the business of publishing or reading the accepted texts about property. The result was one of the most arresting decisions of the early American republic: Johnson v. McIntosh,[49] a John Marshall opinion concerning the validity of opposing claims to land in what is now a large part of Illinois and Indiana. The plaintiffs in this case claimed through Indian tribes, on the basis of deeds made out in the 1770's; the defendants claimed under titles that came from the United States. The Court found for the defendants, holding that the claims through the Indians were invalid, for reasons derived largely from international law rather than from the law of first possession. But tucked away in the case was a first-possession argument that Marshall passed over. The Indians, according to an argument of the claimants from the United States,

49. 21 U.S. (8 Wheat.) 543 (1823).

could not have passed title to the opposing side's predecessors because, "[b]y the law of nature," the Indians themselves had never done acts on the land sufficient to establish property in it. That is to say, the Indians had never really undertaken those acts of possession that give rise to a property right.

Although Marshall based his decision on other grounds, there was indeed something to the argument from the point of view of the common law of first possession. Insofar as the Indian tribes moved from place to place, they left few traces to indicate that they claimed the land (if indeed they did make such claims). From an eighteenth-century political economist's point of view, the results were horrifying. What seemed to be the absence of distinct claims to land among the Indians merely invited disputes, which in turn meant constant disruption of productive activity and dissipation of energy in warfare. Uncertainty as to claims also meant that no one would make any productive use of the land because there is little incentive to plant when there is no reasonable assurance that one will be in possession of the land at harvest time. From this classical economic perspective, the Indians' alleged indifference to well-defined property lines in land was part and parcel of what seemed to be their relatively unproductive use of the earth.

Now it may well be that North American Indian tribes were not so indifferent to marking out landed property as eighteenth-century European commentators supposed. . . . Or it may be that at least some tribes found landed property less important to their security than other forms of property and thus felt no need to assert claims to property in land. But however anachronistic the *Johnson* parties' (ultimately mooted) argument may now seem, it is a particularly striking example of the relativity of the "text" of possession to the interpretative community for that text. It is doubtful whether the claims of any nomadic population could ever meet the common law requirements for establishing property in land. Thus, the audience presupposed by the common law of first possession is an agrarian or a commercial people — a people whose activities with respect to the objects around them require an unequivocal delineation of lasting control so that those objects can be managed and traded.

But perhaps the deepest aspect of the common law text of possession lies in the attitude that this text strikes with respect to the relationship between human beings and nature. At least some Indians professed bewilderment at the concept of owning the land. Indeed they prided themselves on not marking the land but rather on moving lightly through it, living with the land and with its creatures as members of the same family rather than as strangers who visited only to conquer the objects of nature. The doctrine of first possession, quite to the contrary, reflects the attitude that human beings are outsiders to nature. It gives the earth and its creatures over to those who mark them so clearly as to transform them, so that no one else will mistake them for unsubdued nature.

We may admire nature and enjoy wildness, but those senti-ments find little resonance in the doctrine of first possession. Its texts are those of cultivation, manufacture, and development. We cannot have our fish both loose and fast, as Melville might have said,[61] and the common law of first possession makes a choice. The common law gives preference to those who convince the world that they have caught the fish and hold it fast. This may be a reward to useful labor, but it is more precisely the articulation of a specific vocabulary within a structure of symbols approved and understood by a commercial people. It is this commonly understood and shared set of symbols that gives significance and form to what might seem the quintessentially individualistic act: the claim that one has, by "possession," separated for oneself property from the great com-mons of unowned things.

NOTES AND QUESTIONS ON FIRST POSSESSION

1. Rose presents the meaning of "possession" as culturally rela-tive. Is it? Is Sugden more accurate when he suggests that some in-dicia of ownership are "found everywhere"? Consider the Native American blazes on trees, described in the selection from Demsetz, supra p. 148: Would those be recognized as property claims every-where? What about a wall or a fence? Are these universally recog-nizable assertions of ownership? If so, would this mean that possession is not culturally relative after all?

2. Even if one supposes that the specific indicia of property are relative, how do those indicia begin and evolve? Who thought of putting a chair in the shovelled-out parking place and how did oth-ers decipher its meaning? Are there similarities between these sig-naling devices and the more general evolution of language? Is there some "deep structure" of property analogous to the "deep struc-ture" that some linguists (notably Noam Chomsky) detect in lan-guage and grammar? See also the selections on informal property rights, infra Chapter 6.

3. Rose slides easily from visible signals of property to "artifi-

61. . . . . Moby-Dick, ch. 89 ("Fast-Fish and Loose-Fish") (1st ed. London, 1851). . . .

cial" systems of property designation, such as recording systems. Are these really so similar? Might the intervention of legal institutions make the latter "marking" devices differ with respect to costs, effectiveness, and responsiveness to change?

4. Richard Epstein, in Possession as the Root of Title, 13 Ga. L. Rev. 1221 (1979), asserts that the question of what counts as "possession" is the "little question," whereas he himself is interested in the "big question": Why does possession serve as the basis of title? Is he right — that is, is Rose wasting her time on a relatively trivial issue in discussing the meaning of "possession"? Does her concentration on a silly issue like fox hunting suggest that she is? Or is Epstein himself skirting around an issue central to his "big question"?

5. Does this selection overly romanticize Native Americans' relationships to nature? Lewis and Clark's Journals reported that Plains Indians routinely killed far more animals than they ate (for example, by herding buffalo over cliffs), and deliberately set fires to tall pine trees to watch them explode. More recent historical work confirms that Indians used fire extensively as a wildlife management agent, and apparently hunted some prehistoric animals to extinction. See, for instance, Stephen J. Pyne, Fire in America: A Cultural History of Wildland and Rural Fire 71-76 (1982); Albert E. Cowdrey, This Land, This South: An Environmental History 12-15 (1983). Does all this mean that Indians had a more callous and instrumental attitude toward nature than Rose suggests? If so, is it fair to suggest that the common law of property has a uniquely instrumental and domineering attitude toward nature?

6. An academic literature loosely described as "ecofeminism" also explores the relationship of nature to property. A classic work is Carolyn Merchant, The Death of Nature (1980), arguing that the post-Renaissance development of male-dominated, rationalistic, scientific thought has contributed to an estrangement from nature in modern Western thinking; interestingly enough, Merchant identifies rationalistic science with capitalist property. Are science, capitalism, and property all tied together in an instrumental and domineering attitude toward nature? Or is the "conquest of nature" simply part of what all people do in their use of natural resources? See James R. McGoodwin, Crisis in the World's Fisheries (1990), detailing attitudes and practices in small fishing communities around the world; see also Bonnie McCay & James Acheson, The Question of the Commons (1990), in which several essays deal with indigenous practices and attitudes about wildlife, particularly Raymond Hames, Game Conservation or Efficient Hunting? (at 92-107) and James G. Carrier, Marine Tenure and Conservation in Papua, New Guinea: Problems in Interpretation (at 142-67).

Property Rules, Liability Rules, and Adverse Possession*

Thomas W. Merrill

The law of adverse possession tends to be regarded as a quiet backwater. Both judicial opinions and leading treatises treat the legal doctrine as settled. The theory underlying the doctrine, although routinely discussed in the opening weeks of first-year property courses, is only rarely aired in the law reviews any more. Indeed, the most frequently cited articles on adverse possession date from the 1930s and earlier. Perhaps most tellingly, adverse possession seems to have completely escaped the attention of the modern law and economics movement — almost a sure sign of obscurity in today's legal-academic world.

Nevertheless, two recent events — one academic, the other judicial — are sufficiently challenging to our conventional understanding of adverse possession that they deserve comment. The academic event is the publication of a law review article by Professor Richard Helmholz of the University of Chicago concerning the state of mind that a possessor must have before he can obtain title by adverse possession.[3] Earlier treatments of this subject tended to proceed normatively, asserting the "correct" rule based on considerations of policy. Helmholz, however, is interested in determining what state of mind is actually demanded by courts before they will award title by adverse possession. To this end, he has surveyed "the bulk" of all reported cases dealing with adverse possession decided since 1966. His conclusion is rather startling. Although academic commentators generally argue that the subjective mental state of the possessor should be irrelevant, Helmholz finds that "where courts allow adverse possession to ripen into title, bad faith on the part of the possessor seldom exists. Where the possessor knows that he is trespassing, valid title does not accrue to him simply by the passage of years."

If nothing else, Helmholz's study casts doubt on whether we should take the common law test for acquiring title by adverse possession at face value. According to the common law, adverse possession requires, in addition to the running of the statute of limitations, that the possession be (1) actual, (2) open and notorious, (3) exclusive, (4) continuous, and (5) hostile under a claim of right. The common law test does not demand subjective good faith belief on

*Source: 79 Nw. U. L. Rev. 1122-1128, 1133-1135, 1152-1153 (1984-1985).
    3. Helmholz, Adverse Possession and Subjective Intent, 61 Wash. U. L.Q. 331 (1983).

the part of the possessor that he is entitled to the property. Never-theless, it appears that judges and juries rather consistently manipu-late the five standard elements in such a way as to award title to the possessor who entered the property in good faith, i.e., without ac-tual knowledge of the paramount title of the true owner, and to deny title to the possessor who entered in bad faith, i.e., with actual knowledge of the paramount title. Subjective good faith is, then, an unstated sixth element — one which can be overcome perhaps if the equities strongly cut the other way, but a presumptive element all the same. This conclusion, which Helmholz convincingly demon-strates, suggests the need to reassess the common law doctrine.

The judicial event which challenges our traditional understand-ing of adverse possession is a decision of the California Supreme Court, Warsaw v. Chicago Metallic Ceilings, Inc.,[10] concerning a first cousin of adverse possession — prescriptive easements.[11] The plain-tiff had constructed a large commercial building with a narrow driveway that left insufficient room for delivery trucks to turn around and back up to its loading dock. Consequently, trucks regu-larly drove onto a vacant portion of the defendant's land next door in order to make this maneuver. The plaintiff was aware of the prob-lem, and tried several times, without success, to purchase an ease-ment from the defendant. Later, the defendant decided to develop its land, erecting a pad of earth (and, after the plaintiff was denied a preliminary injunction, a warehouse) at the point where the trucks turned onto its property. The plaintiff sued, contending that the construction interfered with an easement it had acquired by pre-scription. The trial court sustained this contention, finding that the plaintiff had used the subject property for the statutory period of five years, and had satisfied all of the other elements necessary for prescription. The defendant was ordered to remove the pad of earth and the structure.

What is significant about *Warsaw* is the debate about remedies which took place on appeal. The court of appeal, although sustain-ing the finding that the plaintiff had satisfied the requirements for prescription, declared that the plaintiff could obtain a prescriptive easement and force the defendant to remove the improvements, only if the *plaintiff* agreed to pay the defendant the fair market value of the easement thus acquired. The California Supreme Court like-

10. 35 Cal. 3d 564, 676 P.2d 584, 199 Cal. Rptr. 773 (1984).
11. Prescriptive easements involve nonpossessory *use* of property which rip-ens into an easement, as opposed to possession of property which ripens into a fee simple. 7 R. Powell, Real Property ¶1026 (P. Rohan ed. 1977). Generally speaking, the same legal requirements apply to both adverse possession and prescriptive ease-ments, although the non-possessory nature of an easement generally means that the continuity and exclusivity elements must be interpreted differently.

wise upheld the finding that the plaintiff had satisfied the requirements for prescription, but overturned this novel form of relief.

The significance of the debate in *Warsaw* emerges in terms of the typology of legal rules introduced by Calabresi and Melamed. Traditionally, adverse possession and prescription have reflected what Calabresi and Melamed call a system of "property rules." That is, before judgment the true owner's (TO's) interest is protected by a property rule: no one — including the adverse possessor (AP) — can take it from the TO without his consent. After entry of judgment awarding the AP title by adverse possession, the AP's interest is protected by a property rule: no one — including the TO — can take it from the AP without his consent. The court of appeal's decision in *Warsaw*, however, suggests a different kind of scheme. Before judgment, the TO's entitlement would be protected, as before, by a property rule. But after judgment, the entitlement would remain with the TO, protected now by what Calabresi and Melamed call a "liability rule." In other words, after judgment the TO would keep the property, but the AP could take it away from the TO without his consent by paying the TO the fair market value of the property taken.

In what follows, I will suggest that the research of Professor Helmholz and the remedial innovation proposed in *Warsaw* are related. After all, *Warsaw* is, in Professor Helmholz's terminology, a clear case of bad faith — there is no question that the plaintiff knew that its trucks were encroaching on land belonging to the defendant. In light of Professor Helmholz's study, therefore, it is somewhat surprising that the California courts ruled in favor of the plaintiff in the first place. This may explain why a majority of the judges who heard the *Warsaw* case, even if they felt constrained to hold that the plaintiff had established an easement by prescription, were sympathetic to the idea of making the plaintiff pay for the easement so acquired — a liability rule. More generally, it suggests that liability rules may be an appropriate mediating device between the traditional policies supporting the institution of adverse possession — all of which apply whether the possessor is acting in good faith or in bad faith — and the evident reluctance of courts to "reward" bad faith possessors by giving the AP an entitlement protected by a property rule. . . .

I.   The Theory of Adverse Possession . . .

The assignment of entitlements in the period before the statute of limitations runs need not detain us for long. There is no question about who gets the entitlement during this period: Courts uniformly and automatically award it to the TO. The reasons for this are generally the same as those which support a system of private property rights, as opposed to one which recognizes only possessory, i.e., squatter's rights. First, there is a strong economic justification. If the state did not protect title but only the fact of possession, no one would ever be secure in leaving valuable things unattended, or entrusting them to someone else through lease or bailment.[17] The result would undoubtedly be over-investment in security devices, and under-investment in the cultivation and development of natural resources. In addition, there is a derivative justification based upon civic values: Cultural diversity, countervailing centers of political power, and independent institutions of scholarly inquiry may require larger accumulations of private wealth than would be possible under a system of mere possessory rights.[18] Finally, and again derivatively, there is a justification based on human personality: Accumulated material wealth may be important to an individual's identity and plans for the future, and property rights in material things protect these interests.[19] All of this, with varying degrees of emphasis on different aspects of the justification for property rights, has rarely been a matter of controversy, at least within the Anglo-American legal tradition.[20]

The problem comes in determining who should get the entitlement to the property *after* the statute of limitations runs. Clearly, courts often award the entitlement to the possessor rather than to the title holder during this period — that's what adverse possession is all about. But as Professor Helmholz's study reminds us, courts may also grant the entitlement to the TO. Given the strong case for maintaining a system of property rights, a threshold question is why we are *ever* justified in shifting the entitlement from the TO to the AP after the passage of a number of years. Surprisingly, there is very little systematic discussion of this fundamental issue in the legal literature. Nevertheless, it is possible, with some effort, to glean from that literature four different, and yet essentially complementary, rationales for the institution of adverse possession[.] . . . the problem of lost evidence, the desirability of quieting titles, the interest in discouraging sleeping owners, and the reliance interests of AP's and interested third persons. The important thing to note about

17. See 2 W. Blackstone, Commentaries ch. 1 (1766).
18. See M. Friedman, Capitalism and Freedom ch. 1 (1962); Reich, The New Property, 73 Yale L.J. 733 (1964).
19. Cf. Radin, Property and Personhood, 34 Stan. L. Rev. 957 (1982) (contrasting property for personhood and "fetishistic," i.e., purely accumulative, property).
20. Even the Marxist critique of private property advocates state or collectively owned property — not a system of possessory rights — as an alternative. As Demsetz has pointed out, state or collectively owned property is in many respects more like private property than possessory rights.

these rationales is that, at least at the level of general justification, they are mutually supportive. One can like some and dislike others, or one can subscribe to all four, and the result is still the same — the entitlement should be transferred to the AP after the statute of limitations runs. Indeed, standing alone some of these rationales may appear too weak to overcome the presumption in favor of a system of property rights rather than of possessory rights. But taken together, they represent a rather imposing case for transferring the entitlement to the AP after a significant period of time has elapsed.

All of this makes Professor Helmholz's study the more puzzling. The traditional theories suggest that the entitlement should be transferred to the AP after the expiration of the limitations period, and provide no basis for distinguishing between the good faith and bad faith possessor. Yet Professor Helmholz's findings about the importance of subjective intent cast considerable doubt on whether the traditional theories provide a complete account of the relevant concerns. Of course, his findings do not necessarily mean that the proclivities of judges and juries who decide adverse possession cases are correct. One could argue that judges and juries, absorbed in an ex post analysis of the facts of particular controversies, simply have failed to appreciate the strength of the systemic justifications for the institution of adverse possession. But it is probably unwise to denounce the voice of collective experience. A better approach would be to ask whether the inclination of the courts has some justification of its own — a justification which perhaps the legal literature has overlooked. If such a countervailing rationale exists, then the question of assigning the entitlement after the statute of limitations runs may not be so simple after all.

Actually, it is not hard to identify a countervailing concern: the interest in punishing or deterring those who engage in purely coercive transfers of property. This concern can be stated in terms of incentives. Purely coercive transfers of property are socially undesirable because they undermine incentives for productive activity, stimulate excessive precautionary measures, and generally destroy the fabric of human relations. What then will be the effect on the incidence of this activity if the dispossessor can, after the passage of a certain period of time, obtain title to the property? Obtaining title constitutes a powerful reward for such a coerced transfer. With title, the dispossessor no longer has to fear legal retribution from the TO (or the state), and can develop, sell, subdivide, or borrow against the property at will. One would expect a potential dispossessor, in calculating whether to seize someone else's property, to balance this potential reward against the probability of apprehension and the severity of the penalty if caught. If we assume any degree of rationality at all (and decisions about taking property are generally "rational," i.e., economically motivated) then the potential reward, even if it is several years in coming, should lead to a higher incidence of coerced transfers than we would expect to find in the absence of such a reward.

In the period before the statute of limitations runs, the concern with punishing or deterring coerced transfers is much in evidence. Intentional dispossession of property — whether in the form of trespass or theft — generally is regarded as a felony punishable by imprisonment. Moreover, the TO has an impressive array of civil remedies to recover the property or its value in money, often fortified by statutory provisions for multiple or punitive damages. After the statute runs, however, the concern with punishing or deterring coerced transfers disappears; or at least it *seems* to disappear in the common law doctrine and traditional legal commentary on adverse possession.

For present purposes, what is especially promising about the interest in punishing or deterring coerced transfers is that it provides a basis for distinguishing between the good faith and bad faith possessor, and thus for explaining the findings of Professor Helmholz. . . .

. . . I suggested that courts manipulate the common law doctrine of adverse possession in order to punish or deter those who intentionally dispossess others of their property. A less drastic means of achieving a similar end would be to apply a liability rule in cases of bad faith possession. A rule of limited indemnification would in effect impose a fine on bad faith dispossessors equal to the value of the property at the time of original entry. Squatters and thieves would know that, even if they could obtain title to property after the passage of the statute of limitations and the satisfaction of the common law's five elements, they would have to pay for their gain. Consequently, the incentives to engage in coerced transfers would be reduced.

There are several advantages to reflecting our disapproval of the bad faith possessor at the stage of remedy rather than entitlement. First, in cases where the TO has disappeared or the dispossession occurred so long ago that evidence of the mental state of the possessor has been lost or forgotten, an action for indemnification would simply fail, leaving the main purposes of the system of adverse possession intact. Conversely, if subjective bad faith were an express requirement for obtaining title by adverse possession, the difficulties of proof associated with this element could interfere measurably with the functions of adverse possession.

Second, by limiting the issue of subjective intent to the remedial stage, we would strengthen the extent to which AP's and interested third parties could rely on an AP's continued possession of the property. Consider the case, probably not that unusual, where the AP has some inkling that the title rests in someone else — in other words, where the evidence of bad faith is ambiguous — and yet the TO has not filed an action to regain possession. If the subjective intent of the AP were a relevant issue at the stage of entitlement, then the AP would face considerable uncertainty. If he should go ahead and improve or develop the property, he could have his entire interest wiped out by a subsequent action by the TO for possession. However, if the issue of subjective intent were relevant only to the question of remedy, the worst that could happen in this situation would be that the AP would have to pay the fair market value as of the date of original entry (plus prejudgment interest). This should encourage AP's to improve and develop the property, safe in the knowledge that they would be assured at least continued possession of the property and the value of the improvements. In addition, interested third parties (who do not know whether the AP acquired the property in good faith or bad faith) should have greater confidence that the AP will remain in possession.

Finally, and perhaps most importantly, if courts knew that the bad faith possessor would be faced with an action for indemnification, they might not feel compelled to manipulate the traditional common law doctrine in order to "punish" those who acquired the property in bad faith, and "reward" those who acquired it innocently. Adoption of the limited indemnification requirement would permit the basic entitlement determination rule to take on a more mechanical cast, reducing the need for litigation to establish title by adverse possession, at least in cases where the TO has disappeared or there is no question that the AP acted in good faith. Admittedly, there is an element of speculation here. But it stands to reason that judges and juries would be much more willing to apply a mechanical rule at the stage of entitlement if they knew that there was a way of "doing justice" at the stage of remedy. Certainly, it is hard to imagine that this reform would produce greater uncertainty than exists today, when the official doctrine says one thing and the results reached by the courts say another.

NOTES AND QUESTIONS ON
ADVERSE POSSESSION

1. Why are judges and juries generally unsympathetic to would-be adverse possessors who knew of, or believed in, the true owner's superior title? In particular, how much do you suppose judges and juries are influenced by what Merrill identifies as the

economic inefficiencies of coerced transfer? In their hostility to such adverse possessors, are they simply indifferent to the "desert" theory, that is, the idea that property should reward useful labor?

2. Merrill lists several rationales against shifting ownership: securing titles, encouraging investment, diffusing political power, and protecting personal projects. Can you think of ways in which some or all of these same rationales speak for adverse possession? Is this an instance in which, as the Critical Legal Studies scholars assert more generally, the legal rationales are indeterminate? Does Helmholz's study of the ways judges and juries actually behave support the charge of legal indeterminacy?

3. Doesn't Merrill's proposed solution encourage willful trespass? Note that in the *Warsaw* case that serves as his central example, the plaintiff would be entitled to "buy" an easement in the end, even though the defendant refused to sell. Is this solution simply a variation on eminent domain, which in most jurisdictions is only granted for projects that have an arguable public purpose? See the dissent in the much-cited Boomer v. Atlantic Cement Co., 309 N.Y.S.2d 312 (N.Y. 1970), and the selection by Calabresi and Melamed, infra p. 236.

4. Suppose that the true owner (TO1) sells to TO2 after an adverse possessor (AP) has trespassed on a portion of the property for the statutory period (so that under the Merrill proposal AP acquires an interest in the property but has to pay compensation). Who should receive the compensation, TO1 or TO2? On what does your answer depend? Does this problem suggest why courts do not necessarily find liability rules an attractive alternative to property rules?

5. If you have a taste for obscurantism, consider the rules concerning "accretion" and "avulsion," which govern ownership of riparian land that has been physically gained or lost on account of a transfer by the flow of water. In the case of accretion — a slow buildup — the legal boundaries move with nature and the property right goes to the recipient owner. In the case of avulsion — a sudden shift — riparian owners can claim to the old watercourse boundaries so that the property right stays with the first owner. In neither case do human actions do anything to bring about the land alterations. How might liability rules alter the existing doctrines? Is there a better case for a liability rule to protect the owner who has lost land by accretion, or the owner who has lost by avulsion? Why?

6. Speaking of flowing water, when all is said and done, is it not true that adverse possession is a "quiet backwater"? Many cases exemplify mistakes or petty overreaching between neighbors; do many of our property transactions depend on solutions to these be-

haviors? Indeed, is there reason to think that the doctrine of adverse possession is simply an artifact of our untidy system of land records? Could the whole doctrine be eliminated with more strict recording requirements, as is the case in jurisdictions that rely on the Torrens system of land registration? What problems might arise? For some of these, see Rose, Crystals and Mud, infra p. 320.

Chapter 4

The Coase Theorem and its Limitations

The Problem of Social Cost*

Ronald H. Coase

I. The Problem To Be Examined

This paper is concerned with those actions of business firms which have harmful effects on others. The standard example is that of a factory the smoke from which has harmful effects on those occupying neighbouring properties. The economic analysis of such a situation has usually proceeded in terms of a divergence between the private and social product of the factory, in which economists have largely followed the treatment of Pigou in The Economics of Welfare. The conclusions to which this kind of analysis seems to have led most economists is that it would be desirable to make the owner of the factory liable for the damage caused to those injured by the smoke, or alternatively, to place a tax on the factory owner varying with the amount of smoke produced and equivalent in money terms to the damage it would cause, or finally, to exclude the factory from residential districts (and presumably from other areas in which the emission of smoke would have harmful effects on others). It is my contention that the suggested courses of action are inappropriate, in that they lead to results which are not necessarily, or even usually, desirable.

*Source: 3 J. L. & Econ. 1-3, 6-8, 13-19 (1960).

II. The Reciprocal Nature of the Problem

The traditional approach has tended to obscure the nature of the choice that has to be made. The question is commonly thought of as one in which A inflicts harm on B and what has to be decided is: How should we restrain A? But this is wrong. We are dealing with a problem of a reciprocal nature. To avoid the harm to B would inflict harm on A. The real question that has to be decided is: Should A be allowed to harm B or should B be allowed to harm A? The problem is to avoid the more serious harm. I instanced in my previous article[2] the case of a confectioner the noise and vibrations from whose machinery disturbed a doctor in his work. To avoid harming the doctor would inflict harm on the confectioner. The problem posed by this case was essentially whether it was worth while, as a result of restricting the methods of production which could be used by the confectioner, to secure more doctoring at the cost of a reduced supply of confectionery products. Another example is afforded by the problem of straying cattle which destroy crops on neighbouring land. If it is inevitable that some cattle will stray, an increase in the supply of meat can only be obtained at the expense of a decrease in the supply of crops. The nature of the choice is clear: meat or crops. What answer should be given is, of course, not clear unless we know the value of what is obtained as well as the value of what is sacrificed to obtain it. To give another example, Professor George J. Stigler instances the contamination of a stream.[3] If we assume that the harmful effect of the pollution is that it kills the fish, the question to be decided is: Is the value of the fish lost greater or less than the value of the product which the contamination of the stream makes possible. It goes almost without saying that this problem has to be looked at in total *and* at the margin.

III. The Pricing System with Liability for Damage

I propose to start my analysis by examining a case in which most economists would presumably agree that the problem would be solved in a completely satisfactory manner: when the damaging business has to pay for all damage caused *and* the pricing system works smoothly (strictly this means that the operation of a pricing system is without cost).

A good example of the problem under discussion is afforded by

2. Coase, The Federal Communications Commission, 2 J. Law & Econ. 26-27 (1959).
3. G.J. Stigler, The Theory of Price 105 (1952).

the case of straying cattle which destroy crops growing on neighbouring land. Let us suppose that a farmer and a cattle-raiser are operating on neighbouring properties. Let us further suppose that, without any fencing between the propeties, an increase in the size of the cattle-raiser's herd increases the total damage to the farmer's crops. What happens to the marginal damage as the size of the herd increases is another matter. This depends on whether the cattle tend to follow one another or to roam side by side, on whether they tend to be more or less restless as the size of the herd increases and on other similar factors. For my immediate purpose, it is immaterial what assumption is made about marginal damage as the size of the herd increases.

To simplify the argument, I propose to use an arithmetical example. I shall assume that the annual cost of fencing the farmer's property is $9 and that the price of the crop is $1 per ton. Also, I assume that the relation between the number of cattle in the herd and the annual crop loss is as follows:

Number in Herd (Steers)	Annual Crop Loss (Tons)	Crop Loss per Additional Steer (Tons)
1	1	1
2	3	2
3	6	3
4	10	4

Given that the cattle-raiser is liable for the damage caused, the additional annual cost imposed on the cattle-raiser if he increased his herd from, say, 2 to 3 steers is $3 and in deciding on the size of the herd, he will take this into account along with his other costs. That is, he will not increase the size of the herd unless the value of the additional meat produced (assuming that the cattle-raiser slaughters the cattle), is greater than the additional costs that this will entail, including the value of the additional crops destroyed. Of course, if, by the employment of dogs, herdsmen, aeroplanes, mobile radio and other means, the amount of damage can be reduced, these means will be adopted when their cost is less than the value of the crop which they prevent being lost. Given that the annual cost of fencing is $9, the cattle-raiser who wished to have a herd with 4 steers or more would pay for fencing to be erected and maintained, assuming that other means of attaining the same end would not do so more cheaply. When the fence is erected, the marginal cost due to the liability for damage becomes zero, except to the extent that an increase in the size of the herd necessitates a stronger and therefore more expensive fence because more steers are liable to lean against it at the same time. But, of course, it may be cheaper for the cattle-raiser not to fence and to pay for the damaged crops, as in my arithmetical example, with 3 or fewer steers. . . .

IV. The Pricing System with No Liability for Damage

I now turn to the case in which, although the pricing system is assumed to work smoothly (that is, costlessly), the damaging business is not liable for any of the damage which it causes. This business does not have to make a payment to those damaged by its actions. I propose to show that the allocation of resources will be the same in this case as it was when the damaging business was liable for damage caused. As I showed in the previous case that the allocation of resources was optimal, it will not be necessary to repeat this part of the argument.

I return to the case of the farmer and the cattle-raiser. The farmer would suffer increased damage to his crop as the size of the herd increased. Suppose that the size of the cattle-raiser's herd is 3 steers (and that this is the size of the herd that would be maintained if crop damage was not taken into account). Then the farmer would be willing to pay up to $3 if the cattle-raiser would reduce his herd to 2 steers, up to $5 if the herd were reduced to 1 steer and would pay up to $6 if cattle-raising was abandoned. The cattle-raiser would therefore receive $3 from the farmer if he kept 2 steers instead of 3. This $3 foregone is therefore part of the cost incurred in keeping the third steer. Whether the $3 is a payment which the cattle-raiser has to make if he adds the third steer to his herd (which it would be if the cattle-raiser was liable to the farmer for damage caused to the crop) or whether it is a sum of money which he would have received if he did not keep a third steer (which it would be if the cattle-raiser was not liable to the farmer for damage caused to the crop) does not affect the final result. In both cases $3 is part of the cost of adding a third steer, to be included along with the other costs. If the increase in the value of production in cattle-raising through increasing the size of the herd from 2 to 3 is greater than the additional costs that have to be incurred (including the $3 damage to crops), the size of the herd will be increased. Otherwise, it will not. The size of the herd will be the same whether the cattle-raiser is liable for the damage caused to the crop or not.

It may be argued that the assumed starting point — a herd of

3 steers — was arbitrary. And this is true. But the farmer would not wish to pay to avoid crop damage which the cattle-raiser would not be able to cause. For example, the maximum annual payment which the farmer could be induced to pay could not exceed $9, the annual cost of fencing. And the farmer would only be willing to pay this sum if it did not reduce his earnings to a level that would cause him to abandon cultivation of this particular tract of land. Furthermore, the farmer would only be willing to pay this amount if he believed that, in the absence of any payment by him, the size of the herd maintained by the cattle-raiser would be 4 or more steers. Let us assume that this is the case. Then the farmer would be willing to pay up to $3 if the cattle-raiser would reduce his herd to 3 steers, up to $6 if the herd were reduced to 2 steers, up to $8 if one steer only were kept and up to $9 if cattle-raising were abandoned. It will be noticed that the change in the starting point has not altered the amount which would accrue to the cattle-raiser if he reduced the size of his herd by any given amount. It is still true that the cattle-raiser could receive an additional $3 from the farmer if he agreed to reduce his herd from 3 steers to 2 and that the $3 represents the value of the crop that would be destroyed by adding the third steer to the herd. Although a different belief on the part of the farmer (whether justified or not) about the size of the herd that the cattle-raiser would maintain in the absence of payments from him may affect the total payment he can be induced to pay, it is not true that this different belief would have any effect on the size of the herd that the cattle-raiser will actually keep. This will be the same as it would be if the cattle-raiser had to pay for damage caused by his cattle, since a receipt foregone of a given amount is the equivalent of a payment of the same amount.

It might be thought that it would pay the cattle-raiser to increase his herd above the size that he would wish to maintain once a bargain had been made, in order to induce the farmer to make a larger total payment. And this may be true. It is similar in nature to the action of the farmer (when the cattle-raiser was liable for damage) in cultivating land on which, as a result of an agreement with the cattle-raiser, planting would subsequently be abandoned (including land which would not be cultivated at all in the absence of cattle-raising). But such manoeuvres are preliminaries to an agreement and do not affect the long-run equilibrium position, which is the same whether or not the cattle-raiser is held responsible for the crop damage brought about by his cattle.

It is necessary to know whether the damaging business is liable or not for damage caused since without the establishment of this initial delimitation of rights there can be no market transactions to transfer and recombine them. But the ultimate result (which maximizes the value of production) is independent of the legal position if the pricing system is assumed to work without cost.

V. The Problem Illustrated Anew . . .

Judges have to decide on legal liability but this should not confuse economists about the nature of the economic problem involved. In the case of the cattle and the crops, it is true that there would be no crop damage without the cattle. It is equally true that there would be no crop damage without the crops. The doctor's work would not have been disturbed if the confectioner had not worked his machinery; but the machinery would have disturbed no one if the doctor had not set up his consulting room in that particular place. . . . If we are to discuss the problem in terms of causation, both parties cause the damage. If we are to attain an optimum allocation of resources, it is therefore desirable that both parties should take the harmful effect (the nuisance) into account in deciding on their course of action. It is one of the beauties of a smoothly operating pricing system that, as has already been explained, the fall in the value of production due to the harmful effect would be a cost for both parties. . . .
. . . [I]t has to be remembered that the immediate question faced by the courts is *not* what shall be done by whom *but* who has the legal right to do what. It is always possible to modify by transactions on the market the initial legal delimitation of rights. And, of course, if such market transactions are costless, such a rearrangement of rights will always take place if it would lead to an increase in the value of production.

VI. The Cost of Market Transactions Taken into Account

The argument has proceeded up to this point on the assumption (explicit in Sections III and IV and tacit in Section V) that there were no costs involved in carrying out market transactions. This is, of course, a very unrealistic assumption. In order to carry out a market transaction it is necessary to discover who it is that one wishes to deal with, to inform people that one wishes to deal and on what terms, to conduct negotations leading up to a bargain, to draw up the contract, to undertake the inspection needed to make sure that the terms of the contract are being observed, and so on. These opera-

tions are often extremely costly, sufficiently costly at any rate to prevent many transactions that would be carried out in a world in
which the pricing system worked without cost.

In earlier sections, when dealing with the problem of the rearrangement of legal rights through the market, it was argued that
such a rearrangement would be made through the market whenever
this would lead to an increase in the value of production. But this
assumed costless market transactions. Once the costs of carrying out
market transactions are taken into account it is clear that such a rearrangement of rights will only be undertaken when the increase
in the value of production consequent upon the rearrangement is
greater than the costs which would be involved in bringing it about.
When it is less, the granting of an injunction (or the knowledge that
it would be granted) or the liability to pay damages may result in an
activity being discontinued (or may prevent its being started) which
would be undertaken if market transactions were costless. In these
conditions the inital delimitation of legal rights does have an effect
on the efficiency with which the economic system operates. One arrangement of rights may bring about a greater value of production
than any other. But unless this is the arrangement of rights established by the legal system, the costs of reaching the same result by
altering and combining rights through the market may be so great
that this optimal arrangement of rights, and the greater value of production which it would bring, may never be achieved. . . .

The discussion of the problem of harmful effects in this section
(when the costs of market transactions are taken into account) is extremely inadequate. But at least it has made clear that the problem
is one of choosing the appropriate social arrangement for dealing
with the harmful effects. All solutions have costs and there is no
reason to suppose that government regulation is called for simply
because the problem is not well handled by the market or the firm.
Satisfactory views on policy can only come from a patient study of
how, in practice, the market, firms and governments handle the
problem of harmful effects. Economists need to study the work of
the broker in bringing parties together, the effectiveness of restrictive covenants, the problems of the large-scale real-estate development company, the operation of Government zoning and other
regulating activities. It is my belief that economists, and policymakers generally, have tended to over-estimate the advantages
which come from governmental regulation. But this belief, even if
justified, does not do more than suggest that government regulation
should be curtailed. It does not tell us where the boundary line
should be drawn. This, it seems to me, has to come from a detailed

investigation of the actual results of handling the problem in different ways. . . .

NOTES AND QUESTIONS ON THE COASE THEOREM

1. Although The Problem of Social Cost received little acclaim in the mid-1960s, by the 1970s and 1980s it had become the most cited article on law. It is regarded as the genesis of two highly influential concepts: the "Coase Theorem" and "transaction costs" (although neither phrase actually appears in the article). Coase's major writings are collected in Ronald Coase, The Firm, the Market, and the Law (1988), a corpus of work that won him the Nobel Prize in Economic Science in 1991. Before being influenced by the pages that follow, try to articulate Coase's central, and quite counterintuitive, insight in The Problem of Social Cost.

2. Is the practical upshot of Coase's analysis that legal decisions are unimportant? Or rather that, when comparing alternative rules, one should focus on the relative levels of transaction costs that parties would have to bear in bargaining to effect a transfer of entitlements? Coase himself has spoken on the matter: "The world of zero transaction costs has often been described as a Coasian world. Nothing could be further from the truth. It is the world of modern economic theory, one which I was hoping to persuade economists to leave." The Firm, the Market, and the Law 174 (1988). In effect, Coase revealed the importance of transaction costs by assuming them away, much as economists came to better understand the significance of restraints on trade by devising models of perfect competition.

3. The *strong* version of the Coase Theorem, sometimes called the "invariance" proposition, asserts that, in a world of zero transaction costs, a change in legal rules would have no effect on the allocation of resources. To use Coase's example, the imposition of liability for cattle trespass would not cause cattle-raisers to reduce the size of their herds or to install more fencing. It is now universally agreed that the strong version of the theorem is untenable because changes in law may have "wealth effects." For instance, the imposition of liability on ranchers might result in a reduction of the wealth of individuals who own land especially suited for ranching. Because of these wealth effects, an allocation of resources that had previously been efficient might no longer be so. For example, if owners of ranchland were to be the primary purchasers of cowboy boots, a

drop in their wealth would lead to a drop in the optimal output of cowboy boots. On the general point, see Harold Demsetz, When Does the Rule of Liability Matter, 1 J. Legal Stud. 13 (1972), and the discussions by Kennedy and Michelman, supra pp.65–69, and Calabresi and Melamed, infra pp.240–241.

More plausible to many economists is the *weak* version of the Coase Theorem, often called the "efficiency" proposition. This weak form holds that, regardless of initial legal entitlements, in a world of zero transaction costs individuals would bargain with one another to garner all possible gains from trade (in economic jargon, move to the Pareto frontier). What is the difference between these two formulations? Why is the second version weaker than the first?

4. The demise in 1976 of the Reserve Clause in major league baseball gave rise to a spirited debate over the realism of various versions of the Coase Theorem. The Reserve Clause prohibited a veteran player from negotiating with teams other than his current one. In When Does the Rule of Liability Matter?, 1 J. Legal Stud. 13, 16-18 (1972), Harold Demsetz, embracing a strong version of the Coase Theorem, argued that the Reserve Clause did not affect the pairing of players with teams, although it did reduce the salaries of veteran players. According to Demsetz's reasoning, if, say, Pete Rose meshed most efficiently with the Cincinnati Reds, market transactions would eventually put him there, Reserve Clause or not.

In Consumption Theory, Production Theory, and Ideology in the Coase Theorem, 52 S. Cal. L. Rev. 669 (1979), Mark Kelman observed that during 1976-1977, the first two years after the demise of the Reserve Clause, *all* 20 players who had declared themselves free agents changed teams. Kelman argued that this pattern refuted Demsetz's prediction. Kelman was promptly challenged in Matthew Spitzer & Elizabeth Hoffman, A Reply to Kelman . . . , 53 S. Cal. L. Rev. 1187 (1980). Spitzer and Hoffman asserted that a broader look at 1967-1977 data indicated that the elimination of the Reserve Clause had not significantly increased the *rate* at which players moved from one major league team to another. Spitzer and Hoffman's analysis implied that the 20 free agents who had changed teams in 1976-1977 had recognized that they were no longer efficiently paired with their old team and in effect had "traded" themselves. Kelman's rejoinder appears at 53 S. Cal. L. Rev. 1215 (1980).

For evidence that the demise of the Reserve Clause led to more long-term guaranteed contracts, see Kenneth Lehn, Property Rights, Risk Sharing, and Player Disability in Major League Baseball, in Sportometrics 35 (Brian L. Goff & Robert D. Tollison eds. 1990). Lehn argues that free-agentry made players wealthier, increasing their demand for arrangements that insured them against risks of injury.

5. The Problem of Social Cost eventually spawned a huge literature, much of it attacking one or another of Coase's assumptions. The next three readings explore, in turn, the realism of:

a. Coase's sense of how people bargain;
b. Coase's notion that the legal system is the basic source of initial entitlements; and
c. Coase's view that "A receipt foregone of a given amount is the equivalent of the payment of the same amount."

The Cost of Coase*

Robert Cooter

III. Bargaining and the Coase Theorem

Coase gave his name to a fundamental theorem on externalities and tort law, but he left to others the job of stating exactly what the theorem says. The basic idea of the theorem is that the structure of the law which assigns property rights and liability does not matter so long as transaction costs are nil; bargaining will result in an efficient outcome no matter who bears the burden of liability. The conclusion may be drawn that the structure of law should be chosen so that the transaction costs are minimized, because this will conserve resources used up by the bargaining process and also promote efficient outcomes in the bargaining itself.

It has been suggested that the Coase Theorem is a tautology, like the proposition "All husbands are married." But a tautology conveys no information to someone who is competent in the language, whereas the Coase Theorem is the basis for a theory of externality and the evolution of property rights. Most discussions of the Coase Theorem do not treat it as an empty tautology; rather, it is taken to suggest a definitive approach to policy and legislation — use the law to lubricate private bargaining. In order to account for the Coase Theorem's power, it must be regarded as being what its name proclaims, a theorem not a tautology.

It is helpful to keep in mind the distinction between them. A tautology is true by virtue of the definition of words. A theorem is true by virtue of its deduction from the assumptions of a theory.

*Source: 11 J. Legal Stud. 1, 14-20 (1982).

Tautologies are based upon linguistic conventions and theorems are based upon theoretical assumptions. The power of Coase's Theorem is explained by the fact that it is treated as if it were an economic theorem, that is, a proposition deduced from standard economic assumptions. The proof has never been constructed, but there is widespread conviction that it could be constructed if sufficient care were taken in arranging the assumptions.

We shall argue that the central version of the Coase Theorem cannot be deduced from economic assumptions. The widespread belief to the contrary is symptomatic of confusion about bargaining. This confusion results in blindness toward certain outcomes of policy. We shall try to restore accurate vision by explaining the relations among liability law, bargaining, and the economic assumptions of rational behavior.

Bargaining Problem

The Coase Theorem identifies a set of conditions under which the legal assignment of liability makes no difference. The phrase "makes no difference" has two interpretations: (*i*) the allocation of resources is invariant, or (*ii*) the allocation of resources is efficient. There was a confused debate about invariance verses efficiency, but now there is agreement that the invariance version is untenable.[13] It is the efficiency version which we shall consider.

There is no agreed-upon interpretation of the conditions suggested by Coase under which the rule of liability does not affect efficiency. One tradition of exegesis interprets Coase as requiring competitive markets, so that no one has any bargaining power. For example, Richard Zerbe has offered the following statement of the Coase Theorem: "In a world of perfect competition, perfect information, and zero transaction costs, the allocation of resources will be efficient and invariant with respect to legal rule of liability."[14] We have already observed that the invariance interpretation is discredited, so the phrase "and invariant" should be deleted. The idea is that a complete set of markets can be achieved by liability law, even in the presence of externalities, and that these markets are efficient when competitive.

This form of the Coase Theorem is true. . . .

Another interpretation of the Coase Theorem does not mention a requirement of competitive markets. For example, Polinsky has

13. See comments by Bruce Ackerman, in Economic Foundations of Property Law 23 (Bruce Ackerman ed. 1975).
14. Richard O. Zerbe, The Problem of Social Cost: Fifteen Years Later, Theory and Measurement of Economic Externalities 29 (Steven A.Y. Lin ed. 1976).

offered this compact statement of Coase's Theorem: "If transaction costs are zero the structure of the law does not matter because efficiency will result in any case."[15] The meaning of transaction costs is not well-standardized in the literature. Calabresi says, "By transaction costs, I have in mind costs like those of getting large numbers of people together to bargain, and the cost of excluding freeloaders."[16] The transaction costs of bargaining refer to the cost of communicating among the parties (including the value of time used up in sending messages), making side payments (the cost of the transaction, not the value of what is exchanged), and the cost of excluding people from sharing in the benefits exchanged by the parties. In the case of contingent commodities, the cost of obtaining information on the actions of the players is also treated as a transaction cost, so the inefficiencies from moral hazard and adverse selection are swept under the blanket of transaction costs. We shall not quarrel with the expansion of transaction costs to cover such diverse phenomena. Our objection is more fundamental.

The mechanism for achieving efficiency in the absence of competitive markets is bargaining. For example, Calabresi formulated the Coase Theorem as follows: "If one assumes rationality, no transaction costs, and no legal impediments to bargaining, *all* misallocation of resources would be fully cured in the market by bargains."[17] This formulation apparently presupposes a general proposition about bargaining, namely, "Bargaining games with zero transaction costs reach efficient solutions."[18]

In order to evaluate this interpretation of Coase, we must explain the place of bargaining in game theory. A zero-sum game is a game in which total winnings minus total losses equals zero. Poker is an example. A zero-sum game is a game of pure redistribution, because nothing is created or destroyed. By contrast, a coordination game is a game in which the players have the same goal. For example, if a phone conversation is cut off, then the callers face a coordination problem. The connection cannot be restored unless someone dials, but the call will not go through if both dial at once. The players win or lose as a team, and winning is productive, so coordination games are games of pure production.

A bargaining game involves distribution and production. Typi-

15. A. Mitchell Polinsky, Economic Analysis as a Potentially Defective Product: A Buyer's Guide to Posner's Economic Analysis of Law, 87 Harv. L. Rev. 1165 (1974).

16. Guido Calabresi, Transaction Costs, Resource Allocation, and Liability Rules — A Comment, 11 J. Law & Econ. 67 (1968).

17. Calabresi, supra note 16, at 68.

18. Donald H. Regan, The Problem of Social Cost Revisited, 15 J. Law & Econ. 427 (1972).

cally, there is something to be divided called the *stakes*. For example, one person may have a car to sell and the other may have money to spend. The stakes are the money and the car. If the players can agree upon a price for the car, then both of them will benefit. The *surplus* is the joint benefits from cooperation, for example, consumer's surplus plus seller's surplus in our example of the car. If the players cannot agree upon how to divide the stakes, then the surplus will be lost. In brief, bargaining games are games in which production is contingent upon agreement about distribution.

The bargaining version of the Coase Theorem takes an optimistic attitude toward the ability of people to solve this problem of distribution. The obstacles to cooperation are portrayed as the cost of communicating, the time spent negotiating, the cost of enforcing agreements, etc. These obstacles can all be described as transaction costs of bargaining. Obviously, we can conceive of a bargaining game in which these costs are nil.

A pessimistic approach assumes that people cannot solve the distribution problem, even if there are no costs to bargaining. According to this view, there is no reason why rationally self-interested players should agree about how to divide the stakes. The distribution problem is unsolvable by rational players. To eliminate the possibility of noncooperation, we would have to eliminate the problem of distribution, that is, to convert the bargaining game into a coordination game. But it makes no sense to speak about a bargaining game without a problem of distribution.

Our example of selling a car illustrates the collision of these two viewpoints. The costs of communicating, writing a contract, and enforcing its terms are the transaction costs of buying or selling a car. These costs sometimes constitute an obstacle to exchange. However, there is another obstacle of an entirely different kind, namely the absence of a competitive price. The parties must haggle over the price until they can agree upon how to distribute the gains from trade. There is no guarantee that the rational pursuit of self-interest will permit agreement. If we interpret zero transaction costs to mean that there is no dispute over price, then we have dissolved the bargaining game.

The polar opposite of the optimistic bargaining theorem can be stated as follows: "Bargaining games have noncooperative outcomes even when the bargaining process is costless." This line of thought suggests the polar opposite of the Coase Theorem: "Private bargaining to redistribute external costs will not achieve efficiency unless there is an institutional mechanism to dictate the terms of the contract." We have already discussed one institutional mechanism to achieve efficiency, namely a competitive market, which eliminates the power of parties to threaten each other. Another such institution is compulsory arbitration.

The conception of law which is the polar opposite to Coase is articulated in Hobbes and is probably much older. It is based upon the belief that people will exercise their worst threats against each other unless there is a third party to coerce both of them. The third party for Hobbes is the prince or leviathan — we would say dictatorial government — who has unlimited power relative to the bargainers. Without his coercive threats, life would be "nasty, brutish, and short."[19] We shall refer to the polar opposite of the Coase Theorem as the Hobbes Theorem.

The Coase Theorem identifies the problem of externalities with the cost of the bargaining process, whereas the Hobbes Theorem identifies the problem with the absence of an authoritative distribution of the stakes. We shall argue that both theorems are false. However, they are illuminating falsehoods because they offer a guide to structuring law in the interests of efficiency.

In real situations faced by policymakers, transaction costs are positive. The Coase Theorem suggests that the role of law is to assign entitlements to the party who values them the most, so that the costly process of exchanging the entitlement is unnecessary. There are many similar versions of this proposition, for example, liability for accidents should be assigned to the party who can prevent them at lowest cost, or the cost of breach of contract should be assigned to the party who is the best insurer against nonperformance. If the party who values the entitlement the most cannot be identified, then it should be assigned to the party who can initiate an exchange at the least cost.[20]

The Hobbes Theorem suggests that the role of law is to minimize the inefficiency that results when bargaining fails, by restricting the threats which the parties can make against each other. In the jargon of game theory, law increases the value of the noncooperative solution by eliminating elements of the payoff matrix with low value. This function is obvious in criminal law, where threats of violence against property or persons are punished. This function of law

19. In a state of nature men live in "continual fear, and danger of violent death; and the life of man [is] solitary, poor, nasty, brutish, and short." Thomas Hobbes, Leviathan 100 (Collier-MacMillan ed. 1973).

20. "Suppose we are not sure whether rubber bumpers or wearing fluorescent clothing is the 'cheapest way' of handling the car-pedestrian accident problem. In this case it may become necessary to consider the following question: Is an erroneous placing of liability on car owners or an erroneous placing of liability on pedestrians more likely to be corrected in the market? Whether car owners (or car makers) can bribe pedestrians more cheaply than pedestrians can bribe car owners or makers, becomes the relevant issue." Calabresi, supra note 16, at 72.

is also apparent in regulation of collective bargaining and strike activity. We claim that the same principle is at work where the threat is, say, to pollute a stream, to not perform on a contract, or to not take precautions against accidents. . . .

The Coase Theorem and the Hobbes Theorem have contradictory implications for the size of government. We can see this point most clearly by considering the policy implications in the ideal world of zero transaction costs. According to the Coase Theorem, there is no continuing need for government under these conditions. Like the deist god, the government retires from the scene after creating some rights over externalities, and efficiency is achieved regardless of what rights were created. According to the Hobbes Theorem, the coercive theats of government or some similar institution are needed to achieve efficiency when externalities create bargaining situations, even though bargaining is costless. Like the theist god, the government continuousy monitors private bargaining to insure its success.

The Coase Theorem represents extreme optimism about private cooperation and the Hobbes Theorem represents extreme pessimism. Perhaps the Coase Theorem is more accurate than the Hobbes Theorem in the sense that gains from trade in bargaining situations are more often realized than not, or perhaps the Hobbes Theorem is more accurate from the perspective of lawyers who must pick up the pieces when cooperation fails. We shall not attempt an allocation of truth. The strategic considerations are not normally insurmountable, as suggested by Hobbes, or inconsequential, as suggested by Coase. An informed policy choice must balance the Coase Theorem against the Hobbes Theorem in light of the ability of the parties to cooperate.

NOTES AND QUESTIONS ON TRANSACTION COSTS AND BARGAINING

1. How should one "allocate the truth" between the Coase Theorem and the Hobbes Theorem? When a customer bargains with the proprietor of the only hardware store in a small town are the two likely to resolve cooperatively what Cooter calls the "distribution problem"? What about a professional team trying to sign a star athlete it has drafted? Divorcing parents fighting over child custody? A pedestrian pleading with an armed robber not to take a wallet containing personal papers? More generally, under what sort

of circumstances are bargainers most likely to resolve the distribution problem? The selection by Robert Axelrod, infra p.275, explores the issue of cooperation.

2. Cooter cites, in footnote 20, an early version of Guido Calabresi's influential recommendations about how entitlements should be allocated, given that transaction costs in reality are positive. Calabresi's most compact statement is that it is advantageous for a legal system to allocate risks of losses to the party "in the best position to make the cost-benefit analysis between accident costs and accident avoidance costs and to act on that decision once it is made." See Guido Calabresi & Jon T. Hirschoff, Toward a Test for Strict Liability in Torts, 81 Yale L.J. 1055, 1060 (1972). For the richest version of Calabresi's normative scheme, see The Costs of Accidents 26-31 (1970).

Can legislators and judges make practical use of Calabresi's abstract recommendations? In the first paragraph of "The Problem of Social Cost," Coase asserts that it is generally "inappropriate" to make the owner of a polluting factory liable to those injured by its smoke. Why might the Calabresian approach suggest a contrary result under these exact circumstances? On the wisdom of emission fees on polluters, see the selection by Thomas Schelling, infra p.532.

3. Coase's primary example is worth revisiting. If transaction costs are indeed positive, should cattle-owners be liable for cattle trespass? There is a surprisingly rich and diverse body of law on the issue. See Glanville Williams, Liability for Animals (1939); Kenneth Vogel, The Coase Theorem and California Animal Trespass Law, 16 J. Legal Stud. 149 (1987); and the book excerpted in the next selection.

Order Without Law: How Neighbors Settle Disputes *

Robert C. Ellickson

[This work describes the resolution of animal-trespass disputes in a rural portion of Shasta County, located at the northern end of California's Central Valley. This county contains both "open range," within which owners of livestock are generally *not* liable for damage that their trespassing cattle cause upon unfenced land, and also "closed range," within which they *are* liable for that damage.

*Source: pp. 52-62 (1991).

Before reading the selection, try to anticipate to what extent trespass law actually affects how Shasta County cattle ranchers interact with their rural neighbors, many of whom live on smaller "ranchettes."]

The Settlement of Trespass Disputes

If Shasta County residents were to act like the farmer and the rancher in Coase's parable, they would settle their trespass problems in the following way. First, they would look to the formal law to determine who had what entitlements. They would regard those substantive rules as beyond their influence (as "exogenous," to use the economists' adjective). When they faced a potentially costly interaction, such as a trespass risk to crops, they would resolve it "in the shadow of" the formal legal rules. Because transactions would be costless, enforcement would be complete: No violation of an entitlement would be ignored. For the same reason, two neighbors who interacted on a number of fronts would resolve their disputes front by front, rather than globally.

The field evidence casts doubt on the realism of each of these literal features of the parable. Because Coase himself was fully aware that transactions are costly and thus that the parable was no more than an abstraction, the contrary evidence in no way diminishes his monumental contribution in "The Problem of Social Cost." Indeed the evidence is fully consistent with Coase's central idea that, regardless of the content of law, people tend to structure their affairs to their mutual advantage. Nevertheless, the findings reported here may serve as a caution to law-and-economics scholars who have underestimated the impact of transaction costs on how the world works.

Norms, Not Legal Rules, Are the Basic Sources of Entitlements

In rural Shasta County, where transaction costs are assuredly not zero, trespass conflicts are generally resolved not *in* "the shadow of the law" but, rather, *beyond* that shadow. Most rural residents are consciously committed to an overarching norm of cooperation among neighbors. In trespass situations, their applicable particularized norm, adhered to by all but a few deviants, is that an owner of livestock is responsible for the acts of his animals. Allegiance to this norm seems wholly independent of formal legal entitlements. Most cattlemen believe that a rancher should keep his animals from eating a neighbor's grass, regardless of whether the range is open or closed. Cattlemen typically couch their justifications for the norm in moral terms. Marty Fancher: "Suppose I sat down [uninvited] to a dinner your wife had cooked?" Dick Coombs: It "isn't right" to get free pasturage at the expense of one's neighbors. Owen Shellworth: "[My cattle] don't belong [in my neighbor's field]." Attorney-rancher Pete Schultz: A cattleman is "morally obligated to fence" to protect his neighbor's crops, even in open range. . . .

Incomplete Enforcement: The Live-and-Let-Live Philosophy

The norm that an animal owner should control his stock is modified by another norm that holds that a rural resident should put up with ("lump") minor damage stemming from isolated trespass incidents. The neighborly response to an isolated infraction is an exchange of civilities. A trespass victim should notify the animal owner that the trespass has occurred and assist the owner in retrieving the stray stock. Virtually all residents have telephones, the standard means of communication. A telephone report is usually couched not as a complaint but rather as a service to the animal owner, who, after all, has a valuable asset on the loose. Upon receiving a telephone report, a cattleman who is a good neighbor will quickly retrieve the animals (by truck if necessary), apologize for the occurrence, and thank the caller. The Mortons and the Shellworths, two ranching families in the Oak Run area particularly esteemed for their neighborliness, have a policy of promptly and apologetically responding to their neighbors' notifications of trespass.

Several realities of country life in Shasta County help explain why residents are expected to put up with trespass losses. First, it is common for a rural landowner to lose a bit of forage or to suffer minor fence damage. The area northeast of Redding lies on a deer migration route. During the late winter and early spring thousands of deer and elk move through the area, easily jumping the barbed-wire fences. Because wild animals trespass so often, most rural residents come to regard minor damage from alien animals not as an injurious event but as an inevitable part of life.

Second, most residents expect to be on both the giving and the receiving ends of trespass incidents. Even the ranchette owners have, if not a few hobby livestock, at least several dogs, which they keep for companionship, security, and pest control. Unlike cattle, dogs that trespass may harass, or even kill, other farm animals. If trespass risks are symmetrical, and if victims bear all trespass losses, accounts balance in the long run. Under these conditions, the advantage of reciprocal lumping is that no one has to expend time or money to settle disputes.

The norm of reciprocal restraint that underlies the "live-and-let-live" philosophy also calls for ranchers to swallow the costs of boarding another person's animal, even for months at a time. A cattleman often finds in his herd an animal wearing someone else's brand. If he recognizes the brand he will customarily inform its owner, but the two will often agree that the simplest solution is for the animal to stay put until the trespass victim next gathers his animals, an event that may be weeks or months away. The cost of "cutting" a single animal from a larger herd seems to underlie this custom. Thus, ranchers often consciously provide other people's cattle with feed worth perhaps as much as $10 to $100 per animal. Although Shasta County ranchers tend to regard themselves as financially pinched, even ranchers who know that they are legally entitled to recover feeding costs virtually never seek monetary compensation for boarding estrays. The largest ranchers northeast of Redding who were interviewed reported that they had never charged anyone or been charged by anyone for costs of that sort. Even when they do not know to whom a stray animal belongs, they put the animal in their truck the next time they take a load of animals to the auction yard at Cottonwood and drop it off without charge so that the brand inspector can locate the owner.

Mental Accounting of Interneighbor Debts

Residents who own only a few animals may of course be unable to see any average reciprocity of advantage in a live-and-let-live approach to animal trespass incidents. This would be true, for example, of a farmer whose fields frequently suffered minor damage from incursions by a particular rancher's livestock. Shasta County norms entitle a farmer in that situation to keep track of those minor losses in a mental account, and eventually to act to remedy the imbalance.

A fundamental feature of rural society makes this enforcement system feasible: Rural residents deal with one another on a large number of fronts, and most residents expect those interactions to continue far into the future. In sociological terms, their relationships are "multiplex," not "simplex." In game-theoretic terms, they are engaged in iterated, not single-shot, play.[51] They interact

---

51. The law-and-society literature has long emphasized that law is not likely to be important to parties enmeshed in a continuing relationship. For example, Marc Galanter has observed: "In the American setting, litigation tends to be between parties who are strangers. Either they never had a mutually beneficial continuing relationship, as in the typical automobile case, or their relationship — marital, commercial, or organizational — is ruptured. In either case, there is no anticipated

on water supply, controlled burns, fence repairs, social events, staffing the volunteer fire department, and so on. Where population densities are low, each neighbor looms larger. Thus any trespass dispute with a neighbor is almost certain to be but one thread in the rich fabric of a continuing relationship.

A person in a multiplex relationship can keep a rough mental account of the outstanding credits and debts in each aspect of that relationship. Should the aggregate account fall out of balance, tension may mount because the net creditor may begin to perceive the net debtor as an overreacher. But as long as the aggregate account is in balance, neither party need be concerned that particular subaccounts are not. For example, if a rancher were to owe a farmer in the trespass subaccount, the farmer could be expected to remain content if that imbalance were to be offset by a debt he owed the rancher in, say, the water-supply subaccount.

The live-and-let-live norm also suggests that neighbors should put up with minor imbalances in their aggregate accounts, especially when they perceive that their future interactions will provide adequate opportunities for settling old scores. Creditors may actually prefer having others in their debt. For example, when Larry Brennan lost seven tons of baled hay to Frank Ellis' cattle in open range, Brennan (although he did not know it) had a strong legal claim against Ellis for intentional trespass. Brennan estimated his loss at between $300 and $500, hardly a trivial amount. When Ellis learned of Brennan's loss he told Brennan to "come down and take some hay" from Ellis' barn. Brennan reported that he declined this offer of compensation, partly because he thought he should not have piled the bales in an unfenced area, but also because he would rather have Ellis in debt to him than be in debt to Ellis. Brennan was willing to let Ellis run up a deficit in their aggregate interpersonal accounts because he thought that as a creditor he would have more leverage over Ellis' future behavior.

The Control of Deviants: The Key Role of Self-Help

The rural Shasta County population includes deviants who do not adequately control their livestock and run up excessive debts in their informal accounts with their neighbors. Frank Ellis, for ex-

---

future relationship. In the American setting, unlike some others, resort to litigation is viewed as an irreparable breach of the relationship." Marc Galanter, "Reading the Landscape of Disputes: What We Know and Don't Know (and Think We Know) about Our Allegedly Contentious and Litigious Society," 31 UCLA L. Rev. 4, 24-25 (1983). . . .

ample, was notoriously indifferent about his reputation among his neighbors. In general, the traditionalists who let their animals loose in the mountains during the summer are less scrupulous than the modernists are in honoring the norms of neighborliness. This is likely due to the fact that traditionalists have less complex, and shorter-lived, interrelationships with the individuals who encounter their range cattle.

To discipline deviants, the residents of rural Shasta County use the following four types of countermeasures, listed in escalating order of seriousness: (1) self-help retaliation; (2) reports to county authorities; (3) claims for compensation informally submitted without the help of attorneys; and (4) attorney-assisted claims for compensation. The law starts to gain bite as one moves down this list.

Self-help. Not only are most trespass disputes in Shasta County resolved according to extralegal rules, but most enforcement actions are also extralegal. A measured amount of self-help — an amount that would serve to even up accounts — is the predominant and ethically preferred response to someone who has not taken adequate steps to prevent his animals from trespassing.

The mildest form of self-help is truthful negative gossip. This usually works because only the extreme deviants are immune from the general obsession with neighborliness. Although the Oak Run-Round Mountain area is undergoing a rapid increase in population, it remains distinctly rural in atmosphere. People tend to know one another, and they value their reputations in the community. Some ranching families have lived in the area for several generations and include members who plan to stay indefinitely. Members of these families seem particularly intent on maintaining their reputations as good neighbors. Should one of them not promptly and courteously retrieve a stray, he might fear that any resulting gossip would permanently besmirch the family name.

Residents of the Northeastern Sector foothills seem quite conscious of the role of gossip in their system of social control. One longtime resident, who had lived for many years in a suburb of a major California urban area, observed that people in the Oak Run area "gossip all the time," much more than in the urban area. Another reported intentionally using gossip to sanction a traditionalist who had been "impolite" when coming to pick up some stray mountain cattle; he reported that application of this self-help device produced an apology, an outcome itself presumably circulated through the gossip system.

The furor over Frank Ellis's loose cattle in the Oak Run area induced area residents to try a sophisticated variation of the gossip sanction. The ranchette residents who were particularly bothered by

Ellis's cattle could see that he was utterly indifferent to his reputation among them. They thought, however, that as a major rancher, Ellis would worry about his reputation among the large cattle operators in the county. They therefore reported Ellis's activities to the Board of Directors of the Shasta County Cattlemen's Association. This move proved unrewarding, for Ellis was also surprisingly indifferent to his reputation among the cattlemen.

When milder measures such as gossip fail, a person is regarded as being justifed in threatening to use, and perhaps even actually using, tougher self-help sanctions. Particularly in unfenced country, a victim may respond to repeated cattle trespasses by herding the offending animals to a location extremely inconvenient for their owner. Another common response to repeated trespasses is to threaten to kill a responsible animal should it ever enter again. Although the killing of trespassing livestock is a crime in California, six landowners — not noticeably less civilized than the others — unhesitatingly volunteered that they had issued death threats of this sort. These threats are credible in Shasta County because victims of recurring trespasses, particularly if they have first issued a warning, feel justified in killing or injuring the mischievous animals.[58] Despite the criminality of the conduct (a fact not necessarily known to the respondents), I learned the identity of two persons who had shot trespassing cattle. Another landowner told of running the steer of an uncooperative neighbor into a fence. The most intriguing report came from a rancher who had had recurrent problems with a trespassing bull many years before. This rancher told a key law enforcement official that he wanted to castrate the bull — "to turn it into a steer." The official replied that he would turn a deaf ear if that were to occur. The rancher asserted that he then carried out his threat.

It is difficult to estimate how frequently rural residents actually resort to violent self-help. Nevertheless, fear of physical retaliation is undoubtedly one of the major incentives for order in rural Shasta County. Ranchers who run herds at large freely admit that they worry that their trespassing cattle might meet with violence. One traditionalist reported that he is responsive to complaints from ran-

58. Violent self-help — occasionally organized on a group basis as vigilante justice — was a tradition in the nineteenth-century American West. "The laws [in Wyoming] appeared to require that a farmer fence his land to keep cattle out, but many a farmer preferred to save the cost of a fence, then wait until cattle came in his land, and with a shot or two secure a winter's supply of beef." Daniel J. Boorstin, The Americans: The Democratic Experience 30 (1973). See also Ernest Staples Osgood, The Day of the Cattleman (1929), at 157-160 (lynching of horse thieves); at 242 (killing of trespassing cattle); and at 252-253 (describing how large cattle companies mobilized an army to invade Johnson County, Wyoming, to prevent small ranchers from using violent self-help against the companies' cattle).

chette owners because he fears they will poison or shoot his stock. A judge for a rural district of the county asserted that a vicious animal is likely to "disappear" if its owner does not control it. A resident of the Oak Run area stated that some area residents responded to Frank Ellis's practice of running herds at large by rustling Ellis's cattle. He suggested that Ellis print tee shirts with the inscription: "Eat Ellis Beef. Everyone in Oak Run Does!"

Complaints to public officials. The longtime ranchers of Shasta County pride themselves on being able to resolve their problems on their own. Except when they lose animals to rustlers, they do not seek help from public officials. Although ranchette owners also use the self-help remedies of gossip and violence, they, unlike the cattlemen, sometimes respond to a trespass incident by contacting a county official who they think will remedy the problem. These calls are usually funneled to the animal control officer or brand inspector, who both report that most callers are ranchette owners with limited rural experience. As already discussed, these calls do produce results. The county officials typically contact the owner of the animal, who then arranges for its removal. Brad Bogue, the animal control officer, reported that in half the cases the caller knows whose animal it is. This suggests that callers often think that requests for removal have more effect when issued by someone in authority.

Mere removal of an animal may provide only temporary relief when its owner is a mountain lessee whose cattle have repeatedly descended upon the ranchettes. County officials therefore use mild threats to caution repeat offenders. In closed range, they may mention both their power to impound the estrays and the risk of criminal prosecution. These threats appear to be bluffs; as noted, the county never impounds stray cattle when it can locate an owner, and it rarely prosecutes cattlemen (and then only when their animals have posed risks to motorists). In open range, county officals may deliver a more subtle threat: not that they will initiate a prosecution, but that, if the owner does not mend his ways, the Board of Supervisors may face insuperable pressure to close the range in the relevant area. Because cattlemen perceive that a closure significantly diminishes their legal entitlements in situations where motorists have collided with their livestock, this threat can catch their attention.

A trespass victim's most effective protest is one delivered directly to his elected county supervisor — the person best situated to change stray-cattle liability rules. Many Shasta County residents are aware that traditionalist cattlemen fear the supervisors more than they fear law enforcement authorities. Thus in 1973 the alfalfa farmer John Woodbury made his repeated phone calls about mountain cattle not to Brad Bogue but to Supervisor John Caton. When a supervisor receives many calls from trespass victims, his first instinct is to mediate the crisis. Supervisor Norman Wagoner's standard procedure was to assemble the ranchers in the area and advise them to put pressure on the offender or else risk the closure of the range. Wagoner's successor, Supervisor John Caton, similarly told Frank Ellis that he would support a closure at Oak Run unless Ellis built three miles of fence along the Oak Run Road. If a supervisor is not responsive to a constituent's complaint, the constituent may respond by circulating a closure petition, as Doug Heinz eventually did in Oak Run.

The rarity of claims for monetary relief. Because Shasta County residents tend to settle their trespass disputes beyond the shadow of the law, one might suspect that the norms of neighborliness include a norm against the invocation of formal legal rights. And this norm is indeed entrenched. Owen Shellworth: "I don't believe in lawyers [because there are] always hard feeligs [when you litigate]." Tony Morton: "[I never press a monetary claim because] I try to be a good neighhbor." Norman Wagoner: "Being good neighbors means no lawsuits." Although trespasses are frequent, Shasta County's rural residents virtually never file formal trespass actions against one another. John Woodbury, for example, made dozens of phone calls to Supervisor John Caton, but never sought monetary compensation from the traditionalists whose cattle had repeatedly marauded his alfalfa field. Court records and conversations with court clerks indicate that in most years not a single private lawsuit seeking damages for either trespass by livestock or the expense of boarding estrays is filed in the county's courts. Not only do the residents of the Northeastern Sector foothills refrain from filing formal lawsuits, but they are also strongly disinclined to submit informal monetary claims to the owners of trespassing animals.

The landowners who were interviewed clearly regard their restraint in seeking monetary relief as a mark of virtue. When asked why they did not pursue meritorious legal claims arising from trespass or fence-finance disputes, various landowners replied: "I'm not that kind of guy"; "I don't believe in it"; "I don't like to create a stink"; "I try to get along." The landowners who attempted to provide a rationale for this forbearance all implied the same one, a long-term reciprocity of advantage. Ann Kershaw: "The only one that makes money [when you litigate] is the lawyer." Al Levitt: "I figure it will balance out in the long run." Pete Schultz: "I hope they'll do the same for me." Phil Ritchie: "My family believes in 'live and let live.'"

Mutual restraint save parties in a long-term relationship the costs of going through the formal claims process. Adjoining land-owners who practice the live-and-let-live approach are both better off whenever the negative externalities from their activities are roughly in equipoise. Equipoise is as likely in closed range as in open. Landowners with property in closed range — the ones with the greatest formal legal rights — were the source of half of the quotations in the prior two paragraphs.

When a transfer *is* necessary to square unbalanced accounts, rural neighbors prefer to use in-kind payments, not cash. Shasta County landowners regard a monetary settlement as an arms' length transaction that symbolizes an unneighborly relationship. Should your goat happen to eat your neighbor's tomatoes, the neighborly thing for you to do would be to help replant the tomatoes; a transfer of money would be too cold and too impersonal. When Kevin O'Hara's cattle went through a break in a fence and destroyed his neighbor's corn crop (a loss of less than $100), O'Hara had to work hard to persuade the neighbor to accept his offer of money to compensate for the damages. O'Hara insisted on making this payment because he "felt responsible" for his neighbor's loss, a feeling that would not have been in the least affected had the event occurred in open instead of closed range. There can also be social pressure against offering monetary settlements. Bob Bosworth's father agreed many decades ago to pay damages to a trespass victim in a closed-range area just south of Shasta County; other cattlemen then rebuked him for setting an unfortunate precedent. The junior Bosworth, in 1982 the president of the Shasta County Cattlemen's Association, could recall no other out-of-pocket settlement in a trespass case.

Trespass victims who sustain an unusually large loss are more likely to take the potentially deviant step of making a claim for monetary relief. Among those interviewed were adjusters for the two insurance companies whose liability policies would be most likely to cover losses from animal trespass. The adjusters' responses suggest that in a typical year these companies receive fewer than ten trespass damage claims originating in Shasta County. In the paradigmatic case, the insured is not a rancher but rather a ranchette owner, whose family's horse has escaped and trampled a neighboring homeowner's shrubbery. The claimant is typically not represented by an attorney, a type of professional these adjusters rarely encounter. The adjusters also settle each year two or three trespass claims that homeowners or ranchette owners have brought against the ranchers. Ranchers who suffer trespasses virtually never file claims against other's insurance companies. An adjuster for the company that insures most Shasta County ranchers stated that he could not recall, in his twenty years of adjusting, a single claim by a rancher for compensation for trespass damage.

Attorney-assisted claims. The landowners, particularly the ranchers, express a strong aversion to hiring an attorney to fight one's battles. To hire an attorney is to escalate a conflict. A good neighbor does not do such a thing because the "natural working order" calls for two neighbors to work out their problems between themselves. The files in the Shasta County courthouses reveal that the ranchers who honor norms of neighborliness — the vast majority — are not involved in cattle-related litigation of any kind.

NOTES AND QUESTIONS ON INFORMAL NORMS

1. This selection's central theme is that neighbors are often inclined to trump formal law with their own informal norms. This finding is consistent with a critique of "legal centralism" that Law and Society scholars have embraced for many years. These "legal pluralists" assert that in practice people derive entitlements not only from the state but also from other sources. See, for example, Marc Galanter, Justice in Many Rooms: Courts, Private Ordering, and Indigenous Law, 19 J. Legal Pluralism 1 (1981).

Does the legal-pluralist thesis demolish Coase's analysis, or could Coase readily accommodate it by revising his statements that imply that law is the source of entitlements? Does a practicing lawyer have to be sensitive to the influence of nonlegal sources of rules? Does the legal-pluralist thesis hold lessons for what law schools should teach? Does the Shasta County aphorism, "Being good neighbors means no lawsuits," necessarily imply that the practice of law is ignoble? That litigious people are deviants? For more on informal property rights, see Acheson, supra p.141, and the selections in Chapter 6, infra.

2. In other portions of his Shasta County study, Ellickson reports that rural residents worry far more that wayward livestock will collide with highway motorists than that animals will trespass on cropland. The ruralites unhesitatingly turn to the legal system to resolve highway claims (which commonly are high-stakes disputes between strangers), but seldom use the legal system to resolve animal-trespass disputes (which commonly are low-stakes affairs arising between neighbors engaged in continuing dealings).

Footnote 51 of the selection quotes Galanter's assertion that law is primarily important when disputants lack a future relationship. If this is true, in what contexts is, say, adverse-possession law likely to be irrelevant? Landlord-tenant law? Nuisance law? The law governing relations among concurrent owners?

3. Regardless of what the formal law provides, Shasta County residents are reportedly a norm that an owner of livestock is responsible for the acts of his animals. Why did they embrace that particular norm, as opposed to, for example, a norm obligating cropgrowers to fence out others' livestock? Ellickson speculates that a fencing-out norm *did* prevail in Shasta County during the nineteenth century, when the population was less dense, fencing more expensive, and highways free of motorists. Order Without Law 185-188 (1991). This thesis that norms evolve adaptively echoes Demsetz's notions about the evolution of property rights, supra p.148. In the excerpts provided, did either Demsetz or Ellickson identify an institutional mechanism that would generate this upbeat result?

4. Shasta County residents are reported to use mild forms of violence to enforce their norms. Are their violent acts legally privileged forms of self-help? How great is the danger that self-help violence will trigger an escalating feud? Did Acheson's lobstermen feud too much? Recall Cooter's discussion of Hobbes's view that the state must act to limit the private exercise of violence. Was Hobbes too pessimistic about the chances for cooperation in the absence of a state? Is it significant that Shasta County residents developed their norms while under the umbrella of an established government?

5. Why might neighbors in Shasta County prefer to square unbalanced accounts with gifts and other in-kind payments, as opposed to cash transfers? Are urbanites just as likely to do this? See also Margaret Radin on alienability, infra p.336. More broadly, how generalizable are the Shasta County findings?

The Endowment Effect and Evidence of Nonreversible Indifference Curves*

Jack L. Knetsch

[Students who have not studied economics may be unfamiliar with the core idea that Knetsch challenges in this selection, an idea that Coase implicitly embraced in The Problem of Social Cost. The MIT Dictionary of Modern Economics (4th ed. 1992) defines an *in-*

*Source: 79 Am. Econ. Rev. 1277-1283 (1989).

difference curve as "A curve showing the locus of combinations of the amounts of two goods, say *X* and *Y,* such that the individual is indifferent between any combination on that curve."]

Indifference curves are normally taken to indicate corresponding tradeoffs of goods *A* for *B* or *B* for *A* over the same interval: "the rate of commodity substitution at a point on an indifference curve is the same for movements in either direction" (James Henderson and Richard Quandt, 1971, p.12). However, recent empirical findings of asymmetric evaluations of gains and losses imply that the presumed reversibility may not accurately reflect preferences, and that people commonly make choices that differ depending on the direction of proposed trades.

The evidence from a wide variety of tests is consistent with the suggestions of Daniel Kahneman and Amos Tversky (1979), and Richard Thaler (1980), that losses from a reference position are systematically valued far more than commensurate gains. The minimum compensation people demand to give up a good has been found to be several times larger than the maximum amount they are willing to pay for a commensurate entitlement. For example, when questioned about the possible destruction of a duck habitat, hunters responded that they would be willing to pay an average of $247 to prevent its loss but would demand $1044 to accept it (Judd Hammack and Gardner Brown, 1974). Respondents in another study demanded payments to accept various levels of visibility degradation that were from 5 to over 16 times higher than their valuations based on payment measures. Similar large differences in valuations of a wide variety of goods and entitlements have been reported in numerous survey studies.

These valuation differences based on responses to hypothetical survey questions prompted further, more severe, tests of the disparity using a variety of real exchange experimental designs. The results have been much the same. Even when exchanges of real goods and actual cash payments motivated the evaluations, the compensation demanded to give up an entitlement has been reported to far exceed the comparable payment measure of value. . . .

. . . Other more recent tests of the evaluation disparities, or endowment effects, have shown that the observed disparities between evaluations of entitlements are not the result of wealth effects or income constraints, strategic behavior, or transactions costs, and that the differences persist over repeated binding iterations of market trials (Knetsch, Thaler, and Kahneman, 1988).

The purpose here is to report the results of more direct tests of the reversibility of indifference curves. A variety of test designs were used in these exercises, but in each case one-half of a sample of participants were offered one good or money for another good, and the other half were offered a similar trade but in the opposite direction.

I.   Test 1: Exchanges of Two Goods

A straightforward preference exercise involving a choice between two goods was conducted with three comparable groups of University of Victoria students.

In one class, 76 participants were given a coffee mug and were then asked to complete a short questionnaire. The students had the mug in their possession while they answered the written questions. After the questionnaires were completed, the experimenter showed the participants a 400-gram Swiss chocolate bar and told them they could have one in exchange for their mug.[3] Participants were informed that they could either keep their mugs, or have a chocolate bar. They were instructed to hold up a colored paper with the word "trade" marked on it if they preferred the candy to their mug and wished to make an exchange. All desired trades were made immediately by one of four experimenters present, there was no uncertainty of receiving the other good and no effort was required beyond raising the paper to indicate a willingness to make an exchange.

The 87 participants in the second group were offered an opportunity to make the opposite trade of giving up a candy bar, which had been given them initially, for a mug. All conditions were the same except for the direction of the exchange offer.

The 55 people in the third group were simply offered a choice between receiving a candy bar or mug.

The choices presented to people in each of the first two groups differed only in terms of which good they had to give up to obtain the other — incentives were compatible and there were no income, or wealth, effect possibilities, nor any wealth constraints. However, contrary to the expectation of an equal proportion favoring one good over the other in each group, based on the conventional assertion of economic theory and practice, the different initial entitlements and subsequent direction of potential trades heavily influenced the participants' valuations of the two goods.

---

3. Participants were familiar with both the mugs and the candy bars. The mugs were sold in the University bookstore for $4.95 and the candy bars were available in local shops for around $6.

The preferences indicated by the choices were:

Group	Proportion Favoring (In Percent)		N
	Mug Over Candy	Candy Over Mug	
1. Give up mug to obtain candy	89	11	76
2. Give up candy to obtain mug	10	90	87
3. No initial entitlement	56	44	55

When given a simple choice without a prior entitlement or reference position, 56 percent of the participants (Group 3) selected a mug in preference to a candy bar. But only 10 percent valued a mug more than a candy bar when they had to give up the candy to obtain a mug (Group 2), while 89 percent of those who initially received a mug (Group 1) declined to give it up for a candy bar. The preferences for a mug over a candy bar varied from 10 to 89 percent depending entirely on the reference position of the endowment at the time of the valuations.

In this simple experiment, participants' preferences were not independent of the direction of the exchanges, as is commonly assumed. They expressed a dramatic asymmetry in valuations by weighing the loss of giving up their initial or reference entitlement far more heavily than the foregone gains of not obtaining the alternative entitlement.

II. Test 2: Minimum Acceptable Exchanges

The symmetry of exchange preferences was further tested in a second experiment involving real goods and actual cash payments. As in the first test, the design of this experiment also precluded the influence of a wealth constraint and the possibility of an income, or wealth, effect. The participants were 80 students in five tutorial groups of an introductory pre-principles economics class at Simon Fraser University. The exercise was repeated in the five tutorial meetings in a single afternoon.

Forty-one individuals in three of the groups were first given two 100-gram Swiss chocolate candy bars.[4] They were then asked to state the smallest amount of money they would accept to give up both of their candy bars.

The 39 members of the other two tutorial groups were each given two single-dollar bills. They were then asked the minimum number of chocolate bars they would require to give up their two dollars. The initial offering of money or candy bars was alternated over the five participating groups.

The method of obtaining the declarations of minimum acceptable trades was designed so that stating the smallest compensation each participant would agree to was in the person's best interest. To ensure that the individuals understood that this was the case, a preliminary instruction and screening test was conducted so that they could demonstrate their understanding before becoming participants in the real exchange exercise. This preliminary test involved a hypothetical, induced, or prescribed, value and the identical bidding mechanism that was used to reveal preferences in the subsequent real good exchange.

All participants were given the same form for the preliminary demonstration and screening test:

THIS FIRST PART OF THIS EXERCISE IS HYPOTHETICAL ONLY; NO ACTUAL PAYMENTS WILL BE MADE. HOWEVER, DEPENDING ON THE RESPONSE OF PARTICIPANTS IN THIS GROUP, A SECOND PART MAY BE CONDUCTED IN WHICH ACTUAL PAYMENTS WILL BE MADE.

IF THE SECOND PART IS CONDUCTED, YOU CAN ONLY WIN, YOU CANNOT LOSE.

Assume that the person conducting this exercise will pay you $2.50 for the ticket attached to this sheet.

Now assume that before you redeem the ticket you are given an opportunity to sell it. The price you will be offered for it will be determined by a random draw of one of six cards with the dollar amounts: $0, $1, $2, $3, $4, or $5 on them.

What is the smallest of these offer prices you would accept to give up your ticket?

$_____ (use only whole dollars — i.e., no cents). If the offer price on the randomly drawn card is the same or higher than the price you stated above, you will receive the amount of money on the card in exchange for your ticket. If the offer price on the card is lower than your indicated minimum selling price, you will keep the ticket (and turn it in for the $2.50).

After the participants read the instructions for the preliminary test, the experimenter gave a further explanation and answered

4. These candy bars sell for around $2 each in most shops.

questions. Participants then completed the forms. The experimenter checked the forms to ensure that at least 75 percent of the individuals knew how to respond in a way that served their best interest (by stating $3 as the minimum acceptable price). If more than 25 percent failed to answer in this way the experiment was terminated for that whole group.[6]

Of the 80 individuals in the five groups that went on to the second part involving the real exchanges, only 14 (18 percent) failed to answer the first part correctly.[7] Before proceeding with the second part, the experimenter explained the bidding mechanism again, and pointed out the reasons why other answers could work to the disadvantage of the respondent. These further explanations, and the screening of participants by their demonstrated ability to reveal their true minimum values in this market, ensured that individuals participating in the real exchange experiment fully understood the value revealing incentives of the bidding procedure.

Participants in the second, real exchange, part of the experiment were given their endowment of either candy bars or dollar bills and were told that these were theirs to keep. Those with an entitlement of candy bars then received the following second form:

THIS SECOND PART WILL INVOLVE REAL PAYMENTS. THERE ARE NO RIGHT OR WRONG ANSWERS. YOUR RESPONSE SHOULD REFLECT ONLY YOUR OWN PREFERENCES.

You have been given 2 candy bars. They are yours to keep. However, if you like — and the choice is entirely yours — you may be able to trade the 2 candy bars for money. We want to know about your personal preferences in terms of the smallest number of dollars you would accept to give up the two candy bars.

The amount you will be offered to give up your 2 candy bars will be determined in the same way as it was in Part 1 of this exercise. That is, an offer price, in dollars, will be determined by a random draw of one of the six cards with amounts ranging from $0 to $5.

If you are willing to give up the 2 candy bars for $5 or less, write the smallest of these offer prices that you would accept to give up both of the candy bars in the blank below.

If it would take more than $5 for you to agree to give up your two candy bars, then write a 6 in the blank, and you will then keep your candy bars.

$____ (use only whole dollars — i.e., no cents). If the offer amount on the randomly drawn card is the same or higher than the number you have written above, you will receive the amount of

---

6. This occurred in four other groups.

7. All but 3 of the 14 individuals answering incorrectly specified a selling price *lower* than the most profitable one, an error that would bias the results toward lower evaluations of the initial entitlements and symmetry and away from the much higher values of losses subsequently revealed.

money on the card in exchange for your 2 candy bars. If the offer on the card is lower than the number you have written above you will be allowed to keep the candy bars.

Individuals receiving an initial endowment of money were given a comparable form.

The bid procedure was then explained yet again and questions answered. The random draw of the card was made after the forms were completed, and exchanges were made according to the indicated minimum acceptable trades.

The results again demonstrated a strong aversion to giving up an initial entitlement.

The participants' dollar value of the candy bars is given either by the minimum amount demanded to give them up, or by the number of candy bars required to give up dollars. The proportions of the two samples valuing a candy bar equal to or greater than $1 and $2 are given in the following tabulation.

	Proportion of Individuals Valuing Candy Bar Equal to or More than:	
Group	$1	$2
1. Give Up Money to Get Candy Bars (N = 39)	33%	8%
2. Give Up Candy Bars to Get Money (N = 41)	95%	37%
Chi-Squared Value	35.05	9.57

The participants valued the candy or money significantly more when considering the prospect of giving it up than they did when they had the opportunity to acquire either in exchange for their original entitlement. The average evalutations of the candy bars, based on the responses of all of the participants in each original endowment group, were approximately $1.83 with the entitlement and $0.90 without it. That is, the people starting with the candy bars valued them at a little over twice as much as the people did who were given money.

As in the earlier test, the relative preferences of participants in this exercise depended on reference entitlements and the subsequent direction of trade offers. . . .

The results of the exercises reported here are consistent with other empirical tests of people's evaluations. The greater value ascribed to entitlements that might be lost over ones that might be gained gives rise to the disparity between bid and offer values. This appears to be similar to the observed nonreversibility of indifference curves in the data reported here. . . .

The widespread irreversibility of indifference curves would not imply that people will not make any trades, or that consumers will not change future consumption patterns in response to changing relative prices. However, the presence of irreversibilities would imply that fewer trades will be made than predicted by standard assumptions, and they offer little assurance that the shifts in future consumption will be as complete or as prompt as would be expected if indifference curves were reversible.

In a similar way, the presence of irreversibilities also suggests that common presumptions of the potential gains from trade may often be overstated. . . . And the commonly observed aversion to giving up concessions in negotiations may well be due to a similar asymmetry in valuations of gains and losses.

NOTES AND QUESTIONS ON LOSS AVERSION

1. Cognitive psychologists Daniel Kahneman and Amos Tversky can be credited with many of the pathbreaking advances on loss aversion. Among their many works, see Prospect Theory: An Analysis of Decision under Risk, 47 Econometrica 263 (1979). The blossoming research on the topic is accessibly reviewed in Daniel Kahneman, Jack L. Knetsch & Richard H. Thaler, The Endowment Effect, Loss Aversion, and Status Quo Bias, 5 J. Econ. Perspectives 193 (1991).

2. In Consumption Theory, Production Theory, and Ideology in the Coase Theorem, 52 S. Cal. L. Rev. 669 (1979), cited supra p.208, Mark Kelman argues that the Kahneman-Tversky findings undercut the strong version of the Coase Theorem. If individuals treat the loss of an item as a more momentous event than forgoing the gain of the same item, initial allocations of entitlements will have some tendency to persist. This flypaper tendency is due not just to the transaction costs of exchange, but also to loss aversion, which biases individuals toward maintaining the status quo. In Kelman's eyes, the Coase Theorem embodies the "Chicago School" ideology that state activism is invariably misguided. According to Kelman, Chi-

cagoans think that "the market, like an untameable river, will knock out attempts to alter its course." Kelman himself believes that phenomena such as loss aversion lend significance to legal decisions. Would Coase disagree?

3. Does the Knetsch selection help reveal the sources of what might be called "psychological ownership" — that is, the disposition to regard the deprivation of an item as a loss, as opposed to a forgone gain? In the mug experiments reported by Knetsch, of what significance was physical possession? The passage of time? Perceptions of legal or other normative title? Past outlays of effort and expense? Are the influences of these factors likely to be universalistic, or to vary appreciably from one culture to the next?

4. Consider the political implications of loss aversion. Does it help explain why Congress has been reluctant to close military bases, end agricultural subsidies, and privatize public housing? Does it explain why legislators require employers to withhold estimated income-tax liabilities from employees' paychecks? Why the local officials who support growth controls rarely push to reduce current populations? See generally Roger G. Noll & James E. Krier, Some Implications of Cognitive Psychology for Risk Regulation, 19 J. Legal Stud. 747 (1990), an exploration of the political implications of a number of psychological phenomena.

Does loss aversion make any cost-benefit analysis indeterminate, and hence useless as an instrument of policy analysis? Compare Duncan Kennedy, Cost/Benefit Analysis of Entitlement Problems: A Critique, 33 Stan. L. Rev. 387 (1981) with Richard S. Markovits, Duncan's Do Nots, 36 Stan. L. Rev. 1169 (1984).

5. What are the implications for legal doctrine? If loss aversion creates a status quo bias, does it help explain the rule of *stare decisis*? Why a minor physical taking is usually more constitutionally suspect than a regulatory restriction that drastically reduces future development opportunities? In adverse possession cases, why the law eventually favors the claims of the adverse possessor, as opposed to those of the original owner? See David Cohen & Jack L. Knetsch, Judicial Choice and Disparities Between Measures of Economic Values, 30 Osgoode Hall L.J. 737 (1992); Robert C. Ellickson, Bringing Culture and Human Frailty to Rational Actors, 65 Chi.-Kent L. Rev. 23, 35-39 (1989).

6. The theory of loss aversion is hardly universally embraced. Some critics have attacked its proponents' methodologies; others have pointed to evidence that market participants learn through experience to suppress loss aversion. Edmund W. Kitch succinctly summarizes these criticisms under the entry *framing hypothesis* in

the New Palgrave Dictionary of Money & Finance 184 (1992). For a more comprehensive review of the literature, pro and con, see Elizabeth Hoffman & Matthew L. Spitzer, Willingness to Pay vs. Willingness to Accept: Legal and Economic Implications, 71 Wash. U. L.Q. 59 (1993).

Chapter 5

Property Rules, Liability Rules

Property Rules, Liability Rules, and Inalienability: One View of the Cathedral*

Guido Calabresi & A. Douglas Melamed

I. Introduction

Only rarely are Property and Torts approached from a unified perspective. Recent writings by lawyers concerned with economics and by economists concerned with law suggest, however, that an attempt at integrating the various legal relationships treated by these subjects would be useful both for the beginning student and the sophisticated scholar.[1] By articulating a concept of "entitlements" which are protected by property, liability, or inalienability rules, we present one framework for such an approach. We then analyze aspects of the pollution problem to demonstrate how the model enables us to perceive relationships which have been ignored by writers in those fields.

The first issue which must be faced by any legal system is one we call the problem of "entitlement." Whenever a state is presented with the conflicting interests of two or more people, or two or more

---

*Source: 85 Harv. L. Rev. 1089-1199, 1105-1127 (1972).
1. See, e.g., Michelman, Pollution as a Tort: A Non-Accidental Perspective on Calabresi's Costs, 80 Yale L.J. 647 (1971) (analysis of three alternative rules in pollution problems); Demsetz, Toward a Theory of Property Rights, 57 Am. Econ. Rev. 347 (1967) (Vol. 2 — Papers and Proceedings) (analysis of property as a means of cost internalization which ignores liability rule alternatives).

groups of people, it must decide which side to favor. Absent such a decision, access to goods, services, and life itself will be decided on the basis of "might makes right" — whoever is stronger or shrewder will win. Hence the fundamental thing that law does is to decide which of the conflicting parties will be entitled to prevail. The entitlement to make noise versus the entitlement to have silence, the entitlement to pollute versus the entitlement to breathe clean air, the entitlement to have children versus the entitlement to forbid them — these are the first order of legal decisions.

Having made its initial choice, society must enforce that choice. Simply setting the entitlement does not avoid the problem of "might makes right"; a minimum of state intervention is always necessary. Our conventional notions make this easy to comprehend with respect to private property. If Taney owns a cabbage patch and Marshall, who is bigger, wants a cabbage, he will get it unless the state intervenes. But it is not so obvious that the state must also intervene if it chooses the opposite entitlement, communal property. If large Marshall has grown some communal cabbages and chooses to deny them to small Taney, it will take state action to enforce Taney's entitlement to the communal cabbages. The same symmetry applies with respect to bodily integrity. Consider the plight of the unwilling ninety-eight-pound weakling in a state which nominally entitles him to bodily integrity but will not intervene to enforce the entitlement against a lustful Juno. Consider then the plight — absent state intervention — of the ninety-eight-pounder who desires an unwilling Juno in a state which nominally entitles everyone to use everyone else's body. The need for intervention applies in a slightly more complicated way to injuries. When a loss is left where it falls in an auto accident, it is not because God so ordained it. Rather it is because the state has granted the injurer an entitlement to be free of liability and will intervene to prevent the victim's friends, if they are stronger, from taking compensation from the injurer. The loss is shifted in other cases because the state has granted an entitlement to compensation and will intervene to prevent the stronger injurer from rebuffing the victim's requests for compensation.

The state not only has to decide whom to entitle, but it must also simultaneously make a series of equally difficult second order decisions. These decisions go to the manner in which entitlements are protected and to whether an individual is allowed to sell or trade the entitlement. In any given dispute, for example, the state must decide not only which side wins but also the kind of protection to grant. It is with the latter decisions, decisions which shape the subsequent relationship between the winner and the loser, that this article is primarily concerned. We shall consider three types of entitlements — entitlements protected by property rules, entitlements protected by liability rules, and inalienable entitlements. The categories are not, of course, absolutely distinct; but the categorization is useful since it reveals some of the reasons which lead us to protect certain entitlements in certain ways.

An entitlement is protected by a property rule to the extent that someone who wishes to remove the entitlement from its holder must buy it from him in a voluntary transaction in which the value of the entitlement is agreed upon by the seller. It is the form of entitlement which gives rise to the least amount of state intervention: Once the original entitlement is decided upon, the state does not try to decide its value.[7] It lets each of the parties say how much the entitlement is worth to him, and gives the seller a veto if the buyer does not offer enough. Property rules involve a collective decision as to who is to be given an initial entitlement but not as to the value of the entitlement.

Whenever someone may destroy the initial entitlement if he is willing to pay an objectively determined value for it, an entitlement is protected by a liability rule. This value may be what it is thought the original holder of the entitlement would have sold it for. But the holder's complaint that he would have demanded more will not avail him once the objectively determined value is set. Obviously, liability rules involve an additional stage of state intervention: Not only are entitlements protected, but their transfer or destruction is allowed on the basis of a value determined by some organ of the state rather than by the parties themselves.

An entitlement is inalienable to the extent that its transfer is not permitted between a willing buyer and a willing seller. The state intervenes not only to determine who is initially entitled and to determine the compensation that must be paid if the entitlement is taken or destroyed, but also to forbid its sale under some or all circumstances. Inalienability rules are thus quite different from property and liability rules. Unlike those rules, rules of inalienability not only "protect" the entitlement; they may also be viewed as limiting or regulating the grant of the entitlement itself.

It should be clear that most entitlements to most goods are mixed. Taney's house may be protected by a property rule in situa-

---

7. A property rule requires less state intervention only in the sense that intervention is needed to decide upon and enforce the initial entitlement but not for the separate problem of determining the value of the entitlement. Thus, if a particular property entitlement is especially difficult to enforce — for example, the right to personal security in urban areas — the actual amount of state intervention can be very high and could, perhaps, exceed that needed for some entitlements protected by easily administered liability rules.

tions where Marshall wishes to purchase it, by a liability rule where the government decides to take it by eminent domain, and by a rule of inalienability in situations where Taney is drunk or incompetent. This article will explore two primary questions: (1) In what circumstances should we grant a particular entitlement? and (2) In what circumstances should we decide to protect that entitlement by using a property, liability, or inalienability rule?

II.   The Setting of Entitlements

What are the reasons for deciding to entitle people to pollute or to entitle people to forbid pollution, to have children freely or to limit procreation, to own property or to share property? They can be grouped under three headings: economic efficiency, distributional preferences, and other justice considerations.

A.   Economic Efficiency

Perhaps the simplest reason for a particular entitlement is to minimize the administrative costs of enforcement. This was the reason Holmes gave for letting the costs lie where they fall in accidents unless some clear societal benefit is achieved by shifting them. By itself this reason will never justify any result except that of letting the stronger win, for obviously that result minimizes enforcement costs. Nevertheless, administrative efficiency may be relevant to choosing entitlements when other reasons are taken into account. This may occur when the reasons accepted are indifferent between conflicting entitlements and one entitlement is cheaper to enforce than the others. It may also occur when the reasons are not indifferent but lead us only slightly to prefer one over another and the first is considerably more expensive to enforce than the second.

But administrative efficiency is just one aspect of the broader concept of economic efficiency. Economic efficiency asks that we choose the set of entitlements which would lead to that allocation of resources which could not be improved in the sense that a further change would not so improve the condition of those who gained by it that they could compensate those who lost from it and still be better off than before. This is often called Pareto-optimality. To give two examples, economic efficiency asks for that combination of entitlements to engage in risky activities and to be free from harm from risky activities which will most likely lead to the lowest sum of accident costs and of costs of avoiding accidents. It asks for that form of property, private or communal, which leads to the highest product for the effort of producing.

Recently it has been argued that on certain assumptions, usually termed the absence of transaction costs, Pareto-optimality or economic efficiency will occur regardless of the initial entitlement. For this to hold, "no transaction costs" must be understood extremely broadly as involving both perfect knowledge and the absence of any impediments or costs of negotiating. Negotiation costs include, for example, the cost of excluding would-be freeloaders from the fruits of market bargains.[13] In such a frictionless society, transactions would occur until no one could be made better off as a result of further transactions without making someone else worse off. This, we would suggest, is a necessary, indeed a tautological, result of the definitions of Pareto-optimality and of transaction costs which we have given.

Such a result would not mean, however, that the *same* allocation of resources would exist regardless of the initial set of entitlements. Taney's willingness to pay for the right to make noise may depend on how rich he is; Marshall's willingness to pay for silence may depend on his wealth. In a society which entitles Taney to make noise and which forces Marshall to buy silence from Taney, Taney is wealthier and Marshall poorer than each would be in a society which had the converse set of entitlements. Depending on how Marshall's desire for silence and Taney's for noise vary with their wealth, an entitlement to noise will result in negotiations which will lead to a different quantum of noise than would an entitlement to silence. This variation in the quantity of noise and

13. The freeloader is the person who refuses to be inoculated against smallpox because, given the fact that almost everyone else is inoculated, the risk of smallpox to him is less than the risk of harm from the inoculation. He is the person who refuses to pay for a common park, though he wants it, because he believes that others will put in enough money to make the park available to him. The costs of excluding the freeloader from the benefits for which he refused to pay may well be considerable as the two above examples should suggest. This is especially so since these costs may include the inefficiency of pricing a good, like the park once it exists, above its marginal cost in order to force the freeloader to disclose his true desire to use it — thus enabling us to charge him part of the cost of establishing it initially.

It is the capacity of the market to induce disclosure of individual preferences which makes it theoretically possible for the market to bring about exchanges leading to Pareto-optimality. But the freeloader situation is just one of many where no such disclosure is achieved by the market. If we assume perfect knowledge, defined more broadly than is normally done to include knowledge of individual preferences, then such situations pose no problem. This definition of perfect knowledge, though perhaps implicit in the concept of no transaction costs, would not only make reaching Pareto-optimality easy through the market, it would make it equally easy to establish a similar result by collective fiat. . . .

silence can be viewed as no more than an instance of the well accepted proposition that what is a Pareto-optimal, or economically efficient, solution varies with the starting distribution of wealth. Pareto-optimality is optimal *given* a distribution of wealth, but different distributions of wealth imply their own Pareto-optimal allocation of resources.

All this suggests why distributions of wealth may affect a society's choice of entitlements. It does not suggest why *economic efficiency* should affect the choice, if we assume an absence of any transaction costs. But no one makes an assumption of no transaction costs in practice. Like the physicist's assumption of no friction or Say's law in macro-economics, the assumption of no transaction costs may be a useful starting point, a device which helps us see how, as different elements which may be termed transaction costs become important, the goal of economic efficiency starts to prefer one allocation of entitlements over another.

Since one of us has written at length on how in the presence of various types of transaction costs a society would go about deciding on a set of entitlements in the field of accident law, it is enough to say here: (1) that economic efficiency standing alone would dictate that set of entitlements which favors knowledgeable choices between social benefits and the social costs of obtaining them, and between social costs and the social costs of avoiding them; (2) that this implies, in the absence of certainty as to whether a benefit is worth its costs to society, that the cost should be put on the party or activity best located to make such a cost-benefit analysis; (3) that in particular contexts like accidents or pollution this suggests putting costs on the party or activity which can most cheaply avoid them; (4) that in the absence of certainty as to who that party or activity is, the costs should be put on the party or activity which can with the lowest transaction costs act in the market to correct an error in entitlements by inducing the party who can avoid social costs most cheaply to do so; and (5) that since we are in an area where by hypothesis markets do not work perfectly — there are transaction costs — a decision will often have to be made on whether market transactions or collective fiat is most likely to bring us closer to the Pareto-optimal result the "perfect" market would reach.

Complex though this summary may suggest the entitlement choice to be, in practice the criteria it represents will frequently indicate which allocations of entitlements are most likely to lead to optimal market judgments between having an extra car or taking a train, getting an extra cabbage and spending less time working in the hot sun, and having more widgets and breathing the pollution that widget production implies. Economic efficiency is not, however, the sole reason which induces a society to select a set of entitlements. Wealth distribution preferences are another, and thus it is to distributional grounds for different entitlements to which we must now turn.

B. Distributional Goals

There are, we would suggest, at least two types of distributional concerns which may affect the choice of entitlements. These involve distribution of wealth itself and distribution of certain specific goods, which have sometimes been called merit goods.

All societies have wealth distribution preferences. They are, nonetheless, harder to talk about than are efficiency goals. For efficiency goals can be discussed in terms of a general concept like Pareto-optimality to which exceptions — like paternalism — can be noted. Distributional preferences, on the other hand, cannot usefully be discussed in a single conceptual framework. There are some fairly broadly accepted preferences — caste preferences in one society, more rather than less equality in another society. There are also preferences which are linked to dynamic efficiency concepts — producers ought to be rewarded since they will cause everyone to be better off in the end. Finally, there are a myriad of highly individualized preferences as to who should be richer and who poorer which need not have anything to do with either equality or efficiency — silence lovers should be richer than noise lovers because they are worthier.

Difficult as wealth distribution preferences are to analyze, it should be obvious that they play a crucial role in the setting of entitlements. For the placement of entitlements has a fundamental effect on a society's distribution of wealth. It is not enough, if a society wishes absolute equality, to start everyone off with the same amount of money. A financially egalitarian society which gives individuals the right to make noise immediately makes the would-be noisemaker richer than the silence loving hermit. Similarly, a society which entitles the person with brains to keep what his shrewdness gains him implies a different distribution of wealth from a society which demands from each according to his relative ability but gives to each according to his relative desire. One can go further and consider that a beautiful woman or handsome man is better off in a society which entitles individuals to bodily integrity than in one which gives everybody use of all the beauty available. . . .

III.   Rules for Protecting and Regulating Entitlements

Whenever society chooses an initial entitlement it must also determine whether to protect the entitlement by property rules, by liability rules, or by rules of inalienability. In our framework, much of what is generally called private property can be viewed as an entitlement which is protected by a property rule. No one can take the entitlement to private property from the holder unless the holder sells it willingly and at the price at which he subjectively values the property. Yet a nuisance with sufficient public utility to avoid injunction has, in effect, the right to take property with compensation. In such a circumstance the entitlement to the property is protected only by what we call a liability rule: An external, objective standard of value is used to facilitate the transfer of the entitlement from the holder to the nuisance. Finally, in some instances we will not allow the sale of the property at all, that is, we will occasionally make the entitlement inalienable.

This section will consider the circumstances in which society will employ these three rules to solve situations of conflict. Because the property rule and the liability rule are closely related and depend for their application on the shortcomings of each other, we treat them together. We discuss inalienability separately.

A.   Property and Liability Rules

Why cannot a society simply decide on the basis of the already mentioned criteria who should receive any given entitlement, and then let its transfer occur only through a voluntary negotiation? Why, in other words, cannot society limit itself to the property rule? To do this it would need only to protect and enforce the initial entitlements from all attacks, perhaps through criminal sanctions, and to enforce voluntary contracts for their transfer. Why do we need liability rules at all?

In terms of economic efficiency the reason is easy enough to see. Often the cost of establishing the value of an initial entitlement by negotiation is so great that even though a transfer of the entitlement would benefit all concerned, such a transfer will not occur. If a collective determination of the value were available instead, the beneficial transfer would quickly come about.

Eminent domain is a good example. A park where Guidacres, a tract of land owned by 1,000 owners in 1,000 parcels, now sits would, let us assume, benefit a neighboring town enough so that the 100,000 citizens of the town would each be willing to pay an average of $100 to have it. The park is Pareto-desirable if the owners of the tracts of land in Guidacres actually value their entitlements at less than $10,000,000 or an average of $10,000 a tract. Let us assume that in fact the parcels are all the same and all the owners value them at $8,000. On this assumption, the park is, in economic efficiency terms, desirable — in values foregone it costs $8,000,000 and is worth $10,000,000 to the buyers. And yet it may well not be established. If enough of the owners hold-out for more than $10,000 in order to get a share of the $2,000,000 that they guess the buyers are willing to pay over the value which the sellers in actuality attach, the price demanded will be more than $10,000,000 and no park will result. The sellers have an incentive to hide their true valuation and the market will not succeed in establishing it.

An equally valid example could be made on the buying side. Suppose the sellers of Guidacres have agreed to a sales price of $8,000,000 (they are all relatives and at a family banquet decided that trying to hold out would leave them all losers). It does not follow that the buyers can raise that much even though each of 100,000 citizens *in fact* values the park at $100. Some citizens may try to free-load and say the park is only worth $50 or even nothing to them, hoping that enough others will admit to a higher desire and make up the $8,000,000 price. Again there is no reason to believe that a market, a decentralized system of valuing, will cause people to express their true valuations and hence yield results which all would *in fact* agree are desirable.

Whenever this is the case an argument can readily be made for moving from a property rule to a liability rule. If society can remove from the market the valuation of each tract of land, decide the value collectively, and impose it, then the holdout problem is gone. Similarly, if society can value collectively each individual citizen's desire to have a park and charge him a "benefits" tax based upon it, the freeloader problem is gone. If the sum of the taxes is greater than the sum of the compensation awards, the park will result.

Of course, one can conceive of situations where it might be cheap to exclude all the freeloaders from the park, or to ration the park's use in accordance with original willingness to pay. In such cases the incentive to free-load might be eliminated. But such exclusions, even if possible, are usually not cheap. And the same may be the case for the market methods which might avoid the holdout problem on the seller side.

Moreover, even if holdout and freeloader problems can be met feasibly by the market, an argument may remain for employing a liability rule. Assume that in our hypothetical, freeloaders can be excluded at the cost of $1,000,000 and that all owners of tracts in

Guidacres can be convinced, by the use of $500,000 worth of advertising and cocktail parties, that a sale will only occur if they reveal their true land valuations. Since $8,000,000 plus $1,500,000 is less than $10,000,000, the park will be established. But if collective valuation of the tracts and of the benefits of the prospective park would have cost less than $1,500,000, it would have been inefficient to establish the park through the market — a market which was not worth having would have been paid for.[36]

Of course, the problems with liability rules are equally real. We cannot be at all sure that landowner Taney is lying or holding out when he says his land is worth $12,000 to him. The fact that several neighbors sold identical tracts for $10,000 does not help us very much; Taney may be sentimentally attached to his land. As a result, eminent domain may grossly undervalue what Taney would actually sell for, even if it sought to give him his true valuation of his tract. In practice, it is so hard to determine Taney's true valuation that eminent domain simply gives him what the land is worth "objectively," in the full knowledge that this may result in over or under compensation. The same is true on the buyer side. "Benefits" taxes rarely attempt, let alone succeed, in gauging the individual citizen's relative desire for the alleged benefit. They are justified because, even if they do not accurately measure each individual's desire for the benefit, the market alternative seems worse. For example, fifty different households may place different values on a new sidewalk that is to abut all the properties. Nevertheless, becaue it is too difficult, even if possible, to gauge each household's valuation, we usually tax each household an equal amount.

The example of eminent domain is simply one of numerous instances in which society uses liability rules. Accidents is another. If we were to give victims a property entitlement not to be acci-

---

36. It may be argued that, given imperfect knowledge, the market is preferable because it places a limit — the cost of establishing a market — on the size of the possible loss, while the costs of coercion cannot be defined and may be infinite. This may be true in some situations but need not always be the case. If, for example, we know that the holdouts would sell for $500,000 more than is offered, because they recently offered the land at that higher price, coercing them to sell at an objectively determined price between the seller's offer and the purchaser's offer cannot result in more than $500,000 in harm. Thus, the costs of coercion would also not be infinite. Nor is it an answer to say that the man who would sell for a higher price but is coerced for a lower one suffers an indefinite nonmonetary cost in addition to the price differential simply because he is coerced and resents it. For while this may well be true, the same nonmonetary resentment may also exist in those who desire the park and do not get it because the market is unable to pay off those who are holding out for a greater than actual value. In other words, unascertainable resentment costs may exist as a result of either coercion or market failure.

dentally injured we would have to require all who engage in activities that may injure individuals to negotiate with them before an accident, and to buy the right to knock off an arm or a leg. Such pre-accident negotiations would be extremely expensive, often prohibitively so. To require them would thus preclude many activities that might, in fact, be worth having. And, after an accident, the loser of the arm or leg can always very plausibly deny that he would have sold it at the price the buyer would have offered. Indeed, where negotiations after an accident do occur — for instance pretrial settlements — it is largely because the alternative is the collective valuation of the damages.

It is not our object here to outline all the theoretical, let alone the practical, situations where markets may be too expensive or fail and where collective valuations seem more desirable. Economic literature has many times surrounded the issue if it has not always zeroed in on it in ways intelligible to lawyers. It is enough for our purposes to note that a very common reason, perhaps the most common one, for employing a liability rule rather than a property rule to protect an entitlement is that market valuation of the entitlement is deemed inefficient, that is, it is either unavailable or too expensive compared to a collective valuation.

We should also recognize that efficiency is not the sole ground for employing liability rules rather than property rules. Just as the initial entitlement is often decided upon for distributional reasons, so too the choice of a liability rule is often made because it facilitates a combination of efficiency and distributive results which would be difficult to achieve under a property rule. As we shall see in the pollution context, use of a liability rule may allow us to accomplish a measure of redistribution that could only be attained at a prohibitive sacrifice of efficiency if we employed a corresponding property rule.

More often, once a liability rule is decided upon, perhaps for efficiency reasons, it is then employed to favor distributive goals as well. Again accidents and eminent domain are good examples. In both of these areas the compensation given has clearly varied with society's distributive goals, and cannot be readily explained in terms of giving the victim, as nearly as possible, an objectively determined equivalent of the price at which he would have sold what was taken from him.

It should not be surprising that this is often so, even if the original reason for a liability rule is an efficiency one. For distributional goals are expensive and difficult to achieve, and the collective valuation involved in liability rules readily lends itself to promoting distributional goals. This does not mean that distributional goals are always well served in this way. Ad hoc decision-making is always troublesome, and the difficulties are especially acute when the settlement of conflicts between parties is used as a vehicle for the solution of more widespread distributional problems. Nevertheless, distributional objectives may be better attained in this way than otherwise.

B. Inalienable Entitlements

Thus far we have focused on the questions of when society should protect an entitlement by property or liability rules. However, there remain many entitlements which involve a still greater degree of societal intervention: The law not only decides who is to own something and what price is to be paid for it if it is taken or destroyed, but also regulates its sale — by, for example, prescribing preconditions for a valid sale or forbidding a sale altogether. Although these rules of inalienability are substantially different from the property and liability rules, their use can be analyzed in terms of the same efficiency and distributional goals that underlie the use of the other two rules.

While at first glance efficiency objectives may seem undermined by limitations on the ability to engage in transactions, closer analysis suggests that there are instances, perhaps many, in which economic efficiency is more closely approximated by such limitations. This might occur when a transaction would create significant externalities — costs to third parties.

For instance, if Taney were allowed to sell his land to Chase, a polluter, he would injure his neighbor Marshall by lowering the value of Marshall's land. Conceivably, Marshall could pay Taney not to sell his land; but, because there are many injured Marshalls, freeloader and information costs make such transactions practically impossible. The state could protect the Marshalls and yet facilitate the sale of the land by giving the Marshalls an entitlement to prevent Taney's sale to Chase but only protecting the entitlement by a liability rule. It might, for instance, charge an excise tax on all sales of land to polluters equal to its estimate of the external cost to the Marshalls of the sale. But where there are so many injured Marshalls that the price required under the liability rule is likely to be high enough so that no one would be willing to pay it, then setting up the machinery for collective valuation will be wasteful. Barring the sale to polluters will be the most efficient result because it is clear that avoiding pollution is cheaper than paying its costs — including its costs to the Marshalls.

Another instance in which external costs may justify inalienability occurs when external costs do not lend themselves to collective measurement which is acceptably objective and nonarbitrary. This nonmonetizability is characteristic of one category of external costs which, as a practical matter, seems frequently to lead us to rules of inalienability. Such external costs are often called moralisms.

If Taney is allowed to sell himself into slavery, or to take undue risks of becoming penniless, or to sell a kidney, Marshall may be harmed, simply because Marshall is a sensitive man who is made unhappy by seeing slaves, paupers, or persons who die because they have sold a kidney. Again Marshall could pay Taney not to sell his freedom to Chase the slaveowner; but again, because Marshall is not one but many individuals, freeloader and information costs make such transactions practically impossible. Again, it might seem that the state could intervene by objectively valuing the external cost to Marshall and requiring Chase to pay that cost. But since the external cost to Marshall does not lend itself to an acceptable objective measurement, such liability rules are not appropriate.

In the case of Taney selling land to Chase, the polluter, they were inappropriate because we *knew* that the costs to Taney and the Marshalls exceeded the benefits to Chase. Here, though we are not certain of how a cost-benefit analysis would come out, liability rules are inappropriate because any monetization is, by hypothesis, out of the question. The state must, therefore, either ignore the external costs to Marshall, or if it judges them great enough, forbid the transaction that gave rise to them by making Taney's freedom inalienable.

Obviously we will not always value the external harm of a moralism enough to prohibit the sale. And obviously also, external costs other than moralisms may be sufficiently hard to value to make rules of inalienability appropriate in certain circumstances; this reason for rules of inalienability, however, does seem most often germane in situations where moralisms are involved.

There are two other efficiency reasons for forbidding the sale of entitlements under certain circumstances: self paternalism and true paternalism. Examples of the first are Ulysses tying himself to the mast or individuals passing a bill of rights so that they will be prevented from yielding to momentary temptations which they deem harmful to themselves. This type of limitation is not in any real sense paternalism. It is fully consistent with Pareto-efficiency criteria, based on the notion that over the mass of cases no one knows better than the individual what is best for him or her. It merely allows the individual to choose what is best in the long run rather than in the short run, even though that choice entails giving up some short run freedom of choice. Self paternalism may cause us to require certain conditions to exist before we allow a sale of an entitlement; and it may help explain many situations of inalienability, like the invalidity of contracts entered into when drunk, or under undue influence or coercion. But it probably does not fully explain even these.

True paternalism brings us a step further toward explaining such prohibitions and those of broader kinds — for example the prohibitions on a whole range of activities by minors. Paternalism is based on the notion that at least in some situations the Marshalls know better than Taney what will make Taney better off. Here we are not talking about the offense to Marshall from Taney's choosing to read pornography, or selling himself into slavery, but rather the judgment that Taney was not in the position to choose best for himself when he made the choice for erotica or servitude. The first concept we called a moralism and is a frequent and important ground for inalienability. But it is consistent with the premises of Pareto-optimality. The second, paternalism, is also an important economic efficiency reason for inalienability, but it is not consistent with the premises of Pareto-optimality: The most efficient pie is no longer that which costless bargains would achieve, because a person may be better off if he is prohibited from bargaining.

Finally, just as efficiency goals sometimes dictate the use of rules of inalienability, so, of course, do distributional goals. Whether an entitlement may be sold or not often affects directly who is richer and who is poorer. Prohibiting the sale of babies makes poorer those who can cheaply produce babies and richer those who through some nonmarket device get free an "unwanted" baby. Prohibiting exculpatory clauses in product sales makes richer those who were injured by a product defect and poorer those who were not injured and who paid more for the product because the exculpatory clause was forbidden. Favoring the specific group that has benefited may or may not have been the reason for the prohibition on bargaining. What is important is that, regardless of the reason for barring a contract, a group did gain from the prohibition.

This should suffice to put us on guard, for it suggests that direct distributional motives may lie behind asserted nondistributional grounds for inalienability, whether they be paternalism, self paternalism, or externalities. This does not mean that giving weight to distributional goals is undesirable. It clearly is desirable where on efficiency grounds society is indifferent between an alienable and an inalienable entitlement and distributional goals favor one approach or the other. It may well be desirable even when distributional goals are achieved at some efficiency costs. The danger may be, however, that what is justified on, for example, paternalism grounds is really a hidden way of accruing distributional benefits for a group whom we would not otherwise wish to benefit. For example, we may use certain types of zoning to preserve open spaces on the grounds that the poor will be happier, though they do not know it now. And open spaces may indeed make the poor happier in the long run. But the zoning that preserves open space also makes housing in the suburbs more expensive and it may be that the whole plan is aimed at securing distributional benefits to the suburban dweller regardless of the poor's happiness.

IV. The Framework and Pollution Control Rules

Nuisance or pollution is one of the most interesting areas where the question of who will be given an entitlement, and how it will be protected, is in frequent issue. Traditionally, and very ably in the recent article by Professor Michelman, the nuisance-pollution problem is viewed in terms of three rules.[53] First, Taney may not pollute unless his neighbor (his only neighbor let us assume), Marshall, allows it (Marshall may enjoin Taney's nuisance). Second, Taney may pollute but must compensate Marshall for damages caused (nuisance is found but the remedy is limited to damages). Third, Taney may pollute at will and can only be stopped by Marshall if Marshall pays him off (Taney's pollution is not held to be a nuisance to Marshall). In our terminology rules one and two (nuisance with injunction, and with damages only) are entitlements to Marshall. The first is an entitlement to be free from pollution and is protected by a property rule; the second is also an entitlement to be free from pollution but is protected only by a liability rule. Rule three (no nuisance) is instead an entitlement to Taney protected by a property rule, for only by buying Taney out at Taney's price can Marshall end the pollution.

The very statement of these rules in the context of our framework suggests that something is missing. Missing is a fourth rule representing an entitlement in Taney to pollute, but an entitlement which is protected only by a liability rule. The fourth rule, really a kind of partial eminent domain coupled with a benefits tax, can be stated as follows: Marshall may stop Taney from polluting, but if he does he must compensate Taney.

As a practical matter it will be easy to see why even legal writ-

53. See Michelman, supra n.1.

ers as astute as Professor Michelman have ignored this rule. Unlike the first three it does not often lend itself to judicial imposition for a number of good legal process reasons. For example, even if Taney's injuries could practicably be measured, apportionment of the duty of compensation among many Marshalls would present problems for which courts are not well suited. If only those Marshalls who voluntarily asserted the right to enjoin Taney's pollution were required to pay the compensation, there would be insuperable free-loader problems. If, on the other hand, the liability rule entitled one of the Marshalls alone to enjoin the pollution and required all the benefited Marshalls to pay their share of the compensation, the courts would be faced with the immensely difficult task of determining who was benefited how much and imposing a benefits tax accordingly, all the while observing procedural limits within which courts are expected to function.

The fourth rule is thus not part of the cases legal scholars read when they study nuisance law, and is therefore easily ignored by them. But it is available, and may sometimes make more sense than any of the three competing approaches. Indeed, in one form or another, it may well be the most frequent device employed. To appreciate the utility of the fourth rule and to compare it with the other three rules, we will examine why we might choose any of the given rules.

We would employ rule one (entitlement to be free from pollution protected by a property rule) from an economic efficiency point of view if we believed that the polluter, Taney, could avoid or reduce the costs of pollution more cheaply than the pollutee, Marshall. Or to put it another way, Taney would be enjoinable if he were in a better position to balance the costs of polluting against the costs of not polluting. We would employ rule three (entitlement to pollute protected by a property rule) again solely from an economic efficiency standpoint, if we made the converse judgment on who could best balance the harm of pollution against its avoidance costs. If we were wrong in our judgments and if transactions between Marshall and Taney were costless or even very cheap, the entitlement under rules one or three would be traded and an economically efficient result would occur in either case. If we entitled Taney to pollute and Marshall valued clean air more than Taney valued the pollution, Marshall would pay Taney to stop polluting even though no nuisance was found. If we entitled Marshall to enjoin the pollution and the right to pollute was worth more to Taney than freedom from pollution was to Marshall, Taney would pay Marshall not to seek an injunction or would buy Marshall's land and sell it to someone who would agree not to seek an injunction. As we have assumed no one else was hurt by the pollution, Taney could now pollute even though the initial entitlement, based on a wrong guess of who was the cheapest avoider of the costs involved, allowed the pollution to be enjoined. Wherever transactions between Taney and Marshall are easy, and wherever economic efficiency is our goal, we could employ entitlements protected by property rules even though we would not be sure that the entitlement chosen was the right one. Transactions as described above would cure the error. While the entitlement might have important distributional effects, it would not substantially undercut economic efficiency.

The moment we assume, however, that transactions are not cheap, the situation changes dramatically. Assume we enjoin Taney and there are 10,000 injured Marshalls. Now *even if* the right to pollute is worth more to Taney than the right to be free from pollution is to the sum of the Marshalls, the injunction will probably stand. The cost of buying out all the Marshalls, given holdout problems, is likely to be too great, and an equivalent of eminent domain in Taney would be needed to alter the initial injunction. Conversely, if we denied a nuisance remedy, the 10,000 Marshalls could only with enormous difficulty, given free loader problems, get together to buy out even one Taney and prevent the pollution. This would be so even if the pollution harm was greater than the value to Taney of the right to pollute.

If, however, transaction costs are not symmetrical, we may still be able to use the property rule. Assume that Taney can buy the Marshalls' entitlements easily because holdouts are for some reason absent, but that the Marshalls have great freeloader problems in buying out Taney. In this situation the entitlement should be granted to the Marshalls unless we are sure the Marshalls are the cheapest avoiders of pollution costs. Where we do not know the identity of the cheapest cost avoider it is better to entitle the Marshalls to be free of pollution because, even if we are wrong in our initial placement of the entitlement, that is, even if the Marshalls are the cheapest cost avoiders, Taney will buy out the Marshalls and economic efficiency will be achieved. Had we chosen the converse entitlement and been wrong, the Marshalls could not have bought out Taney. Unfortunately, transaction costs are often high on both sides and an initial entitlement, though incorrect in terms of economic efficiency, will not be altered in the market place.

Under these circumstances — and they are normal ones in the pollution area — we are likely to turn to liability rules whenever we are uncertain whether the polluter or the pollutees can most cheaply avoid the cost of pollution. We are only likely to use liability rules where we are uncertain because, if we are certain, the costs of liability rules — essentially the costs of collectively valuing the damages to all concerned plus the cost in coercion to those who would not sell at the collectively determined figure — are unnecessary. They are unnecessary because transaction costs and bargaining barriers become irrelevant when we are certain who is the cheapest cost avoider; economic efficiency will be attained without transactions by making the correct initial entitlement.

As a practical matter we often are uncertain who the cheapest cost avoider is. In such cases, traditional legal doctrine tends to find a nuisance but imposes only damages on Taney payable to the Marshalls. This way, if the amount of damages Taney is made to pay is close to the injury caused, economic efficiency will have had its due; if he cannot make a go of it, the nuisance was not worth its costs. The entitlement to the Marshalls to be free from pollution unless compensated, however, will have been given *not* because it was thought that polluting was probably worth less to Taney than freedom from pollution was worth to the Marshalls, nor even because on some distributional basis we preferred to charge the cost to Taney rather than to the Marshalls. It was so placed *simply because we did not know* whether Taney desired to pollute more than the Marshalls desired to be free from pollution, and the only way we thought we could test out the value of the pollution was by the only liability rule we thought we had. This was rule two, the imposition of nuisance damages on Taney. At least this would be the position of a court concerned with economic efficiency which believed itself limited to rules one, two, and three.

Rule four gives at least the possibility that the opposite entitlement may also lead to economic efficiency in a situation of uncertainty. Suppose for the moment that a mechanism exists for collectively assessing the damage resulting to Taney from being stopped from polluting by the Marshalls, and a mechanism also exists for collectively assessing the benefit to each of the Marshalls from such cessation. Then — assuming the same degree of accuracy in collective valuation as exists in rule two (the nuisance damage rule) — the Marshalls would stop the pollution if it harmed them more than it benefited Taney. If this is possible, then even if we thought it necessary to use a liability rule, we would still be free to give the entitlement to Taney or Marshall for whatever reasons, efficiency or distributional, we desired.

Actually, the issue is still somewhat more complicated. For just as transaction costs are not necessarily symmetrical under the two converse property rule entitlements, so also the liability rule equivalents of transaction costs — the cost of valuing collectively and of coercing compliance with that valuation — may not be symmetrical under the two converse liability rules. Nuisance damages may be very hard to value, and the costs of informing all the injured of their rights and getting them into court may be prohibitive. Instead, the assessment of the objective damage to Taney from foregoing his pollution may be cheap and so might the assessment of the relative benefits to all Marshalls of such freedom from pollution. But the opposite may also be the case. As a result, just as the choice of which property entitlement may be based on the asymmetry of transaction costs and hence on the greater amenability of one property entitlement to market corrections, so might the choice between liability entitlements be based on the asymmetry of the costs of collective determination.

The introduction of distributional considerations makes the existence of the fourth possibility even more significant. One does not need to go into all the permutations of the possible tradeoffs between efficiency and distributional goals under the four rules to show this. A simple example should suffice. Assume a factory which, by using cheap coal, pollutes a very wealthy section of town and employs many low income workers to produce a product purchased primarily by the poor; assume also a distributional goal that favors equality of wealth. Rule one — enjoin the nuisance — would possibly have desirable economic efficiency results (if the pollution hurt the homeowners more than it saved the factory in coal costs), but it would have disastrous distribution effects. It would also have undesirable efficiency effects if the initial judgment on costs of avoidance had been wrong and transaction costs were high. Rule two — nuisance damages — would allow a testing of the economic efficiency of eliminating the pollution, even in the presence of high transaction costs, but would quite possibly put the factory out of business or diminish output and thus have the same income distribution effects as rule one. Rule three — no nuisance — would have favorable distributional effects since it might protect the income of the workers. But if the pollution harm was greater to the homeowners than the cost of avoiding it by using a better coal, and if transaction costs — holdout problems — were such that homeowners could not unite to pay the factory to use better coal, rule three would have unsatisfactory efficiency effects. Rule four — payment of damages to the factory after allowing the homeowners to compel it to use better coal, and assessment of the cost of these damages to the homeowners — would be the only one which would accomplish both the distributional and efficiency goals. . . .

Thus far in this section we have ignored the possibility of employing rules of inalienability to solve pollution problems. A general policy of barring pollution does seem unrealistic. But rules of inalienability can appropriately be used to limit the levels of pollution and to control the levels of activities which cause pollution.

One argument for inalienability may be the widespread existence of moralisms against pollution. Thus it may hurt the Marshalls — gentlemen farmers — to see Taney, a smoke-choked city dweller, sell his entitlement to be free of pollution. A different kind of externality or moralism may be even more important. The Marshalls may be hurt by the expectation that, while the present generation might withstand present pollution levels with no serious health dangers, future generations may well face a despoiled, hazardous environmental condition which they are powerless to reverse. And this ground for inalienability might be strengthened if a similar conclusion were reached on grounds of self paternalism. Finally, society might restrict alienability on paternalistic grounds. The Marshalls might feel that although Taney himself does not know it, Taney will be better off if he really can see the stars at night, or if he can breathe smogless air.

Whatever the grounds for inalienability, we should reemphasize that distributional effects should be carefully evaluated in making the choice for or against inalienability. Thus the citizens of a town may be granted an entitlement to be free of water pollution caused by the waste discharges of a chemical factory; and the entitlement might be made inalienable on the grounds that the town's citizens really would be better off in the long run to have access to clean beaches. But the entitlement might also be made inalienable to assure the maintenance of a beautiful resort area for the very wealthy, at the same time putting the town's citizens out of work.

V. The Framework and Criminal Sanctions

Obviously we cannot canvass the relevance of our approach through many areas of the law. But we do think it beneficial to examine one further area, that of crimes against property and bodily integrity. The application of the framework to the use of criminal sanctions in cases of theft or violations of bodily integrity is useful in that it may aid in understanding the previous material, especially as it helps us to distinguish different kinds of legal problems and to identify the different modes of resolving those problems.

Beginning students, when first acquainted with economic efficiency notions, sometimes ask why ought not a robber be simply charged with the value of the thing robbed. And the same question is sometimes posed by legal philosophers. If it is worth more to the robber than to the owner, is not economic efficiency served by such a penalty? Our answers to such a question tend to move quickly into very high sounding and undoubtedly relevant moral considerations. But these considerations are often not very helpful to the questioner because they depend on the existence of obligations on individuals not to rob for a fixed price and the original question was why we should impose such obligations at all.

One simple answer to the question would be that thieves do not get caught every time they rob and therefore the costs to the thief must at least take the unlikelihood of capture into account. But that would not fully answer the problem, for even if thieves were caught every time, the penalty we would wish to impose would be greater than the objective damages to the person robbed.

A possible broader explanation lies in a consideration of the difference between property entitlements and liability entitlements. For us to charge the thief with a penalty equal to an objectively determined value of the property stolen would be to convert all property rule entitlements into liability rule entitlements.

The question remains, however, why *not* convert all property rules into liability rules? The answer is, of course, obvious. Liability rules represent only an approximation of the value of the object to its original owner and willingness to pay such an approximate value is no indication that it is worth more to the thief than to the owner. In other words, quite apart from the expense of arriving collectively at such an objective valuation, it is no guarantee of the economic efficiency of the transfer. If this is so with property, it is all the more so with bodily integrity, and we would not presume collectively and objectively to value the cost of a rape to the victim against the benefit to the rapist even if economic efficiency is our sole motive. Indeed when we approach bodily integrity we are getting close to areas where we do not let the entitlement be sold at all and where economic efficiency enters in, if at all, in a more complex way. But even where the items taken or destroyed are things we do allow to be sold, we will not without special reasons impose an objective selling price on the vendor.

Once we reach the conclusion that we will not simply have liability rules, but that often, even just on economic efficiency grounds, property rules are desirable, an answer to the beginning student's question becomes clear. The thief not only harms the victim, he undermines rules and distinctions of significance beyond the specific case. Thus even if in a given case we can be sure that the value of the item stolen was no more than X dollars, and even if the thief has been caught and is prepared to compensate, we would not be content simply to charge the thief X dollars. Since in the majority of cases we cannot be sure of the economic efficiency of the transfer by theft, we must add to each case an undefinable kicker which represents society's need to keep all property rules from being changed at will into liability rules. In other words, we impose criminal sanctions as a means of deterring future attempts to convert property rules into liability rules.

The first year student might push on, however, and ask why we treat the thief or the rapist differently from the injurer in an auto accident or the polluter in a nuisance case. Why do we allow liability rules there? In a sense, we have already answered the question. The only level at which, before the accident, the driver can negotiate for the value of what he might take from his potential victim is one at which transactions are too costly. The thief or rapist, on the other hand, could have negotiated without undue expense (at least if the good was one which we allowed to be sold at all) because we assume he knew what he was going to do and to whom he would do it. The case of the accident is different because knowledge exists only at the level of deciding to drive or perhaps to drive fast, and at that level negotiations with potential victims are usually not feasible.

The case of nuisance seems different, however. There the polluter knows what he will do and, often, whom it will hurt. But as we have already pointed out, freeloader or holdout problems may often preclude any successful negotiations between the polluter and the victims of pollution; additionally, we are often uncertain who is the cheapest avoider of pollution costs. In these circumstances a liability rule, which at least allowed the economic efficiency of a proposed transfer of entitlements to be tested, seemed appropriate, even though it permitted the nonaccidental and unconsented taking of an entitlement. It should be emphasized, however, that where transaction costs do not bar negotiations between polluter and victim, or where we are sufficiently certain who the cheapest cost avoider is, there are no efficiency reasons for allowing intentional takings, and property rules, supported by injunctions or criminal sanctions, are appropriate.

NOTES AND QUESTIONS ON THE DISTINCTION BETWEEN PROPERTY RULES AND LIABILITY RULES

1. At places Calabresi and Melamed (C & M) imply that lawmakers should *first* decide which party in a dispute to favor, and *then* decide how to protect that favored party. At other places they

argue that these decisions are to be made simultaneously. Which approach is likely to lead to better results? Are lawmakers wiser to consider rights in the abstract, or always with an eye to interrelated remedial issues?

2. The private law of property shifts from property-rule to liability-rule protection when it:

   a. entitles a single concurrent owner to force a partition sale of co-owned real estate;

   b. provides only monetary relief to owners of lands flooded by a millpond created by a private dam (an innovation of the Mill Acts, enacted as early as the eighteenth century); and

   c. restricts nuisance plaintiffs to the remedy of damages.

Under what circumstances would C & M support these shifts to liability rules?

3. According to C & M's analysis, should a local government be entitled to exercise the power of eminent domain when it wishes to acquire (and preserve) the birthplace of a former President? When it wishes to widen Main Street? When it wishes to acquire commercial space to house its planning department? See Thomas W. Merrill, The Economics of Public Use, 72 Cornell L. Rev. 61 (1986).

4. The Kwakiutl institution of potlatching lent protection to a tribal subgroup's territorial fishing rights, but only on the condition that the subgroup share its rich salmon harvests with neighbors suffering from poor harvests. See supra p.170, Note 5. Is potlatching an illustration of C & M's "rule four," in that a subgroup was entitled to prevent encroachments on its territory, but only if the subgroup paid off impecunious would-be encroachers?

5. At places C & M imply that inalienability rules are *alternatives* to property rules and liability rules. In the usual case, property rules and liability rules govern the remedies A has against B when B interferes with A's entitlements; inalienability rules, by contrast, are rights that the *state* has against A to prevent A from consensually making deals with the likes of B. In light of this difference, are C & M wise to treat the three sorts of rules as members of the same set? For more on issues of alienability, see the selection by Radin, infra p.336.

6. On the functions of criminal law, see Alvin Klevorick, Legal Theory and the Economic Analysis of Torts and Crimes, 85 Colum. L. Rev. 905 (1985).

7. In an example on p.254, C & M state that the proper outcome of a pollution dispute might depend on a comparison of the wealth

of the homeowners suffering from the pollution and the wealth of the polluting factory's workers and customers. By contrast, in the sources cited supra pp.113-114, Note 7, both Polinsky and Kaplow & Shavell contend that distributional goals are invariably better achieved by means of broad taxation and welfare programs, rather than through private adjudication. Who has the better of this debate? Whose approach is more congruent with the letter of nuisance doctrine? With nuisance law "in action"?

A License to Steal*

Arthur Hoppe

The revolutionary nature of Mr. Nixon's current Great American Revolution is even more revolutionary than appeared at first glance.

Did you see his Economic Report to Congress? Down in it he suggests that polluters be licensed in return for a fee.

"This charge would be sufficiently high to encourage substantial control of sulphur oxide emissions (or whatever)," says the report, "and the consequent reductions of damage to health and property should substantially exceed the control costs."

Now this is certainly a revolutionary concept. But why limit it to pollution? Properly expanded, it could lead to a new Federal Licensing Bureau, which might even take in enough money to balance the budget.

SCENE: The new Federal Licensing Bureau. A bored clerk is approached by a middle-aged applicant who looks nervous.
Applicant: I'd like to apply for a license to emit sulphur oxides. I have this small backyard smelter and. . . .
Clerk: Okay. That'll be $10,000.
Applicant: Did you say $10,000? That's exorbitant!
Clerk: Look Mac, sulphur oxides aggravate lung diseases, dissolve nylon stockings, peel paint and create killer fogs. The right to do all that doesn't come cheap.
Applicant: I'm sorry, I didn't realize. . . .
Clerk: Remember, it's high fees that reduce damage to health and property. Now if you want something cheap I can let

*Source: San Francisco Chronicle, Feb. 8, 1971.

you have a license good for tossing three beer cans and a sandwich wrapper out your car window. That's only ten bucks.

Applicant: Littering? I don't know, there doesn't seem to be much profit in it.

Clerk: Ah, you're looking for a profit? Confidentially, I think our best buy is a Mugging License. It entitles you to hit three old ladies over the head in the park of your choice and snatch their purses. Most guys come out ahead on this one.

Applicant (surprised):   Hitting old ladies over the head? That sounds anti-social somehow.

Clerk (shrugging):   It's no different than a license to poison people's lungs. And it's only $100.

Applicant (indignant):   That's highway robbery!

Clerk: Nope. Highway Robbery is $200. But it's a non-renewable, nontransferable, one-shot deal.

Applicant: I hate to risk that kind of money.

Clerk: Tell you what. Get a group of your friends together and take out a License to Riot. You can burn and loot five stores in the ghetto of your choice. The fee's relatively low because it's part of our Urban Renewal Program.

Applicant (shaking his head):   It seems like these days people are getting away with murder.

Clerk: Not unless they got 50,000 bucks, buddy. Remember, we got to keep the charges sufficiently high to encourage control of everyone's criminal instincts.

Applicant (appalled):   What kind of concept is that? It just means the rich can get away with crimes like poisoning people's lungs that the poor can't afford to commit.

Clerk (yawning):   So what else is new? Next.

NOTES AND QUESTIONS ON THE MORALITY OF LICENSING HARMS

How is the problem of regulating sulphur dioxide different from the problems regulated by Hoppe's Federal Licensing Bureau? When considering the distinctions among the activities Hoppe discusses, evaluate which (if any) of them *ought* to be licensed through monetary fees. Compare Thomas Schelling's thoughts on putting prices on pollution, infra. p.532.

Trespass, Nuisance, and the Costs of Determining Property Rights*

Thomas W. Merrill

The right to exclude intrusions by others, we have it on high authority, is "one of the most essential sticks in the bundle of rights that are commonly characterized as property."[1] Yet the right to exclude is not one right; it is itself a collection or "bundle" of rights. With respect to property in land, for example, the right to exclude depends to a large extent on whether the intrusion in question is subject to the common law of trespass or of nuisance. Generally speaking, when the intrusion is governed by trespass, then there is no exception for de minimis harms, a rule of strict liability applies, and the landholder can obtain an injunction to prevent future invasions. When the intrusion is governed by nuisance, however, then there will be no liability absent a showing of substantial harm, as a rule the landholder must show that the costs of the intrusion outweigh its benefits, and even then the party subject to the interference may be awarded only damages rather than an injunction for future harms. Thus, the right of a landholder to exclude means one thing with respect to certain intrustions — those subject to the law of trespass — but something altogether different with respect to others — those subject to the law of nuisance.

How do we account for the use of these different legal standards in defining a landholder's right to exclude intrusions by others? And how do we explain the legal system's differentiation between those intrusions subject to the rule of trespass and those subject to nuisance? In this article, I will apply a simple economic model in an effort to answer these questions. The central thesis is that when the costs of transacting are low, the legal system will gravitate toward rules that determine entitlements at a low cost — such as the strict liability rule of trespass. The combination of low transaction costs and low entitlement-determination costs will maximize the extent to which conflicts between competing uses of land can be resolved by market transactions. In contrast, when the costs of transacting are apt to be high, the legal system will incline toward rules for the determination of entitlements that are more expensive — such as the balancing or cost-benefit approach of nuisance.

*Source: 14 J. Legal Stud. 13-26, 35-48 (1985).
1. Kaiser Aetna v. United States, 444 U.S. 164, 176 (1979); see also Pruneyard Shopping Center v. Robins, 447 U.S. 74, 82 (1979).

When market mechanisms fail, these more expensive entitlement-determination rules are necesary in order to give judges the needed discretion to adopt what they perceive as the best "compromise" solution (the efficient solution) to land use disputes.

Although I will use this economic model primarily to explain the differences between trespass and nuisance and the sorts of intrusions covered by each action, the model has the potential for broader application. In Section IV, I will survey some other issues involving the rights to exclude, use, and transfer property and will suggest that the relationship between transaction costs and entitlement-determination costs can account for some of the legal doctrine in these areas. Finally, although the main thrust of the article is positive in its orientation, in Section V I will raise some normative issues for those who believe that the legal system should be concerned, at least in part, with the maximization of social utility or wealth. Here, I argue that low-cost mechanical entitlement-determination rules play an important role in facilitating the exchange and modification of property rights — a role often overlooked by commentators who view them simply as decisional rules to be applied in litigation.

I. Trespass and Nuisance

Although trespass and nuisance are both concerned with the right to exclude intrusions by others, they govern different sorts of physical phenomena. Trespass applies to relatively gross invasions by tangible objects — persons, cars, buildings and the like. Nuisance applies to more indirect and intangible interferences — noise, odor, smoke, funeral homes, and so forth. For the moment, we need not consider the exact line of demarcation between the underlying phenomena or the rationale for that line. I will return to this issue and discuss it at length in Section III. It is first necessary to understand the legal consequences of classifying a given interference as being subject to the rule of either trespass or nuisance.

For this purpose, it is useful to refer to some simple examples drawn from recent cases. Suppose A and B are adjacent landholders. In case 1,[5] B has a long driveway which runs along his common border with A. At the end of this driveway, B has a loading dock. In order for B's trucks to turn around and unload at the loading dock, B's agents must drive onto and back off from A's property. An intrusion of this sort — the repeated driving of trucks on and off a

5. Warsaw v. Chicago Metallic Ceilings, Inc., 35 Cal. 3d 564 (1984).

neighbor's property — is the sort of gross, tangible invasion that is governed by the law of trespass. In case 2,[6] B has a factory which makes a great deal of noise when in operation; A has a family residence. For many years, B operates only one eight-hour shift, which does not unduly disturb A. Subsequently, in an effort to increase production, B starts operating three shifts around the clock. As a consequence, A can no longer sleep at night. This kind of intrusion — the repeated invasion of a neighbor's peace and quiet by sound waves — is governed by the law of nuisance.

In terms of both substantive and remedial doctrine, there are major differences in the law that will be applied in case 1 and case 2. Substantively, the principal distinction is the standard of care that courts apply in determining whether the interference is actionable; that is, whether A's property interest includes the right to exclude B's offending intrusion or B's property interest includes the right to engage in the offending intrusion free of any exclusion from A. These disparities are most pronounced with respect to intentional intrusions — a category which includes not only actions in which B specifically intends to interfere with A's interest in land, but also actions undertaken by B which B knows will interfere with A's interest. Thus, if B directs his agents to back up their trucks to the loading dock, knowing that they must drive on A's property to do so, B will be chargeable with an intentional intrusion, even though he harbors no specific intent to injure A. Similarly, if B knows that his factory makes enough noise to disturb sleeping neighbors, his decision to operate the factory at night constitutes an intentional interference, even though he has no specific intent to disturb anyone's sleep.

Intentional intrusions subject to the rule of trespass are governed by a standard of care which is "exceptionally simple and exceptionally rigorous." In order to establish an actionable trespass, all that A need show is that B is responsible for an invasion of the column of space that defines A's possessory interest under the ad coelum rule. No weighing or balancing of costs and benefits is involved. Thus, one who commits an act which qualifies as an intentional trespass is subject to liability whether or not the benefits of the interfering act — either to B or to the community at large — are greater than the harm imposed on A. Indeed, according to the Restatement of Torts, B will be subject to liability "irrespective of whether he thereby causes harm to any legally protected interest of the other." Therefore, in case 1 the action of B's agents in driving on

6. Wilson v. Interlake Steel Co., 32 Cal. 3d 229 (1982).

and off A's driveway will be considered an actionable trespass, even if these invasions are shown to be only "trifling inconveniences" that do not interfere with A's use and enjoyment of his property.

Intentional harms subject to the law of nuisance, in contrast, are governed by a standard of care that is neither so simple nor so rigorous. Indeed, some commentators have despairingly described the legal doctrine surrounding the concept of nuisance as an "impenetrable jungle." Nevertheless, the description of the standard of care set forth in the Restatement of Torts, which is widely followed by American courts, provides at least an appropriate reference point for comparison to the law of trespass. According to the Restatement, "[t]here is liability for a nuisance only to those to whom it causes significant harm, of a kind that would be suffered by a normal person in the community or by property in normal condition and used for a normal purpose." Clearly, then, a mere "trifling inconvenience" is not actionable. In addition, an intentional nuisance will result in liability only if it is "unreasonble." The primary definition of "unreasonable," again according to the Restatement, is that "the gravity of the harm outweighs the utility of the actor's conduct." Following the Restatement in case 2, therefore, A will have to show not only that the loss of sleep would represent a "significant harm" to a person of normal sensitivities, but also that the harm to A and similarly situated neighbors is greater than the benefits that accrue to B and society generally from increased production and employment at the factory.

In addition, trespass and nuisance differ in terms of the remedies available once an actionable interference is established. Here, perhaps the most important distinction involves the standards for issuance of an injunction. With respect to intentional trespasses, courts will generally issue an injunction against recurring invasions without engaging in any "balancing of equities" — a weighing of the relative strength of A's interest, B's interest, and other possible societal interests — before granting the requested relief. With respect to intentional nuisances, however, almost all courts will engage in some such balancing exercise before issuing an injunction against future interferences. While they may not refer to the process as "balancing the equities," the weighing process nearly always takes place just the same.

Once an injunction is ruled out, either because the intrusion is a nonrecurring one or because of an unfavorable balance of equities, still differences persist, though perhaps less significant, in the standards governing the award of damages. Where the intrusion is a trespass, and A cannot show actual damages, courts generally award the plaintiff at least nominal damages. Failure to show actual damages in nuisance, in contrast, usually results in the denial of all relief (because of the failure to satisfy the "substantial harm" requirement for liability). Moreover, whether or not actual damages are incurred, punitive damages are more likely to be awarded for an intentional trespass than they are for an intentional nuisance.

Given these differences, how should we characterize the distinction between trespass and nuisance? The distinction does not really correspond to that drawn by Calabresi and Melamed between "property rules" and "liabililty rules."[27] To be sure, in its remedial dimension the law of intentional trespass approximates a property rule — injunctive relief more or less follows automatically from liability, at least where the intrusion is a recurring one. But the law of intentional nuisance is neither a property rule nor a liability rule, but sometimes one and sometimes the other — depending on how the court comes out in its "balancing of equities." Moreover, the property rule/liability rule distinction goes only to the question of remedies to protect substantive rights. As we have just seen, however, trespass and nuisance differ not only in terms of remedies but also in terms of the standards applied to establish substantive rights — whether or not A has the right to exclude intrusions by B in the first place.

A more central theme running through the differences between trespass and nuisance concerns the degree of discretion given to courts when resolving questions that involve both substantive and remedial entitlements. Indeed, entitlement-determination rules can be viewed as falling on a spectrum ranging from "mechanical" rules — those which afford little discretion to courts in the establishment of entitlements — to "judgmental" rules — those which afford very broad discretion to courts in determining entitlements.[28] From this perspective, trespass would have to be regarded as the quintessential mechanical entitlement-determination rule. If an interference with an interest in land potentially qualifies as a trespass, all A must show to obtain an injunction barring B from future interference is that B is responsible for recurring invasions of the imaginary column of space which defines A's possessory interest. Once the prescribed

27. Guido Calabresi & A. Douglas Melamed, Property Rules, Liability Rules, and Inalienability: One View of the Cathedral, 85 Harv. L. Rev. 1089, 1092 (1972).

28. The distinction between mechanical rules and judgmental rules is similar to the more commonly encountered distinction between rules and standards or rules and principles. See Isaac Ehrlich & Richard A. Posner, An Economic Analysis of Legal Rulemaking, 3 J. Legal Stud. 257 (1974); Douglas G. Baird & Robert Weisberg, Rules, Standards, and the Battle of the Forms: A Reassessment of § 2-207, 68 Va. L. Rev. 1217 (1982). I use the judgmental/mechanical terminology, however, in order to avoid any implication that mechanical rules necessarily derive from, or are otherwise logically related to, judgmental rules.

invasions are shown, both the substantive right and the remedy follow mechanically — with little room for judicial discretion.

The law of nuisance, in contrast, reflects a judgmental entitlement-determination rule. If interferences with an interest in land potentially qualify as a nuisance, then in order to obtain an injunction barring future invasions, A must (at least if we follow the Restatement account) satisfy a court (1) that he has sustained substantial harm from the interference; (2) that the harm to A and similarly situated persons outweighs the benefit to B and society generally if B is allowed to interfere; and (3) that an injunction against future interference by B is consistent with the balance of equities. These factors, especially factors (2) and (3), are highly judgmental; accordingly, they entail the exercise of a considerable degree of discretion on the part of the court. Moreover, even if the court does not follow the cost-benefit approach of the Restatement in determining the question of substantive entitlement, nuisance still falls at the judgmental end of the spectrum, in part because inquiries (1) and (3) — especially (3) — still involve a significant degree of discretion. In addition, even aside from the cost-benefit calculus espoused by the Restatement, the substantive law of nuisance contains a bewildering array of Latin maxims, conflicting formulations of the standard of care, and defenses and quasi defenses. All of these, taken together, confer a very broad discretion on courts as to how they come out in particular controversies.

If the mechanical/judgmental distinction accurately captures the core contrast between trespass and nuisance, then the question becomes, Why would a common-law system develop two sets of rules — one mechanical and the other judgmental — for determining the right of a landholder to exclude interference by others? In the next section, I will consider whether economic analysis can supply a hypothesis that would account for this phenomenon.

II.   Transaction Costs and Entitlement-Determination Costs ...

Transaction costs, as I will use the term, consist of the resources that must be expended in order to enter into and enforce contracts for the exchange or modification of property rights. ...

Entitlement-determination costs, in contrast to transaction costs, are the resources that must be expended in order to establish who has the property right that is the subject of the exchange. A simple illustration of entitlement-determination costs is provided by the sale of the proverbial Blackacre in fee simple. B can purchase Blackacre from A only if A has something called "title." In order to establish that A has title to the property, some trained expert — a lawyer or the employee of an abstract or title insurance company — must examine A's deed (if any) and the chain of title, and then pass judgment on whether A has marketable title to Blackacre. If the title examination process reveals a "cloud" on A's title, A (or B) may have to go to court and litigate the question whether A has title. The costs incurred in the process of satisfying B (or B's lender) that A has title to Blackacre are entitlement-determination costs.

For present purposes, the magnitude of entitlement-determination costs can be seen as primarily a function of whether the rules for determining property rights are mechanical or judgmental. Mechanical rules — such as the law of intentional trespass — are predictable and relatively inexpensive to apply: Generally speaking, they can be applied by laymen with little or no input from lawyers or judges. (This is probably the principal reason why the tax code, which relies on large-scale compliance by individuals not trained in the law, consists largely of mechanical rules.) In contrast, judgmental rules — such as the law of intentional nuisance — are unpredictable and relatively expensive to apply. Judgmental rules require a large input of legal advice and possibly even a judicial trial (or legislative or administrative action) before the assignment of property rights can be established. There is, however, another side to the distinction between these rules. Mechanical rules, being rigid and inflexible, may often produce results that, unless subsequently modified by the affected parties, are perceived as being unjust, unfair, or inefficient. On the other hand, although judgmental rules are more expensive, they are also inherently flexible, and thus can be manipulated by courts to achieve results which are "just," "fair," or "efficient."

. . .[O]ne can easily determine the pattern that should emerge from a common-law system that (we may assume by hypothesis) seeks to fashion legal rules promoting economic efficiency. First, one would predict that when transaction costs are low, such a legal system would tend to adopt mechanical entitlement-determination rules. Mechanical rules entail lower entitlement-determination costs than judgmental rules, and coupling low transaction costs with low entitlement-determination costs should maximize mutually beneficial exchange or modification of property rights. But when transaction costs are high, market exchange is unlikely to take place, regardless of the choice of entitlement-determination rule. In these circumstances, the economically efficient choice will depend on a comparison of two variables: the increase in entitlement-determination costs entailed by a shift from a mechanical to a judgmental rule versus the potential efficiency gains from allowing the court (or some other collective decision maker) to exercise discretion in resolving the dispute, rather than adhering to whatever solution is dictated by a mechanical rule. If the magnitude of the latter is larger than that of the former (which in many situations I suspect it would be), then in high-transaction-cost situations it will be economically efficient for a legal system to adopt judgmental entitlement-determination rules.

In principle, these considerations are easy to apply to the law of trespass and nuisance. Trespass is clearly a mechanical entitlement-determination rule, and thus one would expect the law of trespass to apply to disputes with low transaction costs. Nuisance, under either the Restatement formulation or the doctrinal obscurantism and inconsistency of the cases generally, is clearly a judgmental entitlement-determination rule. Hence, one would expect the law of nuisance to apply to disputes characterized by high transaction costs. . . .

IV. Other Applications . . .

The right to exclude suggests several situations where the mechanical standard of trespass seems to be required, but in fact the law adopts a judgmental rule. Airplane overflights provide a particular striking illustration of this sort of "exception" to the ordinary rules. Under a literal application of the ad coelum rule, an overflight would constitute a trespass under any of the three traditional threshold tests: it involves an actual, direct, and visible entry into the column of space belonging to the surface owner. Acquisition of the appropriate easements to permit an overflight, however, would obviously entail monumental transaction costs. The owner of the airplane would have great difficulty identifying the various parcels of property traversed by the flight path; the number of parties with which agreements would have to be negotiated would be immense; and the parties would face formidable difficulty detecting and proving violations. The model clearly suggests that the mechanical entitlement-determination rule of trespass is inappropriate in this context.

The common law could have solved the problem of overflights by simply tinkering with the ad coelum rule. Trespass (unlike nuisance) is available only to one who is a "possessor" (as opposed to merely a nonpossessing owner) of land, and courts could have held that although the holder of the surface rights "owns" up to the heavens, he does not possess any more of the column of space than he has occupied (for example, by building a skyscraper). Thus, the surface owner would be left with an action for nuisance, which would ultimately fail because of the absence of significant harm. For whatever reason, the common law did not tend to adopt this neat solution, preferring instead an ad hoc exception for overflights. As the Restatement dutifully notes: "Flight by aircraft in the air space above the land of another is a trespass if, but only if, (*a*) it enters into the immediate reaches of the air space next to the land, and (*b*) it interferes *substantially* with the other's *use and enjoyment* of his land." Predictably, in a high-transaction-cost situation, the mechanical entitlement-determination rule of trespass has been replaced by a judgmental standard that looks very much like the law of nuisance.

Another exception, again consistent with the model, involves unintentional trespasses. Suppose *A* and *B* are driving cars that collide on a public highway, and the force of the collision propels *B*'s car onto *C*'s land, damaging the lawn and bushes. This, like most problems involving traffic accidents, is a high-transaction-cost situation. Advance negotiations between *B* and *C* are out of the question, since the costs to *B* of identifying and negotiating with all possessors of land onto which he may some day be forced to drive his car would be prohibitive. Thus in this situation, the model would predict that the law would apply a judgmental rather than a mechanical entitlement-determination rule.

In fact, the modern trend has been to reject a mechanical rule when the intrusion is neither intended nor known to be substantially certain to follow from the defendant's act, even though historically all trespasses were governed by one standard. According to the Restatement, for example, an unintentional trespass is actionable only if the invasion causes "harm" and only if the defendant acted "recklessly or negligently, or as a result of an abnormally dangerous activity."[84] Standards like "recklessness" and "negligence" (or "abnormally dangerous activity" for that matter) involve judgmental rather than mechanical entitlement-determination rules. Hence, as the model would predict, trespasses that tend to involve high transaction costs are governed by judgmental entitlement-determination rules.[85]

The converse situation also exists: cases in which one might as-

84. Restatement (Second) of Torts § 165 (1965).

85. Other "exceptions" to the standard mechanical rule of trespass can be explained in terms of the potential for strategic bargaining created when one or more parties stand in a monopoly or near-monopoly position relative to other parties. I would include within this category such diverse things as the qualified privilege for entry under circumstances of emergency, see Ploof v. Putnam, 81 Vt. 471 (1908); the privilege for entry by government service workers into migrant labor camps, see State v. Shack, 58 N.J. 297 (1971); the doctrine of easement by necessity or implication, for example, Adams v. Cullen, 44 Wash. 2d 502 (1954); and the grant of the power of eminent domain to private entrepreneurs to allow them to assemble large tracts of land, Poletown Neighborhood Council v. City of Detroit, 410 Mich. 616 (1981).

sume that a judgmental entitlement-determination rule would apply, yet which are in fact governed by a mechanical standard such as strict liability. One illustration of this is innocent building encroachments — cases in which the defendant erects a structure in the belief that it is on his own land, but it turns out to be on someone else's. At the time of construction, the encroachment is not intentional, and hence one might suppose that the intrusion would be subjected to the judgmental rule of unintentional trespass. Nevertheless, both the case law[86] and the Restatement[87] are quite clear in treating innocent building encroachments as an intentional trespass, subject to a rule of strict liability.

This is consistent with the model. Unlike other sorts of unintentional trespass, building encroachments involve low transaction costs, at least when viewed *ex ante* — before the encroachment takes place. If the builder needs to purchase an additional strip of land from a neighbor, the costs of identification, coordination, and enforcement should all be low. Nor would we expect to find insuperable problems of strategic bargaining here, given that the builder has the options of redesigning or relocating the building or moving elsewhere. Of course, if we view the situation ex post, after the encroaching structure is built, there is an obvious potential for strategic bargaining: the neighbor now has a monopoly on something the builder desperately needs — title to the land on which the building sits. But it makes sense to adopt an entitlement-determination rule keyed to the ex ante situation. The costs to the builder of acquiring the necessary information to avoid an encroachment are almost certainly quite low relative to the value of the building itself: all he has to do is commission a lot survey before construction begins. Thus, adopting an entitlement-determination rule that treats the builder as if he had knowlege creates a powerful incentive for the builder to make sure he *does* have knowledge. A mechanical rule of strict liability therefore performs two functions here: It has an in terrorem effect that induces the builder to find out whether he needs to negotiate with a neighbor, and it provides a baseline princple from which those negotiations can take place.[88]

Another illustration is provided by the common-law doctrine related to straying livestock. The common law did not treat straying

86. See Geragosian v. Union Reality Co., 289 Mass. 104 (1935); Pile v. Pedrick, 167 Pa. 296 (1895).

87. Restatement (Second) of Torts § 164 (1965).

88. Although innocent encroachments are uniformly subject to a rule of strict liability, there is a discernible trend toward applying the "balancing of equities" before enjoining the builder to remove the structure. See Annot., 28 A.L.R.2d 679, 705 (1953). To the extent courts follow this approach, they dilute the incentive effects created by a property rule, and increase entitlement determination costs, because of the difficulty of distinguishing between wilful and innocent encroachments.

livestock as a simple case of intentional trespass, perhaps because the wandering of livestock did not fit neatly within the direct versus indirect threshold test traditionally favored by English courts. Nevertheless, the common law was quite firm in subjecting straying cases to a rule of strict liability similar to the law of intentional trespass. In fact, the law here was, if anything, more mechanical than ordinary trespass, given the availability of the self-help remedy of distress damage feasant, which allows a landholder to hold intruding animals as security for compensation. Application of mechanical rules here is predictable, given the nature of disputes involving straying livestock. Domestic animals such as cattle and sheep are unlikely to stray very far, and identification of the possessory interests with which they are likely to interfere should not be difficult. Moreover, contractual solutions to straying problems (such as an informal agreement to fence) are unlikely to require elaborate enforcement mechanisms. Thus, the use of mechanical entitlement-determination rules renders a common "spillover" problem virtually self-regulating.

To be sure, the fact that a mechanical entitlement-determination rule is approprite in this context does not resolve the question of which party should have the entitlement. Interestingly, there has been a split in positions, with England and most eastern states adopting a fencing-in rule and many western states adopting a fencing-out rule. The difference can be explained in terms of which baseline rule is likely to require the fewest contractual modifications. Thus, where there are many farmers and few ranchers, a fencing-in rule is appropriate; conversely, when there are many ranchers and few farmers, a fencing-out rule makes more sense. Indeed, as western states have become more cultivated, many have enacted legislation returning to the English rule. . . .

Turning to issues involving the right to consume or use property, there is also evidence of the transaction-cost/entitlement-determination-cost model at work. For example, much of the doctrine used to resolve conflicts arising when ownership of property is divided among two or more persons can be explained by the model. With respect to concurrent interests — such as tenancies in common or joint tenancies — common-law courts have long been reluctant to arbitrate disputes concerning the use or consumption of property. Instead, courts have followed the rule that any concurrent owner can, at any time and for any reason, petition for partition of the property. The partition action is a mechanical entitlement-determination rule, in that the right to obtain partition is virtually absolute — the court will generally entertain no objections or defenses from the other concurrent owners. This is as one would expect, given that the costs of reaching a mutual accommodation among concurrent owners (who are often members of the same family, such as husband and wife or siblings) should be low. Indeed, when the number of concurrent owners gets too large, the law of partition tends to favor the transformaton of the pattern of ownership into one where the transaction costs are more manageable.

When the ownership of property is divided over time, however, the common law embraces quite different principles. For example, when ownership of a parcel is divided between a life estate and one or more remainders, the law of partition does not apply to resolve disputes over the use or consumption of the property. Instead, courts apply a judgmental entitlement-determination rule known as the law of waste. Application of a judgmental rule when interests are divided over time is consistent with the model, because future interest holders are likely to be dispersed and numerous, and in many cases are not even born. Thus the transaction-cost barriers involved in negotiating a settlement between holders of the life estate and the remaindermen may be prohibitive. A judgmental rule is necessary in these situations to insure an efficient solution to disputes over the use of the property. . . .

V. Some Normative Implications

Even if the common law has taken transaction costs into account in setting entitlement-determination rules, it has not done so perfectly. Only an extreme determinist would assert that common-law rules evolve in such a way that they always reflect the best of all possible worlds. The dimensional test for differentiating between trespass and nuisance is a case in point. Although the test does fairly well in singling out a class of low-transaction-cost disputes for mechanical rules, it is underinclusive. There are clearly many nuisance disputes that must be characterized as involving low transaction costs, and yet they are handled by an extremely judgmental standard that tends to frustrate negotiated solutions.

One possible way to improve on the underinclusiveness of the dimensional test would be to generate two sets of nuisance rules — one for relatively high-transaction-cost situations, another for relatively low-transaction-cost situations. Such a bifurcation could perhaps be achieved via the ancient distinction between public and private nuisance. . . .

More generally, the transaction-cost/entitlement-determination-cost model provides an important justification for mechanical legal rules, which have been in vague disrepute for some time. Part of the legacy of the legal realist movement is that legal rules are viewed as "policy tools," and legal scholars demand that every rule have some "policy justification." Mechanical rules tend to fare rather badly in such an environment, particularly when viewed solely as decisional rules for use in litigation, rather than as rules designed to avoid recourse to litigation. The reason should not be hard to see. Mechanical rules — such as the dimensional test for determining the boundary between trespass and nuisance — are crude and inflexible and often seem to produce unfair (or inefficient) results in particular cases. This leads commentators to question the desirability of such rules and to urge other rules — typically multifactorial balancing tests — in their place. Such "reform," however, may only make negotiated solutions to resource use disputes harder to reach, thus undermining the general efficiency of the economic system.

Related to this is a point about the distributional consequences of mechanical and judgmental rules. Generally speaking, laymen tend to prefer mechanical rules, even if they seem silly or inefficient, whereas spokesmen for the legal community — including leading academics and judges — tend to prefer judgmental rules. This is as one would predict, assuming that laymen prefer private solutions to resource disputes that minimize the demand for lawyers and litigation, whereas the legal community prefers collective solutions that increase the demand. Thus, if one believes that we have too many lawyers or too much litigation, not only should one ask that legislatures exercise restraint in replacing common-law rules with regulatory schemes; one should also demand that *courts* exercise restraint in replacing mechanical entitlement-determination rules with judgmental entitlement-determination rules.

On the other side of the ledger, judgmental rules have also recently come under criticism from legal scholars. For example, two of the areas touched upon in this paper — nuisance and takings law — are notorious for their doctrinal confusion and "ad hocery." Academics with a more theoretical bent — those whom Bruce Ackerman calls "scientific policymakers" — have been understandably frustrated by this state of affairs, and have sought to create new conceptual systems from first principles to reform these areas of the law. Yet these efforts, however interesting and commendable, have to a certain extent missed the point: Doctrinal confusion, question-begging Latin phrases, and unpredictable balancing tests may be functional. That is, what the system builder perceives as unprincipled decision making may in fact function as a relatively inexpensive judgmental entitlement-determination rule. Why relatively inexpensive? Because doctrinal indeterminacy affords a judge the discretion to manipulate legal rules to achieve the result he intuits to be most fair (or efficient), without having to articulate all the factors that go into the development of that conclusion. In contrast, an internally coherent system created from first principles — cost-benefit analysis immediately comes to mind — may permit an equally wide range of results but will likely require a time-consuming (and thus expensive) examination and articulation of the factors that go into the formulation of the result.

I do not want to be understood to be saying that unprincipled decision making is a good thing. My point is simply that the persistence of unprincipled decision making should not come as a surprise. Principled decision making, like other social goods, is costly, and the more resources devoted to any one particular good, the less will be left for other ends that a rational society may desire to pursue.

NOTES AND QUESTIONS ON TRESPASS AND NUISANCE

1. According to Merrill, in contexts involving large numbers of parties or other sources of high transaction costs, a legal system is more likely to resort to "judgmental," as opposed to "mechanical," rules. Calabresi and Melamed imply that judges are more likely to move from property rules to liability rules as transaction costs increase. Can these two points be melded into the broader proposition that state officials more likely to become involved in high-transaction-cost disputes than in low-transaction-cost disputes?

2. Does the Merrill selection help explain why nuisance law inherently tends to be an "impenetrable jungle," as William Prosser once called it?

3. Do you agree with Merrill's statement that "mechanical rules . . . are predictable and relatively inexpensive to apply"? If the tax code is so mechanical, why are there so many members of the tax bar?

4. Does Merrill persuasively explain why courts might apply judgmental rules when a motorist unintentionally drives onto Blackacre, and mechanical rules when a builder unintentionally places a wall that encroaches on Blackacre? In fact, the legal rules on these issues are not tidy. See, for example, the source cited in Merrill's footnote 88, and Cal. Civ. Proc. Code §§871.1 to 871.7 (West 1993) (articulating judgmental rules to be applied when improvements have been placed in good faith on another's land).

5. Does Merrill adequately explain why partition actions are authorized when property is owned concurrently, but not when ownership of property is divided over time, say between a life tenant and a remainderman? Some states entitle life tenants to seek partition. See, for instance, Cal. Code Civ. Proc. §872.210(a)(2) (West 1993). Would Merrill disapprove?

Chapter 6

Property Rights
that Arise Outside
the Legal System

The Evolution of Cooperation*

Robert Axelrod

Under what conditions will cooperation emerge in a world of egoists without central authority? This question has intrigued people for a long time. And for good reason. We all know that people are not angels, and that they tend to look after themselves and their own first. Yet we also know that cooperation does occur and that our civilization is based upon it. But, in situations where each individual has an incentive to be selfish, how can cooperation ever develop?

The answer each of us gives to this question has a fundamental effect on how we think and act in our social, political, and economic relations with others. And the answers that others give have a great effect on how ready they will be to cooperate with us.

The most famous answer was given over three hundred years ago by Thomas Hobbes. It was pessimistic. He argued that before governments existed, the state of nature was dominated by the problem of selfish individuals who competed on such ruthless terms that life was "solitary, poor, nasty, brutish, and short" (Hobbes 1651/ 1962, p.100). In his view, cooperation could not develop without a central authority, and consequently a strong government was nec-

* Source: 3-12, 19-21, 30-35 (1984).

essary. Ever since, arguments about the proper scope of government have often focused on whether one could, or could not, expect cooperation to emerge in a particular domain if there were not an authority to police the situation. . . .

A good example of the fundamental problem of cooperation is the case where two industrial nations have erected trade barriers to each other's exports. Because of the mutual advantages of free trade, both countries would be better off if these barriers were eliminated. But if either country were to unilaterally eliminate its barriers, it would find itself facing terms of trade that hurt its own economy. In fact, whatever one country does, the other country is better off retaining its own trade barriers. Therefore, the problem is that each country has an incentive to retain trade barriers, leading to a worse outcome than would have been possible had both countries cooperated with each other.

This basic problem occurs when the pursuit of self-interest by each leads to a poor outcome for all. To make headway in understanding the vast array of specific situations which have this property, a way is needed to represent what is common to these situations without becoming bogged down in the details unique to each. Fortunately, there is such a representation available: the famous *Prisoner's Dilemma* game.

In the Prisoner's Dilemma game, there are two players. Each has two choices, namely cooperate or defect. Each must make the choice without knowing what the other will do. No matter what the other does, defection yields a higher payoff than cooperation. The dilemma is that if both defect, both do worse than if both had cooperated. This simple game will provide the basis for the entire analysis used in this book.

The way the game works is shown in figure 1. One player chooses a row, either cooperating or defecting. The other player simultaneously chooses a column, either cooperating or defecting. Together, these choices result in one of the four possible outcomes shown in that matrix. If both players cooperate, both do fairly well. Both get *R*, the *reward for mutual cooperation*. In the concrete illustration of figure 1 the reward is 3 points. This number might, for example, be a payoff in dollars that each player gets for that outcome. If one player cooperates but the other defects, the defecting player gets the *temptation to defect*, while the cooperating player gets the *sucker's payoff*. In the example, these are 5 points and 0 points respectively. If both defect, both get 1 point, the *punishment for mutual defection*.

What should you do in such a game? Suppose you are the row player, and you think the column player will cooperate. This means that you will get one of the two outcomes in the first column of

---

Figure 1
The Prisoner's Dilemma

		Column Player	
		Cooperate	*Defect*
Row Player	*Cooperate*	$R = 3, R = 3$ Reward for mutual cooperation	$S = 0, T = 5$ Sucker's payoff, and temptation to defect
	Defect	$T = 5, S = 0$ Temptation to defect and sucker's payoff	$P = 1, P = 1$ Punishment for mutual defection

Note: The payoffs to the row chooser are listed first.

---

figure 1. You have a choice. You can cooperate as well, getting the 3 points of the reward for mutual cooperation. Or you can defect, getting the 5 points of the temptation payoff. So it pays to defect if you think the other player will cooperate. But now suppose that you think the other player will defect. Now you are in the second column of figure 1, and you have a choice between cooperating, which would make you a sucker and give you 0 points, and defecting, which would result in mutual punishment giving you 1 point. So it pays to defect if you think the other player will defect. This means that it is better to defect if you think the other player will cooperate, *and* it is better to defect if you think the other player will defect. So no matter what the other player does, it pays for you to defect.

So far, so good. But the same logic holds for the other player too. Therefore, the other player should defect no matter what you are expected to do. So you should both defect. But then you both get 1 point which is worse than the 3 points of the reward that you both could have gotten had you both cooperated. Individual rationality leads to a worse outcome for both than is possible. Hence the dilemma.

The Prisoner's Dilemma is simply an abstract formulation of some very common and very interesting situations in which what is best for each person individually leads to mutual defection, whereas everyone would have been better off with mutual cooperation. The definition of Prisoner's Dilemma requires that several relationships hold among the four different potential outcomes. The first relationship specifies the order of the four payoffs. The best a player can do is get T, the temptation to defect when the other player cooperates.

The worst a player can do is get S, the sucker's payoff for cooperating while the other player defects. In ordering the other two outcomes, R, the reward for mutual cooperation, is assumed to be better than P, the punishment for mutual defection. This leads to a preference ranking of the four payoffs from best to worst as T, R, P, and S.

The second part of the definition of the Prisoner's Dilemma is that the players cannot get out of their dilemma by taking turns exploiting each other. This assumption means that an even chance of exploitation and being exploited is not as good an outcome for a player as mutual cooperation. It is therefore assumed that the reward for mutual cooperation is greater than the average of the temptation and the sucker's payoff. This assumption, together with the rank ordering of the four payoffs, defines the Prisoner's Dilemma.

Thus two egoists playing the game *once* will both choose their dominant choice, defection, and each will get less than they both could have gotten if they had cooperated. If the game is played a known finite number of times, the players still have no incentive to cooperate. This is certainly true on the last move since there is no future to influence. On the next-to-last move neither player will have an incentive to cooperate since they can both anticipate a defection by the other player on the very last move. Such a line of reasoning implies that the game will unravel all the way back to mutual defection on the first move of any sequence of plays that is of known finite length (Luce and Raiffa 1957, pp. 94-102). This reasoning does not apply if the players will interact an indefinite number of times. And in most realistic settings, the players cannot be sure when the last interaction between them will take place. As will be shown later, with an indefinite number of interactions, cooperation can emerge. The issue then becomes the discovery of the precise conditions that are necessary and sufficient for cooperation to emerge.

In this book I will examine interactions between just two players at a time. A single player may be interacting with many others, but the player is assumed to be interacting with them one at a time. The player is also assumed to recognize another player and to remember how the two of them have interacted so far. This ability to recognize and remember allows the history of the particular interaction to be taken into account by a player's strategy.

A variety of ways to resolve the Prisoner's Dilemma have been developed. Each involves allowing some additional activity that alters the strategic interaction in such a way as to fundamentally change the nature of the problem. The original problem remains, however, because there are many situations in which these remedies are not available. Therefore, the problem will be considered in its fundamental form, without these alterations.

1. There is no mechanism available to the players to make enforceable threats or commitments (Schelling 1960). Since the players cannot commit themselves to a particular strategy, each must take into account all possible strategies that might be used by the other player. Moreover the players have all possible strategies available to themselves.

2. There is no way to be sure what the other player will do on a given move. This eliminates the possibility of metagame analysis which allows such options as "make the same choice as the other is about to make." It also eliminates the possibility of reliable reputations such as might be based on watching the other player interact with third parties. Thus the only information available to the players about each other is the history of their interaction so far.

3. There is no way to eliminate the other player or run away from the interaction. Therefore each player retains the ability to cooperate or defect on each move.

4. There is no way to change the other player's payoffs. The payoffs already include whatever consideration each player has for the interests of the other.

Under these conditions, words not backed by actions are so cheap as to be meaningless. The players can communicate with each other only through the sequence of their own behavior. This is the problem of the Prisoner's Dilemma in its fundamental form.

What makes it possible for cooperation to emerge is the fact that the players might meet again. This possibility means that the choices made today not only determine the outcome of this move, but can also influence the later choices of the players. The future can therefore cast a shadow back upon the present and thereby affect the current strategic situation.

But the future is less important than the present — for two reasons. The first is that players tend to value payoffs less as the time of their obtainment recedes into the future. The second is that there is always some chance that the players will not meet again. An ongoing relationship may end when one or the other player moves away, changes jobs, dies, or goes bankrupt. . . .

The next chapter explores the emergence of cooperation through a study of what is a good strategy to employ if confronted with an iterated Prisoner's Dilemma. This exploration has been done in a novel way, with a computer tournament. Professional game theorists were invited to submit their favorite strategy, and each of these decision rules was paired off with each of the others to see which would do best overall. Amazingly enough, the winner was the simplest of all strategies submitted. This was TIT FOR TAT, the strategy which cooperates on the first move and then does whatever the other player did on the previous move. A second round of the tournament was conducted in which many more entries were submitted by amateurs and professionals alike, all of whom were aware of the results of the first round. The result was another victory for TIT FOR TAT! The analysis of the data from these tournaments reveals four properties which tend to make a decision rule successful: avoidance of unnecessary conflict by cooperating as long as the other player does, provocability in the face of an uncalled for defection by the other, forgiveness after responding to a provocation, and clarity of behavior so that the other player can adapt to your pattern of action.

These results from the tournaments demonstrate that under suitable conditions, cooperation can indeed emerge in a world of egoists without central authority. To see just how widely these results apply, a theoretical approach is taken in chapter 3. A series of propositions are proved that not only demonstrate the requirements for the emergence of cooperation but also provide the chronological story of the evolution of cooperation. Here is the argument in a nutshell. The evolution of cooperation requires that individuals have a sufficiently large chance to meet again so that they have a stake in their future interaction. If this is true, cooperation can evolve in three stages.

1. The beginning of the story is that cooperation can get started even in a world of unconditional defection. The development *cannot* take place if it is tried only by scattered individuals who have virtually no chance to interact with each other. However, cooperation can evolve from small clusters of individuals who base their cooperation on reciprocity and have even a small proportion of their interactions with each other.

2. The middle of the story is that a strategy based on reciprocity can thrive in a world where many different kinds of strategies are being tried.

3. The end of the story is that cooperation, once established on the basis of reciprocity, can protect itself from invasion by less cooperative strategies. Thus, the gear wheels of social evolution have a ratchet.

Chapters 4 and 5 take concrete settings to demonstrate just how widely these results apply. Chapter 4 is devoted to the fascinating case of the "live and let live" system which emerged during the trench warfare of World War I. In the midst of this bitter conflict, the front-line soldiers often refrained from shooting to kill — provided their restraint was reciprocated by the soldiers on the other side. What made this mutual restraint possible was the static nature of trench warfare, where the same small units faced each other for extended periods of time. The soldiers of these opposing small units actually violated orders from their own high commands in order to achieve tacit cooperation with each other. A detailed look at this case shows that when the conditions are present for the emergence of cooperation, cooperation can get started and prove stable in situations which otherwise appear extraordinarily unpromising. . . .

. . . Two important facts about non-zero-sum settings . . . have to be taken into account. First, the proposition of the previous chapter demonstrates that what is effective depends not only upon the characteristics of a particular strategy, but also upon the nature of the other strategies with which it must interact. The second point follows directly from the first. An effective strategy must be able at any point to take into account the history of the interaction as it has developed so far.

A computer tournament for the study of effective choice in the iterated Prisoner's Dilemma meets these needs. In a computer tournament, each entrant writes a program that embodies a rule to select the cooperative or noncooperative choice on each move. The program has available to it the history of the game so far, and may use this history in making a choice. If the participants are recruited primarily from those who are familiar with the Prisoner's Dilemma, the entrants can be assured that their decision rule will be facing rules of other informed entrants. Such recruitment would also guarantee that the state of the art is represented in the tournament.

Wanting to find out what would happen, I invited professional game theorists to send in entries to just such a computer tournament. It was structured as a round robin, meaning that each entry was paired with each other entry. As announced in the rules of the tournament, each entry was also paired with its own twin and with RANDOM, a program that randomly cooperates and defects with equal probability. Each game consisted of exactly two hundred moves. The payoff matrix for each move was the familiar one described in chapter 1. It awarded both players 3 points for mutual cooperation, and 1 point for mutual defection. If one player defected while the other player cooperated, the defecting player received 5 points and the cooperating player received 0 points.

No entry was disqualified for exceeding the allotted time. In fact, the entire round robin tournament was run five times to get a more stable estimate of the scores for each pair of players. In all, there were 120,000 moves, making for 240,000 separate choices.

The fourteen submitted entries came from five disciplines: psychology, economics, political science, mathematics, and sociology. . . .

One remarkable aspect of the tournament was that it allowed people from different disciplines to interact with each other in a common format and language. Most of the entrants were recruited from those who had published articles on game theory in general or the Prisoner's Dilemma in particular.

TIT FOR TAT, submitted by Professor Anatol Rapoport of the University of Toronto, won the tournament. This was the simplest of all submitted programs and it turned out to be the best!

TIT FOR TAT, of course, starts with a cooperative choice, and thereafter does what the other player did on the previous move. This decision rule is probably the most widely known and most discussed rule for playing the Prisoner's Dilemma. It is easily understood and easily programmed. It is known to elicit a good degree of cooperation when played with humans (Oskamp 1971; W. Wilson 1971). As an entry in a computer tournament, it has the desirable properties that it is not very exploitable and that it does well with its own twin. It has the disadvantage that it is too generous with the RANDOM rule, which was known by the participants to be entered in the tournament.

In addition, TIT FOR TAT was known to be a powerful competitor. In a preliminary tournament, TIT FOR TAT scored second place; and in a variant of that preliminary tournament, TIT FOR TAT won first place. All of these facts were known to most of the people designing programs for the Computer Prisoner's Dilemma Tournament, because they were sent copies of a description of the preliminary tournament. Not surprisingly, many of them used the TIT FOR TAT principle and tried to improve upon it.

The striking fact is that *none* of the more complex programs submitted was able to perform as well as the original, simple TIT FOR TAT.

This result contrasts with computer chess tournaments, where complexity is obviously needed. For example, in the Second World Computer Chess Championships, the least complex program came in last (Jennings 1978). It was submitted by Johann Joss of the Eidgenossishe Technische Hochschule of Zurich, Switzerland, who also submitted an entry to the Computer Prisoner's Dilemma Tournament. His entry to the Prisoner's Dilemma Tournament was a small modification of TIT FOR TAT. But his modification, like the others, just lowered the performance of the decision rule.

Analysis of the results showed that neither the discipline of the author, the brevity of the program — nor its length — accounts for a rule's relative success. What does?

Before answering this question, a remark on the interpretation of numerical scores is in order. In a game of 200 moves, a useful benchmark for very good performance is 600 points, which is equivalent to the score attained by a player when both sides always cooperate with each other. A useful benchmark for very poor performance is 200 points, which is equivalent to the score attained by a player when both sides never cooperate with each other. Most scores range between 200 and 600 points, although scores from 0 to 1000 points are possible. The winner, TIT FOR TAT, averaged 504 points per game.

Surprisingly, there is a single property which distinguishes the relatively high-scoring entries from the relatively low-scoring entries. This is the property of being *nice*, which is to say never being the first to defect. (For the sake of analyzing this tournament, the definition of a nice rule will be relaxed to include rules which will not be the first to defect before the last few moves, say before move 199.)

Each of the eight top-ranking entries (or rules) is nice. None of the other entries is. There is even a substantial gap in the score between the nice entries and the others. The nice entries received tournament averages between 472 and 504, while the best of the entries that were not nice received only 401 points. Thus, not being the first to defect, at least until virtually the end of the game, was a property which, all by itself, separated the more successful rules from the less successful rules in this Computer Prisoner's Dilemma Tournament.

Each of the nice rules got about 600 points with each of the other seven nice rules and with its own twin. This is because when two nice rules play, they are sure to cooperate with each other until virtually the end of the game. Actually the minor variations in endgame tactics did not account for much variation in the scores.

Since the nice rules all got within a few points of 600 with each other, the thing that distinguished the relative rankings among the nice rules was their scores with the rules which are not nice. This much is obvious. What is not obvious is that the relative ranking of the eight top rules was largely determined by just two of the other seven rules. These two rules are *kingmakers* because they do not do very well for themselves, but they largely determine the rankings among the top contenders.

The most important kingmaker was based on an "outcome maximization" principle originally developed as a possible interpretation of what human subjects do in the Prisoner's Dilemma laboratory experiments (Downing 1975). This rule, called DOWNING, is a particularly interesting rule in its own right. It is well worth studying as an example of a decision rule which is based upon a quite sophisticated idea. Unlike most of the others, its logic is not just a variant of TIT FOR TAT. Instead it is based on a deliberate attempt to understand the other player and then to make the choice that will yield the best long-term score based upon this understanding. The idea is that if the other player does not seem responsive to what DOWNING is doing, DOWNING will try to get away with whatever it can by defecting. On the other hand, if the other player does seem responsive, DOWNING will cooperate. To judge the other's responsiveness, DOWNING estimates the probability that the other player cooperates after it (DOWNING) cooperates, and also the probability that the other player cooperates after DOWNING defects. For each move, it updates its estimate of these two conditional probabilities and then selects the choice which will maximize its own long-term payoff under the assumption that it has correctly modeled the other player. If the two conditional probabilities have similar values, DOWNING determines that it pays to defect, since the other player seems to be doing the same thing whether DOWNING cooperates or not. Conversely, if the other player tends to cooperate after a cooperation but not after a defection by DOWNING, then the other player seems responsive, and DOWNING will calculate that the best thing to do with a responsive player is to cooperate. Under certain circumstances, DOWNING will even determine that the best strategy is to alternate cooperation and defection.

At the start of a game, DOWNING does not know the values of these conditional probabilities for the other players. It assumes that they are both .5, but gives no weight to this estimate when information actually does come in during the play of the game.

This is a fairly sophisticated decision rule, but its implementation does have one flaw. By initially assuming that the other player is unresponsive, DOWNING is doomed to defect on the first two moves. These first two defections led many other rules to punish DOWNING, so things usually got off to a bad start. But this is precisely why DOWNING served so well as a kingmaker. First-ranking TIT FOR TAT and second-ranking TIDEMAN AND CHIERUZZI both reacted in such a way that DOWNING learned to expect that defection does not pay but that cooperation does. All of the other nice rules went downhill with DOWNING. . . .

NOTES AND QUESTIONS ON GAME THEORY AND THE ITERATED PRISONER'S DILEMMA

1. Axelrod's computer tournament was far tidier than human affairs. The payoff matrix did not vary from round to round. Each pair of entrants knew they would play one-against-the-other for ex-

actly 200 rounds. No contestant could find out the choices a competitor had made in his prior encounters with other entrants. Do these sorts of simplifications limit the lessons one can draw from Axelrod's results? Or does simplification help reveal, to quote Axelrod, the "fundamental form" of the problem of cooperation?

For criticism of the Axelrod format, see, for instance, Jack Hirshleifer & Juan Carlos Martinez Coll, What Strategies Can Support the Evolutionary Emergence of Cooperation?, 32 J. Conflict Resolution 367 (1988), who showed that TIT FOR TAT was dominated by "mean" strategies in elimination games, in which only winners move on. See also Anthony de Jasay, Social Contract, Free Ride: A Study of the Public Goods Problem 64-65 (1989), predicting that single-minded rational actors will always "take the money and run" when interactions are not repeated. Do these criticisms make the phenomenon of cooperation even more mysterious?

2. In Axelrod's tournament a player tended to prosper by being:

a. nice (that is, not the first to defect);
b. immediately prepared to punish a defection; and
c. willing to forgive another's past defections once accounts had been squared.

Aside from the issue of whether rational actors would choose these tactics, do they constitute a sound approach to the game of life? What truth is there in baseball manager Leo Durocher's adage, "Nice guys finish last"?

3. Can Axelrod's work shed light on the landlord-tenant relationship? A landlord and tenant are situated in a repeated game. Each may be tempted to defect — typically, the tenant by failing to pay rent when due, and the landlord, by breaching obligations to maintain the premises. The payoffs in a landlord-tenant relationship, however, are not necessarily structured like those of a Prisoner's Dilemma. Is landlord-tenant law usefully viewed as an attempt to alter the payoff structure in order to elicit cooperation between landlords and tenants?

Game theory suggests that cooperation is most likely to break down toward the end of a relationship. Is this true in the case of leaseholds? How might landlords employ security deposits to prevent tenants from chiseling at the end of the term on rent obligations? How might tenants (or lawmakers) prevent landlords from wrongfully withholding the return of security deposits?

Reputational concerns can deter opportunism. For example, a

landlord might refrain from mistreating current tenants because prospective tenants might learn of the misconduct. What might a university's student government do to enhance local landlords' reputational concerns? Conversely, in many urban markets commercial firms will provide to landlords, for a fee, reports on prospective tenants' prior involvements in housing litigation. What sorts of tenants might be *helped* by the existence of these firms?

In an ambitiously broad study of an actual housing market, the Rand Corporation found landlord-tenant relations in Brown County, Wisconsin, to be "relaxed and comfortable." Rand Corporation, Second Annual Report of the Housing Assistance Supply Experiment 69 (R-1959-HUD May 1976). Why might reported appellate cases provide a distorted lens on landlord-tenant relationships? What effect does rent control have on the level of cooperation between landlords and tenants? On rent control, see infra pp. 404–423.

4. Recall Acheson's description, supra p.141, of how the lobster gangs of Maine created property rights in congestible fisheries. Under what conditions can the users of a limited-access commons employ strategies similar to TIT FOR TAT to forestall the sort of "tragedy" that Garrett Hardin thought to be inexorable? Of what relevance are studies of the evolution of property rights within preliterate societies? See, for example, Robert Cooter, Inventing Market Property: The Land Courts of Papua New Guinea, 25 Law & Soc'y Rev. 759 (1991); Michael J. Trebilcock, Communal Property Rights: The Papua New Guinea Experience, 34 U. Toronto L. Rev. 377 (1984).

In a laboratory experiment involving human subjects, Ostrom, Walker, and Gardner (OWG) simulated exploitation of a common-pool resource. The pool was vulnerable to excessive depletion unless all eight possible appropriators cooperated to limit their rates of extraction. OWG manipulated from session to session the ability of the appropriators to communicate with one another and to sanction those who overdrew from the common pool. Generally, provision of opportunities for both communication and sanctioning fostered cooperative behavior. OWG conclude:

> Policymakers responsible for the governance and management of small-scale [common-pool resources] should *not* presume that the individuals involved are caught in an inexorable tragedy from which there is no escape. Individuals may be able to arrive at joint strategies to manage these resources more efficiently. To accomplish this task, they must have sufficient information to pose and solve the allocation problems they face. They must also have an arena where they can discuss joint strategies and perhaps implement monitoring and sanctioning. In other words, when individuals are given an opportunity to restructure their own situation, they frequently — but not al-

ways — use this opportunity to make credible commitments and achieve higher joint outcomes without an external enforcer.

Elinor Ostrom, James Walker & Roy Gardner, Covenants with and without a Sword: Self-Governance is Possible, 86 Am. Pol. Sci. Rev. 404, 414 (1992). What are the implications for natural resources law? For land use regulation?

5. Axelrod's book helped trigger a boom in academic work on cooperation, much of it from a game-theoretic perspective. For law students, an especially suitable introduction to game theory is Douglas G. Baird, Robert H. Gertner & Randel C. Picker, Game Theory and the Law (1994).

Entitlements, Rights, and Fairness: An Experimental Examination of Subjects' Concepts of Distributive Justice[*]

Elizabeth Hoffman & Matthew L. Spitzer

I. Introduction

The research reported in this paper arose from a previous experimental study conducted by the authors.[1] That study involved bargains struck between two subjects who had opposing payoff functions and full information of one another's payoffs. By a flip of a coin one participant could choose a noncooperative outcome, unilaterally: The winner of the coin toss could simply choose an outcome which gave him $12 and left the other subject nothing, whether or not the loser agreed. However, if the two subjects cooperated, they could obtain from the experimenter $14, which could be split between the subjects in any mutually agreed-on manner. Cooperative game theory predicts that the subjects will cooperate and divide the rewards $13 to $1 (the Nash bargaining solution: an even division of the $2 gain from trade). Under no circumstances should the winner of the coin flip settle for less than $12, according to game theory. In our experiments all of the subject pairs chose the joint profit-maximizing outcome, which the theory predicts, but they then divided the rewards $7 to $7. In effect, each winner of a

* Souce: 14 J. Legal Stud. 259-284 (1985).
    1. Elizabeth Hoffman & Matthew L. Spitzer, The Coase Theorem: Some Experimental Tests, 25 J. Law & Econ. 73 (1982).

coin flip agreed to take $5 *less* than the $12 that he could have obtained *without* the other subject's cooperation.

These results often startle economists (ourselves included), who usually assume that individuals will generally behave in a self-regarding manner. However, if one is willing to hypothesize that subjects behave "as if" they distribute the payoffs in accord with their perceptions of fairness, the results can be rationalized. In particular, we can construct a model based on the following set of related assumptions:

Model 1:
1. Each subject would concur with a particular concept of fairness in distribution (also known as a theory of distributive justice).
2. Each subject perceives the experimental institutions as triggering a particular aspect of his concept of justice, indicating which distribution or set of distributions is fair within that experiment.
3. The subject implements his perceptions of a fair distribution.

In the results reported above, we hypothesize that subjects behave in accord with a theory of distributive justice that says that flipping a coin is not a just way of allocating unequal property entitlements. Subjects perceived no morally justified difference between themselves, even though one "legally" owned a substantial property entitlement and the other did not. Because they were "morally equal," an equal split seemed to be the only fair allocation.

If this explanation of subject behavior is correct, then by systematically varying the experimental institutions and observing how subjects' payoff distributions change, we should be able to infer which theories of distributive justice subjects hold. We consider, in particular, three different candidates for subjects' concepts of fairness, drawn from three major families of theories of distributive justice: utilitarian, egalitarian, and natural law/desert. Specifically, we consider the self-regarding, economic man paradigm from utilitarian theory, an extreme egalitarian theory of equal sharing, and the Lockean theory of earned desert.

Each of the experiments reported in this paper allocated entitlements in a different manner and then allowed subjects to divide the value of those entitlements. The results suggest that subjects behaved in accord neither with the self-regarding utilitarian theory nor with the egalitarian theory of distributive justice, but rather in accord with the Lockean theory of earned desert. These experimental results show strongly that different methods of assigning property entitlements lead to significant differences in the frequency of self-regarding versus equal payoff divisions. Subjects appeared to treat their entitlements as rights to unequal payoff divisions when the experimental institutions led them to believe that they had "earned" those entitlements. Subjects continued to maximize joint profits (chose efficient outcomes) in all versions of the experiment.

Both behavioral scientists and lawyers should be interested in the results reported below. Experimental economists and psychologists should be particularly intrigued by the results, for they help to trace out the domain within which one may safely utilize the postulate of self-regarding behavior. Legal theorists may also be interested in property entitlements and moral rules for allocating payments. A large group of scholars believe that the law should (or does) reflect widely held moral norms. Hence, it is important to learn of their content.[5] Application of the information provided by the experiments reported herein may suggest important policies for shaping the law.

We must note, however, that substantial difficulties may plague any such applications of our results to the law. For example, an individual's beliefs about morality may determine his behavior. But there is a substantial amount of experimental evidence tending to show that the correlation between an individual's moral behavior (cheating, for example) in one situation and moral behavior in similar (but not identical) situations tends to be positive and significant, but small in size. Therefore, one should be very careful about predicting behavior generated by moral norms (for example, cheating is bad) over different sorts of situations. To the extent that one can make such predictions, however, they can help inform fundamental policy choices. In the final section of this paper we explore some

5. Norms may be a product of nature or of socialization processes. Sociobiologists argue that a mechanism of natural selection provides survival advantages to those who hold certain moral beliefs. See generally, Edward O. Wilson, On Human Nature (1978) at 5. See also Paul H. Rubin, Evolved Ethics and Efficient Ethics, 3 J. Econ. Behav. & Organization 161 (1982), contending, inter alia, that modern man's disposition to share wealth with his less fortunate fellows (and his disposition to dislike wealthy individuals) can be explained as the product both of kin selection procedures, id. at 165, and primitive insurance ("reciprocal altruism") against "unlucky" events, such as poor animal hunts, in primitive hunter-gatherer tribes. Rubin contends that both of these traits probably produced survival advantages in primitive tribes and that these traits survive today as "ethical intuitions" that are counterproductive for our modern social organization. Others argue that beliefs about morality are produced by the socialization process. See, for example, Barry Holden, Liberal Democracy and the Social Determination of Ideas, 25 Nomos: Liberal Democracy 289 (J. Roland Pennock & John W. Chapman eds. 1983), discussing Marxist critiques of liberal democratic theory.

possible legal applications and discuss problems involved in using them to inform policy.

II.   Theories of Distributive Justice

A.   Utilitarian

Utilitarian theories assert that people ought to act so as to maximize some function which is monotonically increasing in the utility of each of the members of society (for example, sums or products of individual utility functions). We consider only one version of utilitarianism: Each person's utility is independent of any other person's utility and each person weights his own utility more heavily than the utility of anyone else. This self-regarding version of utilitarianism suggests that subjects will regard any distribution in which they have more money as more desirable. This belief will lead subjects to act so as to maximize their own holdings, appearing to be "greedy."

This version of utilitarianism generates the paradigm of the "economic man," who under most economic and game-theoretic models makes self-regarding decisions about whatever entitlements he is endowed with. Where property rights are well defined, the rational economic agent is assumed to enter only into bargains that he believes will leave him no worse off than if he had not traded at all. In particular, he does not give away claims to resources unless he gets some commensurate reward in return. Altruism may exist, but it is generally ignored in economic and game-theoretic modeling.[9]

B.   Egalitarian

Egalitarian theories all posit that a just distribution gives everyone an equal share of resources. The theories differ over *what* exactly should be equalized. For example, needs theories claim that people who are equal in terms of their needs for resources should get equal holdings. One such theory is the psychologist's attempt to create an inventory or hierarchy of basic needs. A second is the analysis of

9. Altruism is used only to mean interdependent utility functions. That is, one person is made happier by another person becoming happier, without any change in the first person's private holdings. The few economists who have developed models that allow for altruism include Gary S. Becker, A Treatise on the Family (1981); Mordecai Kurz, Altruistic Equilibria, in Economic Progress, Private Values, and Public Policy (Bela Belassa & Richard Nelson eds. 1977). . . .

human needs in recent Roman Catholic social encyclicals. Roman Catholicism builds theories of rights and justice on assessments of dignity, which is achieved by satisfying natural human needs. Third, Marxian political theory offers to make need the measure of right, but insists that this is impossible, not only in capitalist society, but also in the first phases of communist society. Hence, "From each according to his ability, to each according to his needs," applies in the later phases of communist society only.[12] Fourth, liberal political theory has tried to link distributive justice to the satisfaction of minimum needs. Rawls's *Theory of Justice,* for example, tolerates inequality between persons only where the inequality will redound to the benefit of the worst-off person in society.

Our experiments explore the very simplest form of egalitarianism: equal sharing regardless of other characteristics. This version of egalitarianism is championed by many psychologists, who argue from theory and experimental evidence that a norm favoring equality or payment according to need is so strong that people will only deviate from it in limited circumstances.[15] Subjects who hold such beliefs should always split payoffs equally, regardless of how they obtained those payoffs. This is, of course, exactly what subjects did in our original set of experiments.

C. Natural Law/Desert

Natural law/desert theories assert that, as a matter of natural law, someone or other *deserves* resources. The only variant of this group of theories of distributive justice that we explore is Locke's.[17] The Lockean theory posits that an individual deserves, as a matter of natural law, a property entitlement in resources that have been accumulated or developed through the individual's expenditure of effort. The individual deserves the entitlement because he has "mixed his labor" with the resource. A subject who holds a Lockean theory of distributive justice will behave in a self-regarding manner whenever he perceives that he has "mixed his labor" with a resource.

A literature in social psychology, termed equity theory, seems to fit with the Lockean theory. Equity theory argues, from first prin-

12. See, for example, Karl Marx, Critique of the Gotha Program, in Karl Marx and Frederick Engels: Basic Writings on Politics and Philosophy 112, 119 (Lewis S. Feuer ed. 1959).

15. See Morton Deutsch, Equity, Equality, and Need: What Determines Which Value Will Be Used as the Basis of Distributive Justice, 31 J. Soc. Issues 137 (No. 3, 1975). . . .

17. John Locke, Second Treatise of Civil Government, ch. 5 (1978).

ciple and experimental evidence, that people allocate payments so as to equalize individual ratios between payments and intrinsic inputs.[19] Unfortunately, equity theory provides, in general, no testable hypotheses. Equity theorists commonly define "intrinsic inputs" to include difficulty of the work, the time spent, the amount of work completed, and salient personal characteristics such as intelligence, family name, or social status. "Payments" include both benefits and harms produced by the experimental situation. However, because many of the inputs are not observable, and because of the difficulty of predicting, in general, which characteristics will be salient, one cannot construct the ratios between inputs and payments to test the behavioral predictions.

Despite these formidable empirical obstacles, equity theory is not completely useless. In certain experimental settings subjects behave as if the amount of effort is the only salient input and as if equal ratio payment should guide their behavior. Experimental subjects who are paid more than equal coworkers frequently give some of their payoffs to the lower-paid coworkers, thereby restoring an equitable ratio of payments to inputs.

D. Non-Value-oriented Explanations

The three classes of theories of distributive justice discussed above — utilitarian, egalitarian, and natural law/desert — all represent value-oriented explanations. In contrast, we classify purely authoritarian and sociobiological explanations of morally relevant behavior as non value oriented. The purely authoritarian explanation posits that people will behave as if they are morally justified in treating their entitlements as rights whenever an authority (herein termed a *moral authority*) tells them that their entitlements are rights. The moral authority may, of course, refer to value-oriented theories when telling people to believe that a certain distribution is just. For example, an authority might tell people that they are justified in acting in a self-regarding fashion because each of them has special needs. Nonetheless, a moral authority need not resort to such an

---

19. Note that this rule is equivalent to an economic rule which allocates rewards to keep the ratios of payments to the *average* product of labor equal. . . . This is in contrast to the *efficient* payment rule which equates the ratios of wages and *marginal* products of labor. . . . The ideal of equity theory was originally formalized by J.S. Adams, Inequity in Social Exchange, in Advances in Experimental Social Psychology (Leonard Berkowitz ed. 1965), and by George Caspar Homans, Social Behavior: Its Elementary Forms (1961). The idea is based on an Aristotelian notion of social justice. Subsequent researchers have refined the equal ratio formula, but the basic idea remains a cornerstone of equity theory. See, for example, John C. Allessio, Another Folly for Equity Theory, 43 Soc. Psychology Q. 336 (1980). . . .

approach. It might, instead, merely tell people that a certain distribution is just, and make no reference whatsoever to any value-oriented theory. Similarly, the sociobiological theory posits that genetic material governs much morally relevant behavior and that genes producing behavior that enhances survivability of the line (maximizes inclusive fitness across generations) will eventually predominate.

The experimental design described below introduces a treatment variable that may be interpreted as a form of moral authority. The instructions in some of the experiments *tell* the subjects that they have "earned" their entitlements. If the authoritarian theory has an explanatory power, subjects thus instructed should be more willing to treat their entitlements as legitimate rights. The design has no features which could be interpreted in the context of a sociobiological model.

III. Experimental Design

A. General

All the experiments reported here involved two people who were fully informed about one another's payoffs. Bargaining was face to face and public and involved more money than most students can earn for an hour's work in their next-best alternative employment. Side payments were allowed. Contracts were in writing and strictly enforced. All payments were made in public. Subjects were given no motivational instructions: that is, they were not told what their objectives should be in choosing numbers or in forming contracts.

B. Experimental Instructions

1. *Game-Trigger, Moral Authority Experiments.* As the subjects arrived at a designated room they were randomly assigned the letters *A* or *B*. Each pair was placed in a separate room, with a monitor being the only other person present. The monitor provided the following set of instructions to the subjects, who first read them silently and then listened to the monitor read them aloud.

Instructions

General
   You are about to participate in an experiment in decision-making. The purpose of the experiment is to gain insight into certain

features of complex economic processes. If you follow the instructions carefully, you might earn a considerable amount of money. You will be paid in cash at the end of the experiment.

Specific Instructions to Participants
   You are person _____. The other participant is person _____.
   This experiment requires that two decisions be made. Each decision will involve choosing a number. The number chosen will correspond to an actual dollar amount which will be paid to you at the end of this experiment. The number and corresponding payoffs for the first decision are on page five of these instructions; the number and payoffs for the second decision are on page six. Pages five and six list not only the value of each number to you (under column _____), but also the value of each number to the other participant (under column _____).
   Before each decision, both participants *A* and *B* will play a game. Whoever wins this game earns the right to be designated "controller" for that decision. The rules of this preliminary game are as follows.

/ / / / / / / / / / / / / / / / /

Above here is a picture of 17 vertical hash marks. Each player must, on each turn, cross out 1, 2, 3, *or* 4 hash marks. After a player has crossed out as many hash marks as he or she wishes, it is the other player's turn to cross out 1, 2, 3, *or* 4 hash marks. The game continues until all hash marks have been crossed out. The person who crosses out the last hash mark *loses* the game. *A* will go first on the first decision, *B* will go first on the second decision.

Example: A goes first and crosses out 4 marks

/////// / / / / / / / / / / / / /

   Then B crosses out 4 marks

/////////////// / / / / / / / / /

   Then A crosses out 4 marks

/////////////////////// / / / / /

   Then B crosses out 4 marks

/////////////////////////////// /

A must cross out the last mark on his turn, so *A* loses the game and *B* has earned the position of the controller.
   If you win the game and are designated controller, you may, if you wish, choose any number you like by filling out the form on page seven and giving it to the monitor. However, if you lose the preliminary game and are not designated controller, you may still attempt to influence the controller to form a *joint agreement* and choose some

other number. In order to induce the controller to reach an acceptable *joint agreement,* you may offer to pay part of your earnings to the controller.

Example: Assume that *A* wins the preliminary game and earns the position of controller for the first decision. Assume also the following payoffs for *A* and *B*.

Number	A's Payoff	B's Payoff
1	$4	$1
2	5	2
3	3	5

Once *A* has become controller, he or she may choose number 2 without consulting *B*. However, *B* may attempt to persuade *A* to join in a joint decision to choose another number and/or division of payoffs. If a joint agreement is reached, *both* parties must sign the agreement form on page seven, stating both what the chosen number will be and how much money will be transferred from one participant's earnings to the other's. For example, *A* and *B* might sign the agreement form on page seven choosing number 3 and directing that $2.00 be paid from *B* to *A*. Once the agreement form is signed the monitor will note that for this decision *A* is to be paid $5.00 at the end of the experiment, representing the $3.00 original payoff for the number 3 plus the $2.00 transferred from *B*, and that *B* is to be paid $3.00, representing the $5.00 original payoff less the $2.00 transferred to *A*.

The monitor can only enforce written decisions recorded on the form set out on page 7. You are, however, free to make any other sort of informal agreement that you wish.

No physical threats are allowed. If any party makes a physical threat, the threatened party will get his or her maximum payoff and the threatening party will get nothing.

Are there any questions? We ask you to answer the questions on the attached sheet to make sure you understand the instructions.

Questions

(Refer to your payoffs on page 5 [listed immediately below])
1. Number _____ makes me the most money. Number _____ makes me the least money.
2. If I become controller, I can make $_____ even if the other person doesn't agree.
3. If *A* and *B* reach a joint decision to choose number 4 and *B* pays *A* $2.00, I make $_____.
4. If I am the controller, I may choose the number which corresponds to my maximum payoff without making a joint agreement with the other participant, TRUE or FALSE? _____
5. Which of the following do you prefer? _____
   a) $1.50 for sure.
   b) A fair coin toss which pays $0 for heads and $11 for tails.

Payoff Sheet

Decision #1

Number	A's Payoff	B's Payoff
1	$0.00	$12.00
2	4.00	10.00
3	6.00	6.00
4	7.50	4.00
5	9.00	2.50
6	10.50	1.00
7	12.00	0.00

Decision #2

Number	A's Payoff	B's Payoff
1	$0.00	$12.50
2	1.50	11.00
3	3.00	9.50
4	4.50	8.00
5	6.00	6.50
6	10.00	5.00
7	11.50	1.50
8	13.00	0.00

Agreement Form

Decision _____

Number Chosen _____

$_____ to be paid from _____ to _____

Signed: _____

A

_____

B

In essence, these instructions told subjects that they had to choose a number between 1 and 7 (decision 1) or 1 and 8 (decision 2) and that they would be paid in cash according to the discrete payoff functions given on pages 5 and 6 of the instructions. In addition, one subject won, by playing the hash mark game, the right to choose the number unilaterally and was told that he had *earned* that right by winning the game.

After reading the instructions and examining their payoffs, subjects were tested on their understanding of the rules and the consequences of decisions they might make. After both subjects had answered all of the questions correctly, and after the monitor had answered all the subjects' remaining uncertainties about the rules of the game, the subjects played the hash mark game. The winner of the game was told orally that he had earned the right to be controller. The subjects were then instructed to proceed with the experiment (by choosing a number).

2. *Coin-Flip, Moral Authority Experiments.* This set of instructions resembled the previous experiment in all respects save one. The controller was chosen by a flip of a coin instead of by winning the hash mark game. However, the winner of the coin flip was still told by the experimenter that he had earned the property entitlement. The instructions for this experiment were identical to the above instructions except for the section on the hash mark game. In place of the section beginning, "Before each decision, both participants *A* and *B* will play a game," and ending, ". . . choose any number you like by filling out the form on page seven and giving it to the monitor," the new instructions say,

> Before each decision, the monitor will flip a coin. Whoever wins this coin toss earns the right to become "controller" for that decision. If you win the coin toss and are designated controller, you may, if you wish, choose any number you like by filling out the form on page seven and giving it to the monitor.

3. *Game-Trigger, No Moral Authority Experiments.* The next set of experiments also resembled the game-trigger, moral authority experiments in almost all respects. The difference is that whenever the moral authority instructions say "earns the right" or "earns the position," the no moral authority instructions simply say "is designated." In addition, the example and the questions suggest that less moral authority is given to the controller. . . .

4. *Coin-Flip, No Moral Authority Experiments.* These experiments resemble the game-trigger, no moral authority experiments in the same way that the coin-flip moral authority experiments resemble the game-trigger moral authority experiments. The only difference between the coin-flip, no moral authority experiments and the game-trigger, no moral authority experiments is that subjects were told that one subject would be designated controller by a flip of a coin. There was no reference to a hash mark game.

C. Subjects

The subjects were upper-level economics and management majors and management graduate students at Purdue University and law students, upper-level arts and sciences students, and university staff at the University of Southern California. They were recruited in classes and by telephone and told only that they would participate in an economic decision. They were promised $4 per hour *plus* their earnings. Extra subjects were recruited in case of no-shows and paid at least $2 just for showing up. All subjects were inexperienced in this particular kind of experiment and friends were not allowed to participate together. After each experiment, we explained the nature of the experiment and the scientific importance of not telling their friends about it. Later subjects appeared to be as naive about the experiment as earlier subjects had been, and there did not seem to be any time trend in the results.

D.   Correspondence between Experimental Institutions and Theories of Distributive Justice

Assumption 2 of our model requires that subjects perceive the features of the experiment to trigger their beliefs about distributive justice. Therefore, we must inquire about the reasonableness of our experimental treatments. We argue below that the game trigger would lead a Lockean to believe that the winner could treat his entitlements as rights, but that a coin flip would not. We also argue that our moral authority instructions might trigger, as a matter of blind (non-value-oriented) faith, the belief that one is justified in treating the entitlements as rights. However, we also recognize that the moral authority instructions could be reinforcing latent Lockean beliefs. . . .

IV.   Experimental Results

Table 1 summarizes the results of all eighty-two experimental decisions. Notice first that 91 percent of the decisions are joint profit maximizing. Thus these results are generally consistent with those we have already reported. Second, there appear to be significant differences in the payoff divisions among at least three of the four experimental treatments. Looking first at the extremes, in the no moral authority experiments, 61 percent of the decisions are nearly equal splits. However, in the game-trigger, moral authority experiments more than half of the divisions give the controller more than his individual maximum and 68 percent give the controller at least his individual maximum. Only 32 percent are within $1 of an equal split. The other experimental treatment is intermediate: 50 percent of the coin-flip, moral authority decisions are within $1 of an equal

Table 1
Summary of Experimental Results

Experiment	Number of Decisions (N)	Number of Joint Maxima (N_1)	Equal Split (N_2)	Equal ± $1.00 (N_3)	Division of Payments			
					Controller Receives his Maximum (N_4)	Controller Receives more than Maximum (N_5)	Halfway between Equal and Controller Max (N_6)	Other (N_7)
A. Coin flip:								
1. No moral authority	22	20	10	4	3	3	2	0
2. Moral authority	20	19	9	1	5	1	2	2
B. Game trigger:								
1. No moral authority	22	18	9	4	2	4	3	0
2. Moral authority	22	21	4	3	3	12	0	0
Total	86	78	32	12	13	20	7	2

split, while 30 percent give the controller at least his individual maximum.

[The authors' discussion of the statistical significance of these results has been omitted.]

V. Discussion of Results

The results first suggest that subjects behaved as Lockeans instead of utilitarians or egalitarians, in that they tended to regard the position of controller as a justified right to a greater extent after playing the hash mark game than after a coin flip. Utilitarian subjects should have behaved in a greedy fashion in both game-trigger and coin-flip experiments, whereas egalitarian subjects should have equal split in both. In sum, we would argue that the subjects behaved as Lockeans, except where there was no obvious morally relevant distinction between themselves, at which time they fell back to egalitarian norms. . . .

Interpreting the moral authority results is less clear cut. They may, as suggested above, show that subjects can be prodded to regard entitlements as rights, without reference to a value-oriented theory of fairness (authoritarian explanation). Such an explanation gains plausibility from the significance of the moral authority instructions with the coin-flip experiments, since a Lockean would be hard-pressed to find morally justified rights.

However, the alternative interpretation, that the moral authority instructions legitimized a Lockean set of values in the subjects, cannot be ruled out. The combination of the moral authority and the game-trigger treatments produced the highest greed index. Perhaps subjects basically thought as Lockeans, but were uncomfortable with the Lockean result that some people end up with a larger slice of the pie. Therefore, it is possible that the moral authority instructions reinforced the Lockean tendency to regard "earned" entitlements as rights. . . .

NOTES AND QUESTIONS ON NORMS OF DISTRIBUTIVE JUSTICE

1. Under what circumstances do Hoffman and Spitzer (H & S) anticipate that an individual will prefer a relatively egalitarian distribution of benefits in lieu of a split that maximizes personal gain?

Do H & S's findings undermine the model of human motivation prevalent in economic analysis?

Based on H & S, would one expect the winner of the grand prize in a lottery to share the prize? A farmer to share mineral deposits discovered on the back forty? A chemist to decline to patent a breakthrough drug discovered by fluke? A singer born with a world-class voice to forgo appearance fees? How, if at all, are these outcomes distinguishable from those produced by coin flips? Under what circumstances, if any, should utilitarians and Lockeans regard an equal split as the proper default rule for distribution? Review the selections on distributive justice, supra Part 1. D.

2. H & S's experiments involved the splitting of small sums. Would you anticipate the same results if the sums had been increased a thousand-fold?

Suppose H & S had deliberately selected A's of high social status and B's of low social status. Would that have affected the subjects' propensities to share?

3. Do legal choices, say on issues such as the degree of progressivity of the income tax and the allocation of voting rights, significantly shape citizens' perceptions of distributive fairness? Or do concepts of justice derive mainly from nonlegal influences? More generally, how culturally contingent are Lockeanism and other norms of distributive justice? On this question, examine footnote 5 in H & S and the selection by James Q. Wilson, supra p.114. How significant is it that the experimenters' assertions of "moral authority" seemed to influence the subjects?

4. H & S's results suggest the importance of *first-party* systems of social control, that is, self-enforced constraints on egoism. Lawyers are mainly used to thinking of *third-party* social controls — rewards and punishment that external agents administer. Consider how a society might attempt to reduce littering. Possible third-party controls include both legal sanctions, such as criminal fines for littering, and social sanctions, such as ostracism of litterers. First-party controls, by contrast, would be created through the inculcation of norms against littering in the course of child-rearing, education, and other processes of socialization. An individual who had internalized an anti-littering norm would feel guilty if he were to violate it, even in an instance where there was no risk of detection by others. On first-party social controls, see Robert C. Ellickson, Bringing Culture and Human Frailty to Rational Actors: A Critique of Classical Law and Economics, 65 Chi.-Kent L. Rev. 23, 43-54 (1989) (noting advantages of self-executing systems of civic virtue).

Were third-party controls subtly built into the H & S experiments insofar as choices and bargains were made public? Might the subjects' choices have been influenced by their perceptions of onlookers' norms, in this case those of the experimenters? See Philip Pettit, *Virtus Normativa:* Rational Choice Perspectives, 100 Ethics 725 (1990).

To Each Less than She Needs, From Each More than She Can Do: Allocations, Entitlements and Value*

Hanna Papanek

Differential morbidity and mortality rates between males and females in southern Asia indicate starkly how inequalities in resource allocation affect women's survival chances. The purpose of this chapter is to bring together two areas of scholarship that are beginning to show signs of convergence: (1) studies by demographers, economists, nutritionists, and health specialists that provide concrete data to document these inequalities and (2) explorations into women's sense of self-worth, their feelings about their place in family and society, and the social learning of gender differences and gender relations. Using Asia as the focus in this chapter, I will relate ideas about socially and culturally formed "entitlements" to resource shares to ideas about the process of socialization for inequality.

Gender and Inequality

Gender differences, based on the social construction of biological sex distinctions, are one of the great "fault lines" of societies — those marks of difference among categories of persons that govern the allocation of power, authority, and resources. . . .

. . . Both gender differences and gender relations are of special importance within domestic groups, and it is within the household that children first learn their significance. The adults and older children who consciously and unconsciously teach them also reinforce their own learning in the process.

How a group or society distributes available resources among

* Source: In Persistent Inequalities (Irene Tinker ed. 1990), 167-173.

members reflects not only power and authority relations but also the moral basis of the group, its consensus about distributive justice, and its implicit priorities. Uncovering these implicit priorities is especially important in the case of gender-based inequalities for, having been learned from a very early age, they are unusually resistant to change later on. The relations between males and females are also so full of ambivalences and contradictions that change can be resisted at every turn. For example, cultural ideals in many societies prescribe high respect for women, especially mothers, yet in the same society, social norms accord women little power and authority and smaller shares of available resources. In addition, if the process of socialization for inequality has been successful, most people will not perceive inequalities for what they are — or, if they do, will argue for their moral rightness.

Children are taught very early in life about distributive justice in terms of differences in gender and age. When some get more food on their plate and others less, when some are sent to school and others not, children can see, in dramatic ways, what the differences are between boys and girls in their societies. These are lessons that they will remember, even those rebels who carry their anger over unjust treatment into adult activism for a cause. The way children are taught about shares and inequalities based on gender and age is a crucial part of the way they learn their place in family and society. The "compulsory emotions" — the way one is supposed to feel — play an important role in this learning.

Resource allocation processes within groups are, of course, closely linked to power and authority relations, but the linkage is not always obvious. Bigger shares of resources may signal a difference in power or status, rewarding those who are singled out for "the lion's share." Being able to look forward to getting bigger shares when one is older or more successful may be a goad for getting ahead or a solace while one waits, as in the stereotypical notion of the South Asian daughter-in-law in a patrilineal household who waits resentfully, doing the hard work of the house, until she can unload it on her successor. But age can also bring responsibilities, as in the equally stereotypical case of elder brothers in South Asia who forgo their privileges in favor of younger siblings for whom they are newly responsible. The expectation that mothers will sacrifice themselves for their children is another stereotype — and not only in South Asia.

. . . I emphasize resource allocations within households from the perspective of sociocultural *entitlements* to resource shares. These entitlements are based on social consensus and form an important process of childhood socialization. As noted in more detail in the sections that follow, the didactic function of entitlements has much to do with learning how one is valued by others and how one values oneself. Power and authority are also closely related to entitlements — both as a means for obtaining consensus on larger entitlements and as a reward.

A focus on social learning of inequalities is crucial to the process of change — whether this change comes about through major reorganizations of societies or by way of individuals and groups changing their ideas and behavior. One of the tasks of research on inequality is also to explain its persistence so that active attempts toward change can be more effective.

A perspective on resource entitlements and social learning, finally, helps to uncover some of the processes of women's complicity in their own inequality. The "secondary" socialization of adult women that I discuss later in this essay indicates how and why women often teach their children inequality, even if this involves their own remembered pain. . . .

Empirically measurable indicators of inequality are the first step in developing such criteria. The last two decades have seen an unprecedented accumulation of evidence about gender-based inequalities in resource allocations and access to opportunities in countries around the world. In South Asia, researchers often began by focusing on the very distorted sex ratio (proportion of males and females in a population), largely due to the excess of female over male mortality. In the most basic sense — survival — females are disadvantaged. . . . In Bangladesh, for example, detailed observations have shown that females receive less food than males in intrahousehold resource allocations and less medical care.

Other studies have focused on women's employment. . . .

In literacy and education, females are disadvantaged throughout South Asia, except in Sri Lanka and parts of southern India, but are being educated in much larger numbers in Southeast Asian countries. In South Asia, girls attend school in smaller numbers and for shorter periods than boys, with the differences most marked in Pakistan. Literacy rates are heavily skewed as a result. There are sharp differences between urban and rural areas throughout the region, in this respect, and these differences reflect not only class distinctions but also differences in family strategies of survival and mobility. Where there are no acceptable job opportunities for educated women, families must think twice before investing scarce resources in educating daughters.

In short, social scientists (both within these societies and outside them) have invoked criteria of equality that may run counter to the conventional wisdom in these societies to document inequalities between males and females in the allocation of the most basic resources. These include inequalities in food intake, medical care, and education. . . .

Value, Self-Worth, and Empowerment

Explanations of allocational inequalities in recent studies often focus on the presumed value of women in terms of the anticipated returns to female labor. In the case of excess female mortality in India, there has been a tendency to find causal connections between levels of female participation in remunerated labor (especially in agriculture) and female survival chances. For example, Barbara D. Miller argued that "where FLP [female labor force participation] is high, there will *always* be high preservation of female life, but where FLP is low, female children may *or* may not be preserved (1981: 117). Miller based her conclusions on extensive comparisons of ethnographic and statistical sources, but problems of interpretation remain. . . .

[P]roblems in linking women's value to labor force participation arise with respect to women's indispensable — indeed "priceless" — work in household maintenance and home production. Even if a particular woman can be dispensed with, women's labor in food preparation, water and fuel collection, house maintenance, and care of children and the sick or elderly remains crucial in the absence of institutional substitutes. Many societies allow widowers to remarry quickly but often frown on the remarriage of widows and divorced women. If the value of women was measured in terms of their indispensability to the household, therefore, it might be set very high. Something else is clearly involved here.

On the borderline between strictly material and what might be called "symbolic" work lies a range of activities in the social, political, and economic realms. . . . They include unpaid assistance in the work of an earning member of the household, as in the "two-person careers" of men in professional occupations (Papanek 1973); participation in children's schooling that directly assists the efforts of teachers or is linked to upward social mobility efforts; direct "status politics" in the community; and performance of religious rituals tied to family status in the community. . . .

Social and Cultural Entitlements to Resource Shares

Women, like men, get a sense of their value to others from the way they are treated by them — a process that begins in early childhood and continues throughout life. Explicitly, as well as covertly, people get messages from those around them on which to base a sense of their value to others; in turn, their sense of self-worth is, at least in part, a reflection of the value they feel they have for others. These messages may be concrete — say, receiving smaller shares of household resources than others — but they may also be interpreted in such positively compensatory ways that some household members can still *feel* valued in spite of being shortchanged (according to outside assessments). More likely, both women and men get ambiguous messages about their value to others from their material shares and the sociocultural interpretations of the rightness of these shares. . . .

The links between resource shares and feelings of self-worth are particularly important if one is interested in changing persistent inequalities. People who are consistently shortchanged may be feeling so powerless in their situations that specific attention must be paid to mobilizing solidarity among people in similar situations. Enhanced feelings of self-worth can result from efforts to mobilize a group and from experiencing — often for the first time — that even the powerless can sometimes succeed in changing their situations.

One way of conceptualizing these linkages with a view to changing inequalities is to focus on the concept of entitlements, both in their objective, material form and in the social norms and cultural values that perpetuate differential entitlements. In this second sense, these entitlements represent the social consensus about the value of specific categories of persons as expressed in the norms governing "who gets what and why." As used here, the term "entitlement" refers to the socially and culturally recognized rights of specific categories of persons to particular resource shares. These rights are expressed in common statements, such as "a man needs more food than a woman because . . . or "a girl does not have to be as well educated as a boy because. . . ." The resources available to be shared include material resources, such as food, clothing, and shelter, as well as the resources devoted to the development of individual capacities, which result from adequate health care, education, and other ways of developing necessary skills.

The concept of entitlement to resource shares embodies the ideas of distributional justice shared by members of a group or society and can therefore be seen as a central part of its moral basis. How this concensus is developed is a process that begins in childhood as a critical feature of the process of socialization. . . .

. . . Since [the] intrahousehold allocation process is of major importance in socialization for inequality and reflects the internal power relations within the household, I will stress three distinct aspects: (1) the objective consequences of an allocational pattern in terms of differences among household members in nutritional status, morbidity, mortality, and skill acquisition; (2) the psychosocial consequences for individuals in terms of how they feel about themselves and how they relate to others; and (3) the moral basis of the group of society that is reflected in the norms that govern sharing of resources. Except for the first aspect, on which there is considerable empirical evidence (especially from parts of South Asia), the discussion I present here emphasizes issues for research on the basis of their relevance to potential change in persistent inequalities. . . .

My emphasis on social and cultural elements in the consensus about entitlements leads directly to consideration of the way gender differences are learned (and taught) in a particular group. For example, when children are told that "girls need less food than boys," they are learning something important about the value of persons and not only about feeling hungry.

For the most part, allocational inequalities have been studied largely through their objective outcomes or in terms of material differences in resource shares. The "explanations" offered to justify them are equally important, especially for those who seek to change persistent inequalities. For example, in the Indian Punjab, boys customarily get curds, the richer and more valued food, while girls get buttermilk. This is said to be based on Punjabi beliefs that rich foods are needed to withstand cold winter weather. What does this explanation imply about the effect of cold on females and about women's capacity for suffering? Similarly, in Meerut District (Uttar Pradesh, India), men and women from different castes told researchers that girls and boys got different kinds of food because rich, "heat-producing" foods like butter, milk, and meat hasten the onset of puberty in girls. Parents are, in any case, anxious about protecting the sexuality of their daughters and find this reason persuasive. The implications for physical growth are clear, but what about the psychological messages carried by these food restrictions?

The mother who follows these precepts acts according to group norms and it not simply expressing a personal preference. Of course, preference for sons is in the self-interest of all mothers in a society that measures the status of women by their reproductive performance. Sons are supposed to support parents in their old age, whereas daughters have gone to another patrilineage. But a third reason, never mentioned by researchers on son-preference, is the fact that a woman can gain the household assistance of a daughter-in-law *only* by having a son; her own daughters will marry out. The mother need not explain or justify her actions in giving better food to sons but would most likely have a lot of explaining to do in the community if she acted otherwise.

Ideas about entitlement are also part of a larger cultural repertoire containing many other ideas about the relative value of categories of persons. Entitlement ideas, in short, constitute part of a system of beliefs about distributional justice. Unequal allocations of resources not only have objective effects but also fulfill a crucial didactic function. They teach children about their rights and privileges in concrete ways that are understandable even to the very young.

Later on in a child's life, these ideas and actions are elaborated into more complex statements that fulfill multiple goals. For example, telling a child that "men work harder than women and that's why they need more (or better) food" not only justifies unequal resource allocations but also says something about the value of a task and of the person carrying it out. Children know that their mothers are always busy and that their work is often arduous. Women's work is also more salient to children because it is always visible, whereas that of men may not be. But differential entitlements put another face on the reality that children see. The work of men is socially defined as more valuable, not only in words but also in terms of the concrete reward that is explicitly linked to the value of the work and of the worker.

Girls may also receive another message from adults, however, when unequal resource allocations are explained to them in *compensatory* terms that reflect an underlying cultural ambivalence about the value of people and tasks. For example, an elderly Javanese woman recalled from her own childhood that girls were taught to restrain themselves not only with respect to food but also in the enjoyment of other pleasures in life. Her mother told her that girls needed to develop more inhibitions — also in self-expression — because "women set the norms for civilization because men cannot control themselves." Women's role in educating children, for instance, was defined as having more spiritual value than men's role in making a living. . . . Ideas about entitlements, as in this instance, are not only culturally sanctioned but also sanctified in spiritual terms, a frequent occurrence in other societies where women are charged with greater responsibilities for maintaining a family's social and religious status.

Unequal entitlements are often based on *imputed needs* that differ for categories of persons. The anthropologist Leela Dube (personal communication, December 23, 1987) linked these imputed needs to the anticipated life trajectories of different categories of individuals; these are, in turn, reflected in the care and respect given by others. Dube also notes that the greater entitlement of one person often becomes the increased responsibility for care given by another. A male infant's entitlement to more food and more careful nurturance (as in parts of India and Bangladesh) becomes the responsibility of his caretaker, usually a female adult or child. The importance of differential entitlements to nurturance is dramatically illustrated in the many studies of neglect of female children in parts of India. . . .

Differences in imputed needs can also come to include a broad spectrum of ideas about physiological and psychological processes in women and men. The presumed inability of men to control their sexual impulses is coupled in many societies with restrictions on women's behavior and an emphasis on female self-restraint in sexual matters (for added discussion of this point see Papanek 1988 and references cited there). In addition, notions of women's greater ability in self-restraint are found with reference to other physiological processes (e.g., excretion) and women's presumed greater ability to tolerate pain. These imputed needs — or lack thereof — have obvious implications for personal and public health in addition to their clear relevance to systems of strict sex segregation. But all of these ideas about imputed needs coupled with differences in entitlements are also another kind of social construction of physical realities that plays a role in the perpetuation of inequality.

The didactic importance of entitlements — in the sociocultural sense used here — is especially clear in situations of competition for household resources. Siblings, for example, may be particularly strongly affected by differential resource allocations, as when girls and boys in the same household receive different amounts and kinds of food, health care, and education, and when these differences are explained to them in terms of their entitlements. Much other learning about their society is the likely outcome. . . .

References
Miller, Barbara D., 1981. The Endangered Sex: Neglect of Female Children in Rural North India. Ithaca, N.Y.: Cornell Univ. Press.
Papanek, Hanna, 1973. Men, Women and Work: Reflections on the Two Person Career. American Journal of Sociology 78 (4) 852-872.
Papanek, Hanna, 1988. Afterword: Caging the Lion: A Fable for Our Time, in Rokeya Sakhawat Hossain, Sultan's Dream. New York: Feminist Press, 58-85.

NOTES AND QUESTIONS ON GENDER-BASED ENTITLEMENTS

1. Is it appropriate to analyze intimate intrafamilial relations by focusing on ideas of entitlement? Is a property-rights approach too hard-edged and "arms-length" to render a realistic picture of these relationships? Or, as Papanek argues, does a failure to notice differential entitlements only naturalize and perpetuate intrafamilial inequalities? For this debate in the context of divorce settlement, see Milton Regan, Spouses and Strangers, 82 Geo. L.J. 2303 (1994), and cf. Carol M. Rose, Rhetoric and Romance, 82 Geo. L.J. 2409 (1994).

2. Does Papanek's analysis have any bearing on gender relations in more developed economies? Are there identifiable gender-based differences in intrafamilial entitlements in "first-world" societies, comparable to the differences that she discusses in developing countries? Amartya Sen, More than 100 Million Women Are Missing, N.Y. Rev. of Books, Dec. 20, 1990, at 61, argues that the more developed countries exhibit the same kinds of phenomena, though to a less severe degree. For other discussions, see, for example, Viviana Zelizer, The Social Meaning of Money: 'Special Monies,' 95 Am. J. Soc. 342, 352-367 (1989) (gender differences in intrafamilial wealth, symbolized in "pin money"); Mary Louise Fellows, Wills and Trusts: 'The Kingdom of the Fathers,' 10 L. & Inequality 137 (1991) (history of gender differences in inheritance); Paula England & George Farkas, Households, Employment, and Gender (1986) (inequalities in employment, domestic housework); but see Jerry A. Jacobs, Revolving Doors: Sex Segregation and Women's Careers (1989) 41-43 (education outlays similar for both genders in the modern U.S.).

3. If there are differences in entitlements based on gender, how do these differences begin and continue? For a theoretical perspective from classical contractarianism, see Carol Pateman, The Sexual Contract 39-76 (1982). More practically, Papanek discusses the self-perpetuation of such differences through the effects on the individual sense of self-worth and through social conceptions of justice. But she also mentions other institutions that maintain gendered differences of entitlement. For example, how does the common marriage custom dictating that the wife join her husband's household enlist the self-interest of parents in favoring sons over daughters?

4. Upon what general theory of property does Papanek's approach rest? That is, what does she see as the source of entitlements generally? She does not appear to follow the strict labor or desert theory, discussed in the Hoffman and Spitzer selection, supra p.287. As Papanek points out, a woman's labor often enhances other people's

entitlements rather than her own; Papanek seems to argue that entitlements are based on general cultural expectations. Are these cultural expectations in some way utilitarian or rational, particularly after a given distribution has fallen into place? For example, if a given culture excludes women from the professions and trades, does it become rational to concentrate family resources on male children? See Gary Becker, A Treatise on the Family 180, 192 (enlarged ed. 1991). If so, are members of inegalitarian cultures trapped, in the sense that rational actors within the cultures have little choice but to replicate the distributional patterns that favor male family members? See Robert Sugden, Contractarianism and Norms, 100 Ethics 768, 779-782 (1990); Carol M. Rose, Women and Property: Gaining and Losing Ground, 78 Va. L. Rev. 421 (1992). Could the same be said of unequal distributional patterns between social groups other than men and women? That is, might inequalities be perpetuated by economic decisions that seem rational within the confines of the sytem? Sugden, Contractarianism, supra, argues that discrimination patterns may be self-perpetuating. See also Ian Ayres, Fair Driving: Gender and Race Discrimination in Retail Car Negotiations, 104 Harv. L. Rev. 817, 827-836, 850-851 (1991), arguing that discriminatory practices in car sales result from sellers' self-fulfilling prophecies in identifying some customers as "suckers."

5. Is the family the primary source of concepts of justice, imparting ideas not only of gender roles but of hierarchical ordering in other spheres? See Susan Moller Okin, Justice, Gender and the Family (1989). If so, does Rawls also need a theory of the family?

6. Is it possible that gender differences in entitlements result from differences in men's and women's bargaining strategies? There is a modest but growing literature that explores gender relations in the light of bargaining models. See Amartya Sen, Gender and Cooperative Conflicts, in Persistent Inequalities (Irene Tinker ed., 1990), linking women's lesser entitlements to bargaining disadvantages in intrafamilial "cooperative conflicts"; Sugden, Contractarianism, supra, using the example of cultural gender expectations to illustrate that bargains may yield systematically unequal outcomes for the parties; Lloyd Cohen, Marriage, Divorce, and Quasi-Rents; or, 'I Gave Him the Best Years of My Life,' 16 J. Legal Stud. 267 (1987), analyzing gender-based inequalities in marriage partnerships by analogy to "quasi-rents" in corporate dealings; Rose, Women and Property, supra, exploring a real or purported gender difference in a "taste for cooperation," the effects of such a difference on bargaining, and ultimate outcomes in the areas of employment, housework, and domestic violence. See also Martha Nussbaum, Justice for

Women! 39 N.Y. Rev. of Books 43, Oct. 8, 1992 (review of Okin, supra), commenting on Rawls's Theory of Justice and arguing that distributional schemes must include a theory of bargaining. Bargaining models are of course only a very small part of the now-vast literature on gender equality and inequality.

Chapter 7

Transacting and Trading

A. Ground Rules for Exchange

Filling Gaps in Incomplete Contracts: An Economic Theory of Default Rules*

Ian Ayres & Robert Gertner

The legal rules of contracts and corporations can be divided into two distinct classes. The larger class consists of "default" rules that parties can contract around by prior agreement, while the smaller, but important, class consists of "immutable" rules that parties cannot change by contractual agreement. Default rules fill the gaps in incomplete contracts; they govern unless the parties contract around them. Immutable rules cannot be contracted around; they govern even if the parties attempt to contract around them. For example, under the Uniform Commercial Code (U.C.C.) the duty to act in good faith is an immutable part of any contract, while the warranty of merchantability is simply a default rule that parties can waive by agreement . . .[10]

---

* Source; 99 Yale L.J. 87-100, 125-127 (1989).
10. . . . This default rule/immutable rule dichotomy also pervades other areas of the law that have contractual components. In the law of divorce, for example, wealth accrued before marriage is allocated according to default rules that can be altered in pre-nuptial agreements, while income earned after marriage is immutably divided. Similarly, the repayment priorities set by state debtor-creditor law can, like default rules, be reordered through private contract. The laws of intestacy are also default rules: they fill any testamentary gap, but can be contracted around.

There is surprising consensus among academics at an abstract level on two normative bases for immutability. Put most simply, immutable rules are justifiable if society wants to protect (1) parties within the contract, or (2) parties outside the contract. The former justification turns on parentalism; the latter on externalities. Immutable rules displace freedom of contract. Immutability is justified only if unregulated contracting would be socially deleterious because parties internal or external to the contract cannot adequately protect themselves. With regard to immutable rules, the disagreement among academics is not over this abstract theory, but whether in particular contexts parentalistic concerns or externalities are sufficiently great to justify the use of immutable rules.

When the preconditions for immutability are not present, the normative legal analysis devolves to the choice of a default rule. Yet academics have paid little attention about how to choose among possible default rules. The law-and-economics movement has fought long and hard to convince courts to restrict the use of immutable rules, but has lost most of its normative energy in constructing a theory of default choice. Economists seem to believe that, even if lawmakers choose the wrong default, at worst there will be increased transaction costs of a second order of magnitude.

Few academics have gone beyond one-sentence theories stipulating that default terms should be set at what the parties would have wanted. . . .

This Article provides a theory of how courts and legislatures should set default rules. We suggest that efficient defaults would take a variety of forms that at times would diverge from the "what the parties would have contracted for" principle. To this end, we introduce the concept of "penalty defaults." Penalty defaults are designed to give at least one party to the contract an incentive to contract around the default rule and therefore to choose affirmatively the contract provison they prefer. In contrast to the received wisdom, penalty defaults are purposefully set at what the parties would not want — in order to encourage the parties to reveal information to each other or to third parties (especially the courts). . . .

An essential component of our theory of default rules is our explicit consideration of the sources of contractual incompleteness. We distinguish between two basic reasons for incompleteness. Scholars have primarily attributed incompleteness to the costs of contracting. Contracts may be incomplete because the transaction costs of explicitly contracting for a given contingency are greater than the benefits. These transaction costs may include legal fees, negotiation costs, drafting and printing costs, the costs of researching the effects and probability of a contingency, and the costs to the parties and the courts of verifying whether a contingency occurred. Rational parties will weigh these costs against the benefits of contractually addressing a particular contingency. . . . Scholars who attribute contractual incompleteness to transaction costs are naturally drawn toward choosing defaults that the majority of contracting parties "would have wanted" because these majoritarian defaults seem to minimize the costs of contracting.

We show, however, that this majoritarian "would have wanted" approach to default selection is, for several reasons, incomplete. First, the majoritarian approach fails to account for the possibly disparate costs of contracting and of failing to contract around different defaults. For example, if the majority is more likely to contract around the minority's preferred default rule (than the minority is to contract around the majority's rule), then choosing the minority's default may lead to a larger set of efficient contracts. Second, the received wisdom provides little guidance about how tailored or particularized the "would have wanted" analysis should be. Finally, the very costs of ex ante bargaining may encourage parties to inefficiently shift the process of gap filling to ex post court determination. If it is costly for the courts to determine what the parties would have wanted, it may be efficient to choose a default rule that induces the parties to contract explicitly. In other words, penalty defaults are appropriate when it is cheaper for the parties to negotiate a term ex ante than for the courts to estimate ex post what the parties would have wanted. Courts, which are publicly subsidized, should give parties incentives to negotiate ex ante by penalizing them for inefficient gaps.

This Article also proposes a second source of contractual incompleteness that is the focus of much of our analysis. We refer to this source of incompleteness as strategic. One party might strategically withhold information that would increase the total gains from contracting (the "size of the pie") in order to increase her private share of the gains from contracting (her "share of the pie"). By attempting to contract around a certain default, one party might reveal information to the other party that affects how the contractual pie is split. Thus, for example, the more informed party may prefer to have inefficient precaution rather than pay a higher price for the good. While analysts have previously explained incomplete contracting solely in terms of the costs of writing additional provisions, we argue that contractual gaps can also result from strategic behavior by relatively informed parties. By changing the default rules of the game, lawmakers can importantly reduce the opportunities for this rent-seeking, strategic behavior. In particular, the possibility of strategic incompleteness leads us to suggest that efficiency-minded lawmakers should sometimes choose penalty defaults that induce knowledgeable parties to reveal information by contracting around the default penalty. The strategic behavior of the parties in forming the contract can justify strategic contractual interpretations by courts. . . .

[I.] B.   Toward a More General Theory of Penalty Defaults

Penalty defaults, by definition, give at least one party to the contract an incentive to contract around the default. From an efficiency perspective, penalty default rules can be justified as a way to encourage the production of information. The very process of "contracting around" can reveal information to parties inside or outside the contract. Penalty defaults may be justified as 1) giving both contracting parties incentives to reveal information to third parties, especially courts, or 2) giving a more informed contracting party incentives to reveal information to a less informed party. . . .

In some situations it is reasonable to expect one party to the contract to be systematically informed about the default rule and the probability of the relevant contingency arising. If one side is repeatedly in the relevant contractual setting while the other side rarely is, it is a sensible presumption that the former is better informed than the latter. Consider, for example, the treatment of real estate brokerage commissions when a buyer breaches a purchase contract. Such contracts typically include a clause which obligates the purchaser to forfeit some given amount of "earnest" money if she breaches the agreement. How should the earnest money be split between the seller and the broker if their agency contract does not address this contingency? Some courts have adopted a "what the parties would have wanted" approach and have awarded all the earnest money to the seller. We agree with this outcome, but for different reasons. The real estate broker will more likely be informed about the default rule than the seller. Indeed, the seller may not even consider the issue of how to split the earnest money in case of default. Therefore, if the efficient contract would allocate some of the earnest money to the seller, the default rule should be set against the broker to induce her to raise the issue. Otherwise, if the default rule is set to favor the broker, a seller may not raise the issue, and the broker will be happy to take advantage of the seller's ignorance. By setting the default rule in favor of the uninformed party, the courts induce the informed party to reveal information, and, consequently, the efficient contract results.

Although social welare may be enhanced by forcing parties to reveal information to a subsidized judicial system, it is more problematic to understand why society would have an efficiency interest in inducing a relatively informed party to a transaction to reveal information to the relatively uninformed party. After all, if revealing information is efficient because it increases the value created by the contract, one might initially expect that the informed party will have a sufficient private incentive to reveal information — the incentive of splitting a bigger pie. This argument ignores the possibility, however, that revealing information might simultaneously increase the total size of the pie and decrease the share of the pie that the relatively informed party receives. If the "share-of-the-pie effect" dominates the "size-of-the-pie effect," informed parties might rationally choose to withhold relevant information.[57]

Parties may behave strategically not only because they have superior information about the default, but also because they have superior information about other aspects of the contract. We suggest that a party who knows that a particular default rule is inefficient may choose not to negotiate to change it. The knowledgeable party may not wish to reveal her information in negotiations if the information would give a bargaining advantage to the other side.

How can it be that by increasing the total gains from contracting (the size-of-the-pie effect) the informed party can end up with a smaller share of the gains (the share-of-the-pie effect)? This Article demonstrates how relatively informed parties can sometimes benefit by strategically withholding information that, if revealed, would increase the size of the pie. A knowledgeable buyer, for example, may prefer to remain indistinguishable from what the seller wrongly perceives to be the class of similarly situated buyers. By blending in with the larger class of contractors, a buyer or a seller may receive a cross-subsidized price because the other side will bargain as if she is dealing with the average member of the class. A knowledgeable party may prefer to remain in this inefficient, but cross-subsidized, contractual pool rather than move to an efficient, but unsubsidized, pool. If contracting around the de-

---

57. Withholding socially valuable private information to obtain private gains is common. Companies may withhold information about innovations from competitors to increase profits; car buyers may withhold information about particular options or accessories that they value if this information signals to car dealers a greater willingness to pay for the underlying automobile; and professional athletes may withhold information about injuries to increase their salaries, even though as a result their team may inefficiently hire reserves.

fault sufficiently reduces this cross-subsidization, the share-of-the-pie effect can exceed the size-of-the-pie effect because the informed party's share of the default pie was in a sense being artifically cross-subsidized by other members of the contractual class. Under this scenario, withholding information appears as a kind of rent-seeking in which the informed party foregoes the additional value attending the revealed information to get a larger piece of the contractual pie. . . .

C. Legal Responses to Contracting Around Immutable Rules

An important difference between default and immutable rules is that if parties attempt to contract around a default rule and fail, they will simply be bound by the default, whereas if parties attempt to contract around an immutable rule and fail, the law may choose to penalize the attempt by imposing a penalty different from (and, from the parties' ex ante perspective, worse than) the immutable standard. From an ex ante perspective the possibility of receiving this ex post penalty is just another expected cost of contracting around the default rule.

The legal response to parties who try to contract around immutable rules can also be given a default interpretation. . . .

This . . . tension arises with covenants not to compete. Courts have established an immutable rule that parties cannot make covenants of unreasonable duration. In Fullerton Lumber Co. v. Torborg, for example, the Supreme Court of Wisconsin held that a ten-year covenant was unreasonable but then struggled in deciding whether it should reformulate the contract to impose a duty not to compete for a reasonable period or penalize the employer for transgressing the immutable limitation by allowing the former employee to compete immediately.

If the goal of an immutable rule is to discourage people from even attempting to contract around a provision, then it would seem that the penalty reconstruction would be the favored result. This is again analogous to our earlier discussion of penalty defaults, in which we suggested that courts should choose the penalty that provided "least cost deterrence." The difference is that in the earlier discussion the penalties were attempting to deter gaps and here the penalties are attempting to promote gaps (that is, deter contracting around). The preference for penalty defaults to fill the gaps left in unconscionable contracts may justify the common law "blue pencil" test which simply enforces contracts after the offending provision has been struck (with a blue pencil).

NOTES AND QUESTIONS ON DEFAULT RULES

1. Though Ayres and Gertner's (A & G) article concerns contracts rather than property, they use an example from real estate sales. Can you think of other areas in which their analysis might sort out the rules of property law?

Consider, for example, a landlord's implied warranty of habitability: Is this a conventional fallback rule, a penalty default rule, or an immutable rule? That is, does it reflect (a) a best guess about what most landlords and tenants would agree to, (b) an inducement to landlords (or tenants) to disclose information about expectations for repair, or (c) an ironclad rule that overrides any bargain to which the parties may agree? What are the arguments for and against each possibility? Which view should prevail, and why?

Compare the builder selling a house to a consumer: Does the builder implicitly warrant the house's habitability? If so, is the warranty a fallback rule, a penalty default, or an immutable rule? Compare, finally, the homeowner-seller: Should contract rules imply a warranty? What kind of rule should apply?

2. What accounts for changes in default rules over time? See, for example, the transformations in the law of caveat emptor described in the next selection. Why might the law shift from a default rule that penalizes buyers who fail to investigate fully the condition of the property, to a default rule that penalizes sellers who fail to disclose information?

3. Isn't it slightly odd to find a civil court's rule described as a "penalty" when these same courts often frown on any effort by the parties to build penalties into contracts? Are penalties nevertheless a pervasive aspect of the civil law, as A & G suggest? If so, why would civil law judges try to disguise this fact? If penalties are present in the civil law, how should the size of the penalty be set? Are the considerations the same as, or different from, those that govern the penalties meted out in the criminal law?

4. What precisely is the point of immutable rules? A & G mention two standard justifications: preventing externalities (protecting third parties) and parentalism (protecting the parties in the bargain). The externality argument seems straightforward, but why should courts indulge in parentalism? Why might courts try to discourage ostensibly willing parties from bargaining over certain items of property (such as parts of one's body), or transferring some property separately from other property (such as an apartment without a warranty of quality)? Does the idea of immutable bargaining rules suggest that some property is inalienable? For a

further discussion of inalienability, see the selection from Radin, Market-Inalienability, infra p.336.

Crystals and Mud in Property Law*

Carol M. Rose

Property law, and especially the common law of property, has always been heavily laden with hard-edged doctrines that tell everyone exactly where they stand. Default on paying your loan installments? Too bad, you lose the thing you bought and your past payments as well. Forget to record your deed? Sorry, the next buyer can purchase free of your claim, and you are out on the street. Sell that house with the leak in the basement? Lucky you, you can unload the place without having to tell the buyer about such things at all.

In a sense, hard-edged rules like these — rules that I call "crystals" — are what property is all about. If, as Jeremy Bentham said long ago, property is "nothing but a basis of expectation,"[1] then crystal rules are the very stuff of property: Their great advantage, or so it is commonly thought, is that they signal to all of us, in a clear and distinct language, precisely what our obligations are and how we may take care of our interests. Thus, I should inspect the property, record my deed, and make my payments if I don't want to lose my home to unexpected physical, legal, or financial impairments. I know where I stand and so does everyone else, and we can all strike bargains with each other if we want to stand somewhere else.

Economic thinkers have been telling us for at least two centuries that the more important a given kind of thing becomes for us, the more likely we are to have these hard-edged rules to manage it. We draw these ever-sharper lines around our entitlements so that we know who has what, and so that we can trade instead of getting into the confusions and disputes that would only escalate as the goods in question became scarcer and more highly valued.

At the root of these economic analyses lies the perception that it costs something to establish clear entitlements to things, and we won't bother to undertake the task of removing goods from an

---

* Source: 40 Stan. L. Rev. 577-590, 596-604 (1988).
    1. J. Bentham, Theory of Legislation, Principles of the Civil Code, pt. 1, ch. 8, at 68 (Baxi ed. . . . 1975).

ownerless "commons" unless it is worth it to us to do so. What makes it worth it? Increasing scarcity of the resource, and the attendant conflicts over it. To use the example given by Harold Demsetz, one of the most notable of the modern economists telling this story, when the European demand for fur hats increased demand for (and scarcity of) fur-bearing animals among Indian hunters, the Indians developed a system of property entitlements to the animal habitat.[6] . . . In effect, as our competition for a resource raises the costs of conflict about it, those conflict costs begin to outweigh the costs of taking it out of the commons and establishing clear property entitlements. We establish a system of clear entitlements so that we can barter and trade for what we want instead of fighting.

The trouble with this "scarcity story" is that things don't seem to work this way, or at least not all the time. Sometimes we seem to substitute fuzzy, ambiguous rules of decision for what seem to be perfectly clear, open and shut, demarcations of entitlements. I call this occurrence the substitution of "mud" rules for "crystal" ones.

Thus, in the examples with which I began, we find that, over time, the straightforward common law crystalline rules have been muddied repeatedly by exceptions and equitable second-guessing, to the point that the various claimants under real estate contracts, mortgages, or recorded deeds don't know quite what their rights and obligations really are . . .

. . . [A] move to the uncertainty of mud seems disruptive to the very practice of a private property/contractual exchange society. Thus, it is hardly surprising that we individually and collectively attempt to clear up the mud with new crystal rules — as when private parties contract out of ambiguous warranties, or when legislatures pass new versions of crystalline record systems — only to be overruled later, when courts once again reinstate mud in a different form.

These odd permutations on the scarcity story must give us pause. Why should we shift back and forth instead of opting for crystal when we have greater scarcity? Is there some advantage to mud rules that the courts are paying attention to? And if so, why do we not opt for mud rules instead? . . .

I.   From Crystal to Mud and Back: Three Examples

From all appearances, and despite the obvious advantages of crystalline property rules for the smooth flow of trade and commerce,

---

6. Demsetz, [Toward a Theory of Property Rights, 57 Am. Econ. Rev. Proc. 347 (Pap. & Prac. 1967)].

we seem to be caught in an era of intractable and perhaps even increasing muddiness. One could choose any number of areas to see this, and I will briefly discuss only a few, namely the examples with which I began. . . .

A.   The Demise of Caveat Emptor

For several hundred years, and right up to the last few decades, caveat emptor was the staple fare of the law of real estate purchases, at least for buildings already constructed. The purchaser was deemed perfectly capable of inspecting the property and deciding for himself whether he wanted it, and if anyone were foolish enough to buy a pig in a poke, he deserved what he got. Short of outright fraud that would mislead the buyer, the seller had no duties to disclose anything at all.

One chink in this otherwise smooth wall was the doctrine of "latent defects," which, like the exception for fraud, suggested that perhaps the buyer really can't figure things out entirely. For some time now, in at least some states, a seller has had to tell a buyer about material problems with the property known to the seller but undiscoverable by the purchaser upon reasonable inspection. The doctrine began to raise a few problems of muddiness: What defects are "material"? What does the seller "know"? To what extent should the buyer "reasonably" have to inspect for herself?

Within the last few decades, the movement to mud in this area has become even more pronounced as some courts and legal commentators maintain that builder/vendors implicitly warrant a new house "habitable." But what does habitability mean? Is the house's habitability coterminous with the local housing code, or does "habitability" connote some less definite standard? What if the defects were obvious, and just what does "obvious" mean, anyway? We don't know until we litigate the issues.

Even if builder/vendors' warranties do muddy up property rights, there are some plausible reasons for them. After all, the builder/vendors are professionals, and they should know more about their own construction; they even might have avoided the problems in the first place by building more carefully. It is somewhat more difficult to extend those arguments to sellers who are themselves merely homeowners instead of builder/vendors, yet we find that even these nonprofessional sellers have increasing obligations to anticipate the buyers' desires, and to inform buyers about disagreeable factors that might make the buyers think twice. A California court, for example, has ruled that the sellers had to inform the buyer that a mass murder had taken place a decade previously in a particular house.[28] The courts now seem to presume a buyer who can't figure out much at all, and to protect that buyer they have adopted a mud standard: like good neighbors, sellers must tell buyers about any "material" defects — whatever those may be. . . .

But there is a countermove as well: Even if the legal rules have moved toward mud, private bargainers often try to install their own little crystalline systems through contractual waivers of warranties or disclosure duties (for example, the "as is" or "no warranty" sale). These private efforts in effect move things into the pattern of a circle, from crystal to mud and back to crystal. And the circle turns once again when the courts ban such waivers, as they sometimes do, and firmly re-establish a rule of mud — only to be followed by even more artful waivers.

The back-and-forth pattern of crystal and mud is even more evident in the next example, the loan secured by landed property — a form of real estate transaction whose history has often been described as resembling a seesaw.

B. Of Mortgages and Mud

Early common law mortgages were very crystalline indeed. They had the look of pawnshop transactions and were at least sometimes structured as conveyances: I borrow money from you, and at the same time I convey my land to you as security for my loan. If all goes well, I pay back my debt on the agreed "law day," and you reconvey my land back to me. But if all does not go well and I cannot pay on the appointed day, then, no matter how heartrending my excuse, I lose my land to you and, presumably, any of the previous payments I might have made. As the fifteenth century commentator Littleton airily explained, the name "mortgage" derived from the rule that, if the debtor "doth not pay, then the land which he puts in pledge . . . is gone from him for ever, and so dead.[35]

This system had the advantage of great clarity, but it sometimes must have seemed very hard on mortgage debtors to the advantage of scoundrelly creditors. Littleton's advice about the importance of specifying the precise place and time for repayment, for example, conjures up images of a wily creditor hiding in the woods on the repayment day to frustrate repayment; presumably, the unfound creditor could keep the property. But by the seventeenth century, the intervention of courts of equity had

28. Reed v. King, . . . 193 Cal. Rptr. 130 (Cal App. 1983).
35. Littleton's Tenures, . . . at §332.

changed things. By the eighteenth and nineteenth centuries, the equity courts were regularly giving debtors as many as three or four "enlargements" of the time in which they might pay and redeem the property before the final "foreclosure," even when the excuse was lame. One judge explained that an equity court might well grant more time even after the "final" order of "foreclosure absolute," depending on the particular circumstances.[39]

The muddiness of this emerging judicial remedy argued against its attractiveness. Chief Justice Hale complained in 1672 that, "[b]y the growth of Equity on Equity, the Heart of the Common Law is eaten out, and legal Settlements are destroyed; . . . as far as the Line is given, Man will go; and if an hundred Years are given, Man will go so far, and we know not whither we shall go."[40] Instead of a precise and clear allocation of entitlements between the parties, the "equity of redemption" and its unpredictable foreclosure opened up vexing questions and uncertainties: How much time should the debtor have for repayment before the equitable arguments shifted to favor the creditor? What sort of excuses did the debtor need? Did it matter that the property, instead of dropping in the lap of the creditor, was sold at a foreclosure sale?

But as the courts moved towards muddiness, private parties attempted to bargain their way out of these costly uncertainties and to reinstate a crystalline pattern whereby lenders could get the property immediately upon default without the costs of foreclosure. How about a separate deal with the borrower, for example, whereby he agrees to convey any equitable interest to the lender in case of default? Nothing doing, said the courts, including the United States Supreme Court, which in 1878 stated flatly that a mortgagor could not initially bargain away his "equity of redemption."[45] Well, then, how about an arrangement whereby it looks as if the lender already owns the land, and the "borrower" only gets title if he lives up to his agreement to pay for it by a certain time? This seemed more promising: In the 1890s California courts thought it perfectly correct to hold the buyer to his word in such an arrangement, and to give him neither an extension nor a refund of past payments. By the 1960s, however, they were changing their minds about these "installment land contracts." After all, these deals really had exactly the same effect as the old-style mortgages — the defaulting buyer could lose everything if he missed a payment, even the very last payment. Human vice and error

39. Campbell v. Holyland, 7 Ch. D. 166, 172 (1876). . . .
40. Roscarrick v. Barton, 22 Eng. Rep. 769, 770 (1672).
45. Peugh v. Davis, 96 U.S. 332, 337 (1878).

seemed to put the crystal rule in jeopardy: In a series of cases culminating with a default by a "willful but repentant" little old lady who had stopped paying when she mistakenly thought that she was being cheated, the California Supreme Court decided to treat these land contracts as mortgages in disguise.[48] It gave the borrower "relief from forfeiture" — a time to reinstate the installment contract or get back her past payments.

With mortgages first and mortgage substitutes later, we see a back-and-forth pattern: crisp definition of entitlements, made fuzzy by accretions of judicial decisions, crisped up again by the parties' contractual arrangements, and once again made fuzzy by the courts. Here we see private parties apparently following the "scarcity story" in their private law arrangements: when things matter, the parties define their respective entitlements with ever sharper precision. Yet the courts seem at times unwilling to follow this story or to permit these crystalline definitions, most particularly when the rules hurt one party very badly. The cycle thus alternates between crystal and mud.

But the subject matter that has truly defied the scarcity story, often to the despair of property professors, has not been mortgages or mortgage substitutes. It has been the recording system, to which I now turn.

C. Broken Records

In establishing recording systems, legislatures have lent support to private parties' efforts to sharpen the definition of their entitlements. The *raison d'etre* of such systems is to clarify and perfectly specify landed property rights for the sake of easy and smooth transfers of land.

But the Anglo-American recording system in fact has been a saga of frustrated efforts to make clear who has what in land transfers. Common law transfers of land required a certain set of formalities between the parties, but thereafter, conflicting claims were settled by the age-old principle, "first in time, first in right." Thus, on Tuesday I might sell my farm to you, and on Wednesday I might wrongfully purport to sell it once again to innocent Farmer Brown. Poor Farmer Brown remains landless even though he knew nothing about the prior sale to you and indeed had no way of knowing about it. This outcome was hardly satisfactory from a property rights perspective. "First in time, first in right" may work well enough in a community where everyone knows all about everyone else's trans-

---

48. MacFadden v. Walker, . . . 97 Cal. Rptr. 537 (Cal. 1971).

actions, but outside that context, the doctrine does little to put people on notice of who owns what, and the opportunities for conflicting claims are endless.

But the efforts to remedy this flaw have gone through new cycles of certainty and uncertainty. Henry VIII attempted — without great success — to establish public registration of land claims through the Statute of Enrollments in 1536. Versions of the Statute resurfaced in Massachusetts' 1640 recording act and in other seventeenth and eighteenth century colonial recording acts, all of which were much more widely (though still somewhat irregularly) applied than their Henrician model had been.

Henry's Statute and its original American counterparts reflected an emphatically crystalline view of property. Their literal language suggests that they were versions of what has come to be called a "race" statute: the first purchaser to record (the winner of the "race" to the registry) can hold this title against all other claimants, whether or not he was in fact the first to purchase. In such a system, the official records become an unimpeachable source of information about the status of land ownership; the law counts the record owner, and only the record owner, as the true owner. The purchaser can buy in reliance on the records without fear of divestment by some unknown interloper, and without the need to make some cumbersome extra-record search for such potential interlopers.

This system was too crystalline to last. The characters to muck up this crystalline system by now should be sounding familiar: ninnies, hard-luck cases, and the occasional scoundrels who take advantage of them. What are we to do, for example, with the silly fellow who buys an interest in property but simply forgets to record? Or with the more conscientious one who does attempt to record his interest, but whose records wind up in the wrong book? Or with the lost soul whose impeccably correct filing is dropped behind the radiator by the neglectful clerk? Some courts take a hard line, perhaps concluding that the first owner was in a better position than our innocent outsider — that is, the next purchaser — to detect and correct the flaws in the records. But our sympathies for the luckless unrecorded owner put pressure on the recording system that would divest him in favor of the later-arriving outsider.

Our sympathies are all the greater when the outsider is not so innocent after all. What shall we do, say, when the unrecorded first buyer is snookered out of his claim by a later purchaser who knows perfectly well that the land had already been sold? Shall we allow this nasty second buyer to perfect a claim simply because he carefully follows the official recording rules? This thought was too much for the courts of equity, and too much for American legislatures as well. By the early nineteenth century, the British equity courts had imported an element of non-record "notice" into what had initially been a "race" system. Under these doctrines, the later purchaser could take free of the prior claims only if he did not *know* about those prior claims, either from the records or from non-record facts that should put him "on notice." American legislatures followed this move to such a degree that, at present, only a handful of states maintain a race system with any rigor. The other states deny the subsequent claim of the person who had or should have had notice of the earlier claim.

This development means mud: What "should" a purchaser know about, anyway? To be sure, if someone is living on the land, perhaps the potential purchaser should make a few inquiries about the occupant's status. But what if the "occupant's" acts are more ambiguous, consisting of, say, shovelling some manure onto the contested land? Well, said one court, a buyer should have asked about the source of all that manure — and since he didn't, and thus did not find out about the manure shoveller's prior but unrecorded claim, the later buyer did not count as an innocent; his title was a nullity.

With the emergence of this judicial outlook, the crystalline idea of the recording system has come full cycle back to mud. To be sure, the recording system can give one a fair guess about the legal status of any given property. But by the end of the last century, as a Massachusetts court put it, "it would be seldom that a case could occur where some state of facts might not be imagined which, if it existed, would defeat a title." Thus, the test of a title's "marketability" became a question of whether the title was subject to "reasonable" doubt — a matter, of course, for the discretion of the court. In the meantime, a whole title insurance industry sprang up to calm the fears of would-be purchasers who wanted to avoid questions about which doubts were reasonable and which were not. It is this industry, in a sense, that once again makes crystals out of the recording system's mud; and according to the reformers, it is this industry that now stands in the way of a more rational method of cleaning up the mess once and for all.

Yet one must wonder whether cleaning up the mess might not just repeat the cycle of mud/crystal/mud. One of the most popular suggestions for reform is the so-called "Torrens" system, named for someone who thought that shipping registry methods could be used beneficially in real estate. In this system, all claims on a given property — sales, liens, easements, etc. — are first registered and then incorporated in a certificate. Torrens registration echoes eerily the colonial "race" statutes: No unregistered claim counts, and the owner's certificate for a given property acts as the complete record of everything that anyone might claim.

Well, perhaps not everything. Government liens, fraudulent transactions, and, according to some courts, even simple errors or neglect in registration can produce unregistered claims that count. Hence this neo-race system provides no complete relief from the recording system's mud. Even after we look at the Torrens certificate, we still have to be on the lookout for the G-men, the forgers, and the ninnies who neglected to register their claims properly. Not a lot of mud, to be sure, but just wait. In some jurisdictions with a long history of Torrens registration, courts have in effect reestablished a "notice" system, defeating the interest of one who registers his claim when he knows about a prior unregistered one — or merely when he *should* have known about the prior claim. This practice, of course, means that the registry and certificate no longer count as the complete source of information about a property's title status.

The most striking aspect of these developments is that first the title recording acts, and later the registration systems, represented deliberate choices to establish crystalline rules for the sake of simplicity and ease of land sales and purchases. People who failed to use the records or registries were supposed to lose their claims, no matter how innocent they might have been, and no matter how nastily their opponents might have behaved. Yet these very crystalline systems have drifted back into mud through the importation of equitable ideas of notice — only to be replaced by new crystalline systems in the form of private contract or public legislation.

All these examples put the scarcity story to the test: What has happened to that story, according to which our rules should become more crystalline as resources become more scarce and more valuable? Why instead do we shift back and forth between hard-edged, yes-or-no crystalline rules and discretion-laden, post hoc muddy rules? Why do we have, over time, *both* mud *and* crystal rules with respect to the very same things, without any notable relation to their scarcity or plenty? The following section runs through a few theories that might help to explain this mystery.

[The second part of the article discusses several alternative explanations. Two opposing arguments suggest that one side or the other has been simply mistaken; some commentators associated with the law-and-economics movement argue that "mud" rules are mistaken because they impede trade; an opposing argument, associated with the critical legal studies movement, argues that crystal rules are mistaken because they send the wrong message about social norms — that is, one of unrestrained self-interest. The article puts both of these positions to one side because the historic see-saw record suggests that, mistaken or not, we are not likely to have much choice about having both crystals and mud. The author also questions a third argument — that crystal rules are associated with low transactions costs and muddy ones with high transactions costs; again the historic record seems not to bear this out. She then rejects an historical theory that crystal rules were associated with an effort to instill labor discipline, since the correlation seems weak in different times and places.

The article finds more promising an analogy to Alfred Hirschman's Shifting Involvements (1982), an economic history of social movements, which argues that as people become satiated with public affairs they move to private satisfactions, and vice versa.]

Might this process parallel the shift between mud and crystal in property law? Hirschman's book suggests that where we see recurring patterns, we might look for some internal — or as some theorists say, endogenous — factors that lead to these circular patterns. Does such an account apply to the oscillation between crystal and mud in our definitions of entitlements? We can see its application in one area at least: the recording system, where we have so often resolved uncertainty with a crystalline system, only to muddy it so thoroughly over time that we have to start all over again with a newly-minted set of clear rules.

Let us suppose that we have a system for the clarification of property titles. Might we have a tendency to overuse the system, so that in the end it becomes so hopelessly bogged down in detail that the purpose of clarity is defeated? Certainly our traditional land records have this quality. Some early cases permitted only fee interests to be recorded, but it was the very attractiveness of the system that created pressure to allow the recordation of other interests; liens, for example, or easements. Indeed, some claims may be in the records even though they are not legally recordable. Then too, many claims are recorded and just stay put over time, and sometimes even conflict with other recorded claims. The layers of these recorded but unextinguished claims can grow so thick that it hardly seems worth the time to go back and check them all. So, in a sense, we treat our clarifying systems — in this case the recording mechanisms — as a kind of "commons." The resulting system overload, in turn, creates a certain disgust with the lush proliferation of records. In fact, one of our current recording reforms would simply extinguish claims that have not been asserted during a given period.

Thus, the very attractiveness of making clear one's claims by recording them defeats the purpose of the system, that is, to clarify all claims against a given property. One sees the same pattern in the excessively long contracts that attempt to specify all possible contingencies and that no one actually reads; however comforting it might be to "have it in writing," it really isn't worth the effort to nail down everything, and the overly precise contract may wind up being just as opaque as — and perhaps even more arbitrary than — the one that leaves adjustments to the contingencies of future relations.

The trouble, then, is that an attractively simple legal device draws in too many users, or too complex a set of uses. And that, of course, is where the simple rule becomes a booby trap. It is this booby trap aspect of what seems to be clear, simple rules — the scenario of disproportionate loss by some party — that seems to drive us to muddy up crystal rules with the exceptions and the post hoc discretionary judgments. I turn now to the subject of disproportionate loss, the subject to which some courts apply the shorthand label of "forfeiture."

III.   Forfeiture as Overload: The Problem and the Players

A strong element of moral judgment runs through the cases in which mud supersedes crystal. These cases are often rife with human failings — sloth and forgetfulness on the one hand, greed and self-dealing on the other. These vices put pressure on our efforts to elaborate clear and distinct property specifications, and make judges and others second guess the deals that call for a pound of flesh.

Perhaps we can get at this human element by thinking not about moral qualities that are at issue, but rather about the pound of flesh. We have already seen that in the decisions about mortgages and installment land contracts, there lurks a deep antipathy to what is explicitly called the debtor's "forfeiture." The same antipathy to "forfeiture" — a loss disproportionate to the lapse — also appears in our other examples. Thus, the non-recording (or improperly recording, or negligently recording) owner would lose the very property itself; thus, the non-inspecting (or imperfectly inspecting, or negligently inspecting) buyer would get stuck with a house that may be flooded twice a week with the neighbor's sewage.

Our law seems to find these dramatic losses abhorrent. James Gordley has written convincingly that unequal exchanges have been overwhelmingly disfavored in the western legal tradition,[117] and his work suggests that rules leading to forfeitures and penalties generally are unstable in our law. Why is this so? Gordley argues that, traditionally, exchanges centering more or less around a mar-

---

117. Gordley, Equality in Exchange, 69 Calif. L. Rev. 1587 (1981).

ket price counted as "equal." Such exchanges taken collectively restored the costs to the seller, and beyond that, Gordley argues, the law has had no reason to enforce what he calls random redistributions. . . .

Forfeiture might be seen as a symptom of the overloading of crystal rules. Crystalline property doctrines yield fixed consequences, and their predictability makes these doctrines attractive; but for that very reason they may be overused or overloaded in contexts that make them *un*predictable and counterproductive.

Consider the way that the enforcement of a penalty affects the incentives of persons on either side of a property entitlement. If we were to enforce penalties against defaulters or violators, the persons involved undoubtedly would be especially careful about avoiding violations. But perhaps they would be *too* careful, and try to live up to their obligations even when circumstances changed radically, and when everyone would really be better off if someone defaulted and paid normal damages for whatever harm their default caused another. Penalties might also affect the behavior of the non-defaulting parties. Because they would gain much more than damages if penalties were enforced, unscrupulous dealers might expend efforts to find trading partners who would *fail* rather than succeed, or take measures to make them trip up, in order to take the penalty proceeds and run. These victims are the people that petty con artists in my hometown of Chicago might call "mopes," a term that undoubtedly could include the unsuspecting house purchasers who overestimate their ability to live up to the loan payments, or who never suspect that there might be rats in the basement, or who don't have a clue that they have to record their titles.

Fools on the one side and sharp dealers on the other, then, are central players in the crystal-to-mud story, because they are the characters most likely to have a leading role in the systematic overloading of crystalline rules. From this perspective, as indeed the more sophisticated economic analyses tell us, crystalline rules seem less the king of the efficiency mountain than we may normally assume. One can argue that elaborate ex post allocations of responsibilities might be efficient too, even if they make people's entitlements fuzzier ex ante. The very knowledge than one cannot gull someone else, and get away with it, makes it less likely that anyone will dissipate time and effort in trying to find the gullible. This knowledge will also reassure those of us who fear we may be made fools; we can go about our business and take part in the world of trade without cowering at home because we think we need to hire a lawyer and an accountant every time we leave the car at a commercial parking lot.

How can we fit these factors together with the scarcity story about property rights? According to that story, the driving force toward crystalline rules is the competition for resources hitherto unowned — in other words, overuse of a "commons" in a given resource. The conflicts and waste from commons overuse induce us to define boundaries around entitlements to that we can trade our entitlements instead of fighting over them.

But the driving force of the movement to mud rules seems to be an overuse in the "commons" of the crystal rules themselves: We are tempted to take rules that are simple and informative in one context — as, for example, "first in time, first in right" may be in a small community — and extend them to different or more complex situations, where the consequences may be unexpected and confusing. It is in these "overload" situations that crystal rules may ultimately impede trade. Not only might sharp dealers seek out situations in which trade will fail (allowing them to collect a forfeiture from the mopes), but the mopes themselves may be frightened out of dealing altogether. Simple boundaries and simple remedies, it turns out, may yield radically unexpected results, and may destroy the confidence we need for trade, rather than fostering it. It is forfeiture, the prospect of dramatic or disproportionate loss, that brings this home; and forfeiture — and the detailed ways in which it might have been avoided — can only be known to us ex post.

IV. The Context of Forfeiture: Crystals and Mud as Institutional Responses to Estrangement

What can be said to generalize the context of forfeiture, where crystal rules are overloaded? Where is it in our commercial life, for example, that we find the invocation of those crystalline rules at the cost of great forfeiture to another? Stewart Macaulay's work on contracts suggests that forfeitures and penalties are called for in one context in particular: where the parties have no longterm relationship with each other.[128] . . .

Macaulay's work, as well as that of Ian Macneil,[132] suggests that crystalline rules (and their attendant forfeitures) are only designed for people who see each other on a one-time basis, and whose temptations to dupe each other, or simply to play commercial hardball, might be strongest. By way of contrast, where two persons are members of the same community, religion, family, or ongoing business

128. See Macaulay, Elegant Models, Empirical Pictures and the Complexity of Contract, 11 Law & Soc'y Rev. 507, 509 (1977).
132. See Macneil [The Many Futures of Contract, 47 S. Cal. L. Rev. 691 (1974)].

deal, there are inducements to cooperation and trust that are entirely independent of the enforcement of crystalline rules.

Modern game-theorist mathematicians buttress this point, telling us that if we can arrange things in such a manner that we have repeated contact with our opposite numbers, then we can enforce cooperation through the game of "tit for tat." Recent historical work supports the point from another direction, telling us that prior to the eighteenth century, much European commerce was dominated by Jewish and Quaker merchants, whose family and religious connections could assure their mutual reliability.

Recent historical literature also suggests that as modern property and contract law developed, it became possible for people to do business with each other on the basis of sheer promises even though they had none of these familial or other longterm relationships. The legal categories of contract acted as an artificial, officially sponsored surety for the confidence and trust that would otherwise come only through the constraints of community, religion, and family. The enforceability of clear rules enables us to deal with the world of strangers apart from these communities and to arrange our affairs with persons whom we do not know, and never expect to see again. We can do so, we think, because rules are rules are rules — we all know them, and know what to expect. Crystalline rules thus seem to perform the service of creating a context in which strangers can deal with each other in confidence.

But what is easily overlooked is that mud rules, too, attempt to recreate an underlying non-legal trading community in which confidence is possible. In those communities, the members tend to readjust for future complications, rather than drive hard bargains. Mud rules mimic a pattern of post hoc readjustments that people *would* make if they were in an ongoing relationship with each other. People in such relationships would hardly dupe their trading partners out of their titles, sell them defective goods, or fail to make minor readjustments on debts. If they did such things, they would lose a trading partner (or suffer denunciation in church, or become black sheep), and everyone would know it.

Now we can see why crystal and mud are a matched pair. Both are distilled from a kind of non-legal commercial context where people already in some relationship arrive at more or less imperfect understandings at the outset and expect post hoc readjustments when circumstances require. Just as the parties call on courts to enforce promises and protect entitlements that would otherwise be enforced by the threat of informal sanctions, so too do they call on the courts to figure out the post hoc readjustments that would otherwise have been made by the parties themselves.

In our one-time dealings with strangers a wedge appears that splits a trading relationship into ex ante and ex post, crystals and mud. These dealings are the situations in which it seems most important to have clear definitions of obligations, but in which it is also important to have some substitute for the pattern of ongoing cooperation that would protect us against sudden and unexpected loss.

The split between crystals and mud from one-time dealings also falls along divisions in our legal institutions. We call for crystals when we are in what Mel Eisenberg has called our "rulemaking" mode, that is, when private parties make contracts with strangers or when legislatures make prospective law for an unknown future.[137] We call for mud and exceptions only later, after things have gone awry, but at that point we stand before judges.

. . . [J]udges, who see everything ex post, really cannot help but be influenced by their ex post perspectives. They lean ever so slightly to mud, in order to save the fools from forfeiture at the hands of scoundrels. Indeed, if judges have even an occasional preference for post hoc readjustments, to avoid forfeiture, this preference will gradually place an accretion of mud rules over people's crystalline arrangements. These considerations suggest a modification of claims about the efficiency of common law adjudication. We are more likely to find that judicial solutions veer towards mud rules, while it is legislatures that are more apt to join with private parties as "rulemakers" with a tilt towards crystal. . . .

[The last part of the article suggests that the choice between crystals and mud may have very little practical effect on vast parts of commercial life, given the predominating characteristics of repeat play and longterm relations in commercial dealings; the impact of the debate, the author suggests, may be largely a matter of rhetoric, and of the kinds of things people like to believe about the society they live in.]

NOTES AND QUESTIONS ON OSCILLATIONS IN LEGAL RULES

1. Rose's approach suggests pessimism about lasting reform in certain legal areas, particularly our messy land records system. Is she overly gloomy? Might there be room for improvement, in which the "mud" is cabined and restrained in a generally "crystalline" system like Torrens registration, subject to exceptions for fraud and perhaps

---

137. . . . [S]ee Eisenberg, Private Ordering Through Negotiation: Dispute-Settlement and Rulemaking, 89 Harv. L. Rev. 637, 664-665 (1976).

a small number of other information sources outside the formal records? Can computers help to sort out the recording system? For an interesting and informative discussion of the potential impact of computer technology, see John L. McCormack, Torrens and Recording: Land Title Assurance in the Computer Age, 18 Wm. Mitchell L. Rev. 61 (1992).

2. If courts are reluctant to permit forfeitures or penalties, how can they themselves impose the remedies that Ayres and Gertner, Filling Gaps, supra p.313, call "penalty default rules," effectively punishing knowledgeable parties for failing to reveal information? How do court-imposed "penalty default rules" differ from the forfeitures that Rose describes?

3. What is so problematic about forfeiture? Why does the prospect of forfeiture seem to ring so many emotional bells that it can cause judges to muddy perfectly clear rules, presumably to the collective detriment of future bargaining? Might this reaction stem from "loss aversion" or "endowment effects" — that is, attachments to the things that one has (as opposed to things one might have in the future)? Recall the discussion of coffee mugs and candy bars in Knetsch, Endowment Effect, supra p.226.

If loss aversion creates an urge to make rules muddy with ex post doctrines such as "unconscionability," does loss aversion dissipate total social wealth? Or does loss aversion instead suggest a hidden efficiency argument for muddy rules? On this issue, consider a famous article, with a title almost as catchy as The Tragedy of the Commons: George Akerlof, The Market for 'Lemons': Quality Uncertainty and the Market Mechanism, 84 Q.J. Econ. 488 (1970). Akerlof argued that certain kinds of markets (for instance, used car sales) cannot easily assure customers against defects; hence customers are frightened away, and both they and potential sellers miss opportunities for mutually beneficial sales. By extension, if customers are truly loss averse, such "markets for lemons" might tarnish the image of markets generally, and frighten customers away from transactions even in more reliable markets; see Carol Rose, Giving Some Back — A Reprise, 44 Fla. L. Rev. 365, 374-375 (1992). How might muddy rules help overcome customer fears, restore confidence in markets, and open up opportunities for beneficial trades?

4. At the end of this selection, Rose mentions the highly contested hypothesis that common law adjudication leads to the emergence of efficient rules. For some arguments in favor of this position, see, for example, George Priest, The Common Law Process and the Selection of Efficient Rules, 6 J. Legal Stud. 65 (1977); Paul H. Rubin, Why is the Common Law Efficient?, 6 J. Legal Stud. 51 (1977). Rose, however, suggests that the oscillating patterns in property law cast

doubt on this theory of evolutionary efficiency in common law adjudication, since courts play the role of muddying the crystalline rules previously established by private bargains and legislation.

Surprisingly, oscillations in legal rules have attracted little attention in legal academic literature. One exception is Jason Scott Johnston, Uncertainty, Chaos, and the Torts Process: An Economic Analysis of Legal Form, 76 Cornell L. Rev. 341 (1991). Johnston finds a similar back-and-forth pattern in the law of torts. He disagrees with Rose's institutional bifurcation, however, and concludes that the courts engage in this pattern on their own, without the input of other actors that normally operate from an ex ante perspective, such as private bargainers and legislatures. Why might private bargains have relatively little impact in the torts context? Be that as it may, does Johnston's conclusion mean that Rose is mistaken and that courts sometimes can see matters from a systematically ex ante perspective? Compare Duncan Kennedy, Form and Substance in Common Law Adjudication, 89 Harv. L. Rev. 1685 (1976), which sees all legal rhetoric as choosing between "rules" that reflect individualist concerns, and "standards" that reflect altruistic preferences.

B.   Markets and Morals

Market-Inalienability*

Margaret Jane Radin

Since the declaration of "unalienable rights" of persons at the founding of our republic, inalienability has had a central place in our legal and moral culture. Yet there is no one sharp meaning for the term "inalienable." Sometimes inalienable means nontransferable, sometimes only nonsalable. Sometimes inalienable means nonrelinquishable by a rightholder; sometimes it refers to rights that cannot be lost at all. In this Article I explore nonsalability, a species of inalienability I call market-inalienability. Something that is market-inalienable is not to be sold, which in our economic system means it is not to be traded in the market.

Controversy over what may be bought and sold — for example,

* Source: 100 Harv. L. Rev. 1849-1851, 1855-1858, 1870-1873, 1877-1881, 1885 (1987).

blood or babies — pervades our news. Although some scholars have considered whether such things may be traded in markets, they have not focused on the phenomenon of market-inalienability. About fifteen years ago, for example, Richard Titmuss advocated in his book, *The Gift Relationship*,[6] that human blood should not be allocated through the market; others disagreed. More recently, Elisabeth Landes and Richard Posner suggested the possibility of a thriving market in infants,[8] yet most people continue to believe that infants should not be allocated through the market. What I believe is lacking, and wish to supply, is a general theory that can illuminate these debates. Two possibilities for filling this theoretical gap are traditional liberalism and modern economic analysis, but in this Article I shall find them both wanting.

The most familiar context of inalienability is the traditional liberal triad: the rights to life, liberty, and property. To this triad, liberalism juxtaposes the most familiar context of alienability: traditional property rights. Although the right to hold property is considered inalienable in traditional liberalism, property rights themselves are presumed fully alienable, and inalienable property rights are exceptional and problematic.

Economic analysis, growing out of the liberal tradition, tends to view all inalienabilities in the way traditional liberalism views inalienable property rights. When it does this, economic analysis holds fast to one strand of traditional liberalism, but it implicitly rejects — or at least challenges — another: the traditional distinction between inalienable and alienable kinds of rights. In conceiving of all rights as property rights that can (at least theoretically) be alienated in markets, economic analysis has (at least in principle) invited markets to fill the social universe. It has invited us to view all inalienabilities as problematic.

In seeking to develop a theory of market-inalienability, I argue that inalienabilities should not always be conceived of as anomalies, regardless of whether they attach to things traditionally thought of as property. Indeed, I try to show that the characteristic rhetoric of economic analysis is morally wrong when it is put forward as the sole discourse of human life. My general view deviates not only from the traditional conception of the divide between inalienable and alienable kinds of rights, but also from the traditional conception of alienable property. Instead of using the categories of economics or those of traditional liberalism, I think that we should evaluate

6. . . . (1971).
8. See Landes & Posner, The Economics of the Baby Shortage, 7 J. Legal Stud. 323 (1978). . . .

inalienabilities in connection with our best current understanding
of the concept of human flourishing. . . .

I. Market-Inalienability and Noncommodification . . .

B. The Commodification Issue

Market-inalienability often expresses an aspiration for noncommodification. By making something nonsalable, we proclaim that it
should not be conceived of or treated as a commodity. . . .

How are we to determine the extent to which something ought
to be noncommodified, so that we can determine to what extent
market-inalienability is justified? Because the question asks about
the appropriate relationship of particular things to the market, normative theories about the appropriate social role of the market
should be helpful in trying to answer it. We can think of such theories as ordered on a continuum stretching from universal noncommodification (nothing in markets) to universal commodification
(everything in markets). On this continuum, Karl Marx's theory can
symbolize the theoretical pole of universal noncommodification,
and Richard Posner's can be seen as close to the opposite theoretical
pole.[38] Distributed along the continuum are theorists we may call
pluralists — those who see a normatively appropriate but limited
realm for commodification coexisting with one or more nonmarket
realms. Pluralists often see one other normative realm besides that
of the market, and partition the social world into markets and politics, markets and rights, or markets and families; but pluralists also
may envision multiple nonmarket realms. For a pluralist, the crucial
question is how to conceive of the permissible scope of the market.
An acceptable answer would solve problems of contested commodification. . . .

III. The Critique of Universal Commodification

A traditional critical response to universal commodification, at least
since Marx, has been a global rejection of commodification. Universal decommodification or noncommodification maintains that the
market ought not to exist and that social interactions involving production and consumption should be reconceived in a nonmarket
way. Even if one rejects that ideal, however, as I do because of a
problem of transition, the critique of universal commodification of-

---

38. . . . See R. Posner, [Economic Analysis of Law (2d ed. 1977)], at 29-33.

fers a crucial insight: a world in which human interactions are conceived of as market trades is different from one in which they are not. Rhetoric is not just shaped by, but shapes, reality.

A. Universal Noncommodification

Universal noncommodification holds that the hegemony of profit-maximizing buying and selling stifles the individual and social potential of human beings through its organization of production, distribution, and consumption, and through its concomitant creation and maintenance of the person as a self-aggrandizing profit- and preference-maximizer. Anticommodifiers tend to assume that we are living under a regime of universal commodification, with its attendant full-blown market methodology and market rhetoric. They also tend to assume that universal commodification is a necessary concomitant of commodification in the narrower sense — the existence of market transactions under capitalism. Anticommodifiers link rhetoric and reality in their assumption that our material relationships of production and exchange are interwoven with our discourse and our understanding of ourselves and the world.

1. Alienability and Alienation: The Problem of Fetishism. For critics of the market society, commodification simultaneously expresses and creates alienation. The word "alienation" thus harbors an ironic double meaning. Freedom of alienation is the paramount characteristic of liberal property rights, yet Marx saw a necessary connection between this market alienability and human alienation. In his early writings, Marx analyzed the connection between alienation and commodity production in terms of estranged labor; later he introduced the notion of commodity festishism. In his treatment of estranged labor, Marx portrayed workers' alienation from their own human self-activity as the result of producing objects that became market commodities. By objectifying the labor of the worker, commodities create object-bondage and alienate workers from the natural world in and with which they should constitute themselves by creative interaction. Ultimately, laboring to produce commodities turns the worker from a human being into a commodity, "indeed the most wretched of commodities."[81] Marx continued:

> The worker becomes an ever cheaper commodity the more commodities he creates. With the *increasing value* of the world of things proceeds in direct proportion the *devaluation* of the world of men.

---

81. Marx, Economic and Philosophical Manuscripts of 1844, in The Marx-Engels Reader 70 (R. Tucker 2d ed. 1984).

> Labour produces not only commodities; it produces itself and the worker as a *commodity* — and does so in the proportion in which it produces commodities generally.

Commodification brings about an inferior form of human life. As a result of this debasement, Marx concluded that people themselves, not just their institutions, must change in order to live without the market. To reach the post-capitalist stage, "the alteration of men on a mass scale is necessary."[84]

The fetishism of commodities represents a different kind of human subjection to commodities (or a different way of looking at human subjection to commodities). By fetishism Marx meant a kind of projection of power and action onto commodities. This projection reflects — but disguises — human social interactions. Relationships between people are disguised as relationships between commodities, which appear to be governed by abstract market forces. I do not decide what objects to produce, rather "the market" does. Unless there is a demand for paperweights, they will have no market value, and I cannot produce them for sale. Moreover, I do not decide what price to sell them for, "the market" does. At market equilibrium, I cannot charge more nor less than my opportunity costs of production without going out of business. In disequilibrium, my price and profit are still set by "the market"; my price depends upon how many of us are supplying paperweights in relation to how many people want to buy them and what they are willing to pay for them. Thus, the market value of my commodity dictates my actions, or so it seems. As Marx put it, "[producers'] own social action takes the form of the action of objects, which rule the producers instead of being ruled by them."[87] . . .

B.   The Moral and Political Role of Rhetoric . . .

"The word is not the thing," we were taught, when I was growing up. Rhetoric is not reality; discourse is not the world. Why should it matter if someone conceptualizes the entire human universe as one giant bundle of scare goods subject to free alienation by contract, especially if reasoning in market rhetoric can reach the same result that some other kind of normative reasoning reaches on the other grounds? Consider three possible answers: It matters because the rhetoric might lead less-than-perfect practitioners to wrong answers in sensitive cases; it matters because the rhetoric

---

84. Marx, The German Ideology: Part I, in The Marx-Engels Reader, . . . at 193. . . .

87. 1 K. Marx [Capital . . . (S. Moore & E. Aveling trans., 1984], at 79.

itself is insulting or injures personhood regardless of the result; or — the implicit philosophical commitment of the anticommodifiers — it matters because *there is no such thing as two radically different normative discourses reaching the "same" result.*

1. Risk of Error. The rhetoric of commodification might lead imperfect practitioners to wrong answers, even if the sophisticated practitioner would not be misled. In other words, commodification-talk creates a serious risk of error in certain cases. . . .

2. Injury to Personhood. In some cases market discourse itself might be antagonistic to interests of personhood. Recall that Posner conceives of rape in terms of a marriage and sex market. Posner concludes that "the prevention of rape is essential to protect the marriage market . . . and more generally to secure property rights in women's persons."[109] Calabresi and Melamed also use market rhetoric to discuss rape.[110] In keeping with their view that "property rules" are prima facie more efficient than "liability rules" for all entitlements, they argue that people should hold a "property rule" entitlement in their own bodily integrity. Further, they explain criminal punishment by the need for an "indefinable kicker," an extra cost to the rapist "which represents society's need to keep all property rules from being changed at will into liability rules." Unlike Posner's view, Calabresi and Melamed's can be understood as pluralist, but like Posner's, their view conceives of rape in market rhetoric. Bodily integrity is an owned object with a price.

What is wrong with this rhetoric? The risk-of-error argument . . .is one answer. Unsophisticated practitioners of cost-benefit analysis might tend to undervalue the "costs" of rape to the victims. But this answer does not exhaust the problem. Rather, for all but the deepest enthusiast, market rhetoric seems intuitively out of place here, so inappropriate that it is either silly or somehow insulting to the value being discussed.

One basis for this intuition is that market rhetoric conceives of bodily integrity as a fungible object. A fungible object is replaceable with money or other objects; in fact, possessing a fungible object is the same as possessing money. A fungible object can pass in and out of the person's possession without effect on the person as long as its market equivalent is given in exchange. To speak of personal attributes as fungible objects — alienable "goods" — is in-

109. R. Posner, [Economic Analysis of Law, 2d ed. 1977], at 202.
110. Calabresi & Melamed, [Property Rules, Liability Rules, and Inalienabilty: One View of the Cathedral, 85 Harv. L. Rev. 1089 (1972)], at 1124-1127.

tuitively wrong. Thinking of rape in market rhetoric implicitly conceives of as fungible something that we know to be personal, in fact conceives of as fungible property something we know to be too personal even to be personal property. Bodily integrity is an attribute and not an object. We feel discomfort or even insult, and we fear degradation or even loss of the value involved, when bodily integrity is conceived of as a fungible object.

Systematically conceiving of personal attributes as fungible objects is threatening to personhood, because it detaches from the person that which is integral to the person. Such a conception makes actual loss of the attribute easier to countenance. For someone who conceives bodily integrity as "detached," the same person will remain even if bodily integrity is lost; but if bodily integrity cannot be detached, the person cannot remain the same after loss. Moreover, if my bodily integrity is an integral personal attribute, not a detachable object, then hypothetically valuing my bodily integrity in money is not far removed from valuing *me* in money. For all but the universal commodifier, that is inappropriate treatment of a person. . . .

3. *"The Texture of the Human World."** Market rhetoric, if adopted by everyone, and in many contexts, would indeed transform the texture of the human world. This rhetoric leads us to view politics as just rent seeking, reproductive capacity as just a scarce good for which there is high demand, and the repugnance of slavery as just a cost. To accept these views is to accept the conception of human flourishing they imply, one that is inferior to the conception we can accept as properly ours. An inferior conception of human flourishing disables us from conceptualizing the world rightly. Market rhetoric, the rhetoric of alienability of all "goods," is also the rhetoric of alienation of ourselves from what we can be as persons.

One way to see how universal market rhetoric does violence to our conception of human flourishing is to consider its view of personhood. In our understanding of personhood we are committed to an ideal of individual uniqueness that does not cohere with the idea that each person's attributes are fungible, that they have a monetary equivalent, and that they can be traded off against those of other people. Universal market rhetoric transforms our world of concrete persons, whose uniqueness and individuality is expressed in specific personal attributes, into a world of disembodied, fungible, attribute-less entities possessing a wealth of alienable, sever-

* This phrase comes from H. Putnam, Reason, Truth and History 139-141 (1981).

able "objects." This rhetoric reduces the conception of a person to an abstract, fungible unit with no individuating characteristics.

Another way to see how universal market rhetoric does violence to our conception of human flourishing is to consider its view of freedom. Market rhetoric invites us to see the person as a self-interested maximizer in all respects. Freedom or autonomy, therefore, is seen as individual control over how to maximize one's overall gains. In the extreme, the ideal of freedom is achieved through buying and selling commodified objects in order to maximize monetizable wealth. As we have seen, Marx argued with respect to those who produce and sell commodities that this is not freedom but fetishism; what and how much is salable is not autonomously determined. Whether or not we agree with him, it is not satisfactory to think that marketing whatever one wishes defines freedom. Nor is it satisfactory to think that a theoretical license to acquire all objects one may desire defines freedom. . . .

NOTES AND QUESTIONS ON INALIENABILITY AND COMMODIFICATION

1. Blackstone and Posner both generally favored the alienability of resources, on the ground that trades can be expected to benefit both buyers and sellers. See supra pp.37 and 45. To what extent does Radin succeed in refuting their analysis?

2. Radin's article revisits an issue discussed by Rose in Property as Storytelling and in Crystals and Mud, supra p.20 and p.320: Why does rhetoric matter? Why is the "texture of the world" inferior if market rhetoric is used in domains that Radin regards as inappropriate? In a passage not reproduced here, Radin cites the potential damage that a child might suffer from thinking that she might be bought or sold like "fungible" property. How does the example illuminate Radin's objections to market rhetoric?

3. Note that property rhetoric is not necessarily *commodification* rhetoric. Might one think of the parent-child relationship as a trusteeship, which is of course a kind of property relation?

4. Environmental law is another area in which the rhetoric of commodification is highly controversial. The selection by Schelling, Prices as Regulatory Instruments, infra p.532, gives the major arguments favoring pricing approaches to pollution; but environmentalists often argue that these devices convey the morally objectionable impression that one may buy the right to do a wrong. Could Radin use this as an example of the effects of inappropriate rhetoric?

5. Does Radin overly romanticize intimate domains, and thus risk misunderstanding the ways that participants actually interact? Recall that Papanek, To Each Less than She Needs, supra, analyzed the family in terms of the allocation of entitlements among the members. Which approach is more realistic?

6. Does Radin really reject Richard Posner's analogy of rape laws to the prohibitions on theft? Or does she rather reject the suggestion that the rights-holder is in some kind of "market"? In several passages not given here, Radin notes that some matters, including most body parts, may not be legally sold, even though they may be given away. Might such gift-but-not-sale rules aim to prevent a particularly horrifying form of theft? Is there an analogy between a prohibition on the sale of kidneys and the international prohibition on the sale of elephant tusks?

7. What is the actual effect of making something inalienable? Consider once again children, and the effect of a child's inalienability on an abusive parent: Might such a child be better off if the parent could sell him or her? Might alienability mean that such children would be less likely to be abused in the first place? Does inalienability really send the signal that something is priceless, or rather that it is valueless?

8. Toward the end of the full article, Radin states that a genuine concern for the avoidance of inappropriate commodification will entail some form of wealth redistribution and income maintenance. Why?

9. Suppose we were to go to the opposite extreme from universal commodification: What would "universal noncommodification" look like? Any transfers would presumably take the form of gifts. Anthropologists who study gift-giving and -receiving behavior have often noted a similarity to commercial transactions, particularly when the parties are entangled in complex and multi-layered gift-*exchange* relationships. On these accounts, gift exchange stems not from pure altruism but rather from calculation, concerns about reciprocity, and even rudimentary ideas of interest payment. The classic statement of this position is Marcel Mauss, The Gift: Forms and Functions of Exchange in Archaic Societies (Ian Cunnison trans., 1967) (1925). If gift-giving is calculated and self-interested, why do many observers hold to the view that gift exchanges are more rhetorically and socially acceptable than exchanges mediated through money? Consider Ellickson's discussion of exchanges among Shasta County neighbors, supra p.224. Why does anyone care about forms and labels if both gifts and commercial trades are simply devices for mutually beneficial exchange?

Other authors have taken the position that gift-giving and market exchange are quite different. A classic is cited by Radin: Richard Titmuss, The Gift Relationship: From Human Blood to Social Policy (1971). Titmuss studied British blood collection and argued not only that most blood is donated altruistically, but that such blood is markedly superior to blood purchased from donors. But see Rueben A. Kessel, Transfused Blood, Serum Hepatitis, and The Coase Theorem, 17 J.L. & Econ. 265 (1974), attributing the superior quality of donated blood to the exemption of suppliers of defective blood from ordinary products liability rules. (Is blood sale another instance of a "Market for Lemons"? See Note 3 after the preceding selection.) Another fascinating sociological study of modern gift-giving, also rejecting the self-interest model, is David Cheal, The Gift Economy (1988); see also Carol M. Rose, Giving, Trading, Thieving, and Trusting, 44 Fla. L. Rev. 295 (1992), stressing the importance of what seems to be an irrational element of altruism not only in gifts but in commercial transactions as well.

10. For the other leading work on the topic (published shortly before Radin's article), see Susan Rose-Ackerman, Inalienability and the Theory of Property Rights, 85 Colum. L. Rev. 931 (1985). For Radin's most recent views on this subject, see her Market-Rhetoric and Reality: Commodification in Words and the World (Harvard, forthcoming).

Rival Interpretations of Market Society: Civilizing, Destructive, or Feeble?*

Albert O. Hirschman

Introduction

Once upon a time, not all that long ago, the social, political and economic order under which men and women were living was taken for granted. Among the people of those idyllic times many of course were poor, sick, or oppressed, and consequently unhappy; no doubt, others managed to feel unhappy for seemingly less cogent reasons; but most tended to attribute their unhappiness either to concrete and fortuitous happenings — ill luck, ill health, the machinations of enemies, an unjust master, lord or ruler — or to remote, general and unchangeable causes, such as human nature or the will of God. The

* Source: 20 J. Econ. Lit. 1463-1474 (1982).

idea that the social order — intermediate between the fortuitous and the unchangeable — may be an important cause of human unhappiness became widespread only in the modern age, particularly in the eighteenth century. Hence Saint-Just's famous phrase: "The idea of happiness is new in Europe" — it was then novel to think that happiness could be *engineered* by changing the social order, a task he and his Jacobin companions had so confidently undertaken. . . . In any event, the idea of a perfectible society was not to be nipped in the bud; to the contrary, it experienced a most vigorous development, and, soon after the French Revolution, reappeared in the guise of powerful critiques of the social and economic order — capitalism — emerging at the beginning of the nineteenth century. . . .

I. The Doux-commerce Thesis

To begin, let me briefly evoke the complex of ideas and expectations which accompanied the expansion of commerce and the development of the market from the sixteenth to the eighteenth centuries. Here I must return to a principal theme of The Passions and the Interests (Hirschman, 1977), with the hope of placating at least partially those of my readers who complained that, with the book tracing ideological developments in some detail only up to Adam Smith, they were left guessing what happened next, in the age — our own — that *really* mattered to them. My book dwelt on the favorable side effects that the emerging economic system was imaginatively but confidently expected to have, with respect to both the character of citizens and the characteristics of statecraft. I stressed particularly the latter — the expectation, entertained by Montesquieu and Sir James Steuart, that the expansion of the market would restrain the arbitrary actions and excessive power plays of the sovereign, both in domestic and in international politics. Here I shall emphasize instead the expected effects of commerce on the *citizen* and *civil society*. At mid-eighteenth century it became the conventional wisdom — Rousseau of course rebelled against it — that commerce was a civilizing agent of considerable power and range. Let me again cite Montesquieu's key sentence, which he placed at the very beginning of his discussion of economic matters in the Spirit of the Laws:

> it is almost a general rule that wherever manners are gentle (*moeurs douces*) there is commerce; and wherever there is commerce, manners are gentle [1749, 1961, Vol. 2, p. 8].

Here the relationship between "gentle manners" and commerce is presented as mutually reinforcing, but a few sentences later

Montesquieu leaves no doubt about the predominant direction of the causal link:

> Commerce . . . polishes and softens (*adoucit*) barbaric ways as we can see every day [p. 81].

This way of viewing the influence of expanding commerce on society was widely accepted throughout most of the eighteenth century. It is stressed in two outstanding histories of progress — then a popular genre — William Robertson's View of the Progress of Society in Europe (1769) and Condorcet's Esquisse d'un tableau historique du progrès de l'esprit humain (1793-1794). Robertson repeats Montesquieu almost word by word:

> Commerce . . . softens and polishes the manners of men [p. 67].

and Condorcet, while elsewhere critical of Montesquieu's political ideas also followed his lead in this area quite closely:

> Manners (*moeurs*) have become more gentle (*se sont adoucies*) . . . through the influence of the spirit of commerce and industry, those enemies of the violence and turmoil which cause wealth to flee . . . [Condorcet, 1795, p. 238].

One of the strongest statements comes from Thomas Paine, in The Rights of Man (1792):

> [Commerce] is a pacific system, operating to cordialise mankind, by rendering Nations, as well as individuals, useful to each other. . . . The invention of commerce . . . is the greatest approach towards universal civilization that has yet been made by any means not immediately flowing from moral principles [p. 215].

What was the concrete meaning of all this *douceur*, polish, gentleness, and even cordiality? Through what precise mechanisms was expanding commerce going to have such happy effects? The eighteenth-century literature is not very communicative in this regard, perhaps because it all seemed so obvious to contemporaries. The most detailed account I have been able to find appears in a technical book on commerce first published in 1704 that must have been highly successful as it was reedited repeatedly through the next eighty years.

> Commerce attaches [men] one to another through mutual utility. Through commerce the moral and physical passions are superseded by interest. . . Commerce has a special character which distinguishes it from all other professions. It affects the feelings of men so strongly that it makes him who was proud and haughty suddenly turn supple, bending and servicable. Through commerce, man learns to deliberate, to be honest, to acquire manners, to be prudent and reserved in both

talk and action. Sensing the necessity to be wise and honest in order to succeed, he flees vice, or at least his demeanor exhibits decency and seriousness so as not to arouse any adverse judgement on the part of present and future acquaintances; he would not dare make a spectacle of himself for fear of damaging his credit standing and thus society may well avoid a scandal which it might otherwise have to deplore [Samuel Ricard, 1781, p. 463].

Commerce is here seen as a powerful moralizing agent which brings many nonmaterial improvements to society even though a bit of hypocrisy may have to be accepted into the bargain. Similar modifications of human behavior and perhaps even of human nature are later credited to the spread of commerce and industry by David Hume and Adam Smith: The virtues they specifically mention as being enhanced or brought into the world by commerce and manufacturing are industriousness and assiduity (the opposite of indolence), frugality, punctuality, and, most important perhaps for the functioning of market society, probity.

There is here then the insistent thought that a society where the market assumes a central position for the satisfaction of human wants will produce not only considerable new wealth because of the division of labor and consequent technical progress, but would generate as a by-product, or external economy, a more "polished" human type — more honest, reliable, orderly, and disciplined, as well as more friendly and helpful, ever ready to find solutions to conflicts and a middle ground for opposed opinions. Such a type will in turn greatly facilitate the smooth functioning of the market. In sum, according to this line of reasoning, capitalism which in its early phases led a rather shaky existence, having to contend with a host of pre-capitalist mentalities left behind by the feudal and other "rude and barbarous" epochs, would create, in the course of time and through the very practice of trade and industry, a set of compatible psychological attitudes and moral dispositions, that are both desirable in themselves and conducive to the further expansion of the system. And at certain epochs, the speed and vigor displayed by that expansion lent considerable plausibility to the conjecture.

II. The Self-Destruction Thesis

Whatever became of this brave eighteenth-century vision? I shall reserve this topic for later and turn now to a body of thought which is far more familiar to us than the *doux-commerce* thesis — and happens to be its obverse. According to that view which first became prominent in the nineteenth century, capitalist society, far from fostering *douceur* and other fine attitudes, exhibits a pronounced proclivity toward undermining the moral foundations on which any society, including the capitalist variety, must rest. I shall call this the self-destruction thesis.

This thesis has a fairly numerous ancestry, among both Marxist and conservative thinkers. Moreover, a political economist who was neither has just recently given it renewed prominence and sophisticated treatment. So I shall first present his point of view and then go back to the earlier exponents. In his influential book, Social Limits to Growth (1976), Fred Hirsch dealt at length with what he called "The Depleting Moral Legacy" of capitalism. He argues that the market *undermines* the moral values that are its own essential underpinnings, values that are now said to have been inherited from *preceding* socioeconomic regimes, such as the feudal order. The idea that capitalism depletes or "erodes" the moral foundation needed for its functioning is put forward in the following terms:

> The social morality that has served as an understructure for economic individualism has been a legacy of the precapitalist and preindustrial past. This legacy has diminished with time and with the corrosive contact of the active capitalist values — and more generally with the greater anonymity and greater mobility of industrial society. The system has thereby lost outside support that was previously taken for granted by the individual. As individual behavior has been increasingly directed to individual advantage, habits and instincts based on communal attitudes and objectives have lost out. The weakening of traditional social values has made predominantly capitalist economies more difficult to manage [pp. 117-118].

Once again, one would like to know in more detail how the market acts on values, this time in the direction of "depletion" or "erosion," rather than *douceur*. In developing his argument Hirsch makes the following principal points:

1. The emphasis on self-interest typical of capitalism makes it more difficult to secure the collective goods and cooperation increasingly needed for the proper functioning of the system in its later stages [Chapter 11].
2. With macromanagement, Keynesian or otherwise, assuming an important role in the functioning of the system, the macromanagers must be motivated by 'the general interest' rather than by their self-interest, and the system, being based on self-interest, has no way of generating the proper motivation; to the extent such motivation does exist, it is a residue of previous value systems that are likely to 'erode' [p. 128].

3. Social virtues such as 'truth, trust, acceptance, restraint, obligation,' needed for the functioning of an 'individualistic, contractual
economy' [p. 141] are grounded, to a considerable extent, in religious belief, but 'the individualistic, rationalistic base of the market undermines religious support' [p. 143].

The last point stands in particularly stark contrast to the earlier
conception of commerce and of its beneficial side effects. In the first
place, thinkers of the 17th and 18th centuries took it for granted that
they have to make do with "man as he really is" and that meant to
them with someone who has been proven to be largely impervious
to religious and moralistic precepts. With this realistic-pessimistic
appraisal of human nature, those thinkers proceeded to discover in
"interest" a principle that could replace "love" and "charity" as the
basis for a well-ordered society. Secondly, and most important in the
present context, to the extent that society is in need of moral values
such as "truth, trust, etc." for its functioning, these values were confidently expected to be *generated*, rather than eroded, by the market,
its practices and incentives.

As already noted, Hirsch is only the latest representative of the
idea that the market and capitalism harbor self-destructive proclivities. Let us now trace it back, if only to find out whether contact was
ever made between the two opposite views about the moral effects
of commerce and capitalism that have been spelled out.

The idea that capitalism as a socio-economic order somehow
carries within itself "the seed of its own destruction" is of course a
cornerstone of Marxian thought. But for Marx, this familiar metaphor related to the social and economic working of the system: Some
of its properties, such as the tendency to concentration of capital, the
falling rate of profit, the periodic crises of overproduction, would
bring about, with the help of an ever-more numerous and more
class-conscious and combative proletariat, the socialist revolution.
Thus Marx had little need to discover a more indirect and insidious
mechanism that would operate as a sort of fifth column, by undermining the moral foundations of the capitalist system from within.
Marx did, however, help in forging one key link in the chain of reasoning that would eventually lead to that conception: In the Communist Manifesto and other early writings, Marx and Engels make
much of the way in which capitalism corrodes all traditional values
and institutions such as love, family, and patriotism. Everything
was passing into commerce, all social bonds were dissolved through
money. This perception is by no means original with Marx. Over a
century earlier it was the essence of the *conservative* reaction to the
advance of market society, voiced during the 1730s in England by

the opponents of Walpole and Whig rule, such as Bolingbroke and his circle (Hirschman, 1977, pp. 55-56). The theme was taken up again, from the early nineteenth century on, by the romantic and conservative critics of the Industrial Revolution. Coleridge, for example, wrote in 1817 that the "true seat and sources" of the "existing distress" are to be found in the "Overbalance of the Commercial Spirit" in relation to "natural counter-forces" such as the "ancient feelings of rank and ancestry".

This ability of capitalism to "overbalance" all traditional and "higher" values was not taken as a threat to capitalism itself, at least not right away. The opposite is the case: even though the world shaped by it was often thought to be spiritually and culturally much impoverished, capitalism was viewed as an all-conquering, irresistible force. Its rise was widely expected to lead to a thorough remaking of society: Custom was to be replaced by contract, gemeinschaft by gesellschaft, the traditional by the modern. All spheres of social life, from the family to the state, from traditional hierarchy to longtime cooperative arrangements, were to be vitally affected: Metaphors often used to describe this action of capitalism on ancient social forms ranged from the outright "dissolving" to "erosion," "corrosion," "contamination," "penetration," and "intrusion" by the "juggernaut market."

But once capitalism was thus perceived as an unbridled force, terrifyingly successful in its relentless forward drive, the thought arose naturally enough that, like all great conquerors, it just might break its neck. Being a blind force (recall the expression the "blind market forces") as well as a wild one, capitalism might corrode, not only traditional society and its moral values, but even those essential to its own success and survival. In this manner, to credit capitalism with extraordinary powers of expansion, penetration and disintegration may in fact have been an adroit ideological maneuver for intimating that it was headed for disaster. The maneuver was especially effective in an age which had turned away from the idea of progress as a leading myth and was on the contrary much taken with various myths of self-destruction, from the Nibelungen to Oedipus.

The simplest model for the self-destruction of capitalism might be called, in contrast to the self-reinforcing model of *doux-commerce,* the *dolce vita* scenario. The advance of capitalism requires, so this story begins, that capitalists save and lead a frugal life so that accumulation can proceed apace. However, at some ill-defined point, increases in wealth resulting from successful accumulation will tend to enervate the spirit of frugality. Demands will be made for *dolce vita,* that is for instant, rather than delayed, gratification and when that happens capitalist progress will grind to a halt.

The idea that successful attainment of wealth will undermine the process of wealth-generation is present throughout the eighteenth century from John Wesley to Montesquieu and Adam Smith. With Max Weber's essay on The Protestant Ethic, reasoning along such lines became fashionable once again: Any evidence that the repressive ethic, alleged to be essential for the development of capitalism, may be faltering was then interpreted as a serious threat to the system's survival. Observers as diverse as Herbert Marcuse (1965) and Daniel Bell (1976) have written in this vein, unaware, it would appear, that they were merely refurbishing a well-known, much older morality tale: how the republican virtues of sobriety, civic pride, and bravery — in ancient Rome — led to victory and conquest which brought opulence and luxury, which in turn undermined those earlier virtues and destroyed the republic and eventually the empire.

While appealing in its simple dialectic, that tale has long been discredited as an explanation of Rome's decline and fall. The attempt to account for or to predict the present or future demise of capitalism in almost identical terms richly deserves a similar fate, and that for a number of reasons. Let me just point out one: The key role in this alleged process of capitalism's rise and decline is attributed first to the generation and then to the decline of personal savings so that changes in much more strategic variables, such as corporate savings, technical innovation and entrepreneurial skill, not to speak of cultural and institutional factors, are totally left out of account.

There are less mechanical, more sophisticated forms of the self-destruction thesis. The best known is probably the one put forward by Joseph Schumpeter in Capitalism, Socialism, and Democracy (1942), whose second part is entitled Can Capitalism Survive? Schumpeter's answer to that question was rather negative, not so much, he argued, because of insuperable economic problems encountered or generated by capitalism as because of the growing hostility capitalism meets with on the part of many strata, particularly among the intellectuals. It is in the course of arguing along these lines that Schumpeter writes:

> . . . capitalism creates a critical frame of mind which, after having destroyed the moral authority of so many other institutions, in the end turns against its own; the bourgeois finds to his amazement that the rationalist attitude does not stop at the credentials of kings and popes but goes on to attack private property and the whole scheme of bourgeois values [p. 143].

In comparison to the *dolce vita* scenario, this is a much more general argument on self-destruction. But is it more persuasive? Capitalism is here cast in the role of the sorcerer-apprentice who does not know how to stop a mechanism once set in motion — so it demolishes itself along with its enemies. This sort of vision may have appealed to Schumpeter who, after all, came right out of the Viennese *fin-de-siècle* culture for which self-destruction had become something totally familiar, unquestioned, *selbstverständlich*. Those not steeped in that tradition might not find the argument so compelling and might timidly raise the objection that, in addition to the mechanism of self-destruction, elementary forces of reproduction and *self-preservation* also ought to be taken into account. Such forces have certainly appeared repeatedly in the history of capitalism, from the first enactments of factory legislation to the introduction of social security schemes and the experimentation with counter-cyclical macroeconomic policies. . . .

What is surprising . . . is not that these somber ideas about self-destruction arose at the more difficult and somber moments of our century, but that there was a failure to connect them with earlier, more hopeful expectations of a market society bringing forth its own moral foundation, via the generation of *douceur*, probity, trust and so on. One reason for this lack of contact is the low profile of the *doux-commerce* thesis in the nineteenth century, after its period of self-confidence in the preceding century. Another is the transfiguration of that thesis into one in which it was hard to recognize. The story of that low profile and that transfiguration must now be told.

III.   Eclipse of the Doux-commerce Thesis
After the Eighteenth Century

The most plausible explanation for the eclipse of the *doux-commerce* thesis in the nineteenth-century is that it became a victim of the Industrial Revolution. The commercial expansion of the preceding centuries had of course often been violent and had created a great deal of social and human havoc, but this violence and havoc primarily affected the societies that were the objects of European penetration in Africa, Asia, and America. With the Industrial Revolution, the havoc came home. As traditional products were subjected to competitive pressure from ever new "trinkets and baubles," as large groups of laborers were displaced and as their skills became obsolete and as all classes of society were seized by a sudden passion for enrichment, it was widely felt that a new revolutionary force had arisen in the very center of capitalist expansion.

As already noted, that force was often characterized as wild, blind, relentless, unbridled — hence anything but *doux* (gentle and soft). Only with regard to international trade was it still asserted from time to time, usually as an after-thought, that expanding transactions will bring, not only mutual material gains, but also some fine by-products in the cultural and moral realms, such as intellectual cross-fertilization and mutual understanding and peace.[3] Within the boundaries of the nation, the expansion of industry and commerce was widely viewed as contributing to the breakdown of traditional communities and to the loosening and disintegration of social and affective ties, rather than to their consolidation.

To be sure, here and there one can still find echoes of the older idea that civil society is largely held together by the dense network of mutual relations and obligations arising from the market and from its expansion which in turn is fueled by an increasingly fine division of labor. In fact, as soon as the matter is put this way one's thoughts travel to Emile Durkheim and his Division of Labor in Society (1902). Here it was argued, at least in part, that the advanced division of labor of modern society functions as a substitute for the "common consciousness" that so effectively bonded more primitive societies: "it is principally [the division of labor] which holds together social aggregates of the higher type" (p. 148). But in Durkheim's subtle thought, the transactions arising from the division of labor were not by themselves capable of this substitution. The decisive role was played by the many, often *unintended* ties that people take on or fall into in the wake of market transactions and contractual commitments. Here are some formulations of this thought which recur throughout the book:

> We cooperate because we wanted to do so, but our voluntary cooperation creates duties which we did not intend to assume [p. 192].
> The members [of societies with a fine division of labor] are united by ties that go well beyond the ever so brief moments during which exchange actually takes place. . . . Because we exercise this or that domestic or social function, we are caught in a network of obligations which we do not have the right to forsake [p. 207].
> If the division of labor produces solidarity, this is not only because it makes of each person an exchanger (*échangiste*) to speak the language of the economists; it is because the division of labor creates

3. For example, John Stuart Mill writes in Principles of Political Economy (1848): "It is hardly possible to overrate the value, in the present low state of human improvement, of placing human beings in contact with persons dissimilar to themselves, and with modes of thought and action unlike those with which they are familiar. . . . Such communication has always been, and is peculiarly in the present age, one of the primary sources of progress."

among men a comprehensive system of rights and duties which tie them to one another in a durable fashion [pp. 402-403].

So Durkheim's construction is a great deal more complex and roundabout than Montesquieu's (or Sir James Steuart's): Society is *not* held together directly nor is it made peaceful and *doux* by the network of self-interested market transactions alone; for that sort of doctrine Durkheim has some harsh words that contrast sharply with the seventeenth and eighteenth centuries' doctrine about interest:

> While interest brings people closer together, this is a matter of a few moments only; it can only create an external tie among them. . . . The consciences are only in superficial contact; they do not penetrate one another . . . every harmony of interest contains a latent or delayed conflict . . . for interest is what is least constant in the world [pp. 180-181].[4]

Durkheim was thus caught between the older view that interest-oriented action provides a basis for social integration and the more contemporary critique of market society as atomistic and corrosive of social cohesion. He never spelled out in concrete detail how he conceived a "solidary" society to emerge from the division of labor and eventually moved on to a more activist view that no longer counted on this mechanism to achieve social cohesion and instead stressed moral education and political action. But, as shall be argued later, there may be considerable virtue in his ambivalent stance; and the idea that social bonds can be grafted onto economic transactions if conditions are favorable, remains to be explored in depth.

An ambivalence similar to that of Durkheim characterizes the work of his German contemporary, George Simmel. While no one has written more powerfully on the alienating properties of money, Simmel stressed in other writings the integrating functions of various conflicts in modern society. In this connection he gave high marks to competition as an institution that fosters empathy and the building of strong social ties, not of course among the competitors but between them and an important and often overlooked third party — the customer:

> The aim for which competition occurs within a society is presumably always the favor of one or more third persons. Each of the competing parties therefore tries to come as close to that third one as possible. Usually, the poisonous, divisive, destructive effects of com-

4. Compare this text with the exactly opposite seventeenth- and eighteenth-century statements on the constancy and predictability of interest which I reported in The Passions and the Interests (1977, pp. 48-55).

petition are stressed and, in exchange, it is merely pointed out that it improves economic welfare. But in addition, it has, after all, this immense sociating effect. Competition compels the wooer . . . to go out to the wooed, come close to him, establish ties with him, find his strengths and weaknesses and adjust to them . . .

Innumerable times [competition] achieves what usually only love can do: the divination of the innermost wishes of the other, even before he himself becomes aware of them. Antagonistic tension with his competitor sharpens the businessman's sensitivity to the tendencies of the public, even to the point of clairvoyance, in respect to future changes in the public's tastes, fashion, [and] interests. . . . Modern competition is described as the fight of all against all, but at the same time it is the fight *for* all . . .

. . . In short, [competition] is a web of a thousand sociological threads by means of conscious concentration on the will and feeling and thinking of fellowmen. . . . Once the narrow and naive solidarity of primitive social conditions yielded to decentralization . . . man's effort toward man, his adaptation to the other seems possible only at the price of competition, that is, of the simultaneous fight against a fellowman for a third one . . . [Conflict and the Web of Group affiliations, trans. 1955].

Simmel's thought here comes close to that of Durkheim, in that he also uncovers in the structure and institutions of capitalist society a functional equivalent for the simple bonds of custom and religion that (allegedly) held traditional society together. Elsewhere he shows that the advanced division of labor in modern society, and the importance of credit for the functioning of the economy rests on, and promotes, a high degree of truthfulness in social relations. With his effusiveness and vivid imagery, Simmel is perhaps more successful than the austere Durkheim in convincing the reader that some features of market society make for social integration rather than the opposite. . . .

So much for sociology. What about the economists? After all, here was a group of social scientists that had a tradition of either outspokenly criticizing the capitalist system or of defending and praising it. Should not the praisers, at least, have had an interest in keeping alive the thought that the multiple acts of buying and selling characteristic of advanced market societies forge all sorts of social ties of trust, friendliness, sociability, and thus help hold society together? In actual fact, this sort of reasoning is conspicuously absent from the professional economics literature. The reasons are several. First, economists, in their attempt to emulate, in rigor and quantitative precision, the natural sciences, had little use for the necessarily imprecise ("fuzzy") speculations about the effects of economic transactions on social cohesion. Second, those trained in the tradition of classical economics had only scorn for the concern of sociologists over the more disruptive and destructive aspects of capitalism. They saw in such phenomena a short-run cost necessary to achieve superior long-run gains and were not impelled by that sort of critique of capitalism to search for or invoke any compensating positive effects which the expansion of the market might have on social life and ties.

But the principal explanation is supplied by yet another point. Economists who wish the market well have been *unable*, or rather have tied their own hands and denied themselves the opportunity, to exploit the argument about the integrative effect of markets. This is so because the argument cannot be made for the ideal market with perfect competition. The economists' claims of allocative efficiency and all-round welfare maximization are strictly valid only for this market. Involving large numbers of price-taking anonymous buyers and sellers supplied with perfect information, such markets function without any prolonged human or social contact among or between the parties. Under perfect competition there is no room for bargaining, negotiation, remonstration or mutual adjustment and the various operators that contract together need not enter into recurrent or continuing relationships as a result of which they would get to know each other well. Clearly this latter tie-forming effect of markets can be important only when there are substantial departures or "lapses" from the ideal competitive model. But the fact is that such lapses are exceedingly frequent and important. In the face of this situation pro-market economists have either singled out ties among suppliers and, like Adam Smith, have castigated them as "conspiracies against the public"; or, much more frequently, they have belittled the various lapses in an attempt to present the reality of imperfect competition as coming close to the ideal. In this manner, they endeavored to endow the market system with *economic* legitimacy. But, by the same token, they sacrificed the *sociological* legitimacy that could rightfully have been claimed for the way, so unlike the perfect-competition model, most markets function in the real world.

Only in recent years have a number of approaches been developed by economists that do not look at departures from the competitive model as either sinful or negligible. To the contrary, with their stress on transaction costs, limited information and imperfect maximization, these approaches explain and justify the widespread existence of continuing relationships between buyers and sellers, the frequent establishment of hierarchies in preference to markets partly as a result of such "relational exchange," the use of "voice" rather than "exit" to correct mutual dissatisfaction, and similar phenomena that make for meaningful tie-forming interaction between parties to transactions. The stage could thus be set for a partial rehabilitation of the *doux-commerce* thesis. . . .

NOTES AND QUESTIONS ON THE MORAL
QUALITIES OF CAPITALISM

1. Compare the *doux-commerce* notion with Radin's view of "commodification." Might commodification have a human face after all? The historian Thomas L. Haskell has argued (though not without controversy) that the rise of eighteenth-century commerce played a major role in the growth of world-wide philanthropic interests by introducing Europeans to very distant peoples and fostering sympathy for them. See Capitalism and the Origins of the Humanitarian Sensibility (pt. 2), 90 Am. Hist. Rev. 547 (1985).

2. Hirschman's brief history places Radin's views on commodification into an historical context, and reveals that the idea of capitalism's moral corrosiveness has a venerable pedigree. By relativising the thesis, does this historical excursion undermine Radin's argument?

3. Is it true, as the thesis of capitalism's self-destructiveness supposes, that participants in commerce see themselves as relentlessly pursuing direct self-interest? Stewart MacAulay, An Empirical View of Contract, 1985 Wis. L. Rev. 467, argues against this position and stresses that business people in long-term relationships are often willing to give one another needed breaks. Could commerce survive where all participants pursued their own self-interest to the limit? Consider the network of mutual dependency and trust involved in, say, buying an airplane ticket and using it to travel. Why might commerce suffer in markets in which commercial actors can take advantage of one another or their customers? See Akerlof, The Market for 'Lemons,' discussed in the notes to Rose, Crystals and Mud, supra p.335. Why do not all markets have the failings of "markets for lemons"? Why instead (contrary to the self-destructiveness thesis) does trust enable many to operate reasonably well in markets? Consider the selection from Axelrod, The Evolution of Cooperation, supra p.275, stressing that cooperative strategies dominate repeat-play games. Does the view that capitalism is self-destructive implicitly rest on the view that commercial relationships are predominantly short-term, one-shot bargains? Is this a realistic view of commerce? Consider also the selection by Sunstein, supra p.88, stressing the importance of civil institutions in a market economy.

4. At the end of this selection, Hirschman advances the counter-intuitive suggestion that the market's contributions to social cohesion arise from market impediments — that is, transactions costs, information lapses, and the like. Why might such frictions add to

sociability? Might they even keep the whole market machine itself lurching along? See Hirschman's Exit, Voice, and Loyalty: Responses to Decline in Firms, Organizations, and States 43, 55, 83-84 (1970).

5. In Shifting Involvements (1982), Hirschman argues that social interests tend to fluctuate between public affairs and private business. In each case a given individual begins with enthusiasm, then suffers disappointments or boredom, and then shifts to the alternative pursuit, whereupon the cycle repeats itself. If this is an accurate picture, does it suggest that the interests in public affairs and private business are mutually supporting? Should we expect to see, over time, that societies that have the greatest degree of public involvement are those that also have the greatest degree of private initiative? What countries would be good test cases? The United States? Japan? The old Soviet Union (a negative example)? Do these examples bear out the thesis, or do they suggest that the thesis is unduly optimistic?

Chapter 8

Subdividing Property in Time: Of Estates, Landlords and Tenants

A.   Neighbors in Time: Of Future Interests

Economic Analysis of Law *

Richard A. Posner

§3.10   Divided Ownership — Estates in Land

More than one person may have a property right in the same thing. Our common-pool resource was an example; a more traditional one is the different "estates" in land. Property rights in real estate may be divided between a life tenant and a remainderman, between joint tenants (a special type of co-ownership), between a tenant and a landlord, and in other ways. Such divisions (whether concurrent but nonexclusive, or exclusive but time-limited) create incentives for inefficient use similar to those created by the separate ownership of the railroad right-of-way and the adjacent farmland, or the airport and the adjacent residential community. The problem has been discussed extensively in connection with the poverty of Ireland in the

*Source: pp. 71-76 (4th ed. 1992).

nineteenth century.[1] Most farmers were tenants; and it might seem that a tenant would have little incentive to improve the land because any improvement that outlasted the period of the lease would confer an uncompensated benefit on the landlord under the doctrine of fixtures (anything affixed to the property by the tenant becomes the property of the landlord on the expiration of the lease — can you think of an economic reason for this doctrine?). Yet this suggestion seems on its face to violate the Coase Theorem. Why didn't landlords agree in the leases to compensate tenants for improvements, for example by giving the tenant a percentage of the net revenues from the land after the lease expires?

There were and are landlord-tenant sharing agreements, but they don't always do the trick. Sharecropping is common where tenant farming is common. Suppose the landlord agrees to provide the land, seeds, and fertilizer, and the farmer agrees to provide the labor, with the revenues from the sale of the crops to be split 50-50. The results will not be optimal, as a simple example will show. Suppose that if the farmer worked an extra hour every week on improving the land he would increase the dollar value of the farm's output by $2 (net of any additional cost besides his time), and that the opportunity cost — or shadow price — of his time in foregone leisure is only $1.50. Efficiency requires that he work the extra hour, but he will not, because under his deal with the landlord he will receive only $1 for work that costs him $1.50. A more complicated sharing agreement will be required for optimal results, and the more complicated it is the more costly it will be to negotiate and enforce. And the example abstracts from the problem of long-term improvements, by assuming that the tenant will still be around when his improvements come to fruition. He may not be, if the lease is short-term. But this also means that the problem of the tenant's inadequate incentive to improve the land will be less serious the longer the lease; so it is perhaps not surprising that a system of tenant customary rights evolved in Ireland that made it difficult for the landlord to evict the tenant, either directly or indirectly (the latter by jacking up rents until the tenant was forced to abandon the lease). There would still have been a problem of tenant incentives (as we are about to see) if optimal tenant improvements were likely to outlast the tenants' lives; but major capital improvements, the kind most likely to outlast the current tenant, had to be made by the landlords rather than the tenants anyway, because the landlords had the capital. If anything, the problem was not that tenants lacked incentives

1. See, e.g., A.C. Pigou, The Economics of Welfare 174-175, 178-183 (4th ed. 1932); Barbara Lewis Solow, The Land Question and the Irish Economy, 1870-1903 (1971).

to improve the land but that customary tenant rights made it difficult for landlords to recoup the cost of their own improvements by charging higher rents, since the tenant might complain that the rate increase violated his customary rights.

All this suggests that there is no simple solution to the problem of divided ownership except single ownership, but it is not so simple either. If the tenant is demoted to being an employee of the landlord, the problem of divided ownership disappears but is replaced by a quite analogous problem of agent shirking due to the employee's not getting to keep every dollar in added output from working — just like the tenant. And the tenant may be unwilling to buy the farm from the landlord (although this would eliminate the problem of shirking), even if he were able to do so (what would determine whether or not he was able to do so?), because of the additional risk he would incur — illustrating the important point that leasing is a form of risk-spreading.[3]

So there is an important role for law to play in regulating divided ownership. We might expect the courts to interpret leases as if the parties' intent had been that the property would be managed by the lessee as if he were the owner; for that presumably *was* the parties' intent, if they are rational profit-maximizers. As a matter of fact, an interesting common law doctrine, the law of waste, emerged to reconcile the competing interests of life tenants and remaindermen. A life tenant will have an incentive to maximize not the value of the property, that is, the present value of the entire stream of future earnings obtainable from it, but only the present value of the earnings stream obtainable during his expected lifetime. He will therefore want to cut timber before it has attained its mature growth — even though the present value of the timber would be greater if the cutting of some or all of it were postponed — if the added value from waiting would enure to the remainderman. The law of waste forbade this. There might seem to be no need for a law of waste, because the life tenant and the remainderman would negotiate an optimal plan for exploiting the property. But since the tenant and remainderman have only each other to contract with, the situation is again one of bilateral monopoly, and transaction costs may be high. Also, the remaindermen may be children, who do not have the legal capacity to make binding contracts; they may even be unborn children. The problem of bilateral monopoly is less acute in the landlord-tenant case, because the terms of a lease are set before the landlord and tenant become locked into a relationship with each other. Very often a life tenancy is created by will, and the tes-

3. Steven N.S. Cheung, The Theory of Share Tenancy (1969).

tator (for whom estate planning may be a once-in-a-lifetime experience) may not be alert to the potential conflicts between life tenants and remaindermen.

The law of waste has largely been supplanted by a more efficient method of administering property that resembles unitization: the trust. By placing property in trust, the grantor can split the beneficial interest as many ways as he pleases without worrying about divided ownership. The trustee will manage the property as a unit, maximizing its value and allocating that value among the trust's beneficiaries in the proportions desired by the grantor.

The tenant does not always have a shorter time horizon than the owner of the fee simple (in the case of a landlord) or the remainderman (in the case of a life tenancy). Take the case of an oil lease that promises the lessor a fixed royalty per barrel. Unless he expects the rate of increase of the price of oil to exceed the interest rate, he will want the oil pumped as fast as possible, whether or not the field is unitized. That will mean drilling a lot of wells. But the lessee, who has to pay for those wells, will want to pump the oil more slowly so that he can economize on the number of them. He may even drill too few wells, since in deciding how much a new well is worth he will disregard the portion of the revenues that will go to the lessor as a royalty. Therefore, most oil and gas leases contain a "development" clause that requires the lessee to drill a reasonable number of wells — reasonable meaning cost-justified.

An interesting question has arisen in the interpretation of such clauses: whether the lessee, in figuring the costs of a new well, may include not only his drilling and other direct costs but also the reduced revenue from the old wells, since the new well will deplete the pool from which the old wells as well as the new draw. The economic answer, for which there is some judicial support, is yes, because that depletion is a genuine opportunity cost of the new well.

We have thus far been discussing vertical or temporal division of a property right. There is also horizontal division. The extreme example is the communal right, as in the pasture that is shared by a number of farmers. Communal rights differ only in degree from no rights, and thus are inefficient unless the costs of enforcing individual rights are disproportionate to the benefits.[7] Odd as it may sound, communal rights are frequently created by individuals, although in circumstances where the problem of inefficiency is minimized. For example, *A* may leave a plot of land to *B* and *C*, his

---

7. A good example is a supermarket's parking lot: It doesn't pay (outside of Manhattan!) to charge each customer for his use of a space, although doing so would enable the supermarket to have a slightly smaller lot.

children, in undivided joint ownership (a tenancy in common or a joint tenancy). B and C are formally in much the same position as the inhabitants of a society that does not recognize property rights. If B spends money to repair structures on the property, C will share equally in the value of the repairs, and vice versa. Although there are only two parties, there is the familiar bilateral-monopoly problem. But it is mitigated by the familial relationship; we expect more cooperation between persons united by bonds of affection. . . . In addition, the law credits the joint tenant with the value of any improvements he makes to the property up to the amount by which the improvements increase the property's value (why this qualification?). The law also, and wisely, allows any joint tenant to obtain a partition of the property into separate, individually owned parcels; this power eliminates every vestige of bilateral monopoly and communal rights.

Suppose adjacent owners of row houses, who share a party wall, are unable to agree on how to split the cost of replacing the wall, which is in imminent danger of collapse. One of the owners goes ahead and replaces it at his own expense and then sues the other for half the cost. There is a fair amount of judicial authority for allowing the suit, as a way around the bilateral-monopoly problem. . . .

The law's ingenuity is not limitless, and we end this section with a homely example of a case of divided ownership about which the law can do nothing: automobile rentals. As everyone who has ever rented a car well knows, people do not treat the cars they rent with as much care as the cars they own; they are rougher on them, reflecting the foreshortened time horizon of their use. But because the rental company cannot supervise or monitor that use, there is no way in which it can induce the renter to take the right amount of care of the car. Here, then, is a case where transaction costs are high despite fewness of parties and no problem of bilateral monopoly. The problem is that the cost of enforcing the transaction agreed on is prohibitive.

§3.11   Problems in the Transfer of Property Rights

In order to facilitate the transfer of resources from less to more valuable uses, the law should, in principle, make property rights freely transferable. The principle must be qualified, but before doing so we must notice how divided ownership makes transfer difficult in practice even if there is no formal limitation. If 50 different people are joint tenants of a piece of property, a sale of the property will require them to agree both on the price and on the division of the proceeds among them; there will be holdout problems. The elaborate kinship networks of primitive societies forestall the emergence of property rights in such societies. Efficiency requires that property rights be transferable, and if many people have a claim on each piece of property, transfers will be difficult to arrange.

The history of English land law is a history of efforts to make land more easily transferable and hence to make the market in land more efficient. Two doctrines will illustrate this point. The "Rule in Shelley's Case" provided that if a grantor gave a life estate to *A* with the remainder to *A's* heirs, *A* had a fee simple (i.e., full title); the heirs were cut out. If the remainder in *A's* heirs were recognized, it would be very difficult to transfer the property, because his heirs would not be ascertained until his death. The "Doctrine of Worthier Title" provided that if the grantor gave property to *A* for life, with the remainder to the grantor's heirs, the grantor — not his heirs — owned the remainder, and thus could sell it, as his heirs apparent might not be able to do, because of the uncertainty of their interest. For the grantor might have additional children, and they would be his heirs too.

The economic objection to these doctrines (besides their immense complexity, not hinted at in these descriptions) is that they imply that the grantor is not able to trade off the costs of reduced transferability against whatever benefits he derives from dividing ownership in the way the doctrines prevent. This assumption seems paternalistic and hence questionable from an efficiency standpoint. People know their interests better than courts do. But maybe the explanation is, as suggested earlier, that many of these grants are once-in-a-lifetime transactions for the grantor, and he may not have good information about the problems they create. . . .

A further point is that people who create excessively complex interests burden the courts as well as themselves and their grantees, so there is some externality that might warrant public intervention. This point explains the interesting common law presumption that a conveyance of land to a railroad or other right-of-way company (pipeline company, telephone company, etc.) is the conveyance of a right-of-way, that is, of an easement, terminable when the acquirer's use terminates, rather than the conveyance of a fee simple. Transaction costs are minimized by undivided ownership of a parcel of land, and undivided ownership is, in turn, facilitated by the automatic reuniting of divided land once the reason for the division has ceased. If the railroad is the owner of a multitude of skinny strips of land now usable only by the owner of the surrounding or adjacent land, then before that land can be put to its best use there must be expensive and time-consuming negotiation — that or the gradual extinction of the railroad's interest through the operation of the doctrine of adverse possession. It is cleaner to wipe out the railroad's interest upon its abandonment of railroad service.

NOTES AND QUESTIONS ON DIVIDED OWNERSHIP

1. Posner discusses a variety of co-ownership arrangements, including: (1) temporal divisions, between the owner of a present interest and the owner(s) of one or more future interests; (2) trusts, under which a trustee (the "legal owner") manages the trust assets as a fiduciary for the trust's beneficiaries (the "equitable owners"); (3) concurrent estates, under which two or more parties simultaneously share a resource, often (but not always) in equal shares; and (4) the shared regimes that result when an easement or other nonposessory interest is carved out of a fee simple in land.

In all these contexts there are rules of property law that deal with each co-owner's rights and duties against the other co-owner's. To employ Ayres & Gertner's distinction, supra p.313, should these rules be "immutable"? Or, should there be "defaults" that co-owners can contract around?

Does Posner provide persuasive reasons why judges developed the common-law doctrine of waste? Is this doctrine entirely superfluous in a world of default rules because the owner of the future interest can negotiate an express contract that deters opportunism by the owner of the present interest?

2. Posner regards a short-term lease as an arrangement fraught with incentive incompatibilities, at least compared to a trust. Yet short-term leases are far more common than trusts. Why might trusts give rise to greater transaction costs? (The next selection, on farm leases, may help provide an answer.)

3. Posner cites Steven N. S. Cheung's theory that farm sharecropping arrangements enable farmers to spread risks. Recall the sources supra p.170, Note 5, on the risk-spreading advantages of shared ownership. But why wouldn't a farmer prefer to work as the employee of a landowner, an arrangement that would entirely shift the risk of crop failures to the employer? Note Posner's comment about the problem of shirking, and see generally Oliver E. Williamson, The Economic Institutions of Capitalism 215-223 (1985); Keijiro

Otsuka et al., Land and Labor Contracts in Agrarian Economies, 10 J. Econ. Lit. 1965 (1992). Might it be instructive to view farm leases as landlords' instruments for suppressing subordinate classes? Cf. James C. Scott, Weapons of the Weak: Everyday Forms of Peasant Resistance (1985).

4. Is Posner overly eager to discern efficiencies in the common law? Examine his final paragraph, in which he argues that judges correctly construe ambiguous grants to right-of-way companies as easements, an interpretation that subjects these interests to the doctrine of abandonment. Could one just as persuasively argue that this interpretation is inefficient because the doctrine of abandonment engenders wasteful litigation and delays a railroad company's removal of obsolete tracks?

5. In Anglo-American law the basic estate in land is the fee simple. An owner in fee simple, although mortal himself, has ownership rights of infinite duration. Why should those presently alive have property interests that extend beyond their deaths? Note Blackstone's concern, supra p.44, that "endless disturbances" would ensue if a decedent's property were put up for grabs at death. Why wouldn't a rule that a decedent's property escheats to the state entirely allay Blackstone's concern? Compare Demsetz's statement, supra p.154, that one advantage of the fee simple is that it tends to induce an owner making land-use decisions to consider economic conditions that may exist after his death. Do you understand his reasoning? Find it persuasive? Would a society be wiser to dole out only usufructuary rights in land — ones that would terminate when the usufructuary owner died or abandoned the land? How would Posner answer this question?

Infinitely long private-property rights in land were honored in Mesopotamia and ancient Greece, and have evolved within societies on every continent. See Robert C. Ellickson, Property in Land, 102 Yale L.J. 1315, 1364-1371 (1993). Does this history prove the inherent efficiency of the fee simple? The political clout of large landowners?

A society that doles out property for infinite time periods must develop rules to govern inheritance. With remarkably few exceptions, such as Russia in 1918-1922, legal systems enable property owners to pass on property to kin. Do infinite terms of property ownership serve the interests of the young and unborn? With Demsetz's view, compare Mark L. Asher, Curtailing Inherited Wealth, 89 Mich. L. Rev. 69 (1990). Should a legal system identify particular kinfolk as successors as a matter of law, or instead entitle a decedent to designate successors by will? See James M. Buchanan, Rent Seeking, Noncompensated Transfers, and Laws of Succession, 26

J.L. & Econ. 71 (1983) (exploring the risk that testation may prompt the young to fawn for favorable testamentary treatment from the elderly).

The 'Back Forty' on a Handshake: Specific Assets, Reputation, and the Structure of Farmland Contracts *

Douglas W. Allen & Dean Lueck

> It is a common scene in U.S. agriculture: A landowner and a tenant talk for a few minutes over a cup of coffee, then shake hands to clinch a one-year deal to rent a farm or piece of land. No fuss, no bother, no paperwork.
>
> — *Jonathan Knutson,* Ag. Week *(December 11, 1989)*

1. Introduction

Many exchanges are governed by rather complicated contracts that explicitly denote dates, individuals, locations, prices, products, qualities, quantities, and contingencies for changing conditions. Transaction-cost economics has been quite successful in explaining the structure of these contracts. In particular, long-term contracts and vertical relationships have been shown to solve the contracting problems that arise in the presence of durable, transaction-specific assets. As the quote above suggests, Midwest farmers rely on farmland leases that are surprisingly simple. Contrary to focusing on why complex, long-term contracts exist, we ask the alternative and complementary question: Why do simple, short-term contracts arise when real-world contracting is costly?

In states like Nebraska and South Dakota agriculture is by far the dominant industry. On the nearly 100,000 farms in these two states, a typical farmer uses approximately 1,000 acres of farmland and $100,000 worth of farm equipment. The typical value of the land and buildings is between $300,000 and $400,000 per farm. Farmers annually sell an average of over $60,000 in annual crops such as barley, hay, oats, soybeans, and wheat. Like farmers everywhere, those in Nebraska and South Dakota do not always own all of their farmland and often lease land from other landowners. For instance, in

*Source: 8 J.L. Econ. & Org. 366-371, 375 (1992).

1982 only 59 percent of all U.S. farms were completely owner-operated, and only 35 percent of total farm acreage was cultivated by farmers that owned all their land (U.S. Department of Agriculture: Tables 536 and 537).

1.1 Contracts for Farmland

In stark contrast to the size and methods of modern farming, farmland contracts are simple and informal. Rarely are they lengthy, detailed documents, and in many cases they are not even written agreements. We use data from Nebraska and South Dakota and find that 57 percent of all contracts were oral. Those that are written tend to be simple one- or two-page documents that specify only the names of the farmer and the landowner, the dates for which the contract is binding, the location of the land, the terms of the lease in dollars or shares, and possibly conditions for contract renewal. . . . In a few cases, however, the contracts are more detailed and specify such responsibilities as paying land taxes, controlling noxious weeds, penalties for defaulting, renewal conditions, and the fraction of the land that must lie fallow.

Notably, farmland contracts tend not to stipulate in detail how the land will be farmed; rather, they require that the farmer use the land in a "thorough and farmer-like" or a "good and husband-like" manner. Farmland contracts are most often annual agreements subject to automatic renewal unless one party makes an early commitment not to renew. In our sample 65 percent of the contracts are annual. Sometimes the agreements are for several years, but rarely are they longer than five years. They are, however, typically renewed for extended periods, even up to 30 years. The markets that bring farmers and landowners together are as informal as the contracts themselves, with the most common consummation taking place on the front porch. . . .

2. Why Are Farmland Contracts So Simple?

Although farmland contracts are simple agreements, they must still be enforced. One way to enforce an agreement is for the contracting parties to stipulate and police numerous details. A second method is to specify little in an informal agreement and let market forces or the common law do the policing. Our contention is that for farmland contracts, reputations and law effectively enforce the agreements and render detailed, long-term contracts superfluous.

2.1 Specific Assets

Klein, Crawford, and Alchian and Williamson noted that contracting parties with transaction-specific assets put themselves at risk by using short-term contracts because each party could potentially extract the other's quasi-rents once the investments were made. For farmland contracts short-term leases are feasible because in general appropriable quasi-rents are absent.

Consider the assets involved in a farmland lease contract. Landowners bring just one asset to the exchange — land — and this asset is *not* specific to the exchange. There are numerous other farmers who could profitably use the land. Farmers bring several assets to the exchange, most of which are not specific to the farmland transaction. First, the farmer brings his human capital (farming skills), which are specific to the local "area" but are *not* specific to the contracted plot of land. The farmer could profitably farm other plots in the area with his present capital stock. Second, the farmer has his own land and buildings, but these can be sold and are *not* specific to a particular leased plot or leasing agreement. Third, the farmer has equipment such as tractors, cultivators, and combines. Some of these implements are quite specific to the area. For example, a potato picker has little use in western South Dakota where no potatoes are grown. But, like buildings, these machines are *not* specific to the plot in the lease contract.

In a Midwestern farmland contract only investments related to irrigation assets are potentially transaction-specific. Irrigation investments include pumps, underground pipes, wells, and other equipment that is fixed to the land as well as the farmer's skills in using a particular irrigation system on a specific plot of land. These investments are generally owned by the landowner and are not transaction-specific; but because farmers run the system, pay for daily maintenance, and often share in major repair costs, the possibility of contract hazards exists.

The crop investment is not subject to quasi-rent capture because all of the crops in this data set are annual small grains. If crops were long-term investments, such as orchards, contracts would be expected to be much longer.

2.2 Reputation and Repeated Transactions

It is well known that markets can "self-enforce" contracts. Punishment to cheaters, through lost future trade, encourages cooperation between the contract parties (Kreps). This reputation enforcement is most effective where information about cheating is good and a frequent and long-lived relationship is desired. For Midwestern farmland contracts these conditions are met. Farmers are a part of a small "community" of people who have known each other most of their lives. People would be quickly aware of anyone who cheated another and would avoid future dealings with that person. For both a landowner and a farmer there is a long-term interest in maintaining a relationship.[3]

Farmers and landowners develop reputations for honesty, fairness, producing high yields (with share contracts), and consistently demonstrating that they are good at what they do. In small farming communities reputations are well known, especially over time. As a result, over time landowners indirectly monitor farmers by observing the reported output and the quality of the soil.

The importance of repeated dealing and the minor role of transaction-specific assets influences the structure of farmland contracts. Farmer reputations act as a bond. In any growing season a farmer can reduce effort, exploit soil, or underreport the crop. However, over time an accurate assessment is made by the landowner and others in the area as to the farmer's actual behavior. Farmers that attempt to gain at the landowner's expense will find that others may refuse to deal with them in the future.

2.3   The Common Law

When reputations are absent, farmers rely on written agreements more often, but even these contracts remain simple. This simplicity is possible because of the presence of a well-developed body of common law. For example, the prevalence of "good husbandry" clauses point to the law as a contract enforcer, since violation of such a clause provides legal grounds to terminate the lease. The use of good husbandry clauses indicates that some farming practices are similar from plot to plot in the area and that some types of "bad" farming are identifiable, and thus need not be specified in the contract. In both Nebraska and South Dakota, farming is quite homogeneous within a "locale." In such cases the law can implicitly add detail to contracts that appear to be simple.

Although contract disputes rarely end in court, there have been many cases of farming disputes, especially during the first half of this century, that established the meaning of good husbandry. These cases have involved such issues as overgrazing, destruction of trees, permitting noxious weeds to grow, plowing meadowland, removing manure rather than spreading it, damage to buildings because of

---

3. In fact, the mean duration of the contracts in our sample is 11.5 years.

overloading storage areas with crops, and extracting minerals from the soil. By now these practices are routinely held by courts to constitute poor husbandry, thus violating the terms of the farmland lease and allowing for very informal contracts, even when they are in writing.

3. The Variation in Contract Structure

While it is true that farmland contracts are simple, they do vary: Some are oral rather than written, some are one-year rather than multiyear agreements. Given our explanation of the general simplicity of these contracts, we expect that oral contracts will be present when fewer specific assets are present and when farmers have better reputations. Likewise, annual contracts will be chosen over multiyear contracts in similar situations.

The data used to test the various enforcement cost hypotheses are taken from the 1986 Nebraska and South Dakota Land Leasing Survey (Johnson et al.). This survey collected data from farmers and landowners engaged in farmland leasing during the 1986 crop season. Each of the 3104 observations is a single contract between a farmer and a landowner, where each contract is an exchange of rights to a tract of land.

3.1   Oral or Written?

The Statute of Frauds requires that contracts that cannot be performed in one year must be written to be legally enforceable. For farmland contracts the Statute of Frauds implies that all multiyear contracts must be written contracts in order for them to be enforced in a court. If the court was a routine mechanism of enforcement, we would expect to see all multiyear contracts be written. Yet, our sample shows that only 53 percent of multiyear contracts are written, indicating the courts are not often used to enforce contracts. Instead, farmers and landowners prefer to make oral agreements independent of the contract length and rely on the market to enforce the agreements. . . .

4. Conclusion

Contract structure depends largely on the costs of enforcement. These costs vary from case to case and determine the form of contracts. For farmland leases in the American Midwest, contracts are short-term and lack all but the most rudimentary details. We have argued that this simplicity reflects the comparative advantage of enforcing these contracts through the market and the common law. The character of the farming economy — good information about reputations, desired long-term relationships, immobility of farmers and landowners, and few transaction-specific assets — lends itself to the pervasive use of what may seem to be rather naive contracts.

References

Klein, Benjamin, Robert Crawford, and Armen A. Alchian. 1978. Vertical Integration, Appropriable Rents, and the Competitive Contracting Process, 21 Journal of Law and Economics 297-326.

Kreps, David. 1990. Corporate Culture and Economic Theory, in J. Alt and K. Shepsle, eds., Perspectives on Positive Political Economy. Cambridge, England: Cambridge University Press.

Williamson, Oliver E. 1979. Transaction-Cost Economics: The Governance of Contractual Relations, 22 Journal of Law and Economics 233-261.

NOTES AND QUESTIONS ON FARM LEASES

1. Allen and Lueck (A & L) observe that farm leases are extremely common. How might rural landlords and tenants overcome the risks of waste and other shortsighted land uses that Posner thinks are associated with short-term leaseholds?

2. Why might the number of appellate cases involving the meaning of "good husbandry" have declined in Nebraska and South Dakota during the latter half of the twentieth century?

3. A & L report that 47 percent of the multiyear contracts in their sample were oral and therefore unenforceable in court. What does this statistic reveal about the relative importance, in this context, of informal social controls? Are multiyear commercial leases in a suburban shopping center just as likely to be oral? What about orchard leases in rural areas?

B.   Rental Housing Markets

Poor Tenants, Poor Landlords, Poor Policy*

Irving Welfeld

A "Saturday Night Live" routine, in which Eddie Murphy (playing a convicted murderer) recites a poem entitled "Kill My Landlord," tells us a great deal about the public image of American landlords. The owner of rental property operates in a hostile environment. Although his search for profits is no different from that of other providers of goods and services, the landlord is traditionally cast in a uniquely villainous light; he is the fat cat who takes unfair advantage of the little mice who rent from him. The metaphor is unfair, however; many landlords have as good a claim to victim status as their tenants.

The landlord plays an essential role in America's housing system. There is always a substantial number of people who choose not to own, or for whom ownership may not be a good idea. In the pre-condominium past (before 1961), when apartment living and renting were synonymous, the rental sector could count on the newly married, those who were single, and inveterate urbanites. Even today, rental housing is necessary for the highly mobile, the poor, and the financially insecure.

One would assume that the negative image of landlords derives from their rent-gouging practices, and from the high profitability of real-estate investment. But this assumption is not supported by the facts. Reviewing rent increases and the change in the value of rental property in the 1960s and 1970s, Anthony Downs concluded as follows:

> Residential rents did not increase as fast as consumer income, operating costs, or construction costs. . . . The best available estimate is that real rent levels fell about 8.4 percent from 1960 to 1980. . . . In 1980 rents would have had to be 77 percent higher than they actually were to support real market values equivalent to those in 1960. . . . Putting the conclusion another way, the real value of rental housing properties in the United States *sustainable from rents alone* appears to have fallen substantially since 1960 — perhaps by 50 percent or more. The enormous drop results from much faster increases in operating costs and rates than rents.

The phenomenon is not a new one. As Louis Winnick wrote in the 1950s,

*Source: Public Interest 110-117 (No. 92, Summer 1988).

there is little doubt that the present generation of investors as a group has lived through a long period of relatively poor earnings as owners of rental property. On the basis of historical records of operating experience, the free and clear return on residential real estate, related to original acquisition cost, was quite unfavorable from the end of the 1920s to the 1950s.

This suggests that the bad reputation of landlords has more to do with consumer psychology and the nature of the product and service sold than with the economics of rental housing. Roger Starr makes this argument in The End of Rental Housing (The Public Interest, Fall 1979):

> The major difference between landlords and other kinds of entrepreneurs is that the landlords are involved in a long, continuing relationship with their customers, one in which the customer pays over and over again for what he already has — i.e., access to an apartment that in the very nature of things is a little bit older and worse each month. . . . The tenant cannot truly understand why he should be asked to pay again for something the landlord already made. Renewing a lease on an apartment is not like buying a new suit or a steak. . . . Perhaps they cost more than the previous suit or steak — but they are new, and the purchaser is thrilled at the prospect of eating a fresh sirloin, or wearing a new suit for the first time. An economic relationship in which the supplier cannot increase his volume except by raising his unit prices, and the customer has no psychological satisfaction to show for each new expenditure of money, inevitably produces severe tension and government intercession. As society matures and takes the productive process for granted, the intercession inevitably favors the tenant.

The economics of rental property

If tenants misunderstand their landlords, economists are puzzled by them. For landlords have not acted like economic men. Operating costs rose and vacancy rates dropped in the late seventies; but landlords failed to raise rents, so as to maximize the return on their investment. How could they make a living, having ignored the economists' market models?

Landlords act as they do because for the most part they are small-scale operators. While there are few reliable national data on the subject, Anthony Downs hypothesizes that

> ownership is scattered among many small-scale landlords. My impression is based on the high percentage of rental housing containing fewer than five units [60 percent] . . . and [on conversations with] realtors and investors across the nation. . . . Small scale investors who manage their own property rarely take full account of the cost of their time. So they have lower management costs — both apparent and

real — than large scale operators who employ professional management and maintenance personnel.

This subjective impression is supported by a survey of owners in New York City, the area in which one would most expect to find large-scale ownership of property. Arthur D. Little, Inc. found that 60 percent of landlords own only one building. Of those who bought buildings in the last five years, 68 percent own only one building. In over 60 percent of the cases, the owners are making less than a quarter of their income from their rental investment. The majority of the owners had incomes between $10,000 and $40,000.

Small-time operators with only a few units must act much more conservatively than large-scale operators do, or theoretical economic man would. An owner with only a few units has a stronger incentive than a landlord with more units to avoid raising rents so fast that vacancies increase. The turnover of an apartment usually involves the extra cost of repainting and/or redecorating, and the cost of finding a new tenant. More important, a vacancy for a small-time landlord involves the loss of a substantial portion of the income generated by the building. As a result, writes Anthony Downs, "this situation, plus the high rate of normal turnover among renters [in 1980, 37 percent were living in their unit for less than a year] makes most small-scale landlords *turnover minimizers* rather than *rent maximizers.*"

The eighties have seen a major change in the availability of rental housing. In the third quarter of 1987, the vacancy rate was at its highest level in over two decades. Two million and nine hundred thousand year-round rental housing units were vacant — 8.1 percent of the national inventory. In cities, the rate was even higher (8.9 percent). Nevertheless, there are cries of a housing shortage all across the land.

The problems of the poor

An adequate housing supply can coexist with a housing shortage for families and individuals who cannot afford to pay the rent for the available housing. Housing does filter down — but if the landlord's rent roll does not equal his operating expenses, the housing will filter right out of the market.

There is no more graphic illustration of this problem than the *in rem* program in New York City that attempts to prevent the abandonment of properties in serious tax arrears by means of a rapid foreclosure procedure. As of 1984, the city owned 120,000 units. In spite of an ambitious effort to save these units by management and rehabilitation programs, auction sales with favorable financing, and sales of vacant buildings to community organizations at favorable prices (in some cases, involving transfer of ownership to urban homesteaders and tenants, there was no price at all), the city has been left with 74,000 units that are either vacant or so dilapidated that they are effectively lost from the inventory. And for every city-owned unit lost since 1970, two units in the private sector have been lost — amounting to a total loss of over 200,000 units.

At the same time, the city is the home of homeless people, like "Rachel and her children." Even if we add the "housing homeless" to the number of homeless people whose problems cannot be solved by housing alone — we are not now a saner society than we were a generation ago, despite the fact that the number of residents of public psychiatric institutions dropped from 559,000 in 1955 to 122,000 in 1981 — the total number of lost units is approximately four times larger than the number of homeless people.

When things get tough in the rental market in general, they get even tougher for the poor in particular. This is the conclusion of a memorandum from the Harvard-MIT Joint Center for Housing Studies:

> The changes in the rent burden distribution for the poorest households were particularly dramatic. . . . By 1983 the median rent burden for households in this income class had risen to 46 percent of income, and over one-quarter of the households . . . had a rent burden above three-quarters of income. . . . These results must be interpreted with great care. . . . These rent burdens are based on a household's cash income and therefore exclude income in kind, such as food stamps and Medicaid. Between 1974 and 1980, the in-kind benefits . . . increased significantly. As a result, the figures . . . overstate the increase in rent burden as a percent of total income. . . . One study estimates that including all such benefits reduces the median rent burden for the lowest one-fifth of the income distribution from 62 percent to 39 percent.

From the perspective of poor tenants the problem is excessive expenditures. From the perspective of the uneducated landlord (half of New York City's landlords never graduated from high school), the problem is insufficient revenues. The tenants with the highest rent burden are living in the lowest-priced units. In other words, the poor pay less, but doing so hurts them more (see Table I). This can be seen vividly in an area in which, contrary to popular assumption, the median rent is a bit lower than the national average — New York City. (In 1984 the average New York rent was $330; the national average was $331.49.)

New York City is burdened with an arcane and byzantine sys-

Table I.
Rents and Rent Burdens in New York City[a]

Area	Median Gross Rent (In dollars)	Median Renter Income (In dollars)	Rent Burden (In percentage)
South Bronx	263	6,874	47
Northwest Bronx	333	13,984	29
Northeast Bronx	310	12,421	30
North Brooklyn	274	8,968	37
Central Brooklyn	340	11,854	34
South Brooklyn	333	13,938	29
Northwest Manhattan	309	11,235	33
Northeast Manhattan	222	7,071	38
Upper Midtown	463	23,006	24
Lower Midtown	476	26,801	21
Lower Manhattan	291	12,784	27
Northwest Queens	347	15,468	27
Southern Queens	354	15,630	27
Northeast Queens	403	19,648	25
Richmond	373	15,761	29

[a]Source: Michael A. Stegman, Housing in New York: Study of a City, 1984, p. 23.

tem of rent control, rent stabilization, and regulation that is designed to alleviate the plight of the poor and lower-middle-income renter. In practice, however, the greatest benefits of the system are accorded to the rich and famous. As William Tucker writes:

> 135 Central Park West [is] a magnificent ocean-liner of a building with stunning museum-sized apartments that could easily command five to ten thousand on the open market. . . . [The] tenants are all rent regulated. Consequently [the] rent roll looks like this: Carly Simon pays $2208.75 for ten rooms overlooking Central Park; Mia Farrow pays $1870.31 for ten rooms overlooking Central Park; Whitney Ellsworth, publisher of the New York Review of Books, $1587.22 for ten rooms overlooking Central Park; . . . Jean Stein, heir of the MCA fortune, pays $1241.39 for ten rooms overlooking [the park]; James Levine, music director of the Metropolitan Opera, pays $1156.50 for six rooms overlooking the park. . . . Manocherian [the owner] says he

loses $100,000 a year on the building. He keeps it for sentimental reasons (he lives there himself), plus the ever-faint hope that one day one of his tenants' great-grandchildren may die without an heir and the rights to the apartment will revert to one of his own great-grandchildren, who may be able to rent the apartment at something like its market value.

Rent control does not benefit the poor, by contrast, for whom it is almost irrelevant. Given the low income of such a large sector — one quarter of all New York renters were paying at least 50 percent of their income for housing in 1984 — it would be almost impossible for landlords to squeeze out higher rents, even in the absence of rent control. As Michael Stegman, the leading authority on New York City housing, politely wrote in a report to the administrators of the New York City system: "The more serious challenge to maintaining a healthy rental market might result from limited incomes of households who must depend on the rental market to meet their housing needs, rather than from any unresponsiveness of rent regulations to the cost of providing decent housing."

Low-income landlords

The most ominous occurrence in the New York City rental market is the rise in operating and maintenance expenses as a percentage of rent. In an earlier report, Stegman pointed out that this ratio had risen from 55 percent in 1971 to 70 percent in 1981. The rise meant that the percentage of the rent dollar available to cover vacancy losses, pay debt service, and yield a profit had declined from 45 to 30 percent. Table II (which uses 1981 figures) illustrates the devastating effect of this decline on property values.

If we assume no profit, an 11 percent interest rate, and an amortization period of 15 years, $53 would support a $5,000 mortgage. If the potential buyer wanted 10 percent of the rent as profit (a reasonable amount), the resulting $27 for debt service would support a mortgage of about $2,500 a unit. Thus, while apartments along Central Park may be worth up to fifty times the annual rent as cooperatives or condominiums, a seller a few miles uptown who obtains a price *equalling* the annual rent is doing well.

The battered but unsung heroes of the fight to provide housing for the poor are the owners who have kept many of their buildings open despite these adverse economic conditions. They are not absentee landlords living on their suburban estates. Sixty percent of New York building owners own only one building, and 61 percent

Table II. Median Operating and Maintenance Expenses for New York City Landlords, 1981 (In dollars)[a]		
Rent (New York City Median)		265
Taxes, fees, and permits	49	
Labor	30	
Fuel and Utilities	66	
Contractor services	19	
Administration costs	11	
Other	11	
Total operating and maintenance expenses		186
Vacancy losses (assuming 10% vacancy)	26	
Total costs		212
Remaining income available for debt service and profit		53

[a]Source: Stegman, The Dynamics of Rental Housing in New York City, 1982.

of the owners of buildings with fewer than ten apartments live in their building.

These landlords are not wealthy. More than half of them were not born in the United States, and of owners who have bought within the last five years, over 35 percent are either black, Hispanic, or Asian. Thirty percent reported household incomes of under $20,000, and 9 percent incomes of less than $10,000. They did not buy their buildings because real estate provides a tax shelter. Although there are no statistics on the relation between the income of landlords and that of their tenants, people generally have landlords of their own social class.

What keeps these buildings going is quite often the "sweat" — as we saw above, there is very little equity — of the landlords. Thirty-nine percent of all New York City landlords collect the trash themselves (another 5 percent use unpaid relatives); 36 percent clean the public areas; 31.4 percent do minor plumbing repairs; 32 percent do minor electrical repairs; 23 percent repair leaky roofs; 87 percent collect the rent themselves; and 82 percent keep the books themselves. Almost half of the owners spend two to four days a week on the operations of their building, and only 16 percent receive any salary.

Yet in spite of these economies, only a third of the landlords were making money on a consistent basis, with the remainder either breaking even or losing money. Thirteen percent of the owners had to subsidize their buildings' operating expenses every month; and a further 16 percent had to inject cash during the heating season. Since these statistics cover all New York landlords, it is likely that the situation of landlords serving the poorest tenants is even worse. And even though many owners are also spending money on capital improvements, only 20 percent filed for rent increases — in no small part because of the amount of red tape confronting a landlord who asks for one.

The increase of improvements in the bottom end of the market is substantiated by Stegman's analysis: "Of all the units that have been counted as dilapidated at least once since 1978, only 2 percent were dilapidated at the time of all three Housing and Vacancy Surveys. . . . This suggests the chances a housing unit in serious disrepair will ever be improved are very good."

The conclusion to be drawn is that it is possible for landlords to make a modest profit on buildings that serve low-income tenants — if the debt service, taxes, and vacancies are low, and the owner is handy and has time on his hands. Nevertheless, the operation is marginal. All it takes is one major malfunction — a boiler that needs repair, or a roof on which there is no room for new patches — to bring the whole financial structure down, and to put the landlord and his tenants on the street. . . .

NOTES AND QUESTIONS
ON RESIDENTIAL LANDLORDS

1. Many of Welfeld's statistics indicate the *percentage of landlords* possessing some characteristic; for example, "more than half [of landlords] were not born in the United States." Do these statistics necessarily reveal the *percentage of tenants* who have landlords who possess a certain characteristic? Suppose that foreign-born landlords on average own only a few units, while native-born landlords on average own many.

2. Welfeld quotes Anthony Downs's statement that most small-scale landlords are "*turnover minimizers* rather than *rent maximizers*." Downs's assertion is consistent with a number of studies finding that landlords charge long-resident tenants lower rents than they charge new tenants. For a review of the conflicting evidence on the size and existence of this discount, see J. Luis Guasch & Robert C. Marshall, A Theoretical and Empirical Analysis of the Length of Residency Discount in the Rental Housing Market, 22 J. Urb. Econ. 291 (1987). Would one expect a landlord to strive to

minimize the turnover of tenants who failed to pay rent, or committed waste?

3. Median monthly housing rents, measured in 1989 dollars, declined in the United States from $326 in 1967 to $304 in 1980, but then rose to $354 in 1992. The increases during the 1980-1992 period varied significantly by region, with the sharpest jumps in the Northeast (27 percent) and West (23 percent), and the lowest in the South (6 percent) and Midwest (7 percent). See Joint Center for Housing Studies of Harvard University, The State of the Nation's Housing — 1993, Tables A-1 and A-2. Do these statistics vitiate Welfeld's thesis that rental housing is not highly profitable? Is it plausible that legal constraints on the supply of housing are significantly responsible for the greater rent increases in the Northeast and West? See the selection by William Fischel on growth controls, infra p.457.

4. Does Welfeld adequately explore how homelessness could have emerged as a national political issue at a time when the national vacancy rate for rental housing was at its highest levels in decades? Of the many works on homelessness and its causes, two standouts are Christopher Jencks, The Homeless (1994) and Peter H. Rossi, Down and Out in America (1989).

5. George Sternlieb's classic, The Tenement Landlord (1966), depicts slum landlords in Newark, N.J. For a pro-landlord perspective on housing issues, see William Tucker, The Excluded Americans: Homelessness and Housing Policy (1990). For a pro-tenant view, see, for example, Barbara Bezdek, Silence in the Court: Participation and Subordination of Poor Tenants' Voices in Legal Process, 20 Hofstra L. Rev. 533 (1992).

Private Production: Has the Rising Tide Lifted All Boats? *

John C. Weicher

Housing Quality: Lifting the Boats

The United States has enjoyed a steady improvement in the quality of housing throughout the postwar period. By every available measure, the nation has far fewer inadequate housing units than at any previous time and is close to achieving the goal of a "decent home" originally conceived in the late 1940s. . . .

*Source: Housing America's Poor 45-61 (Peter Salins ed. 1987).

Table 3.1.
Measures of Substandard Housing, 1940-1980
(percentage of all occupied housing)

Problem	1940	1950	1960	1970	1980
Substandard	48.6	35.4	16.0	8.4	N.a.
Lacking complete plumbing	44.6	34.0	14.7	5.5	2.2
Dilapidated	18.1[a]	9.1	4.6	3.7	N.a.
Crowding (more than 1.0 persons per room)	20.2	15.8	11.5	8.8	4.2
Severe crowding (more than 1.5 persons per room)	9.0	6.2	3.8	2.0	1.0

Sources: Data are from the following U.S. Bureau of the Census sources: Sixteenth Census of the United States: 1940, Housing, vol. 2, pt. 1; 1950 Census of Housing, vol. 1, pt. 1; 1960 Census of Housing, vol. 2, pt. 1; 1970 Census of Housing: Components of Inventory Change, HD(4)-1; Annual Housing Survey: 1980, United States and Regions, pt. A.
N.a. = not available.
[a]"Needing major repairs" in 1940. . . .

Quality Changes for Special Groups

All these data are aggregate figures. Improvements also have occurred in the housing of various groups that have frequently received special attention in housing policy, although there are numerous gaps in the data available. The best data are presented in Table 3.5 for five major population groups: blacks, Hispanics, residents of rural areas, and two measures of poverty — the bottom quarter of the income distribution and households with real incomes of $10,000 or less in 1980 dollars. The table includes only the two traditional criteria for which there are data in 1980: units lacking complete plumbing and crowding (units with more than one person per room). For the former, disaggregated data are available for blacks and rural residents from 1940 but for income groups only from 1950; for crowding, there are not full data for ethnic groups and income classes until 1960. But the data that are available confirm the pattern of improvement for these groups: from 1940 to 1970, these groups experienced a reduction in the incidence of dilapidated and substandard housing.

Reported changes in some of the most serious defects reported in the Annual Housing Survey further indicate physical improve-

Table 3.5.
Substandard Housing for Special Groups, 1940–1980
(percentage of occupied units)

Panel A: Lacking Complete Plumbing					
Group	1940	1950	1960	1970	1980
Blacks[a]	79.6	70.9	41.9	16.3	6.1
Hispanics	N.a.	N.a.	N.a.	6.6	2.4
Rural residents	74.8	61.6	31.5	13.8	4.8
Lowest quarter of income distribution	N.a.	60.1	33.9[b]	7.9	5.0
Real income below $10,000 in 1980 dollars	N.a.	51.6	30.0[c]	13.0	5.0

Panel B: Crowding			
Group	1960	1970	1980
Blacks[a]	28.3	19.2	9.1
Hispanics	N.a.	25.7	19.2
Rural residents	20.6	9.9	4.7
Lowest quarter of income distribution	12.1	7.1	4.3
Real income below $10,000 in 1980 dollars	12.7	8.5	4.3

Sources: Same as Table 3.1.
N.a. = not available.
[a] Nonwhites in 1940 and 1950.
[b] Estimated; correct percentage lies between 31.2 and 35.2.
[c] Estimated; correct percentage lies between 27.4 and 31.1.

ment in housing for these groups. These figures, published annually since 1973 for blacks and Hispanics but only since 1978 for income classes, are reported in Table [3.6] for the two ethnic groups. In seven of the eight measures, the incidence of a defect declined between 1973 and 1980; the exception, for blacks and Hispanics, is the presence of rats or mice.

The incompleteness of the data for these and other groups do not invalidate the pattern of improvement. Housing for these major groups remains worse than for the nation as a whole. The reason for the higher incidence of housing inadequacy may be that these groups, like many other groups of interest in housing policy, are

Table 3.6.
Incidence of Housing Defects, Black and Hispanic Households,
1973 and 1983 (percentages)

| | Blacks | | Hispanics | |
Defect	1973	1983	1973	1983
Shared or no bathroom	11.0	5.3	5.0	2.6
Shared or no kitchen	7.9	2.8	2.5	1.5
Presence of rats or mice	26.0	26.6	19.9	19.3
Exposed wiring	6.2	4.0	4.7	4.1
Lacking working out- lets in some rooms	12.6	5.8	6.4	4.3
Leaky roof	15.6	12.2	9.9	10.7
Interior wall or ceiling cracks	16.0	15.3	13.0	11.5
Holes in floors	7.2	6.3	4.4	4.3

Source: Annual Housing Survey, Part B, 1973 and 1983.

disproportionately poor. But the incidence of inadequacy is declining rapidly, indicating that housing quality is improving for the disadvantaged in general.

Explaining the Improvement: What Is Lifting the Boats?

There are four common explanations for the postwar improvement in housing quality: rising real incomes for American families including the poor; a falling relative price for housing; a high rate of new private housing production, predominantly for upper-income households, which ultimately results in better housing available to the poor ("filtering"); and government programs to clear slums and subsidize new housing production specifically for the poor.

All of these phenomena have occurred during the postwar period, concurrently with the downward trend in substandard housing (see Table 3.7). It is clear from Table 3.7 that subsidized production programs by themselves were not directly responsible for all or even most of the improvement that occurred. At best, they may have contributed to a looser housing market, reducing the demand for lower-quality housing, thereby making it possible for the poor to afford better housing.

Table 3.7
Trends in Income, Housing Costs, and Construction, 1950-1980

	1950s	1960s	1970s
Median real income			
(percentage change over decade):			
Families	+37.5	+33.9	+ 0.8
Unrelated males	+30.2	+39.4	+13.5
Unrelated females	+31.6	+37.3	+26.9
Real housing costs			
(percentage change over decade):			
Rent (CPI)	+ 5.9	− 8.4	− 18.0
Homeownership (CPI)[a]	+ 3.9[b]	+13.6	+15.1
Homeownership			
(Hendershott and Shilling)	+15.4[c]	− 27.1	− 22.6
New construction			
(millions of units):			
Total units	16.24	16.48	20.52
Total units/net household form	1.59	1.58	1.23
Private units	15.96	15.99	19.45
Subsidized new low-income units	0.29	0.49	1.07
Subsidized existing units	0	0.10	0.77

Sources: U.S. Bureau of the Census, Statistical Abstract of the United States, various editions, for income, CPI housing costs, total new construction, and household formation; Patric H. Hendershott and James D. Shilling, "The Economics of Tenure Choice, 1955-1979," in C. F. Sirmans, ed., Research in Real Estate, vol. 1 (Greenwich, Conn.: JAI Press, 1982), for Hendershott and Shilling measure of homeownership cost; U.S. Department of Housing and Urban Development, HUD Statistical Yearbook, various years, for subsidized units.

[a] The sharp rise in the CPI homeownership index after 1960 is now generally recognized to misrepresent the situation confronting homebuyers: When inflation and the tax treatment of owner-occupied housing are considered, ownership became an increasingly profitable investment after 1965. These factors are omitted in the CPI. The measure developed by Hendershott and Shilling is one of several recent efforts to construct a more appropriate cost index; it is used here because it is available for the longest period.

[b] Covers 1953-1960 period only.

[c] Covers 1955-1960 period only.

The Concept of Filtering

This chapter is concerned with how the housing quality and economic well-being of the poor may be affected by housing policy and changes in the housing market. Therefore, the relevant question is, does the price of the modest but decent housing fall when new construction occurs? If it does, then poor people are better off in a strict economic sense; their housing costs less, and they can buy better housing, more of other goods and services, or both.

The process by which new housing production for the well-to-do results in improvement in housing quality for the poor has been called "filtering." As new housing is built, some families move into it and leave their old housing vacant. The demand for the type of housing they formerly occupied decreases, reducing its price and permitting families with somewhat lower incomes to buy or rent it. In turn, these families move out of housing that is somewhat lower in quality, reducing the demand for that type of housing and enabling families of still lower income to move in. At the bottom of the quality distribution, some households move from substandard to standard housing, and some are able to move out of the worst housing, which then drops out of the stock.

Not all new construction expedites the filtering process. Filtering occurs if there is a reduction in construction costs (because of technological progress or reduced regulation) or if there is an increase in income among the well-to-do. But units built simply to meet growth in a locality do not necessarily make the market looser; there must be construction in excess of net household formation. Also, government subsidy of the price or interest rate is not likely to cause filtering unless the subsidy induces construction that would not otherwise have occurred, using resources that would have been unemployed. This might occur during a recession. But if the resources would have been used in other economic activity, the subsidy is basically an income transfer to the new home buyers (or new apartment renters) from the rest of society, including the families who would move up. Their incomes are lower, so even if the price of better housing is lower, they may not be able to take advantage of it.

It is important to distinguish the filtering concept from general economic growth. Filtering is hypothesized to occur when the incomes of the rich increase, even if the incomes of the poor do not. Economic growth, particularly in this country, results in higher incomes throughout the population. The notion of the "rising tide" usually refers to economic growth in general; an increase in income for the rich alone is more akin to a locomotive pulling the economy. In fact, both may have been occurring recently. During the postwar period, the income distribution seems to have become slightly more equal, then after 1967 slightly more unequal, but the changes are small. Throughout the period, the poor have increasingly lived in better housing, whether or not filtering has been happening.

It is also important to identify other phenomena that are distinct from the filtering process. First is the process whereby a series of individual households replace each other in a sequence of housing moves. Several studies have identified and interviewed in sequence the specific households that moved, starting with the buyers of new houses, to see whether their housing improved. There is a "chain of moves," continuing until the chain ends, when the last family moves to its new home. The best known of these studies is by John Lansing, Charles Clifton, and James C. Morgan, written in 1969.

Second is the process whereby individual housing units deteriorate over time. Vintage models of the housing stock, such as Richard F. Muth's 1973 study, incorporate this basic assumption and trace out its implications. There is also a small but growing body of literature on housing maintenance. . . .

The Economic Argument

There has been some controversy among economists as to whether the rising tide can lift all boats in the long run. This theory was generally accepted during the 1950s, rejected in the 1960s, and resurrected in the mid-1970s. . . .

Empirical Evidence

There have been very few empirical studies of the rising tide hypothesis and no time-series analysis; the data simply do not exist. The research that has been done is cross-sectional; it usually compares either differences in the incidence of substandard housing across cities or metropolitan areas at a particular date or differential changes among cities over a period.

William Grigsby produced the first and for a long time virtually the only empirical study in 1963. He found that rents and house prices increased least during the 1950s in those metropolitan areas with the most new construction. His study was limited to nine areas, however, and he was unable to adjust for quality changes. In the early 1970s, Frank deLeeuw began to develop a housing market model to simulate various housing policy options, using census data for four metropolitan areas as prototypical markets. This model demonstrates that new private construction results in a reduction in the price and quantity of low-quality housing over a decade. More recently, Thomas G. Thibodeau and I have analyzed the Annual Housing Survey data for sixty large metropolitan areas during the early 1970s. We find a very strong negative relationship between private construction during a five-year period and substandard housing at the end of the period and a weaker but still negative effect from units built five to fifteen years earlier. The short-run impact is about one fewer substandard unit at the end of the period for every three to four built during the period. The only contrary evidence is a recent paper by Donald F. Vitaliano, who found no relationship between new private construction and the incidence of low-quality housing five to fifteen years earlier. His analysis is based on a sample of New York State communities of various sizes, rather than large metropolitan areas. There have been no other empirical investigations of the relationship between private new housing construction and the incidence of substandard housing. . . .

Subsidized Production and Quality Improvement: The "Diverted Flow"

Discussions about housing policy often contrast the filtering hypothesis with subsidized production programs such as public housing. The usual assumption is that subsidized production benefits the poor; the burden of proof thus falls on the advocates of filtering to show that new private construction also benefits the poor. In fact, when the same standards are applied to both policies, it is subsidized production that appears to be clearly inferior.

Conventional public housing, the oldest and simplest subsidized production program, has received the most attention. Analysts agree on one fundamental point — households that move directly into public housing clearly benefit. These families are removed from the private housing market and placed in better housing than they previously occupied.

Analysts have reached diverse conclusions about the effects on low-income households that are not assisted and on the housing market generally. Olsen, for example, concludes that all low-income households not assisted by the program are unaffected; they have the same incomes and face the same price for housing of a given quality as they did before the program was established. Ultimately, as many units drop from the private housing stock as there are households occupying public housing. James Sweeney, however, concludes that public housing benefits all low-income households because demand for private low-quality units declines and the rents of these units therefore fall as well; the number of households occupying the lowest quality of housing also falls. But James C. Ohls gets the opposite result. His simulation model indicates that the quality of housing deteriorates on balance for low-income households that are not assisted. Ohls does not attempt to explain his result. It is possible that public housing construction causes a decrease in private construction at the low-cost end of the housing market, leading in the long run to a reduction in the private stock and a fall in its quality. Thus the various studies allow one to conclude that the total reduction in low-quality housing (the marketwide effect) may be greater, the same as, or less than the number of new public housing units.

According to most of these studies, the effects on households other than those directly assisted occur as a result of relative price changes for different qualities of housing. Thus in this important respect, subsidized production, if effective, works to improve housing by the same filtering process as private construction.

Empirical Evidence

Whereas theoretical studies are ambivalent, empirical studies of the relationship between subsidized housing and quality in the private stock generally support the view that subsidized production has an insignificant or negative impact on the incidence of substandard housing. Studies by Davis, Eastman, and Hua and by Hirsch and Law conclude that subsidized production resulted in an improvement in housing quality only when substandard housing was defined differently at the beginning and end of the study period. When the definition was consistent over time, the subsidized production was unrelated to the incidence of low-quality housing.

My own work with Thomas G. Thibodeau (forthcoming), the most extensive study undertaken to date, found an insignificant relationship most of the time, regardless of the definition of inadequacy and using a variety of data sources on subsidized production. Disaggregating by program type and by year of construction did not improve the results. Moreover, even the most generous estimates of the benefits of subsidized production demonstrate less than a unit-for-unit reduction in substandard housing.

These results are unexpected; they fly in the face of economic theory and conventional wisdom — perhaps even of common sense. If subsidized housing helps poor people directly, it is hard to believe that its side effects can be so perverse as to negate its direct benefits and leave the poor as a whole no better off.

An important partial explanation for this apparent contradiction is that public housing occupancy is not restricted to those who have previously lived in substandard housing. Data on federal government programs show that fewer than half of new residents in assisted housing during the late 1960s and early 1970s moved on from substandard housing. Moreover, the program definition of "substandard" is not the same as criteria used in policy analyses but is an elastic, rather vague notion, based on the perceptions of the tenant and the staff of the local housing authority. Thus public housing in the real world may well have different effects from the abstract concept used in most housing market models.

A more general explanation is that subsidized housing production is in large part a substitute for private production that would probably have occurred without the program. The two most detailed studies, by Michael Murray and Craig Swan, conclude that most public housing has simply replaced private new construction in the long run, although the substitution effect takes a few years. If this is true, then one might describe public housing as a "diverted flow," in contrast to the "rising tide" of private production. . . .

Conclusions and Policy Implications

It appears that there is a rising tide, or filtering process, by which new housing built for the well-to-do ultimately results in better housing for the poor. By academic standards, the theoretical and the empirical evidence is not as conclusive as one might wish. Most recent theoretical analyses support the rising tide theory, but the most elegant ones do not definitely establish the proposition, and there is some disagreement. The preponderance of the empirical evidence, however, supports the theory, although there have not been many studies. . . .

NOTES AND QUESTIONS ON HOUSING POLICY

1. Weicher's Table 3.1 portrays steady improvements in housing quality through 1980. Statistics from the 1990 census, available most handily in the annual Statistical Abstract of the United States, suggest a mixed picture for the 1980s. Nationally the percentage of oc-

cupied dwellings lacking complete plumbing was halved from 2.2 percent in 1980 to 1.1 percent in 1990, but the incidence of crowding (more than 1.0 persons per room) rose from 4.2 percent to 4.9 percent during the same period. In 1990, 11.4 percent of occupied units were crowded in California, a state that during the 1980s experienced both sky-high housing prices and a large influx of immigrants.

2. According to "filtering" theory, why does construction of suburban housing for relatively wealthy households help low-income families living in central cities? How plausible is Weicher's paradoxical thesis that poor households as a whole benefit more from new housing built for the well-to-do than they benefit from the production of subsidized housing?

3. Why should the federal government (or a state government) provide low-income households with in-kind housing assistance, as opposed to unrestricted cash aid? For discussion, see Edwin Mills & Bruce Hamilton, Urban Economics 246-248 (4th ed. 1989). If provided at all, should housing subsidies take the form of transportable vouchers granted to households (the Section 8 program), or project subsidies that reduce rents in specific buildings (traditional public housing)? The authors of a leading work on housing economics come down emphatically on the side of vouchers because "Demand-side approaches directly attack the root of the problem in most markets — the inability of some households to afford decent-quality housing at current rents for such." Jerome Rothenberg et al., The Maze of Urban Housing Markets 349-355 (1991). For additional views, some of them more sympathetic to project subsidies, see Building Foundations: Housing and Federal Policy (Denise Di-Pasquale & Langley C. Keyes eds. 1990); Critical Perspectives on Housing (Rachel G. Bratt, Chester Hartman & Ann Meyerson eds. 1986).

4. Many observers assert that the central shelter problem in the United States is not the *condition* of housing, but rather its *affordability*. See, for example, Curtis Berger, Beyond Homelessness: An Entitlement to Shelter, 45 U. Miami L. Rev. 315, 317-324 (1990-1991). But cf. Robert C. Ellickson, The Untenable Case for an Unconditional Right to Housing, 15 Harv. J.L. & Pub. Pol'y. 17, 28-30 (1992). Drawing on Christopher Jencks & Kathryn Edin, The Real Welfare Problem, Am. Prospect, Spring 1990, at 31, Ellickson asserts that many widely cited statistics about poor tenants' rent/income ratios exaggerate the affordability problem because the actual income of welfare families may average on the order of three times what the Census Bureau reports.

C.   Minimum Housing Standards

Economic Analysis of Law *

Richard A. Posner

§16.6   Wealth Redistribution by Liability Rules:
The Case of Housing Code Enforcement

Housing is a traditional service that the government assists the poor to obtain. Various methods of assistance are used. One is to hire contractors to build apartment houses for the government to own and operate, renting apartments to the poor at zero or nominal rentals. Another is to give poor people money that they are allowed to spend only for housing. This method of subsidy has the attractive feature, to an economist, that it preserves a private market in housing — it just gives the poor more effective demand for the housing supplied in that market. It is true that in the short run the effect may simply be to force up rental rates, and hence to make other renters poorer, and landlords richer, as a result of the subsidy. That is the standard short-run response to a surge in demand, reflecting the fact that productive capacity is by definition fixed in the short run. . . . But in the long run the stock of housing will rise and the price will fall back toward (all the way toward?) its level before the subsidy. And public housing has even worse short-run effects than these. In the short run — before the housing is actually built and rented — the poor obtain no benefit from public housing at all. A system of rent supplements or housing vouchers not only is more flexible but works more quickly to help the intended beneficiaries.

Both public housing and rent supplements involve the taxing and spending branches of government rather than the courts. But there is a method of (purportedly) helping the poor to meet their housing needs that centrally involves the courts: the enforcement of housing codes. These codes specify minimum standards of housing — although whether in order to ensure a decent minimum level of safety and sanitation or to subsidize the building trades is a matter of debate. Legal scholarship has been imaginative in suggesting devices by which the violators of housing codes could be subjected to sanctions that would greatly reduce the incidence of violation. To deal with the problem of substandard housing by legal sanction has

---

*Source: pp. 470-474 (4th ed. 1992).

Figure 16.3

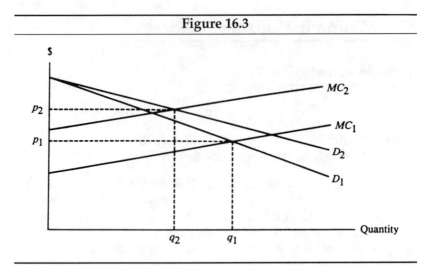

the additional attraction of enabling, or seeming to enable, a principal manifestation of poverty to be eliminated without any public expenditure.

The effects of housing code enforcement are depicted in Figure 16.3. D_1 is the market demand curve for low-income housing before enforcement. It slopes downward because not all tenants would leave if rentals rose as a result of an increase in the landlords' marginal costs. MC_1 is the landlords' pre-enforcement marginal cost curve and is positively sloped to reflect the fact that the creation of low-income rental housing involves the use of some specialized resources — in particular, land — that would be worth less in any other use.

Enforcing the housing code has two main effects on the market depicted in Figure 16.3.[2] By improving the quality of the housing units it increases the demand for them. And by increasing the landlords' maintenance costs, which are marginal costs because they vary with the number of housing units provided, it shifts the marginal cost curve upward. The shift shown in Figure 16.3 is large relative to the shift in the demand curve, on the plausible assumption that if quantity demanded were highly responsive to an increase in the quality of the housing provided, the landlords would upgrade

2. A third effect is a reduction in the rent of land received by the landlords (assuming they are the owners of the land). The irony here is that these "rentiers" include a number of almost-poor people for whom ownership of slum property represents the first stage in the escape from poverty.

quality voluntarily and there would be no need to enforce a housing code. Both demand and supply in Figure 16.3 are depicted as being quite elastic, on the (again plausible) assumptions that slum dwellers lack the resources to pay substantially higher rentals and that slum rentals are already so depressed in relation to costs that a further reduction in those rentals would cause many landlords to withdraw from the low-income housing market (for example, by abandoning their property to the city).

Given these assumptions, housing code enforcement leads to a substantial reduction in the supply of low-income housing (from q_1 to q_2) coupled with a substantial rise in the price of the remaining supply (from p_1 to p_2). The quantity effect is actually understated (though by the same token the price effect is overstated) in Figure 16.3: Some of the higher-quality supply brought forth by housing code enforcement may be rented to the nonpoor.[3] These effects could be offset by rent supplements, but that would deprive the program of its politically attractive quality of entailing no public expenditures.[4]

Admittedly, the magnitude of the effects shown in Figure 16.3 depends on the (arbitrary) location of the curves. It has even been suggested that demand might be perfectly elastic in the relevant region (implying no price effect of housing code enforcement[5]) because the slightest increase would cause many tenants to double up.[6] But since doubling up is costly (it involves forgoing the value of the greater space and privacy of single family occupancy), tenants would surely be willing to pay something to avoid being forced to double up, the something being a somewhat higher rental. This implies a less than perfectly elastic demand. Empirical evidence suggests that Figure 16.3 provides a closer approximation to the actual conditions of the slum housing market than a model which assumes perfect elasticity of demand.

3. Might a covert purpose of housing codes be to increase the supply of middle income housing at the expense of the poor? Cf. George J. Stigler, Director's Law of Public Income Redistribution, 13 J. Law & Econ. 1 (1970).

4. What would be the economic differences between coupling housing code enforcement with rent supplements and a program of rent supplements without code enforcement?

5. There would still be a quantity effect: show this graphically.

6. Bruce Ackerman, Regulating Slum Housing Markets on Behalf of the Poor: Of Housing Codes, Housing Subsidies and Income Redistribution Policy, 80 Yale L.J. 1093 (1971). . . .

One court has suggested that landlords might be forbidden, on a theory of retaliatory eviction, to abandon buildings as an alternative to code compliance if they were "able" to comply. Robinson v. Diamond Housing Corp., 463 F.2d 853, 869 (D.C. Cir. 1972). Would such a prohibition increase or decrease the long-run supply of housing to the poor?

Another suggestion is that the enforcement of a housing code would increase the supply of housing to the poor if enforcers focused their efforts on buildings that landlords were "milking."[8] Milking refers to the practice of maintaining a building at a lower standard than would be appropriate if the landlord intended to keep the building in operation indefinitely. He might have figured for example that because of a changing neighborhood or rising fuel costs he would probably have to abandon the building in five years willy-nilly — by that time his variable costs will exceed his rental income. It may make sense for him, once he has made this calculation, to reduce his expenditures on maintenance at once, since any long-term effects of those expenditures in preserving the building would be of little or no value to him. . . . By reducing those expenditures, he will reduce the quality of the housing, and his rental income will fall, but maybe by less than his expenditures on maintenance fall. An incidental effect may be that he abandons the building even sooner (though this will end his income stream sooner), since those expenditures would have kept the building going a little longer. If the enforcement of the local housing code prevents him from economizing in this manner, maybe he will delay abandonment, since the expenditures he is forced to make may well have some, as it were inadvertent, effect in preserving the building.

All this is terribly "iffy." Even though milking is, doubtless, sometimes rational in the real estate market when all costs and benefits are taken into account, attempting to counteract it through housing code enforcement is as likely to accelerate as to delay abandonment. The costs of compliance with the code are variable costs, which means that, as a first approximation at least, declining rental income and rising variable costs will intersect sooner, leading to earlier abandonment. It is doubtful that a court or legislature could identify those buildings where enforcement of the housing code would delay abandonment through its effect in counteracting milking rather than accelerate it through its effect in making the continued ownership of the building more expensive.

A number of cities have enacted ordinances designed to protect tenants by giving them more procedural rights in the event the landlord tries to evict them, by entitling tenants to withhold rent if landlords fail to make repairs required by the lease, by requiring landlords to pay interest on security deposits, and so forth. The effects are much like those of housing code enforcement: They raise landlords' costs and therefore increase rentals and reduce the

8. Duncan Kennedy, The Effect of the Warranty of Habitability on Low Income Housing: "Milking" and Class Violence, 15 Fla. State U. L. Rev. 485 (1987).

supply of housing (especially rental housing, since such laws encourage conversion to cooperatives and condominiums). From the
standpoint of protecting poor people, the provisions regarding procedural rights and rent withholding are particularly pernicious.
They are rights more likely to be invoked by the poor than by the
rich. They therefore give landlords an added incentive to substitute
toward more affluent tenants, who are less likely to be late with the
rent or to abuse the right to withhold rent.

The reader may be reminded of our analysis . . . of the economic
effects of outlawing efficient but sometimes oppressive methods of
enforcing debts. Both analyses suggest that the use of liability rules
or other legal sanctions to redistribute income from wealthy to poor
is likely to miscarry. A rule of liability is like an excise tax: It induces
a contraction in output and increase in price. . . . The party made
liable, even if not poor himself (but that, as we have seen, is also
possible), may be able to shift much of the liability cost to the poor
through higher prices. The result may be a capricious redistribution
of income and wealth within the class of poor people themselves
and an overall reduction in their welfare.

NOTES AND QUESTIONS ON POSNER
ON HOUSING CODES

1. Examine how Posner draws the two demand curves in Figure 16.3 on p.394. Is it plausible to suppose, as he did, that the individuals who most highly value other attributes of housing place the
lowest value on the benefits of housing code compliance? How did
Posner's placement of the demand curves affect the size of the price
and quantity effects depicted in Figure 16.3?

2. As Posner mentions, Duncan Kennedy has defined "milking" as a landlord's decision to stop maintaining a deteriorating residential building, with the intent of abandoning it within a few years.
Should housing-code officials embrace Kennedy's advice that they
act to prevent milking, or instead let it happen on the theory that
landlords can best decide when investment in upkeep is no longer
cost-effective? Would Posner defend a milking decision that violated a landlord's express warranties of maintenance? Should a
landlord be allowed to obtain a tenant's consent to milking in consideration for charging a low rent?

3. Toward the end of this selection, Posner argues the legal
"provisions regarding procedural rights and rent withholding are
particularly pernicious" for the poor in that they prompt landlords

to shift away from renting to poor households. Is this argument consistent with the position, implied in the first paragraph of Posner's selection, that the supply of housing is highly elastic in the long run? Or does Posner simply think that these sorts of legal measures tend to cost landlords more than they are worth to tenants?

4. A few examples will elucidate the economic concept of elasticity. Price elasticity is measured by the proportional change in quantity divided by the proportional change in price. The supply of a good is highly elastic when a small increase in its market price would sharply increase the quantity supplied. Which is more elastically supplied: corn or coral beaches? The demand for a good is highly inelastic when a large change in price would not greatly affect the quantity demanded. For which is demand more inelastic: corn or cigarettes?

As Posner's discussion indicates, commentators harbor differing conceptions of the long-run elasticities of supply and demand for housing. Those who view the supply as relatively elastic worry most that laws that decimate landlords' returns will lead to housing abandonment. Jerome Rothenberg et al., The Maze of Urban Housing Markets (1991), provides a sophisticated review of research on price elasticities and other economic features of housing markets.

Regulating Slum Housing Markets on Behalf of the Poor [*]

Bruce A. Ackerman

II.   Slumville . . .

Imagine a city called Athens whose slums are concentrated in one geographic area that we shall call Slumville. While the residents of Slumville are extremely mobile within the confines of the slum district, Athenians living outside Slumville are extremely reluctant to move into the area even if there is a significant improvement in housing quality. Of course, if there is an enormous change in the character of the neighborhood, the city's residents may change their view of Slumville. But a moderate change will not lead them to discard their fears about the quality of life, as well as the quality of housing, enjoyed by the area's inhabitants.

While the middle-class Athenian's substantial reluctance to live

*Source: 80 Yale L.J. 1093, 1102-1106 (1971).

in Slumville is fundamental to much of the argument that follows, several additional assumptions will be altered at subsequent stages of this essay. For purposes of the present discussion, then, assume (1) both landlords and tenants act rationally in their self-interest;[11] (2) no landlord or group of landlords has successfully established a monopoly or oligopoly position in the rental market; (3) tenants are aware of the range of prices and quality levels of accommodations offered for rent in Slumville and experience no significant cost in moving from one part of Slumville to another; (4) all of Slumville's accommodations are not only slums, but are *equally* slummy; (5) similarly, all of Slumville's tenants inflict *equal* damage upon the physical structures of the houses in which they reside; (6) a significant number of poor provincials are not entering Athens from the outlands nor are Slumvillites emigrating to the hinterlands; (7) *each* and *every* landlord in Slumville earns a rate of return on his investment which substantially exceeds the return available when the property is used for other purposes; indeed (8) even if the landlords are forced to bring their residential properties up to code, their rate of return would still exceed that available for any other use of the property; and (9) no landlord will find it more profitable to abandon his building entirely when faced with the necessity of investing substantial sums to bring his tenement up to code.

The implications of these last three assumptions can be misunderstood quite easily. They do not imply that the landlords of Slumville are making exceedingly high profits on their original investments. Even if they were only making a very low rate of return after absorbing the costs of code enforcement, my description of Slumville's landlords would still be satisfied if they could only earn an even lower rate of return by converting their land to an alternative commercial use. Similarly, the ninth assumption enumerated above, which stipulates that no buildings be abandoned, does not necessarily suggest the existence of excessive returns. A landlord will seriously consider abandonment only if the discounted present value of the costs code enforcement imposes over time exceeds the capitalized value of the future profits he expects from the building. In other words, even if an investor originally purchased a building for $100,000 and is currently earning only one per cent or $1000 a year in profit before code enforcement, the only financially relevant

---

11. The model under discussion is also restricted to a Slumville composed entirely of renters. While a subsequent portion of the essay considers certain difficulties which arise when owners themselves live in a home rented partly to tenants, considerations of length have made it impossible to consider at this time the full range of complexities raised by the fact that some slumdwellers live in houses which they own.

question for him is the value the market places on the right to receive $1000. If a purchaser is willing to buy this future income stream for $5000, abandonment is irrational unless the anticipated stream of future code costs exceeds this amount after an appropriate discount rate is applied. Thus, the Slumville we have depicted is not one which invokes the legendary exploitative landlord; indeed, our model is compatible with a situation in which each landlord is earning an exceedingly low return on his *original* investment.[14] We have only excluded from consideration in this first simple model those landlords who are in a truly desperate financial situation in which the capitalized value of future profits is lower than the capitalized cost of code repairs.

A.

We are now in a position to trace the economic consequences of a code enforcement program in Slumville. Given the model which has been developed, it follows that when the costs of code improvements are imposed upon Slumville's landlords *none* of them will have an incentive to remove their properties from the rental housing market. For we have stipulated that even after code costs are taken into account, the return on slum investment still exceeds the rate of return available when the land is used for other purposes or not used at all. Since the imposition of code costs upon the landlords does not induce a fall in the supply of housing, rent levels will be determined by the effect of code enforcement upon the demand for housing.

Two different demand responses can be anticipated, depending upon the extent to which the housing code is enforced. First, assume that the code is enforced strictly only in one part (Area X) of Slumville and that the test of Slumville (Area Y) is entirely ignored by the housing code inspectorate. In this case, one would expect that some of the residents of Y will find X a more attractive place than formerly and will bid the rents up in Area X. Those residents of X who find the new rent levels too steep for their taste will of course move to Y, where apartments have been vacated by those moving into the

---

14. Moreover, the relationship which the owner of the fee may have with a mortgage lender is also irrelevant to this analysis. If, for example, code costs will make it unprofitable for the fee owner to meet his mortgage payment, he will simply default and the new owner of the property (generally the mortgagee) will find himself in the same position delineated in the discussion in the text: he will either incur code costs to save the remainder of his $1000 annual income stream or he will withdraw the building from the residential housing market. Since in this introductory analysis we have assumed that this second alternative is not open, only the first alternative remains.

newly improved housing in *X*. Consequently, a program of selective housing code enforcement in Slumville will, in fact, partially fulfill the expectations of those administrators who doubt the desirability of code enforcement: Rents will increase in the target area and tenants who cannot "afford" the higher rents will leave the area to find new abodes in the now slummier sections of Slumville.

B.

If, however, one assumes that the housing code is enforced strictly in all of Slumville, the same result will not follow. Since we have assumed that before the code was enforced, houses in Areas *X* and *Y* were equally dilapidated, the comprehensive enforcement of the code throughout Areas *X* and *Y* will raise the quality of housing in all parts of Slumville to an equal degree, thereby providing no special incentive for a resident of Area *Y* to want to move to Area *X*. Thus, rents will not rise because of competition *among* Slumville residents as occurred in the case of partial code enforcement just discussed.

Indeed rents will not rise *at all* in Slumville if only a single further condition is met. Paradoxically, code enforcements will have "zero rent impact" if and only if there exists a class of Slumville tenants who do *not* believe that code enforcement will significantly improve their lives. A simple mathematical example will make this clear. Assume that, before the code is enforced, two types of families live in Slumville's 100,000 rental units: 90,000 families (the "homelovers") would be willing to pay a significant amount of money for code housing; in contrast, 10,000 families (the "lukewarm" families) would not be willing to pay extra rent for improved housing. This is not to say that even the lukewarm do not recognize that they will benefit from code enforcement — the improvement is simply not significant enough in their minds to warrant allocation of any more of their scarce funds to purchase it.

Now imagine that all of Slumville's landlords seek to pass their code costs on to tenants by raising rents by $25. While the 90,000 homelovers initially respond by paying the premium, the 10,000 lukewarm families act differently. Rather than paying the higher rent, they choose to pair up and share apartments instead, thus leaving 5000 units vacant. The lukewarm families will take this course since they believe that half an apartment at a lower rent is a better deal than a whole apartment at the inflated rental.

When the 10,000 lukewarm families decide to double-up, however, the owners of the 5000 vacant apartments are faced with a serious problem. Since no new residents have (under our assumptions) been attracted to Slumville as a result of code enforcement, there is no reason to expect that they will successfully fill their apartments if they persist in demanding the $25 premium. Rather, a landlord can rent his units in only one of two ways: (a) by inducing one of the homelovers to move by cutting the premium below the $25 level or (b) by cutting the rent sufficiently to induce one of the lukewarm families to prefer an entire apartment to its more crowded quarters. It should be apparent that if a given landlord fills a vacant apartment by offering one of the homelovers a better deal than his present landlord, the competitive dynamic will continue, for the owner of the newly vacated apartment will find himself in the same bleak position as his now successful competitor once occupied. It is only when prices are set low enough to induce the lukewarm families to resume their former habits and live in individual apartments that the economic situation will regain equilibrium. But if a significant number of lukewarm families are willing to spend no additional money for the code improvements, equilibrium will not be attained until the competing landlords absorb all of the code costs and rent all of their units at the pre-code price. Q.E.D. . . .

NOTES AND QUESTIONS ON ACKERMAN ON HOUSING CODES

1. In the latter portions of his lengthy article, Ackerman drops some of the simplifying assumptions that appear in this selection. Which of the assumptions reproduced in the passage are least realistic? Some candidates:

(a)   while tenants are perfectly mobile within Slumville, no migration occurs across Slumville's borders;

(b)   because the return on slum investments is uniformly adequate, code enforcement does not prompt even the most marginally profitable landlords to abandon their buildings; and

(c)   the tenants most tepidly interested in renting in Slumville place no value on code compliance.

Which, if any, of Ackerman's assumptions are essential to his deduced conclusion, in this excerpt, that code enforcement does not push up rents? For a variety of critiques of Ackerman's analysis, see Neil K. Komesar, Return to Slumville, 82 Yale L.J. 1175 (1973) (which is immediately followed by a rejoinder by Ackerman); Werner Z.

Figure 6
The Ackerman model

Hirsch, Joel G. Hirsch & Stephen Margolis, Regression Analysis of the Effects of Habitability Laws Upon Rent: An Empirical Observation on the Ackerman-Komesar Debate, 63 Cal. L. Rev. 1098 (1975); Richard S. Markovits, The Distributive Impact, Allocative Efficiency, and Overall Desirability of Ideal Housing Codes, 89 Harv. L. Rev. 1815 (1976).

2. Examine Figure 6, reprinted from Richard Craswell, Passing On the Costs of Legal Rules: Efficiency and Distribution in Buyer-Seller Relationships, 43 Stan. L. Rev. 361, 381 (1991). Does Craswell's graph accurately capture Ackerman's model in this selection? If so, compare how Ackerman shifts the demand curve from D1 (pre-enforcement) to D2 (post-enforcement) with how Posner makes the same shift in Figure 16.3, supra p.394. How much does one learn from these graphs about urban housing markets? About the nature of legal scholarship?

3. How might the consequences of an implied warranty of habitability differ from the consequences of housing code enforcement? Of the many legal reforms advocated on behalf of tenants, which are most likely to achieve their goals? See generally Edward H. Rabin, The Revolution in Residential Landlord-Tenant Law: Causes and Consequences, 69 Cornell L. Rev. 517 (1984).

4. What would happen if poverty lawyers used every procedural device to delay or prevent evictions within a gentrifying neighborhood? For an optimistic assessment, see Lawrence K. Kolodney, Eviction Free Zones: The Economics of Legal Bricolage in the Fight Against Displacement, 18 Fordham Urb. L.J. 507 (1991).

D.   Rent Control

Rent Control: The International Experience*

Richard Arnott

1. The intellectual background

Until a decade ago, the theoretical literature modeled rent controls as a simple price ceiling (on either a housing unit or a unit of housing service) applied to a product in a perfectly competitive market. Furthermore, the analysis assumed partial equilibrium, which ignored interactions between the housing market and the rest of the economy. Under these assumptions, rent controls are unambiguously harmful. This theoretical conclusion was supported by most of the policy literature, which applied casual empiricism to describe the deleterious effects of first-generation or hard controls in frequently polemical fashion. It is on the basis of this traditional literature that North American economists are virtually unanimous in their opposition to rent controls of almost any form.

In recent years, however, there has been a wave, or at least a swell, of revisionism among housing economists and policy analysts. Most experts of the subject, while not advocating controls, are now considerably more guarded and qualified in their opposition, and some believe that a well designed rent control program can, on balance, be beneficial. I shall discuss four strands of thought that have contributed to this change in point of view.

1. In many jurisdictions, housing economists have been participating in the policy debate on second-generation or soft rent control programs (also termed rent review). Doing so has forced them to address the question, If the political environment is unfavorable to decontrol, then how should the existing rent control program be modified to improve whatever beneficial effects rent control may have, or at least to mitigate the harmful effects? This experience has made housing economists realize that *the effects of a rent control program are sensitive to the details of its provisions* and that *a rent control program is a package of quite disparate policy measures.* As a result, controls are no longer regarded as a monolithic policy which simply imposes a ceiling on rents.

2. Theoretical economic models of the housing market have be-

*Source: 1 J. Real Est. Fin. & Econ. 203-210 (1988).

come considerably more sophisticated in recent years. While these models have received little practical application in housing policy analysis generally and in rent control analysis in particular, they have had some indirect influence through two avenues. First, these models can be reasonably sensitive to the details of a housing policy, and theoretical analyses employing them have reinforced the view that the effects of a policy depend on its particular provisions. Second, the new housing market models contain a significantly different conceptualization of the housing market, which has affected the way some of the younger generation of housing economists perceive the operation of the market.

3. There is increasing unease with the assumption that housing markets are perfectly competitive. While they certainly do exhibit many of the distinguishing features of the classic perfectly competitive market (notably many buyers and sellers and relative ease of entry and exit), they also have significant noncompetitive features: transactions costs (search and mobility costs), inhomogeneity of the product, consumption nonconvexities (because of transport costs, the typical household purchases all of its housing at one location), and asymmetric information (prospective tenants are poorly informed concerning unit characteristics, and landlords are uncertain of the traits of prospective tenants).

A major thrust of recent microeconomic theory has been the analysis of markets with such non-competitive features. It is now well understood that the descriptive properties of such imperfectly competitive markets may be very different from those of perfectly competitive markets. For example, although price is the equilibrating mechanism under perfect competition, under imperfect competition there may be non-price rationing (housing market vacancies may be a manifestation of this). Also, the law of a single price need not hold in an imperfectly competitive market; instead, equilibrium may be characterized by a distribution of prices for a homogeneous product.

The normative properties of perfectly and imperfectly competitive markets may also be markedly different. Perhaps the most celebrated and influential result in modern microeconomic theory is the First Theorem of Welfare Economics: Any perfectly competitive equilibrium is Pareto efficient. This theorem has formed the basis of countless arguments against government intervention, and is the intellectual cornerstone for the majority belief among economists that rent controls are harmful. But the theorem generally does not hold in imperfectly competitive markets, and so the potential scope for ameliorative government intervention may be considerable. The implication of this in the current context is that *because the housing mar-*

ket is imperfectly competitive, there is no a priori presumption that rent controls are harmful; whether in fact they are is an empirical issue and depends on the details of the program.

4. Over the last fifteen years, there have been significant changes in the way economists think about public policy and government intervention. The traditional approach was to: 1) separate equity and efficiency, on the argument that equity considerations were best treated via lump-sum redistribution; 2) employ partial equilibrium analysis, i.e., to examine a market without reference to the rest of the economy; 3) identify classic market failures or inefficiencies (externalities and increasing returns); and 4) to support those government policies (and only those) that corrected classic market failures.

Four serious criticisms have been levelled against this traditional method of public policy analysis.

First, it has been pointed out that lump-sum redistribution is impossible because the government must base redistribution on characteristics of individuals which, because of redistribution, they have an incentive to alter. This abstract statement can be illustrated by reference to the income tax. Suppose individuals differ in terms of ability and that an individual's income is the product of his ability and hours worked. The government would like to redistribute from the more to the less able, since society deems it unfair that a person should live in misery simply because he had the misfortune to be born with little ability. But the government cannot observe ability. It can, however, observe income, and must redistribute on that basis, via an income tax. But the income tax distorts the labor-leisure tradeoff. Since any practical form of redistribution has efficiency costs, equity and efficiency are inextricably intertwined, and so government policies should be evaluated with respect to both their equity and efficiency effects. Rent controls may then be desirable because of their equity benefits, despite their efficiency costs.

Second, it has long been recognized that the conditions under which partial equilibrium analysis is fully valid are very restrictive. In particular, if there are any distortions in the rest of the economy, partial equilibrium efficiency analysis is almost never fully correct since it ignores inter-market efficiency effects. For example, partial equilibrium analysis applied to the pricing of public transit comes up with the result that transit fares should be set equal to marginal cost. When, however, consideration is given to urban auto travel, the result is modified. Because drivers do not pay for the congestion they cause, urban auto travel is typically underpriced, so that more trips are made by car than is efficient. Pricing transit fares below (partial equilibrium) marginal cost causes some drivers to switch to public transit, which reduces the efficiency loss due to underpriced car travel. Such considerations are the subject of the theory of the second best. The first best is to set all prices equal to marginal cost and to redistribute in lump-sum fashion; but given some distortions which cannot be removed, for whatever reason, what is the second best that can be done? Rent controls might be harmful in a first-best or undistorted economy, but, if they reduce the efficiency costs of other distortions in the housing market or of distortions in other markets, they may be desirable on second-best grounds. Second-best arguments work both ways, however; rent controls may be even more harmful in a distorted than in a first-best economy, by exacerbating existing distortions.

Third, the last decade has been a period of extensive and substantial deregulation. The main impetus for this was the recognition of regulatory failure and government failure. Government intervention to correct market failure may be harmful. Not only does government intervention entail administrative and compliance costs, but the intervention process itself is subject to its own kinds of inefficiency: excessive regulation, insufficiently flexible regulation, misregulation, and, in the absence of the discipline of the market, excessive and wasteful spending. Such arguments strengthen the case of those who oppose rent controls.

Fourth, the ideas of James Buchanan and his co-workers are filtering into mainstream economic thought. In the current context, of particular significance are the profound implications of two eminently reasonable statements: 1) a policy will be implemented if and only if it receives political support, and 2) which policies receive political support depends on the constitution, i.e., the body of laws and regulations concerning how social choices are made. The first statement implies that in the determination of optimal policy, account should be taken of political constraints; the second, that if the set of policies chosen is determined by the constitution, then attention should be shifted away from individual policies and instead focused on the design of the constitution. Ironically (since Buchanan is well-known for his opposition to Big Government), the above line of reasoning provides an argument in favor of controls. Rent controls are generally acknowledged to be a highly inefficient method of redistribution. They may, however, be one of the most efficient methods that would receive political support.

To sum up: Ten years ago, almost all North American economists smugly regarded rent controls as the folly of the unenlightened; if all citizens were required to take a course in introductory microeconomics as part of their civics training, rent controls would disappear. Recent developments in economic thought have shaken, though not destroyed, this general belief, and have caused a reassessment and a reevaluation of rent controls, which draws on more sophisticated, but less certain, views of rent controls, the housing market, the economy, and the state. . . .

3. Themes

The Roundtable went on for four days. The topics of the four days were "Description of Different Jurisdictions' Experience" (Los Angeles, Ontario, New York City, the United Kingdom, Sweden, Israel, and Bangalore, India); "What Have We Learned about the Effects of Rent Control;" "Rent Control and Housing Policy;" and "Ontario's Options vis-à-vis Rent Control." The distillation of the discussion at the Roundtable into themes as well as my comments on them are colored by my own perceptions.

3.1 Different jurisdictions' experience

Despite the swell of revisionism referred to earlier concerning the effects and desirability of rent controls, the various jurisdictions' experts were unanimous in their opinion that rent controls have been harmful. In Los Angeles, where they have been mild, they have been an irritant; in Ontario, where they have been in effect for thirteen years and have been moderate, they have had a significant negative impact on the functioning of the market; in New York City, the United Kingdom, Sweden, and Israel, which have had strict controls over a long period, they have severely impeded the functioning of not only the housing market but also the labor market.

The experts were also virtually unanimous on the qualitative impacts of controls: reduced maintenance and accelerated deterioration of the rental housing stock; shrinkage of the private rental housing stock due to demolition, abandonment, conversion, and a fall in the rate of private rental construction; relatedly, a switch towards owner-occupied and public rental housing; mismatch of households to housing units; excess demand phenomena (low vacancy rates, key money and other black and grey market activities); and reduced mobility, which has caused significant distortions in the labor market.

While the evidence provided by each paper was hardly conclusive (e.g., no attempt was made to control for other housing policies or other factors) the unanimity of expert opinion made a strong impression.

A more muted theme was that long-term rent controls, while harmful, are not devastating. Politicians do not stand idly by while the housing market disintegrates; they introduce other policies to

offset the deleterious effects of controls, may turn a blind eye to illegal or quasi-legal housing market activity, and may encourage selective and lax enforcement of the rent control ordinances by, for
example, underfunding.

The "old lady who swallowed a fly," while not so named,
played a role in all the papers. To offset the problems induced by
controls, government intervention in the housing market becomes
increasingly extensive, incursive, and byzantine, until, in some jurisdictions, the rental housing *market* is essentially replaced by government allocation. A related theme is that the longer controls have
been in place, the harder they are to dismantle. Controls confer substantial windfall gains to sitting tenants, which they will fight hard
to retain.

A final theme, which came up throughout the Roundtable, is
that rent control is not a monolithic policy. A rent control policy is a
package of quite disparate provisions that differ substantially from
one jurisdiction to the next. The effects of different jurisdictions'
programs may be significantly different.

Qualifications notwithstanding, the message from the review of
different experiences was clarion: In the jurisdictions surveyed, rent
controls have been harmful and have seriously impeded the functioning of the housing economy. . . .

NOTES AND QUESTIONS ON THE
ECONOMICS OF RENT CONTROL

1. Arnott's essay serves as the introduction to a symposium issue in which members of the Roundtable appraise rent controls in
various locales. The report on Ontario, which adopted rent controls
in 1975, is particularly dramatic. Starts of unsubsidized rental housing fell in that province from an average of 27,999 per year during
1971-1974 (the pre-control period), to an average of 5,512 in
1975-1979. Lawrence B. Smith, An Economic Assessment of Rent
Controls: The Ontario Experience, 1 J. Real Estate Fin. & Econ. 217,
222-223 (1988). What events, other than imposition of rent control,
might have contributed to this sharp falloff?

2. Is it Arnott's thesis that, while economists are less confident
than they used to be that economic *theory* demonstrates the inefficiency of rent control, they are just as confident as ever that empirical *evidence* proves its inefficiency?

3. Arnott asserts that many economists now see efficiency and
equity as "inextricably intertwined." On this point, compare supra

p.113, Note 7 (sources on the relative merits of various methods of income redistribution).

4. Assess Arnott's statement that "Rent controls are generally acknowledged to be a highly inefficient method of redistribution. They may, however, be one of the most efficient methods that would receive political support." Of what plausibility and relevance are the findings in Joseph Gyourko & Peter Linneman, Equity and Efficiency Aspects of Rent Control, 26 J. Urb. Econ. 54 (1989), that the benefits of New York City's rent controls, although slightly progressive, disproportionately favor whites and are highly unequal within income groups?

5. In Note 3, supra pp. 285-286, a residential leasehold is envisioned as a continuing relationship in which both the landlord and tenant are capable of employing informal sanctions, including exiting from the relationship. In practice, rent controls restrict exit opportunities. A landlord is generally prohibited from removing a sitting tenant who tenders the controlled rent. A tenant is unlikely to want to relinquish a dwelling that rents at a below-market rate, especially if the rent regulations have created shortages in the local housing market. By eviscerating social control through the threat of exit, does rent control lessen cooperation between landlords and tenants? For the hypothesis that rent control has made life in New York City more brutish than elsewhere, see Robert C. Ellickson, Rent Control: A Comment on Olsen, 67 Chi.-Kent L. Rev. 947, 948-949 (1991).

6. Edgar O. Olsen, Is Rent Control Good Social Policy?, 67 Chi.-Kent L. Rev. 931 (1991), reviews the voluminous empirical studies on the topic. A comprehensive legal overview is Kenneth K. Baar, Guidelines for Drafting Rent Control Laws, 35 Rutgers L. Rev. 723 (1983).

Residential Rent Control*

Margaret Jane Radin

I.   Introduction: The Standard Economic Analysis . . .

. . . [C]lassic price theory suggests that imposition of rent control will exacerbate the housing shortage that gave rise to the high rents that

*Source: 15 Phil. & Pub. Aff. 350-355, 359-380 (1986).

gave rise to the imposition of rent control, and at the same time will encourage landlords to supply lower-quality housing. No wonder rent control is anathema to economists who espouse this picture. The cure is not only worse than the disease, it is a worse case of the same disease.

From the predictions of this empirical model the normative conclusion that there ought not to be rent control seems, for some, to follow as a matter of course. There is a misallocation of resources when landlords take their units off the market to enter some other business which is less preferred, while people who are willing to rent at the market price cannot find apartments to rent and must go elsewhere. Social welfare is not maximized, and therefore the arrangement is bad.

This is clearly a simple kind of utilitarian analysis. It assumes utility maximization is measured by wealth maximization, and it assumes that housing may be treated normatively like any other market commodity. But even for an economist who accepts both assumptions, the conclusion condemning rent control is too sweeping. If the landlords can collude to extract high prices, then rent control may merely bring prices down to the competitive level. Even if the landlords cannot collude, if they are reaping high "rents" in the economic sense,[3] making them lower prices to the competitive level should result in no restriction of supply or other misallocation of resources.

A more complex ethical analysis might question the two assumptions and find the normative conclusion barring rent control not so obvious. Might the level of efficiency losses be outweighed by other gains? Might some right of tenants "trump" the utility analysis? In this article I focus primarily on challenging the second of the assumptions: the idea that housing is appropriately treated as an ordinary market commodity. In doing so I shall explore a nonutilitarian approach. . . . I shall suggest that the real purpose of rent control is to make it possible for existing tenants to stay where they are, with roughly the same proportion of their income going to rent as they have become used to, and that in light of this purpose rent control might be justified more readily in some particular circumstances or contexts than in others. Thus the analysis I suggest is an

3. Economic rents are "payments to inputs that are above the minimum required to make these inputs available to the industry or to the economy." Edwin Mansfield, Microeconomics: Theory and Applications, 2d ed. (New York: W. W. Norton, 1975), p. 370. Some people might tend to think of economic rents as excess profits, since they are profits above the rate of return required to keep the productive resources allocated to their current use.

all-things-considered weighing of each situation in light of moral factors relevant to the particular situation.

II. Framing Some Normative Issues

To begin, let us introduce some normative approaches to the justice of rent control. To consider approaches other than the simple allocative efficiency model, we must assume that rent control works to some extent, in the sense that tenants are really paying less money for the same thing (or, possibly, less money for a less luxurious but still habitable and adequately maintained dwelling). If rent control doesn't work, it would be hard to justify it merely for the sake of appearances. Hence, we must assume that accompanying circumstances make it impossible for the landlords to reach a new market equilibrium of no benefit to tenants (unacceptable lower quality for the controlled price; or "real" price higher than the controlled nominal price). This in practice will mean that along with rent control there must be concomitant legal safeguards. They might include enactments such as prohibition of disguised pricing; strict housing code enforcement; legal habitability rights; eviction controls; demolition controls; and limitations on conversions to other uses, such as condominiums. The choice of concomitant safeguards may affect the justification of rent control under the circumstances (more about this later).

Assuming that rent control works, the main normative issue seems to be this: where rent control lowers rents at the landlord's expense (that is, thereby decreasing the landlord's profit), is that just? Under one market scenario, landlords are a cartel (oligopoly or shared monopoly). The justice of trustbusting is not disputed very much these days by anyone, whether she is of utilitarian or other ethical persuasion, so I shall pass this as an easy case. That is, I assume it would be just to lower rents from the monopoly price to the competitive price.

The question of economic rents is more interesting. If the market is competitive (not monopolistic), we may assume either (1) that landlords have high economic rents, so that rent control causes a "mere" wealth transfer from landlords to tenants; or (2) that landlords do not have high economic rents, so that there will be some decrease in supply accompanying the wealth transfer. In the second scenario there is an allocative inefficiency; in the first there is not.

A "mere" wealth redistribution between landlords and tenants, if unaccompanied by allocative inefficiencies, should be theoretically acceptable to a "pure" welfare economist, whom I shall call

Posnerian. Only the size of the pie matters, not the size of the pieces held by individuals. If we can assume that landlords are relatively richer than tenants, and if we accept the diminishing marginal utility of money, the wealth will in fact yield more welfare in the hands of the tenants, a situation to be preferred by egalitarians as well as Posnerians.

Someone of libertarian views regarding justice in entitlements, however, might find such redistribution unacceptable even if a welfare gain resulted, simply because it represents nonconsensual governmental alteration of the existing entitlement structure. A hypothetical "pure" libertarian, whom I shall call Nozickian,[7] might well condemn rent control across the board. The Nozickian might argue that unconditional choice of transfer terms is inherent in the concept of property ownership. Alienability is a prime attribute of property in the market society. Another way to put this is that the infrastructure of the market society is not just private property, but private-property-plus-free-contract. This is expressed by Nozick's claim that justice in holdings results from just acquisition and just transfers; that is, entitlement plus alienability. Hence, the Nozickian might argue that landlords have the right to set the price at which they choose to rent their property — period.[9] . . .

In what follows I approach the cluster of normative questions in two ways, one roughly individualist and one roughly group- or community-oriented. Under the first heading we may consider whether a current tenant as an individual has some claim to continuity of residence at a controlled price that takes priority over various individual claims of landlords and would-be tenants. Under the second heading we may consider whether the current tenants as a group or community have a claim that takes priority over claims of the class of would-be tenants and the class of landlords.

7. I refer, of course, to an uncritical reader of Robert Nozick, Anarchy, State, and Utopia (New York: Basic Books, 1974).

9. I should say here that I think such a "pure" Nozickian would be inconsistent with (some of) Nozick's own views. Nozick did recognize, although he did not dwell on the issue, that in the real world the existing entitlement structure can be unjust. Transfers of entitlements occur by rip-offs and fraud as well as free contract. In order to uphold the absolute nature of the rights of private-property-plus-free-contract, a prophylactic corrective justice theory is necessary. Therefore, a Nozickian less oriented solely to an ideal form of entitlement theory might admit that under some circumstances rent control is permitted or required by what Nozick called a theory of rectification. Under nonideal circumstances Nozickian libertarianism does not forbid all forms of redistribution. If the landlords' chain of title to their wealth contains any taint of coercion or conquest, it does not follow that they are entitled to keep it. Nozick did not develop a theory of rectification. For those who consider the bitter details of historical oppression to be the paramount "nonideal" factor for ethics and politics, the requirements of a developed theory of rectification would no doubt engulf most of Nozick's ideal libertarian conclusions.

III.   The Argument From the Tenant as Individual

Most of us, I think, feel that a tenant's interest in continuing to live in an apartment that she has made home for some time seems somehow a stronger or more exigent claim than a commercial landlord's interest in maintaining the same scope of freedom of choice regarding lease terms and in maintaining a high profit margin. Where rising rents are forcing out tenants and where landlords have significant economic rents, that is, one feels the tenant's claim is stronger than the landlord's. Even where significant economic rents are not present, so that some landlords are forced to leave the business, one may still feel that the tenant's expectation or desire to continue in her home is more important than the commercial landlord's expectation or desire to continue in the landlord business over some other business that will yield a better return. We do not recognize any general right to remain in a specific business such that regulation of the industry would be prohibited if regulation would operate to force some of the less efficient suppliers out of that market and into others.

The intuitive general rule is that preservation of one's home is a stronger claim that preservation of one's business, or that noncommercial personal use of an apartment as a home is morally entitled to more weight than purely commercial landlording. I shall discuss shortly a plausible basis for this rule and elaborate what I mean by the distinction between personal and purely commercial holding. It will be helpful first to notice that the exceptions or qualifications that come to mind serve to prove the rule. One class of exceptions involves situations where the landlord's claim seems noncommercial and therefore, more like the tenant's. For example, perhaps the landlord lives on the premises, or perhaps the building constitutes a long-term family business personally maintained by its members. Another class of exceptions involves situations where the tenant's claim is not plausibly that of maintaining an established home; for example, where the tenant is transient. If the landlord appears noncommercial or the tenant's interest is not that of an established home, then the tenant's claim no longer appears obviously weightier than the landlord's. Rent-control ordinances usually exempt transient accommodations and regularly grant special consideration to noncommercial interests of the landlord, such as her desire to move in a family member. Such provisions are responsive to the limits of the intuitive general rule.

The intuitive general rule I just mentioned does not apply to would-be tenants. When we consider people who are tenants elsewhere and wish to become tenants in the rent-controlled community, we are not struck with a similar general intuition of a strong claim. If the claims of would-be tenants seem especially strong, it is likely to be in the situation where large numbers of people work (or perhaps go to school) in the jurisdiction but are unable to find housing there. Their desire to live in the community where they are established in their work (or perhaps their school, but that seems more transient) may seem to make their interest more like that of the current tenants. Unfortunately, many of these people may be losers either way: the vacancies may not exist under rent control but under laissez-faire they would be priced too high. . . .

Let me refer to the situation where the tenant stands to lose an established home and the landlord is purely commercial as "standard circumstances." To the extent there does exist the intuitive appeal for preserving the tenant's home in standard circumstances that I postulate here, it can be understood in terms of the distinction between personal and fungible property that I elaborated in an earlier article.[14] Property that is "personal" in this philosophical sense is bound up with one's personhood, and is distinguishable from property that is held merely instrumentally or for investment and exchange and is therefore purely commercial or "fungible." One way to look at this distinction is to say that fungible property is fully commodified, or represents the ideal of the commodity form, whereas personal property is at least partially noncommodified.

Personal property describes specific categories in the external world in which holders can become justifiably self-invested, so that their individuality and selfhood become intertwined with a particular object. The object then cannot be replaced without pain by money or another similar object of equivalent market value; the particular object takes on unique value for the individual. Only a few special objects or categories of objects are personal property. Other property items, which can be replaced by their equivalents or money at no pain to the holder, are merely fungible, that is not bound up with personhood. When a holding is fungible, the value for the holder is the exchange or market value, not the object per se; one dollar bill is as good as another, or the equivalent in stocks or bonds, or any other item with market value. When a holding is personal, the specific object matters, and the fact that it matters is justifiable. . . .

That the personal/fungible distinction is not really a dichotomy is not troubling in the present context. Given that my view of personhood does not endorse a bright-line distinction between

14. See Margaret Jane Radin, Property and Personhood, Stanford Law Review 34, no. 5 (May 1982): 957.

persons and objects, it does make more sense to think of a continuum that ranges from a thing central to one's being to a thing wholly interchangeable with something else, rather than to think of a personal/fungible dichotomy. But telescoping the continuum to its two end points is useful when referring to situations well accepted as being near one or the other end point of the continuum. The "home" — usually conceived of as an owner-occupied single-family residence — seems to be a paradigm case of personal property in our social context. In this article I wish to suggest that a residential tenancy carries the same moral weight because and insofar as it is the tenant's "home" in the same sense. . . .

The . . . question arises under the personhood argument: Why not tax everyone, and compensate the landlords for having to yield fungible wealth in favor of tenants' personhood interests? But I think it can be answered more readily. It is plausible to maintain that if government must respect equally the personhood of all, it cannot permit forms of fungible property that make full self-development impossible for one class while not being necessary to the self-development of the holders. If the government has erroneously permitted wrongful fungible property, or wrongful commodification, and acts to correct its error, compensation is not appropriate, for reasons analogous to why it is inappropriate to compensate "expropriated" slaveholders or those whose "absolute exclusion" rights were diminished by the 1964 Civil Rights Act. The citizenry as a whole is not required to legitimate (by paying the value of) a benefit that the beneficiary held in error and as a wrong against our ideals of individual worth. Furthermore, if part of the wrong is the fact of commodification, the fact of placing the object in the market realm, then to place a market value on the interest even while decommodifying it seems contradictory or equivocal. If this argument is accepted, there is no corrective justice reason to compensate landlords whose wealth is diminished by rent control. . . .

IV.   The Argument from Tenant Community

The form of personhood argument discussed thus far, as well as the welfare rights argument, is individualistic in flavor. . . .

A different set of arguments may be added by considering an explicit communitarian basis. That is, we must consider the argument from a tenant community. I mean here the situation in which the tenants in a geographical "community" form also a spiritual "community."

Theoretically we might also consider a community including

both landlords and tenants. Although such a world might be far from an ideal world of no inequality or no property, it may nevertheless be one stage closer to the ideal than the usual rent-control situation. In fact rent control with absentee landlords seems intuitively more palatable than rent control with landlords who live on the premises. This could be for individualistic personhood reasons (resident landlords are as personally invested as their tenants), but it could have a communitarian basis as well. I focus primarily on the nonideal case of a tenant community, in what I have called the standard circumstances of dealing with commercial landlords, because it seems to accord with much of the current state of the world. Thus I do not treat the more utopian case of landlord-tenant spiritual community.

Consider the idea that a predominantly tenant community is justified in enacting rent control to avoid dispersion of the community to other and cheaper markets. Under what circumstances would this justification hold? To justify control on this ground would seem to require the general condition (1) that real community (in the spiritual sense) may be preserved even at some expense to fungible property interests of others, at least where the group affirms through local political action like rent control that it seeks continuity; and the specific condition (2) that a particular rent-controlled jurisdiction is indeed such a tenant community. In addition, the argument is strengthened if (3) the community will certainly be dispersed unless rent control is imposed. That is, analogously with the argument from personhood, the argument goes through more readily if tenants are poor, an assumption that is plausible because of the tax structure. Analogously with what was said earlier, the argument does not evaporate if tenants are not down and out. It is perhaps not fair, and harmful to community stability, for the price of community preservation to go up and up; and — the systemic argument — we should err on the side of community preservation because it is an important value.

To take first the general condition (1), it is possible to argue for community either as a good in itself (a species of corporativism) or as something that is valued by all the participants as individuals. Neocorporativist theory is presently murky,[20] though for many people the notion that some human wholes are greater than the sums of their parts seems obvious. One argument is that persons are (partly) *constituted* by communities. To assume that communities are merely of instrumental value to persons seems to contradict this

20. Roberto M. Unger, Knowledge and Politics (New York: Free Press, 1975) is perhaps representative ("theory of organic groups").

by postulating a person wholly separate from the community, capable of receiving the instrumental benefit. Hence, if communities are so constitutive, they must be a good in themselves or at least not totally derivative from individualist values.[21] But even sticking with the individualist base, there are utilitarian and nonutilitarian arguments for preserving community which seem strong enough to hold up against some extent of wealth losses from market distortions. The utilitarian argument is straightforward: We suppose from our knowledge of life in the general society of which we are a part that the personal utility attributable to living in an established close-knit community is very high. The nonutilitarian argument is equally straightforward: We suppose from our knowledge of life in this society that personhood is fostered by living within an established community of other persons.

It is easier to defend long-term rent control by appeal to community than by appeal strictly to the individual interests of present tenants. Relying solely on individual interests seems to imply that rent control is no longer justified when the present tenant dies or moves voluntarily. Communities last beyond the tenure of any one individual. Still, communities too may die of natural causes, so that not even a communitarian-based justification is necessarily permanent in principle.

Assuming that community may be preserved when it exists, at least where the group affirms through local political action like rent control that it seeks continuity, there arises the specific question (2) of when a rent-controlled jurisdiction is in fact such a community. Without a more well-developed theory of community, it is not possible to outline the indicia of community. But it seems there are particular intuitions we can feel fairly confident about, even without a fully developed theory. Sometimes, for example, tenants are primarily members of one ethnic group who interact in ways that form a cohesive and defined group. On the other hand, perhaps a very high turnover rate might convince us we are not dealing with a real community. Sometimes, the case of elderly people on fixed incomes being squeezed out of their long-term homes by younger, wealthier people is especially sympathetic. Of course, the elderly people may have remained strangers to each other during their years of residence, in which case their claims would have to rest on individualism. But it is perhaps more likely that over the years they have developed ties of friendship and support that unite them into a group or community.

21. See, e.g., Ronald R. Garet, Communality and the Existence of Groups, Southern California Law Review 56, no. 5 (July 1983): 1001; Michael J. Sandel, Liberalism and the Limits of Justice (Cambridge: Cambridge University Press, 1982).

There may be many instances where the boundaries of the political jurisdiction are not the same as the boundaries of the spiritual community. Then the normative question becomes whether we may justifiably benefit some nonmembers along with some (or all) members. In addition, there is a "federalism" issue. What circumstances render it appropriate to consider *this* community as the appropriate unit of justice? Political morality might dictate that the appropriate community to preserve is a larger community and not the particular group or locale. If so, we might conclude that the local policy of rent control is causing distortions for the larger community, for example, by making it impossible for workers who need to live near their jobs to move into the local jurisdiction. That might render local rent control unjustified. The workers as would-be tenants might have a stronger claim than some of the present tenants. Lacking good theories of what constitutes a community as an entity, it is hard to know how we would choose the size of the unit whose preservation is a good to be pursued. If a normative concern is to integrate the home and workplace in a single (spiritual and geographic) community, then "bedroom communities" would be disfavored. (They would be relatively disfavored for rent control anyway if all tenants in them are relatively well off.) . . .

V. Some Provisions of Rent-Control Legislation

A survey of rent-control provisions in light of what has been said is now in order. An almost universal companion of rent control is eviction control. The typical rent-control ordinance gives the tenant tantamount to permanent tenure during good behavior. This is in marked contrast to the normal legal rule that periodic tenancies are terminable at will with proper notice, at least if the landlord's motive is not retaliatory. If vacancy decontrol (to be discussed in a moment) is present, eviction control is a necessary safeguard to prevent easy evasion of rent control by landlords. But eviction control represents more than that, as is shown by the fact that it is enacted even without vacancy decontrol. Eviction control demonstrates that rent control is enacted primarily so that tenants may keep their apartments. It is a device to protect the personhood interest of the tenant and the value of community, at least as against commercial landlords. There are almost always exceptions for landlords who wish to move in themselves or their family members, and sometimes for small-scale landlords as well.

Common companions of rent control are condominium-conversion control and demolition control. These prevent landlords from easy exit into another business on the same land; in other words, individual landlords may exit to the widget business by selling their buildings to other landlords, but the number of rental buildings does not decrease. An exception to allow condominium conversion at the instance of tenants themselves might serve the tenants' interest in maintaining their homes.

Two common exemptions in rent-control legislation are vacancy decontrol, permitting the landlord to raise rent to any level she chooses (that is, the "real" price) when a tenant leaves voluntarily or dies, and an exemption for new buildings. The exemption for new buildings may be seen primarily as a method of offsetting the decrease in supply of rental housing that simple price theory predicts. There is no personhood interest to protect in housing that has never been occupied. (Serious problems arise if rent control goes on for a long time and a twenty-year-old building is exempt because it succeeded rent control. Jurisdictions with long-term rent control must adjust such problems from time to time.) Vacancy decontrol seems clearly related to the issue of the individual personhood interest of the established tenant. It is one way of striking a compromise: tenure for a tenant during good behavior, protecting her interest in establishing a home; free choice for the landlord otherwise. Vacancy decontrol seems unresponsive to communitarian concerns, because others of the same spiritual community (for example, adult children of members) may be precluded from moving into the vacancies, so the community may gradually die off as its departing members' decontrolled apartments are filled with (presumably richer) nonmembers. And, of course, vacancy decontrol is terrible for the better world of landlord-tenant community, since the "rational" landlord will be always hoping her long-term tenants will leave.

Previously I have mentioned in passing the occasional exemptions for small-scale landlords, or landlords who live on the premises, which may be attempts to direct rent control only against landlords whose interest is fungible. There are also sometimes exemptions for rented single-family houses and for "luxury units." The luxury-unit exemption is most readily explained in terms of assumptions about tenants' wealth. As we have seen, the easiest case for rent control is where landlords are reaping high economic rents from tenants who stand to lose their homes. The luxury-unit level may represent the legislators' attempt to draw a line between poor tenants who might lose their homes and wealthy tenants who won't. Furthermore, the interest of wealthy tenants is less likely to be personal. Wealthy tenants perhaps rent an apartment merely as [a] pied-à-terre, or for a temporary stay by the beach. There are few if any jurisdictions in which wealthy people, who could be owners, establish their homes as long-term renters. The exemption for single-family homes, where it appears, may be a proxy for the luxury-unit exemption. Depending on the circumstances, it may also carve out a renters' community for protection; for example, a portion of town devoted to multi-unit dwellings. It may also reflect the assumption that rent control is more readily justified as against commercial landlords, whose interest is fungible. Those who rent out single-family dwellings or one half of a duplex are less likely to be commercial landlords; their interest may tend to be personal. . . .

VIII.   Postscript: Exclusion and Pluralism

Finally, the normative examination of rent control brings up the broader issue of community exclusion. The issue is when it is appropriate for a community to make it hard for others to become members. Here the analogy between growth control (exclusionary zoning and servitudes) and rent control (exclusionary pricing?) is striking. Exclusionary zoning refers to local government regulation of lot sizes, unit sizes, household compositions, etc., that has the effect of excluding certain groups, most frequently the less affluent. The same effect can be achieved by complexes of exclusionary servitudes imposed by developers in order to increase the market value of the housing being sold.

Exclusionary zoning and rent control are both acts by local government that have the effect of keeping out would-be entrants. There appears in each case tension between how far we are to pursue our underlying political value of free migration and how far we are to pursue our underlying political values of stability of individuals' homes and local community continuity. Because of the conflicts of values involved, the problems are difficult.

Rent control may be more often justifiable than exclusionary zoning to the extent that rent control protects the homes of poor individuals and communities of poor individuals. In a rising market, a poor person stands to lose her home without rent control (or some other intervention such as an income subsidy offsetting the differential between housing price increases and wage increases). Communities of poor individuals are not likely to be able to regroup elsewhere. Exclusionary zoning, on the other hand, often helps the relatively affluent form enclaves to keep out minority and poor people. They may have an association claim in so doing. But the wealthy do not in general have trouble maintaining their identity and the poor struggle for a place to form theirs. When those doing the excluding are the mainstream of American society and the middle class, their claims of association and personhood may pale beside the claims of personhood and association of the less mainstream and the less fortunate who seek entry. The case against exclusion on the basis of race, for example, has been easy in liberal political theory.

But the tables may be turned. Consider an incorporated town of several hundred black separatists that wishes to exclude whites; consider an incorporated town of several hundred Orthodox Jews that wishes to exclude those of other religions, or at least to ban those who do not observe certain religious rules. Anyone committed to pluralism and the preservation of minority ways cannot be certain this kind of exclusion should be disallowed. The size of the community, its cohesiveness, and its need for exclusionary practices in order to survive as a community might on balance convince us that exclusion is just in these types of cases. Exclusion — whether effected by rent control or other means — is not per se pro- or anti-personhood or pro- or anti-community; the evaluation depends upon the circumstances.

NOTES AND QUESTIONS ON RATIONALES FOR RENT CONTROL

1. Radin calls her approach "nonutilitarian." Would economist Arnott consider Radin's normative criteria irrelevant? Conversely, would Radin reject Arnott's? How should an evaluator of rent control trade off, or rank, diverse considerations such as personal autonomy, community preservation, and efficiency?

2. Radin's analysis is mostly ex post; she seeks to protect tenants who already have apartments, and spiritual communities that already exist. Is this emphasis sound? Consider the relevance of "loss aversion," discussed in the Knetsch selection, supra p.226.

Or is it more sound to reason ex ante — that is, about the sorts of rent regulations that in the long run best enable tenants to enjoy rental arrangements and to live in spiritual communities? Suppose Arnott is correct in his assertion that a rent control measure causes the rental housing stock to shrink and deteriorate. In that case, could the continued commodification of housing, which Radin decries, tend to enhance long-run tenant welfare? Or does this argument reintroduce utilitarian considerations that Radin does not want to consider?

3. Examine Radin's Argument from the Tenant as Individual. How would Radin respond to the suggestion that a tenant desirous

of secure tenure can simply buy a condominium unit or enter into a long-term lease?

Would Radin be satisfied if tenant interests were protected with liability rules, not property rules (to reinvoke Calabresi and Melamed's distinction)? Under a liability-rule approach, a landlord would be empowered to remove a sitting tenant provided the landlord paid the tenant's moving costs and other objective damages.

Does Radin's analysis imply that she disapproves of many exercises of the power of eminent domain? Recall Radin's discussion of this issue in Property and Personhood, supra pp.17-18.

4. Consider Radin's Argument from Tenant Community. Suppose Loraine owns a two-unit structure, occupies the bottom floor herself, and rents out the top floor to Shirley, a tenant. How could city officials determine whether Loraine's neighborhood was a "spiritual community"? Assuming the neighborhood fit that description, how would Radin weigh Loraine's personal interest in controlling her small building against the communitarian advantages of controlling Shirley's rent?

Communities can be viewed dynamically as well as statically. Is a tenant who has moved into a gentrifying neighborhood likely to expect the gentrification to continue, or to cease? If to continue, does rent control serve community values?

Many observers believe that rent controls tend to make landlord-tenant relationships more acrimonious. Should a communitarian be bothered by that, or do only inter-tenant relationships matter?

A university town adopts rent controls. As a result, many former graduate students retain their apartments after their university connections have ceased. Incoming graduate students are therefore forced to live farther from campus. Have the rent controls advanced communitarian objectives?

5. On p.416, Radin concludes that it is just for landlords to bear the costs of tenant-protection measures. Is her reasoning persuasive? Recall the materials on distributive justice, supra Chapter 1.D. For a critique of Radin's analysis, see Timothy J. Brennan, Rights, Market Failure, and Rent Control, 17 Phil. & Pub. Aff. 66 (1988).

Chapter 9

Land Use and the Environment

A. Servitudes and Private Communities

Covenants and Constitutions*

Richard A. Epstein

Covenants and constitutions: strange bedfellows, but more than alliteration unites them. In this brief paper I shall explore the relationship between them. In order to orient the discussion, my use of the term "covenants" includes all forms of servitudes, easements, and restrictions that one person can place on another's lands. "Constitutions" are the documents that identify and entrench the fundamental law of a state or nation, on matters of both structure and individual rights.

At first blush, the two appear to be polar opposites. The law of covenants is the province only of a hardy band of real estate lawyers with the temerity to master a complex and imposing body of rules; vertical and horizontal privity; affirmative and negative covenants; matters in esse and in posse; the touch and concern requirement; notice, actual and constructive; and the ins-and-outs of recordation statutes. Constitutions, by contrast, are the province of us all, the stuff of Senate confirmation hearings, and speak to the eternal and universal truths that bind us into a nation.

Appearances can be deceiving, however. I believe that the law of covenants offers an intelligent blueprint for the analysis of consti-

*Source: 73 Cornell L. Rev. 906-924 (1988).

tutional principles. Covenants may govern party-walls and rights of way over back country roads. Their subject matter may be both well-defined and permanent, and they may bind as few as two parties. But there is nothing about the logic of covenants that restricts them to two-party transactions with simple objectives. Covenants are similar in this regard to corporations, which can be closed or public. There are no external limits on the number of parties who can participate in a contract or on the type of issues that it can govern. The logic of contracting is the logic of unanimous consent. As the number of parties to a system of covenants becomes greater and the issues involved more complex, the polar differences between covenants and constitutions diminish. The closer we look at these covenants, the more they look like mini-constitutions. The common literary image of a constitution as a social contract, or even a social covenant, has more literal truth than is often supposed.

I. Covenants

Let us set the stage for analysis with a short discussion of the function and purpose of covenants. To understand their critical role in modern land transactions, it is best first to envision the circumstances in which covenants have no more than peripheral importance. Thus suppose for the moment that land is a very cheap commodity that can be effectively utilized only if owned in fairly large quantities (say for grazing or farming). Under these circumstances, there may be very little need for any system of covenants at all. Each person can live side by side with his neighbor, and each can rejoice in exclusive ownership of an unencumbered fee simple absolute in possession. The operative principle is that good fences make good neighbors. But this simple property arrangement has its Achilles heel: two people cannot share a single resource. In consequence there might be some underutilization of land. Nonetheless these losses are perhaps smaller than the costs necessary to correct them. Covenants are not cheap to draft and enforce, especially in the era before recordation. So long as transaction costs are positive, the set of efficient solutions cannot involve the realization of all possible gains from trade. Where the gains from trade are smaller than the sum of both sides' transaction costs, then the trade will not take place.

Now let us suppose that the value of land has increased dramatically, whether from an increased demand for farm produce, or from an increased demand for housing in an especially fashionable part of town. Under these circumstances, the balance shifts between the two costs identified above. The losses from the underutilization of land become very large, relative to the transaction costs of creating some legal system that allows more intensive use of the land, and the system of joint control and divided use that it requires. Once the costs of contracting become lower than the economic gains from contracting, we should expect to see voluntary contracts emerge. An increase in the frequency of covenants goes hand in hand with increases in underlying real estate values.

One question is what can the law do in order to minimize the losses from the underutilization of real property. At some macro-level, a wide range of public control devices can have enormous influence on land utilization: systems of zoning, rent control, and taxation are but three types of potent government regulation. But for this discussion on the law of covenants, I shall put those institutional tools aside, and concentrate solely on the private mechanisms of transfer involved in creating complex structures of divided ownership in real property, with reference here only to transactions between neighbors.

Within this narrow focus, what the law can do is to try to reduce the transaction costs of the voluntary arrangements needed to exploit real estate within the confines established by law. The payoff here should be evident: The lower these costs, the more likely it is that private agreements can counteract even small underutilizations of real property. This tendency should be a general social good regardless of the market or regulatory determinants of land value, positive or negative.

A number of legal and institutional developments have fostered desirable voluntary exchanges. It is worthwhile to spend time on two: recordation and common plan building schemes.

A.   Recordation

The system of recordation is an indispensable aid for the effective use of any form of covenant. In the age before recordation, no one could be sure whether a restriction binding upon the immediate parties could also be enforced by or against third parties. The resulting uncertainty was very large, and it fed back into the initial willingness to control land by covenants. As land is permanent, it is only a matter of time before the original parties to the transaction sell their interests or die. Covenantees want to be able to make decisions about the construction of long-term improvements, but cannot do so if the protection they have purchased can be defeated whenever the original covenantor makes a strategic sale to a third party who is then rid of the covenant. The covenantor, for his part, will not be able, ex ante, to command the highest price if he cannot assure the covenantee that his successor in title will be bound by the restriction in question. The first transaction itself may therefore abort, so that the subsequent purchaser is denied the benefit of the purchase that ties the acquisition of the land to acceptance of the servitude. The point remains true, moreover, even if no cash changes hands, as frequently happens when each party's consideration is a reciprocal covenant (such as a covenant not to build above a certain height).

The concern with binding strangers did not preclude the running of covenants before the rise of recordation statutes. Roughly speaking, the rule then was that covenants could only bind subsequent takers if they had notice, actual or constructive, of the covenant.[4] The uncertainties about notice were powerful enough that they doubtless precluded many useful transactions from taking place at all. With recordation, the problem of notice disappears in all but the most unusual case. The covenantee simply records his interest in the appropriate deed or plot index; title companies then memorialize it on their own records; and all subsequent takers are now in position to assess the state of the title, and act accordingly, either by adjusting the purchase price for land to take into account the restrictions that benefit or burden it, or by not purchasing at all. The work is all routine and ministerial — a notable social triumph of the humdrum.

In my view, the recording system renders unnecessary many of the arcane features of the law of covenants that might have made sense in the prior age. The requirement that covenants "touch and concern" the land may well have made sense in an age before recordation; those covenants that did touch and concern the land were more likely to be detected by subsequent purchasers than those that were purely personal to the parties. Similarly, it might have been more difficult from an inspection of the premises to discover whether the seller had undertaken some affirmative obligation to a neighboring landowner. But now that the system of recordation is in place, the notice issue is typically solved in an explicit, sensible, and well-nigh decisive fashion, rendering unnecessary the need for the clumsy proxies that still survive in the law.

The limitation of valid covenants to those that touch and concern land, and the prohibition on affirmative obligations, are not, I believe, of much practical consequence, because there are very few

4. The modern law starts with Tulk v. Moxhay, 2 Ph. 774, 41 Eng. Rep. 1143 (Ch. 1848), which allowed restrictive covenants to run in equity against the purchasers who took with notice of them.

persons who really would want as a business matter to tie either type of undertaking to the ownership of real property — who would want the assignee of a covenantor to prepare his income taxes? Even so, some famous institutional cases have turned on either or both these requirements. Thus the decision in Neponsit Property Owners' Association, Inc. v. Emigrant Industrial Savings Bank[8] was necessary to quell some residual doubt whether the obligation to pay money to a property owners' association touched and concerned the land, or fell afoul of New York's stringent rule against affirmative covenants. Clearly no common ownership association could survive at all without these standard covenants, any more than a government could survive without any power to tax. . . . The result in *Neponsit* is a happy one, but it could have been better reached by jettisoning the older restrictions on covenants, now that recordation statutes are in place.

A contrary position on recordation and notice is taken by Professor Alexander in his provocative paper, Freedom, Coercion, and the Law of Servitudes.[10] His attack takes place on several levels and deserves an answer here. His most general argument is that one cannot assume that interested parties are rational or understand the terms found in covenants. "[P]eople *do* engage in irrational behavior." Stated in this form, the argument extends far more broadly than the law of covenants. Indeed, if treated as a general description of human conduct, it undermines the possibilities of any form of intelligent organization whatsoever. Under this view, private bargains are unacceptable because they are doomed by ignorance and exploitation. Yet by the same token, political solutions are doomed as well, because irrationality is hardly cured in a regime that requires imperfect actors to navigate the many pitfalls of collective action. If people cannot contract intelligently, then how can they vote? The assumption of systemic irrationality is a general nonstarter from which only universal skepticism follows. . . .

B. Common Building Plans

The previous discussion shows how the rules of recordation help facilitate transactions that bind three or more persons. Recordation itself is not sufficient for that purpose and the law has also developed effective rules to allow covenants to be created that benefit and bind a large number of persons, such as the members of a

8. . . . 15 N.E. 2d 793 ([N.Y.] 1938).
10. Alexander, Freedom, Coercion, and the Law of Servitudes, 73 Cornell L. Rev. 883 (1988).

subdivision, condominium, or cooperative. There is an evident transactional problem here if covenants can only exist between two persons in privity. The extent of the difficulty is fully revealed by a simple mathematical calculation. If there are n persons, then there must be pairwise contracts among all of them, so that:

$$\sum_{i=1}^{n} n - 1$$

is the minimum number of separate contracts to bind everyone to everyone else. Alternatively, if it is possible for all persons to bind each other by dealing with a common party (usually the developer) who stands at the middle of the circle, then n contracts (one between each person and the developer) suffice to create a network in which all persons can be bound and benefitted by a set of reciprocal contracts.

Where n is very small, the transactional difference between the two methods of contracting is not significant. In order to contract with a common agent at the middle it is necessary to set up that agent but the costs of that institution can be spread only over a very small number of contracts. If the effort is to link only three people, there will have to be three contracts no matter whether they go around the sides of the triangle or through a fourth point at the middle. The system of three pairwise contracts, moreover, might be cheaper because the costs of setting up the common party at the center are avoided. As the numbers get large, as is typical with modern real estate when land becomes valuable, then there is a pronounced advantage to contracting through the central point. Thus for n equal to 100, the number of pairwise contracts required is, by the well-known formula:

$$\sum_{i=1}^{n} n - 1 = n(n - 1)/2, \text{ equal to } 4950,$$

while the number of contracts through the center is only 100. At that point it would long since have been cost effective to incur the heavy front-end fixed costs of instituting a central party through whom all individual landowners are able to contract. The marginal costs of adding a single new member to the group are low when governance runs through the center, but they would be astronomical if 101 new contracts have to be separately formed. In addition, the costs of maintaining the contract network are reduced as well, for no longer is it necessary to modify, for example, 4950 existing separate contracts. Instead it should be possible to make changes in one single master arrangement in accordance with predetermined decision rules.

The law of covenants had an intuitive sense of the real economies of scale that have developed in this area. The rules for common building plans or schemes allow a promoter to insure that all purchasers of individual units stand in a position of perfect parity with one another, regardless of when they purchase their units, by inserting proper ("intent to run") language in the original deeds and faithfully recording all documents. The flexibility of this way of doing business should be manifest. The developer can now assure the first round of buyers that subsequent takers will be bound; thereafter, the developer can also assure subsequent rounds of buyers that prior takers are bound. Buyers can remain happily ignorant of the details of the scheme, precisely because it works so well. Over time, individual units may fluctuate in value, but these differences can be handled by adjustments in purchase price or financing terms without any alteration of the basic network of covenants.

In effect, the rules show the advantages of standard form contracts when there are a large number of parties. By reducing transaction costs, common building plans effectively allow vast numbers of individuals to make use of certain common areas or to benefit from the mutual restrictions and requirements on use. They become ever more important today when the high price of land makes the ideal of separate and self-contained ownership a luxury that few people who want glamour in the city or quiet at the beach can afford.

Professor Alexander sees in these rules some "particularly insidious form of coercion because it purports to effectuate private intentions rather than acknowledging that private volition is being sacrificed for the sake of some collective good." But where is the coercion or sacrifice? Of coercion there is none, unless the discrete purchase or sale is infected with duress or fraud, issues that the ordinary law of contract can handle (as it has for ages). Of sacrifice there is none either: the system of sequential contracts will only go forward if, at *every* point in the chain, both parties to the contract think that they are better off with the agreement than without it. The constant effort to conflate close choices and hard bargains with coercion is of a piece with the effort to conflate agreement with theft, and scarcity with coercion. Of course there will be some transactions in which prospective consumers find themselves making close marginal calls; that is not evidence of coercion, but only of negatively sloped demand curves.

II.   The Problems of Governance: Externalities, Transaction Costs, and Intergenerational Effects

The combined effect of the recordation and building plan rules should by now be clear. Recordation is an effective way to control the externalities associated with covenants, while building plans reduce the cost of transacting among large numbers of covenantees. Nonetheless several related inquiries need still to be answered: Are there any externalities that recordation does not address? Are there any transactional difficulties that cannot be overcome by the principles of serial contracting made possible by the building plan rules? What implications do these difficulties have for the enforcement of covenants?

The most obvious way in which recordation systems control the problem of externalities is to give notice to the rest of the world of the state of the title of any person whom a network of covenants binds or benefits. Within this framework, some might fear a different kind of externality: that the substance of that network of covenants will be in some way objectionable. This fear is misplaced, because the original developer (like the corporate promoter intent upon maximizing his profit from a venture) has all the right incentives to offer the ideal mix of burdens and benefits. If he offers inferior terms, then his return from sales will suffer because the price that he can command in the market for the units will be reduced. It seems clear from common practice that few developers think that their unit owners are happy with the limited "no invasion" type restrictions that are associated with the common law of nuisance. Nuisance-type prohibitions against noise, smells, and discharges remain part and parcel of any common ownership system, but they do not begin to exhaust the class of restrictions that are routinely included in any common real estate venture. Most planned developments contain detailed restrictions concerning height, decor, and maintenance. These restrictions may look byzantine to an outsider, but they are likely to make sense because the party who imposes them has everything to lose if they are made either too stringent or too relaxed.

Some have questioned whether there are certain kinds of externalities that the above analysis does not reach. Here in particular three types should be discussed: monopoly, discrimination, and intergenerational effects — the last with reference to the doctrine of changed conditions. All involve possible harms to third persons that might not be internalized by an original owner of the land. . . .

A. Monopoly

As regards monopoly, the source of the concern is that the single developer of a large project may be able to exert some market power. The argument is always plausible with regard to land because it is an asset, fixed in location, that can have (almost by definition) only imperfect substitutes located some distance away. The question of monopoly power, however, generates different responses for different kinds of covenants. Those restrictions that are perfectly reciprocal (e.g., that relate to appearance and height) do not seem to raise any concerns under the monopoly model. If there is a monopoly problem in this context, it arises from the ability of the original developer (who may be protected by zoning restrictions on nearby parcels) to extract a monopoly price from his own purchasers. If some form of public control is found necessary, it need not be tied to the law of covenants. For in his efforts to extract monopoly rents, the developer, as already observed, has every incentive to supply the ideal set of restrictions for all his parcels: he can maximize his monopoly return in this way. The proper types of response, therefore, are numerous. The law could place some restrictions on price, for which the risks of overreaction are manifest; it could limit the size of certain subdivisions under common ownership, but only at the cost of some arguable efficiencies in operation; or ideally, it could remove whatever legal restrictions block the entry of other developers into the local market. . . .

B. Antidiscrimination

Restrictive covenants have also been used to exclude persons from certain real estate developments because of their race or religion. As a matter of American constitutional and statutory law, these covenants are now universally regarded as illegal, precisely because of their adverse effects on third parties. My purpose here is not to assess the desirability of the constitutional rules or statutes but only to stress again the general point. Any concern with antidiscrimination is best attacked head on and does not raise any problems with restrictive covenants that are not also found, say, with employment or with housing generally. It is very doubtful, therefore, that any distinctive doctrine of covenant law can begin to reach this issue. Restrictive covenants of this sort touch and concern the land, are negative in effect, are clear as to both intent and meaning, and are capable of recordation. Yet all this only shows that the problem is better handled by other legal rules which have discrimination, race, and religion at their core, and not by the law of covenants.

C. Intergenerational Effects: The Problem of Changed Conditions

The last possible source of externalities has to do with the inter-generational effects of a system of restrictive covenants. Within the traditional legal framework this problem is brought to the fore in connection with the so-called doctrine of changed conditions. This doctrine holds that a restrictive covenant is no longer enforceable, at least without modification, when the social and environmental conditions existing when the covenant was created no longer apply. In effect the doctrine of changed conditions allows the courts to ex-punge covenants from the records, or at least modify their provi-sions, once the court determines that the covenants no longer serve the purposes for which they were first introduced. In one sense, therefore, the doctrine of changed conditions is a slightly more ro-bust form of the doctrine of frustration of purpose as it exists in the general law of contract. But the doctrine of changed conditions has a more distinctive and coercive cast. Courts may invoke it to in-validate covenants notwithstanding the parties' express contractual intent to be bound in perpetuity unless released by contrary unani-mous agreement.

The battleground here is a familiar one: Should the doctrine of changed conditions operate as a plausible default rule or as a rule of public regulation? I have already taken the position that it should fill the former, and more modest, office once the recordation system gives all parties notice of the relevant conditions. So long as all the original parties have themselves taken into account the need for fu-ture change it is highly unlikely that the legal system, which oper-ates with very inexact knowledge of their private preferences and subjective costs, can find a rule that works better than the one that the parties themselves have agreed upon. . . .

This basic point that freedom of contract should govern is, I think, correct, but the matter of holdouts, and the bilateral mo-nopoly problems they generate, does require more discussion. . . .

Initially, it will be instructive to draw some distinctions be-tween the small and large number cases. Where there are, for ex-ample, only two parties to a covenant, there is much to be said for the simple rule that protects it for all time and under all circum-stances. Thus the normal right of way over a servient tenement is generally regarded as valid in perpetuity, just like the fee. To be sure, there can be limitations upon the easement by contract, but as a con-structional matter, the safe preference is to resist the application of the changed circumstances doctrine and to enforce the easement so long as the holder of the dominant tenement has not abandoned its use. The holder of the servient tenement who wants release from the easement must purchase it at an agreed price.

The more difficult issues arise at the other end of the spectrum when the law of covenants is pressed into the service of modern condominium and cooperative associations. In this context, should the doctrine of changed circumstances have greater sway? As is so often the case, it is critical to distinguish between the ex ante and ex post effect of the rules. Ex post it is clearly in some people's interest to have the right to hold out. This right may be awkward to exercise when it is apparent that consent is withheld only to extract a profit from others but it may nonetheless still have real positive value. In many cases the covenant continues to be of some value to a covenantee. As there is no ready market value for the release of the covenant, the holdout can conceal his advantage taking as a defense the subjective value he enjoys in keeping the covenant alive. Others' inability to draw a clear operational line between subjective value (thought good) and holdout value (thought bad) is great enough in practice that the determined and subtle holdout artist has a good deal of room to maneuver before he is detected and perhaps disgraced.

From the ex ante perspective, however, the desirability of allowing holding out takes on a very different complexion. The developer will be able to command less total value from sales if the legal arrangements that he sells give rise to a substantial holdout risk some time in the future. We must assume that holdouts give rise to negative sum games, for if bargaining were costless no one would care about the problem. Confronting any holdout problems consumes administrative resources, and this necessarily reduces the total gains from removing covenants — assuming that it does not block their removal altogether. The developer who can find a way to limit holdout problems will therefore be able to command a higher total price for the units that he sells than one who cannot. We should therefore expect him to take some effort in that direction, even if preventing the holdout problem from arising is itself a task that consumes resources. The gains from investing in legal structure are likely to be substantial.

Just such an effort is made in fashioning the rules whereby covenants can be modified or removed. The holdout problem occurs in its most extreme form when unanimous consent is necessary to release lands from the restrictions imposed by covenants. The problem is identical to that which any organization, governmental or voluntary, faces when it can pass a law or resolution only by unanimous consent. Most voluntary groups recognize this problem. In response to it, they provide *by original unanimous consent* for a set of decision rules that allows some fraction, usually a majority by legal interest or number, to reverse the original decisions. So long as it is not possible to forecast perfectly, some such discretion will be needed in any system of governance. Majority rule can be introduced into networks of covenants that are part and parcel of building plans, and frequently is. In some cases where the restrictions are largely negative in type, it may be possible for any party to the covenants, upon the signature of some fraction of the total units, to free his own unit from the restrictions in question. Thus we can find majority rule provisions for modification without government command. In other cases where the interdependence between the units is greater, it might be necessary for the party to run through formal deliberation in a forum provided for in the original agreements.

The connection between covenants and constitutions should now be explicit. In both cases the ultimate task is to protect individual rights to property without inviting excessive holdout problems. A rule that allowed a majority of unit owners to do whatever it pleased with regard to restrictive covenants in place would rightly be perceived as unfair: there would be too much scope for advantage taking. It would be quite unthinkable for the majority to be able to vote to release all its units from the force of the covenants while continuing to impose those covenants upon others; this would be indistinguishable from a corporation's majority shareholders voting a dividend for themselves and denying it to the minority, or from the majority of citizens voting to confiscate the property of some minority faction. But by the same token, any absolute protection of individual rights with an individual veto re-introduces the same problem of holdout that every system of collective governance wishes to overcome.

We therefore are driven to some mixed system of entrenched rights, compensation tests, and majority rule — all messy, and all necessary. . . .

The choices involved are both vexing and important, and I shall not try to choose in the abstract among veto rights, majority rule, compensation, and their many variations and combinations. Instead my point is more modest. So long as we know that the original owner of the property was aware of these difficulties, then the basic analysis still holds: there is no need for any public doctrine of changed conditions to limit the scope and effect of private covenants. The intermediate solutions found in the standard agreements are likely those that, in the long run, tend to minimize the total breakdown. In this light, it becomes all the more dangerous simply to invalidate a covenant on a wholesale basis, and thereby to ignore the explicit protections that the parties themselves have drafted, including those that allow for introducing some change in the existing structure.

Of course, the parties' inability to draft with perfect foresight and completeness necessarily means that courts will have to engage in some "interstitial legislation" in construing the terms of the basic agreement. No set of agreements governs all contingencies and something has to be done to fill up the gaps. In many instances the theory of the "implied term" does reflect the standard usages of the parties to a transaction. In other cases, the implied term looks more like a judicial invention and less like an explication of the parties' intention. For example, we could say with some confidence that a court's construction of a homeowners' association provision was inconsistent with the parties' intention if it worked a systematic redistribution among the association's members, because such rules, if explicit to the agreement, would reduce the total value of the units sold at the outset. Again, the parallel to basic constitutional interpretation seems too clear to require much elaboration.

At bottom, the problems of homeowners' associations are identical to those of all long term relational contracts: How should the gaps be filled? While there is of necessity some role for judicial intervention, there is an important question as to how much. In one sense the argument turns on *who* can make the best decision about whether to change or enforce covenants.

In many instances this problem might be viewed as one of institutional competence: Do parties by agreement have a better sense of what is going on than do courts? Without majority rule provisions, it could be suggested that courts may do a better job than the parties because courts' information is better, even if their incentive to get things right is weaker. But where the parties have internal governance structures in place, these tend to undercut the judicial advantage by allowing homeowners' associations to defer the time of collective choice until they have the needed information. While there is doubtless some small place for the doctrine of changed conditions to operate on agreements that are incomplete, it should have at best a tiny importance once governance structures are in place. . . .

NOTES AND QUESTIONS ON PRIVATE LAND RESTRICTIONS

1. Is Epstein sweeping too broadly in likening private land restrictions ("covenants") to constitutions, or even in likening simple two-party covenants to more complex multiparty ones? Is a simple two-party covenant, such as a common driveway agreement, really a close relative of the complex covenants of a con-

dominium association or a large planned community such as Columbia, Maryland, or Reston, Virginia? Consider the feasibility of requirements for unanimous consent to alter covenant schemes: Is it important, for example, to have non-unanimous "sunset" rules (such as "changed conditions") to extinguish two-party covenants? Is it important to have them in multiparty contexts? Do constitutions ever contemplate unanimity at all, either at the initiation or amendment stage?

2. Epstein argues that the advent of the recordation system permits courts to dispense with many of the traditional hedges around covenants, on the theory that those hedges were basically aimed at assuring notice to purchasers; presumably recordation now can take over the notice function. Is that all that the hedges can or should do?

On this point, compare the article that Epstein cites: Gregory S. Alexander, Freedom, Coercion, and the Law of Servitudes, 73 Cornell L. Rev. 883 (1988), as well as Alexander's Dilemmas of Group Autonomy: Residential Associations and Community, 75 Cornell L. Rev. 1 (1989). Alexander argues that, among other things, even with formal notice, people may not really understand the covenant obligations that they supposedly undertake when they buy a covenanted property. Does Epstein's answer — that people are generally rational, and that Alexander's argument would deny the possibility of free contract or even intelligent political action — completely dispose of Alexander's argument? Who has the more realistic view of the development firms that in practice draft covenant schemes and the purchasers who buy into condominiums and planned communities? Are covenant arrangements systematically more obscure than ordinary contracts? Does it matter, for example, that in a contractual context, the parties often "cut the deal" themselves, whereas in the covenant context, one often buys a property upon which the deal has already been cut by preceding owners?

3. In opting for nonunanimous consent procedures and other mixed and "messy" systems of governance to avoid holdout problems in planned developments, is Epstein tacitly conceding the strength of Alexander's position — that people don't really know what they are getting into when they buy into condominium associations or other planned developments? Is Epstein's embrace of majority-rule devices a tacit concession that no one can see into the future accurately, even with the most careful planning? For an extensive development of the ways that the shortsightedness problem plays out in older servitude rules, see Stewart E. Sterk, Freedom from Freedom of Contract: The Enduring Value of Servitude Restrictions, 70 Iowa L. Rev. 615 (1985).

4. Epstein also discusses another of Alexander's critiques of

covenants (further developed in Dilemmas of Group Autonomy, supra): Covenants can turn planned communities into "tight little islands" in which

a. internal majorities can coerce internal minorities, and
b. the planned community can unduly insulate itself from outsiders.

With respect to the coercion of insiders, Epstein responds that people are not coerced if they choose to buy into the plan; with respect to discrimination against outsiders, he responds that discrimination can be countered directly by antidiscrimination legislation. Do these answers completely meet Alexander's objections?

What might subject the insider to coercion? Does the homeowner's investment itself make him or her vulnerable to coercion after purchase? Does it matter that the unit owner's investment is in a *home?* Compare Radin, Property and Personhood, supra p.8. Do the possible abuses of majority rule suggest that planned community self-rule should be limited in ways analogous to the constraints on majority rule in political communities? For further debate on this subject, see Robert C. Ellickson, Cities and Homeowners Associations, 130 Pa. L. Rev. 1519 (1982), and Gerald E. Frug, Cities and Homeowners' Associations: A Reply, 130 U. Pa. L. Rev. 1589 (1982).

Why might outsiders suffer from association rules? Do antidiscrimination laws suffice to keep planned development residents from isolating themselves from the larger community? For example, could planned community rules establish de facto income requirements that have discriminatory effects but are beyond the reach of antidiscrimination legislation? Is de facto income discrimination a greater risk in planned communities than in neighborhoods made up by individual sales of homes? In the latter, what role might be played by zoning laws that restrict homes exclusively to single-family houses? See the selections on public land-use controls, infra.

5. Related to Epstein's view is the argument that far from coercing or excluding individuals, covenants assure people a choice from a diverse mosaic of living environments. (Compare the Tiebout Hypothesis discussed in the notes to the selection by Michelman, infra p.514, describing households as "voting with their feet" among local governments.) Are there recognizable "community rights," such that planned communities, in order to retain their distinctiveness, must be entitled to put some constraints on individual behavior? Joseph Sax, Do Communities Have Rights? The National Parks as a Laboratory for New Ideals, 45 U. Pitt. L. Rev. 499 (1984), makes a case for "community rights," though not in the context of covenants.

Is it such a terrible thing to restrain the individual for the sake of the collective, if individuals can choose among many alternative collective lifestyles? Would there be so many alternatives if covenant enforcement were attenuated? Consider, for example, fraternities and sororities, religious communities, and other forms of communal living. Have the participants created their own versions of the "commons," subject to the tragedy of the commons unless the members submit to enforceable rules of cooperation and conformity? How does your answer affect your view of the legal constraints that might be put on planned community self-rule?

B.   Public Land Use Controls

A Walk Along Willow: Patterns of Land Use Coordination in Pre-Zoning New Haven (1870-1926)*

Andrew J. Cappel

. . . [T]he last thirty years have witnessed a lively debate between supporters and opponents of zoning. Supporters base their arguments on the explicit or implicit assumption that rational land use decisions cannot be made without public controls. Without zoning, the argument goes, incompatible uses, such as apartments and commercial or industrial enterprises, would encroach upon low-density residential neighborhoods — thus decreasing residential property values. In addition, uncontrolled development would place severe burdens on school systems, road networks, and other aspects of urban infrastructure and could cause environmental damage. Supporters of zoning buttress their argument by relying on an historical narrative which credits the rise of zoning to the failure of the earlier, unzoned legal regime, based primarily on common law nuisance, to promote adequately coordinated land use.[9]

Opponents of zoning, on the other hand, claim that zoning diverts land to less efficient uses, is costly to administer, and is susceptible to processes of municipal corruption. Critics also argue that

---

*Source: Note, 101 Yale L.J. 617-637 (1991).

9. This narrative was constructed by zoning advocates during the first decades after zoning achieved widespread implementation in the United States. See e.g., Edward M. Bassett, Zoning 22-26 (1936); 1. James Metzenbaum, The Law of Zoning 7-11, 65-68 (2d ed. 1955). . . .

zoning allows communities to exclude racially or economically un-desired groups and may increase the cost of available housing for such groups. They have also cast doubts upon the ability of local authorities to predict future community land use needs accurately when drawing up a comprehensive plan.[11] Suggested reforms range from proposals to curtail sharply the role of government (especially local government) in controlling land use to outright abolition of zoning.

The assumption underlying all of these criticisms is that market forces, in conjunction with popular social and aesthetic norms, will produce a system of satisfactorily coordinated land use without the defects associated with a zoned legal regime. The pioneering work on this subject was done by Bernard Siegan, who studied land use patterns in Houston, the only major unzoned city in the United States.[13] Concentrating on representative types of commercial use, such as gas stations and automobile dealerships, and on selected residential districts, Siegan concluded that Houston had attained roughly the same degree of land use coordination — especially seg-regation of incompatible uses, a traditional objective of zoning — as cities operating under zoned legal regimes.[14] Results of a handful of other studies of land use patterns in major American cities prior to the enactment of zoning ordinances at least partially support the notion that coordinated land use can arise under an unzoned legal system.[15]

All of these studies concern themselves with large, metropoli-tan areas and thus are necessarily impressionistic; moreover, most of them focus only on selected types of land use. In contrast, this Note constitutes the first attempt to look at an unzoned regime on a microlevel, block-by-block. It examines all of the aspects of land use that zoning traditionally regulates: building coverage, height, use, lot size, yards, and setbacks. The goal of this study is not to come to a definitive conclusion concerning the desirability of zoning as com-pared to a less regulated system of land use control. Rather, it seeks

11. See Jan Z. Krasnowiecki, The Fallacy of the End-State System of Land Use Control, Land Use L. & Zoning Dig., Apr. 1986, at 3.
13. Bernard H. Siegan, Non-Zoning in Houston, 13 J.L. & Econ. 71 (1970); Bernard H. Siegan, The Houston Solution: The Case for Removing Public Land Use Controls, Land Use Controls Q., Summer 1970, at 1 [hereinafter Siegan, Houston Solution].
14. See Siegan, Houston Solution, supra note 13, at 1. But cf. John Mixon, Neighborhood Zoning for Houston, 31 S. Tex. L. Rev. 1 (1990). Mixon argues that Houston's unzoned system has failed in important aspects of land use coordina-tion, particularly in preserving residential areas (and residential property values) from damage resulting from the proximity of incompatible commercial and indus-trial uses.
15. See Roger W. Lotchin, San Francisco 1846-1856 (1974): Sam B. Warner, Jr., Streetcar Suburbs (2d ed. 1978) (urban development in Boston, 1870-1900). . . .

to provide empirical evidence, on the microlevel of neighborhood development, of the ways in which a community without zoning succeeded in achieving rational land use coordination. This study offers a contribution to the larger contemporary debate concerning optimal forms of land use control by documenting the following: (1) the degree of land use coordination that can arise under an unzoned legal regime; (2) the extent to which any such coordinated land use may arise from economic and social forces, rather than from formal legal controls; and (3) the circumstances under which public regulations are effective in influencing private choices about land use and the circumstances under which they are relatively ineffective in doing so. In addition, this Note will cast some doubt upon the validity of the prevailing pro-zoning historical narrative: Contrary to this narrative, my research suggests that zoning might not always have been adopted in response to serious failures of the unzoned legal regime.

The subject of my research is New Haven, Connecticut, from 1870 to 1926. The study starts at the same time the city began the largest urban expansion in its history and concludes in 1926 with the enactment of its first zoning ordinance. New Haven offers a number of advantages for a study of this nature. It is representative of medium-sized cities that warmly embraced zoning during the 1920's. As an early, well-developed commercial and industrial center, as well as a center of rail transportation, New Haven possessed an abundance of the types of land uses thought to be incompatible with the preservation of residential neighborhoods. Like most medium-sized and large American cities, New Haven had a heterogeneous population composed of Yankees, Italian and Irish immigrants, and small Jewish and Black communities; it is therefore unlikely that any observed patterns of coordinated land use can be attributed to particular cultural characteristics of individual ethnic groups. Local historians have left extremely thorough documentation of the city's history, and printed records are available for all of the city's Board of Aldermen meetings during the period 1870-1926. Above all, we can trace the development of land use in pre-zoning New Haven through a remarkable series of maps, dated 1886, 1901, and 1923, that were developed for use by fire insurance companies. These maps specify the exact location, height, and mass of every structure in the city, and also specify each structure's use, such as commercial, industrial, or residential, and single or multifamily.

My research has concentrated on a seventeen block, predominantly middle class residential area in the northeast part of the city, between Lawrence and Cold Spring Streets and between Foster and St. Ronan Streets — and in particular, on the "Willow-Canner strip" which consists of the blocks between Willow Street and the south side of Canner from Foster to St. Ronan. On this strip, land use patterns have been analyzed on a lot-by-lot basis. This district has been selected because it is representative of the type of areas opened to development in the post-1870 years and because it is especially well suited for study in conjunction with the fire insurance maps, the first set of which was produced in 1886. Because the northeast residential district was one of the few in the city to remain rural until this time, it offers an exceptional opportunity to follow the growth of a neighborhood from the ground up. . . .

I. Patterns of Land Use

A cursory glance at maps of pre-zoning New Haven reveals an unmistakable pattern: Most industrial and commercial uses were segregated from residential property. In 1912, over sixty percent of manufacturing concerns, including virtually all heavy industry in the city, were located in a relatively small number of locations. . . . Within these areas, industrial concerns tended to group themselves together in discrete units, separated from neighboring housing. The resulting concentration left other portions of the city completely nonindustrial. Thus, in 1923, the northeast residential section of the city contained no manufacturing concerns; factories instead were grouped along its fringes. . . . Similarly, while State Street and the central downtown district were flourishing commercial centers, the area between Lawrence and East Rock Streets possessed only eighteen commercial sites, all but three of which were situated on corners along the north-south thoroughfares of Orange, Anderson, and Foster Streets. These sites did not encroach into the surrounding east-west residential blocks.

Examination of the northeast residential district, in particular of the Willow-Canner strip, reveals other, more subtle patterns of coordinated land use. The very existence of such patterns seems remarkable in light of how most of northeast New Haven was developed in the late nineteenth and early twentieth centuries. There are only occasional examples of developers in the modern sense of the term, who bought large parcels of land on which to build homes for public sale. More commonly, the original rural landowner sold lots directly to individual buyers or to small-scale investors who held the property — generally in groups of four lots or less — for resale. As originally surveyed, lots were of uniform size with fifty-foot frontages, but purchasers could always buy lots with greater or lesser dimensions. After purchase, owners hired their own builders or architects to design and construct their homes. Thus, the high degree of land use coordination that we find in this area cannot, for

Northeast New Haven in 1923

N

→

Single Family

Two Family

Three Family

Apartments

Commercial

Undeveloped

443

the most part, be attributed to the actions of a single planner-owner-builder. New Haven was largely developed house-by-house with the patterns of coordination emerging out of the independent decisions of many individuals.

A. Lot Size

One of the most striking features of the pre-zoning regime was the segregation of lots according to size. From Foster to Orange Streets, lots along Willow and Canner Streets tended to be small, with the majority under 4000 square feet. Sizes increased from Orange to Livingston Streets, where a typical lot measured between 5000 and 7000 square feet. Lots between Livingston and Whitney Avenue ran larger, with half measuring 7000 square feet or more. The largest lots were those from Whitney Avenue to the west, with the majority in excess of 9000 square feet. A glance at the map confirms that this progressive east-west increase in lot size was a dominant characteristic of the entire northeast residential district.

B. Single v. Multifamily Dwellings

The location of single-family houses and two- and three-family "flats" roughly mirrored the segregation of lots, with the number of multifamily homes decreasing from east to west. A number of two-family houses, as well as some three-family, "triple-decker" buildings, were built east of Orange Street. Two-family houses predominated on most blocks between Orange and Livingston Streets, while, moving west, two-family houses appeared less frequently near Whitney Avenue. The area west of Whitney was composed almost exclusively of single-family dwellings.

By 1923, the northeast residential district, like the rest of New Haven, had undergone the phenomenon of multiple unit apartment construction. Here, as with lot size and multifamily home distribution, it is possible to observe a remarkable degree of segregation: While complexes were built along Whitney Avenue and in fringe areas on south Orange and near State, there was no sign of significant encroachment by apartments into the central portion of the residential district.

C. Building Coverage

Despite substantial variations in lot and building size, the houses along Canner and Willow Streets displayed surprising uniformity in building coverage, i.e., the percentage of a lot covered by a structure. Of the 111 sites with reliable documentation, all but twelve had buildings (excluding garages) that covered a third or less of total lot size. In fact, the majority of sites had building coverage of a quarter or less of total lot size, and no building covered more than half its site. Indeed, in the northeast residential district as a whole, only six sites had building coverage greater than fifty percent.

D. Building Height

With the exception of fourteen structures, eight triple-decker residences east of Orange Street, two stores on Foster Street, single houses on Lawrence and Everit Streets, and two apartment complexes on Whitney Avenue (all three stories high), all buildings in the northeast residential district were two and one-half stories or less.

E. Frontyards and Rearyards

Most of the structures on Willow and Canner Streets were generously set back from the street line, often with a notable degree of uniformity. On the north side of Willow Street between Livingston Street and Whitney Avenue, for example, every building was set back exactly twelve feet. On the south side of Canner Street between Whitney and Orange, the closest building stood twelve feet away from the street line, and most of the remaining houses on the block were set back twelve to fifteen feet. Frontyard setbacks were similarly spaced throughout most of the northeast residential district, although the distances diminished somewhat at the eastern edge. Rearyards throughout northeast New Haven were uniformly deeper than thirty feet, and most were greater than forty to fifty feet deep.

F. Sideyards

Sideyards also displayed a great deal of coordination, although it is superficially hard to see. At first glance, the small size of sideyards seems to reflect a weakness in New Haven's pre-zoning regime. In the northeast residential district, sideyards were small: along the Willow-Canner strip, more than half measured five feet or less. If the distance between houses serves as our standard of measure, however, the proportions were more ample. Few houses were closer to one another than ten feet, and most stood much farther apart than that. Indeed, the size of their separation often compared favorably to the fourteen foot minimum enacted under the 1926 zoning ordinance. Even on the small lots east of Orange Street, only two buildings extended to the lot line, and sufficient space normally existed between buildings to ensure adequate air and light. When an early buyer on a block placed his house near the lot edge, the subsequent purchaser of an adjacent lot would often place his house at the extreme opposite edge of his own lot, setting a pattern followed by subsequent purchasers. For example, prior to 1901, houses were built on the right side of lots at 285-287 and 281-283 Willow Street. When owners built in 1906-1907 on the next two adjacent lots, 279 and 277, they likewise positioned their structures at the far right side. Throughout the northeast residential district, whole lines of buildings on adjacent lots owed their site configuration to this same phenomenon. An informal social mechanism was thus created to resolve a complicated coordination problem.

In sum, on the eve of zoning, the northeast sector constituted a predominantly residential district bordered, but largely unencroached upon, by industrial and commercial sites. Lots gradually increased in size on blocks running from east to west, while the incidence of multifamily homes decreased; apartment construction remained largely confined to Whitney Avenue and areas near State Street. Building heights were low, rearyards large, and, with some exceptions, houses were situated in a roughly uniform manner an ample distance from the street. Landowners do not appear to have economized on land costs by erecting large structures on small lots; building coverage was low and remarkably uniform, and sideyards, although sometimes small, were normally sufficient for light and ventilation. Taken together, these patterns reveal a complex system of land use coordination arising out of the gradual processes of neighborhood development.

II.   Land Use Controls Under a Pre-Zoning Legal Regime

The unzoned legal regime, as we have just noted, was capable of producing examples of highly sophisticated land use coordination. What is not clear from the foregoing discussion is the extent to which such coordination arose from the existence of legal rules and regulations as opposed to nonlegal forces. In order to clarify these issues, it is first necessary to outline the essential features of the pre-zoning regime.

A.   Public Law: Municipal Ordinances and Regulations

As was the case elsewhere in the country, New Haven's city government underwent a transformation during the course of the second half of the nineteenth century[52] — expanding, with the creation of most of the major city departments, into roughly its current form. With these changes in the size and organization of city government came a vast enlargement in the extent and scope of municipal legislation. For example, the Building Code, which in 1870 took a mere four pages, comprised seventy-three pages of detailed regulations by 1914. Land use regulations were unusually extensive and often painstakingly detailed, with countless pages in the minutes of city council meetings devoted to such issues as whether to allow erection of billboards, theater marquises, and illuminated signs, and whether to permit building cornices to project over the sidewalk.

This did not constitute regulation in the modern sense of zoning, that is, consciously planned public control over the size and location of all types of public and private land uses. In keeping with nineteenth-century laissez faire doctrines, the city charter largely limited the scope of municipal legislation to matters of public property. To the extent that government authority extended over private property, it was restricted within the confines of the police power: prevention of fire, supervision of building safety, prohibition of private encroachment onto public streets and walks, and abatement of public nuisances.

The ordinances enacted under these charter provisions nevertheless covered a wide range of concerns touching upon problems related to land use coordination and urban development. For example, the city controlled the layout of streets in developing areas and approved the plan for private streets that landowners established before selling their parcels to the public. Similarly, the state controlled the location of street railway lines, which, by tying outlying areas to the downtown, constituted the avenues along which urban development took place.

Even before 1870, New Haven had received state authorization to establish building lines that would provide uniform mandatory minimum setbacks along each block. By 1910, however, it had become clear that the city's efforts to establish minimum legal setbacks had proven ineffective: some areas had no building lines; in other areas, there was widespread encroachment of buildings across the designated lines; and many earlier lines were established without the legally mandated assessment of damages and benefits, and were

52. On the 19th-century transformation of urban local government in the United States, see generally Hendrik Hartog, Public Property and Private Power (1983); Robin L. Einhorn, Property Rules (1991). Einhorn's book also provides a valuable discussion of how pre-zoning legal rules, in particular the use of special assessments to finance public works, influenced development patterns in Chicago during the years 1833-1872. See Einhorn, supra. at 61-187.

therefore unenforceable. Between 1910 and 1914, the Board of Aldermen, assisted by a newly created Commission on Building Lines, established new lines, confirmed or modified hundreds of existing ones, and passed an ordinance requiring that a building line be established for each new street at the time of its initial layout. The city designated some of these lines on its own initiative, but the majority of these lines appear to have been established in response to petitions of local landowners who desired legally mandated setbacks.

Other land use regulations appeared in the Fire and Building Codes. Most of the downtown area was designated a fire district: Within this area, owners were prohibited from erecting new wooden structures; additions to existing wooden buildings were permitted only after the owner had received special approval from the city; and no such addition could extend closer than five feet to the property line. New wooden construction was permitted outside of the fire district, but wooden houses could not be built to a height greater than three floors. In addition, no existing frame building could be converted into flats containing more than three units, and owners were prohibited from constructing multifamily housing in their rearyards. In 1905, the state enacted legislation regulating construction of "tenements" — multifamily dwellings of more than three units — that mandated maximum building coverage (ninety percent of corner lots, seventy-five percent of others), minimum rearyard sizes (ten feet), and, in most cases, minimum sideyards (four feet). At the same time, a municipal ordinance seeking to guarantee minimum levels of light and ventilation in other buildings imposed a maximum ninety-percent limit on building coverage, except for corner lots, throughout the city.

Finally, New Haven's charter empowered the city to abate nuisances injurious to health or offensive to the public. Under this grant, the city was able to regulate particularly hazardous or noxious uses: Tanneries, sellers of gunpowder and inflammable oils, slaughterhouses, and manufacturers of tallow and soap could not occupy a site without obtaining a special license. The minutes of city council meetings occasionally mention citizen complaints concerning smoke and noise were nuisances emanating from nearby railroad tracks or industrial concerns and specify the actions taken by the city for the abatement of these nuisances.

B. Private Law: Nuisance

Where public nuisance action was impossible, either because the harm was confined to a few neighbors or because those affected by the nuisance sought damages as well as abatement, aggrieved owners found a potent source of relief in the law of private nuisance.

In particular, Connecticut law was unusually favorable to local residents in actions against nearby industrial concerns. In Whitney v. Bartholomew, the Connecticut Supreme Court of Errors held that even lawful uses, performed without negligence on the defendant's property, could be considered nuisances if they caused unreasonable damage to a neighbor's health or property.[80] In other decisions, Connecticut courts rejected two common defenses to nuisance actions: plaintiff's coming to the nuisance, and defendant's operating under a city license. To balance the scales somewhat, courts defined "reasonable use" in a flexible manner. Rather than applying an abstract uniform standard, courts held that reasonableness depended not only on the nature of the use, but also on its location; homeowners in industrial districts were expected to endure higher degrees of discomfort from smoke and noise than were their counterparts in more residential areas. Industry was thus protected against sensitive neighbors, and judges had the freedom to allow industrial and residential uses to coexist near one another, while still protecting homeowners from glaring abuses.[84]

III.   Legal and Non-legal Determinants of Coordination

Public and private law in New Haven had the potential to influence land use significantly. By returning to northeast New Haven, this Note analyzes the extent to which the existing patterns of coordination may have arisen as a response to the regulations of this legal regime or, alternatively, to nonlegal factors.

A.   The Role of Law

1.   STREET GRID

When preparing an area for development, owners were required to submit plans for new streets for city approval, and such

---

80. Whitney v. Bartholomew, 21 Conn. 213, 218-219 (1851).

84. In addition to nuisance suits, the existence of private covenants among landowners could have had a significant impact on local land use patterns. By the mid-19th century, Connecticut courts had upheld the enforceability of covenants running with the land. See Wright v. Wright, 21 Conn. 329 (1851). The issue of covenants need not be studied here in detail, however, since restrictive covenants were not employed in New Haven to any significant extent prior to the 1940's as a method of attaining large-scale coordinated land use. Interview with attorneys Paul North, Jr., and Daniel Dennis, Jr., in New Haven, Conn. (Nov. 20, 1990) (authorities on history of New Haven real estate). For example, with the exception of a number of right-of-way easements . . . none of the lots on the Willow-Canner strip is encumbered by title restrictions.

approval was almost invariably granted.[85] City officials seem to have shared with developers and individual buyers a common cultural notion of what a residential street should look like, and City Hall — hoping to increase the rate of private homeownership — provided a layout of streets and blocks that was attractive to potential buyers. A harmonious combination of public regulation and popular expectations thus gave rise to the familiar street grid of small blocks which were easily divisible into the deep rectangular lots favored by most buyers.

2. SEGREGATION OF USES

The pattern of segregation of industry away from residences appears largely to be rooted in the legal regime. Confronted with proresidential nuisance law, industry tended to congregate in isolated districts and blocks. The possibility of a nuisance suit also facilitated coordination between disparate uses by encouraging private abatement agreements. In addition, the flexible juridical notion of "reasonable uses" promoted industrial/residential coordination by stimulating construction of inexpensive housing in strips alongside industrial districts whose low cost compensated for the annoyance of smoke and noise.

There are other examples of segregated uses that are attributable to public decisionmaking. In particular, government control over the location of streetcar lines profoundly influenced patterns of neighborhood development. Apartment buildings appeared near Whitney Avenue and State Street where the presence of streetcars made these areas uniquely well suited for multiunit construction. Similarly, the presence of a streetcar line on State Street stimulated a concentration of commercial establishments there. As a result of such concentration, the remainder of the northeast part of the city was left free for low-density residential use.

3. SETBACKS

Ironically, building lines, the object of so much municipal regulation, played a relatively minor role in neighborhood development. Along the Willow-Canner strip, most residences failed to observe the legal limit, and the same pattern can be seen elsewhere in the city, even after the Board of Aldermen attempted to redesignate the lines between 1910 and 1914. This phenomenon is partly explained by lax municipal enforcement, but it also reflects a deep conflict between municipal law and entrenched building custom. When owners, usually early purchasers on a block, petitioned for a building

---

85. During the period 1870-1926, there was only one case in which the city failed to approve a proposed street plan. . . .

line, the city usually designated one a few feet behind the line of existing structures in order to ensure larger future setbacks. Subsequent purchasers had to choose whether to follow the mandated line or their neighbors' practice. While examples of both decisions exist, the latter is more common, reflecting the dominance of local building customs at the time when most of the northeast residential district was built. The power of this custom was more evident on blocks like those at the east end of Willow Street, where there were predominantly uniform setbacks of six to twelve feet, despite the fact that the law permitted building up to the street line. This suggests that the law was valuable mainly as a reinforcement to local practice, encouraging owners to leave adequate, if not always fully legal, setbacks by building as far from the street as their neighbors. . . .

B. Nonlegal Determinants . . .

Uniformity in height, building coverage, and yards seems largely attributable to purchaser preferences. A number of magazines at the turn of the century published plans and descriptions of idealized detached homes characterized by low height, limited mass, and generous yards of the type found in northeast New Haven. These publications played an important role in shaping popular demand for a certain type of construction. Such uniformity was furthered by the fact that New Haven possessed relatively few residential architects and builders whom owners could ask to design their homes, and they tended to build the same type of house over and over. For example, many of the houses on Willow Street were designed by two men, William Allen and Frank Brown. Coordinated land use was also promoted by private agreements between individuals: when the owner of lots at 344 and 346 Willow Street sold the 346 property in 1924, he included in the sales agreement a provision giving him an eight-foot right-of-way easement over the land directly adjacent to his remaining property, thus preventing the neighbor from building too close to the lot line. In addition, there are examples of informal social norms exerting influence over landowner behavior: archival records reveal instances where individuals encouraged their neighbors to conform to community building standards.

IV. The Introduction of Zoning

In 1926, despite the presence of sophisticated patterns of coordinated land use, New Haven passed its first zoning ordinance. The

question therefore arises whether the introduction of zoning occurred as a response to significant failings of the pre-zoning regime
or was caused by factors having little or nothing to do with actual
conditions of land use in the city. The paucity of source material
makes it impossible to give a conclusive answer to this question, but
some general observations can be made. Initial interest in zoning
appears to have arisen as the result of anxieties associated with the
rapid pace of urban growth in the years after 1870.

In the aftermath of the population and building booms of 1870-
1910, New Haven was confronted with a shortage of land for development in reasonable proximity to downtown. At the same time,
technological advances in transportation and engineering led to the
introduction of automobiles and highrise construction in the city.
As a result, the city began to experience problems of increased traffic, lack of parking, and congestion caused by the construction of
apartments and tall downtown office buildings. Moreover, some
homeowners may have become apprehensive that this congestion
might force commercial enterprises to locate on residential blocks
and thereby cause a decline in nearby residential property values.
Concern about these problems appears to have led to fears that the
formal and informal controls that had formerly determined land use
decisionmaking and safeguarded the interests of property owners
might prove inadequate in the face of large-scale demographic and
technological change. Such fears persuaded important elements of
the city's business and political elites, above all the Chamber of
Commerce, to support the City Plan Commission's proposal to
adopt zoning as part of a broader scheme of planned urban development. Over time, local advocates of urban planning, armed with
theories of the "City Beautiful" movement, which had become
prominent throughout the country after its inception at the 1893 Co-
lumbian Exposition, came to dominate the discussion of land use
controls, and the actual conditions of the city became increasingly
irrelevant. Outside consultants educated residents on the theoretical
superiority of zoned to unzoned land use, and in 1924 the mayor
chided his fellow citizens for failing to adopt the progressive policies already enacted by more enlightened neighbors.

What got lost in this discussion was the fact that the unzoned
system appeared to function fairly well. This was clearly the case in
residential northeast New Haven, where there was no indication of
widespread problems of traffic or of encroachment of high-density
or commercial uses onto residential blocks. The scant evidence also
suggests that problems of land use coordination were also not acute
in the remainder of the city. For example, while several traditionally
poor areas of New Haven had degenerated into slums by the 1920's,
this process or urban decay appears to have been largely self-

contained and did not seem to have spread significantly into surrounding areas. In addition, there is no evidence of widespread popular dissatisfaction with the pre-zoning system. Instead, the mass of small residential and commercial landowners formed some of zoning's most vociferous critics. In 1924, a group of property owners petitioned the Board of Aldermen in opposition to zoning, and public reaction at hearings held in 1925 was overwhelmingly opposed to zoning, as unduly restrictive of owners' rights to find the most profitable use for their properties.

Thus, there never appears to have been a widespread, grass roots perception in New Haven's neighborhoods that the city's pre-zoning regime did not work. Rather, new theories of urban planning fed into and complemented general fears relating to the city's growth and modernization, making zoning supporters view zoning as both necessary and inevitable. The continuing efficacy of the pre-zoning system of land use coordination, however, is confirmed by a glance at provisions of the 1926 zoning ordinance for northeast New Haven: Instead of imposing stricter requirements on the area, the ordinance, with a few exceptions, simply confirmed existing patterns of development. As a result, the great majority of buildings in northeast New Haven were already in substantial compliance with the ordinance's provisions. . . .

. . . Although the results of a single, small-scale study cannot be considered determinative, this study of New Haven casts doubt upon the prevailing assumption that coherent land use cannot take place without the type of planned public regulation represented by zoning. In particular, the results of this survey indicate that where public regulation conflicts with local economic realities or social norms — as was the case with municipal regulation of building lines — such regulation is likely to prove ineffective.[119]

In addition, this study suggests that the introduction of zoning into New Haven was not necessitated by actual conditions of local land use, but rather was the work of certain elites, particularly members of the Chamber of Commerce and City Plan Commission, who were influenced by theories developed as part of the national "City Beautiful" movement. Therefore, in contrast to the narrative traditionally advanced by supporters of zoning, the rapid spread of zoning in the 1920's may well have brought zoning to cities like New Haven where it was not really needed.

---

119. A similar result was reached as part of a study of patterns of urban change in New Haven several decades after the initiation of zoning. It concluded that when a community is confronted with changes either in economic conditions or in popular expectations concerning land use, "zoning probably does little more than slow down the inevitable." David L. Birch et al, Patterns of Urban Change 71-73 (1974).

NOTES AND QUESTIONS ON THE EVOLUTION AND MERITS OF ZONING

1. How representative is New Haven? The neighborhood Cappel describes? A statistical study with results consistent with Cappel's is Daniel P. McMillen & John F. McDonald, Could Zoning Have Increased Land Values in Chicago?, 33 J. Urb. Econ. 167 (1993) ("We can state definitively that zoning did not increase land values in 1920s Chicago. . . .").

2. Does Cappel provide adequate evidence on the relative influence of custom, public and private nuisance law, and prezoning regulations on development in New Haven during 1870-1926? Recall the materials on informal property rights, supra Chapter 6.

3. Cappel's essay indicates the welter of more limited public regulations that preceded zoning. What activities do zoning ordinances govern that these prior legal measures did not? How might one argue that New Haven needed zoning more to control uses with pervasive effects (such as tall buildings) than uses with localized effects (such as backyard garages). Recall Calabresi and Melamed's thoughts on how transaction costs vary with the number of parties, supra p.252.

4. Suppose five individuals, A, B, C, D, and E, each own one of five adjacent and equally sized lots on a blockfront on Poplar Street, which runs east-west. As in the Cappel vignette on p.446, the three middle owners (B, C, and D) all shift the footprints of their houses toward the western portions of their lots. A and E have preexisting houses situated in the middle of their respective lots. How well has the sideyard-setback problem been resolved on Poplar Street? How likely, according to Cappel, is this sort of outcome in the absence of zoning?

5. Cappel's study terminates in 1926. What are its current implications, given intervening legal, social, and technological changes? More specifically, Cappel's New Haven lacked large-scale developers and — perhaps as a result — was almost entirely free of land-use covenants until the 1940s. (See Cappel's footnote 84.) Is zoning more or less necessary when developers are large in scale and subdivision covenants routine? Shopping centers have largely supplanted the sorts of mom-and-pop commercial outlets that appear on Cappel's map. Do bigger stores create a greater need for zoning?

6. Cappel asserts that members of business and political elites brought zoning to New Haven, even though popular opinion was opposed to it. How widespread is popular support for zoning today? Is it significant that the number of localities with zoning ordi-

nances continues to mount, and that scarcely any have repudiated zoning after first embracing it?

William A. Fischel, the Economics of Zoning Laws (1985), comprehensively assesses the institution. Fischel theorizes that local officials "attempt to maximize the net worth of the median voter" in the locality. Id. at 127. If so, zoning officials can be expected to cater entirely to current residents, without regard to the welfare of nonresident households and owners of undeveloped tracts in the locality. Is Fischel's political model realistic?

7. The role of covenants in land use regulation is discussed in the preceding selection by Epstein, and the following selection by Fischel. How easy is it for the residents of an existing neighborhood to create a covenant regime to control future development? Instead of authorizing zoning, should a state legislature authorize the owners of, say, two-thirds of the acreage in a neighborhood to impose covenants that bind the entire neighborhood? Would such a scheme violate one-person, one-vote requirements? More generally, what changes in servitude law would lessen the need for zoning?

8. Although the institution of zoning is firmly ensconced in the United States, a vigorous debate rages over the merits of the institution. Virtually all commentators have been critical of suburbs' exclusionary practices that thwart construction of modest-cost housing. Most observers are comfortable, however, with the basic notion that a local government should tightly control the development of the private lands within its borders. The underlying rationale is that development tends to generate externalities that developers will not adequately take into account. Can this rationale survive the Coasean critique, supra Chapter 4?

For criticism — implicit and explicit — of the soundness of the institution of zoning, see, for example, the sources cited in the Cappel reading; Jane J. Jacobs, The Death and Life of Great American Cities (1961); Robert C. Ellickson, Alternatives to Zoning: Covenants, Nuisance Rules, and Fines as Land Use Controls, 40 U. Chi. L. Rev. 681 (1977); Douglas W. Kmiec, Deregulating Land Use: An Alternative Free Enterprise Development System, 130 U. Pa. L. Rev. 28 (1981).

9. A staunch defense of zoning can be found in Eric Steele, Participation and Rules — The Functions of Zoning, 1986 Am. B. Found. Res. J. 709. Steele studied the piecemeal zoning change process in Evanston, an older suburban city north of Chicago. He came away impressed with the success of zoning as a participatory mechanism:

> ... I suggest that zoning ordinances should be viewed as procedural mechanisms to guarantee the opportunity for community participa-

tion just as much as they are viewed as rules mandating the specific details of physical design. Zoning rules form a checklist of objective physical characteristics that crudely and indirectly try to set out and define minimum standards for ephemeral, subjective, qualitative, environmental characteristics of community life. . . .

The functioning of zoning boards makes far more sense when zoning rules are viewed as a set of criteria to identify which proposed changes may be potentially problematic to the community. The working assumption is that building more of the same is not problematic but building bigger, taller, denser, or for a different use may be damaging and therefore requires review. When potentially problematic proposals are identified, the community is notified and its members are offered the chance to come forward and state their concerns.

Id. at 749. If, as Fischel posits, local officials cater to the median voter in a municipality, does zoning serve all "community" interests? How do zoning's participatory mechanisms compare with those at work when a homeowners' association enforces covenants? When neighbors interact on a customary basis, as Cappel has described? See generally Carol M. Rose, New Models for Local Land Use Decisions, 79 Nw. U. L. Rev. 1155 (1984-1985).

10. Section 3 of the Standard Zoning Enabling Act provides that zoning "regulations shall be made in accordance with a comprehensive plan." Is comprehensive planning desirable? Possible?

The fundamental idea of zoning is that development is best controlled by a set of "self-administering" rules laid down by the legislative body of a municipality long in advance of actual development. The administrative paraphernalia of zoning, and the opinions of the courts, assume that this idea is sound and that it offers a true description of zoning. . . .

The central idea of the planner is that government ought to dictate the future, and zoning is the ultimate expression of this idea. If zoning, in fact, relates to development through a series of amendments and relaxations undertaken pursuant to pressure put upon the system by application or litigation, then the attempt to control the future by describing it in detail, in advance, has failed, and reality looks more like disjointed incrementalism — a theory of planning few planners would want to embrace. . . .

The thesis of this paper is that zoning cannot work, especially in a developing community. . . .

Jan Z. Krasnowiecki, Abolish Zoning, 31 Syracuse L. Rev. 719-720 (1980). Krasnowiecki proposes a law creating "a statutory presumption that any housing project must be approved unless the approving agency gives persuasive reasons why it should not." Id. at 750. Are courts capable of reviewing local decisions under the standard that Krasnowiecki proposes?

11. Daniel R. Mandelker & Roger A. Cunningham, Planning and Control of Land Development 1-24 (3rd ed. 1990), provides a concise review of the policy debate over zoning and planning.

Do Growth Controls Matter? A Review of Empirical Evidence on the Effectiveness and Efficiency of Local Government Land Use Regulations*

William A. Fischel

. . . The focus of this survey is local government control of development, not national environmental policy. Growth control devices include the tightening of traditional zoning laws as well as moratoriums on the extension of water and sewer lines, nonprice rationing of building permits, and tying development permits to the provision of new public facilities. . . . [Some commentators assert] that most of zoning's benefits could be provided by private covenants and nuisance laws. Bernard Siegan's (1972) study of Houston seems to support this claim, insofar as covenants are widely used in that city in lieu of zoning.

The covenant alternative would be most persuasive if it were easy to establish covenants in developed areas that lacked them. Janet Furman Spreyer (1989) demonstrates that they are not. Spreyer found a rare sample that enabled her to compare a zoned area with an unzoned area. The city of Houston, which still has no zoning, surrounds two municipalities that do have zoning. Within Houston are neighborhoods that are subject to private covenants and some that are not. Using a sample of homes that included all three arrangements — (a) zoned, (b) unzoned but covenanted, and (c) unzoned and uncovenanted — Spreyer was able to determine which types of property were most valuable, after accounting for the usual differences.

Spreyer found that unzoned but covenanted properties in Houston had the same value as properties in the zoned cities, but that properties that were both unzoned and uncovenanted were significantly less valuable than either of the others. In symbols, the value of (a)=(b)>(c). (To be precise, Spreyer found no statistically significant difference between (a) and (b), not perfect equality.) This could provide arguments for both sides: People who favor zoning can say it performs as well as covenants but is more easily altered, while people who dislike zoning can say that covenants do just as well as zoning with none of the governmental coercion.

Both debating points miss the cost of forming covenants. If it were easy to establish covenants in already-developed areas (or in areas in which covenants had expired — courts usually limit their duration to less than fifty years), one should observe that uncove-

*Source: pp. 2, 13-19, 23, 29-37, 53-57 (1990).

nanted land (c) has the same value as that subject to covenants (b). All it would take to convert uncovenanted land to covenanted land would be some legal fees to record the covenant in each deed. Since legal fees per housing unit would presumably be small, the reduction in land value caused by lack of covenants should be trivial. Spreyer's result, then, shows that covenants are costly to establish. This is intuitively plausible. Transaction costs of getting *all* people in an existing neighborhood to agree to restrict potential uses of their property are usually prohibitively high.

Simply to say that some zoning may be justified by the lower transaction costs of establishing it is not to say that any type of zoning is justified. Moreover, Spreyer's exclusive attention to single-family homes precludes any efficiency analysis. Lack of covenants might have permitted multifamily homes or commercial uses with values that could have been much greater than the single-family homes they displaced or devalued. But Spreyer's results do suggest that covenants are a realistic alternative to zoning only in undeveloped areas in which a single developer can acquire enough land and impose restrictions prior to sale of the homes themselves. . . .

An important pair of studies by William Stull (1975) and Ronald Lafferty and Ted Frech (1978) [addresses] the interaction between neighborhood spillover effects and local land use controls. . . . Using median home values from a 1960s sample of 40 suburban towns in the Boston metropolitan area, Stull found that nonresidential uses did adversely affect home values. Specifically, the proportion of community land devoted to the multifamily dwellings and to industrial land uses lowered single-family home values. Stull also found that the proportion of land devoted to commercial uses raised median home values when the proportion was low, but that larger proportions lowered home values. His interpretation of this is that community residents like a little commercial development for the convenience of shopping nearby, but regional commercial centers are regarded as a net cost.

Lafferty and Frech undertook to replicate Stull's study with the same sample of Boston suburbs, but they added an insightful twist. They pointed out that the avowed purpose of traditional zoning was not to exclude entire categories of uses, as Stull seemed to imply, but to concentrate them in contiguous zones. Zoning is, in principle, a municipal good-housekeeping rule: a place for everything, and everything in its place. . . . Their critique of Stull is that he looked only at community-wide effects, neglecting the adverse effects of nonresidential properties on individual properties.

To rectify this, Lafferty and Frech employed Stull's sample with an additional variable that measured the *dispersion* of nonresidential

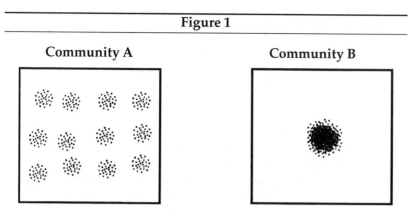

Figure 1

Community A   Community B

Dark areas are nonresidential uses.

land uses. If traditional zoning theory is valid, a community that is half nonresidential but with all stores and factories concentrated in a single district will have higher average home values than similar communities that have permitted their nonresidential uses to be dispersed among the housing developments. (In fact, of course, most of the dispersed nonresidential uses might have predated the existing zoning ordinance.) In Figure 1, Community *A* should have lower average residential values than Community *B*.

Lafferty and Frech found that their dispersion index was an important overall determinant of housing values. The more dispersed a community's nonresidential land uses, the lower the value, on average, of single-family homes. The good-housekeeping theory of zoning is thus supported although the significance level of several individual variables was doubtful. . . .

One issue raised by the studies of Stull and Lafferty and Frech is the effect of undeveloped land on nearby single-family home values. In Stull's specification, a higher proportion of vacant and agricultural land reduced the average value of housing; in Lafferty and Frech's specification, the dispersion rather than the proportion of vacant land reduced the value of housing. (Dispersion is highly correlated with proportion for this variable, though.) Both findings seem entirely at odds with modern growth control rhetoric, in which preservation of open space is the *summum bonum*. If we are to take these results literally, then arguing against further residential development is irrational in the sense that maintaining open space seems to *reduce* average home values.

The problem with this interpretation (which may, even so, be a correct conclusion) is that, in the samples used, vacant land is a residual category that includes swamps and military bases as well as golf courses, parks, and wildlife refuges. Its negative impact, Stull surmises, is due to the uncertainty of future development rather than undesirability of the current use itself (1975, p. 546). Anxieties that the open space may be developed with uses that adversely affect their properties may outweigh homeowners' current enjoyment of open space. In other studies, permanently established greenbelts in other areas of the country are found to have a positive effect on nearby home values, which comports with the rhetoric of most suburban growth control advocates.[19] Thus one cannot infer that growth control is irrational from the Boston suburban studies, though it seems reasonable to surmise . . . that the enthusiasm for open space may often stem from a dislike of a specific proposal than an affection for open space itself. . . .

Gerrit Knaap (1985) conducted a study of the Portland, Oregon, urban growth boundaries. This is of special interest because it involves a modern program of comprehensive growth controls. Oregon state legislation requires that urban areas define growth boundaries around their perimeters to prevent sprawl and preserve farmland. Portland has two such boundaries: an outer perimeter beyond which no development is allowed until the year 2000 and an inner boundary outside of which development can be forbidden at local option until the land inside has been fully developed.

Knaap's 455 observations (from a sample taken during 1980) were undeveloped sites zoned for single-family homes. They were drawn from inside and outside both boundaries. His results showed that in the two Portland-area counties (Washington and Clackamas), land outside the outer growth boundary sold for significantly less than land inside the boundary. Because Knaap had already accounted for distance from the Portland CBD separately, he inferred that the twenty-year delay in development was perceived as a binding constraint and reduced the land values outside the outer boundary. His results for the effects of the inner boundary were mixed. In Washington County, the more affluent of the two counties studied, the inner growth boundary was shown also to be a constraint, but this was not so in Clackamas County. I think this inconsistency may be explained by the fact that the inner boundary may be breached by local government exceptions, which may have been more readily forthcoming in less affluent and more rural Clackamas County. . . .

19. Correll, Lillydahl, and Singell (1978) found this for Boulder, Colorado, and Nelson (1988) found a similar effect for Portland, Oregon.

§6   Growth Controls and Housing Costs . . .

Seymour Schwartz at the University of California at Davis has been a coauthor of numerous studies of growth controls in the 1970s. His first event-study was Petaluma, California, which . . . had enacted a nationally famous growth control law in 1972. It was enacted specifically in reaction to new residential development, which was being built to serve commuters who took Highway 101 south toward San Francisco, forty miles away. The Petaluma Plan limited building permits to a maximum of 500 per year, well below recent and expected demand, and it rationed them with a point system that gave substantial weight to costly design features and developer-provided amenities and services to the community.

Schwartz, Hansen, and Green (1981) found that after several years, Petaluma's standard-unit housing prices had risen eight percent above those of nearby Santa Rosa, which had not adopted growth controls during that period and which had formerly had the same prices. In a follow-up study, Schwartz, Hansen, and Green . . . found that the fraction of Petaluma's housing stock that was affordable to low- and moderate-income households had dropped significantly below that of a control group. The costly design points offered by the plan overwhelmed the few points that developers got for moderate-income housing.

Schwartz, Zorn, and Hansen (1986) also examined the effects of the less famous but nearly as effective growth controls in Davis, California. As in Petaluma, house prices in Davis grew significantly more rapidly than those of a control sample of other Sacramento suburbs after growth controls were implemented. The best estimate given by the study is that growth controls caused prices in Davis to be nine percent higher in 1980 than they would have been without them.

The city of Davis attempted to mandate that the limited number of new units that were built under their controlled-growth program include some units earmarked for low- and moderate-income residents. (As a former resident of Davis, I speculate that they did this to offset the charges that growth management policies are harmful to the poor.) Growth controls were established limiting the number of building permits and requiring builders who did get permits to construct some units earmarked for low-income people.[33] According

33. The tie-in is a frequently employed technique of "inclusionary zoning," and it is the centerpiece of the New Jersey Supreme Court's attempt to promote low-income housing in the suburbs. See Southern Burlington Co. NAACP v. Mt. Laurel

to Zorn, Hansen, and Schwartz (1986), the Davis program was successful in avoiding the skewness of the Petaluma Plan. The limited growth that did occur contained both low-income and high-income housing.

Apparent success with moderate-income housing was accompanied by an unanticipated offset. Housing built in Davis before growth controls were adopted increased both in price and in quality (more space, better accessories). Zorn, Hansen, and Schwartz expressed some puzzlement at the quality increase. They had expected that older housing in Davis would increase in price as a result of the growth controls, but they did not expect the quality increase. My interpretation of this is that older housing in Davis was filtering up rather than down. Since Davis's regulations attempted to suppress construction for the richer side of the market, housing that otherwise would have filtered down was refitted for the more affluent buyers.

The Davis experience shows in a microcosm what econometric studies of public housing have shown at the national level. Construction of a million new public housing units for the poor does not augment the stock of housing for the poor by one million units. Some private housing that would have been built for the poor (e.g., mobile homes) does not get built, and some middle-class units that would have filtered down to the poor are either maintained at a higher level or diverted to other uses.[35] The housing market, like other capital markets, is subject to government crowding effects.

The other group of housing price studies was done by Lawrence Katz and Kenneth Rosen at the University of California, Berkeley. A drawback of the previous studies is their focus on two communities, both of which might be sufficiently unusual to make extrapolations unwarranted. Petaluma was a famous test case, and Davis is a university town known for its attention to environmental amenities. Notoriety itself might have sent housing prices up by signalling to house buyers the existence of an exclusive community.

Katz and Rosen (1987) overcame this problem by selecting a sample of over 1600 single-family home sales from 64 communities in the San Francisco Bay Area during 1979. Of these sales, 175 occurred in communities that had a growth control program (building permit moratorium or a binding rationing system) in effect for at

---

456 A.2d 390 (N.J. 1983). A skeptical evaluation of inclusionary zoning, noting that, outside of New Jersey, it is most common in exclusive communities, is Ellickson (1981).

35. For empirical evidence supporting benefits of the filtering process to the poor, see Weicher and Thibodeau (1988). The national displacement effect was also found in an earlier study by Michael Murray (1983).

least one year in the period 1973-1979. They found that houses selling in the growth controlled communities were 17 to 38 percent more expensive than those in other communities. Katz and Rosen thus corroborated with a broader sample (but with a larger price differential) the results that Schwartz and his coauthors found for Davis and Petaluma. . . .

What conclusions can be drawn from the housing cost studies? Their authors imply that they show that growth controls are undesirable. . . .

Let me take the role of an advocate for growth controls to show the weakness of the inefficiency implication. We know from the studies reviewed . . . above that community and neighborhood amenities raise housing values. Growth controls may create residential amenities, or, for rapidly growing communities, they may prevent impending disamenities. Hence the higher housing prices could be taken as evidence that growth controls do what they are intended to do. . . .

. . . [T]he problem caused by the focus on distributional consequences of growth controls has led to the inference that the higher housing prices that follow their imposition are a measure of their costs. In principle, the opposite is more likely true: The higher prices of housing could be a measure of their benefits. The real problem here is to identify what causes the higher prices. Higher prices of housing — or higher prices of anything else, for that matter — can occur either as a result of supply restriction (an inward shift of the supply curve, showing that lower supplies are provided at all prices) or demand stimulation (an outward shift of the demand curve, showing that higher demand exists at all prices). Inward shifts in supply smell of monopoly, and that is one efficiency objection to growth controls.

Figure 2 illustrates the problem. The panel on the left indicates a supply restriction of S to S^1, which raises the price from P_1 to P_2. The panel on the right shows the effect of making the community more attractive and thus stimulating demand from D to D^1. Just as in the inefficient supply restriction, the demand-stimulating effects of growth controls will make prices increase from P_1 to P_2. Confronted simply with evidence that prices of housing rose as a result of a public growth management program, we cannot say which scenario is the dominant case.

Of course, the two graphs [below] are distinguished by opposite effects on the quantity of housing. The supply restriction reduces the quantity of housing, while the demand stimulation increases it. The problem with evaluating growth controls as a monopoly supply restriction is that it is hard to know what the true supply curve looks

Figure 2

like when conditions naturally change over time. Simply observing that a community declines to allow the same number of building permits as it did in the recent past is not even proof of monopoly action, much less monopoly power. A private firm with output that has expanded by ten percent per year for the last five years may find that it has reached the limits of its managerial capacities and decline to expand any more. This is not monopolistic as long as other firms can enter the industry to meet the new demand.

Growth controls are especially difficult to assess because restriction in housing supply may actually stimulate the demand for housing for reasons that have nothing to do with monopoly. With rising incomes or other shifts in demand, it may be that low-density, high-amenity communities have become relatively scarce. Growth controls may then be seen as a *positive* supply response to such demands. This statement seems odd only if one looks at a single community rather than a system of communities in a larger metropolitan market. Viewed in the metropolitan context, growth controls may be no more anomalous a supply response than a market-driven trend toward larger houses.

The key to this apologia for growth controls is the existence of alternative communities to meet other kinds of demands. If housing consumers in general or low-income people in particular do not have alternative communities in which to locate, then the reduced number of sites in the growth control communities will have extraterritorial effects on the housing market. If the supply of sites is inelastic in communities that lack growth controls, then housing prices in the metropolitan area will rise.[43] Adverse impacts from growth controls can be tested by looking at housing prices outside the restrictive communities: If they have increased, the impacts are adverse, since, presumably, the benefits of growth controls accrue exclusively to the community that enacts them.

Just such a test was conducted by Henry Pollakowski and Susan Wachter (1990). They examined the growth restrictions adopted in Montgomery County, Maryland, the northern suburb of Washington, D.C. The county had seventeen planning districts. Pollakowski and Wachter found that districts adjacent to more restrictive districts had significantly higher housing prices, though the difference was not large. This implies a spillover effect from zoning that is most probably caused by monopolistic scarcity in the more restrictive areas, since the districts were large enough that amenity effects would not have affected adjacent districts significantly.

An indirect way of testing for extraterritorial effects is to ask whether entire metropolitan areas in which some communities have growth controls have higher housing prices than other metropolitan areas. This is an imperfect measure, because some of the increase in housing prices could be due to communities making themselves more attractive relative to others. Hence the metropolitan area average would rise somewhat even under an efficient system of growth controls. One would expect this effect to be small, however, insofar as growth controls are typically adopted by local governments to provide benefits for their own residents, not for the entire metropolitan area.

Two types of studies have attempted to determine the metropolitan-wide effects of growth controls. One tests directly for the influence of growth controls, and the other tests for monopoly power. Both types of studies demonstrate some metropolitan-wide housing price effects, with the strong implication that such effects are net costs. . . .

§9   The Causes and Consequences of Growth Controls

Much of this essay has taken a contrary point of view. To those economists who argue that land use controls are ineffective and unnecessary, I have endeavored to show that empirical economic re-

43. Michael Elliott's (1981) study of California cities and counties shows that geographically isolated communities (e.g., Fresno) that enact growth controls have no effect on housing prices, but when several communities in one area or entire counties adopt controls, the effects are significant.

search does not support either conclusion, and plenty of other research points to the opposite conclusions. To those who criticize growth controls for causing high housing prices, I have pointed out that at least some of the increase in prices could result from amenity creation rather than monopolistic exclusion. On balance, however, I am inclined to believe that most growth controls impose a net cost on society. I believe that the econometric evidence discussed in this paper supports the following three conclusions:

(1) Land use controls, especially overall growth control programs, are important constraints on the land market. This in turn affects housing values, especially in suburban and exurban communities.

(2) Land use controls do provide some benefits that would be difficult to obtain under less coercive conditions. Abolition of zoning and related controls would create a demand for alternative controls, and it is not clear that the alternatives are less costly to administer or more efficient in their effects than zoning.

(3) Growth controls and other aggressive extensions of land use regulations probably impose costs on society that are larger than the benefits they provide. The higher housing prices associated with communities that impose growth controls are more likely the result of wasteful supply constraints than benign amenity production.

The last conclusion is more tentative than the first two because only a few studies have addressed it in a persuasive framework. . . .

Aside from their adverse effects on the cost of housing, inefficiently restrictive growth controls probably cause metropolitan areas to be too spread out. This is not to deny that growth controls may make development in *individual* municipalities more compact. My claim is that such local ordinances cause developers to go to other communities. The most likely alternative sites are in exurban and rural communities, where the political climate, at least initially, is more favorable to development. As the more rural communities become partly developed, the newcomers wrest the political machinery from the pro-growth farmers and business interests. Then these communities, too, adopt growth controls, sending development still farther from employment and commercial centers. Eventually, employment and commercial activities also disperse from traditional population centers as they find that employees and customers are harder to find.

A paradigm of modern growth control policy that illustrates the foregoing argument was recently described by Bob Narus (1990). The fifteen-square-mile town of Lincoln, Massachusetts, has for years limited growth by means of regulation, selective purchase of open land, and legal action to block regional road construction. Yet this very affluent enclave (pop. 5200) is among the few to meet the state's requirement that ten percent of the housing stock be affordable to low- and moderate-income households. Subsidized housing was built by developers as a condition for permission to build more profitable commercial buildings. The affordable units were isolated from the affluent parts of town, in which two-acre building lots recently sold for $350,000.

Its growth controls would have little effect on the housing market if Lincoln were an isolated rural town. Its open spaces, however, are maintained next to the Boston region's major employment corridor, Route 128. The town is only thirteen miles from downtown Boston. If one considers that the average gross density of most new suburbs is about four persons per acre, Lincoln's plan has displaced about 25,000 people. Given that Lincoln is not unique, merely the most successful of a group, I would conclude that at least some of the low-density, sprawling development that occurs well beyond the Route 128 corridor is caused by successful growth management by the close-in suburbs.

The long-run effect of this is a lower standard of living. People will commute more than they otherwise would, which reduces their real incomes unless they enjoy commuting. Dispersion of residences and jobs promotes more automobile travel and longer trips, creating more congestion and pollution (assuming, as is realistic, that cars are not charged for their social costs) and eventually requiring more highway construction.

The more subtle loss from inefficiently dispersed homes and businesses is the loss of agglomeration economies for firms. The basis for urban economies is the advantages of operating a business in the proximity of many other businesses. Location in a city allows firms to have access to a more skilled and flexible labor force. It also permits the face-to-face exchange of ideas, which promotes innovation. Forces that tend to disperse firms erode such advantages and reduce potential output from the industry. Telecommunications allows firms to deal with dispersion more easily now than in the past, and it is probable that advances in the electronic media have induced at least some businesses to leave urban areas without any loss in efficiency. But such firms are still the exception. Face-to-face contact is an essential ingredient of most growing businesses.

Bibliography

Correll, Mark R., Jane H. Lillydahl, and Larry D. Singell. The Effect of Greenbelts on Residential Property Values. Land Economics 54 (May 1978): 207-217.

Ellickson, Robert C. The Irony of 'Inclusionary' Zoning. Southern California Law Review 54 (September 1981): 1167-1216.

Elliott, Michael. The Impact of Growth Control Regulations on Housing Prices in California. AREUEA Journal 9 (Summer 1981): 115-133.

Katz, Lawrence, and Kenneth Rosen. The Interjurisdictional Effects of Growth Controls on Housing Prices. Journal of Law and Economics 30 (April 1987): 149-160.

Knaap, Gerrit J. The Price Effects of Urban Growth Boundaries in Metropolitan Portland, Oregon. Land Economics 61 (February 1985): 28-35.

Lafferty, Ronald N., and H. E. Frech III. Community Environment and the Market Value of Single Family Homes: The Effect of the Dispersion of Land Uses. Journal of Law and Economics 21 (October 1978): 381-394.

Murray, Michael. Subsidized and Unsubsidized Housing Starts: 1961-1977. Review of Economics and Statistics 65 (November 1983): 590-597.

Narus, Bob. The Evolution of Growth Management in Lincoln, Massachusetts. Urban Land (January 1990): 16-19.

Nelson, Arthur C. An Empirical Note on How Regional Urban Containment Policy Influences an Interaction between Greenbelt and Exurban Land Markets. American Planning Association Journal 54 (Spring 1988): 178-184.

Pollakowski, Henry, and Susan M. Wachter. The Effects of Land Use Constraints on Land Values. Land Economics 66 (August 1990).

Schwartz, Seymour I., David D. Hansen, and Richard Green. Suburban Growth Controls and the Price of New Housing. Journal of Environmental Economics and Management 8 (December 1981): 303-320.

Schwartz, Seymour I., Peter M. Zorn, and David E. Hansen. Research Design Issue and Pitfalls in Growth Control Studies. Land Economics 62 (August 1986): 223-233.

Siegan, Bernard H. Land Use Without Zoning. Lexington, Massachusetts: Heath-Lexington Books, 1972.

Spreyer, Janet Furman. The Effect of Land Use Restrictions on the Market Value of Single Family Homes in Houston. Journal of Real Estate Finance and Economics 2 (June 1989): 117-130.

Stull, William J. Community Environment, Zoning, and the Market Value of Single-Family Homes. Journal of Law and Economics 17 (October 1975): 535-557.

Weicher, John C., and Thomas G. Thibodeau. Filtering and Housing Markets: An Empirical Analysis. Journal of Urban Economics 23 (January 1988): 21-40.

Zorn, Peter M., David E. Hansen, and Seymour I. Schwartz. Mitigating the Price Effects of Growth Control: A Cast Study of Davis, California. Land Economics 62 (February 1986): 47-57.

NOTES AND QUESTIONS ON GROWTH CONTROLS

1. As Fischel reports on p.457, Janet Spreyer found that unrestricted land in Houston was less valuable, by roughly equal amounts, than land governed by either covenants or zoning. Do Spreyer's results indicate that nuisance law has been a relatively toothless method of land use regulation in Houston? To what extent do Spreyer's findings cast doubt on Cappel's conclusions about the merits of New Haven's initial zoning ordinance?

2. Is Fischel, an economist, correct in his legal assertion that "courts usually limit [covenants'] duration to less than fifty years"?

3. Fischel reviews a host of sources that indicate that growth controls push up housing prices. Do these studies help explain why local politicians are eager to manage growth? Attempt to restate Fischel's argument that price increases by themselves do not necessarily indicate that growth controls are inefficient. Why does Fischel conclude, from studies such as Pollakowski & Wachter's, that most growth controls nevertheless probably *are* inefficient?

4. Regional and state growth controls, which affect larger markets than local controls do, have also been found to boost housing prices. Much of the increase occurs suddenly, at the time when buyers and sellers first anticipate that the regional controls are in the offing. See, for instance, W. Patrick Beaton, The Impact of Regional Land-Use Controls on Property Values: The Case of the New Jersey Pinelands, 67 Land Econ. 172 (1991); David Dale-Johnson & Hyang K. Yim, Coastal Development Moratoria and Housing Prices, 3 J. Real Est. Fin. & Econ. 165 (1990) (on the consequences of the California Coastal Initiative). What implications do these studies have for the wisdom of state and regional land-use regulation?

5. Fischel's overview generally treats growth controls as binding constraints. Some are not. John D. Landis, Do Growth Controls Work?, 58 J. Am. Planning Ass'n. 489 (1992), reports on growth-control programs in seven mid-size California cities during the

1980s. Landis found that these programs had been too "porous" to have had much effect on housing markets. What inducements might motivate a local government to provide a waiver from an anti-growth measure?

6. Fischel's footnote 33 mentions the "inclusionary zoning" program that New Jersey adopted in the aftermath of the 1983 *Mount Laurel* decision. For a descriptive review of the program's results, see Martha Lamar, Alan Mallach & John M. Payne, *Mount Laurel* at Work: Affordable Housing in New Jersey, 1983-1988, 41 Rutgers L. Rev. 1197 (1989). Of the more than 2,000 occupied *Mount Laurel* units, the authors were able to find ethnic/racial data for 169. "Many developments have very small minority populations and, within that minority population, even smaller numbers of black residents. At least three *Mount Laurel* developments appear to have no black residents; in some other developments the percentage of black homebuyers varies from 1% to 3%. It is likely that the black percentage is larger at Lawrence Square Village, but reliable statistics are not available." Id. at 1256. Should racial integration be an objective of inclusionary zoning? The next two selections address the causes of segregated neighborhoods.

C. Housing Segregation

Cities and Housing*

Richard F. Muth

Racial Segregation and Discrimination

Most of the readers of this book are familiar enough with racial segregation, or separation, in housing that they will not require any documentation of its existence. For those few skeptics, Karl E. Taeuber has demonstrated that in most large cities in the United States around 90 percent of the Negro population would have to move to new residences in order for them to be spatially distributed in the same way as the native white population. He has also shown that little of the Negro segregation vis-à-vis the native white population

*Source: 106-112 (1969).

can be attributed to income and occupational differences. Of course, the residential clustering of certain groups is not limited to Negroes. Many neighborhoods in American cities are noted as the residential locations of various ethnic groups; others are justly characterized as workingmen's neighborhoods, suburbs of younger, middle-income groups with large families, and so forth. However, the residential segregation of Negroes is of great current interest because of the Negro drive for racial equality, and it is frequently alleged to have important effects on the intensity of residential land use and the quality of urban housing. This section, therefore, will be concerned primarily with the residential segregation of Negroes.

It is commonly believed that residential segregation results from the refusal of landlords to rent to Negroes in white areas and of real-estate agents in these areas to deal with potential Negro buyers. Indeed, so-called "open occupancy" legislation would seem to be designed with this hypothesis in mind. While landlords and real-estate agents probably behave as alleged above, it is important to inquire into the reasons for their behavior. One explanation, which I call the seller's preference hypothesis, is that renters or sellers of housing have a unique aversion to dealing with Negroes not shared by the community at large and thus refuse to do so. I find this explanation quite unsatisfying. In the first place, segregation occurs in many other forms where landlords and real-estate agents are not involved. While it might be argued that the failure to serve Negroes in some restaurants and to hire Negroes in some establishments may be due to the aversion of their owners to deal with Negroes, segregation also occurs in churches and country clubs as well as in many fraternal organizations where there is no handy villain to be found. In addition, members of many ethnic groups tend to congregate in cities without apparent coercion. Finally, and most important, if landlords refuse to rent to Negroes because of their own aversion to doing so, they will tend to have a greater number of vacancies in their buildings on the average and earn lower incomes from these buildings than they otherwise would. Similarly, if real-estate agents fail to deal with potential Negro buyers because of their own preferences, they will make fewer sales and earn lower incomes. It would thus be in the interest of renters or sellers of real estate to sell out to others without an aversion to dealing with Negroes; by so doing they could increase their incomes, since potential buyers without these aversions would offer more than the capitalized value of the business to the landlords or real-estate agents who are averse to dealing with Negroes.

An even less satisfying explanation for the residential segregation of Negroes is what might be termed the collusion hypothesis. According to the latter, some landlords and real-estate agents, perhaps in concert with other persons, actively collude to limit the range of residences open to Negroes in order to profit from higher Negro housing prices. To a great extent the collusion hypothesis suffers from the same shortcomings as the seller's preference hypothesis. For it is difficult to account for segregation in non-profit organizations or for the segregation of various other social and ethnic groups on the basis of such a hypothesis. More important, however, is the fact that such collusive agreements, which would necessarily involve literally hundreds of participants in large cities, would be impossibly difficult to administer and enforce without active governmental support. It is almost inconceivable that such a large number of participants could agree upon or carry out a plan for dividing the gains from collusion. Any party to the collusive agreement would stand to benefit by breaking it so long as the other members of the conspiracy were to follow the agreement. Furthermore, if somehow the conspiracy were organized and succeeded for a time in raising housing prices to Negroes, it would be profitable for non-members of the agreement to sell occupancy rights to their properties to Negroes. Thus, such a conspiracy would probably break down quickly.

A much more reasonable explanation for residential segregation is that whites have a greater aversion to living among Negroes than do other Negroes. If so, whites would offer more for housing in predominantly white neighborhoods than would Negroes, and separation of the residential areas of the two groups would result. To see why this is so, consider the residential configuration schematized in Figure 2, where the symbol W stands for a white resident and N for a Negro resident. Suppose that whites are willing to pay more for housing to the right of the line B than are Negroes. Negroes may either be willing to pay more for residences to the left of B or to the right; in the latter case it is only necessary that they be willing to pay less for these residences than white buyers. Under such conditions white buyers will tend to move to the right of line B since they are willing to offer more for occupancy rights to such housing than the Negroes currently living there, and the converse will apply to Negroes. The two groups will thus tend to gravitate into separate residential areas. Note also that the price of housing along the line B will differ from that in the interior of the same area. If whites have an aversion to living in proximity to Negroes, they will inhabit residences along the right of the boundary between the white and Negro areas only at a lower price for housing than in the interior of the

---

Figure 2
Race and Residential Location

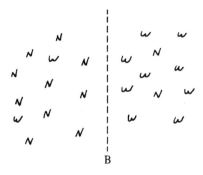

B

---

white area. If, as seems likely, some Negroes are willing to pay more for housing in proximity to whites, or have an aversion to segregation, the price of housing immediately to the left of the line *B* will tend to be greater than in the interior of the Negro area.

This alternative explanation for residential segregation suffers none of the shortcomings of the seller's preference or collusion hypotheses enumerated above. Segregation in stores, eating places, and the like, and in employment may similarly be explained in terms of preferences of customers or employees, as can segregation in religious and fraternal organizations and the residential separation of ethnic groups. The failure of landlords to rent to or real-estate agents to deal with Negroes is also readily understandable in terms of this explanation. The landlord's refusal may be interpreted as based upon a desire to avoid the loss of white tenants, the real-estate agent's, similarly, on the desire to avoid the loss of future business — even if the white seller for whom he is acting as agent has no aversion to selling to a Negro buyer. Under these conditions, no other person would be willing to offer more for the landlord's building or the agent's business and to deal with Negroes, since he would be subject to the same restrictions. Now, it might be argued that landlords and agents act as they do in the mistaken belief that their customers have an aversion to living near Negroes. But this suggestion is subject to the same shortcomings as the seller's preference hypothesis.

If the customer preference hypothesis is correct, then enforced open-occupancy legislation would have little effect on the residential segregation of Negroes. Such legislation might force some landlords who otherwise would not rent to Negroes to do so. But, if their white tenants have an aversion to living among Negroes and comparable housing is available to them elsewhere at the same price, they will tend to move out of the integrated buildings and neighborhoods, and the area will come to be inhabited wholly by Negroes. The enforced open-occupancy legislation would tend primarily to penalize landlords and real-estate agents for catering to the preferences of their customers. Such legislation, however, might tend to make the area inhabited by Negroes grow more rapidly over time by making it easier for them to obtain housing outside existing Negro areas. The effects of other measures to break down the residential segregation of Negroes, such as President Kennedy's famous "stroke of the pen" forbidding refusal to sell federally-assisted housing to Negroes, are likely to have similar effects so long as whites are willing to pay higher prices for housing in proximity to other whites than are Negroes.

As ably pointed out by Becker, the fact of residential segregation need not imply discrimination, or higher prices for housing of comparable quality in the Negro than in the white area. While Negroes and whites may tend to live in separate areas and Negroes may be unable to obtain housing in the interior of the white area at any given time, the relative prices of housing in the two areas depend upon the size and rate of growth of the Negro area in relation to the Negro demand for housing. In fact, if the customer preference hypothesis described above is correct, then under certain circumstances housing prices in the Negro area might even be lower than in the white area. Returning to Figure 2, suppose initially that prices in the interior of the Negro area were the same as in the interior of the white area. Assuming that Negroes prefer integration and whites segregation, prices would then be higher than in the interior on the Negro side of the boundary and lower on the white side.

Thus, at the boundary separating the two areas, housing prices in Negro occupancy would be higher, owners of occupancy rights on the white side of the boundary would have the incentive to sell them to Negroes, and the boundary would tend to shift toward the white area. If there are no external forces to prevent this movement and if the Negro and white demands for housing are changing at the same rate, then as the boundary shifts and the supply of housing to Negroes grows relative to the white supply, housing prices to Negroes will fall relative to those paid by whites. Under such conditions, the only possible equilibrium position is one in which prices are equal on the Negro and white sides of the boundary. Such a situation implies, of course, that housing prices in the interior of the Negro area would be lower than in the interior of the white area.

Of course, in many large cities the Negro population is growing relative to the white population. Under these conditions the Negro demand for housing would grow relative to the white demand for housing, and it could do so at a great enough rate relative to the increase in the size of the Negro area so that any initial price differential for housing in the interior of the two areas would tend to be maintained or even increased over time.

The analysis of the three preceding paragraphs readily suggests why so-called "block-busters" may make money by purchasing occupancy rights to residences on the white side of the boundary and selling these rights to Negroes. Even if housing prices in the interiors of the Negro and white areas were the same, a greater aversion on the part of whites to living among Negroes would imply that at the boundary separating the two areas the Negro price would exceed the white price. Block-busters profit by buying in the lower-price market and selling in the higher-price one. The returns to block-busting may be increased by the refusal of established real-estate agents to handle transactions in racially changing neighborhoods. Their refusal, coupled with a fall-off in demand by white buyers and a lack of knowledge about potential Negro buyers on the part of white sellers, would enable block-busters to purchase occupancy rights from white sellers at a lower price than they otherwise would. There is little reason to expect that block-busters are enabled to sell at an above-normal price to Negro buyers, however, since the alternative opportunities of the latter are in no way restricted by the conditions described in the previous sentence. The refusal of established real-estate agents to take part in transactions in changing neighborhoods would also tend to slow down the expansion of the Negro residential area in the face of a relative growth in Negro demand. For this reason, prices in the Negro area are probably higher than they would otherwise be.

Evidence on housing prices by race is difficult to obtain. Consumer expenditure surveys and census data on average contract rents generally show that Negroes make greater expenditures on housing than do whites at any given income level. Such evidence is frequently taken to mean that housing prices are higher to Negroes than to whites, but this evidence is faulty for several reasons. Data from consumer expenditure studies are frequently distorted by various eligibility requirements for inclusion as well as by the fact that such studies often include repayment of mortgage principal and exclude interest on the owner's equity for those in owner-occupied housing. Census data on average contract rents include, in addition to space rent, any payments for rental of furnishings and for utilities furnished the tenant, and these may differ systematically among various groups. In addition, Negroes tend to have more persons per room, mostly because of their lower incomes, than do whites. Rentals they pay may be larger on this account because of greater costs for utilities and depreciation. But most important is the fact that the effect of price differences on expenditure differences depends critically upon the elasticity of demand for housing. Evidence cited earlier suggests, in fact, that the price elasticity of the demand for housing is at least equal to unity and perhaps even numerically larger. Thus, if housing prices for Negroes were higher than for whites, Negroes would tend to spend the same or less for housing on this account, not more. Even when using census data, it is quite difficult to eliminate the effects of size, condition, and other factors making for differences in quantity purchased as well as such factors as accessibility and neighborhood effects which, apart from race, affect housing prices.

The only convincing previous evidence on the relation of housing prices to race of which I am aware is that provided in a recent study by Martin J. Bailey.* Bailey analyzed the selling prices, as measured by the amount of federal real-estate transfer tax stamps affixed to the deed, of single-family houses in the Hyde Park-Kenwood area of Chicago. In addition to a large number of variables describing the physical characteristics of dwellings and their locations, Bailey included the percentage of the non-white population in the block in which the property was located and also that in the surrounding ring of blocks. For sets of transactions in both the periods 1948-1951 and 1954-1957 his results imply that in the interior of the non-white residential area selling prices were *below* those of comparable properties in the interior of the white area, as these terms are used above. His findings are also consistent with the hypothesis that whites have an aversion to, but non-whites prefer, residential integration. For they imply that on the non-white side of the boundary separating the two residential areas prices are higher than those of comparable properties in the interior of the non-white area, while on the white side of the boundary they are lower than prices in the interior of the white area.

---

*Effects of Race and Other Demographic Factors on the Values of Single-Family Houses, 35 Land Economics 288-292 (Aug. 1959).

NOTES AND QUESTIONS ON CAUSES
OF SEGREGATED HOUSING

1. Fair housing audits, which involve successive inquiries by testers of different races, are often used to detect racial discrimination by landlords, brokers, lenders, and other intermediaries in housing markets. See, for instance, John Yinger, Measuring Racial Discrimination with Fair Housing Audits, 76 Am. Econ. Rev. 881 (1986) (reporting black testers in Boston audits were shown 36.3 percent fewer apartments than their white counterparts). Yinger concludes from his study that "the primary cause of racial discrimination in housing is that housing agents illegally promote their economic interests by catering to the racial prejudice of their current or potential white customers." Would Muth find fault in Yinger's theory?

2. Muth predicts that fair housing legislation will be largely ineffective because, even if intermediaries do not discriminate, prejudiced whites will pay a premium to live in segregated (or nearly segregated) areas. Elaborate Muth's argument and consider whether its assumptions are plausible.

3. Muth argues that in the long run blacks will pay *less* for housing in a prejudiced city than they would in a city without racial prejudice. Do you understand the argument? What are its critical assumptions? Does Muth's argument imply that discrimination in other areas of life also redounds to the economic benefit of blacks?

4. There is an unsettled debate over whether blacks in fact tend to pay less than whites for housing. Studies based on pre-1970 data generally show premium prices in black areas, while studies based on post-1970 data show either black discounts or no difference. See, for example, Daniel N. Chambers, The Racial Housing Price Differential and Racially Transitional Neighborhoods, 32 J. Urb. Econ. 214 (1992); John F. McDonald, Economic Analysis of an Urban Housing Market 54-61 (1979).

5. Between 1960 and 1990 large numbers of black households moved from central cities to suburban areas. For example, by 1992 a majority of blacks in the Washington, D.C., metropolitan area lived outside the District of Columbia. Most of these suburban areas, however, "quickly undergo racial transition to majority-black status after racial integration begins." John Charles Boger, Race and the American City, 71 N.C. L. Rev. 1289, 1310-1313 (1993). Is this demographic trend consistent with Muth's theory?

By most measures, black-white segregation decreased slightly in most U.S. metropolitan areas during both the 1970s and 1980s. See Douglas S. Massey & Nancy A. Denton, American Apartheid

222 (1993); Reynolds Farley & William H. Frey, Changes in the Segregation of Whites from Blacks During the 1980s, 59 Am. Soc. Rev.
23 (1994) (finding greatest decreases in young and growing metropolitan areas in the Sunbelt).

Micromotives and Macrobehavior *

Thomas C. Schelling

Individual Incentives and Collective Results

Economists are familiar with systems that lead to aggregate results that the individual neither intends nor needs to be aware of,
results that sometimes have no recognizable counterpart at the level
of the individual. The creation of money by a commercial banking
system is one; the way savings decisions cause depressions or infla-
tions is another.

Biological evolution is responsible for a lot of sorting and separating, but the little creatures that mate and reproduce and forage
for food would be amazed to know that they were bringing about
separation of species, territorial sorting, or the extinction of species.
Among social examples, the coexistence or extinction of second languages is a phenomenon that, though affected by decrees and school
curricula, corresponds to no conscious collective choice.

Romance and marriage . . . are exceedingly individual and private activities, at least in this country, but their genetic consequences
are altogether aggregate. The law and the church may constrain us
in our choices, and some traditions of segregation are enormously
coercive; but, outside of royal families, there are few marriages that
are part of a genetic plan. When a short boy marries a tall girl, or a
blonde a brunette, it is no part of the individual's purpose to increase genetic randomness or to change some frequency distribution within the population.

Some of the phenomena of segregation may be similarly complex in relation to the dynamics of individual choice. One might
even be tempted to suppose that some "unseen hand" separates
people in a manner that, though foreseen and intended by no one,
corresponds to some consensus or collective preference or popular
will. But in economics we know a great many macro-phenomena,
like depression and inflation, that do not reflect any universal desire

*Source: pp. 140-141, 146-155 (1978).

for lower incomes or higher prices. The same applies to bank failures and market crashes. What goes on in the "hearts and minds"
of small savers has little to do with whether or not they cause a depression. The hearts and minds and motives and habits of millions
of people who participate in a segregated society may or may not
bear close correspondence with the massive results that collectively
they can generate.

A special reason for doubting any social efficiency in aggregate
segregation is that the range of choice is often so meager. The demographic map of almost any American metropolitan area suggests
that it is easy to find residential areas that are all white or nearly so
and areas that are all black or nearly so but hard to find localities in
which neither whites nor nonwhites are more than, say, three-
quarters of the total. And, comparing decennial maps, it is nearly
impossible to find an area that, if integrated within that range, will
remain integrated long enough for a couple to get their house paid
for or their children through school.

Some Quantitative Constraints

Counting blacks and whites in a residential block or on a baseball team will not tell how they get along. But it tells something,
especially if numbers and ratios matter to the people who are moving in or out of the block or being recruited for the team. With quantitative analysis there are a few logical constraints, analogous to the
balance-sheet identities in economics. (Being logical constraints,
they contain no news unless one just never thought of them before.)

The simplest constraint on dichotomous mixing is that, within
a given set of boundaries, not both groups can enjoy numerical superiority. For the whole population the numerical ratio is determined at any given time; but locally, in a city or a neighborhood, a
church or a school or a restaurant, either blacks or whites can be a
majority. But if each insists on being a local majority, there is only
one mixture that will satisfy them — complete segregation.

People who have to choose between polarized extremes — a
white neighborhood or a black, a French-speaking club or one
where English alone is spoken, a school with few whites or one with
few blacks — will often choose in the way that reinforces the polar-
ization. Doing so is no evidence that they prefer segregation, only
that, if segregation exists and they have to choose between exclusive
association, people elect like rather than unlike environments. . . .

Some of the processes may be passive, systemic, unmotivated
but nevertheless biased. If job vacancies are filled by word of mouth
or apartments go to people who have acquaintances in the building,

or if boys can marry only girls they know and can know only girls who speak their language, a biased communication system will preserve and enhance the prevailing homogeneities.

A Self-Forming Neighborhood Model

Some vivid dynamics can be generated by any reader with a half-hour to spare, a roll of pennies and a roll of dimes, a tabletop, a large sheet of paper, a spirit of scientific inquiry, or, lacking that spirit, a fondness for games.

Get a roll of pennies, a roll of dimes, a ruled sheet of paper divided into one-inch squares, preferably at least the size of a checkerboard (sixty-four squares in eight rows and eight columns) and find some device for selecting squares at random. We place dimes and pennies on some of the squares, and suppose them to represent the members of two homogeneous groups — men and women, blacks and whites. French-speaking and English-speaking, officers and enlisted men, students and faculty, surfers and swimmers, the well dressed and the poorly dressed, or any other dichotomy that is exhaustive and recognizable. We can spread them at random or put them in contrived patterns. We can use equal numbers of dimes and pennies or let one be a minority. And we can stipulate various rules for individual decision.

For example, we can postulate that every dime wants at least half its neighbors to be dimes, every penny wants a third of its neighbors to be pennies, and any dime or penny whose immediate neighborhood does not meet these conditions gets up and moves. Then by inspection we locate the ones that are due to move, move them, keep on moving them if necessary and, when everybody on the board has settled down, look to see what pattern has emerged. (If the situation never "settles down," we look to see what kind of endless turbulence or cyclical activity our postulates have generated.)

Define each individual's neighborhood as the eight squares surrounding him; he is the center of a 3-by-3 neighborhood. He is content or discontent with his neighborhood according to the colors of the occupants of those eight surrounding squares, some of which may be empty. We furthermore suppose that, if he is discontent with the color of his own neighborhood, he moves to the nearest empty square that meets his demands.

As to the order of moves, we can begin with the discontents nearest the center of the board and let them move first, or start in the upper left and sweep downward to the right, or let the dimes

---

Figure 3

```
    # O # O # O
  # O # O # O # O
  O # O # O # O #
  # O # O # O # O
  O # O # O # O #
  # O # O # O # O
  O # O # O # O #
    O # O # O #
```

---

move first and then the pennies; it usually turns out that the precise order is not crucial to the outcome.

Then we choose an overall ratio of pennies to dimes, the two colors being about equal or one of them being a "minority." There are two different ways we can distribute the dimes and the pennies. We can put them in some prescribed pattern that we want to test, or we can spread them at random.

Start with equal numbers of dimes and pennies and suppose that the demands of both are "moderate" — each wants something more than one-third of his neighbors to be like himself. The number of neighbors that a coin can have will be anywhere from zero to eight. We make the following specifications. If a person has one neighbor, he must be the same color; of two neighbors, one must be his color; of three, four, or five neighbors, two must be his color; and of six, seven, or eight neighbors, he wants at least three.

It is possible to form a pattern that is regularly "integrated" that satisfies everybody. An alternating pattern does it (Figure 3), on condition that we take care of the corners.

No one can move, except to a corner, because there are no other vacant cells; but no one wants to move. We now mix them up a little, and in the process empty some cells to make movement feasible.

There are 60 coins on the board. We remove 20, using a table of random digits; we then pick 5 empty squares at random and replace a dime or a penny with a 50-50 chance. The result is a board with 64 cells, 45 occupied and 19 blank. Forty individuals are just where they were before we removed 20 neighbors and added 5 new ones. The left side of Figure 4 shows one such result, generated by exactly this process. The #'s are dimes and the O's are pennies; alternatively, the #'s speak French and the O's speak English, the #'s are black and the O's are white, the #'s are boys and the O's are girls, or whatever you please.

The right side of Figure 4 identifies the individuals who are not

---

Figure 4

```
- # - # O # - O        - - - # - # - -
# # # O - O # O        - - - - - - - -
- # O - - # O #        - - - - - - - -
- O # O # O # O        - - # - # - # -
O O O # O O O -        - - - - - - - -
# - # # # - - O        # - - - - - - -
- # O # O # O -        - - O - O - O -
- O - O - - # -        - - - - - - - -
```

---

content with their neighborhoods. Six #'s and three O's want to move; the rest are content as things stand. The pattern is still "integrated"; even the discontent are not without some neighbors like themselves, and few among the content are without neighbors of opposite color. The general pattern is not strongly segregated in appearance. One is hard-put to block out #-neighborhoods or O-neighborhoods at this stage. The problem is to satisfy a fraction, 9 of 45, among the #'s and O's by letting them move somewhere among the 19 blank cells.

Anybody who moves leaves a blank cell that somebody can move into. Also, anybody who moves leaves behind a neighbor or two of his own color; and when he leaves a neighbor, his neighbor loses a neighbor and may become discontent. Anyone who moves gains neighbors like himself, adding a neighbor like them to their neighborhood but also adding one of opposite color to the unlike neighbors he acquires.

I cannot too strongly urge you to get the dimes and pennies and do it yourself. I can show you an outcome or two. A computer can do it for you a hundred times, testing variations in neighborhood demands, overall ratios, sizes of neighborhoods, and so forth. But there is nothing like tracing it through for yourself and seeing the thing work itself out. In an hour you can do it several times and experiment with different rules of behavior, sizes and shapes of boards, and (if you turn some of the coins heads and some tails) subgroups of dimes and pennies that make different demands on the color compositions of their neighborhoods.

Chain Reaction

What is instructive about the experiment is the "unraveling" process. Everybody who selects a new environment affects the environments of those he leaves and those he moves among. There is

---

Figures 5 and 6

```
  # #   O # #              # # # O       O
# # # O O O # #            # # # O   O   O
# # O O       O #          # # O         O
# O   O   O O O            O   O   O   O
O O O # O O O              O O O # O O O
  O # # # O O O              # # # O O O
    # # # #                O # # # # # # #
O O           #            O O       # # #
```

---

a chain reaction. It may be quickly damped, with little motion, or it may go on and on and on with striking results. (The results of course are only suggestive, because few of us live in square cells on a checkerboard.)

One outcome for the situation depicted in Figure 4 is shown in Figure 5. It is "one outcome" because I have not explained exactly the order in which individuals moved. If the reader reproduces the experiment himself, he will get a slightly different configuration, but the general pattern will not be much different. Figure 6 is a replay from Figure 4, the only difference from Figure 5 being in the order of moves. It takes a few minutes to do the experiment again, and one quickly gets an impression of the kind of outcome to expect. Changing the neighborhood demands, or using twice as many dimes as pennies, will drastically affect the results; but for any given set of numbers and demands, the results are fairly stable.

All the people are content in Figures 5 and 6. And they are more segregated. This is more than just a visual impression: We can make a few comparisons. In Figure 4 the O's altogether had as many O's for neighbors as they had #'s; some had more or less than the average, and 3 were discontent. For the #'s the ratio of #-neighbors to O-neighbors was 1:1, with a little colony of #'s in the upper left corner and 6 widely distributed discontents. After sorting themselves out in Figure 5, the average ratio of like to unlike neighbors for #'s and O's together was 2.3:1, more than double the original ratio. And it is about triple the ratio that any individual demanded! Figure 6 is even more extreme. The ratio of like to unlike neighbors is 2.8:1, nearly triple the starting ratio and four times the minimum demanded.

Another comparison is the number who had no opposite neighbors in Figure 4. Three were in that condition before people started moving; in Figure 5 there are 8 without neighbors of opposite color, and in Figure 6 there are 14.

Figure 7

```
# # # # O     O
# # # # O O   O
# # # #     O
  O # O O O   O
O O O # O O O
      # # O
    O # # # O
  O   O # # #
```

What can we conclude from an exercise like this? We may at least be able to disprove a few notions that are themselves based on reasoning no more complicated than the checkerboard. Propositions beginning with "It stands to reason that . . ." can sometimes be discredited by exceedingly simple demonstrations that, though perhaps true, they do not exactly "stand to reason." We can at least persuade ourselves that certain mechanisms could work, and that observable aggregate phenomena could be compatible with types of "molecular movement" that do not closely resemble the aggregate outcomes that they determine.

There may be a few surprises. What happens if we raise the demands of one color and lower the demands of the other? Figure 7 shows typical results. Here we increased by one the number of like neighbors that a # demanded and decreased by one the number that an O demanded, as compared with Figures 5 and 6. By most measures, "segregation" is about the same as in Figures 5 and 6. The differences is in population densities: the O's are spread out all over their territory, while the #'s are packed in tight. The reader will discover, if he actually gets those pennies and dimes and tries it for himself, that something similar would happen if the demands of the two colors were equal but one color outnumbered the other by two or three to one. The minority then tends to be noticeably more tightly packed. Perhaps from Figure 7 we could conclude that if surfers mind the presence of swimmers less than swimmers mind the presence of surfers, they will become almost completely separated, but the surfers will enjoy a greater expanse of water.

Is it "Segregated"?

The reader might try guessing what set of individual preferences led from Figure 4 to the pattern in Figure 8.

The ratio of like to unlike neighbors for all the #'s and O's to-

Figure 8

```
      #  #            #  #
   #  #  #         #  #  #
   #  #  O  O  O  #  O
      O  O  O  O  O  O  O
   O  O  O  #  O  O  O
      O  #  #  #  O  O  O
      #  #  #        O  O
      #  #
```

gether is slightly more than three to one, and there are 6 O's and 8 #'s that have no neighbors of opposite color. The result is evidently segregation; but, following a suggestion of my dictionary, we might say that the process is one of *aggregation*, because the rules of behavior ascribed both to #'s and to O's in Figure 8 were simply that each would move to acquire three neighbors of like color irrespective of the presence or absence of neighbors of opposite color. As an individual motivation, this is quite different from the one that formed the patterns in Figures 5 and 6. But in the aggregate it may be hard to discern which motivation underlies the pattern, and the process, of segregated residence. And it matters!

The first impact of a display like this on a reader may be — unless he finds it irrelevant — discouragement. A moderate urge to avoid small-minority status may cause a nearly integrated pattern to unravel, and highly segregated neighborhoods to form. Even a deliberately arranged viable pattern, as in Figure 3, when buffeted by a little random motion, proves unstable and gives way to the separate neighborhoods of Figures 5 through 8. These then prove to be fairly immune to continued random turnover.

For those who deplore segregation, however, and especially for those who deplore more segregation than people were seeking when they collectively segregated themselves, there may be a note of hope. The underlying motivation can be far less extreme than the observable patterns of separation. What it takes to keep things from unraveling is to be learned from Figure 4; the later figures indicate only how hard it may be to restore such "integration" as would satisfy the individuals, once the process of separation has stabilized. In Figure 4 only 9 of the 45 individuals are motivated to move, and if we could persuade them to stay everybody else would be all right. Indeed, the reader might exercise his own ingenuity to discover how few individuals would need to be invited into Figure 4 from outside, or how few individuals would need to be relocated in Figure 4, to keep anybody from wanting to move. If two lonely #'s join a third lonely #, none of them is lonely anymore, but the first will not move to the second unless assured that the third will arrive, and without some concert or regulation, each will go join some larger cluster, perhaps abandoning some nearby lonely neighbor in the process and surely helping to outnumber the opposite color at their points of arrival.

NOTES AND QUESTIONS
ON NEIGHBORHOOD SORTING

1. The segregated patterns in Schelling's Figures 5 and 6 resulted from preferences to avoid being disproportionately outnumbered by "others." Preferences to be near a certain absolute number of "one's own" produced the segregated pattern in Figure 8. Should opponents of segregation be equally damning of these somewhat different preferences? Could one tell which of the two had segregated a particular neighborhood?

2. Schelling suggests that race-conscious interventions targeted at keeping a few apprehensive households in place might be enough to prevent racial segregation. As a practical matter, could government officials pinpoint the households on the brink of tipping out?

Schelling's idea broaches the legally complex issue of affirmative action. To stem white flight, should a city be empowered to protect homeowners in transitional neighborhoods from declines in property value? Carry out race-conscious affirmative marketing? Entitle landlords and other intermediaries to use "benign quotas" that abet integration? If legal, which of these policies is apt to be most effective? See Comment, The Legality and Efficacy of Homeowners Equity Assurance: A Study of Oak Park, Illinois, 78 Nw. U. L. Rev. 1463 (1984); George C. Galster, Neighborhood Racial Change, Segregationist Sentiments, and Affirmative Marketing Policies, 27 J. Urb. Econ. 344 (1990); Dorn Bishop, Note, Fair Housing and the Constitutionality of Government Measures Affecting Community Ethnicity, 55 U. Chi. L. Rev. 1229-1266 (1988).

3. Not all commentators deplore segregated outcomes. See, for example, Michael R. Tein, Note, The Devaluation of Nonwhite Community in Remedies for Subsidized Discrimination, 140 U. Pa. L. Rev. 1463 (1992). Is there a compelling communitarian defense of racial and ethnic enclaves? How should Fair Housing statutes accommodate the national commitment to an open society with individuals' preferences for clustering with persons like themselves?

Should the developer of a planned community be able to employ covenants to help ensure the community's appeal to particular racial, ethnic, or religious groups? See supra pp.424-439.

D.   The Takings Issue

Property, Utility, and Fairness: Comments on the Ethical Foundations of 'Just Compensation' Law*

Frank I. Michelman

"Taking" is, of course, constitutional law's expression for any sort of publicly inflicted private injury for which the Constitution requires payment of compensation. Whether a particular injurious result of governmental activity is to be classed as a "taking" is a question which usually arises where the nature of the activity and its causation of private loss are not themselves disputed; and so a court assigned to differentiate among impacts which are and are not "takings" is essentially engaged in deciding when government may execute public programs while leaving associated costs disproportionately concentrated upon one or a few persons.

It might be thought remarkable that we tolerate even the raising of such a question. There is, after all, strong appeal in Hobhouse's insistence that a rational social order does not rest "the essential indispensable condition of the happiness of one man on the unavoidable misery of another, the happiness of forty millions of men on the misery of one"; and it is not easy to disagree with his statement that, however temporarily expedient, "it is eternally unjust that one man should die [he means, should be compelled to die] for the people." If deliberate governmental activity foreseeably entails some injurious impact on an established private interest, how can we, without violating Hobhouse's strictures, avoid concluding at once that compensation is in order? Where is the occasion for further classifying such impacts into those which are and those which are not "takings"?

The issues become more distinct if we compare with the uncompromising platform of Hobhouse the worldly wise, tolerant pragmatism of Holmes. Without adverting to questions of "ratio-

*Source: 80 Harv. L. Rev. 1165-1169, 1214-1238, 1245, 1253-1258 (1967).

nality," Holmes is content to lay it down that a government ought not to be called "civilized" if it "sacrifices the citizen more than it can help." He leaves it to us to imagine what he has in mind when he speaks of deliberate public sacrifice of an individual which the government "cannot help." Could we convince Hobhouse that such a case is possible? Would he make exceptions for it if we could? Or would he be bound to conclude that the society which admits to the possibility of "unavoidable" sacrifice must be irrationally organized or motivated?

I believe that the "taking" problem can be reduced to terms which allow us to say that Holmes and Hobhouse are telling different versions of the same truth.

It is debatable whether what follows is an essay in constitutional law. There is no doubt that the problem to be canvassed — what will be called the compensation problem — has received a generous share of attention from courts called upon to interpret and enforce constitutional strictures on public action and from scholars drawn to analysis, appraisal, and rationalization of constitutional doctrine as it materializes from the decisions. More analysis and more criticism will be found in the following pages. Missing, perhaps conspicuously, will be efforts to arrive at a systematic restatement of legal doctrine, or to reformulate doctrine, redirect it, or overhaul it; for what is counselled here is, more than anything else, a deemphasis of reliance on judicial action as a method of dealing with the problem of compensation. . . .

Such questions as those of distinguishing the "police power" from the "power of eminent domain" and of calculating "just compensation" thus seem to derive from a broader question: When a social decision to redirect economic resources entails painfully obvious opportunity costs, how shall these costs ultimately be distributed among all the members of society? Shall they be permitted to remain where they fall initially or shall the government, by paying compensation, make explicit attempts to distribute them in accordance with decisions made by whatever process fashions the tax structure, or perhaps according to some other principle? Shall the losses be left with the individuals on whom they happen first to fall, or shall they be "socialized"? . . .

IV. Utility, Fairness, and Compensation

A. Compensation and Utility

A strictly utilitarian argument leading to the specific identification of "compensable" occasions would have a quasi-mathematical structure. Let us define three quantities to be known as "efficiency gains," "demoralization costs," and "settlement costs." "Efficiency gains" we define as the excess of benefits produced by a measure over losses inflicted by it, where benefits are measured by the total number of dollars which prospective gainers would be willing to pay to secure adoption, and losses are measured by the total number of dollars which prospective losers would insist on as the price of agreeing to adoption. "Demoralization costs" are defined as the total of (1) the dollar value necessary to offset disutilities which accrue to losers and their sympathizers specifically from the realization that no compensation is offered, and (2) the present capitalized dollar value of lost future production (reflecting either impaired incentives or social unrest) caused by demoralization of uncompensated losers, their sympathizers, and other observers disturbed by the thought that they themselves may be subjected to similar treatment on some other occasion. "Settlement costs" are measured by the dollar value of the time, effort, and resources which would be required in order to reach compensation settlements adequate to avoid demoralization costs. Included are the costs of settling not only the particular compensation claims presented, but also those of all persons so affected by the measure in question or similar measures as to have claims not obviously distinguishable by the available settlement apparatus.

A measure attended by positive efficiency gains is, under utilitarian ethics, prima facie desirable. But felicific calculation under the definition given for efficiency gains is imperfect because it takes no account of demoralization costs caused by a capricious redistribution, or alternatively, of the settlement costs necessary to avoid such demoralization costs. When pursuit of efficiency gains entails capricious redistribution, either demoralization costs or settlement costs must be incurred. It follows that if, for any measure, both demoralization costs and settlement costs (whichever were chosen) would exceed efficiency gains, the measure is to be rejected; but that otherwise, since either demoralization costs or settlements costs must be paid, it is the lower of these two costs which should be paid. The compensation rule which then clearly emerges is that compensation is to be paid whenever settlement costs are lower than both demoralization costs and efficiency gains. But if settlement costs, while lower than demoralization costs, exceed efficiency gains, then the measure is improper regardless of whether compensation is paid. The correct utilitarian statement, then, insofar as *the issue of compensability* is concerned, is that compensation is due whenever demoralization costs exceed settlement costs, and not otherwise.

Let us now focus on the problem of appraising demoralization costs. Since we are looking ultimately to the specification of practical methods for identifying compensable occasions, we may begin by saying that it obviously will not do to interview every potential compensation claimant and ask him how demoralized he expects to be if a given measure is adopted without provision for compensation. The objections to such a solution run far deeper than the obvious one about the costs of conducting such interviews. The interviewee probably will not himself know the answer to the question (putting aside the difficulty of his attaching a dollar value to his outrage and his loss of incentive even if he could appraise those subjectively) and, for strategic reasons, would not reveal the true answer if he knew it.

We are compelled, then, to frame the question about demoralization costs in terms of responses we must impute to ordinarily cognizant and sensitive members of society. Utilitarian algebra, it appears, cannot specify a sound compensation practice — the equation cannot be solved for that "value" of compensation which yields a maximum excess of efficiency gains over demoralization or settlement costs — until supposed facts about human psychology and behavior have been plugged into the equation as independent variables.

If we hypothesize a utilitarian defense of currently observable social practices pertaining to compensation, we can make some interesting deductions about the behavioral assumptions which must have entered into the utilitarian calculation. One clear characteristic of current practices is their reflection of a special urgency in the demand for publicly financed compensation when a loss has evidently been occasioned by deliberate social action. Society has not yet placed itself under any systematic discipline designed to assure people of compensation for all economic losses inflicted by forces regarded as beyond social control, such as earthquake or plague. If, then, the just compensation requirement is supposed to rest on strictly utilitarian grounds — if, that is, it is supposed to rest on a purpose of forestalling demoralization which impairs the output of goods — there must be at work a tacit assumption that losses which seem the proximate results of deliberate collective decision have a special counterproductive potency beyond any which may be contained in other kinds of losses. It cannot, in other words, be simply uncertainty — awareness of the possibility of unpredictable and unpreventable future loss — which utilitarians engaged in rationalizing the just compensation practice judge to be intolerably demoralizing.

We are thus led to inquire whether there is any reason to suppose that a visible risk of majoritarian exploitation should have any greater disincentive effect than the ever-present risk that accidents may happen, this being the only supposition which seems, on utilitarian premises, to justify a constitutional guaranty aimed specially against the former sort of risk. If I am able to mobilize my productive faculties under the general conditions of uncertainty which prevail in the universe, why should I be paralyzed by a realization that I am at the mercy of majorities?

There seems only one possible way to defend this behavioral supposition. The defense must begin with an imputation to human actors of a perception that the force of a majority is self-determining and purposive, as compared with other loss-producing forces which seem to be randomly generated. The argument must then proceed to the effect that even though people can adjust satisfactorily to random uncertainty, which can be dealt with through insurance, including self-insurance, they will remain on edge when contemplating the possibility of strategically determined loses. For when the bearing of strategy is evident, one faces the risk of being *systematically* imposed upon, which seems a risk of a very different order from the risk of occasional, accidental injury. One faces also the rational necessity of devoting a large proportion of his energies and resources to counterstrategy aimed at fending off the risk; where the possibility of loss will visibly be determined by strategy, that possibility cannot be conveniently dismissed from consciousness on the ground that, being uncontrollable, it is not worth thinking about.

Whatever the empirical verity of this behavioral picture, it does seem implicit in any attempt to rationalize current compensation practices in utilitarian (product-maximizing) terms. Accordingly, it seems in order to ask what criteria of compensability will emerge if the practice of compensating is taken to have the purpose of quieting people's unease about the possibility of being strategically exploited.

It seems obvious, to begin with, that this unease will be stirred by any spectacle of capricious redistribution which could easily have been avoided. Capricious redistributions will not be tolerated, even as accidental adjuncts of efficiency-dictated measures, when compensation settlements can be reached without much trouble, that is, when settlement costs are low. The clearer it is that the claimant has sustained an injury distinct from those sustained by the generality of persons in society, and the more obviously there appears to be some objectively satisfactory measure of his disproportionate or distinctive injury, the more compelling will his claim to compensation become.

Society, moreover, will have to avoid not only those capricious redistributions which a compensation payment could easily offset, but also those practically noncompensable ones which cannot plausibly be said to be necessitated by the pursuit of efficiency. Thus, measures whose efficiency is open to grave question will have to be rejected unless attended by compensation even though their arguable efficiency is enough to justify their adoption in some form. Payment of compensation in such cases may furnish a necessary assurance that the measure is not simply a disguised attempt to redistribute deliberately, by confirming the hypothesis that society deems the measure a "gainful" (efficient) one in the only ethically sure sense. Therefore, as the collective allocational measure approaches the limit of doubtful efficiency, the claim for compensation will become more compelling.

Other intertwined branches of a compensability inquiry could grow out of a utilitarian purpose to cater to the sense of security by preserving an illusion of long-run indiscriminateness in the distribution of social burdens and benefits. Thus the magnitude of the imposition would plainly be relevant: is it of quotidian variety, or is it once in a lifetime mayhem? But magnitude of individual burden, no matter how purposively conceived, reveals only a fragment, meaningless by itself, of the whole picture. We need additional information. For example, is the burden for which compensation is sought a rare or peculiar one, or do like burdens seem to have been widely, even though not uniformly, scattered about the community? Is there implicit in the measure some reciprocity of burdens coupled with benefits (as, for example, in a measure restricting a large area to residential development) or does it channel benefits and burdens to different persons? How likely does it seem that members of the class burdened by the measure were able to wield enough effective influence in the process leading to its adoption to have extracted some compensatory concession "in kind"?

B. Compensation and Fairness

It is not the purpose of this essay to make a case for utilitarian ethics. Unquestionably, the provisional assumption of a utilitarian stance towards efficiency, property, and security is clarifying to a critical study of actual compensation practices. But there is no basis for concluding that the question of compensability is intelligible only when compensation is regarded as an instrument of utilitarian maximizing. Many observers, though they may admit that the question of compensability can logically be viewed as a question of efficiency, will insist that it can also be viewed as a question of justice to be decided without regard to the effect of the decision on the net social product. We must consider whether, in the name of justice, a person might not claim compensation (or society might not refuse compensation) regardless of the consequences for the net social product.

Since I am not prepared to embark on a general canvassing of philosophies of justice, I have selected for examination one recent, nonmaximizing account of justice which seems to hold forth special promise of illuminating the compensation problem, namely the account given by John Rawls of "justice as fairness."[104]

Rawls's theory attracts our attention because it is concerned with inequalities in the treatment — the quota of powers, honors, and incomes — received by individuals under collectively maintained arrangements. A cogent attempt is made to clarify the idea of justice as the special virtue of social arrangements within which such inequalities become acceptable. They are said to be acceptable — the arrangements producing them are deemed just — if those arrangements are consistent with principles which could command the assent of every member of a group of rational, self-regarding persons, convening under circumstances of mutually acknowledged equality and interdependence, to hammer out principles by which they will judge complaints against whatever rules and institutions may come to characterize their association. All of these persons are presumed to be aware that each is powerless either to impose his preferences on any other or to claim for himself, in advance, any particular position which may be constituted by a rule or institution. Social practices, then, are to be judged by principles which a person would favor if he had to assume that he might occupy the least advantageous position distinguishable under any rule or institution which might emerge. (The model embodies, in effect, the two very broad ethical propositions invoked at the outset of this article — that good is ultimately to be understood in terms of individually experienced satisfactions, and that the respective claims of individuals to satisfaction cannot be ranked.)

Rawls finds that two fundamental principles would emerge from this convention of the circumspect. The first principle is a general presumption that social arrangements should accord no preferences to anyone, but should assure to each participant the maximum liberty consistent with a like liberty on the part of every other participant. The second principle defines a justification for departures from the first: An arrangement entailing differences in treatment is just so long as (a) everyone has a chance to attain the positions to which differential treatments attach, and (b) the arrangement can reasonably be supposed to work out to the advantage of every participant, and especially the one to whom accrues

104. [Ed. Note: See Rawls's book, A Theory of Justice, 1971.]

the least advantageous treatment provided for by the arrangement in question.

For illustration of these principles we may begin by imagining, as a mode of basic organization in which the principle of "equal liberty" is strictly adhered to insofar as economic life is concerned, a society where product is distributed to all in equal shares of purchasing power. If "equal liberty" were an unqualified principle we might have to choose some such form of organization. Rawls's second principle, however, permits us to opt for some other mode of organization which departs from the strict equality principle, as long as the occupant of each position constituted by the preferred mode should be able to see that the arrangement, precisely because it involves inequalities, improves his long-run prospects over what they would have been under the "equality" mode. So, under private property institutions, product is distributed in part according to an inevitably unequal pattern which reflects the fortuity of "factor endowments" — the morally accidental and unequal distribution among individuals of strength, skill, ambition, and ownership of physical resources (and, derivatively, of training, position, and influence). Such inequalities are deemed just, however, as long as it is clear that permitting distribution to take the form of returns to factors of production enhances the volume of production so significantly that (taking into account the society's other distributional practices) even the least well-endowed participant winds up better off than he could reasonably count on being under any version of strict equality. The justice of "capitalism" depends, then, on the beliefs that markets are essential to sound resource allocation, and that allowance of negotiated returns is essential to productive incentive.

Now it is apparent that Rawls's two principles are most immediately adapted to judging fundamental social arrangements — those which establish the various stations in life to which different packages of lifetime expectations are attached — and are not directly applicable either to a particular compensation controversy or to a rule defining with some generality the cases in which compensation is to be paid. For an occasion of compensability is not likely to be an occasion of determining or assigning to stations. It is an interruption or dislocation which, while it may palpably harm the claimant, will probably leave him stationed as before with his basic life prospects unimpaired.

But justice is a virtue of rules, practices, and specific acts occurring within basic distributional frameworks, as well as of the basic frameworks themselves. It is not insuperably difficult to see how Rawls's two principles are to be applied by analogy to test the justice of a compensation practice. Analogous to the equal liberty principle would be a rule forbidding all efficiency-motivated social under-takings, which have the prima facie effect of impairing "liberties" unequally, unless corrective measures (compensation payments) are employed to equalize impacts. The second principle, however, would permit a departure from this uncompromising rule of full compensation if it could be shown that some other rule should be expected to work out best for each person insofar as his interests are affected by the social undertakings giving rise to occasions of compensation.

Although it is not easy to convert Rawls's second principle into a specific test of the fairness of a given compensability decision — in part because the principle is a great deal more complex and subtle than may appear on the surface — it will be worthwhile to make the effort for the added insight it may give us into the idea of fairness as it bears on the compensation problem.

What we want to know, then, is whether a specific decision not to compensate is fair. By the very asking of the question we adopt the vantage point of the disappointed claimant and assume on his part a capacity (a) to appraise his treatment and calculate his advan-tage over a span of time (that is, he is not without patience) and (b) to view the particular decision in question as a specific manifes-tation of a general practice which will be applied consistently to situations involving other people. If he is unable to extend his think-ing in those two dimensions, there is no possibility that immediately disadvantageous treatment will be acceptable to him because it is fair.

The relevant comparison, then, is between the general practices respectively represented by specific decisions to compensate and not to compensate in this particular case; and the crucial question is which of these general practices maximizes our claimant's opportu-nities over the time span covered by his patience, imagination, and ability to project a sense of continuing selfhood. Since, however, the claimant is supposed to understand that he may turn out to be the person who fares worst under whatever compensation scheme is adopted (a fair arrangement, remember, is one which is best for whoever turns out to be worst off), it is more straightforward to ask which of the two practices minimizes his risks.

Previous discussion helps us identify the relevant risks. The risk associated with the more stringent compensation practice is that its settlement costs will force abandonment of efficient projects. Opportunities to augment social output will, then, be missed, and this is matter of concern to our claimant because, no matter what distributional pattern eventuates, if there is more to be shared he stands to get more. The risk associated with the less stringent compensation practice is that of sustaining concentrated losses from efficiency-motivated social projects which otherwise would not have been sustained — losses which may partially or totally exclude their bearer from sharing in the general gains from social activity.

The question, then, is whether the more or the less stringent compensation practice minimizes the sum of these risks; or, re-translating the inquiry into one about the fairness of a particular decision not to compensate, the question is whether the practice represented by such a decision involves a greater or a less total of the two risks — of missed opportunities for augmenting shareable social output and of losses which impair the claimant's participation in such aggregate increments as are achieved — than does the practice represented by the opposite decision. But since a compensation practice is of complex and indeterminate composition — since, that is, its nature cannot be inferred by a simple process of generalizing from a single manifestation — the question of fairness must be reformulated one last time. A decision not to compensate is not unfair as long as the disappointed claimant ought to be able to appreciate how such decisions might fit into a consistent practice which holds forth a lesser long-run risk to people like him that would any consistent practice which is naturally suggested by the opposite decision.

If we set about to make practical use of this approach, we shall find ourselves asking much the same questions to determine whether a compensability decision is fair as were suggested by the utilitarian approach. The relevant risks plainly are minimized by insistence on compensation when settlement costs are low, when efficiency gains are dubious, and when the harm concentrated on one individual is unusually great. They are also minimized if insistence on compensation is relaxed when there are visible reciprocities of burden and benefit, or when burdens similar to that for which compensation is denied are concomitantly imposed on many other people (indicating that settlement costs are high and that those sustaining the burden are probably incurring relatively small net losses — else, being many, they probably could have been mobilized to deflect the measure which burdens them).

It is important, however, to note here the possibility that the utilitarian approach and the fairness approach will yield sharply inconsistent results in some situations. Whether they do will depend on the behavioral assumptions which are plugged into the utilitarian equation, and on whether utilitarian decision makers are required to assume that their decisions will be widely publicized and sensitively construed. Consider first a case involving impact of a superficially unusual sort, perhaps not likely either to cause a great stir in the community or to recur; for example, one in which conservation officials of the United States forbid travel across a wilderness area, first by air and then by overland vehicle, with the result that the claimant is left with no practical access to his small hunting and fishing camp and is forced to close it down. Fairness rather clearly requires compensation here. But the Great Administrator who presides over the utilitarian controls might calculate that, while the settlement costs of recognizing compensability could turn out to be substantial because of a liberalizing effect on precedents governing compensability of access impairments in general, he could reasonably count on holding down the demoralization costs of a failure to compensate either by preventing the matter from becoming widely known or by not revealing the general implications of this particular decision. There is no need for our purposes to delve further into the issue of whether utilitarian decision makers should be deemed free to base their decisions on such speculations about who will find out and how perceptively they will detect and generalize from the decisions' informing principles. If the rule is that publication and perceptive interpretation of decisions must be assumed, then the divergence between utility and fairness will narrow sharply.

Yet even then it may not completely disappear. Even if utilitarian administrators are not permitted to count on keeping secret their decisions, or to disavow the general principles of action implicit in their specific acts, still they must be permitted to take due account of men's psychological makeups so far as those are supposed to be known. If, then, there are circumstances where a decision not to compensate would greatly demoralize men as they are supposed actually to be, even though that decision would be fully acceptable to the patient, far-seeing, reasonable folk who inhabit the fairness model, utility and fairness will yield different results—and utility, oddly enough, will favor the more liberal compensation practice. The significance of this point will emerge in the next section.

V. The Rules of Decision Revisited

A brief recapitulation of the discussion up to this point may be helpful. We have, in effect, been searching for a useful and satisfying way to identify the "evil" supposedly combatted by the constitutional just compensation provisions, and have now suggested equating it with a capacity of some collective actions to imply that someone may be subjected to immediately disadvantageous or painful treatment for no other apparent reason, and in accordance with no other apparent principle, than that someone else's claim to satisfaction has been ranked as intrinsically superior to his own.

The discussion has also shown why avoidance of this evil is not the same thing as avoidance of all social action having capricious redistributive effects. The reasons begin with the universal acknowledgement that some collective constraint on individual free choice is necessary in order to minimize the frustrations produced by people's concurrent quests for fulfillment, and to exploit fully the potential benefits from human interaction; and that social control, therefore, can ultimately lead to fuller achievement by each of his own ends. It is true that collective action which depends for its legitimacy on such understandings must look ultimately to the furtherance of *everyone's* attainment of his own ends, without "discrimination," and that this latter requirement would most obviously be met if a way were found to distribute the benefits and costs associated with each collective measure so that each person would share equally in the net benefit. But such perfection is plainly unattainable. Efficiency-motivated collective measures will regularly inflict on countless people disproportionate burdens which cannot practically be erased by compensation settlements. In the face of this difficulty, it seems we are pleased to believe that we can arrive at an acceptable level of assurance that *over time* the burdens associated with collectively determined improvements will have been distributed "evenly" enough so that everyone will be a net gainer. The function of a compensation practice, as here viewed, is to fulfill a strongly felt need to maintain that assurance at an "acceptable" level — to justify the general expectations of long-run "evenness." If one feels impelled to refer this need back to a social interest in maximizing production, what we have called a utilitarian approach to compensation will be the result. If, however, the need is accepted on its own terms and for its own sake, as simply rooted in the condition of being a human person, then justice or fairness, rather than utility, will seem to be the key to compensation. The two approaches may lead to different results in some situations, but in general decisions made under their guidance turn on much the same factors — the disproportionateness of the harm a measure inflicts on individuals, the likelihood that those harmed were in a position to extract balancing concessions, the clarity with which efficiency demands the measure, and so forth. In what follows, I shall often treat the two approaches as parallel, and use the word "fairness" to signify also that apparent evenhandedness which a utilitarian approach may be understood as requiring.

　　If it truly is important for society to subordinate its pursuit of efficiency to a discipline aimed at preventing outrages to fairness, then it may be worth asking whether the constitutional just compensation provisions present any hazard to sound social functioning. These provisions attract attention as the visible, formal expressions of society's commitment to fairness as a constraint on its pursuit of efficiency. The question is whether their magnetism is an energizing force, or a mesmerizing one. If it induces the habit of waiting upon the courts to administer a fairness discipline, and if courts are less than fully equal to the task or cannot perform it without serious damage to their effectiveness in other spheres, then there is cause for concern.

To argue at length for the unamazing proposition that the true purpose of the just compensation rule is to forestall evils associated with unfair treatment, is to imply that the proposition, for all its obviousness, is insufficiently understood or recognized in practice. We should, then, consider carefully the extent to which the "fairness" or utility rationale is already reflected, even if inexplicitly, in the judicial doctrines which presently compose the main corpus of our just compensation lore. My conclusion is that these doctrines do significantly reflect the line of thought which has been elaborated in these pages, and that this approach, indeed, derives some indirect support from its power to explain much that is otherwise mysterious about the doctrines. Nevertheless, the courts fall too far short of adequate performance to be left without major assistance from other quarters.

A. Physical Invasion

It will be recalled that the factor of physical invasion has a doctrinal potency often troublesome on two counts. First, private losses otherwise indistinguishable from one another may, as in the flight nuisance cases, be classified for compensability purposes according to whether they are accompanied by a physical invasion, even though that seems a purely fortuitous circumstance. Second, purely nominal harms — such as many which accompany street-widenings or subterranean utility installations — are automatically deemed compensable if accompanied by governmental occupation of private property, in apparent contradiction of the principle that the size of the private loss is a critically important variable. Both these seeming oddities may now seem easier to understand.

Actual, physical use or occupation by the public of private property may make it seem rather specially likely that the owner is sustaining a distinctly disproportionate share of the cost of some social undertaking. Moreover, there probably will be no need, in such a case, to trace remote consequences in order to arrive at a reasonable appraisal of the gravity of the owner's loss — a loss which is relatively likely to be practically determinable and expressible as a dollar amount. Furthermore, to limit compensation to those whose possessions have been physically violated, while in a sense arbitrary, may at least furnish a practical, defensible, impersonal line between compensable and noncompensable impositions — one which makes it possible to compensate on some occasions without becoming mired in the impossible task of compensating all disproportionately burdened interests.

The most obvious argument, then, for physical invasion as a discriminant of compensability would be that it combines a capacity to hold down settlement costs — both as to determining liability and as to measuring damages — with at least some tendency to draw the line so that compensable losses do, as a class, exceed in magnitude those deemed noncompensable. To the extent that the physical invasion criterion really does have these attributes, it should satisfy the test of fairness whether viewed as independent of or as subservient to a test of utility.

But this justification for a physical invasion criterion is really rather weak. The capacity for such a criterion to minimize settlement costs is beyond question, but its capacity to distinguish, even crudely, between significant and insignificant losses is too puny to be taken seriously. A rule that no loss is compensable unless accompanied by physical invasion would be patently unacceptable. A physical invasion test, then, can never be more than a convenience for identifying *clearly compensable* occasions. It cannot justify dismissal of any occasion as *clearly noncompensable.* But in that case, the significance of the settlement-cost-saving feature is sharply diminished. We find ourselves accepting the disadvantage of a test requiring compensation on many occasions where losses in truth seem relatively insignificant and bearable, in return for the convenience of having a simple way to identify some — but by no means all — compensable occasions. This seems a questionable bargain.

There may be a way of shoring up the physical invasion test — viewing it as a way of identifying some but not all compensable occasions — if we are inclined to take a utilitarian rather than an "absolute" view of fairness. This requires some reflection on psychic phenomena. Physical possession doubtless is the most cherished prerogative, and the most dramatic index, of ownership of tangible things. Sophisticated rationalizations and assurances of overall evenness which may stand up as long as one's possessions are unmolested may wilt before the stark spectacle of an alien, uninvited presence in one's territory. The psychological shock, the emotional protest, the symbolic threat to all property and security, may be expected to reach their highest pitch when government is an unabashed invader. Perhaps, then, the utilitarian might say that as long as courts must fend with compensability issues, to lay great stress on the polar circumstance of a permanent or regular physical use or occupation by the public is sound judicial practice — even though, at the same time and in a broader view, to discriminate on such a basis seems unacceptably arbitrary.

It is this evident arbitrariness which seems to require outright disapproval of the physical invasion criterion if we judge it by the standards of "absolute" fairness. For, true as may be the utilitarian controller's judgment that physical invasion raises special risks to the sense of security he wishes to inculcate, the rational actors of the fairness model must be expected to see that the relevant comparison is between large losses and small losses — not between those which are and are not accompanied by partial evictions.

B. Diminution of Value

Earlier we found it hard to understand why compensability should be thought to turn on a comparison of the size of the claimant's loss with the preexisting value of that spatially defined piece of property to which the loss in value seems to be specifically attached. It can now be suggested that judicial reliance on such comparisons reflects a utilitarian approach to compensability, as qualified by some special behavioral assumptions.

The method of identifying compensable harms on the basis of the degree to which "the affected piece" of property is devalued offers several parallels to that of discriminating on the basis of physical invasion. Both methods, though they seem obtuse and illogical so long as the purpose of compensation is broadly stated to be that of preventing capricious redistributions, gain in plausibility given the more refined statement that the purpose of compensation is to prevent a special kind of suffering on the part of people who have grounds for feeling themselves the victims of unprincipled exploitation. Moreover, the appeal of both methods rests ultimately in administrative expediency, in their defining classes of cases whose members will (a) usually be easy to identify and (b) usually, under certain behavioral suppositions, present a particularly strong subjective need for compensation.

As applied to the diminution of value test, these statements require explanation. We may begin by noticing a refinement, not mentioned earlier, which might initially seem only to deepen the mystery. It will be recalled that Justice Holmes, writing for the Court in the famous Pennsylvania Coal case,[111] held that a restriction on the extraction of coal, which effectively prevented the petitioner

111. Pennsylvania Coal Co. v. Mahon, 260 U.S. 393 (1922).

from exercising certain mining rights which it owned, was a taking of property and so could be enforced only upon payment of compensation. Holmes intimated strongly that the separation in ownership of the mining rights from the balance of the fee, prior to enactment of the restriction, was critically important to the petitioner's victory. But why should this be so? We can see that if one owns mining rights only, but not the residue of the fee, then a regulation forbidding mining totally devalues the owner's stake in "that" land. But is there any reason why it should matter whether one owns, in addition to mining rights, residuary rights in the same parcel (which may be added to the denominator so as probably to reduce the fraction of value destroyed below what is necessary for compensability) or residuary rights in some other parcel (which will not be added to the denominator)?

The significance of this question is confirmed by its pertinency to many comparable judicial performances. There is, for example, the widespread rule requiring compensation to the owner of an equitable servitude (such as a residential building restriction) when the government destroys the servitude's value by acquiring the burdened land and then using that land in violation of the private restriction embodied in the servitude. Vis-à-vis the servitude owner, the government cannot be said in the narrow sense to have "taken" any property. It has not, as in the air easement cases, engaged in an activity which would be an actionable eviction if privately instigated. It is not affirmatively exploiting any prerogative formerly held by the owner of the servitude. It is simply engaging in activity which, absent the servitude, might have been a nuisance; but government does not usually come under an automatic obligation to compensate whenever it maintains a nuisance. Yet many courts award compensation to persons deprived by government action of the benefits of private building restrictions, without asking any questions about how much value, or what fraction of some value, has been destroyed. Thus, government activity, on land adjacent to the complainant's, which would otherwise give rise to no claim to compensation, may support such a claim if it violates a building restriction of which the complainant is a beneficiary. If a justification exists for such a difference in treatment, it would seem to be that one's psychological commitment to his explicit, formally carved out, appurtenant rights in another's land is much more sharply focused and intense, and much nearer the surface of his consciousness, than any reliance he places on his general claim to be safeguarded against nuisances. This proposition, if valid, would not affect the "fairness" of noncompensation, but it means that a utilitarian, with his eye on the actual long term psychological effects of his decisions, will be wary of denying compensation to the affronted servitude owner. . . .

The "fraction of value destroyed" test, to recapitulate, appears to proceed by first trying to isolate some "thing" owned by the person complaining which is affected by the imposition. Ideally, it seems, one traces the incidence of the imposition and then asks what "thing" is likely to be identified by the owner as "the thing" affected by this measure? Once having thus found the denominator of the fraction, the test proceeds to ask what proportion of the value or prerogatives formerly attributed by the claimant to that thing has been destroyed by the measure. If practically all, compensation is to be paid.

All this suggests that the common way of stating the test under discussion — in terms of a vaguely located critical point on a sliding scale — is misleading (though certainly a true representation of the language repeatedly used by Holmes). The customary labels — magnitude of the harm test, or diminution of value test — obscure the test's foundations by conveying the idea that it calls for an arbitrary pinpointing of a critical proportion (probably lying somewhere between fifty and one hundred percent). More sympathetically perceived, however, the test poses not nearly so loose a question of degree; it does not ask "how much," but rather (like the physical-occupation test) it asks "whether or not": Whether or not the measure in question can easily be seen to have practically deprived the claimant of some distinctly perceived, sharply crystallized, investment-backed expectation.

The nature and relevance of this inquiry may emerge more clearly if we notice one other familiar line of doctrine — that which enjoins special solicitude, when a new zoning scheme is instituted, for "established" uses which would be violations were the scheme applied with full retrospective vigor. The standard practice of granting dispensations for such "nonconforming uses" seems to imply an understanding that simply to ban them without payment of compensation, thus seriously reducing the property's market value, would be wrong and perhaps unconstitutional. But a ban on potential uses not yet established may destroy market value as effectively as does a ban on activity already in progress. The ban does not shed its retrospective quality simply because it affects only prospective uses. What explains, then, the universal understanding that only those nonconforming uses are protected which were demonstrably afoot by the time the regulation was adopted? The answer seems to be that actual establishment of the use demonstrates that the prospect of continuing it is a discrete twig out of his fee simple bundle to which the owner makes explicit reference in his own thinking, so that enforcement of the restriction would, as he looks at the matter, totally defeat a distinctly crystallized expectation. Here, then, is a case in which functional division of spatially unitary property makes the same kind of difference it made in Pennsylvania Coal although the division here exists only within the eye of the beholder whose feelings we are concerned about, and is not reflected in any title papers.

The worth of this kind of analysis in a utilitarian compensation program depends on a number of assumptions which, while not void of plausibility, are surely debatable. The assumptions are (1) that one thinks of himself not just as owning a total amount of wealth or income, but also as owning several discrete "things" whose destinies he controls; (2) that deprivation of one of these mentally circumscribed things is an event attended by pain of a specially acute or demoralizing kind, as compared with what one experiences in response to the different kind of event consisting of a general decline in one's net worth; and (3) that events of the specially painful kind can usually be identified by compensation tribunals with relative ease.

If these propositions are accepted, the parallelism between the physical occupation and diminution of value tests will be clear. Of the three propositions, the second surely is the most suspect. The first seems self-evident, and the third seems probably true. Thus, the claimant in Pennsylvania Coal, which supposed itself to own a mining interest before the incidence of the regulation, owned nothing of consequence afterward, but a residential owner in the regulated district still had essentially what he had before (though its market value may have been reduced). The zoned-out apartment house owner no longer has the apartment investment he depended on, whereas the nearby land speculator who is unable to show that he has yet formed any specific plans for his vacant land still has a package of possibilities with its value, though lessened, still unspecified — which is what he had before.

C. Balancing

Earlier it was argued that while the process of striking a balance between a compensation claimant's losses and "society's" net gains would reveal the efficiency of the measure responsible for those losses and gains, it would be inconclusive as to compensability. By viewing compensation as a response to the demands of fairness we can now see that the "balancing" approach, while certainly inconclusive, is not entirely irrelevant to the compensability issue.

What fairness (or the utilitarian test) demands is assurance that society will not act deliberately so as to inflict painful burdens on some of its members unless such action is "unavoidable" in the interest of long-run, general well-being. Society violates that assurance if it pursues a doubtfully efficient course and, at the same time, refuses compensation for resulting painful losses. In this situation, even a practical impossibility of compensating will leave the sense of fairness unappeased, since it is unfair, and harmful to those expectations of the property owner that society wishes to protect, to proceed with measures which seem certain to cause painful individual losses while not clearly promising any net social improvement. In short, where compensability is the issue the "balancing" test is relevantly aimed at discovering not whether a measure is or is not efficient, but whether it is *so obviously* efficient as to quiet the potential outrage of persons "unavoidably" sacrificed in its interest. This conclusion does not, of course, detract from our earlier conclusion that even the clear and undisputed efficiency of a measure does not sufficiently establish its fairness in the absence of compensation.

D. Harm and Benefit

For clarity of analysis the most important point to be made about asking whether a restrictive measure requires a man to "benefit" his neighbors or only stops him from "harming" them is that this distinction (insofar as it is relevant and valid at all) is properly addressed to an issue different from, and antecedent to, the issue of "compensation" as we have now come to view it. We concluded earlier that the harm-benefit distinction was illusory as long as efficiency was to be taken as the justifying purpose of a collective measure. But we have for many pages past been treating the compensation problem as one growing out of a need to reconcile efficiency with the protection of fair, or socially useful, expectations. The issue we have been trying to clarify does not exist apart from the collective pursuit of efficiency. In this scheme of things, the office of the harm-benefit distinction cannot be to help resolve that issue. But the distinction, properly understood, does have a related use. It helps us to identify certain situations which, although in most obvious respects they resemble paradigm compensability problems, can be treated as raising no compensation issues *because the collective measures involved are not grounded solely in considerations of efficiency.*

The core of truth in the harm-prevention/benefit-extraction test — and the reason for its strong intuitive appeal — emerges when we recognize that some use restrictions can claim a justification having nothing to do with the question of what use of the available resources is the most efficient. If someone, without my consent, takes away a valuable possession of mine, he is said to have stolen and is called a thief. When the theft occurs, society usually will do what it can to make the thief restore to the owner the thing stolen or its equivalent, either because "commutative justice" so requires or because it is felt that there will be an intolerable threat to stable, productive social existence unless society sets its face against the unilateral decisions of thieves that they should have what is in the possession of others. The case is not essentially different if I own a residence in a pleasant neighborhood and you open a brickworks nearby. In pursuit of your own welfare you have by your own fiat deprived me of some of mine. Society, by closing the brickworks, simply makes you give back the welfare you grabbed; and, since you were not authorized in the first place to make distributional judgments as between you and me, you have no claim to compensation. The whole point of society's intervention negates any claim to compensation.

The point, then, is that the appeal of the tendered distinction between antinuisance measures and public benefit measures lies in the fact that the activities curbed by the first sort of measure are much more likely to have been "theft-like" in their origin than are activities restricted by the second sort. Measures of the "public benefit" type can usually be justified *only* in terms of efficiency, a justification which leaves the compensation issue unresolved, while "antinuisance" measures may be justified by considerations of commutative justice, or of the protection of orderly decision making, which negate any possible claim to compensation.

It should be clear, however, that no sharp distinction is thus established between the two types of measures. Activity which is obviously detrimental to others at the time regulations are adopted may have been truly innocent when first instigated. Failure to act upon this plain truth is responsible for some of the most violently offensive decisions not to compensate. The brickyard case is the undying classic. The yard is established out of sight, hearing, and influence of any other activity whatsoever. The city expands, and eventually engulfs the brickyard. The brickmaker is then ordered to desist. That order reduces the market value of his land from 800,000 dollars to 60,000 dollars. There is no question here of disgorging ill-gotten gains: Brick-making is a worthy occupation, and at the time of its establishment the yard generated no nuisance. No incompatibility with any use of other land was apparent. To say that the brickmaker should have foreseen the emergence of the incompatibility is fantastic when the conclusion depending from that premise is that we may now destroy his investment without compensating him. It would be no less erratic for society to explain to a homeowner, as it bulldozed his house out of the way of a new public school or pumping station, that he should have realized from the beginning that congestion would necessitate these facilities and that topographical factors have all along pointed unerringly in the direction of his lot.

Just as the compensation issue raised by an ostensibly nuisance-curbing regulation cannot always be dismissed by assuming that the owner's claim is no stronger than a thief's or a gambler's, so conversely it will often be wholly appropriate to deny compensation because that assumption does hold, even though the measure occasioning the private loss seems to fall within the class of restrictions on "innocent" activity for the enrichment of the public.

Suppose I buy scenic land along the highway during the height of public discussion about the possibility of forbidding all development of such land, and the market clearly reflects awareness that future restrictions are a significant possibility. If restrictions are ultimately adopted, have I a claim to be compensated in the amount of the difference between the land's value with restrictions and its value without them? Surely this would be a weak claim. I bought land which I knew might be subjected to restrictions; and the price I paid should have been discounted by the possibility that restrictions would be imposed. Since I got exactly what I meant to buy, it perhaps can be said that society has effected no redistribution so far as I am concerned, any more than it does when it refuses to refund the price of my losing sweepstakes ticket. . . .

VI. Institutional Arrangements for Securing Just Compensation . . .

A serious objection to the habit of leaving fairness discipline to the courts is that we may thereby miss opportunities to make good use of settlement methods too artificial or innovative for judicial adoption. A court, it seems, must choose between denying all compensation and awarding "just" compensation; the loss is either a "taking" of "property" or it is not. If "just" compensation is essentially incalculable, or if the cost of computing it is very high, the court may be led to classify a situation as noncompensable. If choice must be relegated to this framework, we shall not be able to exploit the substitutability of settlement costs and demoralization costs. It may be that even though that settlement which would reduce demoralization costs to zero would be prohibitively costly, there exists some relatively cheap form of settlement which would reduce demoralization costs so effectively that, by using it, we can reduce the total of settlement plus demoralization costs below what they would be in the absence of any settlement. Such a settlement technique, if one exists, is very likely to require legislative adoption.

For illustration, consider the problem of "relocation payments" to people uprooted by various public development programs, particularly urban renewal. When land is appropriated for clearance and redevelopment, its owner is, of course, compensated in the amount of its "fair market value." But, by the generally received doctrines, tenants are not constitutionally entitled to anything (unless nonsalvageable tenant-owned fixtures are destroyed), and tenant-owners are not constitutionally entitled to be compensated for the disruptive effects of changing neighborhoods and sinking new roots, or even, in case a business is uprooted, for good will destroyed, or, very possibly, for the cash outlay entailed in moving. Justification is not hard to come by for judicial abstinence from such claims. Valuation of good will is a formidable problem. How far away is a person "entitled" to move? How do you translate into dollars the shock of changing neighborhoods and the damnable inconvenience of moving, or appraise the educational damage inflicted by midstream changes in schools? All these problems are multiplied a hundred or a thousandfold where large scale programs scatter large numbers of families. The imponderable and idiosyncratic nature of the losses involved, and the interminable wrangling over amounts which would result from imposing a legal requirement of "just compensation," furnish a classic instance in which compensation claims are defeated largely because of sheer impenetrability.

Yet the violent unfairness of many such operations is manifest. The social gains hoped for from some urban redevelopment programs, while plausible enough to override any "public purpose" objection, nevertheless depend on a still controversial conception. Easily identified, relatively small numbers of people are being handed a distinctly disproportionate and frequently excruciating share of the cost of whatever social gain is involved. Redevelopment has been typically sporadic and probably will be infrequent over the long run — a few explosions here and there in the community in the course of a lifetime. There is no palpable reciprocity; the sufferers rarely double as special gainers, and they must submit to the spectacle of private land developers (or new residents) moving in for what looks like a publicly subsidized benefit. Those dislocated are likely to be members of a social class which comes increasingly to be identified as a faction — "the urban poor." Yet their influence and organization is not so great, certainly less than their numbers might indicate; and so the sense of having bargained for compensatory concessions probably brings little satisfaction. Altogether, the spectacle of uncompensated dislocations under these circumstances is an oppressive one.

Here is a situation in which a legislature can impose a useful fairness discipline which eludes the grasp of courts. There has, indeed, been a steadily expanding congressional solicitude for persons displaced by federally financed redevelopment activities. The first concession was to provide for payment of actual moving expenses occasioned by urban renewal programs. That even this innovation depended upon the exercise of special legislative and administrative capabilities, and would have been much harder to introduce judicially, is suggested by the inclusion of fixed monetary and mileage ceilings, and also of a device to minimize small claims settlement costs by making payments in fixed amounts to compensate for household moving expenses.

Artificial methods have, moreover, been invented for recognizing the existence of essentially unappraisable losses in addition to the expense of moving. Fixed sums are payable to some businesses, without regard to proof of damage, presumably in respect of their destroyed good will and momentum. "Relocation Adjustment Payments" are also available to some displaced households to acknowledge the likelihood of an increase in rental expense as a result of relocation. There has, as yet, been no attempt to recognize by monetary payment the sentimental injury, or the loss of valued society, or the inconvenience and annoyance, which a forced move may occasion, but devices have been recommended for such purposes. . . .

Settlement schemes, whether of legislative or judicial origin, are bound to be imperfect. There will be occasion on which recognition of these imperfections should spell the difference between approving and disapproving some collective undertaking. A danger of automatically entrusting the fairness discipline to courts is that public administrators may fail to take appropriate notice of this problem.

A superhighway, let us assume, is to be built through a densely settled urban area. Three routes are technologically feasible. One would go underground, would be minimally disruptive, and would be frightfully expensive. A second would travel through a university campus, entailing a large compensation liability but not an injury irreparable by money payments. A third would run across blocks of modest dwellings. Compensation liabilities would be incurred, but satisfactory settlements for tenants would be impossible. A fourth alternative would be not to build the highway. In this situation, the planner preoccupied with calculations of comparative costs will have no difficulty seeing the costs entailed by the first, second, and fourth possibilities. But if he is accustomed to transferring all responsibility for the fairness of his decisions to the judiciary, he will fail to take into account a significant cost entailed by the third alternative, that being the demoralization cost, or sense of injustice, remaining after the court has exerted its inadequate, even if maximum, effort to secure the payment of "just compensation." It is the duty of public officials to take such costs into account. . . .

Present in the foregoing discussion (buried in it, if you like) are the makings of a reconciliation between Holmes and Hobhouse.

The Hobhouse dictum that a society cannot be called "rational" if it is unable to avoid choices between public and private ruin can surely claim our support as a statement pertaining to the long run. For a society which finds it "necessary" to sacrifice individuals irrevocably in the interest of the mass must believe in the reality of collective experience, or subscribe to a nonegalitarian ethic, or be unable to see or exploit the mechanisms of compensation — any of which traits would be regarded by most of us as a gross enough deformity to warrant the epithet "irrational."

But the Hobhouse dictum rings false if we have in mind the short run only. Within the confines of a single transaction we may indeed be put to a choice between public good and private security, for the possibility of adjustment through compensation may then be a merely theoretical and not a practical possibility. In such a context the Holmesian conception of a government which "cannot help" sacrificing individuals is meaningful and valid. That Holmes had some inkling of Hobhouse's perception of the long view is indicated by his insistence that civilized governments impose disproportionate hardship on citizens *only* when they cannot help it. That Hobhouse took his stand with specific reference to the long view appears from his choice of metaphor.

NOTES AND QUESTIONS ON MICHELMAN'S ANALYSIS OF TAKINGS

1. Before asking any questions about this article, let us be sure we understand Michelman's utilitarian argument. In that section of the selection, Michelman appears to divide the problem of governmental regulation into two basic elements. First, it must be decided whether the program should be adopted at all. This, Michelman suggests, requires a decision whether the costs of the program are greater than its benefits. In other words, the program should be rejected if *both*:

$$(1)\ B - C - D < 0$$

and

$$(2)\ B - C - S < 0$$

where B = project benefits
       D = demoralization costs
       S = settlement costs
       C = all project costs other than S or D.

It is only after determining that the project's benefits are greater than its costs, that a second question must be reached. This is the question whether those who lose as a result of regulation should be compensated for their losses. Here, Michelman suggests, the fundamental issue is whether D > S, in which case compensation should be paid, or S > D, in which case not.

Given this skeletal outline, consider the following question: Which institutions, in Michelman's judgment, should be involved in resolving the first of the two basic questions? Which, the second? Can the legislature resolve the first question without knowing how the second will be resolved?

2. Although "demoralization costs" is Michelman's phrase, its intellectual source was Jeremy Bentham, who counted among the losses from confiscation not only the direct loss of the confiscated thing itself but also the fear of losing more in the future, the discouragement of friends and well-wishers, and the resulting "deadening of industry." Bentham, Principles of the Civil Code in Theory of Legislation 115-116 (C.K. Ogden, ed. 1987) (1789).

3. Virtually all the writing on "loss aversion" (for instance, Knetsch, Endowment Effect, supra p.226) appeared after Michelman wrote this famous article. Does loss aversion make compensation even more important? Or might loss aversion argue instead for a more relaxed attitude about compensation, on the grounds that people are overly attached to the status quo and demand irrationally high compensation for losses, impeding needed social change? How would you expect loss aversion to affect the *politics* of takings and compensation issues? Roger G. Noll & James E. Krier, Some Implications of Cognitive Psychology for Risk Regulation, 19 J. Leg. Stud. 747, 769 (1992), suggest that the outcomes of political debates may be affected by the ways that the issues are framed, for example, as losses or as gains with respect to what is described as the status quo.

4. Michelman claims that compensation issues (and demoralization costs) are especially likely to arise in the context of losses inflicted by "deliberate social action," since accidental losses are less likely to be seen as the outgrowth of a systematic collective strategy. Why should the source of the loss matter? By analogy, would a loss due to theft cause a farmer more discouragement than a loss from

flooding or insect damage? If human agency is so important, why do governments frequently subsidize flood control and flood insurance, while theft is usually compensated only by private insurance? Is it the *collective* nature of the confiscation, rather than the loss resulting from the confiscation itself, that especially matters in takings jurisprudence?

5. Do owners passively submit to governmental actions that seem to single them out? Note, for example, that arson is a widespread problem among buildings designated for special preservation as historic landmarks. Note also that when California's legal doctrine changed to allow public prescription (technically, implied dedication) of privately-held beaches, some owners used explosives and guard dogs to keep the public off their beach property; see Michael J. O'Flaherty, Note, This Land Is My Land: The Doctrine of Implied Dedication and Its Application to California Beaches, 44 S. Cal. L. Rev. 1092 (1971). Do such self-help efforts suggest other reasons why legislatures might be cautious about seemingly confiscatory measures? Should a "felicific calculus" of the costs and benefits of regulation take account of possible self-help countermeasures?

6. When Michelman revisits the rules of decision in Section V, he appears to present a supplemental reason for noncompensation, stating that "it seems we are pleased to believe that we can arrive at an acceptable level of assurance that *over time* the burdens associated with collectively determined improvements will have been distributed 'evenly' enough so that everyone will be a net gainer." Does this gradual spreading-out of public risks raise other problems? For example, locally-undesirable public facilities are often sited with little or no compensation to neighboring uses. Is a sewage treatment plant in your neighborhood the equivalent of a prison half-way house in someone else's neighborhood? Why have so many neighborhoods joined NIMBY (Not in My Back Yard) movements to avoid *any* unwanted land uses? See Peter Margulies, Building Communities of Virtue: Political Theory, Land Use Policy, and the 'Not in My Backyard' Syndrome, 43 Syr. L. Rev. 945 (1992). Does this phenomenon suggest a distrust of governmental even-handedness? A collective action problem among neighborhoods?

Another issue concerns timing: What is a fair time span within which burdens might be evened out? May the process take several generations? Note the acerbic treatment of remote compensation in the old Wobbly tune: "There'll be pie / in the sky / when you die / by and by." Does the answer depend on the discount rate — that is, how one calculates the present value of future gains and losses?

7. Is Michelman's approach to fairness faithful to Rawls? Michelman seems to consider the condition of persons made worse off as

a result of particular governmental actions. Is this the relevant "worst off" grouping in a Rawlsian scheme? Might Rawls think it appropriate that a better-off group come out worse with respect to a particular measure, if the effect were to advance the larger social welfare and particularly to advance the least advantaged group?

8. How satisfactory do you find Michelman's psychological justification for the "physical invasion" test? Does it suggest some innate human characteristic, such as territoriality? Do you see any relationship between Michelman's psychological explanation and Sugden's description of property based on "association" in the selection from Sugden's Economics of Rights, supra p.172?

9. Michelman identifies a crucial problem in the "diminution of value" test of takings, that is, the choice of the denominator, or the underlying property to which the loss is compared. "How much is taken" entails understanding how much *of what*. Unfortunately, the definition of the "original" or "underlying" property turns out to be quite tricky.

Suppose your corporation owned 1) a beautiful old railroad station in Manhattan, 2) other real estate in the area of the station, and 3) the railroad operation itself. Suppose further that a new city historic-preservation ordinance made it well-nigh impossible for you to redevelop the station to fill up the zoning "envelope" enjoyed by all other owners in the area. If your loss — the value of air space above the station — is to be placed in the numerator, what is the denominator? Should it be the lost airspace itself? The full station site? The corporation's real estate assets in the larger area? All the corporation's assets? Can you see why this issue affects the question of "the extent of the diminution"?

A curiously dismissive treatment of this central issue appears in the case upon which this hypothetical is based, Penn Central Transportation Co. v. City of New York, 438 U.S. 104, 130 (1978); but the problem of defining the underlying property interest is noted in Lucas v. South Carolina Coastal Council, 112 S. Ct. 2886, 2894 n.7 (1992).

10. Consider the "balancing" and "harm and benefit" takings tests that Michelman identifies. With respect to "balancing," do you agree that an owner suffering a property loss might be mollified by the consideration that the loss is offset by a larger public gain?

With respect to "harm and benefit," how does one know whether a building ban along a highway, to use one of Michelman's examples, prohibits harms or forces benefits? Can ordinary language help? Michelman suggests that a brickmaker who moves to a remote location can thereby insulate himself from a later charge that his activity harms the property of newcomers to the area. Is a long-standing harm no longer a harm? Nuisance law may provide a guide. Cases invoking a "coming to the nuisance" defense seem to support this proposition, but some courts are more subtle, allowing "coming to the nuisance" as a defense only in nuisance suits asking for injunctive relief, and not in suits for damages. What is the point of this distinction? Would Calabresi and Melamed approve? For some modern permutations, see Spur Industries, Inc. v. Del E. Webb Dev. Co. 494 P. 2d 700 (Ariz. 1972).

11. Is "exit" a viable self-help solution to threatened takings problems? Can the implicit threat of citizen departures (or ex ante refusals to move in) diminish the risk of confiscatory legislation in the first place? Might this particularly apply to the takings issues presented by local governments, since those governments are most likely to compete for desirable residents? See Vicki Been, Exit as a Constraint on Land Use Exactions: Rethinking the Unconstitutional Conditions Doctrine, 91 Colum. L. Rev. 473 (1991); but for a critique, see Stewart E. Sterk, Competition Among Municipalities as a Constraint on Land Use Exactions, 45 Vand. L. Rev. 831 (1992) (stressing the immobility of real estate assets). Much of the debate on the issue of "regulatory competition" revolves around the seminal article by Charles Tiebout, A Pure Theory of Local Expenditures, 64 J. Pol. Econ. 416 (1956). According to Tiebout, just as firms compete for customers by offering varying packages of goods and services, local governments compete for residents by offering varying regulatory programs and public goods. Tiebout argued that this competition produces ideal results, but only if some highly restrictive conditions are met. Can you guess what some of them are?

Takings, Insurance, and Michelman: Comments on Economic Interpretations of 'Just Compensation' Law*

William A. Fischel & Perry Shapiro

I. The Noncompensation Controversy

Under the takings clause of the Constitution, the state is required to pay just compensation whenever it takes private property for public use. Yet the explicit command of the Fifth Amendment does not foreclose asking whether, on balance, this rule is a good thing. If

*Source: 17 J. Legal Stud. 269-293 (1988).

pressed on the question, most economists and lawyers would, we believe, conclude that the government should pay for the property that it takes. The argument, especially that of economists, might be that forcing the government to pay for the resources it gets promotes efficiency. In a world lacking any compensation requirement, the obvious fear is that private investors will be inhibited by the thought that government will snatch away or unthinkingly destroy the fruits of their venture. The fears of what will happen at the end of the process work themselves into the calculation of property owners at the beginning of that process, so that too little capital will be invested in productive enterprises. The compensation requirement thus serves the dual purpose of offering a substantial measure of protection to private entitlements, while disciplining the power of the state, which would otherwise overexpand unless made to pay for the resources that it consumes.

This conventional economic wisdom has been challenged by Blume, Rubinfeld, and Shapiro (henceforth, BRS).[2] Their article offered a model that proved that compensation for takings is inefficient in that such compensation encourages landowners to overinvest in private capital. The basic logic of their position is that compensation allows landowners to ignore the opportunity cost of their land for efficient government projects. This finding will be called the noncompensation result.

The noncompensation result is not merely an economist's curiosity. Since its articulation in 1984, the BRS result has become the focus of two law journal articles that advance it as the basis for a substantial reevaluation of compensation practice in American law.[3] Two of the authors of the article, Blume and Rubinfeld, have offered an analysis of compensation as insurance, and they have suggested that courts distinguish their awards of compensation on the basis of the risk preferences of those affected by takings. Their rule is that people whose property is taken should be awarded compensation only if they did not have an opportunity to reduce the risk of a taking by purchasing private insurance (presumably available once the rule was adopted) or by spreading risks through diversification and

2. Lawrence E. Blume, Daniel L. Rubinfeld, & Perry Shapiro, The Taking of Land: When Should Compensation Be Paid? 99 Q. J. Econ. 71 (1984).
3. Lawrence E. Blume & Daniel L. Rubinfeld, Compensation for Takings: An Economic Analysis, 72 Cal. L. Rev. 569 (1984); and Louis Kaplow, An Economic Analysis of Legal Transitions, 99 Harv. L. Rev. 509 (1986). Their insurance rationale for takings was anticipated, without extensive analysis, by Richard A. Posner, Economic Analysis of Law 41 n. 1 (2d ed. 1977). Another recent article relies on the BRS noncompensation result to propose modifications of takings jurisprudence, but it does not advance the insurance rationale — Robert Cooter, Unity in Tort, Contract, and Property: The Model of Precaution, 73 Cal. L. Rev. 1 (1985).

contingent contracts. Compensation by government agencies is thus viewed as a last-resort substitute for private insurance. As a practical matter, Blume and Rubinfeld suggest that wealthier people are more likely to be able to insure privately, and thus government compensation for takings might be reserved for poor people.

Louis Kaplow adopts a premise that is similar to that of Blume and Rubinfeld — that compensation serves the function of insurance — but arrives at a different policy conclusion. He argues that because moral hazard problems identified by BRS are less efficiently controlled by the government, only private insurance is needed to provide compensation for takings and, more generally, for all legal transitions, such as tax reform and deregulation. The noncompensation result thus forms an economic rationale for reading the just compensation clause out of the Constitution, although Kaplow professes to be agnostic about the application of his discussion.[5]

In Section II we explore the logic of the noncompensation result using the distinction between property rules and liability rules developed by Calabresi and Melamed.[6] It is shown that the source of the inefficiency created by compensation is similar to the moral hazard found in many other economic policies. Section III explicates Frank Michelman's utilitarian standard and places the noncompensation result in that context.[7] We argue that the insurance model does not fit into this framework because its promoters ignore or misinterpret Michelman's demoralization costs. It is shown that the noncompensation result, which occasioned the development of the insurance model, can be incorporated in Michelman's model, and that it does militate against compensation in many instances. Section IV shows that misinterpretation of demoralization costs is also the source of confusion about whether capitalization of expected takings into land value militates against compensation for purchasers. The conclusions are given in Section V.

II. Compensation and Moral Hazard

A. A Tale of Four Floods

The following example is intended to capture the salient points of the BRS article by extending one of their examples. A family owns

---

5. Kaplow, supra note 3, at 572. . . .
6. . . . . Property Rules, Liability Rules and Inalienability: One View of the Cathedral, 85 Harv. L. Rev. 1089 (1972).
7. Frank Michelman, Property, Utility and Fairness: Comments on the Ethical Foundations of 'Just Compensation' Law, 80 Harv. L. Rev. 1165 (1967).

Table 1		
Summary of the Scenarios in Section II		
Scenario (and Rule)	*Outcome*	*Efficiency*
1. Natural disaster (no compensation)	Campground	Efficient
2. Natural disaster (government compensation)	Hotel	Inefficient
3. Public dam (government compensation)	Hotel	Inefficient
4. Private dam (landowner consent)	Campground	Efficient

land in a river valley on which they contemplate establishing a business to provide overnight accommodations. They must choose between a campground and a hotel. The campground requires investments of small amounts of capital that depreciate quickly. The hotel involves more capital, which lasts longer and provides more guest services per year. Prior to investigating the geology of the region, the family concludes that the hotel is more profitable.

The only thing that would make the hotel less profitable would be to have the level of the river in the valley rise to such an extent that it would inundate the hotel, in which case all capital would be lost because the hotel would be "immovable" (too costly to move). In that case, the campground would have been more profitable, since only a trivial amount of capital would have been lost. What causes the river to rise, and what knowledge the landowners have or should have about such events, will be discussed under different scenarios. It is assumed throughout that the landowners are risk neutral. (The scenarios are summarized in Table 1 to facilitate comparison of the results.)

Scenario 1 involves a natural disaster. The landowners are made aware that there is a 20 percent probability that their land will be inundated when a natural lake is formed as a result of a rockslide on government-owned land downstream from the proposed hotel. Nothing can be done to reduce the probability of this event or to mitigate the damages it will cause once it happens, and the government is known not to be responsible for the consequences of this "act of God." As a result, the landowners decide to build the nondurable hotel (the campground), a decision which is assumed to maximize social welfare.

In scenario 2, suppose that prior to the landowners' decision to build the campground the government enacted a flood compensation bill that offers to pay those affected by natural disasters for the market value of their losses. No payment in advance, other than an increase in taxes spread among all citizens, is necessary to acquire this guarantee of compensation.

This bill will induce the landowners to erect the hotel rather than the campground. This outcome is inefficient because it guides capital into ventures with negative expected value. The risk to the landowner is removed by the promise of compensation, but the cost to society remains, since capital is removed from safer places to riskier ones. The incentive created by the flood compensation bill is an example of moral hazard.[8] Moral hazard arises from any entitlement that divorces the consequences of people's actions from their decisions. The phenomenon is pervasive in any society. Companies that provide fire insurance worry that policyholders may ignore efficient fire prevention measures; payments to victims of pollution may induce them to live too close to its source; and colleges that grant tenure to professors may find that they work relatively little thereafter. As these examples suggest, moral hazard is not confined to insurance companies or to government programs, nor does moral hazard alone deter governments from undertaking otherwise desirable actions.

Scenario 3 assumes that no natural disaster can inundate the land on which the hotel construction is planned, but the land may be submerged by a dam built by a local government granted the power of eminent domain. The government finds it socially profitable to build the dam only if some exogenous event, such as a rise in the price of oil, occurs to make hydropower profitable. Both the would-be hotel owners and the government dam builder know that the probability of such an event is 20 percent (the same as in the natural disaster case), and both parties know that the value of the dam if this event occurs will exceed the value of the durable hotel.

Assume, moreover, that the government does only projects whose benefits exceed their costs, and everyone knows that when oil prices exceed a certain level, the government will build the dam. The government cannot be swayed from this decision by any political activity or legal manipulations. We call this relentless dedication

---

8. Blume & Rubinfeld, supra note 3, at 618 n. 144, use this term, as do BRS, supra note 2, at 86. Moral hazard may also be thought of as an externality in the sense that it induces people to ignore some of the costs of their actions. Kaplow, supra note 3, at 551, uses this term to describe the BRS characterization of compensation. Our subsequent use of the term "moral hazard" in the text refers solely to the landowner incentives identified by BRS.

to benefit/cost principles the Pigovian assumption.[9] It allows the landowners to regard the government's decision to build the dam as an exogenous event. The government will seize the property if the aforementioned increase in oil prices occurs; otherwise the property is safe.

Under these conditions, BRS prove that it is inefficient to compensate the landowner for the taking. "Just compensation" is, under these conditions, a form of moral hazard. Advance knowledge of a rule that the government would pay for damages to structures would be inefficient for the same reason that disaster payments are inefficient in the second scenario: durable private capital is unnecessarily put at risk of destruction. The essence of the BRS result is that government takings are analogous to these problems. We shall examine this analogy in the next scenario and in the next section.

The BRS moral hazard problem could not arise if the private capital could be costlessly removed from the site. This result follows because the social cost of landowners who ignore the possible government taking of their land is not their loss of the land but the destruction of the capital they put there. It follows, then, that there is no inefficiency entailed in paying full compensation for government takings of labor services or portable capital. Indeed, the very mobility of such resources induces rational governments to pay full compensation for their services regardless of any constitutional requirements. This observation helps explain why real estate is the focus of a disproportionate number of taking cases.

The inefficiency of compensation is not necessarily caused by strategy. The BRS result does not depend on landowners' deliberately overbuilding, which would in any event be unprofitable unless compensation for excessive structure were for more than its market value. The BRS efficiency problem is simply that the landowners rationally disregard the probability that the government may have alternative uses for their land that require the destruction or costly removal of private capital. . . .

Scenario 4 involves a private dam. (This case does not track BRS or other aforementioned papers.) It involves the same facts as in scenario 3: A dam will become profitable if and only if there is a rise in oil prices, an exogenous event whose probability is 20 percent. The difference is that the prospective dam builder is a private party who cannot exercise the right of eminent domain.

9. That Pigou may not have been a Pigovian is argued by Victor Goldberg. Pigou on Complex Contracts and Welfare Economics, 3 Res. Law and Econ. 39 (1981). We instead refer to the "Pigovian tradition" identified by Ronald H. Coase, The Problem of Social Cost, 3 J. Law & Econ. 1 (1960).

The government's role is solely to enforce contracts and protect private property from being taken by another without *consent*. Consent implies that ownership of resources is protected by a property rule, meaning that the owner can refuse to trade. The contrasting protection, under the distinctions developed by Calabresi and Melamed, is a liability rule, in which resources must be exchanged as long as the purchaser pays compensation judged by a third party to be equal to the value of the property taken. The typical example of liability rule protection for landowners is eminent domain, under which the government may take their property if it pays for it. It is this rule, of course, that is being examined in this section.

The upstream landowners in the present scenario must give their consent to the building of the dam. What will they do in this situation with regard to their business decision? They will build the campground, just as they would in the case of an uncompensated disaster. This is the efficient decision, which they will make because they can bargain with the dam builder for some of the profits of his dam in exchange for their not building the hotel. (Recall that we assumed that the dam was more profitable than the hotel, so such an exchange is feasible if transaction costs are low enough.)

It would be irrational for the upstream landowners to build the hotel to establish a better bargaining position. Property rule protection puts them in an unimprovable position: they can refuse any offer by the dam builder regardless of the current state of their land. They are thus able to collect all of the surplus value of the dam, and they have no incentive to ignore the probability that a lake may be the most profitable use of their land. This example shows that the BRS result depends on the nature of property rights as well as on the nature of government. Both issues are explored in the next section.

B.   Moral Hazard, Liability Rules, and Pigovianism

The BRS noncompensation result is counterintuitive because most economists expect that attaching market prices to things induces economic agents to behave efficiently. But their result becomes more plausible if we note two differences between their models of takings and ordinary exchange. One of the actors, the government, is constrained by the Pigovian assumption to act optimally. The government does not need to be constrained by prices, since, by assumption, it has all the information and incentives to act correctly. Pigovianism suppresses any concern with inefficient levels of government.

Pigovianism alone is not sufficient to get the counterintuitive result, though, since the landowner could be protected by a property rule against government invasions as well as against invasions by other people. In such a case, the government would have to negotiate with the landowners. Because of the security of their position, the landowners would not be induced to ignore the alternative uses for their land that the government might have in mind. The sufficient (and reasonable) condition for the BRS noncompensation result is that the landowner be protected only by liability rules.

The essential problem of a liability rule is that it attempts to limit the entitlements of private property owners. The economic rationale for a liability rule is that it avoids the holdout problem. Under property rule protection, private landowners may strategically refuse to sell their property at values that may be acceptable to them in ordinary transactions in an effort to extract some of the government's surplus from the project. This is inefficient because some such strategies may result in no exchange at all, or they may involve additional resources not otherwise employed in normal market transactions. This rationale, which we accept for this article, precludes the solution suggested by scenario 4 in the previous section.[14]

Our emphasis on compensation as a liability rule also explains the problem with the traditional argument (in Section I) that compensation will improve the allocation of resources because it protects private property. The answer is that eminent domain itself is, in one perspective, a reduction in property rights, not a protection of them. The Fifth Amendment concludes, "nor shall private property be taken for public use, *without just compensation*" (our emphasis). If this clause were intended solely to protect private property, the last three words would be omitted, and *without the consent of the owner* would be substituted (as it is in the Third Amendment's prohibition of quartering peacetime troops in private homes). Just compensation forces a sale on prearranged terms, something no private person could do without government authority. Those who argue that protecting private property rights improves efficiency are not contradicted by the BRS result; they have only misidentified the just compensation clause as an absolute protection for property rights. . . .

14. Some research has suggested that eminent domain is not less costly to the government than voluntary market transactions. See Patricia Munch. An Economic Analysis of Eminent Domain, 84 J. Pol. Econ. 473 (1976); and A. Mitchell Polinsky, Controlling Externalities and Protecting Entitlements: Property Right, Liability Rule, and Tax Subsidy Approaches, 8 J. Legal Stud. 1 (1979). If these findings held generally, however, governments would forgo the use of eminent domain, and there is little evidence that they do.

III.   Michelman's Demoralization Costs and Insurance

This section explicates Frank Michelman's utilitarian approach to the taking issue and compares it to the view of takings as insurance outlined in Section I. Michelman's article is widely cited, but its economic implications are not fully appreciated.[15] Part of our purpose is to place his contribution in terms of normative economic theory, and part is to show why the aforementioned insurance rationales for takings are inconsistent with Michelman's criteria.

In addition to the utilitarian approach, Michelman advances a Rawlsian fairness criterion, which he implicitly prefers. He suggests, however, that the fairness and utilitarian criteria usually yield the same rules for compensation. For this reason, we confine ourselves in this article to the criterion based on philosophical utilitarianism, which was the original basis of normative economic theory and retains important links to modern welfare economics.

A.   The Utilitarian Standard

According to Michelman, in deciding whether a government action was a taking that requires compensation, a utilitarian would consider three factors: efficiency gains, demoralization costs, and settlement costs. . . .

Michelman combines these factors into a utilitarian "felicific calculation." A government measure whose dollar benefits (B) exceed costs (C) as determined by willingness to pay and be paid, respectively, should nevertheless *not* be adopted if the net benefit is exceeded by both demoralization costs (D) and settlement costs (S). In symbols, a utilitarian does not do the project if $(B - C) <$ min (D, S). Michelman does not say what course should be followed if the government decides to go ahead with a project in which $B < C$. However, in subsequent discussion of demoralization costs, he notes that taking on an inefficient project would raise demoralization costs and compel compensation. This would, as a practical matter, discourage a budget-conscious government from performing such a project.

If net benefits are positive and greater than *either* settlement or demoralization costs (or both), the lower of S or D should be endured by the government. Thus, in this latter situation, if settlement costs are lower than demoralization costs, compensation should

---

15. Michelman, supra note 7, is the most frequently cited (in law journals) article on takings and the eighth most cited law journal article on any subject in the last forty years. Fred Shapiro, The Most Cited Law Review Articles, 73 Cal. Law Rev. 1540 (1985).

be paid in order to avoid the greater cost (demoralization). But if settlement costs are higher than demoralization costs, compensation should be denied on this utilitarian calculus. In symbols, the government should pay if $(B - C) > S$, and $S < D$. On the other hand, the government does *not* have to pay if $(B - C) > D$, and $D < S$.

B. Pareto, Kaldor-Hicks, and Michelman

Michelman's utilitarian standard is sometimes called an efficiency criterion. This can be misleading. It is not a rule that all government decisions must involve Pareto-superior moves, because it allows that in some situations (that is, when $[B - C] > D$, and $D < S$), some people can be left worse off if it is too costly to compensate them. In fact, it may even be possible for the government to make compensation and still do the project profitably $(B > C + S)$ but still not be compelled to pay, because demoralization costs are relatively low $(D < S)$. Thus, Michelman's criterion is more permissive to the government than the Pareto-superiority criterion.

On the other hand, Michelman's standard is less permissive than the Kaldor-Hicks criterion, which says simply that the government should take on projects if the gainers can compensate the losers, but does not require that it actually make the compensation. This is simply Michelman's efficiency gain, that $B > C$. The Kaldor-Hicks criterion was developed in response to the notion that settlement costs of the Pareto-superiority criterion may be so large as to prohibit all projects. But Kaldor-Hicks does not address the troubling possibility that the government may thereby impose large burdens on particular individuals.

Michelman's path-breaking contribution was to define an intermediate standard. The appeal to economists of Michelman's utilitarian formulation is that it offers a coherent, efficiency-based (cost minimization) standard for choosing between the rigid Pareto-superiority criterion, which disallows consideration of settlement costs, and the permissive Kaldor-Hicks criterion, which ignores the distribution of utility gains. . . .

C. Demoralization and Majoritarianism

The source of the demoralization cost for Michelman is the risk of "majoritarian exploitation." He is explicit in keying demoralization costs to the distinction between this political hazard and risk due to random events such as natural disasters. Majoritarianism is said to have greater disincentive effects because of a "perception that the force of a majority is self-determining and purposive. . . .

The argument [for the existence of demoralization costs as distinct from other risks] must then proceed to the effect that even though people can adjust satisfactorily to random uncertainty, which can be dealt with through insurance, including self-insurance, they will remain on edge when contemplating the possibility of strategically determined losses."

Why should people feel worse about majoritarian exploitation than about other hazards? Michelman suggests it is because they are strategically determined. People can adjust to strategic losses, but these adjustments are more costly (or involve greater disutility) than adjustments to random losses, which can be "conveniently dismissed from consciousness on the ground that, being uncontrollable, it is not worth thinking about."

Regardless of the source of demoralization costs, our critical point at this juncture is that Michelman regards them as distinct from natural hazards. This is further emphasized by his list of causes of demoralization costs. They include government actions in which (a) settlement costs are low (that is, people feel worse about not being compensated if it would have been easy to do so); (b) losers perceive that their burdens are large relative to others' (disproportionate impact); (c) the efficiency of the project itself is so doubtful that it is a thin veil for unprincipled redistribution; (d) the loss is not likely to be recouped by benefits tied in some way to the project (that is, lack of reciprocity); (e) those who lose now have little confidence that they will gain from similar projects in the future; (f) losers lack political influence to be able to extract concessions to mitigate their burdens in the future.

Our private analogy of Michelman's demoralization distinction is the difference between one's feelings about a watch that is stolen and a watch that is lost. The watch is gone in both cases, but the very knowledge that it was stolen may make you feel worse and thus expend more real resources in avoiding this particular kind of loss, in part because such deliberate acts may be repeated.[31] The ability to purchase insurance against theft does not dispose of such costs, since insurance simply spreads them out over a period of time through insurance premiums. Note that the stolen watch's demoralization is net of the utility gain of the person who now has the

---

31. The context of the theft may make a difference. A watch left unattended in a public washroom for a time may be stolen, but its owner may feel less demoralized from that than if it were stolen from a bedroom or by an identifiable individual. Surveys of perceptions of fairness indicate that people most strenuously object to transfers that involve deliberate exploitation of one person's utility by another. See Daniel Kahneman. Jack L. Knetsch, & Richard Thaler, Fairness as a Constraint on Profit Seeking, 76 Am. Econ. Rev. 728, 735 (1986).

stolen watch — and what victim has not wished that a thief's booty bring him ill fortune?

The direct disutility of the citizens whose losses are not compensated to their satisfaction is not the only demoralization cost for Michelman's utilitarians. They also count the disappointment of the losers' sympathizers, who are not necessarily losers themselves but who are made anxious (suffer disutility) as a result of the noncompensation. Add to this the "value of lost future production (reflecting either impaired incentives or social unrest) *caused by demoralization* of uncompensated losers, their sympathizers, and other observers disturbed by the thought that they themselves may be subjected to similar treatment on some other occasion."

The emphasis is added to indicate that Michelman considers these long-run costs to be caused specifically by demoralization; they are not merely prudent responses to random risks. These long-run costs arise not only from "impaired incentives" but also from social unrest. Social unrest costs could include direct public and private outlays to guard against antisocial actions, but they could as well include disaffection with the entire political process.

D. Why Insurance Models Overlook Demoralization

Given Michelman's specific disavowal of the analogy of the risk of a taking to the risk of a natural disaster, we must ask why those who advert to Michelman's principles nonetheless adopt the analogy. . . . BRS, Blume and Rubinfeld (in their joint article), Cooter, and Kaplow each adopt, for the noncompensation result, a Pigovian model of government. This model assumes that government is an unimpeachable benefit-cost machine. It does not inquire about the distribution of benefits, nor can it be manipulated by any faction of those governed. Thus, losses incurred by individuals whose property is taken should be regarded as analogous to those that occur through such unsystematic and noncompensable events as market forces or natural events.[37] There are no majoritarian excesses possible, because government decisions do not depend on the will of

---

37. That members of society may regard losses incurred by deliberate acts as worse than those that occur randomly is not to argue that compensation should never be paid to the victims of random events who may not have insured themselves (for example, flood victims or destitute retirees). Our argument is only that the reasons for the latter programs do not rest on demoralization costs, but on something else, perhaps empathy with the victims. While demoralization costs are increased by the empathy of those who see others being involuntarily exploited, the basic source is the losers' knowledge that they are being involuntarily used for another's gain.

anyone, let alone the majority. Demoralization costs in such a world should be zero.

The Pigovian model, which is adopted in most public policy models as an innocent ceteris paribus assumption, turns out to dispose of the taking issue entirely. Since BRS show that settlement costs are always positive (due to the moral hazard problem), $S > D$ for all projects, since $D = 0$ in the Pigovian model. Thus compensation would never be called for in a Pigovian application of Michelman's utilitarian framework.

IV.   The Temporal Error of Insurance and Capitalization

A.   Private Insurance and Demoralization Costs

It has been argued in the previous section that Michelman's utilitarian criterion forms a coherent framework to accommodate the moral hazard issue, and that no additional efficiency rationale is needed. Now we ask whether, if one accepts this conclusion, one could not accept also private insurance for takings, which Kaplow argues is more efficient. If landowners whose property is taken are paid, why should they feel greater loss if the payment comes from private insurance rather than from the public purse? Why does a check from a private insurer not soothe demoralization costs as well as public compensation?

One response to this line of reasoning is its impracticality. Kaplow does not attempt to explain the absence of a private, third-party insurance market for losses not covered by current eminent domain practices. We know of no legal inhibitions on such insurance, and uncompensated costs such as relocation, attorneys' fees, and lost business goodwill are often substantial and accrue to those who seem to be in a poor position to self-insure. An explanation for lack of private taking insurance, suggested to us by Robert Ellickson in a letter, is adverse selection. A public planner might tip off landowners of an impending taking and encourage them to apply for insurance in order to reduce political opposition to his project. Insurance losses would mount as a result, and private insurers would withdraw. Another problem involving purely private insurance against takings is how to secure the assets of insurance companies. If the government can seize any private property without compensation, what would prevent it from seizing the assets of insurance companies?

Even if these practical problems could be overcome, however, there remains a fundamental flaw in relying on private insurance.

Kaplow's proposal looks for the taking at the wrong moment in time. If landowners are risk averse, they can avoid the *risk* of a prospective taking by purchasing insurance or self-insuring. But demoralization costs are not imposed at the moment the property is taken. Demoralization costs, properly understood, arise when landowners *realize* that their wealth is reduced, not when the legal taking occurs. Even if they were risk neutral, so that they had no demand for insurance, landowners would be demoralized by the uncompensated reduction in wealth, which is the value of the property prior to the risk, times the probability that it will be taken. An insurance payment simply spreads this loss over time and reduces variance in the insured's income stream. The existence of insurance does not dispose of the issue of uncompensated transfers of wealth, and it is no more an argument for legalizing uncompensated takings than it is for legalizing the theft of watches.

To drive this point home, consider another analogy. Suppose that copyright laws were suspended. Authors who once relied on royalties from published works would realize at once that their wealth has been reduced. But because not all books may be pirated, there will be uncertainty about future incomes. Risk-averse authors may then insure. They will pay to their insurers premiums, the capitalized value of which is at least equal to the expected loss incurred as a result of copyright suspension. In the end, some authors will receive payments from their insurers for what used to be called copyright infringement. But few economists (and no commercial authors!) would argue that such private insurance amounts to the same thing as copyright law. The fundamental change was the loss of rights previously held. Insurance did not restore those rights. . . .

B.   Capitalization and Notice Arguments against Compensation

Looking at takings at the wrong moment in time is the source of another problem that causes persistent confusion in the takings literature. This is the argument that expectations of a taking are capitalized in the value of property so that purchasers of the property pay less for it and thus should not be compensated. Our argument is that capitalization does not satisfy anxiety about takings because it again views the problem at the wrong moment in time.

If Brennan, expecting that a taking of Alchian's land will not be compensated once Alchian sells it, nonetheless purchases it for $100 instead of the $300 it would command absent the prospective taking, it is true that Brennan does not lose in an expected-value sense if the land is subsequently taken without compensation. But *Alchian* surely lost from the prospective taking. If he had been guaranteed compensation for takings that, like other property entitlements, ran with the land, Brennan would have had to pay Alchian $300.

To say that Brennan should not be compensated because he "moved to the taking" or "purchased with notice" or "assumed the risk" or "had rational expectations" is to make one of *Alchian's* property entitlements inalienable, if Alchian would have received compensation by holding on to it. (If neither Alchian nor Brennan would have been compensated, it is simply a taking of Alchian's property.) Insofar as alienability is regarded as an essential aspect of normal property rights, a rule that purchasers are not compensated is itself a taking of the seller's property.

One of the reasons for confusion about this point is the ambiguity of Michelman's treatment of it. He offers an example in which those who purchase land they know may be taken should not be compensated. His example is a purchaser (our Brennan) of land that is among parcels that are the subject of active public debate to prevent development in order to preserve the scenery along the highway. Michelman indicates that Brennan should not be compensated if the regulations are subsequently adopted because the price he paid for the land reflected the possibility of restrictions.

But it is not clear from the scenic highway example alone whether Michelman believes that the original owner (our Alchian) should have been compensated had he not sold it. If Alchian would not have been entitled to compensation, then there is no reason to compensate Brennan or any other successor in title for the same regulation, and Michelman's example is unexceptionable. If, on the other hand, Alchian would have been compensated but Brennan would not, Michelman makes the error of looking at the taking at the wrong moment in time. The taking's demoralization occurred when Alchian realized that his right to compensation was made inalienable, not when Brennan was denied compensation. . . .

V. Conclusion

Michelman's utilitarian standard offers a method for evaluating compensation questions that is consistent with principles of economic efficiency. It provides a normative guide for when to choose the Pareto-superiority criterion (at least insofar as just compensation is consistent with that criterion) and when to settle for the Kaldor-Hicks criterion. Michelman's framework permits incorporation of the BRS noncompensation result into settlement costs while retaining a view of government more realistic than the Pigovian assumption. Insurance rationales for compensation are inadequate in this framework, because insurance does not address demoralization cost, which plays a pivotal role in Michelman's standard. This is not to argue that the utilitarian standard is the only one consistent with economic reasoning. We argue only that those who advance the insurance rationale for compensation have not addressed the central normative question of compensation, which is when to respect individual property entitlements in a world of less-than-ideal governments.

Failure to address demoralization cost does not itself condemn all insurance rationales for compensation. It may turn out that demoralization is related to risk aversion and can be analyzed with the same methods. We need to know more about the sources of demoralization (if it exists as a distinct cost at all). We also need to know what a "majoritarian" government encompasses and why demoralization costs arise from it rather than from other types of government actions. For this reason, we conclude by pointing out two aspects of Michelman's framework that require more investigation.

"Majoritarianism" points to democratic models, of which there are a wide variety. In a separate article, we model a constitutional choice of compensation levels made in the face of a simple majority-rule government. We find that compensation would be called for if risk-neutral, utility-maximizing constitution framers anticipate a majority rule government rather than a Pigovian government. This suggests a congruence with Michelman's result, although we cannot identify a specific factor in our model analogous to demoralization cost.

We need to know whether decisions of governments that are perceived as dominated by bureaucrats or by special interest groups give rise to demoralization costs in the same way as more obvious examples of majority rule, such as town meetings and plebescites. Existing commentary on this is mixed. Richard Epstein makes no distinction between takings that result from the politics of special interest or majority rule.[54] Taking a little from many people (for example, taxpayers) is regarded as the same as taking a lot from a few people (for example, outvoted owners of undeveloped land). Robert Ellickson, on the other hand, found that just-compensation remedies for excessive suburban zoning laws were especially appropriate because of the majoritarian structure of local government.[55] One reason for this distinction is that in larger governments the special-interest model of politics more likely applies, so that losers from

54. Epstein, [Takings: Private Property and the Power of Eminent Domain (1985)], at 93-96.
55. Robert C. Ellickson, Suburban Growth Controls: An Economic and Legal Analysis, 86 Yale L. J. 385, 404-420 (1977).

uncompensated actions may be less demoralized by failure to compensate because they can recoup their losses in a later coalition.

We suggest that modern survey research and psychological experiments may provide insights into the extent to which random losses differ from government-imposed losses, and how different types of government-imposed losses are perceived by those who bear the costs. . . .

NOTES AND QUESTIONS ON EFFICIENCY AND THE TAKINGS ISSUE

1. Fischel and Shapiro's (F & S) analysis suggests that liability rules (unlike property rules) tend to make landowners ignore the most socially valuable uses of their property; under a liability rule for compensation, they are likely to overexpend on capital projects. This is the moral hazard problem. Does it follow that land should be protected by a property rule instead of a liability rule, either favoring the owner (government may only purchase with the consent of the owner) or favoring the government (government need not compensate and has a property right to use any land at will)? What speaks for an intermediate liability rule instead of one or the other of these property rules? See Calabresi & Melamed, Property Rules, Liability Rules, and Inalienability, supra p.236.

2. F & S stress that Michelman's concept of demoralization costs has special concern for "majoritarian exploitation" of minorities. Is this concern itself well-placed? Compare Bruce Ackerman, Beyond Carolene Products, 98 Harv. L. Rev. 863 (1985), arguing that modern public-choice theory upends the concern about exploitation of small, identifiable minorities. According to this theory, members of such groups are most likely to be able to identify each other, organize around their narrow interests, and influence legislation — unlike the relatively passive members of wide majority groups, who feel costs and benefits only diffusely. Does Ackerman's analysis suggest that "takings" problems (where harms are imposed by the many on the few) are less important than problems of overtaxation (where the few impose costs on the many), even though the latter seem to impose burdens in a wider and more egalitarian way? For more on the relation of public choice considerations to takings law, see Daniel A. Farber, Public Choice and Just Compensation, 9 Const. Commentary 279 (1992).

3. F & S point out an important ambiguity in Michelman's analysis — that is, if purchasers go uncompensated when they know

about potential confiscations, the losses may fall not on them but on their *sellers*. Do you see why? Is this true of any loss from a land use regulation? Might some portion of the loss still fall on purchasers? For an analysis of this question, see Robert C. Ellickson & A. Dan Tarlock, Land Use Controls 735-737 (1981).

4. Does the real estate market itself provide a version of private takings insurance? Could a risk-averse developer protect herself by *leasing* land instead of purchasing? Even in the case of a long-term lease, are there ways in which an owner and a lessee might agree to allocate "takings" risks? For this possibility, and some problems, see Victor P. Goldberg, Thomas C. Merrill & Daniel Unumb, Bargaining in the Shadow of Eminent Domain: Valuing and Apportioning Condemnation Awards Between Landlord and Tenant, 34 U.C.L.A. L. Rev. 1083 (1987).

5. In what ways if any does governmental confiscation resemble normal insurable risks? Can an insurance company predict the probabilities of "takings" risks in a given community in the same way that it predicts, say, the incidence of automobile accidents? If there are differences, how might they affect insurance markets?

In the literature on insurance, Frank Knight, in Risk, Uncertainty, and Profit (1921), drew a well-known distinction between *risk* (which may be estimated probabilistically) and *uncertainty* (which may not). Crudely speaking, risks are thought to be amenable to private insurance, but uncertainties are not, unless they can be grouped in such a way as to permit probabilistic estimates. Can you see why? How do the problem of moral hazard and the related problem of adverse selection (discussed in F&S's text at Part IV. A.) turn risks into uncertainties? For a lucid explanation, see George Priest, Insurability and Punitive Damages, 40 Alabama L. Rev. 1009, 1020 (1989).

Are potential governmental takings risks or uncertainties? Does the answer depend on whether governmental agents correctly weigh costs and benefits on the basis of the public interest (designated by F&S as the "Pigovian assumption")?

6. In discussing copyright laws, F&S suggest that insurance cannot make up for ill-defined or indefensible property rights. Why not?

Might insurance companies themselves take on the role of defending and defining the property rights of the insured? For example, in the eighteenth century, fire insurance companies organized firefighting companies that would respond only to calls from insured property owners. See Fred McChesney, Government Prohibitions on Volunteer Fire Fighting in Nineteenth Century

America: A Property Rights Perspective, 15 J. Legal Stud. 69, 73-75 (1985). Though this particular arrangement died out, can you see the reasons for integrating the services of insurance and property protection? In modern environmental law, insurance companies play a considerable role in "regulating" the activities of insured hazardous waste facilities, linking insurance coverage to compliance with various safety measures; see Steven A. Kunzman, The Insurer as Surrogate Regulator of the Hazardous Waste Industry: Solution or Perversion? 20 The Forum 469 (A.B.A. 1985). How does this role help to control the problems of moral hazard and adverse selection?

Do these examples of insurers' defense and management of property undercut Fischel and Shapiro's argument that insurance cannot take the place of undefended property rights? Would an insurance company be able to prevent the copying of an author's creations? The overregulation of a developer's site?

E.   Environmental Protection

Prices as Regulatory Instruments *

Thomas C. Schelling

Someone who spoils his own land without affecting drainage on other property, runs noisy equipment that no one else can hear, or contaminates his own water supply is not said to create an environmental problem. The problem is said to be environmental when lead and sulfur drift downwind to make somebody sick, an oil spill washes onto a public beach, acid drainage from an abandoned mine destroys marine life, or the burning of fuels changes the regional or global climate. Environmental effects are the consequences that are outside the purview, the cost accounting, the concern, or the responsibility of identifiable producers and consumers. They are outside the pricing system (except when damage suits can make the activities costly).

The activities that have environmental impacts are of many kinds. There are beneficial activities that go unrewarded and harmful ones for which neither price nor penalty is paid. There are some so natural, like the happy voices of children a little too early in the

*Source: In Incentives for Environmental Protection 1-32 (Thomas C. Schelling ed. 1983).

morning, that we hesitate to complain. However, the roar of a motorcycle gets little sympathy. There are individuals who pour crank-
case oil down the storm sewer or throw cigarette butts out the car
window, and there are businesses, large and small, that dump their
waste on land and sea and in the air. There are activities, such as
driving and parking, that are unobjectionable on a modest scale but
on a larger scale cause obstructions. There is illicit disposal of hazardous waste, disposal that is legal but dangerous, and unwitting
disposal of things that prove harmful. There are activities, such as
burning fuel to make electricity, that are bound to continue, the issue being only the scale of the activity. Other activities, such as the
use of certain herbicides or pesticides, need not and ought not to
continue at all. There are damaging activities that are so beneficial
that the harm is incidental and no "problem" is perceived, activities
that pose difficult choices because of disagreement or uncertainty
whether the benefits or the damages are greater, and activities that
almost without question deserve to be discouraged or stopped. And
when all those with any conceivable stake in the matter or any right
to participate get together and determine that some investment in
the environment is not worth the cost or that some depletion is more
than compensated by the benefits, they may count the quorum un-
mindful of all the interested parties who have not been born yet.

Most of us play many roles on the environmental stage. . . . We
complain about the high price of electricity while the utility companies try to keep costs down by avoiding expensive smoke abatement. We patronize an economical laundry that pours chemicals
down the sewer. We pay higher prices for oysters without knowing
that, whether or not the oystermen are suffering from pollution, the
oysters are and it makes them expensive.

It takes some analysis to identify victims and beneficiaries.
When electric utility companies are required for the sake of health,
comfort, and agriculture downwind to clean up the hot gas that
comes out of the smokestacks, it is not easy to figure out who is
going to pay for those downwind benefits. A good guess is that,
taking all the coal-burning electric utilities together, it will not be
their stockholders. Electric rates are set by public boards and commissions that determine what costs are deductible and what rate of
return is appropriate, and most of the cost is passed along to customers. Some of the customers will be industries; they, too, will pass
most of the rate increases along to their customers. If the industries
use much electricity, business may suffer some and wage increases
will be less forthcoming or property-tax assessments less aggressive; and all the results are as complex as locating the ultimate incidence of a tax on electricity or on the coal used in utilities' boilers.

These complications remind us that efforts to preserve or improve the environment, protect against hazards, and abate the degradation of soil and forests and other resources entail a mix of gains and losses and of gainers and losers. And neither the aggregate size of gains and losses nor their distribution among gainers and losers is transparent. The distributional issues — who gains and who loses, by income size or region or occupation — are not easy to discern and are sometimes contrary to intuition. Even the relative magnitudes of gains and losses (those that accrue to individuals and those that are thought of as social values) are not easy to estimate. . . .

. . . [T]he theory with which to think about externalities is well developed. And in theoretical terms it matters little whether the externality in question is one that we would call environmental. Nevertheless, in assessing those impingements of people's activities on the welfare of others that are mediated by the physical environment, there are some elements that the theory of externalities cannot handle. The reason is that the theory is neutral toward the moral significance of activities and events, and excludes values that cannot ultimately be assessed in individual welfare.

Specifically, economic theory evaluates actions by their consequences and by the way the consequences are valued by the people who benefit or suffer, not by whether they are inherently good or evil or according to the spirit in which they are done. However, for many people concerned about the environment, activities are not adequately measured by a summation of individual gains and losses. That there is no one to speak for a particular endangered species or for the Earth itself does not, for some people, imply that, because nobody has a stake in the matter, there is no matter. . . .

Environmental concerns are loaded with additional weight because they occasionally, as with climate, pose the possible risk of irreversible damage of an immensity difficult to agree on. And they entail chemical and biological hazards capable of causing, on a large or a small scale, those most awesome human tragedies, death and fetal abnormality.

Externalities and Social Controls

So it is that people and businesses engage in activities that use up something scarce that doesn't belong to them, spoil something in which others have a legitimate interest, or harm other people directly. Or they do these things immoderately when on a modest scale they might be excused. And they can do it because they do not know they are doing it, or they know but do not care, or they know and care but have a conflicting interest of their own, or they do not know how to moderate their activities or redirect them in less harmful ways. They may enjoy the anonymity that allows them to get away with it, or they may regret their inability to identify their victims and make amends. And activities beneficial to the environment may go unrewarded for similar reasons.

Thus arises the need for some social control, some inducement to curtail or moderate the harmful activities or to enhance the beneficial ones. The generic term *environmental protection* implies that it is the harmful activities that deserve most urgent attention.

Self-controls

For want of a better term we refer to the various ways environmental policy is implemented as *social controls*. The term has to include what might better be called *self-controls*, which are much relied on in social policy. It must include education that generates awareness and knowledge of the consequences of actions or the availability of alternatives. It includes prohibitions, regulations, fees, charges, tax incentives, and methods of enforcement. And it includes what may be done through private negotiation, civil law, and informal cooperative arrangements.

Unquestionably a large part of environmental protection depends on decency, considerateness, and self-control. Some of the most powerful social controls work through habit and etiquette....

Considerateness and self-control deserve emphasis. A propensity for civilized behavior is a precious resource for protecting our environment, and the more overt social controls should be compatible with preserving that widespread sense of personal responsibility on which, especially in densely populated areas, we all depend so much.

Overt controls

The more overt controls take a variety of forms. There are prohibitions on the transport of dangerous chemicals and regulations on where campfires may be lit, when noise may be made, how wastes may be disposed of, how much gas may be emitted, how many deer may be killed, what ingredients may be used in a pesticide, how fast a car may travel, how loud a noise may be, and what unsightly or dangerous objects may not be left in a public place. These can be enforced by fines, imprisonment, tax penalties, or loss of licenses and privileges....

This chapter is about a particular set of measures of social control — measures of a kind familiar in some contexts and unfamiliar, even alien, in others. They are sometimes described as economic incentives, sometimes as measures that work through the price system. A list of measures of this kind would include fees and charges, subsidies, rewards, indemnities, auctions, the assignment of property rights, and the creation of markets. Familiar examples are parking meters and bottle deposits, income-tax credits for home insulation, stimulated markets in recycled paper, and low-interest loans on solar home-heating systems. Less familiar and more controversial are fees, fines, or taxes on the sulfur emissions of electric utilities, on airport noise, and on the venting of noxious fumes. Attempts to generate markets in which new firms that cannot operate without emitting into the atmosphere some quantities of regulated substances can buy the rights of existing and former firms, which in turn discontinue equivalent emissions, are a more recent innovation, as is the proposed "carcass deposit" on new automobiles, which would be refunded at the end of a car's life to whoever disposed of the remains at an approved site.

Pricing systems

The distinguishing characteristic of these measures is not just the payment of money in consideration of damage done, resources depleted, or environmental benefits conferred. . . .

The distinction is illustrated by the difference between a *fee* and a *fine*, or between a *charge* and a *penalty*. It is typical of fees and charges (whether a fee is collected on an activity or paid for its performance) that no moral or legal prejudice attaches to the fee itself or the action on which or for which it is paid. The behavior is discretionary. The fee offers an option: Pay it and deposit your rubbish here or take your rubbish elsewhere. . . .

Decentralized decisions

The essence of a pricing system is that it leaves the decision to pay or not to pay to whoever confronts the price. The price is there to be paid — not to stand as a warning, an act of redemption, or an admission of liability. A pricing mechanism decentralizes the decisions. A central authority may determine the price, but paying or not paying is a decentralized choice. In contrast, a central authority determines that you may not park in front a hydrant — not you, not anybody, not for an hour, not for five minutes, not to make a phone call, not to go to the bathroom. The fine is an enforcement device. It may be calculated to deter; it may be thought commensurate with the offense; but there is no intention that, with the fine for an offense set, it is now freely up to you whether or not to park there. . . .

What is crucial about a price is not merely that it is devoid of ethical significance or that it allows freedom of choice. A price is a *measure*. In the marketplace a price on a voluntary transaction must cover the cost of performance or provision, or represent adequate compensation. The transaction is voluntary. The price paid for a bottle of cola must cover the cost of labor, materials, energy, and anything else that went into producing it, delivering it, and handling it up to the time of sale. If people will not pay enough to cover those costs, we conclude that the drink is not worth what it costs; the labor, materials, and energy will be used elsewhere to produce things that consumers do consider worth the cost. And if the cost of cola delivered to the neighborhood store is well within the prices that consumers will pay, and if no single firm has a monopoly, we expect competition to produce all the cola that people want at a price that covers its cost. . . .

Sometimes prices reflect a scarcity value. Most cities regulate the number of taxicabs. Under the medallion system there is some fixed number of licenses. Medallions are salable, like seats on the stock exchange, and the question of who drives the taxis is thus decentralized to the marketplace. . . .

To translate the examples of cola and medallions into the environmental area, we can think of "bottle bills" requiring a deposit to be paid on returnable containers for beer and soda. Two generations ago beer and soda were sold in returnable containers. Most of us gave little thought to whether, having paid the deposit, we owned the bottles or had merely rented them and pledged with a small deposit to return them. No matter. We paid enough deposit to cover a replacement if we lost or broke or kept the bottle. There were children who would collect bottles for profit if we thought them not worth transporting back to the store. And if we lost or broke one we never had to say we were sorry; the price covered the cost. Neither the store nor the manufacturer cared what we did with the bottle.

But somebody did care, or does now. Broken, the bottle was a nuisance, and intact it was unsightly. If I left a broken bottle on your sidewalk, I had paid for the bottle, but not for cleaning your sidewalk, or repairing your bicycle tire, or treating your dog's paw. But because the bottles cost money I was careful, and if I left behind an unbroken bottle some youngster might retrieve it and redeem it at the store for two cents before it got broken. Now that our standard of living is so high and the technology of disposable containers so cheap that most of us prefer throwaways, the failure of the price of the bottle to reflect the costs of cleaning up or the compensation for damage done is a greater discrepancy than it used to be. The deposit on a returnable container has been reinvented for regulatory use. . . .

Price determination   But how much should the deposit be? At a minimum it should cover the cost of the container, of course; else the consumer is not even paying for the contents. And if, having paid a deposit that covers the replacement cost, consumers husband their bottles and return them faithfully, the problem is solved. If instead they leave them in large numbers at the beach and on the sidewalk, we want a larger deposit to induce a higher rate of return. If we collect a nickel a bottle and it makes no difference, we know that the nuisance of returning empties is equivalent to more than a nickel a bottle for most consumers. Somebody is getting revenue without much being accomplished. We could raise the deposit to $1 a bottle and the return rate might reach 100 percent. . . . But at $5 we would surely not be setting the price at which we are indifferent to whether the consumer forgoes the deposit for the convenience of wasting his bottle or returns it to get his money back.

One other way of deciding on the deposit is to ask at what price people would be indifferent about whether to return the bottle or not. A possibility is that discarded bottles, at a certain price, will be profitably collected by people who retrieve them and bring them to the collection stations. If at 15 cents all the bottles show up, we can excuse the people who leave bottles around, because by forfeiting their deposits they have paid for the cleanup. And if the bottles are not all retrieved but we can afford cleanup crews with the unclaimed deposits, again we may not care whether people return their bottles or pay in advance for the cleanup. These possibilities suggest the kind of deposit we might characterize as a price and why, having set a price, we might be content to let everybody decide for himself whether to pay the price and waste the bottle or save the price and return it.

This discussion does not settle how we should deal with the bottle problem; it only indicates what distinguishes a price system from other modes of regulation, including others that entail payments of money. Specifically, there is no implication here that we have to be ethically neutral about social behavior with beer and soda bottles. Also, there is no *a priori* assurance that any moderate price would cover the cost of cleanup. . . .

Allocating a fixed supply   Taxi medallions have counterparts wherever overcrowding is a problem. . . . With medallions, there is a decision by a central authority on how many cabs might operate, but the question of whose cabs is left to the market. With downtown parking, a central authority may determine how many permits will be issued or how many spaces made available, or exactly where parking will be permitted, and then rather than choose who gets to park or where each person parks, or schedule individuals over the hours of the day or the days of the week, the authorities can let prices take care of those decisions. There are numerous ways. A familiar one is to install meters with rates low enough to keep spaces from going unused but high enough not to attract drivers in numbers much greater than the spaces available. If a uniform meter price leaves outlying spaces unused and centrally located spaces inadequate, higher prices can be set on the meters where spaces are in greater demand. . . .

Discrimination by price   Parking spaces go to the people who can afford them. Whether their parking needs are especially urgent, or driving and parking saves them more money than it saves others, or they are merely wealthier, they get the spaces because they are willing to pay. The apparent discrimination is moderated by the fact that the wealthier the parkers are, the higher the price may go and the more the town can collect. We may nevertheless be tempted to offer spaces free, or at reduced rates, to the poor. A relevant if not decisive consideration should be that because they are poor they would evidently rather have the money than the parking. We might give them parking tokens and expect them to trade them in for cash. If we give them a "property right" that they can enjoy only by driving and parking, they have something less valuable than if they could trade it at a price at which they would rather have the money. . . .

In closing this . . . discussion of bottles and parking, which has been intended only to illuminate what is meant by *prices*, I acknowledge that these examples were picked because they are ideal illustrations that epitomize a wide range of activities to which the same principles apply. However, they are not typical. They are easy cases. . . . In the abstract, the principle applies to Kleenex, cigarette butts, candy wrappers, and eggshells, but we don't expect it to work for them.

Pricing Systems . . .

Two things can be said confidently about extending the price system as a way of bringing environmental problems under control. One is that there is indubitably a role for prices. Numerous successes can be pointed out. A good part of the development of economic institutions has been bringing what used to be externalities into the market system by the conferring and protection of property rights and the enforcement of contracts, by the availability of better information, and by technological development that facilitates marketing. The second is that some environmental problems are bound to remain beyond the reach of even the most ingenious efforts to create or extend markets. Indeed, there is a presumption that it is going to be difficult to bring additional effects into the market system; if it were easy, it would have already been done. . . .

There is great variety in the pricing methods that can be and have been used in regulating activities that affect the environment. In recent years, attention has focused on what are usually called *effluent charges* or *emission charges* (largely because of the dominant importance of air and water pollution from stationary sources, partly because of specific proposals that became controversial). Pricing for environmental protection is not wholly or even mainly about emission charges, but they are currently the most familiar, controversial, and important policy alternatives. . . .

[Instead of levying charges, regulators could impose standards.] The alternative kinds of regulatory standards might be

- a limit on total emissions per day or per year,
- a limit on the emission per unit of legitimate input or output, such as on the sulfur emitted per kilowatt-hour produced, per million BTU of heat used, or per ton of coal burned,
- a prescribed reduction in total emission, or emission per unit, below some traditional level,
- a stipulated change in some input, such as pounds of sulfur per ton of coal or oil consumed, and
- a prescribed change in the mode of combustion or the equipment employed.

These might be varied according to season or wind direction or current air quality, if short-run variation is economical enough to bother with. And the limits may or may not vary with the plant's location; that is, plants located where more people or more crops or more wild animals are affected, or where the people and the crops and the wildlife are more vulnerable, may or may not be regulated differently.

The first thing to ask about a charge system is what the charge is imposed on. A second is what determines the amount of the charge (how many dollars per pound or per cubic foot of something). A third is how the charge will be administered. The object of the charge is to change the quantity, quality, or distribution by time and place of the emission. At the outset we can assume that the desired effects on emissions are basically the same with the charge system as with one of the other kinds of regulation. . . .

For simplicity, imagine a large number of plants (not necessarily identical in what they produce and how they produce it) that all emit a noxious substance. The emissions of each plant are susceptible to measurement, but once in the air the emissions of all the plants become mixed. Damage is not attributable to individual firms, but the emissions of every plant affect the total. How would a charge system work?

This is an easy case. We have an identified culprit (the noxious emission). We can monitor each plant. Only the total of the emissions matters, since the emissions are alike and commingled. All the plants are within a single jurisdiction, the same one in which the victim population resides. Our primary objective is to reduce total emissions, preferably in a manner that treats individual sources "fairly." More accurate[ly], we want to limit the harm the emissions do; but we do that by reducing the emissions.

There are two alternatives to consider in what we know about the "damage function," about the way the severity of the damages relates to the total quantity of the noxious gas. One is that we know how much damage a unit of that noxious substance does, and we can put a money value on that damage. If we can value the damage caused by a pound of the substance without stipulating what the total is to which that pound is added, the damage function must be linear — proportionate to the total quantity. In that case we will probably want to relate the charge to the damage, perhaps charging each plant for its contribution to the damage. The other possibility is that we begin with an idea of how much of the substance we are willing to allow and then set a charge that keeps total emissions within that limit. A possibility is that damages remain moderate up to a certain concentration and thereafter mount rapidly ("nonlinearly") — perhaps after a certain concentration is reached the atmosphere can no longer be refreshed by wind and rain. . . .

Now let us see how the result with a charge system differs from that with the more directly regulatory regime.

In both cases emissions have been reduced. One conspicuous difference is that in one case funds have been collected that are equivalent to the permit price times the remaining quantity of emissions. (And if the price corresponds to an estimate of the damage per pound of emission, the funds are equivalent to the estimated damage.) We will consider in a moment what might usefully be done with those funds. There is also the question of what may legally be done with them — whether they revert to the treasury, are directed by law to particular uses, or go into some environmental-protection budget.

Are emissions in the aggregate reduced the same amount? The answer depends quite simply on whether, if a quantity was determined and the price was allowed to emerge in the market, the quantity was the same that would have been allowed under a regulatory regime. . . .

Several things will be different. A striking difference will likely be that emissions produced by individual firms will not be the same. Indeed, a key result of the charge system is that it concentrates reductions among the firms best able to reduce emissions, since unit costs are higher for the firms least able to get emissions down.

Another likely difference is that the techniques of abatement or the methods of production that give rise to the emission in the first place may differ. Under the charge system each firm is free to reduce emissions the cheapest way it knows how. Under a regulatory regime the technology for abatement might have been specified.

A related difference in the overall result is that under the charge system less of the result was determined by regulation, more by decision of individual firms. . . .

That some firms will prefer a charge system and some will not is easily demonstrated. Suppose emissions with the charge are half the original quantity and the alternative would have been that every firm would have had to reduce emission by half. Firms will reduce emissions if that is cheaper than paying the price and will pay the price if that is cheaper than reducing emissions. Specifically, each firm can be presumed to have reduced emissions as long as reduction was cheaper than paying the price, and to have settled at a level of abatement at which further reduction would have been more costly than the permission to abate. Since the price charged for emissions is (we are assuming here) uniform among firms, all those emissions will have ceased whose elimination was cheaper than the price. So the aggregate abatement will have been achieved at the lowest possible total cost. . . .

The Rationale for Charging

There are several arguments for putting a price on harmful emissions, and, although they are compatible and reinforce each other, they are quite separate.

The market test

As noted above, a price offers an automatic adjustment process — a decentralized decision process — not only inducing the
abatement in those particular firms, uses, or production processes
where abatement can most economically be carried the furthest, but
also providing a measure and a "market test." All abatement that is
cheaper than the price will tend to be undertaken. Abatement that
is so expensive that paying the price is preferable will be avoided,
but only at a cost (paying the price) no less than what any other firm
is expending on actual abatement. . . .

There are at least two fundamental problems with the above
argument. First, if it is denied in principle that the harm and harm-
fulness of the emissions can be gathered into a damage estimate and
expressed as a price per unit of emissions, the argument loses not
only its appeal but its basis. This is not the counterargument that
what is harmed is "priceless" and that abatement should be un-
stinting and without regard to cost comparisons; if the damage is
infinitely large, a prohibitive price is put on the emissions, and emissions cease — if necessary by cessation of the entire process that
gave rise to the emissions. Rather, this counterargument is that the
harm goes beyond the damage. It includes attitudes, responsibilities, and the government's philosophy toward the environment. It
can include an interest in "criminalizing" certain environmental in-
sults. It may reflect a belief that the real or imagined victims of en-
vironmentally transmitted damage, or of harm to the environment
itself, will resent and distrust a policy that appears to make emissions optional, to leave them for the marketplace, or to merchandise
abatement by getting it done by whoever can do it most cheaply.

A second and altogether different objection to the "market test"
is that the costs and damages, even if perfectly measurable in dollars, cannot properly be added together. They cannot be minimized
together because they accrue to different people. If my factory is
causing a farmer (a wholly unrelated individual, possibly unknown
to me) increased costs, reduced productivity, or damages that have
to be repaired, at the rate of $1,000 a month, and I can reduce that
damage by half at a cost of less than $500 to myself, but reducing
damage another 10 percent would cost me substantially more than
$100, why should I be obliged to clean up the first 50 percent and
not further obligated with respect to the other half of the farmer's
damage? True, together we are richer if I abate the first half and stop
there. But there is, in the language of economics, a distributional
dimension of the problem. This makes it inappropriate to do the
arithmetic as though my factory and his farm were both parts of the

same enterprise and together the two parts made more money if abatement went just up to the line where costs and benefits were balanced. . . .

Disposition of proceeds

Meanwhile, back at the agency, the money is coming in. Whose money is it? What should be done with it? Is it a pure byproduct of a regulatory scheme, embarrassing to an agency that has no budgetary authority to spend it and perhaps appearing to be a revenue bonus available to meet public needs? . . . [T]hese funds, generated from a regulatory mechanism that induces an "economical" level of emissions to continue, are equivalent to the costs or damages estimated to be inflicted by those emissions. They ought to be used to complete the transaction by which the emitting firms pay for what they use and what they do. Paying into a public treasury on account of emissions and paying *for* the emissions by paying to repair, indemnify, or forestall the damage are not the same. And getting the benefits to the victim is every bit as important as getting the money from the firm that produces the damage. That is the argument.

It will be the rare environmental externality that permits us, at no exorbitant administrative expense, to identify all the victims and assess their damages individually. We probably have a crude aggregate estimate of damage, and at the level of an individual victim there may be no reliable way of determining how much of any apparent costs is actually due to the regulated emissions. Still, in principle the distributional objection mentioned above could be mitigated if funds were dedicated to completing that transaction. . . .

To recapitulate: There are at least four distinct attractions, separable but compatible, to a charge system. One is to get the abatement allocated among firms so that if some have lower abatement costs than others the cost of any given abatement can be minimized. (This statement can be turned around to read ". . . so that for any given aggregate cost the greatest aggregate abatement can be achieved.") Second, if the price is an approximation of the estimated damage per unit of emission, it offers a market test, revealing the marginal cost of further abatement and inducing the undertaking of abatement where it is no longer less expensive than the costs inflicted by emissions. Third, whoever does the emitting, or whoever purchases the goods and services produced by the emitter, "beneficiary," or "offender," pays the full "social cost" of the goods and services so produced. And fourth, revenue is available that could in principle be used for repair, reparations, and protection, in an amount sufficient to cover the costs inflicted by the emissions if the price has been approximated to those costs (with the "costs" or "damages" augmented by the costs of administering the program).

Focus on damage . . .

Schemes that focus only on the amount of sulfur emitted (irrespective of the target), or on the ambient concentration of a sulfur oxide (irrespective of the exposed populations), deal with a damaging substance but not with the damage. They control the agent but not the effect. Not being concerned with damage, they do not require its identification and measurement.

Pricing schemes, in contrast, require the identification and assessment of damage. They require facing up to questions exactly like this one: Do we want the abatement of noxious substances to be greatest where the exposed and vulnerable population is greatest and least where the exposed and vulnerable population is small, and do we want the emissions to be relocated so that the damage per exposed individual will vary from place to place but the damage for the whole population will be minimized?

NOTES AND QUESTIONS ON PRICING ENVIRONMENTAL PROTECTION

1. If polluters use public resources (like air and water) without payment, could pollution be compared to an implicit public subsidy to polluting firms? Is there an analogy to welfare? Can government now change its policy and restrict or charge for pollution, as if past practices were a public indulgence or "mere largesse" to the polluters? Compare Charles Reich, The New Property, 73 Yale L.J. 733 (1964).

Alternatively, is pollution a case of "first possession"? In that case, are fees on emissions and effluents "takings" of property because they require possessors to pay for what they already own?

Does it matter if a firm constructed its machinery and plant in a permissive regulatory climate, and if retrofit is now very expensive? Should such firms be "grandfathered" out of a new set of regulations and permitted to pollute without paying? Do adverse possession principles apply?

2. Why wouldn't a pricing scheme work as well to reduce candy wrapper trash as it does to encourage bottle returns? Are air pollution emissions more like bottles or candy wrappers? What measures are required to define and enforce property rights for air

emissions? Compare property rights in land: Why do these seem relatively easy? For some ideas and caveats, see Ellickson, Property in Land, supra p.158.

3. Schelling's major ethical claims for pricing seem to be that pricing can yield

a. least-cost environmental improvement, and
b. funds to compensate pollution victims.

Do pricing schemes really provide least-cost environmental improvement? Schelling points out that much environmental protection arises informally, from social practices like good manners and civility. If pricing schemes — unlike fines or prohibitions — treat pollution as morally neutral, might they undermine the moral underpinnings of these social practices and hence wind up costing more? See Carol Rose, Rethinking Environmental Controls, 1991 Duke L.J. 1. Are environmental pricing schemes an example of what Margaret Radin might consider an inappropriate "commodification"? See Radin, Market-Inalienability, supra p.336. What explains the extremely adverse reaction to pricing schemes in Hoppe, A License to Steal, supra p.259?

On the issue of compensating victims, suppose that pricing schemes do save money on pollution abatement, but that some tiny subset of victims cannot be found or compensated except at exorbitantly high costs. Should compensation be disregarded for such victims? Or should pricing schemes themselves be jettisoned, perhaps to be replaced by command-and-control regulation, even though this makes pollution abatement more rigid and expensive? What would Rawlsian principles suggest? See Rawls, A Theory of Justice, supra p.101. For an argument that people are generally willing to forego aggregate efficiency gains in risk regulation for the sake of more equal distribution of risks, see Donald T. Hornstein, Reclaiming Environmental Law: A Normative Critique of Comparative Risk Analysis, 92 Colum. L. Rev. 562 (1992).

4. Will pricing schemes necessarily make the "money come in" so that agencies can compensate victims? The United States' major experiment with such schemes arises from the 1990 Acid Rain amendments to the Clean Air Act. This Act sets an upper limit on the total allowable emission levels of pollutants responsible for acid rain, particularly sulfur dioxide; it also divides up this grand total into a large number of tradeable emission rights. But the Act does not auction or sell the emission rights to firms that need them. Instead, it simply *gives* a quota of emission rights to each major past polluter, notably to the midwestern coal-burning utilities, who are

then entitled to trade the rights among themselves and to other polluting plants. What justification could there be for this windfall to past polluters? What does it do to victim compensation schemes?

Gary Libecap, in Contracting for Property Rights (1989) (discussed in the notes following Demsetz, Toward a Theory of Property Rights, supra p.157), discusses the difficulties of making transitions between resource management schemes, and gives some reasons for paying off past polluters. Are these pay-offs an instance of a political decision to tolerate injustice for the sake of efficiency gains?

5. How can the costs of pollution — or the benefits of abatement — be assessed? For example, could you ask people how much they would pay to keep open an option of a future visit to an unspoiled Grand Canyon? Could you ask how much they would pay simply to know that the Grand Canyon is being preserved? An array of these contingent valuation methods is currently used in environmental law to assess nonmarket values; see Frederick R. Anderson, Natural Resources Damages, Superfund, and the Courts, 16 B.C. Envt'l Aff. L. Rev. 405, 440-452 (1989). Do the results depend on how one frames the question? That is, should one ask people how much they would pay to *obtain* these values, or how much they would take to *sell* or relinquish them? See Knetsch, Endowment Effect, supra p.226.

Are all such questions about "shadow pricing" misplaced? Mark Sagoff, The Economy of the Earth (1988), argues that when people discuss wilderness preservation and other environmental issues they are not concerned about their consumer preferences, but rather about other civic values that are not captured by shadow pricing; but cf. Carol Rose, Environmental Faust Succumbs to Temptations of Economic Mephistopheles, or, Value by Any Other Name is Preference (review), 87 Mich. L. Rev. 1631 (1989).